Marriage-a-la-mode, Plate I.

The English Comédie Humaine
Second Series

ENGLISH HUMORISTS
OF THE
EIGHTEENTH CENTURY

SIR RICHARD STEELE
JOSEPH ADDISON
LAURENCE STERNE
OLIVER GOLDSMITH

ILLUSTRATED AFTER DRAWINGS BY
WILLIAM HOGARTH
SHOWING THE DRESS, MANNERS AND CUSTOMS
OF THAT PERIOD

NEW YORK
The Century Co
1906

Copyright, 1906, by
THE CENTURY CO.

Published April, 1906.

THE DE VINNE PRESS

PUBLISHER'S NOTE.

In this, the initial volume of the second series of the English Comédie Humaine, the delightful sketches and essays of Eighteenth Century Life by the early English humorists and satirists, will be enjoyed as thoroughly by the modern reader as by the society whose shortcomings they aimed to correct; and a sort of visualizing emphasis is given to this unique collection of papers by the remarkable Hogarth drawings.

The papers from The Tatler, and its successor, The Spectator, include some of the best work of both Addison and Steele. In touching on the various social follies of the day with his own exquisitely gentle ridicule, Addison is at his humorous best; while Steele is most felicitous perhaps when he aims at the fashionable absurdities of women which he does in forceful yet sympathetic style.

The Tatler was started in 1709 and in 1711 was merged into The Spectator which in turn survived but a year and a half—a brief life indeed in which to have attained undying fame.

The chief work of Laurence Sterne, the celebrated English novelist and humorist, is "The Life and Opinions of Tristram Shandy, Gentleman," containing nine volumes, and written during the period, 1760 to 1767. In this present volume appear books VI and VII, the first containing the beautiful story of Le Fever, perhaps the most genuinely touching narrative ever penned by the sentimental Sterne; and the second containing the vivacious account of the author's saunterings in France written in his most vivacious and fanciful strain.

"The Citizen of the World; or Letters of a Chinese Philosopher" which rounds out this volume, is Oliver Goldsmith's most brilliant contribution to humorous literature. This collection of letters first appeared in an English newspaper and was issued in book form in 1762. On the surface is gay and sparkling facetiousness, which does not blind one however to the shrewd observation and keen delineation of national character. Beau Tibbs, a prominent character in this work, "is the best comic sketch," says Hazlitt, "since the time of Addison; unrivalled in his fancy, his vanity and his poverty."

CONTENTS.

STEELE	PAGE
From Thackeray's English Humorists	1

The Tatler

No.		PAGE
25	Duelling	43
35	Snuff	45
60	Tom Wildair	47
77	Fashionable affections	49
79	Marriage of Jenny Distaff	52
86	Scene of country etiquette	56
88	A dancing-master practising by book	59
89	Mr. Bickerstaff on himself	33
95	A visit to a friend	39
103	Applications for permission to use canes, etc.	61
104	Mrs. Tranquillus	66
116	The petticoat	70
124	On the lottery	73
126	The prude and the coquette	76
131	Trial of the wine-brewers	80
132	Our club	84
136	Tom Varnish	87
148	Kickshaws	89
151	Beauty unadorned	93
155	The political upholsterer	96
158	Tom Folio	99
160	A visit and letter from the upholsterer	102
165	The critic	104
181	Memories of his childhood	35
192	Characters in a stage-coach	108

vii

CONTENTS.

			PAGE
No.	202	Ambition	111
	208	Flattery as an art	114
	224	On advertisements	117
	249	Adventures of a shilling	120
	254	Frozen words	124
	263	Late hours	127
	264	On long-winded people	130
	266	On the art of growing old	133

ADDISON

From Thackeray's English Humorists ... 137

The Spectator

No.	7	Popular superstitions	149
	9	Clubs	152
	10	The uses of the Spectator	155
	12	Effect of the supernatural on the imagination	158
	15	Dress and show	162
	18	Italian opera	165
	21	Choice of a profession	168
	25	Letter from a valetudinarian	171
	26	Reflections in Westminster Abbey	174
	28	Office for the regulation of signs	177
	34	The club of spectators	180
	35	False wit and humour	183
	37	A lady's library	186
	45	French fashions	190
	49	The coffee-house	193
	69	The Royal Exchange	196
	72	The everlasting club	199
	86	On physiognomy	205
	81	Party patches	202
	90	Adventure of M. Pontignan	208
	102	Exercise of the fan	212

CONTENTS.

		PAGE
No. 105	On pedantry	215
151	The man of pleasure	217
156	A woman's man	221
173	Account of a grinning-match	224
179	Account of a whistling-match	227
195	On temperance	230
198	Character of the salamanders	234
209	Satire on women	237
215	On education	241
251	The cries of London	244
262	The Spectator's success	248
295	Pin-money	251
299	Letter from Sir John Envil	254
317	On waste of time	258
323	A young lady's journal of a week	262
367	Various advantages of the spectators	266
371	Humourous way of sorting companies	268
397	On compassion	272
403	On the death of the King of France	275
435	On female extravagances	278
447	Custom	281
452	On news-writers and readers	284
458	On true and false modesty	288
530	Marriage of Will Honeycomb	291
549	On retirement	293

STERNE AND GOLDSMITH
From Thackeray's English Humorists.................. 297

STERNE
The Story of Le Fever (from the Life and Opinions of Tristram Shandy).. 325
Saunterings in France, Book VII (from the Life and Opinions of Tristram Shandy).. 339

CONTENTS.

GOLDSMITH

Papers from The Citizen of the World: letters from a Chinese philosopher, residing in London, to his friends in the East.

No.		PAGE
1	Introduction	389
2	Arrival of the Chinese philosopher in London. His motives for the journey. Some description of the streets and houses	389
3	The description of London continued. The luxury of the English. Its benefits. The fine gentleman. The fine lady	392
4	English pride. Liberty. An instance of both. Newspapers. Politeness	395
5	English passion for politics. A specimen of a newspaper. Characteristics of the manners of different countries	398
12	The funeral solemnities of the English. Their passion for flattering epitaphs	401
13	An account of Westminster Abbey. (First appearance of the "Man in Black")	404
14	The reception of the philosopher from a lady of distinction	408
21	The philosopher goes to see a play	411
26	The character of the Man in Black; with some instances of his inconsistent conduct	415
27	The history of the Man in Black	418
28	On the great number of old maids and bachelors in London. Some of the causes	423
29	A description of a club of authors	426
30	The proceedings of the club of authors	428
41	The behaviour of the congregation in St. Paul's church at prayers	433
45	The ardour of the people of London in running after sights and monsters	435
46	(The looking-glass of Lao), a dream	439

CONTENTS.

No.		PAGE
51	A bookseller's visit to the Chinese philosopher	443
52	The impossibility of distinguishing men in England by their dress. Two instances of this	446
53	The absurd taste for certain forms of literature	449
54	The character of an important trifler, (Beau Tibbs)	452
55	The character of the trifler continued: with that of his wife, his house, and furniture	455
58	A visitation dinner described	458
64	The great exchange happiness for show. Their folly in this respect of use to society	462
65	The history of a philosophic cobbler	464
71	The shabby Beau, the Man in Black, the Chinese Philosopher, etc., at Vauxhall	466
74	The description of a little great man	470
77	The behaviour of a shopkeeper and his journeyman	473
78	The French ridiculed after their own manner	475
79	The preparations of both theatres, for a winter campaign	477
81	The ladies' trains ridiculed	479
86	The races of Newmarket ridiculed. Description of a cart race	481
88	The ladies advised to get husbands. A story to this purpose	484
90	The English subject to the spleen	487
91	The influence of climate and soil upon the tempers and dispositions of the English	490
96	The condolence and congratulation upon the death of the late king ridiculed. English mourning described	492
98	A description of the courts of justice in Westminster Hall	495
99	A visit from the little Beau. The indulgence with which the fair sex are treated in several parts of Asia	498

CONTENTS.

		PAGE
No. 102	The passion for gaming among ladies ridiculed...	500
105	The intended coronation described..............	501
112	An election described.........................	505
117	A city night-piece...........................	507
119	On the distresses of the poor; exemplified in the life of a private sentinel........................	509
123	The conclusion...............................	513

LIST OF ILLUSTRATIONS
FROM THE WORKS OF
WILLIAM HOGARTH

ILLUSTRATING "THE TATLER"

		FACING PAGE
Marriage à la mode, Plate I		*Frontispiece*
Roast Beef at the Gate of Calais	No. 148	90
The Politician	155	98
The Country Inn Yard	192	108
Modern Midnight Conversation	263	128

ILLUSTRATING "THE SPECTATOR"

Taste in High Life	No. 15	164
Marriage à la mode, Plate IV	45	192
The Rake's Progress, Plate II	151	218
Southwark Fair	173 & 179	226
The Enraged Musician	251	246

ILLUSTRATING "THE CITIZEN OF THE WORLD"

Morning	Letter II	390
Noon	III	394
England, Plate II	IV	396
The Election, Plate II, canvassing for votes	V	400
The Sleeping Congregation	XLI	434
France, Plate I	LXXVIII	476
Marriage à la mode, Plate II	CII	500
The Election, Plate I, the Entertainment	CXII	506

PAPERS FROM

THE TATLER AND THE SPECTATOR

BY SIR RICHARD STEELE AND
JOSEPH ADDISON

WITH INTRODUCTIONS FROM
THACKERAY'S "ENGLISH HUMORISTS"

STEELE

STEELE

FROM THACKERAY'S "ENGLISH HUMORISTS"

WHAT do we look for in studying the history of a past age? Is it to learn the political transactions and characters of the leading public men? is it to make ourselves acquainted with the life and being of the time? If we set out with the former grave purpose, where is the truth, and who believes that he has it entire? What character of what great man is known to you? You can but make guesses as to character more or less happy. In common life don't you often judge and misjudge a man's whole conduct, setting out from a wrong impression? The tone of a voice, a word said in joke, or a trifle in behavior — the cut of his hair or the tie of his neck-cloth may disfigure him in your eyes, or poison your good opinion; or at the end of years of intimacy it may be your closest friend says something, reveals something which had previously been a secret, which alters all your views about him, and shows that he has been acting on quite a different motive to that which you fancied you knew. And if it is so with those you know, how much more with those you don't know? Say, for example, that I want to understand the character of the Duke of Marlborough. I read Swift's history of the times in which he took a part; the shrewdest of observers and initiated, one would think, into the politics of the age — he hints to me that Marlborough was a coward, and even of doubtful military capacity: he speaks of Walpole as a contemptible boor, and scarcely mentions, except to flout it, the great intrigue of the Queen's latter days, which was to have ended in bringing back the Pretender. Again, I read Marlborough's life by a copious archdeacon, who has the command of immense papers, of sonorous language, of what is called the best information; and I get little or no insight into this secret motive which, I believe, influenced the whole of Marlborough's career, which caused his turnings and windings, his opportune fidelity and treason, stopped his army almost at Paris gate, and landed him finally on the Hanoverian side — the winning side: I get, I say, no truth, or only a portion of it, in the narrative of either writer, and believe that Coxe's portrait, or Swift's portrait, is quite unlike the real Churchill. I take this as a single instance, prepared to be as sceptical about any other, and say to the Muse of History, "O venerable daughter of Mnemosyne, I doubt every single statement you ever made since your ladyship was a Muse! For all your grave airs and high pretensions, you are not a whit more trustworthy than some of your lighter sisters on whom your partisans look down. You bid me listen to a general's oration to his soldiers: Nonsense! He no more made it than Turpin made his dying speech at Newgate. You pronounce a panegyric of a hero: I doubt it, and say you flatter outrageously. You utter the condemnation of a loose character: I doubt it, and think you are prejudiced and take the side of the Dons. You offer me an autobiography: I doubt all autobiographies I ever read; except those, perhaps, of Mr. Robinson Crusoe, Mariner, and writers of his class. *These* have no object in setting themselves right with the public or their own consciences; these have no motive for concealment or half-truths; these call for no more confidence than I can cheerfully give, and do not force me to tax my credulity or to fortify it by evidence. I take up a volume of Dr. Smollett, or a volume of the *Spectator*, and say the fiction carries a greater amount of truth in solution than the volume which purports to be all true. Out of the fictitious book I get the expression of the life of the time; of the manners, of the movement, the dress, the pleasures, the laughter, the ridicules of society — the old times live again, and I travel in the old country of England. Can the heaviest historian do more for me?"

As we read in these delightful volumes of the *Tatler* and *Spectator* the past age returns, the England of our ancestors is revivified. The Maypole rises in the Strand again in London; the churches are thronged with daily worshippers; the beaux are gathering in the coffee-houses; the gentry are going to the Drawing-room; the ladies are thronging to the toy-shops; the chairmen are jostling in the streets; the footmen are running with links before the chariots, or fighting round the theatre doors. In the country I see the young Squire riding to Eton with his servants behind him, and Will Wimble, the friend of the family, to see him safe. To make that journey from the Squire's and back, Will is a week on horseback. The coach takes five days between London and Bath. The judges and the bar ride the circuit. If my lady comes to town in her post-chariot, her people carry pistols to fire a salute on Captain Macheath if he should appear, and her couriers ride ahead to prepare apartments for her at the great caravanserais on the road; Boniface receives her under the creaking sign of the "Bell" or the "Ram," and he and his chamberlains bow her up the great stair to the state-apartments, whilst her carriage rumbles into the court-yard, where the "Exeter Fly" is housed that performs the journey in eight days, God willing, having achieved its daily flight of twenty miles, and landed its passengers for supper and sleep. The curate is taking his pipe in the kitchen, where the Captain's man — having hung up his master's half pike — is at his bacon and eggs, bragging of Ramillies and Malplaquet to the town's-folk, who have their club in the chimney-corner. The Captain is ogling the chambermaid in the wooden gallery, or bribing her to know who is the pretty young mistress that has come in the coach. The packhorses are in the great stable, and the drivers and ostlers carousing in the tap. And in Mrs. Landlady's bar, over a glass of strong waters, sits a gentleman of military appearance, who travels with pistols, as all the rest of the world does, and has a rattling gray mare in the stables which will be saddled and away with its owner half an hour before the "Fly" sets out on its last day's flight. And some five miles on the road, as the "Exeter Fly" comes jingling and creaking onwards, it will suddenly be brought to a halt by a gentleman on a gray mare, with a black vizard on his face, who thrusts a long pistol into the coach window, and bids the company to hand out their purses. . . . It must have been no small pleasure even to sit in the great kitchen in those days, and see the tide of humankind pass by. We arrive at places now, but we travel no more. Addison talks jocularly of a difference of manner and costume being quite perceivable at Staines, where there passed a young fellow "with a very tolerable periwig," though, to be sure, his hat was out of fashion, and had a Ramillies cock. I would have liked to travel in those days (being of that class of travellers are who proverbially pretty easy *coram latronibus*) and have seen my friend with the gray mare and the black vizard. Alas! there always came a day in the life of that warrior when it was the fashion to accompany him as he passed — without his black mask, and with a nosegay in his hand, accompanied by halberdiers and attended by the sheriff, — in a carriage without springs, and a clergyman jolting beside him, to a spot close by Cumberland Gate and the Marble Arch, where a stone still records that here Tyburn turnpike stood. What a change in a century; in a few years! Within a few yards of that gate the fields began: the fields of his exploits, behind the hedges of which he lurked and robbed. A great and wealthy city has grown over those meadows. Were a man brought to die there now, the windows would be closed and the inhabitants keep their houses in sickening horror. A hundred years back, people crowded to see that last act of a highwayman's life, and make jokes on it. Swift laughed at him, grimly advising him to provide a Holland shirt and white cap crowned with a crimson or black ribbon for his exit, to mount the cart cheerfully — shake hands with the hangman, and so — farewell. Gay wrote the most delightful ballads, and made merry over the same hero. Contrast these with the writings of our present humorists! Compare those morals and ours — those manners and ours!

We can't tell — you would not bear to be told the whole truth regarding those men and manners. You could no more suffer in a British drawing-room, under the reign of Queen Victoria, a fine gentleman or fine lady of Queen Anne's time, or hear what they heard and said, than you would receive an ancient Briton. It is as one reads about savages, that one contemplates the wild ways, the barbarous feasts, the terrific pastimes, of the men of pleasure of that age. We have our fine gentlemen, and our "fast men"; permit me to give you an idea of one particularly fast nobleman of Queen Anne's days, whose biography has been preserved to us by the law reporters.

In 1691, when Steele was a boy at school, my Lord Mohun was tried by his peers for the murder of William Mountford, comedian. In "Howell's State Trials," the reader will find not only an edifying account of this exceedingly fast nobleman, but of the times and manners of those days. My lord's friend, a Captain Hill, smitten with the charms of the beautiful Mrs. Bracegirdle, and anxious to marry her at all hazards, determined to carry her off, and for this purpose hired a hackney-coach with six horses, and a half-dozen of soldiers, to aid him in the storm. The coach with a pair of horses (the four leaders being in waiting elsewhere) took its station opposite my Lord Craven's house in Drury Lane, by which door Mrs. Bracegirdle was to pass on her way from the theatre. As she passed in company of her mamma and a friend, Mr. Page, the

Captain seized her by the hand, the soldiers hustled Mr. Page and attacked him sword in hand, and Captain Hill and his noble friend endeavored to force Madam Bracegirdle into the coach. Mr. Page called for help: the population of Drury Lane rose: it was impossible to effect the capture; and bidding the soldiers go about their business, and the coach to drive off, Hill let go of his prey sulkily, and waited for other opportunities of revenge. The man of whom he was most jealous was Will Mountford, the comedian; Will removed, he thought Mrs. Bracegirdle might be his: and accordingly the Captain and his lordship lay that night in wait for Will, and as he was coming out of a house in Norfolk Street, while Mohun engaged him in talk, Hill, in the words of the Attorney-General, made a pass and ran him clean through the body.

Sixty-one of my lord's peers finding him not guilty of murder, while but fourteen found him guilty, this very fast nobleman was discharged: and made his appearance seven years after in another trial for murder — when he, my Lord Warwick, and three gentlemen of the military profession, were concerned in the fight which ended in the death of Captain Coote.

This jolly company were drinking together at "Lockit's" in Charing Cross, when angry words arose between Captain Coote and Captain French; whom my Lord Mohun and my Lord the Earl of Warwick and Holland endeavored to pacify. My Lord Warwick was a dear friend of Captain Coote, lent him a hundred pounds to buy his commission in the Guards; once when the captain was arrested for 13$l.$ by his tailor, my lord lent him five guineas, often paid his reckoning for him, and showed him other offices of friendship. On this evening the disputants, French and Coote, being separated whilst they were upstairs, unluckily stopped to drink ale again at the bar of "Lockit's." The row began afresh — Coote lunged at French over the bar, and at last all six called for chairs, and went to Leicester Fields, where they fell to. Their lordships engaged on the side of Captain Coote. My Lord of Warwick was severely wounded in the hand, Mr. French also was stabbed, but honest Captain Coote got a couple of wounds — one especially, "a wound in the left side just under the short ribs, and piercing through the diaphragma," which did for Captain Coote. Hence the trials of my Lords Warwick and Mohun: hence the assemblage of peers, the report of the transaction, in which these defunct fast men still live for the observation of the curious. My

STEELE

Lord of Warwick is brought to the bar by the Deputy Governor of the Tower of London, having the axe carried before him by the gentleman gaoler, who stood with it at the bar at the right hand of the prisoner, turning the edge from him; the prisoner, at his approach, making three bows, one to his Grace the Lord High Steward, the other to the peers on each hand; and his Grace and the peers return the salute. And besides these great personages, august in periwigs, and nodding to the right and left, a host of the small come up out of the past and pass before us — the jolly captains brawling in the tavern, and laughing and cursing over their cups — the drawer that serves, the bar-girl that waits, the bailiff on the prowl, the chairmen trudging through the black lampless streets, and smoking their pipes by the railings, whilst swords are clashing in the garden within. "Help there! a gentleman is hurt!" The chairmen put up their pipes, and help the gentleman over the railings, and carry him, ghastly and bleeding, to the Bagnio in Long Acre, where they knock up the surgeon — a pretty tall gentleman: but that wound under the short ribs has done for him. Surgeon, lords, captains, bailiffs, chairmen, and gentleman gaoler with your axe, where be you now? The gentleman axeman's head is off his own shoulders; the lords and judges can wag theirs no longer; the bailiff's writs have ceased to run; the honest chairmen's pipes are put out, and with their brawny calves they have walked away into Hades — all as irrecoverably done for as Will Mountford or Captain Coote. The subject of our night's lecture saw all these people — rode in Captain Coote's company of the Guards very probably — wrote and sighed for Bracegirdle, went home tipsy in many a chair, after many a bottle, in many a tavern — fled from many a bailiff.

In 1709, when the publication of the *Tatler* began, our great-great-grandfathers must have seized upon that new and delightful paper with much such eagerness as lovers of light literature in a later day exhibited when the Waverley novels appeared, upon which the public rushed, forsaking that feeble entertainment of which the Miss Porters, the Anne of Swanseas, and worthy Mrs. Radcliffe herself, with her dreary castles and exploded old ghosts, had had pretty much the monopoly. I have looked over many of the comic books with which our ancestors amused themselves, from the novels of Swift's coadjutrix, Mrs. Manley, the delectable author of the "New Atlantis," to the facetious productions of Tom

Durfey, and Tom Brown, and Ned Ward, writer of the "London Spy" and several other volumes of ribaldry. The slang of the taverns and ordinaries, the wit of the Bagnios, form the strongest part of the farrago of which these libels are composed. In the excellent newspaper collection at the British Museum, you may see besides, the *Craftsman* and *Postboy* specimens, and queer specimens they are, of the higher literature of Queen Anne's time. Here is an abstract from a notable journal bearing date, Wednesday, October 13th, 1708, and entitled "*The British Apollo; or, curious amusements for the ingenious, by a society of gentlemen.*" The *British Apollo* invited and professed to answer questions upon all subjects of wit, morality, science, and even religion; and two out of its four pages are filled with queries and replies much like some of the oracular penny prints of the present time.

One of the first querists, referring to the passage that a bishop should be the husband of one wife, argues that polygamy is justifiable in the laity. The society of gentlemen conducting the *British Apollo* are posed by this casuist, and promise to give him an answer. Celinda then wishes to know from "the gentlemen," concerning the souls of the dead, whether they shall have the satisfaction to know those whom they most valued in this transitory life. The gentlemen of the *Apollo* give but cold comfort to poor Celinda. They are inclined to think not: for, say they, since every inhabitant of those regions will be infinitely dearer than here are our nearest relatives — what have we to do with a partial friendship in that happy place? Poor Celinda! it may have been a child or a lover whom she had lost, and was pining after, when the oracle of *British Apollo* gave her this dismal answer. She has solved the question for herself by this time, and knows quite as well as the society of gentlemen.

From theology we come to physics, and Q. asks, "Why does hot water freeze sooner than cold?" *Apollo* replies, "Hot water cannot be said to freeze sooner than cold; but water once heated and cold, may be subject to freeze by the evaporation of the spirituous parts of the water, which renders it less able to withsand the power of frosty weather."

The next query is rather a delicate one. "You, Mr. Apollo, who are said to be the God of wisdom, pray give us the reason why kissing is so much in fashion: what benefit one receives by it, and who was the inventor, and you will oblige Corinna." To this

STEELE

queer demand the lips of Phœbus, smiling, answer: "Pretty innocent Corinna! *Apollo* owns that he was a little surprised by your kissing question, particularly at that part of it where you desire to know the benefit you receive by it. Ah! madam, had you a lover, you would not come to *Apollo* for a solution; since there is no dispute but the kisses of mutual lovers give infinite satisfaction. As to its invention, 'tis certain nature was its author, and it began with the first courtship."

After a column more of questions, follow nearly two pages of poems, signed by Philander, Armenia, and the like, and chiefly on the tender passion; and the paper wound up with a letter from Leghorn, an account of the Duke of Marlborough and Prince Eugene before Lille, and proposals for publishing two sheets on the present state of Æthiopia, by Mr. Hill: all of which is printed for the authors by J. Mayo, at the Printing Press against Water Lane in Fleet Street. What a change it must have been — how *Apollo's* cracles must have been struck dumb, when the *Tatler* appeared, and scholars, gentlemen, men of the world, men of genius, began to speak!

Shortly before the Boyne was fought, and young Swift had begun to make acquaintance with English court manners and English servitude, in Sir William Temple's family, another Irish youth was brought to learn his humanities at the old school of Charterhouse, near Smithfield; to which foundation he had been appointed by James Duke of Ormond, a governor of the House, and a patron of the lad's family. The boy was an orphan, and described, twenty years after, with a sweet pathos and simplicity, some of the earliest recollections of a life which was destined to be chequered by a strange variety of good and evil fortune.

I am afraid no good report could be given by his masters and ushers of that thick-set, square-faced, black-eyed, soft-hearted little Irish boy. He was very idle. He was whipped deservedly a great number of times. Though he had very good parts of his own, he got other boys to do his lessons for him, and only took just as much trouble as should enable him to scuffle through his exercises, and by good fortune escape the flogging-block. One hundred and fifty years after, I have myself inspected, but only as an amateur, that instrument of righteous torture still existing, and in occasional use, in a secluded private apartment of the old Charterhouse School; and have no doubt it is the very counterpart, if not the

STEELE

ancient and interesting machine itself, at which poor Dick Steele submitted himself to the tormentors.

Besides being very kind, lazy, and good-natured, this boy went invariably into debt with the tart-woman; ran out of bounds, and entered into pecuniary, or other promissory, engagements with the neighboring lollipop-venders and piemen — exhibited an early fondness and capacity for drinking mum and sack, and borrowed from all his comrades who had money to lend. I have no sort of authority for the statements here made of Steele's early life; but if the child is father of the man, the father of young Steele of Merton, who left Oxford without taking a degree, and entered the Life Guards — the father of Captain Steele of Lucas's Fusiliers, who got his company through the patronage of my Lord Cutts — the father of Mr. Steele the Commissioner of Stamps, the editor of the *Gazette*, the *Tatler*, and *Spectator*, the expelled Member of Parliament, and the author of the "Tender Husband" and the "Conscious Lovers"; if man and boy resembled each other, Dick Steele the schoolboy must have been one of the most generous, good-for-nothing, amiable little creatures that ever conjugated the verb *tupto*, I beat, *tuptomai*, I am whipped, in any school in Great Britain.

Almost every gentleman who does me the honor to hear me will remember that the very greatest character which he has seen in the course of his life, and the person to whom he has looked up with the greatest wonder and reverence, was the head boy at his school. The schoolmaster himself hardly inspires such an awe. The head boy construes as well as the schoolmaster himself. When he begins to speak the hall is hushed, and every little boy listens. He writes off copies of Latin verses as melodiously as Virgil. He is good-natured, and, his own masterpieces achieved, pours out other copies of verses for other boys with an astonishing ease and fluency; the idle ones only trembling lest they should be discovered on giving in their exercises, and whipped because their poems were too good. I have seen great men in my time, but never such a great one as that head boy of my childhood: we all thought he must be Prime Minister, and I was disappointed on meeting him in after life to find he was no more than six feet high.

Dick Steele, the Charterhouse gownboy, contracted such an admiration in the years of his childhood, and retained it faithfully through his life. Through the school and through the world, whithersoever his strange fortune led this erring, wayward, affectionate creature, Joseph Addison was always his head boy. Addison wrote his exercises. Addison did his best themes. He ran Addison's messages: fagged for him and blacked his shoes: to be in Joe's company was Dick's greatest pleasure; and he took a sermon or a caning from his monitor with the most boundless reverence, acquiescence, and affection.

Steele found Addison a stately college Don at Oxford, and himself did not make much figure at this place. He wrote a comedy, which, by the advice of a friend, the humble fellow burned there; and some verses, which I dare say are as sublime as other gentlemen's composition at that age; but being smitten with a sudden love for military glory, he threw up the cap and gown for the saddle and bridle, and rode privately in the Horse Guards, in the Duke of Ormond's troop — the second — and probably, with the rest of the gentlemen of his troop, "all mounted on black horses with white feathers in their hats, and scarlet coats richly laced," marched by King William, in Hyde Park, in November, 1699, and a great show of the nobility, besides twenty thousand people, and above a thousand coaches. "The Guards had just got their new clothes," the *London Post* said: "they are extraordinary grand, and thought to be the finest body of horse in the world." But Steele could hardly have seen any actual service. He who wrote about himself, his mother, his wife, his loves, his debts, his friends, and the wine he drank, would have told us of his battles if he had seen any. His old patron, Ormond, probably got him his cornetcy in the Guards, from which he was promoted to be a captain in Lucas's Fusiliers, getting his company through the patronage of Lord Cutts, whose secretary he was, and to whom he dedicated his work called the "Christian Hero." As for Dick, whilst writing this ardent devotional work, he was deep in debt, in drink, and in all the follies of the town; it is related that all the officers of Lucas's, and the gentlemen of the Guards, laughed at Dick. And in truth a theologian in liquor is not a respectable object, and a hermit, though he may be out at elbows, must not be in debt to the tailor. Steele says of himself that he was always sinning and repenting. He beat his breast and cried most piteously when he *did* repent: but as soon as crying had made him thirsty, he fell to sinning again. In that charming paper in the *Tatler*, in which he records his father's death, his mother's griefs, his own most solemn and tender emotions, he says he is interrupted by the arrival of a hamper of wine, "the same as is to be sold at Garraway's, next week"; upon the receipt of which he sends for three friends, and they fall to instantly, "drinking two bottles apiece, with great benefit to themselves, and not separating till two o'clock in the morning."

His life was so. Jack the drawer was always interrupting it, bringing him a bottle from the "Rose," or inviting him over to a bout there with Sir Plume and Mr. Diver; and Dick wiped his eyes, which were whimpering over his papers, took down his laced hat, put on his sword and wig, kissed his wife and children, told them a lie about pressing business, and went off to the "Rose" to the jolly fellows.

While Mr. Addison was abroad, and after he came home in rather a dismal way to wait upon Providence in his shabby lodging in the Haymarket, young Captain Steele was cutting a much smarter figure than that of his classical friend of Charterhouse Cloister and Maudlin Walk. Could not some painter give an interview between the gallant captain of Lucas's, with his hat cocked, and his lace, and his face too, a trifle tarnished with drink, and that poet, that philosopher, pale, proud, and poor, his friend and monitor of school-days, of all days? How Dick must have bragged about his chances and his hopes, and the fine company he kept, and the charms of the reigning toasts and popular actresses, and the number of bottles that he and my lord and some other pretty fellows had cracked over-night at the "Devil," or the "Garter!" Cannot one fancy Joseph Addison's calm smile and cold gray eyes following Dick for an instant, as he struts down the Mall, to dine with the Guard at St. James's, before he turns with his sober pace and threadbare suit, to walk back to his lodgings up the two pair of stairs? Steele's name was down for promotion, Dick always said himself, in the glorious, pious, and immortal William's last table-book. Jonathan Swift's name had been written there by the same hand too.

Our worthy friend, the author of the "Christian Hero," continued to make no small figure about town by the use of his wits. He was appointed Gazetteer: he wrote, in 1703, "The Tender Husband," his second play, in which there is some delightful farcical writing, and of which he fondly owned in after-life, and when Addison was no more, that there were "many applauded strokes" from Addison's beloved hand. Is it not a pleasant part-

STEELE

nership to remember? Can't one fancy Steele full of spirits and youth, leaving his gay company to go to Addison's lodging, where his friend sits in the shabby sitting-room, quite serene, and cheerful, and poor? In 1704, Steele came on the town with another comedy, and behold it was so moral and religious, as poor Dick insisted, — so dull the town thought, — that the "Lying Lover" was damned.

Addison's hour of success now came, and he was able to help our friend the "Christian Hero" in such a way, that, if there had been any chance of keeping that poor tipsy champion upon his legs, his fortune was safe, and his competence assured. Steele procured the place of Commissioner of Stamps: he wrote so richly, so gracefully often, so kindly always, with such a pleasant wit and easy frankness, with such a gush of good spirits and good humor, that his early papers may be compared to Addison's own, and are to be read, by a male reader at least, with quite an equal pleasure.

After the *Tatler* in 1711, the famous *Spectator* made its appearance, and this was followed, at various intervals, by many periodicals under the same editor — the *Guardian* — the *Englishman* — the *Lover*, whose love was rather insipid — the *Reader*, of whom the public saw no more after his second appearance — the *Theatre*, under the pseudonym of Sir John Edgar, which Steele wrote while Governor of the Royal Company of Comedians, to which post, and to that of Surveyor of the Royal Stables at Hampton Court, and to the Commission of the Peace for Middlesex, and to the honor of knighthood, Steele had been preferred soon after the accession of George I.; whose cause honest Dick had nobly fought, through disgrace, and danger, against the most formidable enemies, against traitors and bullies, against Bolingbroke and Swift in the last reign. With the arrival of the King, that splendid conspiracy broke up; and a golden opportunity came to Dick Steele, whose hand, alas, was too careless to gripe it.

Steele married twice; and outlived his places, his schemes, his wife, his income, his health, and almost everything but his kind heart. That ceased to trouble him in 1729, when he died, worn out and almost forgotten by his contemporaries, in Wales, where he had the remnant of a property.

Posterity has been kinder to this amiable creature; all women especially are bound to be grateful to Steele, as he was the first of our writers who really seemed to admire and respect them. Congreve the Great, who alludes to the low estimation in which women were held in Elizabeth's time, as a reason why the women of Shakspeare make so small a figure in the poet's dialogues, though he can himself pay splendid compliments to women, yet looks on them as mere instruments of gallantry, and destined, like the most consummate fortifications, to fall, after a certain time, before the arts and bravery of the besieger, man. There is a letter of Swift's, entitled "Advice to a very Young Married Lady," which shows the Dean's opinion of the female society of his day, and that if he despised man he utterly scorned women to. No lady of our time could be treated by any man, were he ever so much a wit or Dean, in such a tone of insolent patronage and vulgar protection. In this performance, Swift hardly take pains to hide his opinion that a woman is a fool: tells her to read books, as if reading was a novel accomplishment; and informs her that "not one gentleman's daughter in a thousand has been brought to read or understand her own natural tongue." Addison laughs at women equally; but, with the gentleness and politeness of his nature, smiles at them and watches them, as if they were harmless, half-witted, amusing, pretty creatures, only made to be man's playthings. It was Steele who first began to pay a manly homage to their goodness and understanding, as well as to their tenderness and beauty. In his comedies, the heroes do not rant and rave about the divine beauties of Gloriana or Statira, as the characters were made to do in the chivalry romances and the high-flown dramas just going out of vogue; but Steele admires women's virtue, acknowledges their sense, and adores their purity and beauty, with an ardor and strength which should win the good-will of all women to their hearty and respectful champion. It is this ardor, this respect, this manliness, which makes his comedies so pleasant and their heroes such fine gentlemen. He paid the finest compliment to a woman that perhaps ever was offered. Of one woman, whom Congreve had also admired and celebrated, Steele says, that "to have loved her was a liberal education." "How often," he says, dedicating a volume to his wife, "how often has your tenderness removed pain from my sick head, how often anguish from my afflicted heart! If there are such beings as guardian angels, they are thus employed. I cannot believe one of them to be more good in inclination, or more more charming in form than my wife." His breast seems to warm and his eyes to kindle when he meets with a good and beautiful woman, and it is with his heart as well as with his hat that he salutes her. About children, and all that relates to home, he is not less tender, and more than once speaks in apology of what he calls his softness. He would have been nothing without that delightful weakness. It is that which gives his works their worth and his style its charm. It, like his life, is full of faults and careless blunders; and redeemed, like that, by his sweet and compassionate nature.

We possess of poor Steele's wild and chequered life some of the most curious memoranda that ever were left of a man's biography.*

* The Correspondence of Steele passed after his death into the possession of his daughter Elizabeth, by his second wife, Miss Scurlock, of Carmarthenshire. She married the Hon. John, afterwards third Lord Trevor. At her death, part of the letters passed to Mr. Thomas, a grandson of a natural daughter of Steele's; and part to Lady Trevor's next of kin, Mr. Scurlock. They were published by the learned Nichols — from whose later edition of them, in 1809, our specimens are quoted.

Here we have him, in his courtship — which was not a very long one: —

"To Mrs. Scurlock.

"Aug. 30, 1707.

"Madam, — I beg pardon that my paper is not finer, but I am forced to write from a coffee-house, where I am attending about business. There is a dirty crowd of busy faces all around me, talking of money; while all my ambition, all my wealth, is love! Love which animates my heart, sweetens my humor, enlarges my soul, and affects every action of my life. It is to my lovely charmer I owe, that many noble ideas are continually affixed to my words and actions; it is the natural effect of that generous passion to create in the admirer some similitude of the object admired. Thus, my dear, am I every day to improve from so sweet a companion. Look up, my fair one, to that Heaven which made thee such; and join with me to implore its influence on our tender innocent hours, and beseech the Author of love to bless the rites He has ordained — and mingle with our happiness a just sense of our transient condition, and a resignation to His will, which only can regulate our minds to a steady endeavour to please Him and each other.

"I am for ever your faithful servant,

"Rich. Steele."

Some few hours afterwards, apparently, Mistress Scurlock received the next one — obviously written later in the day: —

"Saturday night (Aug. 30, 1707).

"Dear, Lovely Mrs. Scurlock, — I have been in very good company, where your health, under the character of *the woman I loved best*, has been

STEELE

Most men's letters, from Cicero down to Walpole, or down to the great men of our own time, if you will, are doctored compositions, and written with an eye suspicious towards posterity. That dedication of Steele's to his wife is an artificial performance, possibly; at least, it is written with that degree of artifice which an orator uses in arranging a statement for the House, or a poet employs in preparing a sentiment in verse or for the stage. But there are some 400 letters of Dick Steele's to his wife, which that thrifty woman preserved accurately, and which could have been written but for her and her alone. They contain details of the business, pleasures, quarrels, reconciliations of the pair; they have all the

often drunk; so that I may say that I am dead drunk for your sake; which is more than *I die for you.*

RICH. STEELE."

"To MRS. SCURLOCK.
"Sept. 1, 1707.

"MADAM, — It is the hardest thing in the world to be in love, and yet attend business. As for me, all who speak to me find me out, and I must lock myself up, or other people will do it for me.

"A gentleman asked me this morning, 'What news from Lisbon?' and I answered, 'She is exquisitely handsome.' Another desired to know 'when I had last been at Hampton Court?' I replied, 'It will be on Tuesday come se'nnight.' Pr'ythee allow me at least to kiss your hand before that day, that my mind may be in some composure. O Love!

'A thousand torments dwell about thee,
Yet who could live, to live without thee?'

"Methinks I could write a volume to you; but all the language on earth would fail in saying how much, and with what disinterested passion,

"I am ever yours,
"RICH. STEELE."

Two days after this, he is found expounding his circumstances and prospects to the young lady's mamma. He dates from "Lord Sunderland's office, Whitehall"; and states his clear income at 1,025*l.* per annum. "I promise myself," says he, "the pleasure of an industrious and virtuous life, in studying to do things agreeable to you."

They were married, according to the most probable conjectures, about the 7th Sept. There are traces of a tiff about the middle of the next month; she being prudish and fidgety, as he was impassioned and reckless. General progress, however, may be seen from the following notes. The "house in Bury Street, St. James's" was now taken.

"To MRS. STEELE.
"Oct. 16, 1707.

"DEAREST BEING ON EARTH, — Pardon me if you do not see me till eleven genuineness of conversations; they are as artless as a child's prattle, and as confidential as a curtain-lecture. Some are written from the printing-office, where he is waiting for the proof-sheets of his *Gazette*, or his *Tatler;* some are written from the tavern, whence he promises to come to his wife "within a pint of wine," and where he has given a rendezvous to a friend, or a money-lender: some are composed in a high state of vinous excitement, when his head is flustered with burgundy, and his heart abounds with amorous warmth for his darling Prue: some are under the influence of the dismal headache and repentance next morning: some, alas, are from the lock-up house, where the lawyers have impounded him,

o'clock, having met a school-fellow from India, by whom I am to be informed on things this night which expressly concern your obedient husband,

RICH. STEELE."

"To MRS. STEELE.

"Eight o'clock, FOUNTAIN TAVERN,
Oct. 22, 1707.

"MY DEAR, — I beg of you not to be uneasy; for I have done a great deal of business to-day very successfully, and wait an hour or two about my *Gazette*."

"Dec. 22, 1707.

"MY DEAR, DEAR WIFE, — I write to let you know I do not come home to dinner, being obliged to attend some business abroad, of which I shall give you an account (when I see you in the evening), as becomes your dutiful and obedient husband."

"DEVIL TAVERN, TEMPLE BAR,
Jan. 3, 1707-8.

"DEAR PRUE, — I have partly succeeded in my business to-day, and inclose two guineas as earnest of more. Dear Prue, I cannot come home to dinner. I languish for your welfare, and will never be a moment careless more. Your faithful husband," &c.

"Jan. 14, 1707-8.

"DEAR WIFE, — Mr. Edgecombe, Ned Ask, and Mr. Lumley have desired me to sit an hour with them at the 'George,' in Pall Mall, for which I desire your patience till twelve o'clock, and that you will go to bed," &c.

"GRAY'S INN, Feb. 3, 1708.

"DEAR PRUE, — If the man who has my shoemaker's bill calls, let him be answered that I shall call on him as I come home. I stay here in order to and where he is waiting for bail. You trace many years of the poor fellow's career in these letters. In September, 1707, from which day she began to save the letters, he married the beautiful Mistress Scurlock. You have his passionate protestations to the lady; his respectful proposals to her mamma; his private prayer to Heaven when the union so ardently desired was completed; his fond professions of contrition and promises of amendment, when, immediately after his marriage there began to be just cause for the one and need for the other.

Captain Steele took a house for his lady upon their marriage, "the third door from Germain Street, left hand of Berry Street,"

get Jonson to discount a bill for me, and shall dine with him for that end. He is expected at home every minute.

"Your most humble, obedient servant," &c.

"TENNIS-COURT, COFFEE-HOUSE, May 5, 1708.

"DEAR WIFE, — I hope I have done this day what will be pleasing to you; in the meantime shall lie this night at a baker's, one Leg, over against the 'Devil Tavern,' at Charing Cross. I shall be able to confront the fools who wish me uneasy, and shall have the satisfaction to see thee cheerful and at ease.

"If the printer's boy be at home, send him hither; and let Mrs. Todd send by the boy my night-gown, slippers, and clean linen. You shall hear from me early in the morning," &c.

Dozens of similar letters follow, with occasional guineas, little parcels of tea, or walnuts, &c. In 1709 the *Tatler* made its appearance. The following curious note dates April 7th, 1710: —

"I inclose to you ['Dear Prue'] a receipt for the saucepan and spoon, and a note of 23*l.* of Lewis's, which will make up the 50*l.* I promised for your ensuing occasions.

"I know no happiness in this life in any degree comparable to the pleasure I have in your person and society. I only beg of you to add to your other charms a fearfulness to see a man that loves you in pain and uneasiness, to make me as happy as it is possible to be in this life. Rising a little in a morning, and being disposed to a cheerfulness . . . . would not be amiss."

In another, he is found excusing his coming home, being "invited to supper to Mr. Boyle's." "Dear Prue," he says on this occasion, "do not send after me, for I shall be ridiculous."

and the next year he presented his wife with a country-house at Hampton. It appears she had a chariot and pair, and sometimes four horses: he himself enjoyed a little horse for his own riding. He paid, or promised to pay, his barber fifty pounds a year, and always went abroad in a laced coat and a large black buckled periwig, that must have cost somebody fifty guineas. He was rather a well-to-do gentleman, Captain Steele, with the proceeds of his estates in Barbadoes (left to him by his first wife), his income as a writer of the *Gazette*, and his office of gentleman waiter to his Royal Highness Prince George. His second wife brought him a fortune too. But it is melancholy to relate, that with these houses and chariots and horses and income, the Captain was constantly in want of money, for which his beloved bride was asking as constantly. In the course of a few pages we begin to find the shoemaker calling for money, and some directions from the Captain, who has not thirty pounds to spare. He sends his wife," the beautifullest object in the world," as he calls her, and evidently in reply to applications of her own, which have gone the way of all waste paper, and lighted Dick's pipes, which were smoked a hundred and forty years ago — he sends his wife now a guinea, then a half-guinea, then a couple of guineas, then half a pound of tea; and again no money and no tea at all, but a promise that his darling Prue shall have some in a day or two: or a request, perhaps, that she will send over his night-gown and shaving-plate to the temporary lodging where the nomadic Captain is lying, hidden from the bailiffs. Oh! that a Christian hero and late Captain in Lucas's should be afraid of a dirty sheriff's officer! That the pink and pride of chivalry should turn pale before a writ! It stands to record in poor Dick's own handwriting — the queer collection is preserved at the British Museum to this present day — that the rent of the nuptial house in Jermyn Street, sacred to unutterable tenderness and Prue, and three doors from Bury Street, was not paid until after the landlord had put in an execution on Captain Steele's furniture. Addison sold the house and furniture at Hampton, and, after deducting the sum in which his incorrigible friend was indebted to him, handed over the residue of the proceeds of the sale to poor Dick, who wasn't in the least angry at Addison's summary proceeding, and I dare say was very glad of any sale or execution, the result of which was to give him a little ready money. Having a small house in Jermyn Street for which he couldn't pay, and a country-

STEELE

house at Hampton on which he had borrowed money, nothing must content Captain Dick but the taking, in 1712, a much finer, larger, and grander house, in Bloomsbury Square; where his unhappy landlord got no better satisfaction than his friend in St. James's, and where it is recorded that Dick, giving a grand entertainment, had a half-dozen queer-looking fellows in livery to wait upon his noble guests, and confessed that his servants were bailiffs to a man. "I fared like a distressed prince," the kindly prodigal writes, generously complimenting Addison for his assistance in the *Tatler*,—"I fared like a distressed prince, who calls in a powerful neighbor to his aid. I was undone by my auxiliary; when I had once called him in, I could not subsist without dependence on him." Poor, needy Prince of Bloomsbury! think of him in his palace, with his allies from Chancery Lane ominously guarding him.

All sorts of stories are told indicative of his recklessness and his good humor. One narrated by Dr. Hoadly is exceedingly characteristic; it shows the life of the time: and our poor friend very weak, but very kind both in and out of his cups.

"My father," says Dr. John Hoadly, the Bishop's son, "when Bishop of Bangor, was, by invitation, present at one of the Whig meetings, held at the 'Trumpet,' in Shire Lane, when Sir Richard, in his zeal, rather exposed himself, having the double duty of the day upon him, as well to celebrate the immortal memory of King William, it being the 4th November, as to drink his friend Addison up to conversation pitch, whose phlegmatic constitution was hardly warmed for society by that time. Steele was not fit for it. Two remarkable circumstances happened. John Sly, the hatter of facetious memory, was in the house; and John, pretty mellow, took it into his head to come into the company on his knees, with a tankard of ale in his hand to drink off to the *immortal memory*, and to return in the same manner. Steele, sitting next my father, whispered him — *Do laugh. It is humanity to laugh.* Sir Richard, in the evening, being too much in the same condition, was put into a chair, and sent home. Nothing would serve him but being carried to the Bishop of Bangor's, late as it was. However, the chairmen carried him home, and got him up stairs, when his great complaisance would wait on them down stairs, which he did, and then was got quietly to bed."

There is another amusing story which, I believe, that renowned collector, Mr. Joseph Miller, or his successors, have incorporated

STEELE

into their work. Sir Richard Steele, at a time when he was much occupied with theatrical affairs, built himself a pretty private theatre, and, before it was opened to his friends and guests, was anxious to try whether the hall was well adapted for hearing. Accordingly he placed himself in the most remote part of the gallery, and begged the carpenter who had built the house to speak up from the stage. The man at first said that he was unaccustomed to public speaking, and did not know what to say to his honor; but the good-natured knight called out to him to say whatever was uppermost; and, after a moment, the carpenter began, in a voice perfectly audible: "Sir Richard Steele!" he said, "for three months past me and my men has been a working in this theatre, and we've never seen the color of your honor's money: we will be very much obliged if you'll pay it directly, for until you do we won't drive in another nail." Sir Richard said that his friend's elocution was perfect, but that he didn't like his subject much.

The great charm of Steele's writing is its naturalness. He wrote so quickly and carelessly, that he was forced to make the reader his confidant, and had not the time to deceive him. He had a small share of book-learning, but a vast acquaintance with the world. He had known men and taverns. He had lived with gownsmen, with troopers, with gentlemen ushers of the Court, with men and women of fashion; with authors and wits, with the inmates of the spunging-houses, and with the frequenters of all the clubs and coffee-houses in the town. He was liked in all company because he liked it; and you like to see his enjoyment as you like to see the glee of a boxful of children at the pantomime. He was not of those lonely ones of the earth whose greatness obliged them to be solitary; on the contrary, he admired, I think, more than any man who ever wrote; and full of hearty applause and sympathy, wins upon you by calling you to share his delight and good humor. His laugh rings through the whole house. He must have been invaluable at a tragedy, and have cried as much as the most tender young lady in the boxes. He has a relish for beauty and goodness wherever he meets it. He admired Shakspeare affectionately, and more than any man of his time; and, according to his generous expansive nature, called upon all his company to like what he liked himself. He did not damn with faint praise: he was in the world and of it; and his enjoyment of life presents the strangest contrast to Swift's savage indignation and Addison's lonely serenity.* Permit me to read to you a passage from each writer, curiously indicative of his

* Here we have some of his later letters: —
"To LADY STEELE.
"HAMPTON COURT, March 16, 1716–17.
"DEAR PRUE, — If you have written anything to me which I should have received last night, I beg your pardon that I cannot answer till the next post . . . . Your son at the present writing is mighty well employed in tumbling on the floor of the room and sweeping the sand with a feather. He grows a most delightful child, and very full of play and spirit. He is also a very great scholar: he can read his primer; and I have brought down my Virgil. He makes most shrewd remarks about the pictures. We are very intimate friends and playfellows. He begins to be very ragged; and I hope I shall be pardoned if I equip him with new clothes and frocks, or what Mrs. Evans and I shall think for his service."

"To LADY STEELE.
[UNDATED.]
"You tell me you want a little flattery from me. I assure you I know no one who deserves so much commendation as yourself, and to whom saying the best things would be so little like flattery. The thing speaks for itself, considering you as a very handsome woman that loves retirement — one who does not want wit, and yet is extremely sincere; and so I could go through all the vices which attend the good qualities of other people, of which you are exempt. But, indeed, though you have every perfection, you have an extravagant fault, which almost frustrates the good in you to me; and that is, that you do not love to dress, to appear, to shine out, even at my request, and to make me proud of you, or rather to indulge the pride I have that you are mine. . . .
"Your most affectionate, obsequious husband,
"RICHARD STEELE.
"A quarter of Molly's schooling is paid. The children are perfectly well."

"To LADY STEELE.
"March 26, 1717.
"MY DEAREST PRUE, — I have received yours, wherein you give me the sensible affliction of telling me enow of the continual pain in your head. . . . . When I lay in your place, and on your pillow, I assure you I fell into tears last night, to think that my charming little insolent might be then awake and in pain; and took it to be a sin to go to sleep.
"For this tender passion towards you, I must be contented that your *Prueship* will condescend to call yourself my well-wisher. . . . . "

At the time when the above later letters were written, Lady Steele was in Wales, looking after her estate there Steele, about this time, was much occupied with a project for conveying fish alive, by which, as he constantly assures his wife, he firmly believed he should make his fortune. It did not succeed, however.

Lady Steele died in December of the succeeding year. She lies buried in Westminster Abbey.

peculiar humor: the subject is the same, and the mood the very gravest. We have said that upon all the actions of man, the most trifling and the most solemn, the humorist takes upon himself to comment. All readers of our old masters know the terrible lines of Swift, in which he hints at his philosophy and describes the end of mankind: —

> " Amazed, confused, its fate unknown,
> The world stood trembling at Jove's throne;
> While each pale sinner hung his head,
> Jove, nodding, shook the heavens and said:
> 'Offending race of human kind,
> By nature, reason, learning, blind;
> You who through frailty stepped aside,
> And you who never err'd through pride;
> You who in different sects were shamm'd,
> And come to see each other damn'd;
> (So some folk told you, but they knew
> No more of Jove's designs than you;)
> The world's mad business now is o'er,
> And I resent your freaks no more;
> *I* to such blockheads set my wit,
> I damn such fools — go, go, you're bit!'"

Addison, speaking on the very same theme, but with how different a voice, says, in his famous paper on Westminster Abbey (*Spectator*, No. 26): — "For my own part, though I am always serious, I do not know what it is to be melancholy, and can therefore take a view of nature in her deep and solemn scenes with the same pleasure as in her most gay and delightful ones. When I look upon the tombs of the great, every emotion of envy dies within me; when I read the epitaphs of the beautiful, every inordinate desire goes out; when I meet with the grief of parents on a tombstone, my heart melts with compassion; when I see the tomb of the parents themselves, I consider the vanity of grieving for those we must quickly follow." (I have owned that I do not think Addison's heart melted very much, or that he indulged very inordinately in the "vanity of grieving.") "When," he goes on, "when I see kings lying by those who deposed them: when I consider rival wits placed side by side, or the holy men that divided the world with their contests and disputes, — I reflect with sorrow and astonishment on the little competitions, factions, and debates of mankind. And, when I read the several dates on the tombs of some that died yesterday and some 600 years ago, I consider that Great Day when we shall all of us be contemporaries, and make our appearance together."

Our third humorist comes to speak upon the same subject. You will have observed in the previous extracts the characteristic humor of each writer — the subject and the contrast — the fact of Death, and the play of individual thought, by which each comments on it, and now hear the third writer — death, sorrow, and the grave being for the moment also his theme. "The first sense of sorrow I ever knew," Steele says in the *Tatler*, "was upon the death of my father, at which time I was not quite five years of age: but was rather amazed at what all the house meant, than possessed of a real understanding why nobody would play with us. I remember I went into the room where his body lay, and my mother sat weeping alone by it. I had my battledore in my hand, and fell a beating the coffin, and calling papa; for, I know not how, I had some idea that he was locked up there. My mother caught me in her arms, and, transported beyond all patience of the silent grief she was before in, she almost smothered me in her embraces, and told me in a flood of tears, 'Papa could not hear me, and would play with me no more: for they were going to put him under ground, whence he would never come to us again.' She was a very beautiful woman, of a noble spirit, and there was a dignity in her grief amidst all the wildness of her transport, which methought struck me with an instinct of sorrow that, before I was sensible what it was to grieve, seized my very soul, and has made pity the weakness of my heart ever since."

Can there be three more characteristic moods of minds and men? "Fools, do you know anything of this mystery?" says Swift, stamping on a grave, and carrying his scorn for mankind actually beyond it. "Miserable, purblind wretches, how dare you to pretend to comprehend the Inscrutable, and how can your dim eyes pierce the unfathomable depths of yonder boundless heaven?" Addison, in a much kinder language and gentler voice, utters much the same sentiment: and speaks of the rivalry of wits, and the contests of holy men, with the same sceptic placidity. "Look what a little vain dust we are," he says, smiling over the tombstones; and catching, as is his wont, quite a divine effulgence as he looks heavenward, he speaks, in words of inspiration almost, of "the Great Day, when we shall all of us be contemporaries, and make our appearance together."

The third, whose theme is death, too, and who will speak his word of moral as Heaven teaches him, leads you up to his father's coffin, and shows you his beautiful mother weeping, and himself an unconscious little boy wondering at her side. His own natural tears flow as he takes your hand and confidingly asks your sympathy. "See how good and innocent and beautiful women are," he says; "how tender little children! Let us love these and one another, brother — God knows we have need of love and pardon." So it is each man looks with his own eyes, speaks with his own voice, and prays his own prayer.

When Steele asks your sympathy for the actors in that charming scene of Love and Grief and Death, who can refuse it? One yields to it as to the frank advance of a child, or to the appeal of a woman. A man is seldom more manly than when he is what you call unmanned — the source of his emotion is championship, pity, and courage; the instinctive desire to cherish those who are innocent and unhappy, and defend those who are tender and weak. If Steele is not our friend he is nothing. He is by no means the most brilliant of wits nor the deepest of thinkers: but he is our friend; we love him, as children love their love with an A, because he is amiable. Who likes a man best because he is the cleverest or the wisest of mankind; or a woman because she is the most virtuous, or talks French, or plays the piano better than the rest of her sex? I own to liking Dick Steele the man, and Dick Steele the author, much better than much better men and much better authors.

The misfortune regarding Steele is, that most part of the company here present must take his amiability upon hearsay, and certainly can't make his intimate acquaintance. Not that Steele was worse than his time; on the contrary, a far better, truer, and higher-hearted man than most who lived in it. But things were done in that society, and names were named, which would make you shudder now. What would be the sensation of a polite youth of the present day, if at a ball he saw the young object of his affections taking a box out of her pocket and a pinch of snuff; or if at dinner, by the charmer's side, she deliberately put her knife into her mouth? If she cut her mother's throat with it, mamma would scarcely be more shocked. I allude to these peculiarities of bygone times as an excuse for my favorite, Steele, who was not worse, and often much more delicate than his neighbors.

There exists a curious document descriptive of the manners of the last age, which describes most minutely the amusements and

STEELE

occupations of persons of fashion in London at the time of which we are speaking; the time of Swift, and Addison, and Steele.

When Lord Sparkish, Tom Neverout, and Colonel Alwit, the immortal personages of Swift's polite conversation, came to breakfast with my Lady Smart, at eleven o'clock in the morning, my Lord Smart was absent at the levée. His lordship was at home to dinner at three o'clock to receive his guests; and we may sit down to this meal, like the Barmecide's, and see the fops of the last century before us. Seven of them sat down at dinner, and were joined by a country baronet who told them they kept court hours. These persons of fashion began their dinner with a sirloin of beef, fish, a shoulder of veal, and a tongue. My Lady Smart carved the sirloin, my Lady Answerall helped the fish, and the gallant Colonel cut the shoulder of veal. All made a considerable inroad on the sirloin and the shoulder of veal with the exception of Sir John, who had no appetite, having already partaken of a beefsteak and two mugs of ale, besides a tankard of March beer as soon as he got out of bed. They drank claret, which the master of the house said should always be drunk after fish; and my Lord Smart particularly recommended some excellent cider to my Lord Sparkish, which occasioned some brilliant remarks from that nobleman. When the host called for wine, he nodded to one or other of his guests, and said, "Tom Neverout, my service to you."

After the first course came almond-pudding, fritters, which the Colonel took with his hands out of the dish, in order to help the brilliant Miss Notable; chickens, black puddings, and soup; and Lady Smart, the elegant mistress of the mansion, finding a skewer in a dish, placed it in her plate with the directions that it should be carried down to the cook and dressed for the cook's own dinner. Wine and small beer were drunk during this second course; and when the Colonel called for beer, he called the butler Friend, and asked whether the beer was good. Various jocular remarks passed from the gentlefolks to the servants; at breakfast several persons had a word and a joke for Mrs. Betty, my lady's maid, who warmed the cream and had charge of the canister (the tea cost thirty shillings a pound in those days). When my Lady Sparkish sent her footman out to my Lady Match to come at six o'clock and play at quadrille, her ladyship warned the man to follow his nose, and if he fell by the way not to stay to get up again. And when the gentleman asked the hall-porter if his lady was at home, that functionary replied, with manly waggishness, " She was at home just now, but she's not gone out yet."

After the puddings, sweet and black, the fritters and soup, came the third course, of which the chief dish was a hot venison pasty, which was put before Lord Smart, and carved by that nobleman. Besides the pasty, there was a hare, a rabbit, some pigeons, partridges, a goose, and a ham. Beer and wine were freely imbibed during this course, the gentlemen always pledging somebody with every glass which they drank; and by this time the conversation between Tom Neverout and Miss Notable had grown so brisk and lively, that the Derbyshire baronet began to think the young gentlewoman was Tom's sweetheart; on which Miss remarked, that she loved Tom "like pie." After the goose, some of the gentlemen took a dram of brandy, "which was very good for the wholesomes," Sir John said; and now having had a tolerably substantial dinner, honest Lord Smart bade the butler bring up the great tankard full of October to Sir John. The great tankard was passed from hand to hand and mouth to mouth, but when pressed by the noble host upon the gallant Tom Neverout, he said, "No, faith, my lord; I like your wine, and won't put a churl upon a gentleman. Your honor's claret is good enough for me." And so, the dinner over, the host said, "Hang saving, bring up us a ha'porth of cheese."

The cloth was now taken away, and a bottle of burgundy was set down, of which the ladies were invited to partake before they went to their tea. When they withdrew, the gentlemen promised to join them in an hour: fresh bottles were brought; the "dead men," meaning the empty bottles, removed; and "D'you hear, John? bring clean glasses," my Lord Smart said. On which the gallant Colonel Alwit said, "I'll keep my glass; for wine is the best liquor to wash glasses in."

After an hour the gentlemen joined the ladies, and then they all sat and played quadrille until three o'clock in the morning, when the chairs and the flambeaux came, and this noble company went to bed.

Such were manners six or seven score years ago. I draw no inference from this queer picture — let all moralists here present deduce their own. Fancy the moral condition of that society in which a lady of fashion joked with a footman, and carved a sirloin, and provided besides a great shoulder of veal, a goose, hare, rabbit, chickens, partridges, black puddings, and a ham for a dinner for eight

STEELE

Christians. What — what could have been the condition of that polite world in which people openly ate goose after almond-pudding, and took their soup in the middle of dinner? Fancy a Colonel in the Guards putting his hand into a dish of *beignets d'abricot*, and helping his neighbor, a young lady *du monde!* Fancy a noble lord calling out to the servants, before the ladies at his table, "Hang expense, bring up a ha'porth of cheese!" Such were the ladies of Saint James's — such were the frequenters of "White's Chocolate-House," when Swift used to visit it, and Steele described it as the centre of pleasure, gallantry, and entertainment, a hundred and forty years ago!

Dennis, who ran amuck at the literary society of his day, falls foul of poor Steele, and thus depicts him: — "Sir John Edgar, of the county of —— in Ireland, is of a middle stature, broad shoulders, thick legs, a shape like the picture of somebody over a farmer's chimney — a short chin, a short nose, a short forehead, a broad flat face, and a dusky countenance. Yet with such a face and such a shape, he discovered at sixty that he took himself for a beauty, and appeared to be more mortified at being told that he was ugly, than he was by any reflection made upon his honor or understanding.

"He is a gentleman born, witness himself, of very honorable family; certainly of a very ancient one, for his ancestors flourished in Tipperary long before the English ever set foot in Ireland. He has testimony of this more authentic than the Herald's Office, or any human testimony. For God has marked him more abundantly than he did Cain, and stamped his native country on his face, his understanding, his writings, his actions, his passions, and, above all, his vanity. The Hibernian brogue is still upon all these, though long habit and length of days have worn it off his tongue."

Although this portrait is the work of a man who was neither the friend of Steele nor of any other man alive, yet there is a dreadful resemblance to the original in the savage and exaggerated traits of the caricature, and everybody who knows him must recognize Dick Steele. Dick set about almost all the undertakings of his life with inadequate means, and, as he took and furnished a house with the most generous intentions towards his friends, the most tender gallantry towards his wife, and with this only drawback, that he had not wherewithal to pay the rent when quarter-day came, — so, in his life he proposed to himself the most magnificent schemes of virtue, forbearance, public and private good, and the advancement of his own and the national religion; but when he had to pay for these articles — so difficult to purchase and so costly to maintain — poor Dick's money was not forthcoming: and when Virtue called with her little bill, Dick made a shuffling excuse that he could not see her that morning, having a headache from being tipsy over-night; or when stern Duty rapped at the door with his account, Dick was absent and not ready to pay. He was shirking at the tavern; or had some particular business (of somebody's else) at the ordinary: or he was in hiding, or worse than in hiding, in the lock-up house. What a situation for a man! — for a philanthropist — for a lover of right and truth — for a magnificent designer and schemer! Not to dare to look in the face the Religion which he adored and which he had offended: to have to shirk down back lanes and alleys, so as to avoid the friend whom he loved and who had trusted him; to have the house, which he had intended for his wife, whom he loved passionately, and for her ladyship's company which he wished to entertain splendidly, in the possession of a bailiff's man; with a crowd of little creditors, — grocers, butchers, and small-coal men — lingering round the door with their bills and jeering at him. Alas! for poor Dick Steele! For nobody else, of course. There is no man or woman in *our* time who makes fine projects and gives them up from idleness or want of means. When Duty calls upon *us*, we no doubt are always at home and ready to pay that grim tax-gatherer. When *we* are stricken with remorse and promise reform, we keep our promise, and are never angry, or idle, or extravagant any more. There are no chambers in *our* hearts, destined for family friends and actions, and now occupied by some Sin's emissary and bailiff in possession. There are no little sins, shabby peccadilloes, importunate remembrances, or disappointed holders of our promises to reform, hovering at our steps, or knocking at our door! Of course not. We are living in the nineteenth century; and poor Dick Steele stumbled and got up again, and got into jail and out again, and sinned and repented, and loved and suffered, and lived and died, scores of years ago. Peace be with him! Let us think gently of one who was so gentle: let us speak kindly of one whose own breast exuberated with human kindness.

THE TATLER

THE TATLER

MR. BICKERSTAFF ON HIMSELF

No. 89.] THURSDAY, NOVEMBER 3, 1709. [STEELE.]

> Rura mihi placeant, riguique in evallibus amnes,
> Flumina amem sylvasque inglorius ——
> VIRG. GEORG. ii. 485.
>
> My next desire is, void of care and strife,
> To lead a soft, secure, inglorious life:
> A country cottage near a crystal flood,
> A winding valley, and a lofty wood.

I HAVE received this short epistle from an unknown hand.

"SIR, — I have no more to trouble you with, than to desire you would in your next help me to some answer to the inclosed concerning yourself. In the mean time I congratulate you upon the increase of your fame, which you see has extended itself beyond the bills of mortality."

"SIR, — That the country is barren of news has been the excuse, time out of mind, for dropping a correspondence with our friends in London; as if it were impossible out of a coffee-house to write an agreeable letter. I am too ingenuous to endeavour at the covering of my negligence with so common an excuse. Doubtless, amongst friends, bred, as we have been, to the knowledge of books as well as men, a letter dated from a garden, a grotto, a fountain, a wood, a meadow, or the banks of a river, may be more entertaining than one from Tom's, Will's, White's, or Saint James's. I promise, therefore, to be frequent for the future in my rural dates to you. But for fear you should, from what I have said, be induced to believe I shun the commerce of men, I must inform you, that there is a fresh topic of discourse lately arisen amongst the ingenious in our

THE TATLER

part of the world, and is become the more fashionable for the ladies giving into it. This we owe to Isaac Bickerstaff, who is very much censured by some, and as much justified by others. Some criticise his style, his humour, and his matter; others admire the whole man. Some pretend, from the informations of their friends in town, to decypher the author; and others confess they are lost in their guesses. For my part, I must own myself a professed admirer of the paper, and desire you to send me a complete set, together with your thoughts of the squire and his lucubrations."

There is no pleasure like that of receiving praise from the praiseworthy; and I own it a very solid happiness, that these my lucubrations are approved by a person of so fine a taste as the author of this letter, who is capable of enjoying the world in the simplicity of its natural beauties. This pastoral letter, if I may so call it, must be written by a man who carries his entertainment wherever he goes, and is undoubtedly one of those happy men who appear far otherwise to the vulgar. I dare say, he is not envied by the vicious, the vain, the frolic, and the loud; but is continually blessed with that strong and serious delight, which flows from a well-taught and liberal mind. With great respect to country sports, I may say, this gentleman could pass his time agreeably, if there were not a hare or a fox in his county. That calm and elegant satisfaction which the vulgar call melancholy is the true and proper delight of men of knowledge and virtue. What we take for diversion, which is a kind of forgetting ourselves, is but a mean way of entertainment, in comparison of that which is considering, knowing, and enjoying ourselves. The pleasures of ordinary people are in their passions; but the seat of this delight is in the reason and understanding. Such a frame of mind raises that sweet enthusiasm, which warms the imagination at the sight of every work of nature, and turns all round you into a picture and landscape. I shall be ever proud of advices from this gentleman; for I profess writing news from the learned, as well as the busy world.

As for my labours, which he is pleased to inquire after, if they can but wear one impertinence out of human life, destroy a single vice, or give a morning's cheerfulness to an honest mind; in short, if the world can be but one virtue the better, or in any degree less vicious, or receive from them the smallest addition to their innocent diversions; I shall not think my pains, or indeed my life, to have been spent in vain.

THE TATLER

Thus far as to my studies. It will be expected I should in the next place give some account of my life. I shall therefore, for the satisfaction of the present age, and the benefit of posterity, present the world with the following abridgement of it.

It is remarkable, that I was bred by hand, and eat nothing but milk until I was a twelve-month old; from which time, to the eighth year of my ge, I was observed to delight in pudding and potatoes; and indeed I retain a benevolence for that sort of food to this day. I do not remember that I distinguished myself in any thing at those years, but by my great skill at taw, for which I was so barbarously used, that it has ever since given me an aversion to gaming. In my twelfth year, I suffered very much for two or three false concords. At fifteen I was sent to the university, and staid there for some time ; but a drum passing by, being a lover of music, I inlisted myself for a soldier. As years came on, I began to examine things, and grew discontented at the times. This made me quit the sword, and take to the study of the occult sciences, in which I was so wrapped up, that Oliver Cromwell had been buried, and taken up again, five years before I heard he was dead. This gave me first the reputation of a conjurer, which has been of great disadvantage to me ever since, and kept me out of all public employments. The greater part of my later years has been divided between Dick's coffee-house, the Trumpet in Sheer-lane, and my own lodgings.

MEMORIES OF HIS CHILDHOOD

No. 181.] TUESDAY, JUNE 6, 1710. [STEELE.]

—— Dies, ni fallor, adest, quem semper acerbum,
Semper honoratum, sic dii voluistis habebo.
VIRG. ÆN. v. 49.

And now the rising day renews the year,
A day for ever sad, for ever dear.

THERE are those among mankind, who can enjoy no relish of their being, except the world is made acquainted with all that relates to them, and think every thing lost that passes unobserved;

but others find a solid delight in stealing by the crowd, and modelling their life after such a manner, as is as much above the approbation as the practice of the vulgar. Life being too short to give instances great enough of true friendship or good will, some sages have thought it pious to preserve a certain reverence for the *Manes* of their deceased friends; and have withdrawn themselves from the rest of the world at certain seasons, to commemorate in their own thoughts such of their acquaintance who have gone before them out of this life. And indeed, when we are advanced in years, there is not a more pleasing entertainment, than to recollect in a gloomy moment the many we have parted with, that have been dear and agreeable to us, and to cast a melancholy thought or two after those, with whom, perhaps, we have indulged ourselves in whole nights of mirth and jollity. With such inclinations in my heart I went to my closet yesterday in the evening, and resolved to be sorrowful; upon which occasion I could not but look with disdain upon myself, that though all the reasons which I had to lament the loss of many of my friends are now as forcible as at the moment of their departure, yet did not my heart swell with the same sorrow which I felt at that time; but I could, without tears, reflect upon many pleasing adventures I have had with some, who have long been blended with common earth.

Though it is by the benefit of nature, that length of time thus blots out the violence of afflictions; yet with tempers too much given to pleasure, it is almost necessary to revive the old places of grief in our memory; and ponder step by step on past life, to lead the mind into that sobriety of thought which poises the heart, and makes it beat with due time, without being quickened with desire, or retarded with despair, from its proper and equal motion. When we wind up a clock that is out of order, to make it go well for the future, we do not immediately set the hand to the present instant, but we make it strike the round of all its hours, before it can recover the regularity of its time. Such, thought I, shall be my method this evening; and since it is that day of the year which I dedicate to the memory of such in another life as I much delighted in when living, an hour or two shall be sacred to sorrow and their memory, while I run over all the melancholy circumstances of this kind which have occurred to me in my whole life. The first sense of sorrow I ever knew was upon the death of my father at which time I was not quite five years of age; but was rather amazed at what all the house meant, than possessed with a real understanding why nobody was willing to play with me. I remember I went into the room where his body lay, and my mother sat weeping alone by it. I had my battledore in my hand, and fell a-beating the coffin, and calling papa; for, I know not how, I had some slight idea that he was locked up there. My mother catched me in her arms, and, transported beyond all patience of the silent grief she was before in, she almost smothered me in her embraces; and told me, in a flood of tears, "Papa could not hear me, and would play with me no more, for they were going to put him under ground, whence he could never come to us again." She was a very beautiful woman, of a noble spirit, and there was a dignity in her grief amidst all the wildness of her transport, which, methought, struck me with an instinct of sorrow, that, before I was sensible of what it was to grieve, seized my very soul, and has made pity the weakness of my heart ever since. The mind in infancy is, methinks, like the body in embryo, and receives impressions so forcible, that they are as hard to be removed by reason, as any mark, with which a child is born, is to be taken away by any future application. Hence it is, that good-nature in me is no merit; but having been so frequently overwhelmed with her tears before I knew the cause of any affliction, or could draw defences from my own judgment. I imbibed commiseration, remorse, and an unmanly gentleness of mind, which have since insnared me into ten thousand calamities; from whence I can reap no advantage, except it be, that, in such a humour as I am now in, I can the better indulge myself in the softnesses of humanity, and enjoy that sweet anxiety which arises from the memory of past afflictions.

We, that are very old, are better able to remember things which befel us in our distant youth, than the passages of later days. For this reason it is, that the companions of my strong and vigorous years present themselves more immediately to me in this office of sorrow. Untimely and unhappy deaths are what we are most apt to lament; so little are we able to make it indifferent when a thing happens, though we know it must happen. Thus we groan under life, and bewail those who are relieved from it. Every object that returns to our imagination raises different passions, according to the circumstances of their departure. Who can have lived in an army, and in a serious hour reflect upon the many gay and agreeable men that might long have flourished in the arts of peace, and not join with the imprecations of the fatherless and widow on the tyrant to whose ambition they fell sacrifices? But gallant men, who are cut off by the sword, move rather our veneration than our pity; and we gather relief enough from their own contempt of death, to make that no evil, which was approached with so much cheerfulness, and attended with so much honour. But when we turn our thoughts from the great parts of life on such occasions, and instead of lamenting those who stood ready to give death to those from whom they had the fortune to receive it; I say, when we let our thoughts wander from such noble objects, and consider the havock which is made among the tender and the innocent, pity enters with an unmixed softness, and possesses all our souls at once.

Here (were there words to express such sentiments with proper tenderness) I should record the beauty, innocence and untimely death, of the first object my eyes ever beheld with love. The beauteous virgin! how ignorantly did she charm, how carelessly excel! Oh Death! thou hast right to the bold, to the ambitious, to the high, and to the haughty; but why this cruelty to the humble, to the meek, to the undiscerning, to the thoughtless? Nor age, nor business, nor distress, can erase the dear image from my imagination. In the same week, I saw her dressed for a ball, and in a shroud. How ill did the habit of death become the pretty trifler? I still behold the smiling earth —— A large train of disasters were coming on to my memory, when my servant knocked at my closet-door, and interrupted me with a letter, attended with a hamper of wine, of the same sort with that which is to be put to sale, on Thursday next, at Garraway's coffee-house. Upon the receipt of it, I sent for three of my friends. We are so intimate, that we can be company in whatever state of mind we meet, and can entertain each other without expecting always to rejoice. The wine we found to be generous and warming, but with such an heat as moved us rather to be cheerful than frolicksome. It revived the spirits, without firing the blood. We commended it until two of the clock this morning; and having to-day met a little before dinner, we found, that though we drank two bottles a man, we had much more reason to recollect than forget what had passed the night before.

THE TATLER

A VISIT TO A FRIEND

No. 95.] THURSDAY, NOVEMBER 17, 1709. [STEELE.]

> Interea dulces pendent circum oscula nati,
> Casta pudicitiam servat domus ———
> VIRG. GEORG. ii. 523.

> His cares are eas'd with intervals of bliss;
> His little children, climbing for a kiss,
> Welcome their father's late return at night;
> His faithful bed is crown'd with chaste delight.

THERE are several persons who have many pleasures and entertainments in their possession, which they do not enjoy. It is, therefore, a kind and good office to acquaint them with their own happiness, and turn their attention to such instances of their good fortune as they are apt to overlook. Persons in the married state often want such a monitor; and pine away their days, by looking upon the same condition in anguish and murmur, which carries with it in the opinion of others a complication of all the pleasures of life, and a retreat from its inquietudes.

I am led into this thought by a visit I made an old friend, who was formerly my schoolfellow. He came to town last week with his family for the winter, and yesterday morning sent me word his wife expected me to dinner. I am as it were at home at that house, and every member of it knows me for their well-wisher. I cannot indeed express the pleasure it is, to be met by the children with so much joy as I am when I go thither. The boys and girls strive who shall come first, when they think it is I that am knocking at that door; and that child which loses the race to me runs back again to tell the father it is Mr. Bickerstaff. This day I was led in by a pretty girl, that we all thought must have forgot me; for the family has been out of town these two years. Her knowing me again was a mighty subject with us, and took up our discourse at the first entrance. After which, they began to rally me upon a thousand little stories they heard in the country, about my marriage to one of my neighbour's daughters. Upon which the gentleman, my friend said, "Nay, if Mr. Bickerstaff marries a child of any of his old companions, I hope mine shall have the preference; there is Mrs. Mary is *now sixteen,* and would make him as fine a widow as the best of them. But I know him too well; he is so enamoured with the very memory of those who flourished in our youth, that he will not so much as look upon the modern beauties. I remember, old gentleman, how often you went home in a day to refresh your countenance and dress, when Teraminta reigned in your heart. As we came up in the coach, I repeated to my wife some of your verses on her."

With such reflections on little passages which happened long ago, we passed our time, during a cheerful and elegant meal. After dinner, his lady left the room, as did also the children. As soon as we were alone, he took me by the hand; "Well, my good friend," says he, "I am heartily glad to see thee; I was afraid you would never have seen all the company that dined with you to-day again. Do not you think the good woman of the house a little altered, since you followed her from the play-house to find out who she was for me?" I perceived a tear fall down his cheek as he spoke, which moved me not a little. But, to turn the discourse, I said, "She is not indeed quite that creature she was, when she returned me the letter I carried from you; and told me, 'she hoped, as I was a gentleman, I would be employed no more to trouble her, who had never offended me; but would be so much the gentleman's friend as to dissuade him from a pursuit, which he could never succeed in.' You may remember, I thought her in earnest; and you were forced to employ your cousin Will, who made his sister get acquainted with her, for you. You cannot expect her to be for ever fifteen." — "Fifteen!" replied my good friend: "Ah! you little understand, you that have lived a bachelor, how great, how exquisite a pleasure there is, in being really beloved! It is impossible, that the most beauteous face in nature should raise in me such pleasing ideas, as when I look upon that excellent woman. That fading in her countenance is chiefly caused by her watching with me, in my fever. This was followed by a fit of sickness, which had like to have carried her off last winter. I tell you sincerely, I have so many obligations to her, that I cannot, with any sort of moderation, think of her present state of health. But as to what you say of fifteen, she gives me every day pleasures beyond what I ever knew in the possession of her beauty, when I was in the vigour of youth. Every moment of her life brings me fresh instances of her complacency to my inclinations, and her prudence in regard to my fortune.

Her face is to me much more beautiful than when I first saw it; there is no decay in any feature, which I cannot trace, from the very instant it was occasioned by some anxious concern for my welfare and interests. Thus, at the same time, methinks, the love I conceived towards her for what she was is heightened by my gratitude for what she is. The love of a wife is as much above the idle passion commonly called by that name, as the loud laughter of buffoons is inferior to the elegant mirth of gentlemen. Oh! she is an inestimable jewel. In her examination of her household affairs, she shews a certain fearfulness to find a fault, which makes her servants obey her like children; and the meanest we have has an ingenuous shame for an offence, not always to be seen in children in other families. I speak freely to you, my old friend; ever since her sickness, things that gave me the quickest joy before turn now to a certain anxiety. As the children play in the next room, I know the poor things by their steps, and am considering what they must do, should they lose their mother in their tender years. The pleasure I used to take in telling my boy stories of battles, and asking my girl questions about the disposal of her baby, and the gossiping of it, is turned into inward reflection and melancholy."

He would have gone on in this tender way, when the good lady entered, and with an inexpressible sweetness in her countenance told us, "she had been searching her closet for something very good, to treat such an old friend as I was." Her husband's eyes sparkled with pleasure at the cheerfulness of her countenance; and I saw all his fears vanish in an instant. The lady observing something in our looks which shewed we had been more serious than ordinary, and seeing her husband receive her with great concern under a forced cheerfulness, immediately guessed at what we had been talking of; and applying herself to me, said, with a smile, "Mr. Bickerstaff, do not believe a word of what he tells you; I shall still live to have you for my second, as I have often promised you, unless he takes more care of himself than he has done since his coming to town. You must know, he tells me that he finds London is a much more healthy place than the country; for he sees several of his old acquaintance and schoolfellows are here *young fellows with fair full-bottomed periwigs*. I could scarce keep him this morning from going out *open breasted*." My friend, who is always extremely delighted with her agreable humour, made her sit down with us. She did it with that easiness which is peculiar to women of sense; and, to keep up the good humour she had brought in with her, turned her raillery upon me. "Mr. Bickerstaff, you remember you followed me one night from the play-house; suppose you should carry me thither to-morrow night, and lead me into the front-box." This put us into a long field of discourse about the beauties, who were mothers to the present, and shined in the boxes twenty years ago. I told her, "I was glad she had transferred so many of her charms, and I did not question but her eldest daughter was within half a year of being a Toast."

We were pleasing ourselves with this fantastical preferment of the young lady, when on a sudden we were alarmed with the noise of a drum, and immediately entered my little godson to give me a point of war. His mother, between laughing and chiding, would have put him out of the room; but I would not part with him so. I found upon conversation with him, though he was a little noisy in his mirth, that the child had excellent parts, and was a great master of all the learning on the other side eight years old. I perceived him a very great historian in Æsop's Fables; but he frankly declared to me his mind, "that he did not delight in that learning, because he did not believe they were true"; for which reason I found he had very much *turned* his studies, for about a twelve-month past, into the lives and adventures of don Bellianis of Greece, Guy of Warwick, the Seven Champions, and other historians of that age. I could not but observe the satisfaction the father took in the forwardness of his son; and that these diversions might turn to some profit, I found the boy had made remarks, which might be of service to him during the course of his whole life. He would tell you the mismanagements of John Hickathrift, find fault with the passionate temper in Bevis of Southampton, and loved Saint George for being the champion of England; and by this means had his thoughts insensibly moulded into the notions of discretion, virtue, and honour. I was extolling his accomplishments, when the mother told me, "that the little girl who led me in this morning was in her way a better scholar than he. Betty," says she, "deals chiefly in fairies and sprights; and sometimes in a winter-night will terrify the maids with her accounts, until they are afraid to go up to bed."

I sat with them until it was very late, sometimes in merry, sometimes in serious discourse, with this particular pleasure, which gives the only true relish to all conversation, a sense that every one of us liked each other. I went home, considering the different conditions of a married life and that of a bachelor; and I must confess it struck me with a secret concern, to reflect, that whenever I go off I shall leave no traces behind me.

DUELLING

No. 25.] TUESDAY, JUNE 7, 1709. [STEELE.]

A LETTER from a young lady, written in the most passionate terms, wherein she laments the misfortune of a gentleman, her lover, who was lately wounded in a duel, has turned my thoughts to that subject, and inclined me to examine into the causes which precipitate men into so fatal a folly. And as it has been proposed to treat of subjects of gallantry in the article from hence, and no one point in nature is more proper to be considered by the company who frequent this place than that of duels, it is worth our consideration to examine into this chimerical groundless humour, and to lay every other thought aside, until we have stripped it of all its false pretences to credit and reputation amongst men.

But I must confess, when I consider what I am going about, and run over in my imagination all the endless crowd of men of honour who will be offended at such a discourse; I am undertaking, methinks, a work worthy an invulnerable hero in romance, rather than a private gentleman with a single rapier: but as I am pretty well acquainted by great opportunities with the nature of man, and know of a truth that all men fight against their will, the danger vanishes, and resolution rises upon this subject. For this reason, I shall talk very freely on a custom which all men wish exploded, though no man has courage enough to resist it.

But there is one unintelligible word, which I fear will extremely perplex my dissertation, and I confess to you I find very hard to explain, which is the term "satisfaction." An honest country gentleman had the misfortune to fall into company with two or three modern men of honour, where he happened to be very ill-treated; and one of the company, being conscious of his offence sends a note to him in the morning, and tells him, he was ready to give him satisfaction. "This is fine doing," says the plain fellow; "last night he sent me away cursedly out of humour, and this morning he fancies it would be a satisfaction to be run through the body."

As the matter at present stands, it is not to do handsome actions denominates a man of honour; it is enough if he dares to defend ill ones. Thus you often see a common sharper in competition with a gentleman of the first rank; though all mankind is convinced, that a fighting gamester is only a pickpocket with the courage of an highwayman. One cannot with any patience reflect on the unaccountable jumble of persons and things in this town and nation, which occasions very frequently, that a brave man falls by a hand below that of a common hangman, and yet his executioner escapes the clutches of the hangman for doing it. I shall therefore hereafter consider, how the bravest men in other ages and nations have behaved themselves upon such incidents as we decide by combat; and shew, from their practice, that this resentment neither has its foundation from true reason or solid fame; but is an imposture, made of cowardice, falsehood, and want of understanding. For this work, a good history of quarrels would be very edifying to the public, and I apply myself to the town for particulars and circumstances within their knowledge, which may serve to embellish the dissertation with proper cuts. Most of the quarrels I have ever known, have proceeded from some valiant coxcomb's persisting in the wrong, to defend some prevailing folly, and preserve himself from the ingenuousness of owning a mistake.

By this means it is called "giving a man satisfaction," to urge your offence against him with your sword; which puts me in mind of Peter's order to the keeper, in The Tale of a Tub: "if you neglect to do all this, damn you and your generation for ever: and so we bid you heartily farewell." If the contradiction in the very terms of one of our challenges were as well explained and turned into downright English, would it not run after this manner?

"Sir, — Your extraordinary behaviour last night, and the liberty you were pleased to take with me, makes me this morning give you this, to tell you, because you are an ill-bred puppy, I will meet you in Hyde-park, an hour hence; and because you want both breeding and humanity, I desire you would come with a pistol in your hand, on horseback, and endeavour to shoot me through the head, to teach you more manners. If you fail of doing me this pleasure, I shall say, you are a rascal, on every post in town: and so, sir, if you will not injure me more, I shall never forgive what you have done already. Pray, sir, do not fail of getting everything ready; and you will infinitely oblige, sir, your most obedient humble servant, &c."

SNUFF

No. 35.] THURSDAY, JUNE 30, 1709. [STEELE.]

THERE is a habit or custom which I have put my patience to the utmost stretch to have suffered so long, because several of my intimate friends are in the guilt; and that is, the humour of taking snuff, and looking dirty about the mouth by way of ornament.

My method is, to dive to the bottom of a sore before I pretend to apply a remedy. For this reason, I sat by an eminent story-teller and politician, who takes half an ounce in five seconds, and has mortgaged a pretty tenement near the town, merely to improve and dung his brains with this prolific powder. I observed this gentleman, the other day, in the midst of a story, diverted from it by looking at something at a distance, and I softly hid his box. But he returns to his tale, and, looking for his box, he cries, "And so, sir —" Then, when he should have taken a pinch, "As I was saying —" says he, "has nobody seen my box?" His friend beseeches him to finish his narration: then he proceeds: "And so, sir —— where can my box be?" Then turning to me, "Pray, sir, did you see my box?" "Yes, sir," said I, "I took it to see how long you could live without it." He resumes his tale, and I took notice that his dulness was much more regular and fluent than before. A pinch supplied the place of "As I was saying," and "So, sir"; and he went on currently enough in that style which the learned call the insipid. This observation easily led me into a philosophic reason for taking snuff, which is done only to supply with sensations the want of reflection. This I take to be an εὔρηκα, a nostrum; upon which I hope to receive the thanks of this board; for as it is natural to lift a man's hand to a sore, when you fear anything coming at you; so when a person feels his thoughts are run out, and he has no more to say, it is as natural to supply his weak brain with powder at the nearest place of access, *viz.* the nostrils. This is so evident that nature suggests the use according to the indigence of the persons who take this medicine, without being prepossessed with the force of fashion or custom. For example; the native Hibernians, who are reckoned not much unlike the antient Bœotians, take this specific for emptiness in the head, in greater abundance than any other nation under the sun. The learned Sotus, as sparing as he is in his words, would be still more silent if it were not for this powder.

However low and poor the taking of snuff argues a man to be in his own stock of thoughts, or means to employ his brains and his fingers; yet there is a poorer creature in the world than he, and this is a borrower of snuff; a fellow that keeps no box of his own but is always asking others for a pinch. Such poor rogues put me always in mind of a common phrase among school-boys when they are composing their exercise, who run to an upper scholar, and cry, "Pray give me a little sense." But of all things commend me to the ladies who are got into this pretty help to discourse. I have been these three years persuading Sagissa to leave it off; but she talks so much, and is so learned, that she is above contradiction. However, an accident the other day brought that about, which my eloquence could never accomplish. She had a very pretty fellow in her closet, who ran thither to avoid some company that came to visit her; she made an excuse to go in to him for some implement they were talking of. Her eager gallant snatched a kiss; but, being unused to snuff, some grains from off her upper lip made him sneeze aloud, which alarmed the visitants, and has made a discovery, that profound reading, very much intelligence, and a general knowledge of who and who are together, cannot fill her vacant hours so much, but she is sometimes obliged to descend to entertainments less intellectual.

THE TATLER

TOM WILDAIR

No. 60.] SATURDAY, AUGUST 27, 1709. [STEELE.

TO proceed regularly in the history of my worthies, I ought to give an account of what has passed from day to day in this place; but a young fellow of my acquaintance has so lately been rescued out of the hands of the Knights of the Industry, that I rather choose to relate the manner of his escape from them, and the uncommon way which was used to reclaim him, than to go on in my intended diary.

You are to know then, that Tom Wildair is a student of the Inner Temple, and has spent his time, since he left the university for that place, in the common diversions of men of fashion; that is to say, in whoring, drinking, and gaming. The two former vices he had from his father; but was led into the last by the conversation of a partizan of the Myrmidons who had chambers near him. His allowance from his father was a very plentiful one for a man of sense, but as scanty for a modern fine gentleman. His frequent losses had reduced him to so necessitous a condition, that his lodgings were always haunted by impatient creditors; and all his thoughts employed in contriving low methods to support himself in a way of life from which he knew not how to retreat, and in which he wanted means to proceed. There is never wanting some good-natured person to send a man an account of what he has no mind to hear; therefore many epistles were conveyed to the father of this extravagant, to inform him of the company, the pleasures, the distresses, and entertainments, in which his son passed his time. The old fellow received these advices with all the pain of a parent, but frequently consulted his pillow, to know how to behave himself on such important occasions, as the welfare of his son, and the safety of his fortune. After many agitations of mind, he reflected, that necessity was the usual snare which made men fall into meanness, and that a liberal fortune generally made a liberal and honest mind; he resolved therefore to save him from his ruin, by giving him opportunities of tasting what it is to be at ease, and inclosed to him the following order upon Sir Tristram Cash.

THE TATLER

"Sir, — Pray pay to Mr. Thomas Wildair, or order, the sum of one thousand pounds, and place it to the account of yours,
                                    Humphrey Wildair."

Tom was so astonished with the receipt of this order, that though he knew it to be his father's hand, and that he had always large sums at Sir Tristram's; yet a thousand pounds was a trust of which his conduct had always made him appear so little capable, that he kept his note by him, until he writ to his father the following letter:

"Honoured Father, — I have received an order under your hand for a thousand pounds, in words at length; and I think I could swear it is your own hand. I have looked it over and over twenty thousand times. There is in plain letters, T,h,o,u,s,a,n,d; and after it, the letters P,o,u,n,d,s. I have it still by me, and shall, I believe, continue reading it until I hear from you."

The old gentleman took no manner of notice of the receipt of his letter; but sent him another order for three thousand pounds more. His amazement on this second letter was unspeakable. He immediately double-locked his door, and sat down carefully to reading and comparing both his orders. After he had read them until he was half mad, he walked six or seven turns in his chamber, then opens his door, then locks it again; and, to examine thoroughly this matter, he locks his door again, puts his table and chairs against it; then goes into his closet, and, locking himself in, reads his notes over again about nineteen times, which did but increase his astonishment. Soon after, he began to recollect many stories he had formerly heard of persons, who had been possessed with imaginations and appearances which had no foundation in nature, but had been taken with sudden madness in the midst of a seeming clear and untainted reason. This made him very gravely conclude he was out of his wits; and, with a design to compose himself, he immediately betakes him to his night-cap, with a resolution to sleep himself into his former poverty and senses. To bed therefore he goes at noon-day; but soon rose again, and resolved to visit Sir Tristram upon this occasion. He did so, and dined with the knight, expecting he would mention some advice from his father about paying him money; but no such thing being said, "Look you, Sir Tristram," said he, "you are to know, that an affair has happened, which —" "Look you," says Tristram, "I know, Mr. Wildair, you are going to desire me to advance; but the late call of the bank, where I have not yet made my last payment, has obliged me —" Tom interrupted him, by shewing him the bill of a thousand pounds. When he had looked at it for a convenient time, and as often surveyed Tom's looks and countenance; "Look you, Mr. Wildair, a thousand pounds —" Before he could proceed, he shews him the order for three thousand more — Sir Tristram examined the orders at the light, and finding at the writing the name, there was a certain stroke in one letter, which the father and he had agreed should be to such directions as he desired might be more immediately honoured, he forthwith pays the money. The possession of four thousand pounds gave my young gentleman a new train of thoughts: he began to reflect upon his birth, the great expectations he was born to, and the unsuitable ways he had long pursued. Instead of that unthinking creature he was before, he is now provident, generous, and discreet. The father and son have an exact and regular correspondence, with mutual and unreserved confidence in each other. The son looks upon his father as the best tenant he could have in the country, and the father finds the son the most safe banker he could have in the city.

FASHIONABLE AFFECTATIONS

No. 77.] THURSDAY, OCTOBER 6, 1709. [STEELE.]

AS bad as the world is, I find by very strict observation upon virtue and vice, that if men appeared no worse than they really are, I should have less work than at present I am obliged to undertake for their reformation. They have generally taken up a kind of inverted ambition, and affect even faults and imperfections of which they are innocent. The other day in a coffee-house I stood by a young heir, with a fresh, sanguine, and healthy look, who entertained us with an account of his diet-drinks; though, to my knowledge, he is as sound as any of his tenants.

This worthy youth put me into reflections upon that subject; and I observed the fantastical humour to be so general, that there is hardly a man who is not more or less tainted with it. The first of this order of men are the Valetudinarians, who are never in health; but complain of want of stomach or rest every day until noon, and then devour all which comes before them. Lady Dainty is convinced, that it is necessary for a gentlewoman to be out of order; and, to preserve that character, she dines every day in her closet at twelve, that she may become her table at two, and be unable to eat in public. About five years ago, I remember, it was the fashion to be short-sighted. A man would not own an acquaintance until he had first examined him with his glass. At a lady's entrance into the play-house, you might see tubes immediately levelled at her from every quarter of the pit and side-boxes. However, that mode of infirmity is out, and the age has recovered its sight: but the blind seem to be succeeded by the lame, and a jaunty limp is the present beauty. I think I have formerly observed, a cane is part of the dress of a prig, and always worn upon a button, for fear he should be thought to have an occasion for it, or be esteemed really, and not genteelly, a cripple. I have considered, but could never find out, the bottom of this vanity. I indeed have heard of a Gascon general, who, by the lucky grazing of a bullet on the roll of his stocking, took occasion to halt all his life after. But as for our peaceable cripples, I know no foundation for their behaviour, without it may be supposed that, in this warlike age, some think a cane the next honour to a wooden leg. This sort of affectation I have known run from one limb or member to another. Before the limpers came in, I remember a race of lispers, fine persons, who took an aversion to particular letters in our language. Some never uttered the letter H; and others had as mortal an aversion to S. Others have had their fashionable defect in their ears, and would make you repeat all you said twice over. I know an ancient friend of mine, whose table is every day surrounded with flatterers, that makes use of this, sometimes as a piece of grandeur, and at others as an art, to make them repeat their commendations. Such affectations have been indeed in the world in ancient times; but they fell into them out of politic ends. Alexander the Great had a wry neck, which made it the fashion in his court to carry their heads on one side when they came into the presence. One who thought to outshine the whole court, carried his head so over complaisantly, that this martial prince gave him so great a box on the ear, as set all the heads of the court upright.

This humour takes place in our minds as well as bodies. I

THE TATLER

know at this time a young gentlemen, who talks atheistically all day in coffee-houses, and in his degrees of understanding sets up for a Free-thinker; though it can be proved upon him, he says his prayers every morning and evening. But this class of modern wits I shall reserve for a chapter by itself.

Of the like turn are all your marriage-haters, who rail at the noose, at the words, "for ever and aye," and at the same time are secretly pining for some young thing or other that makes their hearts ache by her refusal. The next to these, are such as pretend to govern their wives, and boast how ill they use them; when at the same time, go to their houses, and you shall see them step as if they feared making a noise, and as fond as an alderman. I do not know but sometimes these pretences may arise from a desire to conceal a contrary defect than that they set up for. I remember, when I was a young fellow, we had a companion of a very fearful complexion, who, when we sat in to drink, would desire us to take his sword from him when he grew fuddled, for it was his misfortune to be quarrelsome.

There are many, many of these evils, which demand my observation; but because I have of late been thought somewhat too satirical, I shall give them warning, and declare to the whole world, that they are not true, but false hypocrites; and make it out that they are good men in their hearts. The motive of this monstrous affectation, in the above-mentioned and the like particulars, I take to proceed from that noble thirst of fame and reputation which is planted in the hearts of all men. As this produces elegant writings and gallant actions in men of great abilities, it also brings forth spurious productions in men who are not capable of distinguishing themselves by things which are really praise-worthy. As the desire of fame in men of true wit and gallantry shews itself in proper instances, the same desire in men who have the ambition without proper faculties, runs wild, and discovers itself in a thousand extravagances, by which they would signalize themselves from others, and gain a set of admirers. When I was a middle-aged man, there were many societies of ambitious young men in England, who, in their pursuits after fame, were every night employed in roasting porters, smoking coblers, knocking down watchmen, overturning constables, breaking windows, blackening sign-posts, and the like immortal enterprizes, that dispersed their reputation throughout the whole kingdom. One could hardly find a knocker at a door in a whole street after a midnight expedition of these *Beaux Esprits*. I was lately very much surprised by an account of my maid, who entered my bed-chamber this morning in a very great fright, and told me, she was afraid my parlour was haunted; for that she had found several panes of my windows broken, and the floor strewed with half-pence. I have not yet a full light into this new way, but am apt to think, that it is a generous piece of wit that some of my contemporaries make use of, to break windows, and leave money to pay for them.

MARRIAGE OF JENNY DISTAFF

No. 79.] TUESDAY, OCTOBER 11, 1709. [STEELE.]

> Felices, ter et amplius,
>   Quos irrupta tenet copula; nec malis
> Divulsus querimoniis,
>   Supremâ citius solvet amor die.
>
> HOR. 1 Od. xiii. 17.
>
> Thrice happy they, in pure delights
> Whom love in mutual bonds unites,
> Unbroken by complaints or strife
> Even to the latest hours of life.

MY sister Jenny's lover, the honest Tranquillus, for that shall be his name, has been impatient with me to dispatch the necessary directions for his marriage; that while I am taken up with imaginary schemes, as he calls them, he might not burn with real desire, and the torture of expectation. When I had reprimanded him for the ardour wherein he expressed himself, which I thought had not enough of that veneration with which the marriage-bed is to be ascended, I told him, "the day of his nuptials should be on the Saturday following, which was the eighth instant." On the seventh in the evening, poor Jenny came into my chamber, and, having her heart full of the great change of life from a virgin condition to that of a wife, she long sat silent. I saw she expected me to entertain her on this important subject, which was too delicate a circumstance for herself to touch upon; whereupon I relieved her modesty in the following manner: "Sister," said I, "you are now going from me: and be contented, that you leave the company of a talkative old man, for that of a sober young one: but take this along with you, that there is no mean in the state you are entering into, but you are to be exquisitely happy or miserable, and your fortune in this way of life will be wholly of your own making. In all the marriages I have ever seen, most of which have been unhappy ones, the great cause of evil has proceeded from slight occasions; and I take it to be the first maxim in a married condition, that you are be above trifles. When two persons have so good an opinion of each other as to come together for life, they will not differ in matters of importance, because they think of each other with respect; and in regard to all things of consideration that may affect them, they are prepared for mutual assistance and relief in such occurrences. For less occasions, they form no resolutions, but leave their minds unprepared.

"This, dear Jenny, is the reason that the quarrel between Sir Harry Willit and his lady, which began about her squirrel, is irreconcilable. Sir Harry was reading a grave author; she runs into his study, and, in a playing humour, claps the squirrel upon the folio: he threw the animal in a rage on the floor; she snatches it up again, calls Sir Harry a sour pedant, without good nature or good manners. This cast him into such a rage, that he threw down the table before him, kicked the book round the room; then recollected himself: 'Lord, madam,' said he, 'why did you run into such expressions? I was,' said he, 'in the highest delight with that author, when you clapped your squirrel upon my book;' and, smiling, added upon recollection, 'I have a great respect for your favourite, and pray let us all be friends.' My lady was so far from accepting this apology, that she immediately conceived a resolution to keep him under for ever; and, with a serious air, replied, 'There is no regard to be had to what a man says, who can fall into so indecent a rage, and such an abject submission, in the same moment, for which I absolutely despise you.' Upon which she rushed out of the room. Sir Harry staid some minutes behind, to think and command himself; after which he followed her into her bed-chamber, where she was prostrate upon the bed, tearing her hair, and naming twenty coxcombs who would have used her otherwise. This provoked him to so high a degree, that he forbore nothing but beating her; and all the servants in the family were at their several stations listening, whilst the best man and woman, the best master and mistress, defamed each other in a way that is not to be repeated even at Billingsgate. You know this ended in an immediate separation: she longs to return home but knows not how to do it: he invites her home every day, and lies with every woman he can get. Her husband requires no submission of her; but she thinks her very return will argue she is to blame, which she is resolved to be for ever, rather than acknowledge it. Thus, dear Jenny, my great advice to you is, be guarded against giving or receiving little provocations. Great matters of offence I have no reason to fear either from you or your husband."

After this, we turned our discourse into a more gay style, and parted: but before we did so, I made her resign her snuff-box for ever, and half drown herself with washing away the stench of the musty.

But the wedding morning arrived, and our family being very numerous, there was no avoiding the inconvenience of making the ceremony and festival more public, than the modern way of celebrating them makes me approve of. The bride next morning came out of her chamber, dressed with all the art and care that Mrs. Toilet, the tire-woman, could bestow on her. She was on her wedding-day three-and-twenty: her person is far from what we call a regular beauty; but a certain sweetness in her countenance, an ease in her shape and motion, with an unaffected modesty in her looks, had attractions beyond what symmetry and exactness can inspire, without the addition of these endowments. When her lover entered the room, her features flushed with shame and joy; and the ingenuous manner, so full of passion and of awe, with which Tranquillus approached to salute her, gave me good omens of his future behaviour towards her. The wedding was wholly under my care. After the ceremony at church, I was resolved to entertain the company with a dinner suitable to the occasion, and pitched upon the Apollo, at the Old-Devil at Temple-Bar, as a place sacred to mirth tempered with discretion, where Ben Jonson and his sons used to make their liberal meetings. Here the chief of the Staffian race appeared; and as soon as the company were come into that ample room, Lepidus Wagstaff began to make me compliments for choosing that place, and fell into a discourse upon the subject of pleasure and entertainment, drawn from the rules of Ben's club, which are in gold letters over the chimney. Lepidus has a way very uncommon, and speaks on subjects on which any man else would certainly offend, with great dexterity. He gave us a large account

THE TATLER

of the public meetings of all the well-turned minds who had passed through this life in ages past, and closed his pleasing narrative with a discourse on marriage, and a repetition of the following verses out of Milton.

> "Hail, wedded love! mysterious law! true source
> Of human offspring, sole propriety
> In paradise, of all things common else.
> By thee adult'rous lust was driven from men
> Among the bestial herds to range; by thee,
> Founded in reason, loyal, just and pure,
> Relations dear, and all the charities
> Of father, son, and brother, first were known.
> Perpetual fountain of domestic sweets,
> Whose bed is undefil'd and chaste pronounc'd,
> Present or past, as saints or patriarchs us'd.
> Here Love his golden shafts employs; here lights
> His constant lamp, and waves his purple wings:
> Reigns here, and revels not in the bought smile
> Of harlots, loveless, joyless, unendear'd,
> Casual fruition; nor in court amours,
> Mix'd dance, or wanton mask, or midnight ball,
> Or serenade, which the starv'd lover sings
> To his proud fair, best quitted with disdain."

In these verses, all the images that can come into a young woman's head on such an occasion are raised; but that in so chaste and elegant a manner, that the bride thanked him for his agreeable talk, and we sat down to dinner.

Among the rest of the company, there was got in a fellow you call a Wag. This ingenious person is the usual life of all feasts and merriments, by speaking absurdities, and putting everybody of breeding and modesty out of countenance. As soon as we sat down, he drank to the bride's diversion that night; and then made twenty double meanings on the word *thing*. We are the best-bred family, for one so numerous, in this kingdom; and indeed we should all of us have been as much out of countenance as the bride, but that we were relieved by an honest rough relation of ours at the lower end of the table, who is a lieutenant of marines. The soldier and sailor had good plain sense, and saw what was wrong as well as another; he had a way of looking at his plate, and speaking aloud in an inward manner; and whenever the Wag mentioned the word *thing*, or the words, *that same*, the lieutenant in that voice cried, "Knock him down." The merry man, wondering, angry, and looking round, was the diversion of the table. When he offered to recover, and say, "To the bride's best thoughts," "Knock him down," says the lieutenant, and so on. This silly humour diverted, and saved us from the fulsome entertainment of an ill-bred coxcomb; and the bride drank the lieutenant's health. We returned to my lodging, and Tranquillus led his wife to her apartment, without the ceremony of throwing the stocking.

SCENE OF COUNTRY ETIQUETTE

No. 86.] THURSDAY, OCTOBER 27, 1709. [ADDISON AND STEELE.]

WHEN I came home last night, my servant delivered me the following letter:

Oct. 24.

"SIR,— I have orders from Sir Harry Quickset, of Staffordshire, Bart., to acquaint you, that his honour Sir Harry himself, Sir Giles Wheelbarrow, Knt., Thomas Rentfree, Esq., justice of the *quorum*, Andrew Windmill, Esq., and Mr. Nicholas Doubt of the Inner Temple, Sir Harry's grandson, will wait upon you at the hour of nine to-morrow morning, being Tuesday the 25th of October, upon business which Sir Harry will impart to you by word of mouth. I thought it proper to acquaint you before-hand so many persons of quality came, that you might not be surprised therewith. Which concludes, though by many years' absence since I saw you at Stafford, unknown,

"Sir, your most humble servant,
"JOHN THRIFTY."

I received this message with less surprise than I believe Mr. Thrifty imagined; for I knew the good company too well to feel any palpitations at their approach: but I was in very great concern how I should adjust the ceremonial, and demean myself to all these great men, who perhaps had not seen anything above themselves for these twenty years last past. I am sure that is the case of Sir Harry. Besides which, I was sensible that there was a great point in adjusting my behaviour to the simple squire, so as to give him satisfaction, and not disoblige the justice of the *quorum*.

THE TATLER

The hour of nine was come this morning, and I had no sooner set chairs (by the stewards' letter) and fixed my tea equipage, but I heard a knock at my door, which was opened, but no one entered; after which followed a long silence, which was broke at last by, "Sir, I beg your pardon; I think I know better:" and another voice, "Nay, good Sir Giles —" I looked out from my window, and saw the good company all with their hats off, and arms spread, offering the door to each other. After many offers, they entered with much solemnity, in the order Mr. Thrifty was so kind as to name them to me. But they are now got to my chamber door, and I saw my old friend Sir Harry enter. I met him with all the respect due to so reverend a vegetable; for you are to know, that is my sense of a person who remains idle in the same place for half a century. I got him with great success into his chair by the fire, without throwing down any of my cups. The knight-bachelor told me, he had a great respect for my whole family, and would, with my leave, place himself next to Sir Harry, at whose right hand he had sat at every quarter-sessions this thirty years, unless he was sick. The steward in the rear whispered the young Templar, "That is true to my knowledge." I had the misfortune, as they stood cheek by jole, to desire the squire to sit down before the justice of the *quorum*, to the no small satisfaction of the former, and resentment of the latter: but I saw my error too late, and got them as soon as I could into their seats. "Well, (said I,) gentlemen, after I have told you how glad I am of this great honour, I am to desire you to drink a dish of tea." They answered, one and all, that "They never drank tea in a morning." "Not in a morning!" said I, staring round me. Upon which the pert jackanapes Nick Doubt tipped me the wink, and put out his tongue at his grandfather. Here followed a profound silence, when the steward in his boots and whip proposed that we should adjourn to some public-house, where everybody might call for what they pleased, and enter upon the business. We all stood up in an instant, and Sir Harry filed off from the left very discreetly, counter-marching behind the chairs towards the door: after him, Sir Giles in the same manner. The simple squire made a sudden start to follow; but the justice of the *quorum* whipped between upon the stand of the stairs. A maid going up with coals made us halt, and put us into such confusion, that we stood all in a heap, without any visible possibility of recovering our order: for the young jackanapes seemed to make a jest of this matter, and had so contrived, by pressing amongst us under pretence of making way, that his grandfather was got into the middle, and he knew nobody was of quality to stir a step, till Sir Harry moved first. We were fixed in this perplexity for some time, till we heard a very loud noise in the street; and Sir Harry asking what it was, I, to make them move, said it was fire. Upon this, all run down as fast as they could, without order or ceremony, till we got into the street, where we drew up in very good order, and filed off down Sheer Lane, the impertinent Templar driving us before him, as in a string, and pointing to his acquaintance who passed by.

I must confess, I love to use people according to their own sense of good breeding, and therefore whipped in between the justice and the simple squire. He could not properly take this ill; but I overheard him whisper the steward, "That he thought it hard that a common conjurer should take place of him, though an elder squire." In this order we marched down Sheer Lane, at the upper end of which I lodge. When we came to Temple Bar, Sir Harry and Sir Giles got over; but a run of coaches kept the rest of us on this side the street: however, we all at last landed, and drew up in very good order before Ben. Tooke's shop, who favoured our rallying with great humanity. From hence we proceeded again, till we came to Dick's Coffee-house, where I designed to carry them. Here we were at our old difficulty, and took up the street upon the same ceremony. We proceeded through the entry, and were so necessarily kept in order by the situation, that we were now got into the coffee-house itself, where, as soon as we arrived, we repeated our civilities to each other; after which, we marched up to the high table, which has an ascent to it enclosed in the middle of the room. The whole house was alarmed at this entry, made up of persons of so much state and rusticity. Sir Harry called for a mug of ale, and Dyer's Letter. The boy brought the ale in an instant: but said, they did not take in the Letter. "No! (says Sir Harry,) then take back your mug; we are like indeed to have good liquor at this house." Here the Templar tipped me a second wink, and if I had not looked very grave upon him, I found he was disposed to be very familiar with me. In short, I observed after a long pause, that the gentlemen did not care to enter upon business till after their morning draught, for which reason

I called for a bottle of mum; and finding that had no effect upon them, I ordered a second, and a third: after which, Sir Harry reached over to me, and told me in a low voice, that the place was too public for business; but he would call upon me again to-morrow morning at my own lodgings, and bring some more friends with him.

A DANCING-MASTER PRACTISING BY BOOK

No. 88.] TUESDAY, NOVEMBER 1, 1709. [ADDISON.]

I WAS this morning awakened by a sudden shake of the house; and as soon as I had got a little out of my consternation, I felt another, which was followed by two or three repetitions of the same convulsion. I got up as fast as possible, girt on my rapier, and snatched up my hat, when my landlady came up to me, and told me that the gentlewoman of the next house begged me to step thither; for that a lodger she had taken in was run mad, and she desired my advice; as indeed everybody in the whole lane does upon important occasions. I am not, like some artists, saucy, because I can be beneficial, but went immediately. Our neighbour told us, she had the day before let her second floor to a very genteel, youngish man, who told her he kept extraordinary good hours, and was generally at home most part of the morning and evening at study; but that this morning he had for an hour together made this extravagant noise which we then heard. I went upstairs with my hand upon the hilt of my rapier, and approached this new logder's door. I looked in at the key-hole, and there I saw a well-made man look with great attention on a book, and on a sudden jump into the air so high, that his head almost touched the ceiling. He came down safe on his right foot, and again flew up, alighting on his left; then looked again at his book, and holding out his right leg, put it into such a quivering motion, that I thought he would have shaked it off. He used the left after the same manner; when on a sudden, to my great surprise, he stooped himself incredibly low, and turned gently on his toes. After this circular motion, he continued bent in that humble posture for some time, looking on his book. After this he recovered himself by a sudden spring, and flew round the room in all the violence and disorder imaginable, till he made a full pause for want of breath. In this interim my woman asked what I thought: I whispered, that I thought this learned person an enthusiast, who possibly had his first education in the peripatetic way, which was a sect of philosophers who always studied when walking. But observing him much out of breath, I thought it the best time to master him if he were disordered, and knocked at his door. I was surprised to find him open it, and say, with great civility and good mien, "That he hoped he had not disturbed us." I believed him in a lucid interval, and desired he would please to let me see his book. He did so, smiling. I could not make anything of it, and therefore asked in what language it was writ. He said, "It was one he studied with great application; but it was his profession to teach it, and could not communicate his knowledge without a consideration." I answered, "That I hoped he would hereafter keep his thoughts to himself; for his meditation this morning had cost me three coffee dishes, and a clean pipe. He seemed concerned at that, and told me he was a dancing-master, and had been reading a dance or two before he went out, which had been written by one who taught at an academy in France. He observed me at a stand, and went on to inform me, "That now articulate motions, as well as sounds, were expressed by proper characters; and that there is nothing so common as to communicate a dance by a letter." I beseeched him hereafter to meditate in a ground-room, for that otherwise it would be impossible for an artist of any other kind to live near him; and that I was sure, several of his thoughts this morning would have shaken my spectacles off my nose, had I been myself at study.

I then took my leave of this virtuoso, and returned to my chamber, meditating on the various occupations of rational creatures.

THE TATLER

APPLICATIONS FOR PERMISSON TO USE CANES, Etc.

No. 103.] TUESDAY, DECEMBER 6, 1709. [ADDISON AND STEELE.]

— Hæ nugæ seria ducunt
In mala, derisum semel exceptumque sinistrê. — HOR.

THERE is nothing gives a man greater satisfaction, than the sense of having despatched a great deal of business, especially when it turns to the public emolument. I have much pleasure of this kind upon my spirits at present, occasioned by the fatigue of affairs which I went through last Saturday. It is some time since I set apart that day for examining the pretensions of several who had applied to me for canes, perspective-glasses, snuff-boxes, orange-flower-waters, and the like ornaments of life. In order to adjust this matter, I had before directed Charles Lillie, of Beaufort Buildings, to prepare a great bundle of blank licences in the following words:

"You are hereby required to permit the bearer of this cane to pass and repass through the streets and suburbs of London, or any place within ten miles of it, without let or molestation: provided that he does not walk with it under his arm, brandish it in the air, or hang it on a button: in which case it shall be forfeited; and I hereby declare it forfeited to any one who shall think it safe to take it from him.

"ISAAC BICKERSTAFFE."

The same form, differing only in the provisos, will serve for a perspective, snuff-box, or perfumed handkerchief. I had placed myself in my elbow-chair at the upper end of my great parlour, having ordered Charles Lillie to take his place upon a joint-stool with a writing-desk before him. John Morphew also took his station at the door; I having, for his good and faithful services, appointed him my chamber-keeper upon court days. He let me know, that there were a great number attending without. Upon which I ordered him to give notice, that I did not intend to sit upon snuff-boxes that day; but that those who appeared for canes might enter. The first presented me with the following petition, which I ordered Mr. Lillie to read.

"To Isaac Bickerstaffe, Esq., Censor of Great Britain.
"The humble Petition of Simon Trippit,
"Showeth,

"That your petitioner having been bred up to a cane from his youth, it is now become as necessary to him as any other of his limbs.

"That a great part of his behaviour depending upon it, he should be reduced to the utmost necessities if he should lose the use of it.

"That the knocking of it upon his shoe, leaning one leg upon it, or whistling with it on his mouth, are such great reliefs to him in conversation, that he does not know how to be good company without it.

"That he is at present engaged in an armour, and must despair of success, if it be taken from him.

"Your petitioner therefore hopes, that (the premises tenderly considered) your Worship will not deprive him of so useful and so necessary a support.

"And your petitioner shall ever," &c.

Upon the hearing of his case, I was touched with some compassion, and the more so, when upon observing him nearer I found he was a prig. I bid him produce his cane in court, which he had left at the door. He did so, and I finding it to be very curiously clouded, with a transparent amber head, and a blue ribbon to hang upon his wrist, I immediately ordered my clerk Lillie to lay it up, and deliver out to him a plain joint, headed with walnut; and then, in order to wean him from it by degrees, permitted him to wear it three days in the week, and to abate proportionably till he found himself able to go alone.

The second who appeared, came limping into the court: and setting forth in his petition many pretences for the use of a cane, I caused them to be examined one by one; but finding him in different stories, and confronting him with several witnesses who had seen him walk upright, I ordered Mr. Lillie to take in his cane, and rejected his petition as frivolous.

THE TATLER

A third made his entry with great difficulty, leaning upon a slight stick, and in danger of falling every step he took. I saw the weakness of his hams; and hearing that he had married a young wife about a fortnight before, I bid him leave his cane, and gave him a new pair of crutches, with which he went off in great vigour and alacrity. This gentleman was succeeded by another, who seemed very much pleased while his petition was reading, in which he had represented, that he was extremely afflicted with the gout, and set his foot upon the ground with the caution and dignity which accompany that distemper. I suspected him for an impostor, and having ordered him to be searched, I committed him into the hands of Dr. Thomas Smith in King Street, (my own corn-cutter,) who attended in an outward room; and wrought so speedy a cure upon him, that I thought fit to send him also away without his cane.

While I was thus dispensing justice, I heard a noise in my outward room; and inquiring what was the occasion of it, my door-keeper told me, that they had taken up one in the very fact as he was passing by my door. They immediately brought in a lively, fresh-coloured young man, who made great resistance with hand and foot, but did not offer to make use of his cane, which hung upon his fifth button. Upon examination, I found him to be an Oxford scholar, who was just entered at the Temple. He at first disputed the jurisdiction of the court; but being driven out of his little law and logic, he told me very pertly, that he looked upon such a perpendicular creature as man to make a very imperfect figure without a cane in his hand. "It is well known (says he) we ought, according to the natural situation of our bodies, to walk upon our hands and feet; and that the wisdom of the ancients had described man to be an animal of four legs in the morning, two at noon, and three at night; by which they intimated, that a cane might very properly become part of us in some period of life." Upon which I asked him, "whether he wore it at his breast to have it in readiness when that period should arrive?" My young lawyer immediately told me, he had a property in it, and a right to hang it where he pleased, and to make use of it as he thought fit, provided that he did not break the peace with it; and further said, that he never took it off his button, unless it were to lift it up at a coachman, hold it over the head of a drawer, point out the circumstances of a story, or for other services of the like nature, that are all within the laws of the land. I did not care for discouraging a young man who, I saw, would come to good; and because his heart was set upon his new purchase, I only ordered him to wear it about his neck, instead of hanging it upon his button, and so dismissed him.

There were several appeared in court, whose pretensions I found to be very good, and therefore gave many their licences upon paying their fees; as many others had their licences renewed, who required more time for recovery of their lameness than I had before allowed them.

Having despatched this set of my petitioners, there came in a well-dressed man, with a glass-tube in one hand and his petition in the other. Upon his entering the room, he threw back the right side of his wig, put forward his right leg, and advancing the glass to his right eye, aimed it directly at me. In the mean while, to make my observations also, I put on my spectacles; in which posture we surveyed each other for some time. Upon the removal of our glasses, I desired him to read his petition, which he did very promptly and easily; though at the same time it set forth, that he could see nothing distinctly, and was within a very few degrees of being utterly blind; concluding with a prayer, that he might be permitted to strengthen and extend his sight by a glass. In answer to this, I told him, he might sometimes extend it to his own destruction. "As you are now (said I) you are out of the reach of beauty; the shafts of the finest eyes lose their force before they can come at you; you cannot distinguish a toast from an orange-wench; you can see a whole circle of beauty without any interruption from an impertinent face to discompose you. In short, what are snares for others" — My petitioner would hear no more, but told me very seriously, "Mr. Bickerstaffe, you quite mistake your man; it is the joy, the pleasure, the employment of my life, to frequent public assemblies, and gaze upon the fair." In a word, I found his use of a glass was occasioned by no other infirmity but his vanity, and was not so much designed to make him see, as to make him be seen and distinguished by others. I therefore refused him a licence for a perspective, but allowed him a pair of spectacles, with full permission to use them in any public assembly as he should think fit. He was followed by so very few of this order of men, that I have reason to hope this sort of cheats are almost at an end.

The orange-flower-men appeared next with petitions, perfumed so strongly with musk, that I was almost overcome with the scent; and for my own sake, was obliged forthwith to licence their handkerchiefs, especially when I found they had sweetened them at Charles Lillie's, and that some of their persons would not be altogether inoffensive without them. John Morphew, whom I have made the general of my dead men, acquainted me, that the petitioners were all of that order, and could produce certificates to prove it if I required it. I was so well pleased with this way of their embalming themselves, that I commanded the abovesaid Morphew to give it in orders to his whole army, that every one who did not surrender himself up to be disposed of by the upholders, should use the same method to keep himself sweet during his present state of putrefaction.

I finished my session with great content of mind, reflecting upon the good I had done; for however slightly men may regard these particularities and little follies in dress and behaviour, they lead to greater evils. The bearing to be laughed at for such singularities, teaches us insensibly an impertinent fortitude, and enables us to bear public censure for things which more substantially deserve it. By this means they open a gate to folly, and oftentimes render a man so ridiculous, as discredit his virtues and capacities, and unqualify them from doing any good in the world. Besides, the giving in to uncommon habits of this nature, is a want of that humble deference which is due to mankind; and (what is worst of all) the certain indication of some secret flaw in the mind of the person that commits them. When I was a young man, I remember a gentleman of great integrity and worth was very remarkable for wearing a broad belt, and a hanger instead of a fashionable sword, though in all other points a very well-bred man. I suspected him at first sight to have something wrong in him, but was not able for a long while to discover any collateral proofs of it. I watched him narrowly for six and thirty years, when at last, to the surprise of everybody but myself, who had long expected to see the folly break out, he married his own cook-maid.

# THE TATLER

MRS. TRANQUILLUS

No. 104.] THURSDAY, DECEMBER 8, 1709. [STEELE.]

———— Garrit aniles
Ex re fabellas ————.   HOR. 2 Sat. vi. 78.

He tells an old wife's tale very pertinently.

MY brother Tranquillus being gone out of town for some days, my sister Jenny sent me word she would come and dine with me, and therefore desired me to have no other company. I took care accordingly, and was not a little pleased to see her enter the room with a decent and matron-like behaviour, which I thought very much became her. I saw she had a great deal to say to me, and easily discovered in her eyes, and the air of her countenance, that she had abundance of satisfaction in her heart, which she longed to communicate. However, I was resolved to let her break into her discourse her own way, and reduced her to a thousand little devices and intimations to bring me to the mention of her husband. But, finding I was resolved not to name him, she began of her own accord. "My husband," said she, "gives his humble service to you;" to which I only answered, "I hope he is well;" and, without waiting for a reply, fell into other subjects. She at last was out of all patience, and said, with a smile and manner that I thought had more beauty and spirit than I had ever observed before in her, "I did not think, brother, you had been so ill-natured. You have seen, ever since I came in, that I had a mind to talk of my husband, and you will not be so kind as to give me an occasion." —"I did not know," said I, "but it might be a disagreeable subject to you. You do not take me for so old-fashioned a fellow as to think of entertaining a young lady with the discourse of her husband. I know, nothing is more acceptable than to speak of one who is to be so; but to speak of one who is so! indeed, Jenny, I am a better bred man than you think me." She shewed a little dislike at my raillery; and, by her bridling up, I perceived she expected to be treated hereafter not as Jenny Distaff, but Mrs. Tranquillus. I was very well pleased with this change in her humour; and, upon talking with her on several subjects, I could not but fancy that

I saw a great deal of her husband's way and manner in her remarks, her phrases, the tone of her voice, and the very air of her countenance. This gave me an unspeakable satisfaction, not only because I had found her an husband, from whom she could learn many things that were laudable, but also because I looked upon her imitation of him as an infallible sign that she entirely loved him.

This is an observation that I never knew fail, though I do not remember that any other has made it. The natural shyness of her sex hindered her from telling me the greatness of her own passion; but I easily collected it from the representation she gave me of his. "I have everything," says she, "in Tranquillus, that I can wish for; and enjoy in him, what indeed you have told me were to be met with in a good husband the fondness of a lover, the tenderness of a parent, and the intimacy of a friend." It transported me to see her eyes swimming in tears of affection when she spoke. "And is there not, dear sister," said I, "more pleasure in the possession of such a man, than in all the little impertinences of balls, assemblies, and equipage, which it cost me so much pains to make you contemn?" She answered, smiling, "Tranquillus has made me a sincere convert in a few weeks, though I am afraid you could not have done it in your whole life. To tell you truly, I have only one fear hanging upon me, which is apt to give me trouble in the midst of all my satisfactions: I am afraid, you must know, that I shall not always make the same amiable appearance in his eyes that I do at present. You know, brother Bickerstaffe, that you have the reputation of a conjurer; and if you have any one secret in your art to make your sister always beautiful, I should be happier than if I were mistress of all the worlds you have shown me in a starry night."—"Jenny," said I, "without having recourse to magic, I shall give you one plain rule, that will not fail of making you always amiable to a man who has so great a passion for you, and is of so equal and reasonable a temper as Tranquillus. Endeavour to please, and you must please; be always in the same disposition as you are when you ask for this secret, and you may take my word, you will never want it. An inviolable fidelity, good humour, and complacency of temper, out-live all the charms of a fine face, and make the decays of it invisible."

We discoursed very long upon this head, which was equally agreeable to us both; for I must confess, as I tenderly love her, I take as much pleasure in giving her instructions for her welfare, as she herself does in receiving them. I proceeded, therefore, to inculate these sentiments, by relating a very particular passage that happened within my own knowledge.

There were several of us making merry at a friend's house in a country village, when the sexton of the parish church entered the room in a sort of surprise, and told us, "that as he was digging a grave in the chancel, a little blow of his pickaxe opened a decayed coffin, in which there were several written papers." Our curiosity was immediately raised, so that we went to the place where the sexton had been at work, and found a great concourse of people about the grave. Among the rest, there was an old woman, who told us, the person buried there was a lady whose name I do not think fit to mention, though there is nothing in the story but what tends very much to her honour. This lady lived several years an exemplary pattern of conjugal love, and, dying soon after her husband, who every way answered her character in virtue and affection, made it her death-bed request, "that all the letters which she had received from him both before and after her marriage should be buried in the coffin with her." These, I found upon examination, were the papers before us. Several of them had suffered so much by time, that I could only pick out a few words; as *my soul! lilies! roses! dearest angel!* and the like. One of them, which was legible throughout, ran thus:

"MADAM, — If you would know the greatness of my love, consider that of your own beauty. That blooming countenance, that snowy bosom, that graceful person, return every moment to my imagination: the brightness of your eyes hath hindered me from closing mine since I last saw you. You may still add to your beauties by a smile. A frown will make me the most wretched of men, as I am the most passionate of lovers."

It filled the whole company with a deep melancholy, to compare the description of the letter with the person that occasioned it, who was now reduced to a few crumbling bones and a little mouldering heap of earth. With much ado I decyphered another letter, which began with, "My dear, dear wife." This gave me a curiosity to see how the style of one written in marriage differed from one written in courtship. To my surprise, I found the fondness rather augmented than lessened, though the panegyric turned upon a different accomplishment. The words were as follows:

"Before this short absence from you, I did not know that I loved you so much as I really do; though, at the same time, I thought I loved you as much as possible. I am under great apprehension, lest you should have any uneasiness whilst I am defrauded of my share in it, and cannot think of tasting any pleasures that you do not partake with me. Pray, my dear, be careful of your health, if for no other reason, but because you know I could not outlive you. It is natural in absence to make professions of an inviolable constancy; but towards so much merit, it is scarce a virtue, especially when it is but a bare return to that of which you have given me such continued proofs ever since our first acquaintance. I am, &c."

It happened that the daughter of these two excellent persons was by when I was reading this letter. At the sight of the coffin, in which was the body of her mother, near that of her father, she melted into a flood of tears. As I had heard a great character of her virtue, and observed in her this instance of filial piety, I could not resist my natural inclination of giving advice to young people, and therefore addressed myself to her. "Young lady," said I, "you see how short is the possession of that beauty, in which nature has been so liberal to you. You find the melancholy sight before you is a contradiction to the first letter that you heard on that subject; whereas you may observe, the second letter, which celebrates your mother's constancy, is itself, being found in this place, an argument of it. But, madam, I ought to caution you, not to think the bodies that lie before you your father and your mother. Know, their constancy is rewarded by a nobler union than by this mingling of their ashes, in a state where there is no danger or possibility of a second separation."

THE TATLER

THE PETTICOAT

No. 116.] THURSDAY, JANUARY 5, 1709–10. [ADDISON.]

―― Pars minima est ipsa puella sui. ― OVID.
The young lady is the least part of herself.

THE court being prepared for proceeding on the cause of the petticoat, I gave orders to bring in a criminal, who was taken up as she went out of the puppet-shew about three nights ago, and was now standing in the street, with a great concourse of people about her. Word was brought me, that she had endeavoured twice or thrice to come in, but could not do it by reason of her petticoat, which was too large for the entrance of my house, though I had ordered both the folding doors to be thrown open for its reception. Upon this, I desired the jury of matrons, who stood at my right-hand, to inform themselves of her condition, and know whether there were any private reasons why she might not make her appearance separate from her petticoat. This was managed with great discretion, and had such an effect, that upon the return of the verdict from the bench of matrons, I issued out an order forthwith, "that the criminal should be stripped of her incumbrances, until she became little enough to enter my house." I had before given directions for an engine of several legs, that could contract or open itself like the top of an *umbrella*, in order to place the petticoat upon it, by which means I might take a leisurely survey of it, as it should appear in its proper dimensions. This was all done accordingly; and forthwith, upon the closing of the engine, the petticoat was brought into court. I then directed the machine to be set upon the table, and dilated in such a manner as to shew the garment in its utmost circumference; but my great hall was too narrow for the experiment; for before it was half unfolded, it described so immoderate a circle, that the lower part of it brushed upon my face as I sat in my chair of judicature. I then inquired for the person that belonged to the petticoat; and, to my great surprise, was directed to a very beautiful young damsel, with so pretty a face and shape, that I bid her come out of the crowd, and seated her upon a little crock at my left hand. "My pretty maid," said I, "do you own yourself to have been the inhabitant of the garment before us?"

The girl, I found, had good sense, and told me with a smile, that, "notwithstanding it was her own petticoat, she should be very glad to see an example made of it; and that she wore it for no other reason, but that she had a mind to look as big and burly as other persons of her quality; that she had kept out of it as long as she could, and until she began to appear little in the eyes of her acquaintance; that, if she laid it aside, people would think she was not made like other women." I always give great allowances to the fair sex upon account of the fashion, and, therefore, was not displeased with the defence of my pretty criminal. I then ordered the vest which stood before us to be drawn up by a pulley to the top of my great hall, and afterwards to be spread open by the engine it was placed upon, in such a manner, that it formed a very splendid and ample canopy over our heads, and covered the whole court of judicature with a kind of silken rotunda, in its form not unlike the cupola of Saint Paul's. I entered upon the whole cause with great satisfaction as I sat under the shadow of it.

The counsel for the petticoat were now called in, and ordered to produce what they had to say against the popular cry which was raised against it. They answered the objections with great strength and solidity of argument, and expatiated in very florid harangues, which they did not fail to set off and furbelow, if I may be allowed the metaphor, with many periodical sentences and turns of oratory. The chief arguments for their client were taken, first, from the great benefit that might arise to our woolen manufactory from this invention, which was calculated as follows. The common petticoat has not above four yards in the circumference; whereas this over our heads had more in the semi-diameter; so that, by allowing it twenty-four yards in the circumference, the five millions of woollen petticoats which, according to Sir William Petty, supposing what ought to be supposed in a well-governed state, that all petticoats are made of that stuff, would amount to thirty millions of those of the ancient mode. A prodigious improvement of the woollen trade! and what could not fail to sink the power of France in a few years.

To introduce the second argument, they begged leave to read a petition of the ropemakers, wherein it was represented, "that the demand for cords, and the price of them, were much risen since this fashion came up." At this, all the company who were present lifted up their eyes into the vault; and I must confess, we did discover many traces of cordage, which were interwoven in the stiffening of the drapery.

A third argument was founded upon a petition of the Greenland trade, which likewise represented the great consumption of whalebone which would be occasioned by the present fashion, and the benefit which would thereby accrue to that branch of the British trade.

To conclude, they gently touched upon the weight and unwieldiness of the garment, which, they insinuated, might be of great use to preserve the honour of families.

These arguments would have wrought very much upon me, as I then told the company in a long and elaborate discourse, had I not considered the great and additional expense which such fashions would bring upon fathers and husbands; and, therefore, by no means to be thought of until some years after a peace. I farther urged, that it would be a prejudice to the ladies themselves, who could never expect to have any money in the pocket, if they laid out so much on the petticoat. To this I added, the great temptation it might give to virgins, of acting in security like married women, and by that means give a check to matrimony, an institution always encouraged by wise societies.

At the same time, in answer to the several petitions produced on that side, I shewed one subscribed by the women of several persons of quality, humbly setting forth, "that, since the introduction of this mode, their respective ladies had, instead of bestowing on them their cast gowns, cut them into shreds, and mixed them with the cordage and buckram, to complete the stiffening of their under petticoats." For which, and sundry other reasons, I pronounced the petticoat a forfeiture: but, to shew that I did not make that judgment for the sake of filthy lucre, I ordered it to be folded up, and sent it as a present to a widow-gentlewoman, who has five daughters; desiring she would make each of them a petticoat out of it, and send me back the remainder, which I design to cut into stomachers, caps, facings of my waistcoat-sleeves, and other garnitures suitable to my age and quality.

I would not be understood, that, while I discard this monstrous invention, I am an enemy to the proper ornaments of the fair sex. On the contrary, as the hand of nature has poured on them such a profusion of charms and graces, and sent them into the world more amiable and finished than the rest of her works; so I would have them bestow upon themselves all the additional beauties that art can supply them with, provided it does not interfere with, disguise, or pervert those of nature.

I consider woman as a beautiful romantic animal, that may be adorned with furs and feathers, pearls and diamonds, ores and silks. The lynx shall cast its skin at her feet to make her a tippet; the peacock, parrot, and swan shall pay contributions to her muff; the sea shall be searched for shells, and the rocks for gems; and every part of nature furnish out its share towards the embellishment of a creature that is the most consummate work of it. All this I shall indulge them in; but as for the petticoat I have been speaking of, I neither can nor will allow it.

ON THE LOTTERY

No. 124.] TUESDAY, JANUARY 24, 1709-10 [STEELE.]

—— Ex humili summa ad fastigia rerum
Extollit, quoties voluit Fortuna jocari.
JUV. SAT. iii. 39.

Fortune can, for her pleasure, fools advance,
And toss them on the wheels of Chance.

I WENT on Saturday last to make a visit in the city; and as I passed through Cheapside, I saw crowds of people turning down towards the Bank, and struggling who should first get their money into the *new-erected lottery*. It gave me a great notion of the credit of our present government and administration, to find people press as eagerly to pay money, as they would to receive it; and, at the same time, a due respect for that body of men who have found out so pleasing an expedient for carrying on the common cause, that they have turned a tax into a diversion. The cheerfulness of spirit, and the hopes of success, which this project has occasioned in this great city, lightens the burden of the war, and puts me in mind of some games which, they say, were invented by wise men, who were lovers of their country, to make their fellow-citizens undergo the tediousness and fatigues of a long siege. I think there is a kind of homage due to fortune, if I may call it so, and that I should be wanting to myself, if I did not lay in my pretences to her favour, and pay my compliments to her by recommending a ticket to her disposal. For this reason, upon my return to my lodgings, I sold off *a couple of globes and a telescope*, which, with the cash I had by me, raised the sum that was requisite for that purpose. I find by my calculations, that it is but *an hundred and fifty thousand to one*, against my being worth a thousand pounds *per annum* for thirty-two years; and if any *Plumb* in the city will lay me an hundred and fifty thousand pounds to twenty shillings, which is an even bet, that I am not this fortunate man, I will take the wager, and shall look upon him as a man of singular courage and fair-dealing; having given orders to Mr. Morphew to subscribe such a policy in my behalf, if any person accepts of the offer. I must confess, I have had such private intimations from the twinkling of a certain star in some of my astronomical observations, that I should be unwilling to take fifty pounds a year for my chance, unless it were to oblige a particular friend.

My chief business at present is, to prepare my mind for this change of fortune: for as Seneca, who was a greater moralist, and a much richer man than I shall be with this addition to my present income, says, *Munera ista Fortunæ putatis? Insidiæ sunt.* "What we look upon as gifts and presents of fortune, are traps and snares which she lays for the unwary." I am arming myself against her favours with all my philosophy; and that I may not lose myself in such a redundance of unnecessary and superfluous wealth, I have determined to settle an annual pension out of it upon a family of Palatines, and by that means give these unhappy strangers a taste of British property. At the same time, as I have an excellent servant-maid, whose diligence in attending me has increased in proportion to my infirmities, I shall settle upon her the revenue arising out of the ten pounds, and amounting to fourteen shillings *per annum;* with which she may retire into Wales, where she was born a gentlewoman, and pass the remaining part of her days in a condition suitable to her birth and quality. It was impossible for me to make an inspection into my own fortune on this occasion, without seeing, at the same time, the fate of others who are embarked in the same adventure. And indeed it was a great pleasure to me to observe, that the war, which generally impoverishes those who furnish out the expense of it, will by this means give estates to some, without making others the poorer for it. I have lately seen several in liveries, who will give as good of their own very suddenly; and took a particular satisfaction in the sight of a young country-wench, whom I this morning passed by as she was whirling her mop, with her petticoats tucked up very agreeably, who, if there is any truth in my art, is within ten months of being the handsomest great fortune in town. I must confess, I was so struck with the foresight of what she is to be, that I treated her accordingly, and said to her, "Pray, young lady, permit me to pass by." I would for this reason advise all masters and mistresses, to carry it with great moderation and condescension towards their servants until next Michaelmas, lest the superiority at that time should be inverted.

I must likewise admonish all my brethren and fellow-adventurers, to fill their minds with proper arguments for their support and consolation in case of ill success. It so happens in this particular, that though the gainers will have reason to rejoice, the losers will have no reason to complain. I remember, the day after the *thousand pound prize* was drawn in the Penny-lottery, I went to visit a splenetic acquaintance of mine, who was under much dejection, and seemed to me to have suffered some great disappointment. Upon inquiry, I found he had put *two-pence* for himself and his son into the lottery, and that neither of them had drawn the thousand pounds. Hereupon this unlucky person took occasion to enumerate the misfortunes of his life, and concluded with telling me, "that he never was successful in any of his undertakings." I was forced to comfort him with the common reflection upon such occasions, "that men of the greatest merit are not always men of the greatest success, and that persons of his character must not expect to be as happy as fools." I shall proceed in the like manner with my rivals and competitors for the *thousand pounds a year*, which we are now in pursuit of; and that I may give general content to the whole body of candidates, I shall allow all that draw prizes to be fortunate, and all that miss them to be wise.

I must not here omit to acknowledge, that I have received several letters upon this subject, but find one common error running through them all, which is, that the writers of them believe their fate in these cases depends upon the astrologer, and not upon the stars; as in the following letter from one, who, I fear, flatters himself with hopes of success which are altogether groundless, since he does not seem to me so great a fool as he takes himself to be.

"SIR,— Coming to town, and finding my friend Mr. Partridge dead and buried, and you the only conjurer in repute, I am under a necessity of applying myself to you for a favour, which nevertheless I confess it would better become a friend to ask, than one who is, as I am, altogether a stranger to you; but poverty, you know, is impudent; and as that gives me the occasion, so that alone could give me the confidence to be thus importunate.

"I am, sir, very poor, and very desirous to be otherwise: I have got ten pounds, which I design to venture in the lottery now on foot. What I desire of you is, that by your art, you will choose such a ticket for me as shall arise a benefit sufficient to maintain me. I must beg leave to inform you, that I am good for nothing, and must therefore insist upon a larger lot than would satisfy those who are capable, by their own abilities, of adding something to what you should assign them; whereas I must expect an absolute independent maintenance, because, as I said, I can do nothing. It is possible, after this free confession of mine, you may think I do not deserve to be rich; but I hope you will likewise observe, I can ill afford to be poor. My own opinion is, that I am well qualified for an estate, and have a good title to luck in a lottery; but I resign myself wholly to your mercy, not without hopes that you will consider, the less I deserve, the greater the generosity in you. If you reject me, I have agreed with an acquaintance of mine to bury me for my ten pounds. I once more recommend myself to your favour, and bid you adieu!"

THE PRUDE AND THE COQUETTE

No. 126.] SATURDAY, JANUARY 28, 1709-10. [STEELE.]

Anguillam caudâ tenes. — T. D'URFEY.

You have got an eel by the tail.

THERE is no sort of company so agreeable as that of women who have good sense without affectation, and can converse with men without any private design of imposing chains and fetters. Belvidera, whom I visited this evening, is one of these.

THE TATLER

There is an invincible prejudice in favour of all she says, from her being a beautiful woman; because she does not consider herself as such when she talks to you. This amiable temper gives a certain tincture to all her discourse, and made it very agreeable to me until we were interrupted by Lydia, a creature who has all the charms that can adorn a woman. Her attractions would indeed be irresistible, but that she thinks them so, and is always employing them in stratagems and conquests. When I turned my eye upon her as she sat down, I saw she was a person of that character, which, for the farther information of my country correspondents, I had long wanted an opportunity of explaining. Lydia is a finished coquette, which is a sect among women of all others the most mischievous, and makes the greatest havoc and disorder in society. I went on in the discourse I was in with Belvidera, without shewing that I had observed anything extraordinary in Lydia: upon which, I immediately saw her look me over as some very ill-bred fellow; and casting a scornful glance on my dress, give a shrug at Belvidera. But, as much as she despised me, she wanted my admiration, and made twenty offers to bring my eyes her way: but I reduced her to a restlessness in her seat, and impertinent playing of her fan, and many other motions and gestures before I took the least notice of her. At last I looked at her with a kind of surprise, as if she had before been unobserved by reason of an ill light where she sat. It is not to be expressed what a sudden joy I saw arise in her countenance, even at the approbation of such a very old fellow: but she did not long enjoy her triumph without a rival; for there immediately entered Castabella, a lady of a quite contrary character, that is to say, as eminent a prude as Lydia is a coquette. Belvidera gave me a glance, which methought intimated, that they were both curiosities in their kind, and worth remarking. As soon as we were again seated, I stole looks at each lady, as if I was comparing their perfections. Belvidera observed it, and began to lead me into a discourse of them both to their faces, which is to be done easily enough; for one woman is generally so intent upon the faults of another, that she has not reflection enough to observe when her own are represented. "I have taken notice, Mr. Bickerstaffe," said Belvidera, "that you have, in some parts of your writings, drawn characters of our sex, in which you have not, to my apprehension, been clear enough and distinct; particularly in those of a Prude and a Coquette." Upon the mention of this, Lydia was roused with the expectation of seeing Castabella's picture, and Castabella, with the hopes of that of Lydia. "Madam," said I to Belvidera, "when we consider nature, we shall often find very contrary effects flow from the same cause. The Prude and Coquette, as different as they appear in their behaviour, are in reality the same kind of women. The motive of action in both is the affectation of pleasing men. They are sisters of the same blood and constitution; only one chooses a grave, and the other a light dress. The Prude appears more virtuous, the Coquette more vicious than she really is. The distant behaviour of the Prude tends to the same purpose as the advances of the Coquette; and you have as little reason to fall into despair from the severity of the one, as to conceive hopes from the familiarity of the other. What leads you into a clear sense of their character is, that you may observe each of them has the distinction of sex in all her thoughts, words, and actions. You can never mention any assembly you were lately in, but one asks you with a rigid, the other with a sprightly air, "Pray, what men were there?" As for Prudes, it must be confessed, that there are several of them who, like hypocrites, by long practice of a false part become sincere; or at least delude themselves into a belief that they are so.

For the benefit of the society of ladies, I shall propose one rule to them as a test of their virtue. I find in a very celebrated modern author, that the great foundress of Pietists, madam de Bourignon, who was no less famous for the sanctity of her life than for the singularity of some of her opinions, used to boast, that she had not only the spirit of continency in herself, but that she had also the power of communicating it to all who beheld her. This the scoffers of those days called, "The gift of infrigidation," and took occasion from it to rally her face, rather than admire her virtue. I would therefore advise the Prude, who has a mind to know the integrity of her own heart, to lay her hand seriously upon it, and to examine herself, whether she could sincerely rejoice in such a gift of conveying chaste thoughts to all her male beholders. If she has any aversion to the power of inspiring so great a virtue, whatever notion she may have of her perfection, she deceives her own heart, and is still in the state of prudery. Some perhaps will look upon the boast of madam de Bourignon, as the utmost ostentation of a Prude.

If you would see the humour of a Coquette pushed to the last excess, you may find an instance of it in the following story: which

I will set down at length, because it pleased me when I read it, though I cannot recollect in what author.

"A young coquette widow in France having been followed by a Gascon of quality, who had boasted among his companions of some favours which he had never received; to be revenged of him, sent for him one evening, and told him, "it was in his power to do her a very particular service." The Gascon, with much profession of his readiness to obey her commands, begged to hear in what manner she designed to employ him. "You know," said the widow, "my friend Belinda; and must often have heard of the jealousy of that impotent wretch her husband. Now it is absolutely necessary, for the carrying on a certain affair, that his wife and I should be together a whole night. What I have to ask of you is, to dress yourself in her night-cloaths, and lie by him a whole night in her place, that he may not miss her while she is with me." The Gascon, though of a very lively and undertaking complexion, began to startle at the proposal. "Nay," says the widow, "if you have not the courage to go through what I ask of you, I must employ somebody else that will." "Madam," says the Gascon, "I will kill him for you if you please; but for lying with him!—— How is it possible to do it without being discovered?" "If you do not discover yourself," says the widow, "you will lie safe enough, for he is past all curiosity. He comes in at night while she is asleep, and goes out in a morning before she awakes; and is in pain for nothing, so he knows she is there." "Madam," replied the Gascon, "how can you reward me for passing a night with this old fellow?" The widow answered with a laugh, "Perhaps by admitting you to pass a night with one you think more agreeable." He took the hint; put on his night-cloaths; and had not been a-bed above an hour before he heard a knocking at the door, and the treading of one who approached the other side of the bed, and who he did not question was the good man of the house. I do not know, whether the story would be better by telling you in this place, or at the end of it, that the person who went to bed to him was our young coquette widow. The Gascon was in a terrible fright every time she moved in the bed, or turned towards him; and did not fail to shrink from her, until he had conveyed himself to the very ridge of the bed. I will not dwell upon the perplexity he was in the whole night, which was augmented, when he observed that it was now broad day, and that the husband did not yet offer to get up and go about his business. All that the Gascon had for it, was to keep his face turned from him, and to feign himself asleep, when, to his utter confusion, the widow at last puts out her arm, and pulls the bell at her bed's head. In came her friend, and two or three companions to whom the Gascon had boasted of her favours. The widow jumped into a wrapping gown, and joined with the rest in laughing at this man of intrigue.

TRIAL OF THE WINE-BREWERS

No. 131.] THURSDAY, FEBRUARY 9, 1709–10. [ADDISON.]

> Scelus est jugulare Falernum,
> Et dare Campano toxica sæva mero.   MART. i. 19.
>
> How great the crime, how flagrant the abuse!
> T' adulterate generous wine with noxious juice.

THERE is in this city a certain fraternity of chemical operators, who work underground in holes, caverns, and dark retirements, to conceal their mysteries from the eyes and observation of mankind. These subterraneous philosophers are daily employed in the transmutation of liquors, and, by the power of magical drugs and incantations, raising under the streets of London the choicest products of the hills and valleys of France. They can squeeze Bordeaux out of the sloe, and draw Champagne from an apple. Virgil, in that remarkable prophecy,

> Incultisque rubens pendebit sentibus uva.
>   VIRG. ECL. iv. 29.
>
> The ripening grape shall hang on every thorn,

seems to have hinted at this art, which can turn a plantation of northern hedges into a vineyard. These adepts are known among one another by the name of Wine-brewers; and, I am afraid, do great injury, not only to her majesty's customs, but to the bodies of many of her good subjects.

Having received sundry complaints against these invisible workmen, I ordered the proper officer of my court to ferret them out of their respective caves, and bring them before me, which was yesterday executed accordingly.

The person who appeared against them was a merchant, who had by him a great magazine of wines, that he had laid in before the war: but these gentlemen, as he said, "had so vitiated the nation's palate, that no man could believe his to be French, because it did not taste like what they sold for such." As a man never pleads better than where his own personal interest is concerned, he exhibited to the court, with great eloquence, "that this new corporation of druggists had inflamed the bills of mortality, and puzzled the college of physicians with diseases, for which they neither knew a name or cure. He accused some of giving all their customers colics and megrims; and mentioned one who had boasted, he had a tun of claret by him, that in a fortnight's time should give the gout to a dozen of the healthfulest men in the city, provided that their constitutions were prepared for it by wealth and idleness. He then enlarged, with a great show of reason, upon the prejudice, which these mixtures and compositions had done to the brains of the English nation; as is too visible, said he, from many late pamphlets, speeches, and sermons, a swell as from the ordinary conversations of the youth of this age. He then quoted an ingenious person, who would undertake to know by a man's writings the wine he most delighted in; and on that occasion named a certain satirist, whom he had discovered to be the author of a lampoon, by a manifest taste of the sloe, which showed itself in it, by much roughness, and little spirit.

In the last place, he ascribed to the unnatural tumults and fermentations which these mixtures raise in our blood, the divisions, heats, and animosities, that reign among us; and, in particular, asserted most of the modern enthusiasms and agitations to be nothing else but the effects of adulterated Port.

The counsel for the Brewers had a face so extremely inflamed, and illuminated with carbuncles, that I did not wonder to see him an advocate for these sophistications. His rhetoric was likewise such as I should have expected from the common draught, which I found he often drank to a great excess. Indeed, I was so surprised at his figure and parts, that I ordered him to give me a taste of his usual liquor; which I had no sooner drunk, but I found a pimple rising in my forehead; and felt such a terrible decay in my understanding, that I would not proceed in the trial until the fume of it was entirely dissipated.

This notable advocate had little to say in the defence of his clients, but that they were under a necessity of making claret, if they keep open their doors; it being the nature of mankind to love everything that is prohibited. He farther pretended to reason, that it might be as profitable to the nation to make French wine as French hats; and concluded with the great advantage that this practice had already brought to part of the kingdom. Upon which he informed the court, that the lands in Herefordshire were raised two years purchase since the beginning of the war.

When I had sent out my summons to these people, I gave, at the same time, orders to each of them to bring the several ingredients he made use of in distinct phials, which they had done accordingly, and ranged them into two rows on each side of the court. The workmen were drawn up in ranks behind them. The merchant informed me, "that in one row of phials were the several colours they dealt in, and in the other, the tastes." He then showed me, on the right-hand, one who went by the name of Tom Tintoret, who, as he told me, "was the greatest master in his colouring of any vintner in London." To give me a proof of his art, he took a glass of fair water; and, by the infusion of three drops out of one of his phials, converted it into a most beautiful pale Burgundy. Two more of the same kind heightened it into perfect Languedoc: from thence it passed into a florid Hermitage: and after having gone through two or three other changes, by the addition of a single drop, ended in a very deep Pontac. This ingenious virtuoso, seeing me very much surprised at his art, told me, that he had not an opportunity of showing it in perfection, having only made use of water for the ground-work of his colouring; but that, if I were to see an operation upon liquors of stronger bodies, the art would appear to a much greater advantage. He added, that he doubted not but it would please my curiosity to see the cyder of one apple take only a vermilion, when another, with a less quantity of the same infusion, would rise into a dark purple, according to the different texture of parts in the liquor. He informed me also, that he could hit the different shades and degrees of red, as they appear in the pink and the rose, the clove and the carnation, as he had Rhenish or Moselle, Perry or White Port, to work in.

I was so satisfied with the ingenuity of this virtuoso, that, after having advised him to quit so dishonest a profession, I promised him, in consideration of his great genius, to recommend him as a partner to a friend of mine, who has heaped up great riches, and is a scarlet-dyer.

The artists on my other hand were ordered, in the second place, to make some experiments of their skill before me: upon which the famous Harry Sippet stepped out, and asked me, "what I would be pleased to drink?" At the same time he filled out three or four white liquors in a glass, and told me, "that it should be what I pleased to call for;" adding very learnedly, "That liquor before him was as the naked substance, or first matter of his compound, to which he and his friend, who stood over-against him, could give what accidents, or form they pleased." Finding him so great a philosopher, I desired he would convey into it the qualities and essence of right Bordeaux. "Coming, coming, sir," said he, with the air of a drawer; and, after having cast his eye on the several tastes and flavours that stood before him, he took up a little cruet, that was filled with a kind of inky juice, and pouring some of it out into the glass of white wine, presented it to me; and told me, "this was the wine, over which most of the business of the last term had been dispatched." I must confess, I looked upon that sooty drug, which he held up in his cruet, as the quintessence of English Bordeaux; and therefore desired him to give me a glass of it by itself, which he did with great unwillingness. My cat at that time sat by me upon the elbow of my chair; and as I did not care for making the experiment upon myself, I reached it to her to sip of it, which had like to have cost her her life; for, notwithstanding it flung her at first into freakish tricks, quite contrary to her usual gravity, in less than a quarter of an hour she fell into convulsions; and, had it not been a creature more tenacious of life than any other, would certainly have died under the operation.

I was so incensed by the tortures of my innocent domestic, and the unworthy dealings of these men, that I told them, if each of them had as many lives as the injured creature before them, they deserved to forfeit them, for the pernicious arts which they used for their profit. I therefore bid them look upon themselves as no better than as a kind of assassins and murderers within the law. However, since they had dealt so clearly with me, and laid before me their whole practice, I dismissed them for that time; with a particular request, that they would not poison any of my friends and acquaintance, and take to some honest livelihood without loss of time.

For my own part, I have resolved hereafter to be very careful in my liquors; and have agreed with a friend of mine in the army, upon their next march, to secure me two hogsheads of the best stomach-wine in the cellars of Versailles, for the good of my Lucubrations, and the comfort of my old age.

OUR CLUB

No. 132.] SATURDAY, FEBRUARY 11, 1709–10. [STEELE.]

Habeo senectuti magnam gratiam, quæ mihi sermonis aviditatem auxit, potionis et cibi sustulit. — TULL. de Sen.

I am much beholden to old age, which has increased my eagerness for conversation in proportion as it has lessened my appetites of hunger and thirst.

AFTER having applied my mind with more than ordinary attention to my studies, it is my usual cusom to relax and unbend it in the conversation of such, as are rather easy than shining companions. This I find particularly necessary for me before I retire to rest, in order to draw my slumbers upon me by degrees, and fall asleep insensibly. This is the particular use I make of a set of heavy honest men, with whom I have passed many hours with much indolence, though not with great pleasure. Their conversation is a kind of preparative for sleep: it takes the mind down from its abstractions, leads it into the familiar traces of thought, and lulls it into that state of tranquillity, which is the condition of a thinking man, when he is but half awake. After this, my reader will not be surprised to hear the account, which I am about to give of a club of my own contemporaries, among whom I pass two or three hours every evening. This I look upon as taking my first nap before I go to bed. The truth of it is, I should think myself unjust to posterity, as well as to the society at the Trumpet, of which I am a member, did not I in some part of my writings give an account of the persons among whom I have passed almost a sixth part of my time for these last forty years. Our club consisted originally of fifteen; but, partly by the severity of the law in arbitrary times, and partly by the natural effects of old age, we are at present reduced to a third

THE TATLER

part of that number: in which, however, we hear this consolation, that the best company is said to consist of five persons, I must confess, besides the aforementioned benefit which I meet with in the conversation of this select society, I am not the less pleased with the company, in that I find myself the greatest wit among them, and am heard as their oracle in all points of learning and difficulty.

Sir Jeoffrey Notch, who is the oldest of the club, has been in possession of the right-hand chair time out of mind, and is the only man among us that has the liberty of stirring the fire. This our foreman is a gentleman of an ancient family, that came to a great estate some years before he had discretion, and run it out in hounds, horses, and cock-fighting; for which reason he looks upon himself as an honest, worthy gentleman, who has had misfortunes in the world, and calls every thriving man a pitiful upstart.

Major Matchlock is the next senior, who served in the last civil wars, and has all the battles by heart. He does not think any action in Europe worth talking of since the fight of Marston Moor; and every night tells us of his having been knocked off his horse at the rising of the London apprentices· for which he is in great esteem among us.

Honest old Dick Reptile is the third of our society. He is a good-natured indolent man, who speaks little himself, but laughs at our jokes; and brings his young nephew along with him, a youth of eighteen years old, to shew him good company, and give him a taste of the world. This young fellow sits generally silent; but whenever he opens his mouth, or laughs at anything that passes, he is constantly told by his uncle, after a jocular manner, "Ay, ay, Jack, you young men think us fools; but we old men know you are."

The greatest wit of our company, next to myself, is a Bencher of the neighbouring Inn, who in his youth frequented the ordinaries about Charing Cross, and pretends to have been intimate with Jack Ogle. He has about ten distichs of Hudibras without book, and never leaves the club until he has applied them all. If any modern wit be mentioned, or any town-frolic spoken of, he shakes his head at the dulness of the present age, and tells us a story of Jack Ogle.

For my own part, I am esteemed among them, because they see I am something respected by others; though at the same time I understand by their behaviour, that I am considered by them as a man of a great deal of learning, but no knowledge of the world;

insomuch, that the Major sometimes, in the height of his military pride, calls me the Philosopher: and Sir Jeoffrey, no longer ago than last night, upon a dispute what day of the month it was then in Holland, pulled his pipe out of his mouth, and cried, "What does the scholar say to it?"

Our club meets precisely at *six o'clock in the evening;* but I did not come last night until half an hour after seven, by which means I escaped the battle of Naseby, which the Major usually begins at about three-quarters after six: I found also, that my good friend the Bencher had already spent three of his distichs; and only waited an opportunity to hear a sermon spoken of, that he might introduce the couplet where "a stick" rhymes to "ecclesiastic." At my entrance into the room, they were naming a red petticoat and a cloak, by which I found that the Bencher had been diverting them with a story of Jack Ogle.

I had no sooner taken my seat, but Sir Jeoffrey, to show his goodwill towards me, gave me a pipe of his own tobacco, and stirred up the fire. I look upon it as a point of morality, to be obliged by those who endeavour to oblige me; and therefore, in requittal for his kindness, and to set the conversation a-going, I took the best occasion I could to put him upon telling us the story of old Gantlett, which he always does with very particular concern. He traced up his descent on both sides for several generations, describing his diet and manner of life, with his several battles, and particularly that in which he fell. This Gantlett was a gamecock, upon whose head the knight, in his youth, had won five hundred pounds, and lost two thousand. This naturally set the Major upon the account of Edge Hill fight, and ended in a duel of Jack Ogle's.

Old Reptile was extremely attentive to all that was said, though it was the same he had heard every night for these twenty years, and, upon all occasions, winked upon his nephew to mind what passed.

This may suffice to give the world a taste of our innocent conversation, which we spun out until about ten of the clock, when my maid came with a lantern to light me home. I could not but reflect with myself, as I was going out, upon the talkative humour of old men, and the little figure which that part of life makes in one who cannot employ his natural propensity in discourses which would make him venerable. I must own, it makes me very melancholy in company, when I hear a young man begin a story; and have often observed, that one of a quarter of an hour long in a man of five-and-twenty, gathers circumstances every time he tells it, until it grows into a long Canterbury tale of two hours by that time he is threescore.

The only way of avoiding such a trifling and frivolous old age is, to lay up in our way to it such stores of knowledge and observation, as may make us useful and agreeable in our declining years. The mind of man in a long life will become a magazine of wisdom or folly, and will consequently discharge itself in something impertinent or improving. For which reason, as there is nothing more ridiculous than an old trifling story-teller, so there is nothing more venerable, than one who has turned his experience to the entertainment and advantage of mankind.

In short, we, who are in the last stage of life, and are apt to indulge ourselves in talk, ought to consider, if what we speak be worth being heard, and endeavour to make our discourse like that of Nestor, which Homer compares to the flowing of honey for its sweetness.

TOM VARNISH

No. 136.] TUESDAY, FEBRUARY 21, 1709-10. [STEELE.]

Deprendi miserum est: Fabio vel judice vincam.
HOR. 1 SAT. ii. ver. ult.

To be surpris'd, is, sure a wretched tale,
And for the truth to Fabius I appeal.

BECAUSE I have a professed aversion to long beginnings of stories, I will go into this at once, by telling you, that there dwells near the Royal Exchange as happy a couple as ever entered into wedlock. These live in that mutual confidence of each other, which renders the satisfaction of marriage even greater than those of friendship, and makes wife and husband the dearest appellations of human life. Mr. Balance is a merchant of good consideration, and understands the world, not from speculation, but practice. His wife is the daughter of an honest house, ever bred in a family-way; and has, from a natural good understanding, and great innocence, a freedom which men of sense know to be the certain sign of virtue, and fools take to be an encouragement to vice.

Tom Varnish, a young gentleman of the Middle-Temple, by the bounty of a good father, who was so obliging as to die, and leave him, in his twenty-fourth year, besides a good estate, a large sum which lay in the hands of Mr. Balance, had by *this means* an intimacy at his house; and being one of those hard students who read plays for the improvement in the law, took his rules of life from thence. Upon mature deliberation, he conceived it very proper, that he, as a man of wit and pleasure of the town, should have an intrigue with *his merchant's* wife. He no sooner thought of this adventure, but he began it by an amorous epistle to the lady, and a faithful promise to wait upon her at a certain hour the next evening, when he knew her husband was to be absent.

The letter was no sooner received, but it was communicated to the husband, and produced no other effect in him, than that he joined with his wife to raise all the mirth they could out of this fantastical piece of gallantry. They were so little concerned at this dangerous man of mode, that they plotted ways to perplex him without hurting him. Varnish comes exactly at his hour; and the lady's well-acted confusion at his entrance gave him opportunity to repeat some couplets very fit for the occasion with very much grace and spirit. His theatrical manner of making love was interrupted by an alarm of the husband's coming; and the wife, in a personated terror, beseeched him, "if he had any value for the honour of a woman that loved him, he would jump out of the window." He did so, and fell upon feather-beds placed on purpose to receive him.

It is not to be conceived how great the joy of an amorous man is, when he has suffered for his mistress, and is never the worse for it. Varnish the next day writ a most elegant billet, wherein he said all that imagination could form upon the occasion. He violently protested, "going out of the window was no way terrible, but as it was going from her;" with several other kind expressions, which procured him a second assignation. Upon his second visit, he was conveyed by a faithful maid into her bed chamber, and left there to expect the arrival of her mistress. But the wench, according to her instructions, ran in again to him, and locked the door after her to keep out her master. She had just time enough to convey the lover into a chest before she admitted the husband and his wife into the room.

You may be sure that trunk was absolutely necessary to be opened; but upon her husband's ordering it, she assured him, "she had taken all the care imaginable in packing up the things with her own hands, and he might send the trunk abroad as soon as he thought fit." The easy husband believed his wife, and the good couple went to bed; Varnish having the happiness to pass the night in the mistress's bedchamber without molestation. The morning arose, but our lover was not well situated to observe her blushes; so that all we know of his sentiments on this occasion is, that he heard Balance ask for the key, and say, "he would himself go with this chest, and have it opened before the captain of the ship, for the greater safety of so valuable a lading."

The goods were hoisted away; and Mr. Balance, marching by his chest with great care and diligence, omitting nothing that might give his passenger perplexity. But, to consummate all, he delivered the chest, with strict charge, "in case they were in danger of being taken, to throw it overboard, for there were letters in it, the matter of which might be of great service to the enemy."

KICKSHAWS

No. 148.] TUESDAY, MARCH 21, 1709-10. [ADDISON.]

—— Gustus elementa per omnia quærunt,
Nunquam animo pretiis obstantibus ——.
JUV. SAT. xi. 14.

They ransack every element for choice
Of every fish and fowl, at any price.

HAVING intimated in my last paper, that I design to take under my inspection the diet of this great city, I shall begin with a very earnest and serious exhortation to all my well-disposed readers, that they would return to the food of their forefathers, and reconcile themselves to beef and mutton. This was the diet which bred that hardy race of mortals who won the fields of Cressy and Agincourt. I need not go up so high as the history of Guy, earl of Warwick, who is well known to have eaten up a dun cow of his own killing. The renowned King Arthur is generally looked upon as the first who ever sat down to a whole roasted ox, which was certainly the best way to preserve the gravy; and it is farther added, that he and his knights sat about it at his round table, and usually consumed it to the very bones before they would enter upon any debate of moment. The Black Prince was a professed lover of the Brisket; not to mention the history of the Surloin, or the institution of the order of Beef-eaters; which are all so many evident and undeniable marks of the great respect, which our warlike predecessors have paid to this excellent food. The tables of the ancient gentry of this nation were covered thrice a day with hot roast beef; and I am credibly informed, by an antiquary who has searched the registers in which the bills of fare of the court are recorded, that instead of tea and bread and butter, which have prevailed of late years, the maids of honour in Queen Elizabeth's time were allowed three rumps of beef for their breakfast. Mutton has likewise been in great repute among our valiant countrymen; but was formerly observed to be the food rather of men of nice and delicate appetites, than those of strong and robust constitutions. For which reason, even to this day, we use the word *Sheep-biter* as a term of reproach, as we do *Beef-eater* in a respectful and honourable sense. As for the flesh of lamb, veal, chicken, and other animals under age, they were the invention of sickly and degenerate palates, according to that wholesome remark of Daniel the historian; who takes notice, that in all taxes upon provisions, during the reigns of several of our kings, there is nothing mentioned besides the flesh of such fowl and cattle as were arrived at their full growth, and were mature for slaughter. The common people of this kingdom do still keep up the taste of their ancestors; and it is to this that we, in a great measure, owe the unparalleled victories that have been gained in this reign: for I would desire my reader to consider, what work our countrymen would have made at Blenheim and Ramillies, if they had been fed with fricassees and ragoûts.

For this reason, we at present see the florid complexion, the strong limb, and the hale constitution, are to be found chiefly among the meaner sort of people, or in the wild gentry who have been educated among the woods or mountains. Whereas many great families are insensibly fallen off from the athletic constitution of their progenitors, and are dwindled away into a pale, sickly, spindle-legged generation of valetudinarians.

I may perhaps, be thought extravagant in my notion; but I must confess, I am apt to impute the dishonours that sometimes

Roast Beef at the Gate of Calais.

happen in great families, to the inflaming kind of diet which is so much in fashion. Many dishes can excite desire without giving strength, and heat the body without nourishing it; as physicians observe, that the poorest and most dispirited blood is most subject to fevers. I look upon a French ragoût to be as pernicious to the stomach as a glass of spirits; and when I have seen a young lady swallow all the instigations of high soups, seasoned sauces, and forced meats, I have wondered at the despair or tedious fighting of her lovers.

The rules among these false Delicates are, to be as contradictory as they can be to nature.

Without expecting the return of hunger, they eat for an appetite, and prepare dishes, not to allay, but to excite it.

They admit of nothing at their tables in its natural form, or without a disguise.

They are to eat of everything before it comes in season, and to leave it off as soon as it is good to be eaten.

They are not to approve anything that is agreeable to ordinary palates; and nothing is to gratify their senses, but what would offend those of their inferiors.

I remember I was last summer invited to a friend's house, who is a great admirer of the French cookery, and, as the phrase is, "eats well." At our sitting down, I found the table covered with a great variety of unknown dishes. I was mightily at a loss to learn what they were, and therefore did not know where to help myself. That which stood before me I took to be a roasted porcupine, however did not care for asking questions; and have since been informed, that it was only a larded turkey. I afterwards passed my eye over several hashes, which I do not know the names of to this day; and, hearing that they were delicacies, did not think fit to meddle with them.

Among other dainties, I saw something like a pheasant, and, therefore desired to be helped to a wing of it; but, to my great surprise, my friend told me it was a rabbit, which is a sort of meat I never cared for. At last I discovered, with some joy, a pig at the lower end of the table, and begged a gentleman that was near it to cut me a piece of it. Upon which the gentleman of the house said, with great civility, "I am sure you will like the pig, for it was whipped to death." I must confess, I heard him with horror, and could not eat of an animal that had died so tragical a death. I was now in great hunger and confusion, when methought I smelled the agreeable savour of roast beef; but could not tell from which dish it arose, though I did not question but it lay disguised in one of them. Upon turning my head, I saw a noble surloin on the side-table smoking in the most delicious manner. I had recourse to it more than once, and could not see without some indignation that substantial English dish banished in so ignominious a manner, to make way for French kickshaws.

The desert was brought up at last, which in truth was as extraordinary as anything that had come before it. The whole, when ranged in its proper order, looked like a very beautiful winter-piece. There were several pyramids of candied sweetmeats, that hung like icicles, with fruits scattered up and down, and hid in an artificial kind of frost. At the same time there were great quantities of cream beaten up into a snow, and near them little plates of sugar-plums, disposed like so many heaps of hail-stones, with a multitude of congelations in jellies of various colours. I was indeed so pleased with the several objects which lay before me, that I did not care for displacing any of them; and was half angry with the rest of the company, that, for the sake of a piece of lemon-peel, or a sugar-plum, would spoil so pleasing a picture. Indeed, I could not but smile to see several of them cooling their mouths with lumps of ice which they had just before been burning with salts and peppers.

As soon as this show was over, I took my leave, that I might finish my dinner at my own house. For as I in everything love what is simple and natural, so particularly in my food; two plain dishes, with two or three good-natured, cheerful, ingenious friends, would make me more pleased and vain, than all that pomp and luxury can bestow. For it is my maxim that "he keeps the greatest table who has the most valuable company at it."

THE TATLER

BEAUTY UNADORNED

No. 151.]   TUESDAY, MARCH 28, 1710.   [STEELE.

—— Ni vis boni
In ipsa inesset forma, hæc formam extinguerent. — TER.

These things would extinguish beauty, if there were not an innate pleasure-giving energy in beauty itself.

WHEN artists would expose their diamonds to an advantage, they usually set them to show in little cases of black velvet. By this means the jewels appear in their true and genuine lustre, while there is no colour that can infect their brightness, or give a false cast to the water. When I was at the opera the other night, the assembly of ladies in mourning made me consider them in the same kind of view. A dress wherein there is so little variety shews the face in all its natural charms, and makes one differ from another only as it is more or less beautiful. Painters are ever careful of offending against a rule which is so essential in all just representations. The chief figure must have the strongest point of light, and not be injured by any gay colourings, that may draw away the attention to any less considerable part of the picture. The present fashion obliges every body to be dressed with propriety, and makes the ladies' faces the principal objects of sight. Every beautiful person shines out in all the excellence with which nature has adorned her; gaudy ribbands and glaring colours being now out of use, the sex has no opportunity given them to disfigure themselves, which they seldom fail to do whenever it lies in their power. When a woman comes to her glass, she does not employ her time in making herself look more advantageously what she really is; but endeavours to be as much another creature as she possibly can. Whether this happens because they stay so long, and attend their work so diligently, that they forget the faces and persons which they first sat down with, or whatever it is, they seldom rise from the toilet the same women they appeared when they began to dress. What jewel can the charming Cleora place in her ears, that can please her beholders so much as her eyes? The cluster of diamonds upon the breast can add no beauty to the fair chest of ivory which supports it. It may indeed tempt a man to steal a woman, but never to love her. Let Thalestris change herself into a motley, party-coloured animal: the pearl necklace, the flowered stomacher, the artificial nosegay, and *shaded furbelow,* may be of use to attract the eye of her beholder, and turn it from the imperfections of her features and shape. But if ladies will take my word for it (and as they dress to please men, they ought to consult our fancy rather than their own in this particular), I can assure them, there is nothing touches our imagination so much as a beautiful woman in a plain dress. There might be more agreeable ornaments found in our own manufacture, than any that rise out of the looms of Persia.

This, I know, is a very harsh doctrine to woman-kind, who are carried away with every thing that is showy, and with what delights the eye, more than any other species of living creatures whatsoever. Were the minds of the sex laid open, we should find the chief idea in one to be a tippet, in another a muff, in a third a fan, and in a fourth a fardingal. The memory of an old visiting lady is so filled with gloves, silks, and ribbands, that I can look upon it as nothing else but a toy-shop. A matron of my acquaintance, complaining of her daughter's vanity, was observing, that she had all of a sudden held up her head higher than ordinary, and *taken an air* that shewed a secret satisfaction in herself, mixed with a scorn of others. "I did not know," says my friend, "what to make of the carriage of this fantastical girl, until I was informed by her eldest sister, that she had a pair of striped garters on." This odd turn of mind makes the sex unhappy, and disposes them to be struck with every thing that makes a show, however trifling and superficial.

Many a lady has fetched a sigh at the *toss* of a wig, and been ruined by the tapping of a snuff-box. It is impossible to describe all the execution that was done by *the shoulder-knot,* while that fashion prevailed, or to reckon up all the virgins that have fallen a sacrifice to a pair of *fringed gloves.* A sincere heart has not made half so many conquests as an *open waistcoat*; and I should be glad to see an able head make so good a figure in a woman's company as a pair of *red heels.* A Grecian hero, when he was asked whether he could play upon the lute, thought he had made a good reply, when he answered, "No; but I can make a great city of a little one." Notwithstanding his boasted wisdom, I appeal to the heart of any Toast in town, whether she would not think the *lutenist* preferable to the statesman? I do not speak this out of any aversion that I have to the sex: on the contrary, I have always had a tenderness for them; but, I must confess, it troubles me very much, to see the generality of them place their affections on improper objects, and give up all the pleasures of life for gewgaws and trifles.

Mrs. Margery Bickerstaff, my great aunt, had a thousand pounds to her portion, which our family was desirous of keeping among themselves, and therefore used all possible means to turn off her thoughts from marriage. The method they took was, in any time of danger, to throw a new gown or petticoat in her way. When she was about twenty-five years of age, she fell in love with a man of an agreeable temper and equal fortune, and would certainly have married him, had not my grandfather, Sir Jacob, dressed her up in a suit of flowered satin; upon which she set so immoderate a value upon herself, that the lover was contemned and discarded. In the fortieth year of her age, she was again smitten; but very luckily transferred her passion to a *tippet*, which was presented to her by another relation who was in the plot. This, with a *white sarsenet hood*, kept her safe in the family until fifty. About sixty, which generally produces a kind of latter spring in amorous constitutions, my aunt Margery had again a colt's tooth in her head; and would certainly have eloped from the mansion-house, had not her brother Simon, who was a wise man and a scholar, advised to dress her in *cherry-coloured ribbands*, which was the only expedient that could have been found out by the wit of man to preserve the thousand pounds in our family, part of which I enjoy at this time.

This discourse puts me in mind of an humourist mentioned by Horace, called Eutrapelus, who, when he designed to do a man a mischief, made him a present of a gay suit; and brings to my memory another passage of the same author, when he describes the most ornamental dress that a woman can appear in with two words, *Simplex Munditiis*, which I have quoted for the benefit of my female readers.

THE TATLER

THE POLITICAL UPHOLSTERER

No. 155.]　　THURSDAY, APRIL 6, 1710.　　[ADDISON.]

　　—— Aliena negotia curat,
Excussus propriis.　　　　　　　　HOR. 3 SAT. ii. 19.

When he had lost all business of his own,
He ran in puest of news through all the town.

THERE lived some years since, within my neighbourhood, a very grave person, an upholsterer, who seemed a man of more than ordinary application to business. He was a very early riser, and was often abroad two or three hours before any of his neighbours. He had a particular carefulness in the knitting of his brows, and a kind of impatience in all his motions, that plainly discovered he was always intent on matters of importance. Upon my inquiry into his life and conversation, I found him to be the greatest newsmonger in our quarter; that he rose before day to read the Postman; and that he would take two or three turns to the other end of the town before his neighbours were up, to see if there were any Dutch mails come in. He had a wife and several children; but was much more inquisitive to know what passed in Poland than in his own family, and was in greater pain and anxiety of mind for King Augustus's welfare, than that of his nearest relations. He looked extremely thin in a dearth of news, and never enjoyed himself in a westerly wind. This indefatigable kind of life was the ruin of his shop; for, about the time that his favourite prince left the crown of Poland, he broke and disappeared.

　　This man and his affairs had been long out of my mind, until about three days ago, as I was walking in St. James's Park, I heard somebody at a distance hemming after me: and who should it be but my old neighbour the upholsterer? I saw he was reduced to extreme poverty, by certain shabby superfluities in his dress; for, notwithstanding that it was a very sultry day for the time of the year, he wore a loose great-coat and a *muff*, with a *long campaign wig* out of curl; to which he had added the ornament of a pair of *black garters buckled under the knee*. Upon his coming to me, I was going to inquire into his present circumstances; but was prevented by his asking me, with a whisper, "whether the last letters brought any accounts that one might rely upon from Bender?" I told him, "None that I heard of;" and asked him, "whether he had yet married his eldest daughter?" He told me, "no. But pray," says he, "tell me sincerely, what are your thoughts of the King of Sweden?" For though his wife and children were starving, I found his chief concern at present was for this great monarch. I told him, "that I looked upon him as one of the first heroes of the age." "But pray," says he, "do you think there is any truth in the story of his wound?" And finding me surprised at the question, "Nay," says he, "I only propose it to you." I answered, "that I thought there was no reason to doubt of it." "But why in the heel," says he, "more than in any other part of the body?" "Because," said I, " the bullet chanced to light there."

This extraordinary dialogue was no sooner ended, but he began to launch out into a long dissertation upon the affairs of the North; and after having spent some time on them, he told me, he was in a great perplexity how to reconcile "The Supplement" with "The English-Post," and had been just now examining what the other papers say upon the same subject. "'The Daily Courant,'" says he, "has these words: 'We have advices from very good hand, that a certain prince has some matters of great importance under consideration.' This is very mysterious; but the Post-boy leaves us more in the dark; for he tells us, 'That there are private intimations of measures taken by a certain prince, which time will bring to light.' Now the 'Post-man,'" says he, "who used to be very clear, refers to the same news in these words; 'The late conduct of a certain prince affords great matter of speculation.' This certain prince," says the upholsterer, "whom they are all so cautious of naming, I take to be ——." Upon which, though there was nobody near us, he whispered something in my ear, which I did not hear, or think worth my while to make him repeat.

We were now got to the upper end of the Mall, where were three or four very odd fellows sitting together upon the bench. These I found were all of them politicians, who used to sun themselves in that place every day about dinner-time. Observing them to be curiosities in their kind, and my friend's acquaintance, I sat down among them.

The chief politician of the bench was a great asserter of paradoxes. He told us, with a seeming concern, "that, by some news he had lately read from Muscovy, it appeared to him that there was a storm gathering in the Black Sea, which might in time do hurt to the naval forces of this nation." To this he added, "that, for his part, he could not wish to see the Turk driven out of Europe, which he believed could not but be prejudicial to our woollen manufacture." He then told us, "that he looked upon those extraordinary revolutions which had lately happened in those parts of the world, to have risen chiefly from two persons who were not much talked of; and those," says he, "are Prince Menzikoff, and the Duchess of Mirandola." He backed his assertions with so many broken hints, and such a show of depth and wisdom, that we gave ourselves up to his opinions.

The discourse at length fell upon a point which seldom escapes a knot of true-born Englishmen, whether, in case of a religious war, the Protestants would not be too strong for the Papists? This we unanimously determined on the Protestant side. One who sat on my right-hand, and, as I found by his discourse, had been in the West Indies, assured us, "that it would be a very easy matter for the Protestants to beat the Pope at sea;" and added, "that whenever such a war does break out, it must turn to the good of the Leeward Islands." Upon this, one who sat at the end of the bench, and as I afterwards found, was the geographer of the company, said, "that in case the Papists should drive the Protestants from these parts of Europe, when the worst came to the worst, it would be impossible to beat them out of Norway and Greenland, provided the Northern crowns hold together, and the czar of Muscovy stand neuter."

He farther told us, for our comfort, "that there were vast tracks of lands about the pole, inhabited neither by Protestants nor Papists, and of greater extent than all the Roman-Catholic dominions in Europe."

When we had fully discussed this point, my friend the upholsterer began to exert himself upon the present negotiations of peace; in which he deposed princes, settled the bounds of kingdoms, and balanced the power of Europe, with great justice and impartiality.

I at length took my leave of the company, and was going away; but had not gone thirty yards, before the upholsterer hemmed again after me. Upon his advancing towards me with a whisper, I expected to hear some secret piece of news, which he had not thought fit to communicate to the bench; but, instead of that, he desired me in my ear to lend him half a crown. In compassion to so needy

The Politician.

a statesman, and to dissipate the confusion I found he was in, I told him, "if he pleased, I would give him five shillings, to receive five pounds of him when the great Turk was driven out of Constantinople;" which he very readily accepted, but not before he had laid down to me the impossibility of such an event, as the affairs of Europe now stand.

This paper I design for the particular benefit of those worthy citizens who live more in a coffee-house than in their shops, and whose thoughts are so taken up with the affairs of the allies, that they forget their custom

TOM FOLIO

No. 158.] THURSDAY, APRIL 13, 1710. [ADDISON.]

Faciunt næ intelligendo, ut nihil intelligant. — TER.

While they pretend to know more than others, they know nothing in reality.

TOM FOLIO is a broker in learning, employed to get together good editions, and stock the libraries of great men. There is not a sale of books begins until Tom Folio is seen at the door. There is not an auction where his name is not heard, and that too in the very nick of time, in the critical moment, before the last decisive stroke of the hammer. There is not a subscription goes forward in which Tom is not privy to the first rough draught of the proposals; nor a catalogue printed, that doth not come to him wet from the press. He is an universal scholar, so far as the title-page of all authors; knows the manuscripts in which they were discovered, the editions through which they have passed, with the praises or censures which they have received from the several members of the learned world. He has a greater esteem for Aldus and Elzevir, than for Virgil and Horace. If you talk of Heredotus, he breaks out into a panegyric upon Harry Stephens. He thinks he gives you an account of an author, when he tells you the subject he treats of, the name of the editor, and the year in which it was printed. Or if you draw him into farther particulars, he cries up the goodness of the paper, extols the diligence of the corrector, and is transported with the beauty of the letter. This he looks upon to be sound learn ing, and substantial criticism. As for those who talk of the fineness of style, and the justness of thought or describe the brightness of any particular passages; nay, though they themselves write in the genius and spirit of the author they admire; Tom looks upon them as men of superficial learning, and flashy parts.

I had yesterday morning a visit from this learned *ideot*, for *that* is the light in which I consider every pedant, when I discovered in him some little touches of the coxcomb, which I had not before observed. Being very full of the figure which he makes in the republic of letters, and wonderfully satisfied with his great stock of knowledge, he gave me broad intimations, that he did not believe in all points as his forefathers had done. He then communicated to me a thought of a certain author upon a passage of Virgil's account of the dead, which I made the subject of a late paper. This thought hath taken very much among men of Tom's pitch and understanding, though universally exploded by all that know how to construe Virgil, or have any relish of antiquity. Not to trouble my reader with it, I found, upon the whole, that Tom did not believe a future state of rewards and punishments, because Æneas, at his leaving the empire of the dead, passed through the gate of ivory, and not through that of horn. Knowing that Tom had not sense enough to give up an opinion which he had once received, that I might avoid wrangling, I told him "that Virgil possibly had his oversights as well as another author." "Ah! Mr. Bickerstaff," says he, "you would have another opinion of him, if you would read him in Daniel Heinsius's edition. I have perused him myself several times in that edition," continued he; "and after the strictest and most malicious examination, could find but two faults in him; one of them is in the Æneids, where there are two commas instead of a parenthesis; and another in the third Georgic, where you may find a semicolon turned upside down." "Perhaps," said I, "these were not Virgil's faults, but those of the transcriber." "I do not design it," says Tom, "as a reflection on Virgil; on the contrary, I know that all the manuscripts declaim against such a punctuation. Oh! Mr. Bickerstaff," says he, "what would a man give to see one simile of Virgil writ in his own hand?" I asked him which was the simile he meant; but was answered, any simile in Virgil. He then told me all the secret history in the commonwealth of learning; of modern pieces that had the names of ancient authors annexed to them; of all the books that were now writing or printing in the several parts of Europe; of many amendments which are made, and not yet puhlished, and a thousand other particulars, which I would not have my memory burdened with for a Vatican.

At length, being fully persuaded that I thoroughly admired him, and looked upon him as a prodigy of learning, he took his leave. I know several of Tom's class, who are professed admirers of Tasso, without understanding a word of Italian: and one in particular, that carries a *Pastor Fido* in his pocket, in which, I am sure, he is acquainted with no other beauty but the clearness of the character.

There is another kind of pedant, who, with all Tom Folio's impertinences, hath greater superstructures and embellishments of Greek and Latin; and is still more insupportable than the other, in the same degree as he is more learned. Of this kind very often are editors, commentators, interpreters, scholiasts, and critics; and, in short, all men of deep learning without common sense. These persons set a greater value on themselves for having found out the meaning of a passage in Greek, than upon the author for having written it; nay, will allow the passage itself not to have any beauty in it, at the same time that they would be considered as the greatest men of the age, for having interpreted it. They will look with contempt on the most beautiful poems that have been composed by any of their contemporaries; but will lock themselves up in their studies for a twelvemonth together, to correct, publish, and expound such trifles of antiquity, as a modern author would be contemned for. Men of the strictest morals, severest lives, and the gravest professions, will write volumes upon an idle sonnet, that is originally in Greek or Latin; give editions of the most immoral authors; and spin out whole pages upon the various readings of a lewd expression. All that can be said in excuse for them is, that their works sufficiently shew they have no taste of their authors; and that what they do in this kind, is out of their great learning, and not out of any levity or lasciviousness of temper.

A pedant of this nature is wonderfully well described in six lines of Boileau, with which I shall conclude his character:

>Un Pedant enyvré de sa vaine science,
>Tout herissé de Grec, tout bouffi d'arrogance.
>Et qui de mille auteurs retenus mot pour mot,
>Dans sa tête entassez n'a souvent fait qu'un sot,
>Croit qu'un livre fait tout, and que sans Aristote
>La raison ne voit goute, and le bon sens radote.

THE TATLER

> Brim-full of learning see that pedant stride,
> Bristling with horrid Greek, and puff'd with pride!
> A thousand authors he in vain has read,
> And with their maxims stuff'd his empty head;
> And thinks that, without Aristotle's rule,
> Reason is blind, and common sense a fool.

A VISIT AND LETTER FROM THE UPHOLSTERER

No. 160.] TUESDAY, APRIL 18, 1710. [ADDISON.]

A COMMON civility to an impertinent fellow, often draws upon one a great many unforeseen troubles; and if one doth not take particular care, will be interpreted by him as an overture of friendship and intimacy. This I was very sensible of this morning. About two hours before day, I heard a great rapping at my door, which continued some time, till my maid could get herself ready to go down and see what was the occasion of it. She then brought me up word, that there was a gentleman who seemed very much in haste, and said he must needs speak with me. By the description she gave me of him, and by his voice, which I could hear as I lay in my bed, I fancied him to be my old acquaintance the upholsterer, whom I met the other day in St. James's Park. For which reason I bid her tell the gentleman, whoever he was, that I was indisposed, that I could see nobody, and that, if he had anything to say to me, I desired he would leave it in writing. My maid, after having delivered her message, told me, that the gentleman said he would stay at the next coffee-house till I was stirring, and bid her be sure to tell me, that the French were driven from the Scarp, and that the Douay was invested. He gave her the name of another town, which I found she had dropped by the way.

As much as I love to be informed of the success of my brave countrymen, I do not care for hearing of a victory before day, and was therefore very much out of humour at this unseasonable visit. I had no sooner recovered my temper, and was falling asleep, but I was immediately startled by a second rap; and upon my maid's opening the door, heard the same voice ask her, if her master was yet up? and at the same time bid her tell me, that he was come on purpose to talk with me about a piece of home-news that everybody in town will be full of two hours hence. I ordered my maid, as soon as she came into the room, without hearing her message, to tell the gentleman, that whatever his news was, I would rather hear it two hours hence than now; and that I persisted in my resolution not to speak with anybody that morning. The wench delivered my answer presently and shut the door. It was impossible for me to compose myself to sleep after two such unexpected alarms; for which reason I put on my clothes in a very peevish humour. I took several turns about my chamber, reflecting with a great deal of anger and contempt on these volunteers in politics, that undergo all the pain, watchfulness, and disquiet of a first minister, without turning it to the advantage either of themselves or their country; and yet it is surprising to consider how numerous this species of men is. There is nothing more frequent than to find a tailor breaking his rest on the affairs of Europe, and to see a cluster of porters sitting upon the ministry. Our streets swarm with politicians, and there is scarce a shop which is not held by a statesman. As I was musing after this manner, I heard the upholsterer at the door delivering a letter to my maid, and begging her, in very great hurry, to give it to her master as soon as ever he was awake, which I opened and found as follows:

"MR. BICKERSTAFFE, — I was to wait upon you about a week ago, to let you know, that the honest gentleman whom you conversed with upon the bench at the end of the Mall, having heard that I had received five shillings of you, to give you a hundred pounds upon the Great Turk's being driven out of Europe, desired me to acquaint you, that every one of that company would be willing to receive five shillings, to pay a hundred pounds on the same conditions. Our last advices from Muscovy making this a fairer bet than it was a week ago, I do not question but you will accept the wager.

"But this is not my present business. If you remember, I whispered a word in your ear as we were walking up the Mall, and you see what has happened since. If I had seen you this morning, I would have told you in your ear another secret. I hope you will be recovered of your indisposition by to-morrow morning, when I will wait on you at the same hour as I did this; my private circumstances being such, that I cannot well appear in this quarter of the town after it is day.

"I have been so taken up with the late good news from Holland, and expectation of further particulars, as well as with other transactions, of which I will tell you more to-morrow morning, that I have not slept a wink these three nights.

"I have reason to believe, that Picardy will soon follow the example of Artois, in case the enemy continue in their present resolution of flying away from us. I think I told you last time we were together my opinion about the Deulle.

"The honest gentlemen upon the bench bid me tell you, they would be glad to see you often among them. We shall be there all the warm hours of the day during the present posture of affairs.

"This happy opening of the campaign will, I hope, give us a very joyful summer; and I propose to take many a pleasant walk with you, if you will sometimes come into the Park; for that is the only place in which I can be free from the malice of my enemies. Farewell till three-a-clock to-morrow morning.

"I am
             Your most humble servant," &c.

"P.S. The king of Sweden is still at Bender."

I should have fretted myself to death at this promise of a second visit, if I had not found in his letter an intimation of the good news which I have since heard at large. I have, however, ordered my maid to tie up the knocker of my door, in such a manner as she would do if I was really indisposed. By which means I hope to escape breaking my morning's rest.

THE CRITIC

No. 165.]   SATURDAY, APRIL 29, 1710.   [ADDISON.]

IT has always been my endeavour to distinguish between realities and appearances, and separate true merit from the pretence to it. As it shall ever be my study to make discoveries of this nature in human life, and to settle the proper distinctions between the virtues and perfections of mankind, and those false colours and resemblances of them that shine alike in the eyes of the vulgar; so I shall be more particularly careful to search into the various merits and pretences of the learned world. This is the more necessary, because there seems to be a general combination among the pedants to extol one another's labours, and cry up one another's parts; while men of sense, either through that modesty which is natural to them, or the scorn they have for such trifling commendations, enjoy their stock of knowledge like a hidden treasure, with satisfaction and silence. Pedantry, indeed, in learning, is like hypocrisy in religion, a form of knowledge without the power of it, that attracts the eyes of common people, breaks out in noise and show, and finds its reward, not from any inward pleasure that attends it, but from the praises and approbations which it receives from men.

Of this shallow species there is not a more importunate, empty, and conceited animal, than that which is generally known by the name of a critic. This, in the common acceptation of the word, is one that, without entering into the sense and soul of an author, has a few general rules, which, like mechanical instruments, he applies to the works of every writer, and as they quadrate with them, pronounces the author perfect or defective. He is master of a certain set of words, as Unity, Style, Fire, Phlegm, Easy, Natural, Turn, Sentiment, and the like; which he varies, compounds, divides, and throws together, in every part of his discourse, without any thought or meaning. The marks you may know him by are, an elevated eye, and dogmatical brow, a positive voice, and a contempt for everything that comes out, whether he has read it or not. He dwells altogether in generals. He praises or dispraises in the lump. He shakes his head very frequently at the pedantry of universities, and bursts into laughter when you mention an author that is known at Will's. He hath formed his judgment upon Homer, Horace, and Virgil, not from their own works, but from those of Rapin and Bossu. He knows his own strength so well, that he never dares praise anything in which he has not a French author for his voucher.

With these extraordinary talents and accomplishments, Sir Timothy Tittle puts men in vogue, or condemns them to obscurity, and sits as judge of life and death upon every author that appears in public. It is impossible to represent the pangs, agonies, and convulsions, which Sir Timothy expresses in every feature of his face, and muscle of his body, upon the reading of a bad poet.

About a week ago I was engaged at a friend's house of mine in an agreeable conversation with his wife and daughters, when, in the height of our mirth, Sir Timothy, who makes love to my friend's eldest daughter, came in amongst us puffing and blowing, as if he had been very much out of breath. He immediately called for a chair, and desired leave to sit down, without any further ceremony. I asked him, "Where he had been? Whether he was out of order?" He only replied, that he was quite spent, and fell a cursing in soliloquy. I could hear him cry, "A wicked rogue! — An execrable wretch! — Was there ever such a monster!" — The young ladies upon this began to be affrighted, and asked, "Whether any one had hurt him?" He answered nothing, but still talked to himself. "To lay the first scene (says he) in St. James's Park, and the last in Northamptonshire!" "Is that all? (says I:) Then I suppose you have been at the rehearsal of the play this morning." "Been! (says he;) I have been at Northampton, in the Park, in a lady's bed-chamber, in a dining-room, everywhere; the rogue has led me such a dance!" — Though I could scarce forbear laughing at his discourse, I told him I was glad it was no worse, and that he was only metaphorically weary. "In short, sir, (says he,) the author has not observed a single unity in his whole play; the scene shifts in every dialogue; the villain has hurried me up and down at such a rate, that I am tired off my legs. I could not but observe with some pleasure, that the young lady whom he made love to, conceived a very just aversion towards him, upon seeing him so very passionate in trifles. And as she had that natural sense which makes her a better judge than a thousand critics, she began to rally him upon this foolish humour. "For my part, (says she,) I never knew a play take that was written up to your rules, as you call them." "How, madam! (says he,) is that your opinion? I am sure you have a better taste." "It is a pretty kind of magic (says she) the poets have to transport an audience from place to place without the help of a coach and horses. I could travel round the world at such a rate. 'Tis such an entertainment as an enchantress finds when she fancies herself in a wood, or upon a mountain, at a feast, or a solemnity; though at the same time she has never stirred out of her cottage." "Your simile, madam, (says Sir Timothy,) is by no means just." "Pray, (says she,) let my similes pass without a criticism. I must confess, (continued she, for I found she was resolved to exasperate him,) I laughed very heartily at the last new comedy which you found so much fault with." "But, madam, (says he,) you ought not to have laughed; and I defy any one to show me a single rule that you could laugh by." "Ought not to laugh! (says she:) Pray who should hinder me?" "Madam, (says he,) there are such people in the world as Rapin, Dacier, and several others, that ought to have spoiled your mirth." "I have heard, (says the young lady,) that your great critics are always very bad poets: I fancy there is as much difference between the works of one and the other, as there is between the carriage of a dancing-master and a gentleman. I must confess, (continued she,) I would not be troubled with so fine a judgment as yours is; for I find you feel more vexation in a bad comedy, than I do in a deep tragedy." "Madam, (says Sir Timothy,) that is not my fault; they should learn the art of writing." "For my part, (says the young lady,) I should think the greatest art in your writers of comedies is to please." "To please!" (says Sir Timothy;) and immediately fell a laughing. "Truly, (says she,) that is my opinion." Upon this, he composed his countenance, looked upon his watch, and took his leave.

I hear that Sir Timothy has not been at my friend's house since this notable conference, to the satisfaction of the young lady, who by this means has got rid of a very impertinent fop.

I must confess, I could not but observe, with a great deal of surprise, how this gentleman, by his ill-nature, folly, and affectation, hath made himself capable of suffering so many imaginary pains, and looking with such a senseless severity upon the common diversions of life.

THE TATLER

CHARACTERS IN A STAGE-COACH

No. 192.] SATURDAY, JULY 1, 1710. [ADDISON.]

Tecum vivere amem,tecum obeam libens. — HOR.

SOME years since I was engaged with a coach full of friends to take a journey as far as the Land's End. We were very well pleased with one another the first day, every one endeavouring to recommend himself by his good humour and complaisance to the rest of the company. This good correspondence did not last long; one of our party was soured the very first evening by a plate of butter which had not been melted to his mind, and which spoiled his temper to such a degree, that he continued upon the fret to the end of our journey. A second fell off from his good humour the next morning, for no other reason that I could imagine, but because I chanced to step into the coach before him, and place myself on the shady side. This, however, was but my own private guess, for he did not mention a word of it, nor indeed of anything else, for three days following. The rest of our company held out very near half the way, when of a sudden Mr. Sprightly fell asleep; and instead of endeavouring to divert and oblige us, as he had hitherto done, carried himself with an unconcerned, careless, drowsy behaviour, till we came to our last stage. There were three of us who still held up our heads, and did all we could to make our journey agreeable; but, to my shame be it spoken, about three miles on·this side Exeter I was taken with an unaccountable fit of sullenness, that hung upon me for above threescore miles; whether it were for want of respect, or from an accidental tread upon my foot, or from a foolish maid's calling me The old Gentleman, I cannot tell. In short, there was but one who kept his good humor to the Land's End.

There was another coach that went along with us, in which I likewise observed, that there were many secret jealousies, heartburnings, and animosities: for when we joined companies at night, I could not but take notice, that the passengers neglected their own company, and studied how to make themselves esteemed by us, who were altogether strangers to them: till at length they grew so well acquainted with us, that they liked us as little as they did one another. When I reflect upon this journey, I often fancy it to be a

The Country Inn Yard.

picture of human life, in respect to the several friendships, contracts, and alliances that are made and dissolved in the several periods of it. The most delightful and most lasting engagements are generally those which pass between man and woman; and yet upon what trifles are they weakened, or entirely broken! Sometimes the parties fly asunder even in the midst of courtship, and sometimes grow cool in the very honey-month. Some separate before the first child, and some after the fifth; others continue good till thirty, others till forty; while some few, whose souls are of an happier make, and better fitted to one another, travel on together to the end of their journey, in a continual intercourse of kind offices and mutual endearments.

When we, therefore, choose our companions for life, if we hope to keep both them and ourselves in good humour to the last stage of it, we must be extremely careful in the choice we make, as well as in the conduct on our own part. When the persons to whom we join ourselves can stand an examination, and bear the scrutiny, when they mend upon our acquaintance with them, and discover new beauties the more we search into their characters, our love will naturally rise in proportion to their perfections.

But because there are very few possessed of such accomplishments of body and mind, we ought to look after those qualifications both in ourselves and others, which are indispensably necessary towards this happy union, and which are in the power of every one to acquire, or at least to cultivate and improve. These, in my opinion, are cheerfulness and constancy. A cheerful temper, joined with innocence, will make beauty attractive, knowledge delightful, and wit good-natured. It will lighten sickness, poverty, and affliction; convert ignorance into an amiable simplicity, and render deformity itself agreeable.

Constancy is natural to persons of even tempers and uniform dispositions, and may be acquired by those of the greatest fickleness, violence, and passion, who consider seriously the terms of union upon which they are come together, the mutual interest in which they are engaged, with all the motives that ought to incite their tenderness and compassion towards those who have their dependence upon them, and are embarked with them for life in the same state of happiness or misery. Constancy, when it grows in the mind upon considerations of this nature, becomes a moral virtue, and a kind of good-nature, that is not subject to any change of health, age, fortune, or any of those accidents which are apt to unsettle the best dispositions that are founded rather in constitution than in reason. Where such a constancy as this is wanting, the most inflamed passion may fall away into coldness and indifference, and the most melting tenderness degenerate into hatred and aversion. I shall conclude this paper with a story that is very well known in the north of England.

About thirty years ago, a packet-boat that had several passengers on board was cast away upon a rock, and in so great danger of sinking, that all who were in it endeavoured to save themselves as well as they could, though only those who could swim well had a bare possibility of doing it. Among the passengers there were two women of fashion, who seeing themselves in such a disconsolate condition, begged of their husbands not to leave them. One of them chose rather to die with his wife, than to forsake her; the other, though he was moved with utmost compassion for his wife, told her, that for the good of their children it was better one of them should live, than both perish. By a great piece of good luck, next to a miracle, when one of our good men had taken the last and long farewell in order to save himself, and the other held in his arms the person that was dearer to him than life, the ship was preserved. It is with a secret sorrow and vexation of mind that I must tell the sequel of the story, and let my reader know, that this faithful pair who were ready to have died in each other's arms, about three years after their escape, upon some trifling disgust, grew to a coldness at first, and at length fell out to such a degree, that they left one another, and parted for ever. The other couple lived together in an uninterrupted friendship and felicity; and, what was remarkable, the husband whom the shipwreck had like to have separated from his wife, died a few months after her, not being able to survive the loss of her.

I must confess, there is something in the changeableness and inconstancy of human nature, that very often both dejects and terrifies me. Whatever I am at present, I tremble to think what I may be. While I find this principle in me, how can I assure myself, that I shall be always true to my God, my friend, or myself? in short, without constancy there is neither love, friendship, or virtue in the world.

THE TATLER

AMBITION

No. 202.]　TUESDAY, JULY 25, 1710.　[STEELE.]

―― Est hic,
Est Ulubris, animus si te non deficit æquus.
HOR. 1 Ep. xi.
True happiness is to no spot confin'd:
If you preserve a firm and equal mind,
'Tis here, 'tis there, and every where. ――

THIS afternoon I went to visit a gentleman of my acquaintance at Mile-End; and passing through Stepney church-yard, I could not forbear entertaining myself with the inscriptions on the tombs and graves. Among others, I observed one with this notable memorial:
"HERE LIES THE BODY OF T. B."

This fanatical desire, of being remembered only by the two first letters of a name, led me into the contemplation of the vanity and imperfect attainments of ambition in general. When I run back in my imagination all the men whom I have ever known and conversed with in my whole life, there are but very few who have not used their faculties in the pursuit of what it is impossible to acquire; or left the possession of what they might have been, at their setting out, masters, to search for it where it was out of their reach. In this thought it was not possible to forget the instance of Pyrrhus, who proposing to himself in discourse with a philosopher, one, and another, and another conquest, was asked, what he would after all that? "Then," says the king, "we will make merry." He was well answered, "What hinders you doing that in the condition you are already?" The restless desire of exerting themselves above the common level of mankind is not to be resisted in some tempers; and minds of this make may be observed in every condition of life. Where such men do not make to themselves, or meet with employment, the soil of their constitution runs into tares and weeds. An old friend of mine, who lost a major's post forty years ago, and quitted, has ever since studied maps, encampments, retreats, and counter-marches; with no other design but to feed his spleen and ill-humour, and furnish himself with matter for arguing against all the successful actions of others. He that, at his first setting out in

THE TATLER

the world, was the gayest man in our regiment; ventured his life with alacrity, and enjoyed it with satisfaction; encouraged men below him, and was courted by men above him, has been ever since the most froward creature breathing. His warm complexion spends itself now only in a general spirit of contradiction; for which he watches all occasions, and is in his conversation still *upon centry*, treats all men like enemies, with every other impertinence of a speculative warrior.

He, that observes in himself this natural inquietude, should take all imaginable care to put his mind in some method of gratification; or he will soon find himself grow into the condition of this disappointed major. Instead of courting proper occasions to rise above others, he will be ever studious of pulling others down to him: it being the common refuge of disappointed ambition, to ease themselves by detraction. It would be no great argument against ambition, that there are such *mortal* things in the disappointment of it; but it certainly is a forcible exception, that there can be no solid happiness in the success of it. If we value popular praise, it is in the power of the meanest of the people to disturb us by calumny. If the fame of being happy, we cannot look into a village, but we see crowds in actual possession of what we seek only the appearance. To this may be added, that there is I know not what malignity in the minds of ordinary men, to oppose you in what they see you fond of; and it is a certain exception against a man's receiving applause, that he visibly courts it. However, this is not only the passion of great and undertaking spirits; but you see it in the lives of such as, one would believe, were far enough removed from the ways of ambition. The rural esquires of this nation even eat and drink out of vanity. A vain-glorious fox-hunter shall entertain half a county, for the ostentation of his beef and beer, without the least affection for any of the crowd about him. He feeds them, because he thinks it a superiority over them that he does so; and they devour him, because they know he treats them out of insolence. This indeed is ambition in grotesque; but may figure to us the condition of politer men, whose only pursuit is glory. When the superior acts out of a principle of vanity, the dependent will be sure to allow it him; because he knows it destructive of the very applause which is courted by the man who favours him, and consequently makes him nearer himself.

But as every man living has more or less of this incentive, which makes men impatient of an inactive condition, and urges men to attempt what may tend to their reputation; it is absolutely necessary they should form to themselves an ambition, which is in every man's power to gratify. This ambition would be independent, and would consist only in acting what, to a man's own mind, appears most great and laudable. It is a pursuit in the power of every man, and is only a regular prosecution of what he himself approves. It is what can be interrupted by no outward accidents; for no man can be robbed of his good intention. One of our society of the Trumpet therefore started last night a notion, which I thought had reason in it. "It is, methinks," said he, "an unreasonable thing, that honest virtue should, as it seems to be at present, be confined to a certain order of men, and be attainable by none but those whom fortune has elevated to the most conspicuous stations. I would have everything to be esteemed as heroic, which is great and uncommon in the circumstances of the man who performs it." Thus there would be no virtue in human life, which every one of the species would not have a pretence to arrive at, and an ardency to exert. Since fortune is not in our power, let us be as little as possible in hers. Why should it be necessary that a man should be rich, to be generous? If we measured by the quality and not the quantity of things, the particulars which accompany an action is what should denominate it mean or great. The highest station of human life is to be attained by each man that pretends to it: for any man can be as valiant, as generous, as wise, and as merciful, as the faculties and opportunities which he has from heaven and fortune will permit. He that can say to himself, "I do as much good, and am as virtuous as my most earnest endeavours will allow me," whatever is his station in the world, is to himself possessed of the highest honour. If ambition is not thus turned, it is no other than a continual succession of anxiety and vexation. But when it has this cast, it invigorates the mind; and the consciousness of its own worth is a reward, which is not in the power of envy, reproach, or detraction, to take from it. Thus the seat of solid honour is in a man's own bosom: and no one can want support who is in possession of an honest conscience, but he who would suffer the reproaches of it for other greatness.

THE TATLER

FLATTERY AS AN ART

No. 208.]   TUESDAY, AUGUST 8, 1710.   [STEELE.]

Si dixeris æstuo, sudat. ——   Juv. Sat. iii. 103.

——If you complain of heat,
They rub th' unsweating brow, and swear they sweat.

AN old acquaintance, who met me this morning, seemed overjoyed to see me, and told me I looked as well as he had known me do these forty years; "but," continued he, "not quite the man you were, when we visited together at lady Brightly's. Oh! Isaac, those days are over. Do you think there are any such fine creatures now living, as we then conversed with?" He went on with a thousand incoherent circumstances, which, in his imagination, must needs please me; but they had the quite contrary effect. The flattery with which he began, in telling me how well I wore, was not disagreeable; but his indiscreet mention of a set of acquaintance we had outlived, recalled ten thousand things to my memory, which made me reflect upon my present condition with regret. Had he indeed been so kind as, after a long absence, to felicitate me upon an indolent and easy old age; and mentioned how much he and I had to thank for, who at our time of day could walk firmly, eat heartily, and converse cheerfully, he had kept up my pleasure in myself. But of all mankind, there are none so shocking as these injudicious civil people. They ordinarily begin upon something, that they know must be a satisfaction; but then, for fear of the imputation of flattery, they follow it with the last thing in the world of which you would be reminded. It is this that perplexes civil persons. The reason that there is such a general outcry among us against flatterers is, that there are so very few good ones. It is the nicest art in this life, and is a part of eloquence which does not want the preparation that is necessary to all other parts of it, that your audience should be your well-wishers: for praise from an enemy is the most pleasing of all commendations.

It is generally to be observed, that the person most agreeable to a man *for a constancy* is he that has no shining qualities, but is a certain degree above great imperfections; whom he can live with as his inferior, and who will either overlook, or not observe his little defects. Such an easy companion as this either now and then throws out a little flattery, or lets a man silently flatter himself in his superiority to him. If you take notice, there is hardly a rich man in the world, who has not such *a led friend* of small consideration, who is a darling for his insignificancy. It is a great ease to have one in our own shape a species below us, and who, without being lifted in our service, is by nature of our retinue. These dependents are of excellent use on a rainy day, or when a man has not a mind to dress; or to exclude solitude, when one has neither a mind to that or to company. There are of this good-natured order, who are so kind as to divide themselves, and do these good offices to many. Five or six of them visit a whole quarter of the town, and exclude the spleen, without fees, from the families they frequent. If they do not prescribe physic, they can be company when you take it. Very great benefactors to the rich, or those whom they call people at their ease, are your persons of no consequence. I have known some of them, by the help of a little cunning, make delicious flatterers. They know the course of the town, and the general characters of persons: by *this means* they will sometimes tell the most agreeable falsehoods imaginable. They will acquaint you, that such a one of a quite contrary party said, "That though you were engaged in different interests, yet he had the greatest respect for your good sense and address." When one of these has a little cunning, he passes his time in the utmost satisfaction to himself and his friends: for his position, is never to report or speak a displeasing thing to his friend. As for letting him go on in an error, he knows, advice against them is the office of persons of greater talents and less discretion.

The Latin word for a flatterer, *assentator*, implies no more than a person that barely consents; and indeed such a one, if a man were able to purchase or maintain him, cannot be bought too dear. Such a one never contradicts you; but gains upon you, not by a fulsome way of commending you in broad terms, but liking whatever you propose or utter; at the same time, is ready to beg your pardon, and gainsay you, if you chance to speak ill of yourself. An old lady is very seldom without such a companion as this, who can recite the names of all her lovers, and the matches refused by her in the days when she minded such vanities, as she is pleased to call them, though she so much approves the mention of them. It is to be noted, that a woman's flatterer is generally elder than herself;

her years serving at once to recommend her patroness's age, and to add weight to her complaisance in all other particulars.

We gentlemen of small fortunes are extremely necessitous in this particular. I have indeed one who smokes with me often; but his parts are so low, that all the incense he does me is to fill his pipe with me, and to be out at just as many whiffs as I take. This is all the praise or assent that he is capable of; yet there are more hours when I would rather be in his company, than in that of the brightest man I know. It would be an hard matter to give an account of this inclination to be flattered; but if we go to the bottom of it, we shall find, that the pleasure in it is something like that of receiving money which lay out. Every man thinks he has an estate of reputation, and is glad to see one that will bring any of it home to him. It is no matter how dirty a bag it is conveyed to him in, or by how clownish a messenger, so the money be good. All that we want, to be pleased with flattery, is to believe that the man is sincere who gives it us. It is by this one accident, that absurd creatures often out-run the most skilful in this art. Their want of ability is here an advantage; and their bluntness, as it is the seeming effect of sincerity, is the best cover to artifice.

Terence introduces a flatterer talking to a coxcomb, whom he cheats out of a livelihood; and a third person on the stage makes on him this pleasant remark, "This fellow has an art of making fools madmen." The love of flattery is, indeed, sometimes the weakness of a great mind; but you see it also in persons, who otherwise discover no manner of relish of any thing above mere sensuality. These latter it sometimes improves; but always debases the former. A fool is in himself the object of pity, until he is flattered. By the force of that, his stupidity is raised into affectation, and he becomes of dignity enough to be ridiculous. I remember a droll, that upon one's saying, "The times are so ticklish, that there must great care be taken what one says in conversation"; answered with an air of surliness and honesty, "If people will be free, let them be so in the manner that I am, who never abuse a man but to his face." He had no reputation for saying dangerous truths; therefore when it was repeated, "You abuse a man but to his face?" "Yes," says he, "I flatter him."

It is indeed the greatest of injuries to flatter any but the unhappy, or such as are displeased with themselves for some infirmity. In this latter case we have a member of our club, who, when Sir Jeffery falls asleep, wakens him with snoring. This makes Sir Jeffery hold up for some moments the longer to see there are men younger than himself among us, who are more lethargic than he is.

When flattery is practised upon any other consideration, it is the most abject thing in nature; nay, I cannot think of any character below the flatterer, except he that envies him. You meet with fellows, prepared to be as mean as possible in their condescensions and expressions; but they want persons and talents to rise up to such a baseness. As a coxcomb is a fool of parts, so is a flatterer a knave of parts.

The best of this order, that I know, is one who disguises it under a spirit of contradiction or reproof. He told an arrant driveller the other day, that he did not care for being in company with him, because he heard he turned his absent friends into ridicule. And upon lady Autumn's disputing with him about something that happened at the Revolution, he replied with a very angry tone, "Pray, madam, give me leave to know more of a thing in which I was actually concerned, than you who were then in your nurse's arms."

ON ADVERTISEMENTS

No. 224. THURSDAY, SEPTEMBER 14, 1710. [ADDISON.]

Materiam superabat opus. —— OVID. Met. ii. 5.
The matter equall'd not the artist's skill.

IT is my custom, in a dearth of news, to entertain myself with those collections of advertisements that appear at the end of all our public prints. These I consider as accounts of news from the little world, in the same manner that the foregoing parts of the paper are from the great. If in one we hear that a sovereign prince is fled from this capital city, in the other we hear of a tradesman who hath shut up his shop, and run away. If in one we find the victory of a general, in the other we see the desertion of a private soldier. I must confess I have a certain weakness in my temper, that is often very much affected by these little domestic occurrences, and have frequently been caught with tears in my eyes over a melancholy advertisement.

But to consider this subject in its most ridiculous lights, advertisements are of great use to the vulgar. First of all, as they are instruments of ambition. A man that is by no means big enough for the Gazette, may easily creep into the advertisements; by which means we often see an apothecary in the same paper of news with a plenipotentiary, or a running-foot-man with an ambassador. An advertisement from Piccadilly goes down to posterity with an article from Madrid, and John Bartlett of Goodman's-fields is celebrated in the same paper with the emperor of Germany. Thus the fable tells us, that the wren mounted as high as the eagle, by getting upon his back.

A second use which this sort of writings hath been turned to of late years, has been the management of controversy; insomuch that above half the advertisements one meets with now-a-days are purely polemical. The inventors of "Strops for razors" have written against one another this way for several years, and that with great bitterness; as the whole argument *pro* and *con* in the case of "the morning gown" is still carried on after the same manner. I need not mention the several proprietors of Dr. Anderson's pills; nor take notice of the many satirical works of this nature so frequently published by Dr. Clark, who has had the confidence to advertise upon that learned knight, my very worthy friend, Sir William Read: but I shall not interpose in their quarrel: Sir William can give him his own in advertisements, that, in the judgment of the impartial, are as well penned as the doctor's.

The third and last use of these writings is to inform the world, where they may be furnished with almost every thing that is necessary for life. If a man has pains in his head, colics in his bowels, or spots in his cloaths, he may here meet with proper cures and remedies. If a man would recover a wife or a horse that is stolen or strayed; if he wants new sermons, electuaries, asses' milk, or anything else, either for his body or his mind; this is the place to look for them in.

The great art in writing advertisements, is the finding out a proper method to catch the reader's eye, without which a good thing may pass over unobserved, or be lost among commissions of bankrupts. Asterisks and hands were formerly of great use for this purpose. Of late years the N. B. has been much in fashion,

THE TATLER

as also little cuts and figures, the invention of which we must ascribe to the author of spring-trusses. I must not here omit the blind Italian character, which, being scarce legible, always fixes and detains the eye, and gives the curious reader something like the satisfaction of prying into a secret.

But the great skill in an advertiser is chiefly seen in the style which he makes use of. He is to mention "the universal esteem, or general reputation," of things that were never heard of. If he is a physician or astrologer, he must change his lodgings frequently; and, though he never saw any body in them besides his own family, give public notice of it, "for the information of the nobility and gentry." Since I am thus usefully employed in writing criticisms on the works of these diminutive authors, I must not pass over in silence an advertisement, which has lately made its appearance, and is written altogether in a Ciceronian manner. It was sent to me, with five shillings, to be inserted among my advertisements; but as it is a pattern of good writing in this way, I shall give it a place in the body of my paper.

"The highest compounded spirit of lavender, the most glorious, *if the expression may be used*, enlivening scent and flavour that can possibly be, which so raptures the spirits, delights the gust, and gives such airs to the countenance, as are not to be imagined but by those that have tried it. The meanest sort of the thing is admired by most gentlemen and ladies; but this far more, as by far it exceeds it, to the gaining among all a more than common esteem. It is sold, in neat flint bottles fit for the pocket, only at the golden Key in Wharton's court, near Holbourn-bars, for three shillings and six-pence, with directions."

At the same time that I recommend the several flowers in which this spirit of lavender is wrapped up, *if the expression may be used*, I cannot excuse my fellow-labourers for admitting into their papers several uncleanly advertisements, not at all proper to appear in the works of polite writers. Among these I must reckon the "Carminative Wind-expelling Pills." If the doctor had called them only his Carminative Pills, he had been as cleanly as one could have wished; but the second word entirely destroys the decency of the first. There are other absurdities of this nature so very gross, that I dare not mention them; and shall therefore dismiss this subject with a public admonition to Michael Parrot, That he do not presume any more to mention a certain worm he knows of, which, by the way, has grown seven feet in my memory; for, if I am not much mistaken, it is the same that was but nine feet long about six months ago.

By the remarks I have here made, it plainly appears that a collection of advertisements is a kind of miscellany; the writers of which, contrary to all authors, except men of quality, give money to the booksellers who publish their copies. The genius of the bookseller is chiefly shewn in his method of ranging and digesting these little tracts. The last paper I took up in my hand places them in the following order: —

The true Spanish blacking for shoes, &c.
The beautifying cream for the face, &c.
Pease and plaisters, &c.
Nectar and Ambrosia, &c.
Four freehold tenements of fifteen pounds *per annum*, &c.
Annotations upon the Tatler, &c.
The present state of England, &c.
A commission of bankruptcy being awarded against B. L., bookseller, &c.

ADVENTURES OF A SHILLING

No. 249.] SATURDAY, NOVEMBER 11, 1710. [ADDISON.]

> Per varios casus, per tot discrimina rerum,
> Tendimus. ——   VIRG.

I WAS last night visited by a friend of mine, who has an inexhaustible fund of discourse, and never fails to entertain his company with a variety of thoughts and hints that are altogether new and uncommon. Whether it were in complaisance to my way of living, or his real opinion, he advanced the following paradox, "That it required much greater talents to fill up and become a retired life, than a life of business." Upon this occasion he rallied very agreeably the busy men of the age, who only valued themselves for being in motion, and passing through a series of trifling and insignificant actions. In the heat of his discourse, seeing a piece of money lying on my table, I defy (says he) any of these active persons to produce half the adventures that this twelvepenny piece has

THE TATLER

been engaged in, were it possible for him to give us an account of his life."

My friend's talk made so odd an impression upon my mind, that soon after I was a-bed I fell insensibly into a most unaccountable reverie, that had neither moral nor design in it, and cannot be so properly called a dream as a delirium.

Methoughts the shilling that lay upon the table reared itself upon its edge, and turning the face towards me, opened its mouth, and in a soft silver sound, gave me the following account of his life and adventures:

"I was born (says he) on the side of a mountain, near a little village of Peru, and made a voyage to England in an ingot, under the convoy of Sir Francis Drake. I was, soon after my arrival, taken out of my Indian habit, refined, naturalized, and put into the British mode, with the face of Queen Elizabeth on one side, and the arms of the country on the other. Being thus equipped, I found in me a wonderful inclination to ramble, and visit all parts of the new world into which I was brought. The people very much favoured my natural disposition, and shifted me so fast from hand to hand, that before I was five years old, I had travelled into almost every corner of the nation. But in the beginning of my sixth year, to my unspeakable grief, I fell into the hands of a miserable old fellow, who clapped me into an iron chest, where I found five hundred more of my own quality who lay under the same confinement. The only relief we had, was to be taken out and counted over in the fresh air every morning and evening. After an imprisonment of several years, we heard somebody knocking at our chest, and breaking it open with a hammer. This we found was the old man's heir, who, as his father lay a dying, was so good as to come to our release: he separated us that very day. What was the fate of my companions I know not: as for myself, I was sent to the apothecary's shop for a pint of sack. The apothecary gave me to an herb-woman, the herb-woman to a butcher, the butcher to a brewer, and the brewer to his wife, who made a present of me to a nonconformist preacher. After this manner I made my way merrily through the world; for, as I told you before, we shillings love nothing so much as travelling. I sometimes fetched in a shoulder of mutton, sometimes a play-book, and often had the satisfaction to treat a Templar at a twelvepenny ordinary, or carry him, with three friends, to Westminster Hall.

"In the midst of this pleasant progress which I made from place to place, I was arrested by a superstitious old woman, who shut me up in a greasy purse, in pursuance of a foolish saying, 'That while she kept a Queen Elizabeth's shilling about her, she should never be without money.' I continued here a close prisoner for many months, till at last I was exchanged for eight and forty farthings.

"I thus rambled from pocket to pocket till the beginning of the civil wars, when, to my shame be it spoken, I was employed in raising soldiers against the king: for being of a very tempting breadth, a sergeant made use of me to inveigle country fellows, and list them in the service of the parliament.

"As soon as he had made one man sure, his way was to oblige him to take a shilling of a more homely figure, and then practise the same trick upon another. Thus I continued doing great mischief to the crown, till my officer, chancing one morning to walk abroad earlier than ordinary, sacrificed me to his pleasures, and made use of me to seduce a milk-maid. This wench bent me, and gave me to her sweetheart, applying more properly than she intended the usual form of, 'To my love and from my love.' This ungenerous gallant marrying her within a few days after, pawned me for a dram of brandy, and drinking me out next day, I was beaten flat with a hammer, and again set a running.

"After many adventures, which it would be tedious to relate, I was sent to a young spendthrift, in company with the will of his deceased father. The young fellow, who I found was very extravagant, gave great demonstrations of joy at the receiving of the will; but opening it, he found himself disinherited and cut off from the possession of a fair estate by virtue of my being made a present to him. This put him into such a passion, that after having taken me in his hand, and cursed me, he squirred me away from him as far as he could fling me. I chanced to light in an unfrequented place under a dead wall, where I lay undiscovered and useless, during the usurpation of Oliver Cromwell.

"About a year after the king's return, a poor cavalier that was walking there about dinner-time, fortunately cast his eye upon me, and, to the great joy of us both, carried me to a cook's shop, where he dined upon me, and drank the king's health. When I came again into the world, I found that I had been happier in my retirement than I thought, having probably, by that means, escaped wearing a monstrous pair of breeches.

THE TATLER

"Being now of great credit and antiquity, I was rather looked upon as a medal than an ordinary coin; for which reason a gamester laid hold of me, and converted me to a counter, having got together some dozens of us for that use. We led a melancholy life in his possession, being busy at those hours wherein current coin is at rest, and partaking the fate of our master, being in a few moments valued at a crown, a pound, or a sixpence, according to the situation in which the fortune of the cards placed us. I had at length the good luck to see my master break, by which means I was again sent abroad under my primitive denomination of a shilling.

"I shall pass over many other accidents of less moment, and hasten to that fatal catastrophe, when I fell into the hands of an artist, who conveyed me under ground, and with an unmerciful pair of shears, cut off my titles, clipped my brims, retrenched my shape, rubbed me to my inmost ring, and, in short, so spoiled and pillaged me, that he did not leave me worth a groat. You may think what a confusion I was in, to see myself thus curtailed and disfigured. I should have been ashamed to have shown my head, had not all my old acquaintance been reduced to the same shameful figure, excepting some few that were punched through the belly. In the midst of this general calamity, when everybody thought our misfortune irretrievable, and our case desperate, we were thrown into the furnace together, and (as it often happens with cities rising out of a fire) appeared with greater beauty and lustre than we could ever boast of before. What has happened to me since this change of sex which you now see, I shall take some other opportunity to relate. In the mean time, I shall only repeat two adventures, as being very extraordinary, and neither of them having ever happened to me above once in my life. The first was, my being in a poet's pocket, who was so taken with the brightness and novelty of my appearance, that it gave occasion to the finest burlesque poem in the British language, entitled from me, 'The Splendid Shilling.' The second adventure, which I must not omit, happened to me in the year 1703, when I was given away in charity to a blind man; but indeed this was by a mistake, the person who gave me having heedlessly thrown me into the hat among a pennyworth of farthings."

THE TATLER

FROZEN WORDS

No. 254.]   THURSDAY, NOVEMBER 23, 1710.   [ADDISON.]

Splendidè mendax ——.   HOR. 2 Od. iii. 35.
Gloriously false ——.

THERE are no books which I more delight in than in travels, especially those that describe remote countries, and give the writer an opportunity of shewing his parts without incurring any danger of being examined or contradicted. Among all the authors of this kind, our renowned countryman, Sir John Mandevile has distinguished himself, by the copiousness of his invention, and the greatness of his genius. The second to Sir John I take to have been, Ferdinand Mendez Pinto, a person of infinite adventure, and unbounded imagination. One reads the voyages of these two great wits, with as much astonishment as the travels of Ulysses in Homer, or of the Red-Cross Knight in Spenser. All is enchanted ground, and fairy-land.

I have got into my hands, by great chance, several *manuscripts* of these two eminent authors, which are filled with greater wonders than any of those they have communicated to the public; and indeed, were they not so well attested, they would appear altogether improbable. I am apt to think the ingenious authors did not publish them with the rest of their works, lest they should pass for fictions and fables: a caution not unnecessary, when the reputation of their veracity was not yet established in the world. But as this reason has now no farther weight, I shall make the publick a present of these curious pieces, at such times as I shall find myself unprovided with other subjects.

The present paper I intend to fill with an *extract* from Sir John's Journal, in which that learned and worthy knight gives an account of the freezing and thawing of several short speeches, which he made in the territories of *Nova Zembla*. I need not inform my reader, that the author of Hudibras alludes to this strange quality in that cold climate, when, speaking of abstracted notions cloathed in a visible shape, he adds that apt similè,

"Like words congeal'd in northern air."

Not to keep my reader any longer in suspense, the relation put into modern language, is as follows:

"We were separated by a storm in the latitude of *seventy-three*, insomuch, that only the ship which I was in, with a Dutch and French vessel, got safe into a creek of *Nova Zembla*. We landed, in order to refit our vessels, and store ourselves with provisions. The crew of each vessel made themselves a cabin of turf and wood, at some distance from each other, to fence themselves against the inclemencies of the weather, which was severe beyond imagination. We soon observed, that in talking to one another we lost several of our words, and could not hear one another at above two yards distance, and that too when we sat very near the fire. After much perplexity, I found that our words froze in the air before they could reach the ears of the persons to whom they were spoken. I was soon confirmed in this conjecture, when, upon the increase of the cold, the whole company grew dumb, or rather deaf; for every man was sensible, as we afterwards found, that he spoke as well as ever; but the sounds no sooner took air than they were condensed and lost. It was now a miserable spectacle to see us nodding and gaping at one another, every man talking, and no man heard. One might observe a seaman that could hail a ship at a league's distance, beckoning with his hand, straining his lungs, and tearing his throat; but all in vain:

'—— Nec vox nec verba sequuntur.
'Nor voice, nor words ensued.

"We continued here three weeks in this dismal plight. At length, upon a turn of wind, the air about us began to thaw. Our cabin was immediately filled with a dry clattering sound, which I afterwards found to be the crackling of consonants that broke above our heads, and were often mixed with a gentle hissing, which I imputed to the letter *s*, that occurs so frequently in the English tongue. I soon after felt a breeze of whispers rushing by my ear; for those, being of a soft and gentle substance, immediately liquefied in the warm wind that blew across our cabin. These were soon followed by syllables and short words, and at length by entire sentences, that melted sooner or later, as they were more or less congealed; so that we now heard everything that had been *spoken* during the whole three weeks that we had been *silent*, if I may use that expression. It was now very early in the morning, and yet, to my surprise, I heard somebody say, 'Sir John, it is midnight, and time for the ship's crew to go to-bed.' This I knew to be the pilot's voice; and, upon recollecting myself, I concluded that he had spoken the words to me some days before, though I could not hear them until the present thaw. My reader will easily imagine how the whole crew was amazed to hear every man talking, and see no man opening his mouth. In the midst of this great surprise we were all in, we heard a volley of oaths and curses, lasting for a long while, and uttered in a very hoarse voice, which I knew belonged to the boatswain, who was a very choleric fellow, and had taken his opportunity of cursing and swearing at me, when he thought I could not hear him; for I had several times given him the strappado on that account, as I did not fail to repeat it for these pious soliloquies, when I got him on ship-board.

"I must not omit the names of several beauties in Wapping, which were heard every now and then, in the midst of a long sigh that accompanied them; as, 'Dear Kate!' 'Pretty Mrs. Peggy!' 'When shall I see my Sue again!' This betrayed several amours which had been concealed until that time, and furnished us with a great deal of mirth in our return to England.

"When this confusion of voices was pretty well over, though I was afraid to offer at speaking, as fearing I should not be heard, I proposed a visit to the Dutch cabin, which lay about a mile farther up in the country. My crew were extremely rejoiced to find they had again recovered their hearing; though every man uttered his voice with the same apprehensions that I had done,

'―――― Et timidè verba intermissa retentat.'
'And try'd his tongue, his silence softly broke.'

"At about half-a-mile's distance from our cabin we heard the groanings of a bear, which at first startled us; but, upon enquiry, we were informed by some of our company, that he was dead, and now lay in salt, having been killed upon that very spot about a fortnight before, in the time of the frost. Not far from the same place, we were likewise entertained with some posthumous snarls, and barkings of a fox.

"We at length arrived at the little Dutch settlement; and, upon entering the room, found it filled with sighs that smelt of brandy, and several other unsavoury sounds, that were altogether inarticulate. My valet, who was an Irishman, fell into so great a rage at what he heard, that he drew his sword; but not knowing where to lay the blame, he put it up again. We were stunned with these confused noises, but did not hear a single word until about half-an-hour after; which I ascribed to the harsh and obdurate sounds of that language, which wanted more time than ours to melt, and become audible.

"After having here met with a very hearty welcome, we went to the cabin of the French, who, to make amends for their three weeks silence, were talking and disputing with greater rapidity and confusion than I ever heard in an assembly, even of that nation. Their language, as I found, upon the first giving of the weather, fell asunder and dissolved. I was here convinced of an error, into which I had before fallen; for I fancied, that for the freezing of the sound, it was necessary for it to be wrapped up, and, as it were, preserved in breath; but I found my mistake when I heard the sound of a kit playing a minuet over our heads. I asked the occasion of it; upon which one of the company told me that it would play there above a week longer; 'for,' says he, 'finding ourselves bereft of speech, we prevailed upon one of the company, who had his musical instrument about him, to play to us from morning to night; all which time was employed in dancing in order to dissipate our chagrin, & *tuer le temps.*'"

Here Sir John gives very good philosophical reason, why the kit could not be heard during the frost; but, as they are something prolix, I pass them over in silence, and shall only observe, that the honourable author seems, by his quotations, to have been well versed in the antient poets, which perhaps raised his fancy above the ordinary pitch of historians, and very much contributed to the embellishment of his writings.

LATE HOURS

No. 263.] THURSDAY, DECEMBER 14, 1710. [STEELE.]

Minimâ contentos nocte Britannos. Juv. Sat. ii. 161.
Britons contented with the shortest night.

AN old friend of mine being lately come to town, I went to see him on Tuesday last about eight o'clock in the evening, with a design to sit with him an hour or two, and talk over old stories; but, upon enquiry after him, I found he was gone to-bed. The next morning, as soon as I was up and dressed, and had dispatched a little business, I came again to my friend's house about eleven o'clock, with a design to renew my visit; but, upon asking for him, his servant told me he was just *sat* down to dinner. In short, I found that my old-fashioned friend religiously adhered to the example of his forefathers, and observed the same hours that had been kept in the family ever since the Conquest.

It is very plain, that the night was much longer formerly in this island than it is at present. By the night, I mean that portion of time which nature has thrown into darkness, and which the wisdom of mankind had formerly dedicated to rest and silence. This used to begin at eight o'clock in the evening, and conclude at six in the morning. The curfeu, or eight o'clock bell, was the signal throughout the nation for putting out their candles and going to-bed.

Our grandmothers, though they were wont to sit up the last in the family, were all of them fast asleep at the same hours that their daughters are busy at crimp and basset. Modern statesmen are concerting schemes, and engaged in the depth of politics at the time when their forefathers were laid down quietly to rest, and had nothing in their heads but dreams. As we have thus thrown business and pleasure into the hours of rest, and by that means made the natural night but half as long as it should be, we are forced to piece it out with a great part of the morning; so that near two-thirds of the nation lie fast asleep for several hours in broad daylight. This irregularity is grown so very fashionable at present, that there is scarce a lady of quality in Great Britain that ever saw the sun rise. And, if the humour increases in proportion to what it has done of late years, it is not impossible but our children may hear the bell-man going about the streets at nine o'clock in the morning, and the watch making their rounds until eleven. This unaccountable disposition in mankind to continue awake in the night, and sleep in the sunshine, has made me enquire, whether the same change of inclination has happened to any other animals? For this reason, I desired a friend of mine in the country to let me know, whether the lark rises as early as he did formerly; and whether the cock begins to crow at his usual hour. My friend has answered me, "that his poultry are as regular as ever, and that all the birds and beasts of his neighbourhood keep the same hours that they have observed in the memory of man; and the same which, in all probability, they have kept for these five thousand years."

Modern Midnight Conversation.

THE TATLER

If you would see the innovations that have been made among us in this particular, you may only look into the hours of colleges, where they still *dine at eleven*, and *sup at six*, which were doubtless the hours of the whole nation at the time when those places were founded. But at present, the courts of justice are scarce opened in Westminster-hall at the time when William Rufus used to go to dinner in it. All business is driven forward. The land-marks of our fathers, if I may so call them, are removed, and planted farther up into the day; insomuch, that I am afraid our clergy will be obliged, if they expect full congregations, not to look any more upon ten o'clock in the morning as a canonical hour. In my own memory, the dinner has crept by degrees from *twelve* o'clock to *three*, and where it will fix nobody knows.

I have sometimes thought to draw up a memorial in the behalf of supper against dinner, setting forth, that the said dinner has made several encroachments upon the said supper, and entered very far upon his frontiers; that he has banished him out of several families, and in all has driven him from his head quarters, and forced him to make his retreat into the hours of midnight: and, in short, that he is now in danger of being entirely confounded and lost in a breakfast. Those who have read Lucian, and seen the complaints of the letter T against S, upon account of many injuries and usurpations of the same nature, will not, I believe, think such a memorial forced and unnatural. If dinner has been thus postponed, or, if you please, kept back from time to time, you may be sure that it has been in compliance with the other business of the day, and that supper has still observed a proportionable distance. There is a venerable proverb, which we have all of us heard in our infancy of " putting the children to-bed, and laying the goose to the fire." This was one of the jocular sayings of our forefathers, but may be properly used in the literal sense at present. Who would not wonder at this perverted relish of those who are reckoned the most polite part of mankind, that prefer sea-coals and candles to the sun, and exchange so many cheerful morning hours, for the pleasures of midnight revels and debauches? If a man was only to consult his health, he would choose to live his whole time, if possible, in day-light; and to retire out of the world into silence and sleep, while the raw damps and unwholesome vapours fly abroad, without a sun to disperse, moderate, or controul them. For my own part, I value an hour in the morning as much as common libertines do an hour at midnight. When I find myself awakened into being, and perceive my life renewed within me, and at the same time see the whole face of nature recovered out of the dark uncomfortable state in which it lay for several hours, my heart overflows with such secret sentiments of joy and gratitude, as are a kind of implicit praise to the great author of nature. The mind, in these early seasons of the day, is so refreshed in all its faculties, and borne up with such new supplies of animal spirits, that she finds herself in a state of youth, especially when she is entertained with the breath of flowers, and melody of birds, the dews that hang upon the plants, and all those other sweets of nature that are peculiar to the morning.

It is impossible for a man to have this relish of being, this exquisite taste of life, who does not come into the world before it is in all its noise and hurry; who loses the rising of the sun, the still hours of the day, and, immediately upon his first getting up, plunges himself into the ordinary cares or follies of the world.

ON LONG-WINDED PEOPLE

No. 264.] DECEMBER 16, 1710. [STEELE.]

Favete linguis. Hor. Od. iii. 2. 2.
Favour your tongues.

BOCCALINI, in his "Parnassus," indicts a laconic writer for speaking that in three words which he might have said in two, and sentences him for his punishment to read over all the works of Guicciardini. This Guicciardini is so very prolix and circumstantial in his writings, that I remember our countryman, doctor Donne, speaking of that majestic and concise manner in which Moses has described the creation of the world, adds, "that if such an author as Guicciardini were to have written on such a subject, the world itself would not have been able to have contained the books that gave the history of its creation."

I look upon a tedious talker, or what is generally known by the name of a story-teller, to be much more insufferable than even a prolix writer. An author may be tossed out of your hand, and thrown aside when he grows dull and tiresome; but such liberties are so far from being allowed towards your orators in common conversation, that I have known a challenge sent a person for going out of the room abruptly, and leaving a man of honour in the midst of a dissertation. This evil is at present so very common and epidemical, that there is scarce a coffee-house in town that has not some speakers belonging to it, who utter their political essays, and draw parallels out of Baker's "Chronicle," to almost every part of her majesty's reign. It was said of two ancient authors, who had very different beauties in their style, "that if you took a word from one of them, you only spoiled his eloquence; but if you took a word from the other, you spoiled his sense." I have often applied the first part of this criticism to several of these coffee-house speakers whom I have at present in my thoughts, though the character that is given to the last of those authors, is what I would recommend to the imitation of my loving countrymen. But it is not only public places of resort, but private clubs and conversations over a bottle, that are infested with this loquacious kind of animal, especially with that species which I comprehend under the name of a story-teller. I would earnestly desire these gentlemen to consider, that no point of wit or mirth at the end of a story can atone for the half hour that has been lost before they come at it. I would likewise lay it home to their serious consideration, whether they think that every man in the company has not a right to speak as well as themselves? and whether they do not think they are invading another man's property, when they engross the time which should be divided equally among the company to their own private use?

What makes this evil the much greater in conversation is, that these humdrum companions seldom endeavour to wind up their narrations into a point of mirth or instruction, which might make some amends for the tediousness of them; but think they have a right to tell any thing that has happened within their memory. They look upon matter of fact to be a sufficient foundation for a story, and give us a long account of things, not because they are entertaining or surprising, but because they are true.

My ingenious kinsman, Mr. Humphrey Wagstaff, used to say, "the life of man is too short for a story-teller."

Methusalem might be half an hour in telling what o'clock it was: but as for us postdiluvians, we ought to do everything in haste; and in our speeches, as well as actions, remember that our time is short.

A man that talks for a quarter of an hour together in company, if I meet him frequently, takes up a great part of my span. A quarter of an hour may be reckoned the eight-and-fortieth part of a day, a day the three hundred and sixtieth part of a year, and a year the threescore and tenth part of life. By this moral arithmetic, supposing a man to be in the talking world one third part of the day, whoever gives another a quarter of an hour's hearing, makes him a sacrifice of more than the four hundred thousandth part of his conversable life.

I would establish but one great general rule to be observed in all conversation, which is this, "that men should not talk to please themselves, but those that hear them." This would make them consider, whether what they speak be worth hearing; whether there be either wit or sense in what they are about to say; and, whether it be adapted to the time when, the place where, and the person to whom, it is spoken.

For the utter extirpation of these orators and story-tellers, which I look upon as very great pests of society, I have invented a watch which divides the minute into twelve parts, after the same manner that the ordinary watches are divided into hours: and will endeavour to get a patent, which shall oblige every club or company to provide themselves with one of these watches, that shall lie upon the table, as an hour-glass is often placed near the pulpit, to measure out the length of a discourse.

I shall be willing to allow a man one round of my watch, that is, a whole minute, to speak in; but if he exceeds that time, it shall be lawful for any of the company to look upon the watch, or to call him down to order.

Provided, however, that if any one can make it appear he is turned of threescore, he may take two, or, if he pleases, three rounds of the watch without giving offence. Provided, also, that this rule be not construed to extend to the fair sex, who shall still be at liberty to talk by the ordinary watch that is now in use. I would likewise earnestly recommend this little automaton, which may be easily carried in the pocket without any incumbrance, to all such as are troubled with this infirmity of speech, that upon pulling out their watches, they may have frequent occasion to consider what they are doing, and by that means cut the thread of the story short, and hurry to a conclusion. I shall only add, that this watch, with a paper of directions how to use it, is sold at Charles Lillie's.

THE TATLER

I am afraid a Tatler will be thought a very improper paper to censure this humour of being talkative; but I would have my readers know that there is a great difference between *tattle* and *loquacity*, as I shall show at large in a following lucubration; it being my design to throw away a candle upon that subject, in order to explain the whole art of tattling in all its branches and subdivisions.

ON THE ART OF GROWING OLD

No. 266.] THURSDAY, DECEMBER 21, 1710. [STEELE.]

Rideat et pulset lasciva decentiùs ætas.
HOR. 2 Ep. ii. ult.

Let youth, more decent in their follies, scoff
The nauseous scene, and hiss thee reeling off.

IT would be a good appendix to "The art of Living and Dying," if any one would write "The Art of growing Old," and teach men to resign their pretensions to the pleasures and gallantries of youth, in proportion to the alteration they find in themselves by the approach of age and infirmities. The infirmities of this stage of life would be much fewer, if we did not affect those which attend the more vigorous and active part of our days; but instead of studying to be wiser, or being contented with our present follies, the ambition of many of us is also to be the same sort of fools we formerly have been. I have often argued, as I am a professed lover of women, that our sex grows old with a much worse grace than the other does; and have ever been of opinion that there are more well-pleased old women, than old men. I thought it a good reason for this, that the ambition of the fair sex being confined to advantageous marriages, or shining in the eyes of men, their parts were over sooner and consequently the errors in the performance of them. The conversation of this evening has not convinced me of the contrary; for one or two fop-women shall not make a balance for the crowds of coxcombs among ourselves, diversified according to the different pursuits of pleasure and business.

Returning home this evening a little before my usual hour, I scarce had seated myself in my easy chair, stirred the fire, and stroked my cat, but I heard somebody come rumbling up stairs. I saw my door opened, and a human figure advancing towards me, so fantastically put together, that it was some minutes before I discovered it to be my old and intimate friend Sam Trusty. Immediately I rose up, and placed him in my own seat; a compliment I pay to few. The first thing he uttered was, "Isaac, fetch me a cup of your cherry-brandy before you offer to ask any question." He drank a lusty draught, sat silent for some time, and at last broke out; "I am come," quoth he, "to insult thee for an old fantastic dotard, as thou art, in ever defending the women. I have this evening visited two widows, who are now in that state I have often heard you call an *after-life;* I suppose you mean by it, an existence which grows out of past entertainments, and is an untimely delight in the satisfactions which they once set their hearts upon too much to be ever able to relinquish. Have but patience," continued he, "until I give you a succinct account of my ladies, and of this night's adventure. They are much of an age, but very different in their characters. The one of them, with all the advances which years have made upon her, goes on in a certain romantic road of love and friendship which she fell into in her teens; the other has transferred the amorous passions of her first years to the love cronies, petts, and favourites, with which she is always surrounded; but the genius of each of them will best appear by the account of what happened to me at their houses. About five this afternoon, being tired with study, the weather inviting, and time lying a little upon my hands, I resolved at the instigation of my evil genius, to visit them; their husbands having been our contemporaries. This I thought I could do without much trouble; for both live in the very next street. I went first to my lady Camomile; and the butler, who had lived long in the family, and seen me often in his master's time, ushered me very civilly into the parlour, and told me, though my lady had given strict orders to be denied, he was sure I might be admitted, and bid the black boy acquaint his lady, that I was come to wait upon her. In the window lay two letters, one broke open, the other fresh sealed with a wafer: the first directed to the divine Cosmelia, the second to the charming Lucinda; but both by the indented characters, appeared to have been writ by very unsteady hands. Such uncommon addresses increased my curiosity, and put me upon asking my old friend the butler, if he knew who those persons were? "Very well," says he, "this is from Mrs. Furbish to my lady, an old school-fellow and a great crony of her ladyship's; and this the answer." I enquired in what country she lived. "Oh dear!" says he, "but just by, in the neighbourhood. Why, she was here all this morning, and that letter came and was answered within these two hours. They have taken an odd fancy, you must know, to call one another hard names; but, for all that, they love one another hugely." By this time the boy returned with his lady's humble service to me, desiring I would excuse her; for she could not possibly see me, nor any body else, for it was opera night."

"Methinks," says I, "such innocent folly as two old women's courtship to each other, should rather make you merry than put you out of humour." "Peace, good Isaac," says he, "no interruption, I beseech you. I got soon to Mrs. Feeble's, she that was formerly Betty Frisk; you must needs remember her; Tom Feeble of Brazen Nose fell in love with her for her fine dancing. Well, Mrs. Ursula, without farther ceremony, carries me directly up to her mistress's chamber, where I found her environed by four of the most mischievous animals that can ever infest a family; an old shock dog with one eye, a monkey chained to one side of the chimney, a great grey squirrel to the other, and a parrot waddling in the middle of the room. However, for a while, all was in a profound tranquillity. Upon the mantel-tree, for I am a pretty curious observer, stood a pot of lambetive electuary, with a stick of liquorice, and near it a phial of rose-water, and powder of tutty. Upon the table lay a pipe filled with betony and colt's foot, a roll of wax-candle, a silver spitting-pot, and a Seville orange. The lady was placed in a large wicker-chair, and her feet wrapped up in flannel, supported by cushions; and in this attitude, would you believe it, Isaac, was she reading a romance with spectacles on. The first compliments over, as she was industriously endeavouring to enter upon conversation, a violent fit of coughing seized her. This awaked Shock, and in a trice the whole room was in an uproar; for the dog barked, the squirrel squealed, the monkey chattered, the parrot screamed, and Ursula, to appease them, was more clamorous than all the rest. You, Isaac, who know how any harsh noise affects my head, may guess what I suffered from the hideous din of these discordant sounds. At length all was appeased, and quiet restored: a chair was drawn for me; where I was no sooner seated, but the parrot fixed his horny beak, as sharp as a pair of sheers, in one of my heels, just above the shoe. I sprung from the place with an unusual agility, and so, being within the monkey's reach, he snatches off my new bob-wig, and throws it upon two apples that were roasting by a sullen sea-coal fire. I was nimble enough to save it from any farther damage than singeing the foretop. I put it on; and composing myself as well as I could, I drew my chair towards the other side of the chimney. The good lady, as soon as she had recovered breath, employed it in making a thousand apologies, and, with great eloquence, and numerous train of words, lamented my misfortune. In the middle of her harangue, I felt something scratching near my knee, and feeling what it should be, found the squirrel had got into my coat-pocket. As I endeavoured to remove him from his burrow, he made his teeth meet through the fleshy part of my forefinger. This gave me an unexpressible pain. The Hungary water was immediately brought to bathe it, and goldbeater's skin applied to stop the blood. The lady renewed her excuses; but being now out of all patience, I abruptly took my leave, and hobbling downstairs with heedless haste, I set my foot full in a pail of water, and down we came to the bottom together." Here my friend concluded his narrative, and, with a composed countenance, I began to make him compliments of condolence; but he started from his chair, and said, "Isaac, you may spare your speeches, I expect no reply. When I told you this, I knew you would laugh at me; but the next woman that makes me ridiculous shall be a young one."

ADDISON

ADDISON

From THACKERAY'S "ENGLISH HUMORISTS"

ADDISON'S father was a clergyman of good repute in Wiltshire, and rose in the church. His famous son never lost his clerical training and scholastic gravity, and was called "a parson in a tye-wig" in London afterwards at a time when tye-wigs were only worn by the laity, and the fathers of theology did not think it decent to appear except in a full bottom. Having been as school at Salisbury, and the Charterhouse, in 1687, when he was fifteen years old, he went to Queen's College, Oxford, where he speedily began to distinguish himself by the making of Latin verses. The beautiful and fanciful poem of "The Pigmies and the Cranes," is still read by lovers of that sort of exercise; and verses are extant in honor of King William, by which it appears that it was the loyal youth's custom to toast that sovereign in bumpers of purple Lyæus: many more works are in the Collection, including one on the Peace of Ryswick, in 1697, which was so good that Montague got him a pension of 300*l.* a year, on which Addison set out on his travels.

During his ten years at Oxford, Addison had deeply imbued himself with the Latin poetical literature, and had these poets at his fingers' ends when he travelled in Italy. His patron went out of office, and his pension was unpaid: and hearing that this great scholar, now eminent and known to the literati of Europe (the great Boileau, upon perusal of Mr. Addison's elegant hexameters, was first made aware that England was not altogether a barbarous nation) — hearing that the celebrated Mr. Addison, of Oxford, proposed to travel as governor to a young gentleman on the grand tour, the great Duke of Somerset proposed to Mr. Addison to accompany his son, Lord Hartford.

Mr. Addison was delighted to be of use to his Grace, and his lordship his Grace's son, and expressed himself ready to set forth. His Grace the Duke of Somerset now announced to one of the

ADDISON

most famous scholars of Oxford and Europe that it was his gracious intention to allow my Lord Hartford's tutor one hundred guineas per annum. Mr. Addison wrote back that his services were his Grace's, but he by no means found his account in the recompense for them. The negotiation was broken off. They parted with a profusion of *congées* on one side and the other.

Addison remained abroad for some time, living in the best society of Europe. How could he do otherwise? He must have been one of the finest gentlemen the world ever saw: at all moments of life serene and courteous, cheerful and calm. He could scarcely ever have had a degrading thought. He might have omitted a virtue or two, or many, but could not have had many faults committed for which he need blush or turn pale. When warmed into confidence, his conversation appears to have been so delightful that the greatest wits sat rapt and charmed to listen to him. No man bore poverty and narrow fortune with a more lofty cheerfulness. His letters to his friends at this period of his life, when he had lost his Government pension and given up his college chances, are full of courage and a gay confidence and philosophy: and they are none the worse in my eyes, and I hope not in those of his last and greatest biographer (though Mr. Macauley is bound to own and lament a certain weakness for wine, which the great and good Joseph Addison notoriously possessed, in common with countless gentlemen of his time), because some of the letters are written when his honest hand was shaking a little in the morning after libations to purple Lyæus over-night. He was fond of drinking the healths of his friends: he writes to Wyche, of Hamburg, gratefully remembering Wyche's "hoc." "I have been drinking your health to-day with Sir Richard Shirley," he writes to Bathurst. "I have lately had the honor to meet my Lord Effingham at Amsterdam, where we have drunk Mr. Wood's health a hundred times in excellent champagne," he writes again. Swift describes him over his cups, when Joseph yielded to a temptation which Jonathan resisted. Joseph was of a cold nature, and needed perhaps the fire of wine to warm his blood. If he was a parson, he wore a tye-wig, recollect. A better and more Christian man scarcely ever breathed than Joseph Addison. If he had not that little weakness for wine — why, we could scarcely have found a fault with him, and could not have liked him as we do.

At thirty-three years of age, this most distinguished wit, scholar, and gentleman was without a profession and an income. His

ADDISON

book of "Travels" had failed: his "Dialogues on Medals" had no particular success; his Latin verses, even though reported the best since Virgil, or Statius at any rate, had not brought him a Government place, and Addison was living up three shabby pairs of stairs in the Haymarket (in a poverty over which old Samuel Johnson rather chuckles), when in these shabby rooms an emissary from Government and Fortune came and found him. A poem was wanted about the Duke of Marlborough's victory of Blenheim. Would Mr. Addison write one? Mr. Boyle, afterwards Lord Carleton, took back the reply to the Lord Treasurer Godolphin, that Mr. Addison would. When the poem had reached a certain stage, it was carried to Godolphin; and the last lines which he read were these: —

> "But, O my Muse! what numbers wilt thou find
> To sing the furious troops in battle join'd?
> Methinks I hear the drum's tumultuous sound
> The victor's shouts and dying groans confound;
> The dreadful burst of cannon rend the skies,
> And all the thunder of the battle rise.
> 'Twas then great Marlborough's mighty soul was proved,
> That, in the shock of charging hosts unmoved,
> Amidst confusion, horror, and despair,
> Examined all the dreadful scenes of war:
> In peaceful thought the field of death surveyed,
> To fainting squadrons sent the timely aid,
> Inspired repulsed battalions to engage,
> And taught the doubtful battle where to rage.
> So when an angel, by divine command,
> With rising tempests shakes a guilty land
> (Such as of late o'er pale Britannia passed),
> Calm and serene he drives the furious blast;
> And, pleased the Almighty's orders to perform,
> Rides in the whirlwind and directs the storm."

Addison left off at a good moment. That simile was pronounced to be of the greatest ever produced in poetry. That angel, that good angel, flew off with Mr. Addison, and landed him in the place of Commissioner of Appeals — vice Mr. Locke providentially promoted. In the following year Mr. Addison went to Hanover with Lord Halifax, and the year after was made Under Secretary of State. O angel visits! you come "few and far between" to literary gentlemen's lodgings! Your wings seldom quiver at second-floor windows now!

ADDISON

You laugh? You think it is in the power of few writers now-a-days to call up such an angel? Well, perhaps not; but permit us to comfort ourselves by pointing out that there are in the poem of the "Campaign" some as bad lines as heart can desire: and to hint that Mr. Addison did very wisely in not going further with my Lord Godolphin than that angeli al simile. Do allow me, just for a little harmless mischief, to read you some of the lines which follow. Here is the interview between the Duke and the King of the Romans after the battle: —

> "Austria's young monarch, whose imperial sway
> Sceptres and thrones are destined to obey,
> Whose boasted ancestry so high extends
> That in the Pagan Gods his lineage ends,
> Comes from afar, in gratitude to own
> The great supporter of his father's throne.
> What tides of glory to his bosom ran
> Clasped in th' embraces of the godlike man!
> How were his eyes with pleasing wonder fixt,
> To see such fire with so much sweetness mixt!
> Such easy greatness, such a graceful port,
> So turned and finished for the camp or court!"

How many fourth-form boys at Mr. Addison's school of Charterhouse could write as well as that now? The "Campaign" has blunders, triumphant as it was; and weak points like all campaigns.

In the year 1713 "Cato" came out. Swift has left a description of the first night of the performance. All the laurels of Europe were scarcely sufficient for the author of this prodigious poem. Laudations of Whig and Tory chiefs, popular ovations, complimentary garlands from literary men, translations in all languages, delight and homage from all — save from John Dennis in a minority of one. Mr. Addison was called the "great Mr. Addison" after this. The Coffee-house Senate saluted him Divus: it was heresy to question that decree.

Meanwhile he was writing political papers and advancing in the political profession. He went Secretary to Ireland. He was appointed Secretary of State in 1717. And letters of his are extant, bearing date some year or two before, and written to young Lord Warwick, in which he addresses him as "my dearest lord," and asks affectionately about his studies, and writes very prettily about nightingales and birds'-nests, which he has found at Fulham for his lordship. Those nightingales were intended to warble in the ear

ADDISON

of Lord Warwick's mamma. Addison married her ladyship in 1716; and died at Holland House three years after that splendid but dismal union.

But it is not for his reputation as the great author of "Cato" and the "Campaign," or for his merits as Secretary of State, or for his rank and high distinction as my Lady Warwick's husband, or for his eminence as an Examiner of political questions on the Whig side, or a Guardian of British liberties, that we admire Joseph Addison. It is as a Tatler of small talk and a Spectator of mankind, that we cherish and love him, and owe as much pleasure to him as to any human being that ever wrote. He came in that artificial age, and began to speak with his noble, natural voice. He came, the gentle satirist, who hit no unfair blow; the kind judge who castigated only in smiling. While Swift went about, hanging and ruthless — a literary Jeffreys — in Addison's kind court only minor cases were tried: only peccadilloes and small sins against society: only a dangerous libertinism in tuckers and hoops; or a nuisance in the abuse of beaux' canes and snuff-boxes. It may be a lady is tried for breaking the peace of our sovereign lady Queen Anne, and ogling too dangerously from the side-box; or a Templar for beating the watch, or breaking Priscian's head: or a citizen's wife for caring too much for the puppet-show, and too little for her husband and children: every one of the little sinners brought before him is amusing, and he dismisses each with the pleasantest penalties and the most charming words of admonition.

Addison wrote his papers as gayly as if he was going out for a holiday. When Steele's "Tatler" first began his prattle, Addison, then in Ireland, caught at his friend's notion, poured in paper after paper, and contributed the stores of his mind, the sweet fruits of his reading, the delightful gleanings of his daily observation, with a wonderful profusion, and as it seemed an almost endless fecundity. He was six-and-thirty years old: full and ripe. He had not worked crop after crop from his brain, manuring hastily, subsoiling indifferently, cutting and sowing and cutting again, like other luckless cultivators of letters. He had not done much as yet; a few Latin poems — graceful prolusions; a polite book of travels; a dissertation on medals, not very deep; four acts of a tragedy, a great classical exercise; and the "Campaign," a large prize poem that won an enormous prize. But with his friend's discovery of the "Tatler," Addison's calling was found, and the most delightful talker in the world began to speak. He does not go very deep: let gentlemen of a profound genius, critics accustomed to the plunge of the bathos, console themselves by thinking that he *couldn't* go very deep. There are no traces of suffering in his writing. He was so good, so honest, so healthy, so cheerfully selfish, if I must use the word. There is no deep sentiment. I doubt, until after his marriage, perhaps, whether he ever lost his night's rest or his day's tranquillity about any woman in his life; whereas poor Dick Steele had capacity enough to melt, and to languish, and to sigh, and to cry his honest old eyes out, for a dozen. His writings do not show insight into or reverence for the love of women, which I take to be, one the consequence of the other. He walks about the world watching their pretty humors, fashions, follies, flirtations, rivalries; and noting them with the most charming archness. He sees them in public, in the theatre, or the assembly, or the puppet-show; or at the toyshop higgling for gloves and lace; or at the auction, battling together over a blue porcelain dragon, or a darling monster in Japan; or at church, eyeing the width of their rivals' hoops, or the breadth of their laces, as they sweep down the aisles. Or he looks out of his window at the "Garter" in St. James's Street, at Ardelia's coach, as she blazes to the drawing-room with her coronet and six footmen; and remembering that her father was a Turkey merchant in the city, calculates how many sponges went to purchase her ear-ring, and how many drums of figs to build her coach-box; or he demurely watches behind a tree in Spring Garden as Saccharissa (whom he knows under her mask) trips out of her chair to the alley where Sir Fopling is waiting. He sees only the public life of women. Addison was one of the most resolute club-men of his day. He passed many hours daily in those haunts. Besides drinking — which, alas! is past praying for — you must know it, he owned, too, ladies, that he indulged in that odious practice of smoking. Poor fellow! He was a man's man, remember. The only woman he *did* know, he didn't write about. I take it there would not have been much humor in that story.

He likes to go and sit in the smoking-room at the "Grecian," or the "Devil"; to pace 'Change and the Mall — to mingle in that great club of the world — sitting alone in it somehow: having goodwill and kindness for every single man and woman in it — having need of some habit and custom binding him to some few; never doing any man a wrong (unless it be a wrong to hint a little doubt about a man's parts, and to damn him with faint praise); and so he looks on the world and plays with the ceaseless humors of all of us — laughs the kindest laugh — points our neighbor's foible or eccentricity out to us with the most good-natured, smiling confidence; and then, turning over his shoulder, whispers *our* foibles to our neighbor. What would Sir Roger de Coverley be without his follies and his charming little brain-cracks? If the good knight did not call out to the people sleeping in church, and say "Amen" with such a delightful pomposity: if he did not make a speech in the assize-court *àpropos de bottes*, and merely to show his dignity to Mr. Spectator: if he did not mistake Madam Doll Tearsheet for a lady of quality in Temple Garden: if he were wiser than he is: if he had not his humor to salt his life, and were but a mere English gentleman and game-preserver — of what worth were he to us? We love him for his vanities as much as his virtues. What is ridiculous is delightful in him; we are so fond of him because we laugh at him so. And out of that laughter, and out of that sweet weakness, and out of those harmless eccentricities and follies, and out of that touched brain, and out of that honest manhood and simplicity — we get a result of happiness, goodness, tenderness, pity, piety; such as, if my audience will think their reading and hearing over, doctors and divines but seldom have the fortune to inspire. And why not? Is the glory of Heaven to be sung only by gentlemen in black coats? Must the truth be only expounded in gown and surplice, and out of those two vestments can nobody preach it? Commend me to this dear preacher without orders — this parson in the tye-wig. When this man looks from the world, whose weaknesses he describes so benevolently, up to the Heaven which shines over us all, I can hardly fancy a human face lighted up with a more serene rapture: a human intellect thrilling with a purer love and adoration than Joseph Addison's. Listen to him: from your childhood you have known the verses: but who can hear their sacred music without love and awe? —

> " Soon as the evening shades prevail,
> The moon takes up the wondrous tale,
> And nightly to the listening earth
> Repeats the story of her birth;
> Whilst all the stars that round her burn,
> And all the planets in their turn,
> Confirm the tidings as they roll,
> And spread the truth from pole to pole.

ADDISON

> What though, in solemn silence, all
> Move round the dark terrestrial ball;
> What though no real voice nor sound
> Amid their radiant orbs be found;
> In reason's ear they all rejoice,
> And utter forth a glorious voice,
> For ever singing as they shine,
> The hand that made us is divine."

It seems to me those verses shine like the stars. They shine out of a great deep calm. When he turns to Heaven a Sabbath comes over that man's mind: and his face lights up from it with a glory of thanks and prayer. His sense of religion stirs through his whole being. In the fields, in the town: looking at the birds in the trees: at the children in the streets: in the morning or in the moonlight: over his books in his own room: in a happy party at a country merry-making or a town assembly, good-will and peace to God's creatures, and love and awe of Him who made them, fill his pure heart and shine from his kind face. If Swift's life was the most wretched, I think Addison's was one of the most enviable. A life prosperous and beautiful — a calm death — an immense fame and affection afterwards for his happy and spotless name.

THE SPECTATOR

THE SPECTATOR

POPULAR SUPERSTITIONS

No. 7.]   THURSDAY, MARCH 8, 1710–11.   [ADDISON.]

> Somnia, terrores magicos, miracula, sagas,
> Nocturnos lemures, portentaque Thessala rides?
> HOR. 2 Ep. ii. 208.
>
> Visions, and magic spells, can you despise,
> And laugh at witches, ghosts, and prodigies?

GOING yesterday to dine with an old acquaintance, I had the misfortune to find his whole family very much dejected. Upon asking him the occasion of it, he told me that his wife had dreamt a very strange dream the night before, which they were afraid portended some misfortune to themselves or to their children. At her coming into the room, I observed a settled melancholy in her countenance, which I should have been troubled for, had I not heard from whence it proceeded. We were no sooner sat down, but, after having looked upon me a little while, "My dear," said she, turning to her husband, "you may now see the stranger that was in the candle last night." Soon after this, as they began to talk of family affairs, a little boy at the lower end of the table told her that he was to go into join-hand on Thursday. "Thursday!" says she; "no, child; if it please God you shall not begin upon Childermas-day; tell your writing-master that Friday will be soon enough." I was reflecting with myself on the oddness of her fancy, and wondering that anybody would establish it as a rule, to lose a day in every week. In the midst of these my musings, she desired me to reach her a little salt upon the point of my knife, which I did in such a trepidation and hurry of obedience that I let it drop by the way; at which she immediately startled, and said it fell towards her. Upon this I looked very blank; and, observing the concern of the whole table, began to consider myself, with some confusion, as a person who had brought a disaster upon the family. The lady, however, recovering herself after a little space, said to her husband with a sigh, "My dear, misfortunes never come single." My friend, I found, acted but an under part at his table; and, being a man of more good-nature than understanding, thinks himself obliged to fall in with all the passions and humours of his yoke-fellow. "Do not you remember, child," says she, "that the pigeon-house fell the very afternoon that our careless wench spilt the salt upon the table?" — "Yes," says he, "my dear; and the next post brought us an account of the battle of Almanza." The reader may guess at the figure I made after having done all this mischief. I dispatched my dinner as soon as I could with my usual taciturnity; when, to my utter confusion, the lady seeing me quitting [wiping] my knife and fork, and laying them across one another upon my plate, desired me that I would humour her so far as to take them out of that figure, and place them side by side. What the absurdity was which I had committed I did not know, but I suppose there was some traditionary superstition in it; and therefore, in obedience to the lady of the house, I disposed of my knife and fork in two parallel lines, which is the figure I shall always lay them in for the future, though I do not know any reason for it.

It is not difficult for a man to see that a person has conceived an aversion to him. For my own part, I quickly found, by the lady's looks, that she regarded me as a very odd kind of fellow, with an unfortunate aspect: for which reason I took my leave immediately after dinner, and withdrew to my own lodgings. Upon my return home, I fell into a profound contemplation on the evils that attend these superstitious follies of mankind; how they subject us to imaginary afflictions, and additional sorrows, that do not properly come within our lot. As if the natural calamities of life were not sufficient for it, we turn the most indifferent circumstances into misfortunes, and suffer as much from trifling accidents as from real evils. I have known the shooting of a star spoil a night's rest; and have seen a man in love grow pale, and lose his appetite, upon the plucking of a merry-thought. A screech-owl at midnight has alarmed a family more than a band of robbers; nay, the voice of a cricket hath struck more terror than the roaring of a lion. There is nothing so inconsiderable, which may not appear dreadful to an imagination that is filled with omens and prognostics: a rusty nail or a crooked pin shoot up into prodigies.

THE SPECTATOR

I remember I was once in a mixed assembly, that was full of noise and mirth, when on a sudden an old woman unluckily observed there were thirteen of us in company. This remark struck a panic terror into several who were present, insomuch that one or two of the ladies were going to leave the room; but a friend of mine, taking notice that one of our female companions was big with child, affirmed there were fourteen in the room, and that, instead of portending one of the company should die, it plainly foretold one of them should be born. Had not my friend found this expedient to break the omen, I question not but half the women in the company would have fallen sick that very night.

An old maid that is troubled with the vapours produces infinite disturbances of this kind among her friends and neighbours. I know a maiden aunt of a great family, who is one of these antiquated Sybils, that forebodes and prophesies from one end of the year to the other. She is always seeing apparitions and hearing death-watches; and was the other day almost frightened out of her wits by the great house-dog that howled in the stable at a time when she lay ill of the toothache. Such an extravagant cast of mind engages multitudes of people, not only in impertinent terrors, but in supernumerary duties of life; and arises from that fear and ignorance which are natural to the soul of man. The horror with which we entertain the thoughts of death (or indeed of any future evil), and the uncertainty of its approach, fill a melancholy mind with innumerable apprehensions and suspicions, and consequently dispose it to the observation of such groundless prodigies and predictions. For as it is the chief concern of wise men to retrench the evils of life by the reasonings of philosophy, it is the employment of fools to multiply them by the sentiments of superstition.

For my own part, I should be very much troubled were I endowed with this divining quality, though it should inform me truly of everything that can befall me. I would not anticipate the relish of any happiness, nor feel the weight of any misery, before it actually arrives.

I know but one way of fortifying my soul against these gloomy presages and terrors of mind; and that is, by securing to myself the friendship and protection of that Being who disposes of events and governs futurity. He sees, at one view, the whole thread of my existence, not only that part of it which I have already passed through, but that which runs forward into all the depths of eternity.

THE SPECTATOR

When I lay me down to sleep, I recommend myself to his care; when I awake, I give myself up to his direction. Amidst all the evils that threaten me, I will look up to him for help; and question not but he will either avert them, or turn them to my advantage. Though I know neither the time nor the manner of the death I am to die, I am not at all solicitous about it; because I am sure that He knows them both, and that He will not fail to comfort and support me under them.

CLUBS

No. 9.] SATURDAY, MARCH 10, 1710 – 11. [ADDISON.]

>   —— Tigris agit rabidâ cum tigride pacem
>   Perpetuam, sævis inter se convenit ursis.
>
>   JUV. Sat. xv. 163.
>
>   Tiger with tiger, bear with bear, you'll find
>   In leagues offensive and defensive join'd.

MAN is said to be a sociable animal, and, as an instance of it, we may observe that we take all occasions and pretensions of forming ourselves into those little nocturnal assemblies, which are commonly known by the name of clubs. When a set of men find themselves agree in any particular, though never so trivial, they establish themselves into a kind of fraternity, and meet once or twice a week upon the account of such a fantastic resemblance. I know a considerable market-town in which there was a club of fat men, that did not come together (as you may well suppose) to entertain one another with sprightliness and wit, but to keep one another in countenance. The room where the club met was something of the largest, and had two entrances; the one by a door of moderate size, and the other by a pair of folding doors. If a candidate for this corpulent club could make his entrance through the first, he was looked upon as unqualified; but if he stuck in the passage, and could not force his way through it, the folding doors were immediately thrown open for his reception, and he was saluted as a brother. I have heard that this club, though it consisted but of fifteen persons, weighed above three ton.

THE SPECTATOR

In opposition to this society, there sprung up another composed of scarecrows and skeletons, who, being very meagre and envious, did all they could to thwart the designs of their bulky brethren, whom they represented as men of dangerous principles, till at length they worked them out of the favour of the people, and consequently out of the magistracy. These factions tore the corporation in pieces for several years, till at length they came to this accommodation: that the two bailiffs of the town should be annually chosen out of the two clubs; by which means the principal magistrates are at this day coupled like rabbits, one fat and one lean.

Every one has heard of the club, or rather the confederacy, of the Kings. This grand alliance was formed a little after the return of King Charles the Second, and admitted into it men of all qualities and professions, provided they agreed in this surname of King, which, as they imagined, sufficiently declared the owners of it to be altogether untainted with republican and anti-monarchical principles.

A Christian name has likewise been often used as a badge of distinction, and made the occasion of a club. That of the George's, which used to meet at the sign of the George on St. George's day, and swear, "Before George," is still fresh in every one's memory.

There are at present in several parts of this city what they call street clubs, in which the chief inhabitants of the street converse together every night. I remember, upon my inquiring after lodgings in Ormond Street, the landlord, to recommend that quarter of the town, told me there was at that time a very good club in it; he also told me, upon further discourse with him, that two or three noisy country squires, who were settled there the year before, had considerably sunk the price of house-rent; and that the club (to prevent the like inconveniences for the future) had thoughts of taking every house that became vacant into their own hands, till they had found a tenant for it of a sociable nature and good conversation.

The Hum-Drum club, of which I was formerly an unworthy member, was made up of very honest gentlemen of peaceable dispositions, that used to sit together, smoke their pipes, and say nothing till midnight. The Mum club (as I am informed) is an institution of the same nature, and as great an enemy to noise.

After these two innocent societies, I cannot forbear mentioning a very mischievous one, that was erected in the reign of King Charles the Second: I mean the club of Duellists, in which none was to be admitted that had not fought his man. The president of it was said to have killed half-a-dozen in single combat; and, as for the other members, they took their seats according to the number of their slain. There was likewise a side-table, for such as had only drawn blood, and shewn a laudable ambition of taking the first opportunity to qualify themselves for the first table. This club, consisting only of men of honour, did not continue long, most of the members of it being put to the sword, or hanged, a little after its institution.

Our modern celebrated clubs are founded upon eating and drinking, which are points wherein most men agree, and in which the learned and illiterate, the dull and the airy, the philosopher and the buffoon, can all of them bear a part. The Kit-cat itself is said to have taken its original from a mutton-pie. The Beef-steak and October clubs are neither of them averse to eating and drinking, if we may form a judgment of them from their respective titles.

When men are thus knit together by a love of society, not a spirit of faction, and do not meet to censure or annoy those that are absent, but to enjoy one another; when they are thus combined for their own improvement, or for the good of others, or at least to relax themselves from the business of the day, by an innocent and cheerful conversation, there may be something very useful in these little institutions and establishments.

I cannot forbear concluding this paper with a scheme of laws that I met with upon a wall in a little alehouse. How I came thither I may inform my reader at a more convenient time. These laws were enacted by a knot of artizans and mechanics, who used to meet every night; and, as there is something in them which gives us a pretty picture of low life, I shall transcribe them word for word.

RULES.

To be observed in the Two-penny club, erected in this place for the preservation of friendship and good neighbourhood.

I. Every member at his first coming in shall lay down his two-pence.

II. Every member shall fill his pipe out of his own box.

III. If any member absents himself, he shall forfeit a penny for the use of the club, unless in case of sickness or imprisonment.

IV. If any member swears or curses, his neighbour may give him a kick upon the shins.

V. If any member tells stories in the club that are not true, he shall forfeit for every third lie a halfpenny.

VI. If any member strikes another wrongfully, he shall pay his club for him.

VII. If any member brings his wife into the club, he shall pay for whatever she drinks or smokes.

VIII. If any member's wife comes to fetch him home from the club, she shall speak to him without the door.

IX. If any member calls another a cuckold, he shall be turned out of the club.

X. None shall be admitted into the club that is of the same trade with any member of it.

XI. None of the club shall have his clothes or shoes made or mended, but by a brother member.

XII. No non-juror shall be capable of being a member.

The morality of this little club is guarded by such wholesome laws and penalties, that I question not but my reader will be as well pleased with them, as he would have been with the *Leges Convivales* of Ben Jonson, the regulations of an old Roman club cited by Lipsius, or the rules of a *Symposium* in an ancient Greek author.   C.

THE USES OF THE SPECTATOR

No. 10.]   MONDAY, MARCH 12, 1710-11.   [ADDISON.]

> Non aliter quam qui adverso vix flumine lembum
> Remigiis subigit: si brachia forte remisit,
> Atque illum in præceps prono rapit alveus amni. — VIRG.

IT is with much satisfaction that I hear this great city inquiring day by day after these my papers, and receiving my morning lectures with a becoming seriousness and attention. My publisher tells me, that there are already three thousand of them distributed every day: so that if I allow twenty readers to every paper, which I look upon as a modest computation, I may reckon about threescore thousand disciples in London and Westminster, who I hope will take care to distinguish themselves from the thoughtless herd of their ignorant and unattentive brethren. Since I have raised to myself so great an audience, I shall spare no pains to make their instruction agreeable, and their diversion useful. For which reasons I shall endeavour to enliven morality with wit, and to temper wit with morality, that my readers may, if possible, both ways find their account in the speculation of the day. And to the end that their virtue and discretion may not be short, transient, intermitting starts of thought, I have resolved to refresh their memories from day to day, till I have recovered them out of that desperate state of vice and folly into which the age is fallen. The mind that lies fallow but a single day, sprouts up in follies that are only to be killed by a constant and assiduous culture. It was said of Socrates that he brought Philosophy down from Heaven, to inhabit among men; and I shall be ambitious to have it said of me, that I have brought Philosophy out of closets and libraries, schools and colleges, to dwell in clubs and assemblies, at tea-tables and in coffee-houses.

I would therefore in a very particular manner recommend these my speculations to all well-regulated families that set apart an hour in every morning for tea and bread and butter; and would earnestly advise them for their good to order this paper to be punctually served up, and to be looked upon as a part of the tea equipage.

Sir Francis Bacon observes, that a well-written book, compared with its rivals and antagonists, is like Moses's serpent, that immediately swallowed up and devoured those of the Egyptians. I shall not be so vain as to think that, where the SPECTATOR appears, the other public prints will vanish; but shall leave it to my readers' consideration, whether, is it not much better to be let into the knowledge of one's self, than to hear what passes in Muscovy or Poland; and to amuse ourselves with such writings as tend to the wearing out of ignorance, passion, and prejudice, than such as naturally conduce to inflame hatreds, and make enmities irreconcilable?

In the next place, I would recommend this paper to the daily perusal of those gentlemen whom I cannot but consider as my good brothers and allies, I mean the fraternity of Spectators, who live in the world without having anything to do in it; and either by the affluence of their fortunes, or laziness of their dispositions, have no other business with the rest of mankind, but to look upon them. Under this class of men are comprehended all contemplative tradesmen, titular physicians, fellows of the Royal Society, Templars that are not given to be contentious, and statesmen that are out of business; in short, every one that considers the world as a theatre, and desires to form a right judgment of those who are the actors on it.

There is another set of men that I must likewise lay a claim to, whom I have lately called the blanks of society, as being altogether unfurnished with ideas, till the business and conversation of the day has supplied them. I have often considered these poor souls with an eye of great commiseration, when I have heard them asking the first man they have met with, whether there was any news stirring? and by that means gathering together materials for thinking. These needy persons do not know what to talk of, till about twelve a clock in the morning; for by that time they are pretty good judges of the weather, know which way the wind sits, and whether the Dutch mail be come in. As they lie at the mercy of the first man they meet, and are grave or impertinent all the day long, according to the notions which they have imbibed in the morning, I would earnestly entreat them not to stir out of their chambers till they have read this paper, and do promise them that I will daily instil into them such sound and wholesome sentiments, as shall have a good effect on their conversation for the ensuing twelve hours.

But there are none to whom this paper will be more useful, than to the female world. I have often thought there has not been sufficient pains taken in finding out proper employments and diversions for the fair ones.

Their amusements seem contrived for them, rather as they are women, than as they are reasonable creatures; and are more adapted to the sex than to the species. The toilet is their great scene of business, and the right adjusting of their hair the principal employment of their lives. The sorting of a suit of ribbons is reckoned a very good morning's work; and if they make an excursion to a mercer's or a toy-shop, so great a fatigue makes them unfit for anything else all the day after. Their more serious occupations are sewing and embroidery, and their greatest drudgery, the preparation of jellies and sweet-meats. This, I say, is the state of ordinary women; though I know there are multitudes of those of a more elevated life and conversation, that move in an exalted sphere of knowledge and virtue, that join all the beauties of the mind to the ornaments of dress, and inspire a kind of awe and respect, as well as love, into their male beholders. I hope to increase the number of these by publishing this daily paper, which I shall always endeavour to make an innocent if not an improving entertainment, and by that means at least divert the minds of my female readers from greater trifles. At the same time, as I would fain give some finishing touches to those which are already the most beautiful pieces in human nature, I shall endeavour to point out all those imperfections that are the blemishes, as well as those virtues which are the embellishments, of the sex. In the mean while I hope these my gentle readers, who have so much time on their hands, will not grudge throwing away a quarter of an hour in a day on this paper, since they may do it without any hindrance to business.

I know several of my friends and well-wishers are in great pain for me, lest I should not be able to keep up the spirit of a paper which I oblige myself to furnish every day: but to make them easy in this particular, I will promise them faithfully to give it over as soon as I grow dull. This I know will be matter of great raillery to the small wits; who will frequently put me in mind of my promise, desire me to keep my word, assure me that it is high time to give over, with many other pleasantries of the like nature, which men of a little smart genius cannot forbear throwing out against their best friends, when they have such a handle given them of being witty. But let them remember that I do hereby enter my caveat against this piece of raillery.

EFFECT OF THE SUPERNATURAL ON THE IMAGINATION

No. 12.] WEDNESDAY, MARCH 14, 1710-11. [ADDISON.]

—— Veteres avias tibi de pulmone revello.
PERS. Sat. v. 92.

I root th' old woman from thy trembling heart.

AT my coming to London, it was some time before I could settle myself in a house to my liking. I was forced to quit my first lodgings, by reason of an officious landlady, that would be asking me every morning how I had slept. I then fell into an honest family, and lived very happily for above a week; when my landlord, who was a jolly, good-natured man, took it into his head that I wanted company, and therefore would frequently come into my chamber to keep me from being alone. This I bore for two or three days; but telling me one day that he was afraid I was melancholy, I thought it was high time for me to be gone, and accordingly took new lodgings that very night. About a week after, I found my jolly landlord, who, as I said before, was an honest, hearty man, had put me into an advertisement of the *Daily Courant*, in the following words: "Whereas a melancholy man left his lodgings on Thursday last in the afternoon, and was afterwards seen going towards Islington; if any one can give notice of him to R. B., fishmonger in the Strand, he shall be very well rewarded for his pains." As I am the best man in the world to keep my own counsel, and my landlord the fishmonger not knowing my name, this accident of my life was never discovered to this very day.

I am now settled with a widow woman, who has a great many children, and complies with my humour in everything. I do not remember that we have exchanged a word together these five years; my coffee comes into my chamber every morning without asking for it; if I want fire, I point to my chimney; if water, to my bason; upon which my landlady nods, as much as to say she takes my meaning, and immediately obeys my signals. She has likewise modelled her family so well, that when her little boy offers to pull me by the coat, or prattle in my face, his eldest sister immediately calls him off, and bids him not to disturb the gentleman. At my first entering into the family, I was troubled with the civility of their rising up to me every time I came into the room; but my landlady observing that upon these occasions I always cried Pish, and went out again, has forbidden any such ceremony to be used in the house; so that at present I walk into the kitchen or parlour without being taken notice of or giving any interruption to the business or discourse of the family. The maid will ask her mistress (though I am by) whether the gentleman is ready to go to dinner, as the mistress (who is indeed an excellent housewife) scolds at the servants as heartily before my face as behind my back. In short, I move up and down the house, and enter into all companies, with the same liberty as a cat or any other domestic animal, and am as little suspected of telling anything that I hear or see.

I remember last winter there were several young girls of the neighbourhood sitting about the fire with my landlady's daughters, and telling stories of spirits and apparitions. Upon my opening the door the young women broke off their discourse, but my landlady's daughters telling them that it was nobody but the gentleman (for that is the name which I go by in the neighbourhood as well as in the family), they went on without minding me. I seated myself by the candle that stood on a table at one end of the room; and pretending to read a book that I took out of my pocket, heard several dreadful stories of ghosts as pale as ashes that had stood at the feet of a bed, or walked over a churchyard by moonlight, and of others that had been conjured into the Red Sea, for disturbing people's rest, and drawing their curtains at midnight; with many other old women's fables of the like nature. As one spirit raised another, I observed that at the end of every story the whole company closed their ranks, and crowded about the fire. I took notice in particular of a little boy, who was so very attentive to every story, that I am mistaken if he ventures to go to bed by himself this twelvemonth. Indeed they talked so long, that the imaginations of the whole assembly were manifestly crazed, and I am sure will be the worse for it as long as they live. I heard one of the girls, that had looked upon me over her shoulder, asking the company how long I had been in the room, and whether I did not look paler than I used to do. This put me under some apprehensions that I should be forced to explain myself if I did not retire; for which reason I took the candle in my hand, and went up into my chamber, not without wondering at this unaccountable weakness in reasonable creatures, that they should love to astonish and terrify one another. Were I a father, I should take a particular care to preserve my children from these little horrors of imagination, which they are apt to contract when they are young, and are not able to shake off when they are in years. I have known a soldier that has entered a breach, affrighted at his own shadow, and look pale upon a little scratching at his door, who the day before had marched up against a battery of cannon. There are instances of persons who have been terrified, even to distraction, at the figure of a tree, or the shaking of a bulrush. The truth of it is, I look upon a sound imagination as the greatest blessing of life, next to a clear judgment and a good conscience. In the meantime, since there are very few whose minds are not more or less subject to these dreadful thoughts and apprehensions, we ought to arm ourselves against them by the dictates of reason and religion, "to pull the old woman out of our hearts" (as Persius expresses it in the motto of my paper), and extinguish those impertinent notions which we imbibed at a time that we were not able to judge of their absurdity. Or, if we believe, as many wise and good men have done, that there are such phantoms and apparitions as those I have been speaking of, let us endeavour to establish to ourselves an interest in Him who holds the reins of the whole creation in His hand, and moderates them after such a manner, that it is impossible for one being to break loose upon another without His knowledge and permission.

For my own part, I am apt to join in opinion with those who believe that all the regions of nature swarm with spirits; and that we have multitudes of spectators on all our actions, when we think ourselves most alone; but instead of terrifying myself with such a notion, I am wonderfully pleased to think that I am always engaged with such an innumerable society, in searching out the wonders of the creation, and joining in the same consort of praise and adoration.

Milton has finely described this mixed communion of men and spirits in paradise; and had doubtless his eye upon a verse in old Hesiod, which is almost word for word the same with his third line in the following passage: —

> —— "Nor think, though men were none,
> That heav'n would want spectators, God want praise:
> Millions of spiritual creatures walk the earth
> Unseen, both when we wake and when we sleep;
> All these with ceaseless praise his works behold
> Both day and night. How often from the steep
> Of echoing hill or thicket have we heard
> Celestial voices to the midnight air,
> Sole, or responsive each to other's note,
> Singing their great Creator? Oft in bands,
> While they keep watch, or nightly rounding walk,
> With heav'nly touch of instrumental sounds,
> In full harmonic number join'd, their songs
> Divide the night and lift our thoughts to heav'n."

C.

THE SPECTATOR

DRESS AND SHOW

No. 15.] SATURDAY, MARCH 17, 1710-11. [ADDISON.]

Parva leves capiunt animos ——
OVID, Ars. Am. i. 159.

Light minds are pleas'd with trifles.

WHEN I was in France, I used to gaze with great astonishment at the splendid equipages and party-coloured habits of that fantastic nation. I was one day in particular contemplating a lady that sat in a coach adorned with gilded cupids, and finely painted with the Loves of Venus and Adonis. The coach was drawn by six milk-white horses, and loaded behind with the same number of powdered footmen. Just before the lady were a couple of beautiful pages, that were stuck among the harness, and, by their gay dresses and smiling features, looked like the elder brothers of the little boys that were carved and painted in every corner of the coach.

The lady was the unfortunate Cleanthe, who afterwards gave an occasion to a pretty melancholy novel. She had, for several years, received the addresses of a gentleman, whom, after a long and intimate acquaintance, she forsook, upon the account of this shining equipage, which had been offered to her by one of great riches, but a crazy constitution. The circumstances in which I saw her, were, it seems, the disguises only of a broken heart, and a kind of pageantry to cover distress; for in two months after she was carried to her grave with the same pomp and magnificence, being sent thither partly by the loss of one lover, and partly by the possession of another.

I have often reflected with myself on this unaccountable humour in womankind, of being smitten with every thing that is showy and superficial; and on the numberless evils that befall the sex from this light fantastical disposition. I myself remember a young lady that was very warmly solicited by a couple of importunate rivals, who, for several months together, did all they could to recommend themselves by complacency of behaviour and agreeableness of conversation. At length, when the competition was doubtful, and the lady undetermined in her choice, one of the young lovers very luckily bethought himself of adding a supernumerary lace to his liveries, which had so good an effect that he married her the very week after.

The useful conversation of ordinary women very much cherishes this natural weakness of being taken with outside and appearance. Talk of a new-married couple, and you immediately hear whether they keep their coach and six, or eat in plate. Mention the name of an absent lady, and it is ten to one but you learn something of her gown and petticoat. A ball is a great help to discourse, and a birthday furnishes conversation for a twelvemonth after. A furbelow of precious stones, a hat buttoned with a diamond, a brocade waistcoat or petticoat, are standing topics. In short, they consider only the drapery of the species, and never cast away a thought on those ornaments of the mind that make persons illustrious in themselves and useful to others. When women are thus perpetually dazzling one another's imaginations, and filling their heads with nothing but colours, it is no wonder that they are more attentive to the superficial parts of life, than the solid and substantial blessings of it. A girl who has been trained up in this kind of conversation, is in danger of every embroidered coat that comes in her way. A pair of fringed gloves may be her ruin. In a word, lace and ribands, silver and gold galloons, with the like glittering gewgaws, are so many lures to women of weak minds or low educations, and, when artificially displayed, are able to fetch down the most airy coquette from the wildest of her flights and rambles.

True happiness is of a retired nature, and an enemy to pomp and noise; it arises, in the first place, from the enjoyment of one's self; and, in the next, from the friendship and conversation of a few select companions; it loves shade and solitude, and naturally haunts groves and fountains, fields and meadows; in short, it feels every thing it wants within itself, and receives no additions from multitudes of witnesses and spectators. On the contrary, false happiness loves to be in a crowd, and to draw the eyes of the world upon her. She does not receive any satisfaction from the applauses which she gives herself, but from the admiration which she raises in others. She flourishes in court and palaces, theatres and assemblies, and has no existence but when she is looked upon.

Aurelia, though a woman of great quality, delights in the privacy of a country life, and passes away a great part of her time in her own walks and gardens. Her husband, who is her bosom friend and companion in her solitudes, has been in love with her ever since he knew her. They both abound with good sense, consummate virtue, and a mutual esteem; and are a perpetual entertainment to one another. Their family is under so regular an economy, in its hours of devotion and repast, employment and diversion, that it looks like a little commonwealth within itself. They often go into company, that they may return with the greater delight to one another; and sometimes live in town, not to enjoy it so properly as to grow weary of it, that they may renew in themselves the relish of a country life. By this means they are happy in each other, beloved by their children, adored by their servants, and are become the envy, or rather the delight, of all that know them.

How different to this is the life of Fulvia! she considers her husband as her steward, and looks upon discretion and good housewifery as little domestic virtues unbecoming a woman of quality. She thinks life lost in her own family, and fancies herself out of the world, when she is not in the ring, the playhouse, or the drawing-room. She lives in a perpetual motion of body, and restlessness of thought, and it is never easy in any one place, when she thinks there is more company in another. The missing of an opera·the first night, would be more afflicting to her than the death of a child. She pities all the valuable part of her own sex, and calls every woman of a prudent, modest, and retired life, a poor-spirited unpolished creature. What a mortification would it be to Fulvia, if she knew that her setting herself to view is but exposing herself, and that she grows contemptible by being conspicuous?

I cannot conclude my paper, without observing, that Virgil has very finely touched upon this female passion for dress and show, in the character of Camilla; who, though she seems to have shaken off all the other weaknesses of her sex, is still described as a woman in this particular. The poet tells us, that, after having made a great slaughter of the enemy, she unfortunately cast her eye on a Trojan who wore an embroidered tunic, a beautiful coat of mail, with a mantle of the finest purple. "A golden bow," says he, "hung upon his shoulder; his garment was buckled with a golden clasp, and his head covered with a helmet of the same shining metal." The Amazon immediately singled out this well-dressed warrior, being seized with a woman's longing for the pretty trappings that he was adorned with:

Taste in High Life.

THE SPECTATOR

> ———Totumque incauta per agmen
> Fœmineo prædæ et spoliorum ardebat amore."

This heedless pursuit after these glittering trifles, the poet (by a nice concealed moral) represents to have been the destruction of his female hero.   C.

ITALIAN OPERA

No. 18.]   WEDNESDAY, MARCH 21, 1710–11. •   [ADDISON.]

> — Equitis quoque jam migravit ab aure voluptas
> Omnis ad incertos oculos et gaudia vana. — HOR.
>
> But now our nobles too are fops and vain,
> Neglect the sense, but love the painted scene.

IT is my design in this paper to deliver down to posterity a faithful account of the Italian Opera, and of the gradual progress which it has made upon the English stage: For there is no question but our great grandchildren will be very curious to know the reason why their forefathers used to sit together like an audience of foreigners in their own country, and to hear whole plays acted before them in a tongue which they did not understand.

Arsinoe was the first opera that gave us a taste of Italian music. The great success this opera met with, produced some attempts of forming pieces upon Italian plans, which should give a more natural and reasonable entertainment than what can be met with in the elaborate trifles of that nation. This alarmed the poetasters and fiddlers of the town, who were used to deal in a more ordinary kind of ware; and therefore laid down an established rule, which is received as such to this day, *That nothing is capable of being well set to music, that is not nonsense.*

This maxim was no sooner received, but we immediately fell to translating the Italian operas; and as there was no great danger of hurting the sense of those extraordinary pieces, our authors would often make words of their own which were entirely foreign to the meaning of the passages they pretended to translate; their chief care being to make the numbers of the English verse answer to those of the Italian, that both of them might go to the same tune. Thus the famous song in *Camilla*,

> "Barbara si t' intendo," &c.
> "Barbarous woman, yes, I know your meaning,"

which expresses the resentments of an angry lover, was translated into that English lamentation —

> "Frail are a lover's hopes," &c.

And it was pleasant enough to see the most refined persons of the British nation dying away and languishing to notes that were filled with a spirit of rage and indignation. It happened also very frequently, where the sense was rightly translated, the necessary transposition of words which were drawn out of the phrase of one tongue into that of another, made the music appear very absurd in one tongue that was very natural in the other. I remember an Italian verse that ran thus word for word,

> "And turn'd my rage into pity;"

which the English for rhyme sake translated,

> "And into pity turn'd my rage."

By this means the soft notes that were adapted to pity in the Italian, fell upon the word rage in the English; and the angry sounds that were turned to rage in the original, were made to express pity in the translation. It oftentimes happened likewise, that the finest notes in the air fell upon the most insignificant words in the sentence. I have known the word *and* pursued through the whole gamut, have been entertained with many a melodious *the*, and have heard the most beautiful graces, quavers and divisions bestowed upon *then*, *for*, and *from;* to the eternal honour of our English particles.

The next step to our refinement, was the introducing of Italian actors into our opera; who sung their parts in their own language, at the same time that our countrymen performed theirs in our native tongue. The king or hero of the play generally spoke in Italian, and his slaves answered him in English: the lover frequently made his court, and gained the heart of his princess in a language which she did not understand. One would have thought it very difficult to have carried on dialogues after this manner, without an interpreter between the persons that conversed together; but this was the state of the English stage for about three years.

At length the audience grew tired of understanding half the opera, and therefore to ease themselves entirely of the fatigue of thinking, have so ordered it at present that the whole opera is performed in an unknown tongue. We no longer understand the language of our own stage; insomuch that I have often been afraid, when I have seen our Italian performers chattering in the vehemence of action, that they have been calling us names, and abusing us among themselves; but I hope, since we do put such an entire confidence in them, they will not talk against us before our faces, though they may do it with the same safety as if it were behind our backs. In the meantime I cannot forbear thinking how naturally an historian, who writes two or three hundred years hence, and does not know the taste of his wise fore-fathers, will make the following reflection, *In the beginning of the eighteenth century, the Italian tongue was so well understood in* England, *that operas were acted on the public stage in that language.*

One scarce knows how to be serious in the confutation of an absurdity that shews itself at the first sight. It does not want any great measure of sense to see the ridicule of this monstrous practice; but what makes it the more astonishing, it is not the taste of the rabble, but of persons of the greatest politeness, which has established it.

If the Italians have a genius for music above the English, the English have a genius for other performances of a much higher nature, and capable of giving the mind a much nobler entertainment. Would one think it was possible (at a time when an author lived that was able to write the *Phædra* and *Hippolitus*) for a people to be so stupidly fond of the Italian opera, as scarce to give a third day's hearing to that admirable tragedy? Music is certainly a very agreeable entertainment, but if it would take the entire possession of our ears, if it would make us incapable of hearing sense, if it would exclude arts that have a much greater tendency to the refinement of human nature: I must confess I would allow it no better quarter than *Plato* has done, who banishes it out of his commonwealth.

At present, our notions of music are so very uncertain, that we do not know what it is we like, only, in general, we are transported with any thing that is not English: so if it be of a foreign growth, let it be Italian, French, or High-Dutch, it is the same thing. In short, our English music is quite rooted out, and nothing yet planted in its stead.

When a royal palace is burnt to the ground, every man is at liberty to present his plan for a new one; and though it be but indifferently put together, it may furnish several hints that may be of use to a good architect. I shall take the same liberty in a following paper, of giving my opinion upon the subject of music, which I shall lay down only in a problematical manner to be considered by those who are masters in the art. C.

CHOICE OF A PROFESSION

No. 21.] SATURDAY, MARCH 24, 1710-11. [ADDISON.]

—— Locus est et pluribus umbris.
HOR. 1 Ep. v. 28.

There's room enough, and each may bring his friend.

I AM sometimes very much troubled when I reflect upon the three great professions of divinity, law, and physic; how they are each of them overburdened with practitioners, and filled with multitudes of ingenious gentlemen that starve one another.

We may divide the clergy into generals, field-officers, and subalterns. Among the first we may reckon bishops, deans, and archdeacons. Among the second are doctors of divinity, prebendaries, and all that wear scarfs. The rest are comprehended under the subalterns. As for the first class, our constitution preserves it from any redundancy of incumbents, notwithstanding competitors are numberless. Upon a strict calculation it is found that there has been a great exceeding of late years in the second division, several brevets having been granted for the converting of subalterns into scarf-officers; insomuch that within my memory the price of lustring is raised above two-pence in a yard. As for the subalterns, they are not to be numbered. Should our clergy once enter into the corrupt practice of the laity, by the splitting of their freeholds, they would be able to carry most of the elections in England.

THE SPECTATOR

The body of the law is no less encumbered with superfluous members, that are like Virgil's army, which he tells us was so crowded many of them had not room to use their weapons. This prodigious society of men may be divided into the litigious and peaceable. Under the first are comprehended all those who are carried down in coach-fulls to Westminster-hall every morning in term time. Martial's description of this species of lawyers is full of humour:

> "Iras et verba locant."

"Men that hire out their words and anger;" that are more or less passionate according as they are paid for it, and allow their client a quantity of wrath proportionable to the fee which they receive from him. I must, however, observe to the reader, that above three parts of those whom I reckon among the litigious are such as are only quarrelsome in their hearts, and have no opportunity of shewing their passion at the bar. Nevertheless as they do not know what strifes may arise, they appear at the Hall every day, that they may shew themselves in a readiness to enter the lists, whenever there shall be occasion for them.

The peaceable lawyers are, in the first place, many of the benchers of the several inns of court, who seem to be the dignitaries of the law, and are endowed with those qualifications of mind that accomplish a man rather for a ruler than a pleader. These men live peaceably in their habitations, eating once a day, and dancing once a year, for the honour of their respective societies.

Another numberless branch of peaceable lawyers are those young men who, being placed at the inns of court in order to study the laws of their country, frequent the play-house more than Westminster-hall, and are seen in all public assemblies, except in a court of justice. I shall say nothing of those silent and busy multitudes that are employed within doors in the drawing up of writings and conveyances; nor of those greater numbers that palliate their want of business with a pretence to such chamber practice.

If, in the third place, we look into the profession of physic, we shall find a most formidable body of men. The sight of them is enough to make a man serious; for we may lay it down as a maxim that when a nation abounds in physicians it grows thin of people. Sir William Temple is very much puzzled to find out a reason why the Northern Hive, as he calls it, does not send out such prodigious swarms, and overrun the world with Goths and Vandals, as it did formerly; but had that excellent author observed that there were no students in physic among the subjects of Thor and Woden, and that this science very much flourishes in the north at present, he might have found a better solution for this difficulty than any of those he has made use of. This body of men in our own country may be described like the British army in Cæsar's time: some of them slay in chariots, and some on foot. If the infantry do less execution than the charioteers, it is because they cannot be carried so soon into all quarters of the town, and despatch so much business in so short a time. Besides this body of regular troops, there are stragglers who, without being duly listed and enrolled, do infinite mischief to those who are so unlucky as to fall into their hands.

There are, besides the above-mentioned, innumerable retainers to physic who, for want of other patients, amuse themselves with the stifling of cats in an air-pump, cutting up dogs alive, or impaling of insects upon the point of a needle for microscopical observations; besides those that are employed in the gathering of weeds, and the chase of butterflies: not to mention the cockleshell-merchants and spider-catchers.

When I consider how each of these professions is crowded with multitudes that seek their livelihood in them, and how many men of merit there are in each of them who may be rather said to be of the science than the profession, I very much wonder at the humour of parents who will not rather choose to place their sons in a way of life where an honest industry cannot but thrive, than in stations where the greatest probity, learning, and good sense may miscarry. How many men are country curates that might have made themselves aldermen of London, by a right improvement of a smaller sum of money than what is usually laid out upon a learned education? A sober frugal person, of slender parts and a slow apprehension, might have thrived in trade though he starves upon physic; as a man would be well enough pleased to buy silks of one, whom he would not venture to feel his pulse. Vagellius is careful, studious, and obliging, but withal a little thick-skulled; he has not a single client, but might have had abundance of customers. The misfortune is, that parents take a liking to a particular profession, and therefore desire their sons may be of it; whereas, in so great an affair of life, they should consider the genius and abilities of their children more than their own inclinations.

THE SPECTATOR

It is the great advantage of a trading nation, that there are very few in it so dull and heavy who may not be placed in stations of life which may give them an opportunity of making their fortunes. A well-regulated commerce is not, like law, physic, or divinity, to be overstocked with hands; but, on the contrary, flourishes by multitudes, and gives employment to all its professors. Fleets of merchantmen are so many squadrons of floating shops, that vend our wares and manufactures in all the markets of the world, and find out chapmen under both the tropics. C.

LETTER FROM A VALETUDINARIAN

No. 25.] THURSDAY, MARCH 29, 1711. [ADDISON.]

—— Ægrescitque medendo.
VIRG. ÆN. xii. 46.

And sickens by the very means of health.

THE following letter will explain itself, and needs no apology: —

"SIR, — I am one of that sickly tribe who are commonly known by the name of Valetudinarians; and do confess to you, that I first contracted this ill habit of body, or rather of mind, by the study of physic. I no sooner began to peruse books of this nature, but I found my pulse was irregular; and scarce ever read the account of any disease that I did not fancy myself afflicted with. Dr. Sydenham's learned treatise of fevers threw me into a lingering hectic, which hung upon me all the while I was reading that excellent piece. I then applied myself to the study of several authors, who have written upon phthisical distempers, and by that means fell into a consumption; till at length, growing very fat, I was in a manner shamed out of that imagination. Not long after this I found in myself all the symptoms of the gout, except pain; but was cured of it by a treatise upon the gravel, written by a very ingenious author, who (as it is usual for physicians to convert one distemper into another) eased me of the gout by giving me the stone. I at length studied myself into a complication of distempers; but accidentally taking into my hand that ingenious discourse written by Sanctorius, I was resolved to direct myself by a scheme of rules, which I had collected from his observations. The learned world are very well acquainted with that gentleman's invention; who, for the better carrying on of his experiments, contrived a certain mathematical chair, which was so artificially hung upon springs, that it would weigh anything as well as a pair of scales. By this means he discovered how many ounces of his food passed by perspiration, what quantity of it was turned into nourishment, and how much went away by the other channels and distributions of nature.

"Having provided myself with this chair, I used to study, eat, drink, and sleep in it; insomuch that I may be said, for these three last years, to have lived in a pair of scales. I compute myself, when I am in full health, to be precisely two hundredweight, falling short of it about a pound after a day's fast, and exceeding it as much after a very full meal; so that it is my continual employment to trim the balance between these two volatile pounds in my constitution. In my ordinary meals I fetch myself up to two hundredweight and half a pound; and if, after having dined, I find myself fall short of it, I drink just so much small beer, or eat such a quantity of bread, as is sufficient to make me weight. In my greatest excesses I do not transgress more than the other half-pound; which, for my health's sake, I do the first Monday in every month. As soon as I find myself duly poised after dinner, I walk till I have perspired five ounces and four scruples; and when I discover by my chair, that I am so far reduced, I fall to my books, and study away three ounces more. As for the remaining parts of the pound, I keep no account of them. I do not dine and sup by the clock, but by my chair; for when that informs me my pound of food is exhausted, I conclude myself to be hungry, and lay in another with all diligence. In my days of abstinence I lose a pound and a half, and on solemn fasts am two pound lighter than on other days in the year.

"I allow myself, one night with another, a quarter of a pound of sleep, within a few grains more or less; and if, upon my rising, I find that I have not consumed my whole quantity, I take out the rest in my chair. Upon an exact calculation of what I expended and received the last year, which I always register in a book, I find the medium to be two hundredweight, so that I cannot discover that I am impaired one ounce in my health during a whole twelvemonth. And yet, Sir, notwithstanding this my great care to ballast myself equally every day, and to keep my body in its proper poise, so it is that I find myself in a sick and languishing condition. My complexion is grown very sallow, my pulse low, and my body hydropical. Let me, therefore, beg you, Sir, to consider me as your patient, and to give me more certain rules to walk by than those I have already observed, and you will very much oblige,

Your humble Servant."

This letter puts me in mind of an Italian epitaph, written on the monument of a valetudinarian: "*Stavo ben, ma per star meglio, sto qui:*" which it is impossible to translate. The fear of death often proves mortal, and sets people on methods to save their lives, which infallibly destroy them. This is a reflection made by some historians, upon observing that there are many more thousands killed in a flight than in a battle; and may be applied to those multitudes of imaginary sick persons that break their constitutions by physic, and throw themselves into the arms of death, by endeavouring to escape it. This method is not only dangerous, but below the practice of a reasonable creature. To consult the preservation of life, as the only end of it; to make our health our business; to engage in no action that is not part of a regimen, or course of physic, are purposes so abject, so mean, so unworthy human nature, that a generous soul would rather die than submit to them. Besides, that a continual anxiety for life vitiates all the relishes of it, and casts a gloom over the whole face of nature; as it is impossible we should take delight in anything that we are every moment afraid of losing.

I do not mean, by what I have here said, that I think any one to blame for taking due care of their health. On the contrary, as cheerfulness of mind and capacity for business are in a great measure the effects of a well-tempered constitution, a man cannot be at too much pains to cultivate and preserve it. But this care, which we are prompted to, not only by common sense, but by duty and instinct, should never engage us in groundless fears, melancholy apprehensions, and imaginary distempers, which are natural to every man who is more anxious to live than how to live. In short, the preservation of life should be only a secondary concern, and the direction of it our principal. If we have this frame of mind, we shall take the best means to preserve life, without being over solicitous about the event; and shall arrive at that point of felicity which

Martial has mentioned as the perfection of happiness, of neither fearing nor wishing for death.

In answer to the gentleman, who tempers his health by ounces and by scruples, and instead of complying with those natural solicitations of hunger and thirst, drowsiness, or love of exercise, governs himself by the prescriptions of his chair, I shall tell him a short fable. Jupiter, says the mythologist, to reward the piety of a certain countryman, promised to give him whatever he would ask. The countryman desired that he might have the management of the weather in his own estate. He obtained his request; and immediately distributed rain, snow, and sunshine among his several fields, as he thought the nature of the soil required. At the end of the year, when he expected to see a more than ordinary crop, his harvest fell infinitely short of that of his neighbours. Upon which (says the fable) he desired Jupiter to take the weather again into his own hands, or that otherwise he should utterly ruin himself.

C.

REFLECTIONS IN WESTMINSTER ABBEY

No. 26.] FRIDAY, MARCH 30, 1711. [ADDISON.]

> Pallida mors æquo pulsat pede pauperum tabernas
>   Regumque turres, O beate Sexti.
> Vitæ summa brevis spem nos vetat inchoare longam,
>   Jam te premet nox, fabulæque manes,
> Et domus exilis Plutonia.   HOR. 1 Od. iv. 13.
>
> With equal foot, rich friend, impartial fate
> Knocks at the cottage, and the palace gate:
> Life's span forbids thee to extend thy cares,
> And stretch thy hopes beyond thy years:
> Night soon will seize, and you must quickly go
> To story'd ghosts, and Pluto's house below.

WHEN I am in a serious humour, I very often walk by myself in Westminster Abbey; where the gloominess of the place, and the use to which it is applied, with the solemnity of the building, and the condition of the people who lie in it, are apt to fill the mind with a kind of melancholy, or rather thoughtfulness, that is not disagreeable. I yesterday passed a whole afternoon in the churchyard, the cloisters, and the church, amusing myself with the tomb-stones and inscriptions that I met with in those several regions of the dead. Most of them recorded nothing else of the buried person, but that he was born upon one day, and died upon another: the whole history of his life being comprehended in those two circumstances that are common to all mankind. I could not but look upon these registers of existence, whether of brass or marble, as a kind of satire upon the departed persons; who left no other memorial of them, but that they were born, and that they died. They put me in mind of several persons mentioned in the battles of heroic poems, who have sounding names given them, for no other reason but that they may be killed, and are celebrated for nothing but being knocked on the head.

"Glaucumque, Medontaque, Thersilochumque."

"Glaucus, and Medon, and Thersilochus." — Virg.

The life of these men is finely described in holy writ by "the path of an arrow," which is immediately closed up and lost.

Upon my going into the church, I entertained myself with the digging of a grave; and saw in every shovel-full of it that was thrown up, the fragment of a bone or skull intermixt with a kind of fresh mouldering earth, that some time or other had a place in the composition of an human body. Upon this I began to consider with myself, what innumerable multitudes of people lay confused together under the pavement of that ancient cathedral; how men and women, friends and enemies, priests and soldiers, monks and prebendaries, were crumbled amongst one another, and blended together in the same common mass; how beauty, strength, and youth, with old age, weakness, and deformity, lay undistinguished in the same promiscuous heap of matter.

After having thus surveyed this great magazine of mortality, as it were in the lump, I examined it more particularly by the accounts which I found on several of the monuments which are raised in every quarter of that ancient fabric. Some of them were covered with such extravagant epitaphs, that if it were possible for the dead person to be acquainted with them, he would blush at the praises which his friends have bestowed on him. There are others so excessively modest, that they deliver the character of the person departed in Greek or Hebrew, and by that means are not understood once in a twelvemonth. In the poetical quarter, I found there were poets who had no monuments, and monuments which had no poets. I observed, indeed, that the present war had filled the church with many of these uninhabited monuments, which had been erected to the memory of persons whose bodies were, perhaps, buried in the plains of Blenheim, or in the bosom of the ocean.

I could not but be very much delighted with several modern epitaphs, which are written with great elegance of expression and justness of thought, and therefore do honour to the living as well as to the dead. As a foreigner is very apt to conceive an idea of the ignorance or politeness of a nation from the turn of their public monuments and inscriptions, they should be submitted to the perusal of men of learning and genius before they are put in execution. Sir Cloudesley Shovel's monument has very often given me great offence. Instead of the brave, rough, English admiral, which was the distinguishing character of that plain, gallant man, he is represented on his tomb by the figure of a beau, dressed in a long periwig, and reposing himself upon velvet cushions under a canopy of state. The inscription is answerable to the monument; for, instead of celebrating the many remarkable actions he had performed in the service of his country, it acquaints us only with the manner of his death, in which it was impossible for him to reap any honour. The Dutch, whom we are apt to despise for want of genius, show an infinitely greater taste of antiquity and politeness in their buildings and works of this nature, than what we meet with in those of our own country. The monuments of their admirals, which have been erected at the public expense, represent them like themselves, and are adorned with rostral crowns and naval ornaments, with beautiful festoons of sea-weed, shells, and coral.

But to return to our subject. I have left the repository of our English kings for the contemplation of another day, when I shall find my mind disposed for so serious an amusement. I know that entertainments of this nature are apt to raise dark and dismal thoughts in timorous minds and gloomy imaginations; but for my own part, though I am always serious, I do not know what it is to be melancholy; and can therefore take a view of nature in her deep and solemn scenes, with the same pleasure as in her most gay and delightful ones. By this means I can improve myself with those objects, which others consider with terror. When I look upon the tombs of the great, every emotion of envy dies in me; when I read the epitaphs of the beautiful, every inordinate desire goes out;

THE SPECTATOR

when I meet with the grief of parents upon a tomb-stone, my heart melts with compassion: when I see the tomb of the parents themselves, I consider the vanity of grieving for those whom we must quickly follow. When I see kings lying by those who deposed them, when I consider rival wits placed side by side, or the holy men that divided the world with their contests and disputes, I reflect with sorrow and astonishment on the little competitions, factions, and debates of mankind. When I read the several dates of the tombs, of some that died yesterday, and some six hundred years ago, I consider that great day when we shall all of us be contemporaries, and make our appearance together.   C.

OFFICE FOR THE REGULATION OF SIGNS

No. 28.] MONDAY, APRIL 2, 1711. [ADDISON.]

— Neque semper arcum
Tendit Apollo.— HOR.

I SHALL here present my reader with a letter from a projector, concerning a new office which he thinks may very much contribute to the embellishment of the city, and to the driving barbarity out of our streets. I consider it as a satire upon projectors in general, and a lively picture of the whole art of modern criticism.

"SIR, — Observing that you have thoughts of creating certain officers under you, for the inspection of several petty enormities which you yourself cannot attend to; and finding daily absurdities hung upon the sign-posts of this city, to the great scandal of foreigners, as well as those of our own country, who are curious spectators of the same: I do humbly propose, that you would be pleased to make me your Superintendent of all such figures and devices as are or shall be made use of on this occasion; with full powers to rectify or expunge whatever I shall find irregular or defective. For want of such an officer, there is nothing like sound literature and good sense to be met with in those objects, that are everywhere thrusting themselves out to the eye, and endeavouring to become visible. Our streets are filled with blue boars, back swans, and red lions; not to mention flying pigs, and hogs in armour, with many other creatures more extraordinary than any in the deserts of Afric. Strange! that one who has all the birds and beasts in nature to choose out of, should live at the sign of an *Ens Rationis!*

"My first task therefore should be, like that of Hercules, to clear the city from monsters. In the second place I would forbid, that creatures of jarring and incongruous natures should be joined together in the same sign; such as the bell and the neat's-tongue, the dog and grid-iron. The fox and goose may be supposed to have met; but what has the fox and the seven stars to do together? And when did the lamb and dolphin ever meet, except upon a signpost? As for the cat and fiddle, there is a conceit in it; and therefore I do not intend that anything I have here said should affect it. I must however observe to you upon this subject, that it is usual for a young tradesman, at his first setting up, to add to his sign that of the master whom he served; as the husband, after marriage, gives a place to his mistress's arms in his own coat. This I take to have given rise to many of those absurdities which are committed over our heads; and, as I am informed, first occasioned the three nuns and a hare, which we see so frequently joined together. I would therefore establish certain rules, for the determining how far one tradesman may give the sign of another, and in what cases he may be allowed to quarter it with his own.

"In the third place, I would enjoin every shop to make use of a sign which bears some affinity to the wares in which it deals. What can be more inconsistent than to see a bawd at the sign of the angel, or a tailor at the lion? A cook should not live at the boot, nor a shoemaker at the roasted pig; and yet, for want of this regulation, I have seen a goat set up before the door of a perfumer, and the French king's head at a sword-cutler's.

"An ingenious foreigner observes, that several of those gentlemen who value themselves upon their families, and overlook such as are bred to trade, bear the tools of their forefathers in their coats of arms. I will not examine how true this is in fact: but though it may not be necessary for posterity thus to set up the sign of their forefathers, I think it highly proper for those who actually profess the trade, to show some such marks of it before their doors.

"When the name gives an occasion for an ingenious sign-post, I would likewise advise the owner to take that opportunity of letting the world know who he is. It would have been ridiculous for the ingenious Mrs. Salmon to have lived at the sign of the trout; for which reason she has erected before her house the figure of the fish that is her namesake. Mr. Bell has likewise distinguished himself by a device of the same nature: and here, sir, I must beg leave to observe to you, that this particular figure of a bell has given occasion to several pieces of wit in this kind. A man of your reading must know that Able Drugger gained great applause by it in the time of Ben Johnson. Our apocryphal heathen god is also represented by this figure; which, in conjunction with the dragon, makes a very handsome picture in several of our streets. As for the Bell Savage, which is the sign of a savage man standing by a bell, I was formerly very much puzzled upon the conceit of it, till I accidentally fell into the reading of an old romance translated out of the French; which gives an account of a very beautiful woman who was found in a wilderness, and is called in the French *La Belle Sauvage;* and is everywhere translated by our countrymen the Bell Savage. This piece of philology will, I hope, convince you that I have made sign-posts my study, and consequently qualified myself for the employment which I solicit at your hands. But before I conclude my letter, I must communicate to you another remark which I have made upon the subject with which I am now entertaining you, namely, that I can give a shrewd guess at the humour of the inhabitant by the sign that hangs before his door. A surly, choleric fellow generally makes choice of a bear; as men of milder dispositions frequently live at the lamb. Seeing a punch-bowl painted upon a sign near Charing-Cross, and very curiously garnished, with a couple of angels hovering over it, and squeezing a lemon into it, I had the curiosity to ask after the master of the house, and found upon inquiry, as I had guessed by the little *agrémens* upon his sign, that he was a Frenchman. I know, sir, it is not requisite for me to enlarge upon these hints to a gentleman of your great abilities; so, humbly recommending myself to your favour and patronage,

"I remain," &c

I shall add to the foregoing letter another, which came to me by the same penny-post.

"Honoured Sir, — Having heard that this nation is a great encourager of ingenuity, I have brought with me a rope-dancer that was caught in one of the woods belonging to the Great Mogul.

THE SPECTATOR

He is by birth a monkey; but swings upon a rope, takes a pipe of tobacco, and drinks a glass of ale, like any reasonable creature. He gives great satisfaction to the quality; and if they will make a subscription for him, I will send for a brother of his out of Holland that is a very good tumbler; and also for another of the same family, whom I design for my merry-andrew, as being an excellent mimic, and the greatest droll in the country where he now is. I hope to have this entertainment in a readiness for the next winter; and doubt not but it will please more than the opera or puppet-show. I will not say that a monkey is a better man than some of the opera heroes; but certainly he is a better representative of a man than the most artificial composition of wood and wire. If you will be pleased to give me a good word in your paper, you shall be every night a spectator at my show for nothing.

"I am," &c.

THE CLUB OF SPECTATORS

No. 34.] MONDAY, APRIL 9, 1711. [ADDISON.]

—— parcit
Cognatis maculis similis fera —Juv.

THE club of which I am a member is very luckily composed of such persons as are engaged in different ways of life, and deputed as it were out of the most conspicuous classes of mankind: by this means I am furnished with the greatest variety of hints and materials, and know everything that passes in the different quarters and divisions, not only of this great city, but of the whole kingdom. My readers, too, have the satisfaction to find, that there is no rank or degree among them who have not their representative in this club, and that there is always somebody present who will take care of their respective interests, that nothing may be written or published to the prejudice or infringement of their just rights and privileges.

I last night sate very late in company with this select body of friends, who entertained me with several remarks which they and others had made upon these my speculations, as also with the various success which they had met with among their several ranks and degrees of readers. Will. Honeycomb told me, in the softest manner he could, that there were some ladies (but for your comfort, says Will., they are not those of the most wit) that were offended at the liberties I had taken with the opera and the puppet-show; that some of them were likewise very much surprised, that I should think such serious points as the dress and equipage of persons of quality proper subjects for raillery.

He was going on, when Sir Andrew Freeport took him up short, and told him, that the papers he hinted at had done great good in the city, and that all their wives and daughters were the better for them: and further added, that the whole city thought themselves very much obliged to me for declaring my generous intentions to scourge vice and folly as they appear in a multitude, without condescending to be a publisher of particular intrigues and cuckoldoms. In short, says Sir Andrew, if you avoid that foolish beaten road of falling upon aldermen and citizens, and employ your pen upon the vanity and luxury of courts, your paper must needs be of general use.

Upon this my friend the Templar told Sir Andrew, That he wondered to hear a man of his sense talk after that manner; that the city had always been the province for satire; and that the wits of King Charles's time jested upon nothing else during his whole reign. He then showed, by the examples of Horace, Juvenal, Boileau, and the best writers of every age, that the follies of the stage and court had never been accounted too sacred for ridicule, how great soever the persons might be that patronized them. But after all, says he, I think your raillery has made too great an excursion in attacking several persons of the inns of court; and I do not believe you can show me any precedent for your behaviour in that particular.

My good friend Sir Roger de Coverley, who had said nothing all this while, began his speech with a pish! and told us, that he wondered to see so many men of sense so very serious upon fooleries. Let our good friend, said he, attack every one that deserves it: I would only advise you, Mr. Spectator, applying himself to me, to take care how you meddle with country squires: they are the ornaments of the English nation; men of good heads and sound bodies! and, let me tell you, some of them take it ill of you, that you mention fox-hunters with so little respect.

Captain Sentry spoke very sparingly on this occasion. What he said was only to command my prudence in not touching upon the army, and advised me to continue to act discreetly in that point.

By this time I found every subject of my speculations was taken away from me, by one or other of the club; and began to think myself in the condition of the good man that had one wife who took a dislike to his grey hairs, and another to his black, till by their picking out what each of them had an aversion to, they left his head altogether bald and naked.

While I was thus musing with myself, my worthy friend the clergyman, who, very luckily for me, was at the club that night, undertook my cause. He told us, that he wondered any order of persons should think themselves too considerable to be advised: that it was not quality, but innocence, which exempted men from reproof: that vice and folly ought to be attacked wherever they could be met with, and especially when they were placed in high and conspicuous stations of life. He further added, that my paper would only serve to aggravate the pains of poverty, if it chiefly exposed those who are already depressed, and in some measure turned into ridicule, by the meanness of their conditions and circumstances. He afterwards proceeded to take notice of the great use this paper might be of to the public, by reprehending those vices which are too trivial for the chastisement of the law, and too fantastical for the cognizance of the pulpit. He then advised me to prosecute my undertaking with cheerfulness, and assured me, that whoever might be displeased with me, I should be approved by all those whose praises do honour to the persons on whom they are bestowed.

The whole club pays a particular deference to the discourse of this gentleman, and are drawn into what he says, as much by the candid, ingenious manner with which he delivers himself, as by the strength of argument and force of reason which he makes use of. Will. Honeycomb immediately agreed, that what he had said was right; and that for his part, he would not insist upon the quarter which he had demanded for the ladies. Sir Andrew gave up the city with the same frankness. The Templar would not stand out: and was followed by Sir Roger and the Captain: who all agreed that I should be at liberty to carry the war into what quarter I pleased; provided I continued to combat with criminals in a body, and to assault the vice without hurting the person.

THE SPECTATOR

This debate, which was held for the good of mankind, put me in mind of that which the Roman triumvirate were formerly engaged in, for their destruction. Every man at first stood hard for his friend, till they found that by this means they should spoil their proscription: and at length, making a sacrifice of all their acquaintance and relations, furnished out a very decent execution.

Having thus taken my resolutions to march on boldly in the cause of virtue and good sense, and to annoy their adversaries in whatever degree or rank of men they may be found, I shall be deaf for the future to all the remonstrances that shall be made to me on this account. If Punch grows extravagant, I shall reprimand him very freely: if the stage becomes a nursery of folly and impertinence, I shall not be afraid to animadvert upon it. In short, if I meet with anything in city, court, or country, that shocks modesty or good manners, I shall use my utmost endeavours to make an example of it. I must, however, entreat every particular person, who does me the honour to be a reader of this paper, never to think himself, or any one of his friends or enemies, aimed at in what is said: for I promise him, never to draw a faulty character which does not fit at least a thousand people; or to publish a single paper that is not written in the spirit of benevolence, and with a love to mankind.

FALSE WIT AND HUMOUR

No. 35.]   TUESDAY, APRIL 10, 1711.   [ADDISON.]

Risu inepto res ineptior nulla est.— MART.

AMONG all kinds of writing, there is none in which authors are more apt to miscarry than in works of humour, as there is none in which they are more ambitious to excel. It is not an imagination that teems with monsters, an head that is filled with extravagant conceptions, which is capable of furnishing the world with diversions of this nature; and yet, if we look into the productions of several writers, who set up for men of humour, what wild irregular fancies, what unnatural distortions of thought, do we meet with? If they speak nonsense, they believe they are talking humour; and when they have drawn together a scheme of absurd, inconsistent ideas, they are not able to read it over to themselves without laughing. These poor gentlemen endeavour to gain themselves the reputation of wits and humourists, by such monstrous conceits as almost qualify them for Bedlam; not considering that humour should always lie under the check of reason, and that it requires the direction of the nicest judgment, by so much the more as it indulges itself in the most boundless freedoms. There is a kind of nature that is to be observed in this sort of compositions, as well as in all other; and a certain regularity of thought which must discover the writer to be a man of sense, at the same time that he appears altogether given up to caprice. For my part, when I read the delirious mirth of an unskilful author, I cannot be so barbarous as to divert myself with it, but am rather apt to pity the man, than to laugh at anything he writes.

The deceased Mr. Shadwell, who had himself a great deal of the talent which I am treating of, represents an empty rake, in one of his plays, as very much surprised to hear one say that breaking of windows was not humour; and I question not but several English readers will be as much startled to hear me affirm, that many of those raving incoherent pieces, which are often spread among us, under odd chimerical titles, are rather the offsprings of a distempered brain, than works of humour.

It is indeed much easier to describe what is not humour, than what is; and very difficult to define it otherwise than as Cowley has done wit, by negatives. Were I to give my own notions of it, I would deliver them after Plato's manner, in a kind of allegory, and by supposing Humour to be a person, deduce to him all his qualifications, according to the following genealogy. Truth was the founder of the family, and the father of Good Sense. Good Sense was the father of Wit, who married a lady of a collateral line, called Mirth, by whom he had issue Humour. Humour therefore being the youngest of this illustrious family, and descended from parents of such different dispositions, is very various and unequal in his temper; sometimes you see him putting on grave looks and a solemn habit, sometimes airy in his behaviour, and fantastic in his dress: insomuch that at different times he appears as serious as a judge, and as jocular as a merry-andrew. But as he has a great deal of the mother in his constitution, whatever mood he is in, he never fails to make his company laugh.

But since there is an imposter abroad, who takes upon him the name of this young gentleman, and would willingly pass for him in the world; to the end that well-meaning persons may not be imposed upon by cheats, I would desire my readers, when they meet with this pretender, to look into his parentage, and to examine him strictly, whether or no he be remotely allied to Truth, and lineally descended from Good Sense; if not, they may conclude him a counterfeit. They may likewise distinguish him by a loud and excessive laughter, in which he seldom gets his company to join with him. For as True Humour generally looks serious, while everybody laughs about him, False Humour is always laughing, whilst everybody about him looks serious. I shall only add, if he has not in him a mixture of both parents, that is, if he would pass for the offspring of Wit without Mirth, or Mirth without Wit, you may conclude him to be altogether spurious and a cheat.

The imposter of whom I am speaking, descends originally from Falsehood, who was the mother of Nonsense, who was brought to bed of a son called Frenzy, who married one of the daughters of Folly, commonly known by the name of Laughter, on whom he begot that monstrous infant of which I have been here speaking. I shall set down at length the genealogical table of False Humour, and, at the same time, place under it the genealogy of True Humour, that the reader may at one view behold their different pedigrees and relations.

FALSEHOOD.
NONSENSE.
FRENZY. ——— LAUGHTER.
FALSE HUMOUR.
TRUTH.
GOOD SENSE.
WIT. ——— MIRTH.
HUMOUR.

I might extend the allegory, by mentioning several of the children of False Humour, who are more in number than the sands of the sea, and might in particular enumerate the many sons and daughters which he has begot in this island. But as this would be a very invidious task, I shall only observe in general, that False Humour differs from the True as a monkey does from a man.

First of all, He is exceedingly given to little apish tricks and buffooneries.

Secondly, He so much delights in mimicry, that it is all one to him whether he exposes by it vice and folly, luxury and avarice; or, on the contrary, virtue and wisdom, pain and poverty.

Thirdly, He is wonderfully unlucky, insomuch that he will bite the hand that feeds him, and endeavour to ridicule both friends and foes indifferently. For having but small talents, he must be merry where he *can*, not where he *should*.

Fourthly, Being entirely void of reason, he pursues no point either of morality or instruction, but is ludicrous only for the sake of being so.

Fifthly, Being incapable of anything but mock-representations, his ridicule is always personal, and aimed at the vicious man, or the writer; not at the vice, or at the writing.

I have here only pointed at the whole species of false humourists; but as one of my principle designs in this paper is to beat down that malignant spirit which discovers itself in the writings of the present age, I shall not scruple, for the future, to single out any of the small wits that infest the world with such compositions as are ill-natured, immoral, and absurd. This is the only exception which I shall make to the general rule I have prescribed myself, of attacking multitudes; since every honest man ought to look upon himself as in a natural state of war with the libeller and lampooner, and to annoy them wherever they fall in his way. This is but retaliating upon them, and treating them as they treat others.

A LADY'S LIBRARY

No. 37.] THURSDAY, APRIL 12, 1711. [ADDISON.]

— Non illa colo calathisve Minervæ
Fœmineas assueta manus.—VIRG.

SOME months ago, my friend Sir Roger, being in the country, enclosed a letter to me, directed to a certain lady whom I shall here call by the name of Leonora, and as it contained matters of consequence, desired me to deliver it to her with my own hand. Accordingly I waited upon her ladyship pretty early in the morning, and was desired by her women to walk into her lady's library, till

THE SPECTATOR

such time as she was in readiness to receive me. The very sound of a lady's library gave me a great curiosity to see in it; and as it was some time before the lady came to me, I had an opportunity of turning over a great many of her books, which were ranged together in a very beautiful order. At the end of the folios (which were finely bound and gilt) were great jars of China placed one above another in a very noble piece of architecture. The quartos were separated from the octavos by a pile of smaller vessels, which rose in a delightful pyramid. The octavos were bounded by tea-dishes of all shapes, colours, and sizes, which were so disposed on a wooden frame, that they looked like one continued pillar indented with the finest strokes of sculpture, and stained with the greatest variety of dyes. That part of the library which was designed for the reception of plays and pamphlets, and other loose papers, was enclosed in a kind of square, consisting of one of the prettiest grotesque works that ever I saw, and made up of scaramouches, lions, monkeys, mandarines, trees, shells, and a thousand other odd figures in China ware. In the midst of the room was a little Japan table, with a quire of gilt paper upon it, and on the paper a silver snuff-box made in the shape of a little book. I found there were several counterfeit books upon the upper shelves, which were carved in wood, and served only to fill up the numbers, like fagots in the muster of a regiment. I was wonderfully pleased with such a mixt kind of furniture, as seemed very suitable to both the lady and the scholar, and did not know at first whether I should fancy myself in a grotto, or in a library.

Upon my looking into the books, I found there were some few which the lady had bought for her own use, but most of them had been got together, either because she had heard them praised, or because she had seen the authors of them. Among several that I examined I very well remember these that follow:

Ogilby's Virgil.
Dryden's Juvenal.
Cassandra.
Cleopatra.
Astræa.
Sir Isaac Newton's Works.
The Grand Cyrus; with a pin stuck in one of the middle leaves.

THE SPECTATOR

Pembroke's Arcadia.
Locke of Human Understanding; with a paper of patches in it.
A spelling-book.
A Dictionary for the explanation of hard words.
Sherlock upon Death.
The Fifteen Comforts of Matrimony.
Sir William Temple's Essays.
Father .Malbranche's Search after Truth, translated into English.
A Book of Novels.
The Academy of Compliments.
Culpepper's Midwifery.
The Ladies' Calling.
Tales in Verse by Mr. Durfey: bound in red leather, gilt on the back, and doubled down in several places.
All the Classic Authors, in wood.
A set of Elzivir's, by the same hand.
Clelia: which opened of itself in the place that describes two lovers in a bower.
Baker's Chronicle.
Advice to a Daughter.
The new Atalantis, with a Key to it.
Mr. Steele's Christian Hero.
A Prayer-book; with a bottle of Hungary water by the side of it.
Dr. Sacheverell's Speech.
Fielding's Trial.
Seneca's Morals.
Taylor's holy Living and Dying.
La Ferte's Instructions for Country Dances.

I was taking a catalogue in my pocket-book of these, and several other authors,. when Leonora entered, and, upon my presenting her with a letter from the Knight, told me, with an unspeakable grace, that she hoped Sir Roger was in good health. I answered *yes;* for I hate long speeches, and after a bow or two retired.

Leonora was formerly a celebrated beauty, and is still a very lovely woman. She has been a widow for two or three years, and being unfortunate in her first marriage, has taken a resolution never to venture upon a second. She has no children to take care of, and leaves the management of her estate to my good friend Sir Roger. But as the mind naturally sinks into a kind of lethargy and falls asleep, that is not agitated by some favourite pleasures and pursuits, Leonora has turned all the passions of her sex into a love of books and retirement. She converses chiefly with men, as she has often said herself,) but it is only in their writings; and admits of very few male-visitants, except my friend Sir Roger, whom she hears with great pleasure, and without scandal. As her reading has lain very much among romances, it has given her a very particular turn of thinking, and discovers itself even in her house, her gardens, and her furniture. Sir Roger has entertained me an hour together with a description of her country seat, which is situated in a kind of wilderness, about an hundred miles distant from London, and looks like a little enchanted palace. The rocks about her are shaped into artificial grottoes, covered with woodbines and jessamines. The woods are cut into shady walks, twisted into bowers, and filled with cages of turtles. The springs are made to run among pebbles, and by that means taught to murmur very agreeably. They are likewise collected into a beautiful lake, that is inhabited by a couple of swans, and empties itself by a little rivulet which runs through a green meadow, and is known in the family by the name of The Purling Stream. The Knight likewise tells me, that this lady preserves her game better than any of the gentlemen in the country. "Not (says Sir Roger) that she sets so great a value upon her partridges and pheasants, as upon her larks and nightingales. For she says that every bird which is killed in her ground, will spoil a concert, and that she shall certainly miss him the next year."

When I think how oddly this lady is improved by learning, I look upon her with a mixture of admiration and pity. Amidst these innocent entertainments which she has formed to herself, how much more valuable does she appear than those of her sex who employ themselves in diversions that are less reasonable, though more in fashion! What improvements would a woman have made, who is so susceptible of impressions from what she reads, had she been guided to such books as have a tendency to enlighten the understanding and rectify the passions, as well as to those which are of little more use than to divert the imagination!

But the manner of a lady's employing herself usefully in reading shall be the subject of another paper, in which I design to recommend such particular books as may be proper for the improvement of the sex. And as this is a subject of a very nice nature, I shall desire my correspondents to give me their thoughts upon it.

FRENCH FASHIONS

No. 45.] SATURDAY, APRIL 21, 1711. [ADDISON.]

Natio Comœda est — JUV.

THERE is nothing which I more desire than a safe and honourable peace, though at the same time I am very apprehensive of many ill consequences that may attend it. I do not mean in regard to our politics, but to our manners. What an inundation of ribbons and brocades will break in upon us! what peals of laughter and impertinence shall we be exposed to! For the prevention of these great evils, I could heartily wish that there was an act of parliament for prohibiting the importation of French fopperies.

The female inhabitants of our island have already received very strong impressions from this ludicrous nation, though by the length of the war (as there is no evil which has not some good attending it) they are pretty well worn out and forgotten. I remember the time when some of our well-bred country-women kept their *valet de chambre*, because, forsooth, a man was much more handy about them than one of their own sex. I myself have seen one of these male Abigails tripping about the room with a looking-glass in his hand, and combing his lady's hair a whole morning together. Whether or no there was any truth in the story of a lady's being got with child by one of these her handmaids, I cannot tell; but I think at present the whole race of them is extinct in our own country.

About the time that several of our sex were taken into this kind of service, the ladies likewise brought up the fashion of receiving visits in their beds. It was then looked upon as a piece of ill-breeding for a woman to refuse to see a man because she was not stirring; and a porter would have been thought unfit for his place, that could have made so awkward an excuse. As I love to see everything that

THE SPECTATOR

is new, I once prevailed upon my friend Will. Honeycomb to carry me along with him to one of these travelled ladies, desiring him, at the same time, to present me as a foreigner who could not speak English, that so I might not be obliged to bear a part in the discourse. The lady, though willing to appear undrest, had put on her best looks, and painted herself for our reception. Her hair appeared in a very nice disorder, as the night-gown which was thrown upon her shoulders was ruffled with great care. For my part, I am so shocked with everything which looks immodest in the fair sex, that I could not forbear taking off my eye from her when she moved in her bed, and was in the greatest confusion imaginable every time she stirred a leg or an arm. As the coquets, who introduced this custom, grew old, they left it off by degrees; well knowing that a woman of threescore may kick and tumble her heart out, without making any impressions.

Sempronia is at present the most profest admirer of the French nation, but is so modest as to admit her visitants no further than her toilet. It is a very odd sight that beautiful creature makes, when she is talking politics with her tresses flowing about her shoulders, and examining that face in the glass, which does such execution upon all the male standers-by. How prettily does she divide her discourse between her woman and her visitants! What sprightly transitions does she make from an opera or a sermon, to an ivory comb or a pincushion! How have I been pleased to see her interrupted in an account of her travels by a message to her footman! and holding her tongue in the midst of a moral reflection by applying the tip of it to a patch!

There is nothing which exposes a woman to greater dangers, than that gaiety and airiness of temper, which are natural to most of the sex. It should be therefore the concern of every wise and virtuous woman, to keep this sprightliness from degenerating into levity. On the contrary, the whole discourse and behaviour of the French is to make the sex more fantastical, or (as they are pleased to term it) more awakened, than is consistent either with virtue or discretion. To speak loud in public assemblies, to let every one hear you talk of things that should only be mentioned in private, or in whisper, are looked upon as parts of a refined education. At the same time, a blush is unfashionable, and silence more ill-bred than anything that can be spoken. In short, discretion and modesty, which in all other ages and countries have been regarded as the greatest ornaments of the fair sex, are considered as the ingredients of narrow conversation and family behaviour.

Some years ago I was at the tragedy of Macbeth, and unfortunately placed myself under a woman of quality that is since dead; who, as I found by the noise she made, was newly returned from France. A little before the rising of the curtain, she broke out into a loud soliloquy, "When will the dear witches enter?" and immediately upon their first appearance, asked a lady that sat three boxes from her, on her right hand, if those witches were not charming creatures. A little after, as Betterton was in one of the finest speeches of the play, she shook her fan at another lady, who sat as far on the left hand, and told her with a whisper, that might be heard all over the pit, we must not expect to see Balloon to-night. Not long after, calling out to a young baronet by his name, who sat three seats before me, she asked him whether Macbeth's wife was still alive; and before he could give an answer, fell a talking of the ghost of Banquo. She had by this time formed a little audience to herself, and fixed the attention of all about her. But as I had a mind to hear the play, I got out of the sphere of her impertinence, and planted myself in one of the remotest corners of the pit.

This pretty childishness of behaviour is one of the most refined parts of coquetry, and is not to be attained in perfection by ladies that do not travel for their improvement. A natural and unconstrained behaviour has something in it so agreeable, that it is no wonder to see people endeavouring after it. But at the same time, it is so very hard to hit, when it is not born with us, that people often make themselves ridiculous in attempting it.

A very ingenious French author tells us, that the ladies of the court of France, in his time, thought it ill-breeding, and a kind of female pedantry, to pronounce an hard word right; for which reason they took frequent occasion to use hard words, that they might show a politeness in murdering them. He further adds, that a lady of some quality at court, having accidentally made use of an hard word in a proper place, and pronounced it right, the whole assembly was out of countenance for her.

I must, however, be so just to own, that there are many ladies who have travelled several thousands of miles without being the worse for it, and have brought home with them all the modesty, discretion, and good sense, that they went abroad with. As, on the contrary, there are great numbers of travelled ladies, who have

Marriage-a-la-mode, Plate IV.

lived all their days, within the smoke of London. I have known a woman that never was out of the parish of St. James's betray as many foreign fopperies in her carriage, as she could have gleaned up in half the countries of Europe.

THE COFFEE-HOUSE

No. 49.] THURSDAY, APRIL 26, 1711. [STEELE.]

―― Hominem pagina nostra sapit. —MART.

Men and their manners I describe.

IT is very natural for a man who is not turned for mirthful meetings of men, or assemblies of the fair sex, to delight in that sort of conversation which we find in coffee-houses. Here a man of my temper is in his element; for, if he cannot talk, he can still be more agreeable to his company, as well as pleased in himself, in being only a hearer. It is a secret known but to few, yet of no small use in the conduct of life, that when you fall into a man's conversation, the first thing you should consider is, whether he has a greater inclination to hear you, or that you should hear him. The latter is the more general desire, and I know very able flatterers that never speak a word in praise of the persons from whom they obtain daily favours, but still practise a skilful attention to whatever is uttered by those with whom they converse. We are very curious to observe the behaviour of great men and their clients; but the same passions and interests move men in lower spheres; and I (that have nothing else to do but make observations) see in every parish, street, lane, and alley of this populous city, a little potentate that has his court and his flatterers, who lay snares for his affection and favour, by the same arts that are practised upon men in higher stations.

In the place I most usually frequent, men differ rather in the time of day in which they make a figure, than in any real greatness above one another. I, who am at the coffee-house at six in the morning, know that my friend Beaver, the haberdasher, has a levee of more undissembled friends and admirers than most of the courtiers or generals of Great Britain. Every man about him has, perhaps, a newspaper in his hand; but none can pretend to guess what step will be taken in any one court of Europe till Mr. Beaver has thrown down his pipe, and declares what measures the allies must enter into upon this new posture of affairs. Our coffee-house is near one of the inns of court, and Beaver has the audience and admiration of his neighbours from six till within a quarter of eight, at which time he is interrupted by the students of the house; some of whom are ready dressed for Westminster at eight in a morning, with faces as busy as if they were retained in every cause there; and others come in their night-gowns to saunter away their time as if they never designed to go thither. I do not know that I meet in any of my walks, objects which move both my spleen and laughter so effectually as those young fellows at the Grecian, Squire's, Searle's, and all other coffee-houses adjacent to the law, who rise early for no other purpose but to publish their laziness. One would think that these young virtuosos take a gay cap and slippers, with a scarf and party-coloured gown, to be ensigns of dignity; for the vain things approach each other with an air which shows they regard one another for their vestments. I have observed that the superiority among these proceeds from an opinion of gallantry and fashion. The gentleman in the strawberry sash, who presides so much over the rest, has, it seems, subscribed to every opera this last winter, and is supposed to receive favours from one of the actresses.

When the day grows too busy for these gentlemen to enjoy any longer the pleasures of their deshabille, with any manner of confidence, they give place to men who have business or good sense in their faces, and come to the coffee-house either to transact affairs, or enjoy conversation. The persons to whose behaviour and discourse I have most regard, are such as are between these two sorts of men; such as have not spirits too active to be happy, and well pleased in a private condition; nor complexions too warm to make them neglect the duties and relations of life. Of these sort of men consist the worthier part of mankind; of these are all good fathers, generous brothers, sincere friends, and faithful subjects. Their entertainments are derived rather from reason than imagination; which is the cause that there is no impatience or instability in their speech or action. You see in their countenances they are at home, and in quiet possession of the present instant as it passes, without desiring to quicken it by gratifying any passion, or prosecuting any new design. These are the men formed for society, and those little communities which we express by the word neighbourhoods.

The coffee-house is the place of rendezvous to all that live near it, who are thus turned to relish calm and ordinary life. Eubulus presides over the middle hours of the day, when this assembly of men meet together. He enjoys a great fortune handsomely, without launching into expense; and exerts many noble and useful qualities, without appearing in any public employment. His wisdom and knowledge are serviceable to all that think fit to make use of them; and he does the office of a counsel, a judge, an executor, and a friend to all his acquaintance, not only without the profits which attend such offices, but also without the deference and homage which are usually paid to them. The giving of thanks is displeasing to him. The greatest gratitude you can show him, is to let him see you are the better man for his services; and that you are as ready to oblige others, as he is to oblige you.

In the private exigencies of his friends he lends, at legal value, considerable sums, which he might highly increase by rolling in the public stocks. He does not consider in whose hands his money will improve most, but where it will do most good.

Eubulus has so great an authority in his little diurnal audience, that when he shakes his head at any piece of public news, they all of them appear dejected; and, on the contrary, go home to their dinners with a good stomach and cheerful aspect when Eubulus seems to intimate that things go well. Nay, their veneration towards him is so great, that when they are in other company they speak and act after him; are wise in his sentences, and are no sooner sat down at their own tables, but they hope or fear, rejoice or despond, as they saw him do at the coffee-house. In a word, every man is Eubulus as soon as his back is turned.

Having here given an account of the several reigns that succeed each other from daybreak till dinner-time, I shall mention the monarchs of the afternoon on another occasion, and shut up the whole series òf them with the history of Tom the Tyrant; who, as first minister of the coffee-house, takes the government upon him between the hours of eleven and twelve at night, and gives his orders in the most arbitrary manner to the servants below him, as to the disposition of liquors, coal, and cinders.　　　　　　　　　R.

THE SPECTATOR

THE ROYAL EXCHANGE

No. 69.] SATURDAY, MAY 19, 1711. [ADDISON.]

> Hic segetes, illic veniunt feliciùs uvæ:
> Arborei fœtus alibi, atque injussa virescunt
> Gramina. Nonne vides, croceos ut Tmolus odores,
> India mittit ebur, molles sua thura Sabæi?
> At Chalybes nudi ferrum, virosaque Pontus
> Castorea, Eliadum palmas Epirus equarum?
> Continuo has leges æternaque fœdera certis
> Imposuit natura locis —
> VIRG. Georg. i. 54.

> This ground with Bacchus, that with Ceres suits;
> That other loads the trees with happy fruits;
> A fourth with grass, unbidden, decks the ground:
> Thus Tmolus is with yellow saffron crown'd;
> India black ebon and white iv'ry bears;
> And soft Idume weeps her od'rous tears:
> Thus Pontus sends her beaver stones from far;
> And naked Spaniards temper steel for war:
> Epirus for th' Elean chariot breeds
> (In hopes of palms) a race of running steeds.
> This is th' original contract; these the laws
> Impos'd by nature, and by nature's cause.
> DRYDEN.

THERE is no place in the town which I so much love to frequent as the Royal Exchange. It gives me a secret satisfaction, and in some measure gratifies my vanity, as I am an Englishman, to see so rich an assembly of countrymen and foreigners consulting together upon the private business of mankind, and making this metropolis a kind of *emporium* for the whole earth. I must confess I look upon high-change to be a great council, in which all considerable nations have their representatives. Factors in the trading world are what ambassadors are in the politic world: they negotiate affairs, conclude treaties, and maintain a good correspondence between those wealthy societies of men that are divided from one another by seas and oceans, or live on the different extremities of a continent. I have often been pleased to hear disputes adjusted between an inhabitant of Japan and an alderman of London, or to see a subject of the Great Mogul entering into a league with one of the Czar of Muscovy. I am infinitely delighted in mixing with these several ministers of commerce, as they are distinguished by their different walks and different languages. Sometimes I am jostled among a body of Armenians; sometimes I am lost in a crowd of Jews; and sometimes make one in a groupe of Dutchmen. I am a Dane, Swede, or Frenchman at different times; or rather fancy myself like the old philosopher, who, upon being asked what countryman he was, replied, that he was a citizen of the world.

Though I very frequently visit this busy multitude of people, I am known to nobody there but my friend Sir Andrew, who often smiles upon me as he sees me bustling in the crowd, but at the same time connives at my presence without taking any farther notice of me. There is, indeed, a merchant of Egypt, who just knows me by sight, having formerly remitted me some money to Grand Cairo; but as I am not versed in the modern Coptic, our conferences go no farther than a bow and a grimace.

This grand scene of business gives me an infinite variety of solid and substantial entertainments. As I am a great lover of mankind, my heart naturally overflows with pleasure at the sight of a prosperous and happy multitude, insomuch that at many public calamities I cannot forbear expressing my joy with tears that have stolen down my cheeks. For this reason I am wonderfully delighted to see such a body of men thriving in their own private fortunes, and at the same time promoting the public stock; or, in other words, raising estates for their own families, by bringing into their country whatever is wanting, and carrying out of it whatever is superfluous.

Nature seems to have taken a particular care to disseminate her blessings among the different regions of the world, with an eye to this mutual intercourse and traffic among mankind, that the natives of the several parts of the globe might have a kind of dependence upon one another, and be united together by their common interest. Almost every degree produces something peculiar to it. The food often grows in one country, and the sauce in another. The fruits of Portugal are corrected by the products of Barbadoes, and the infusion of a China plant is sweetened by the pith of an Indian cane. The Philippic islands give a flavour to our European bowls. The single dress of a woman of quality is often the product of a hundred climates. The muff and the fan come together from the different ends of the earth. The scarf is sent from the torrid zone, and the tippet from beneath the pole. The brocade petticoat rises out of the mines of Peru, and the diamond necklace out of the bowels of Indostan.

If we consider our own country in its natural prospect, without any of the benefits and advantages of commerce, what a barren, uncomfortable spot of earth falls to our share! Natural historians tell us, that no fruit grows originally among us besides hips and haws, acorns, and pig-nuts, with other delicacies of the like nature; that our climate, of itself, and without the assistance of art, can make no farther advances towards a plum than to a sloe, and carries an apple to no greater perfection than a crab; that our melons, our peaches, our figs, our apricots, and cherries, are strangers among us, imported in different ages, and naturalized in our English gardens; and that they would all degenerate and fall away into the trash of our own country, if they were wholly neglected by the planter, and left to the mercy of our sun and soil. Nor has traffic more enriched our vegetable world, than it has improved the whole face of nature among us. Our ships are laden with the harvest of every climate. Our tables are stored with spices, and oils, and wines. Our rooms are filled with pyramids of China, and adorned with the workmanship of Japan. Our morning's draught comes to us from the remotest corners of the earth. We repair our bodies by the drugs of America, and repose ourselves under Indian canopies. My friend Sir Andrew calls the vineyards of France our gardens; the spice-islands, our hot-beds; the Persians, our silk-weavers; and the Chinese, our potters. Nature, indeed, furnishes us with the bare necessaries of life, but traffic gives us a great variety of what is useful, and at the same time supplies us with everything that is convenient and ornamental. Nor is it the least part of this our happiness, that whilst we enjoy the remotest products of the North and South, we are free from those extremities of weather which give them birth; that our eyes are refreshed with the green fields of Britain, at the same time that our palates are feasted with fruits that rise between the tropics.

For these reasons, there are not more useful members in a commonwealth than merchants. They knit mankind together in a mutual intercourse of good offices, distribute the gifts of nature, find work for the poor, add wealth to the rich, and magnificence to the great. Our English merchant converts the tin of his own country into gold, and exchanges his wool for rubies. The Mahometans are clothed in our British manufacture, and the inhabitants of the frozen zone warmed with the fleeces of our sheep.

When I have been upon the 'Change, I have often fancied one of our old kings standing in person where he is represented in effigy, and looking down upon the wealthy concourse of people with which that place is every day filled. In this case, how would he be surprised to hear all the languages of Europe spoken in this little spot of his former dominions, and to see so many private men, who in his time would have been the vassals of some powerful baron, negotiating like princes for greater sums of money than were formerly to be met with in the royal treasury! Trade, without enlarging the British territories, has given us a kind of additional empire. It has multiplied the number of the rich, made our landed estates infinitely more valuable than they were formerly, and added to them an accession of other estates as valuable as the lands themselves. C.

THE EVERLASTING CLUB

No. 72.] WEDNESDAY, MAY 23, 1711. [ADDISON.]

— Genus immortale manet, multosque per annos
Stat fortuna domus, et avi numerantur avorum.
                              VIRG. Georg. iv. 208.

Th' immortal line in sure succession reigns,
The fortune of the family remains,
And grandsire's grandsons the long list contains.

HAVING already given my reader an account of several extraordinary clubs both ancient and modern, I did not design to have troubled him with any more narratives of this nature; but I have lately received information of a club, which I can call neither ancient nor modern, that I dare say will be no less surprising to my reader than it was to myself; for which reason I shall communicate it to the public as one of the greatest curiosities in its kind.

A friend of mine complaining of a tradesman who is related to him, after having represented him as a very idle worthless fellow, who neglected his family and spent most of his time over a bottle, told me, to conclude his character, that he was a member of the

Everlasting Club. So very odd a title raised my curiosity to inquire into the nature of a club that had such a sounding name; upon which my friend gave me the following account:

The Everlasting Club consists of a hundred members, who divide the whole twenty-four hours among them in such a manner, that the club sits day and night from one end of the year to another; no party presuming to rise till they are relieved by those who are in course to succeed them. By this means a member of the Everlasting Club never wants company; for though he is not upon duty himself, he is sure to find some who are; so that if he be disposed to take a whet, a nooning, an evening's draught, or a bottle after midnight, he goes to the club, and finds a knot of friends to his mind.

It is a maxim in this club that the steward never dies; for as they succeed one another by way of rotation, no man is to quit the great elbow-chair which stands at the upper end of the table, till his successor is in readiness to fill it; insomuch that there has not been a *sede vacante* in the memory of man.

This club was instituted towards the end (or, as some of them say, about the middle) of the civil wars, and continued without interruption till the time of the great fire, which burnt them out, and dispersed them for several weeks. The steward at that time maintained his post till he had like to have been blown up with a neighbouring house (which was demolished in order to stop the fire); and would not leave the chair at last, till he had emptied all the bottles upon the table, and received repeated directions from the club to withdraw himself. This steward is frequently talked of in the club, and looked upon by every member of it as a greater man than the famous captain mentioned in my Lord Clarendon, who was burnt in his ship because he would not quit it without orders. It is said that towards the close of 1700, being the great year of Jubilee, the club had it under consideration whether they should break up or continue their session; but after many speeches and debates, it was at length agreed to sit out the other century. This resolution passed in a general club *nemine contradicente.*

Having given this short account of the institution and continuation of the Everlasting Club, I should here endeavour to say something of the manners and characters of its several members, which I shall do according to the best light I have received in this matter.

It appears by their books in general, that, since their first institution, they have smoked fifty tons of tobacco, drank thirty thousand butts of ale, one thousand hogsheads of red port, two hundred barrels of brandy, and a kilderkin of small beer. There has been likewise a great consumption of cards. It is also said that they observe the law in Ben Jonson's club, which orders the fire to be always kept in (*focus perennis esto*), as well for the convenience of lighting their pipes, as to cure the dampness of the club-room. They have an old woman in the nature of a vestal, whose business it is to cherish and perpetuate the fire which burns from generation to generation, and has seen the glass-house fires in and out above a hundred times.

The Everlasting Club treats all other clubs with an eye of contempt, and talks even of the Kit-Cat and October as a couple of upstarts. Their ordinary discourse (as much as I have been able to learn of it) turns altogether upon such adventures as have passed in their own assembly; of members who have taken the glass in their turns for a week together, without stirring out of the club; of others who have smoked a hundred pipes at a sitting; of others who have not missed their morning's draught for twenty years together. Sometimes they speak in raptures of a run of ale in king Charles's reign; and sometimes reflect with astonishment upon games at whist, which have been miraculously recovered by members of the society, when in all human probability the case was desperate.

They delight in several old catches, which they sing at all hours to encourage one another to moisten their clay, and grow immortal by drinking; with many other edifying exhortations of the like nature.

There are four general clubs held in a year, at which times they fill up vacancies, appoint waiters, confirm the old firemaker or elect a new one, settle contributions for coals, pipes, tobacco, and other necessaries.

The senior member has outlived the whole club twice over, and has been drunk with the grandfathers of some of the present sitting members.   C.

THE SPECTATOR

PARTY PATCHES

No. 81.]   SATURDAY, JUNE 2, 1711.   [ADDISON.

    Qualis ubi audito venantum murmure Tigris
    Horruit in maculas.— STATIUS.

    As when the tigress hears the hunter's din,
    Dark angry spots distain her glossy skin.

ABOUT the middle of last winter I went to see an opera at the theatre in the Haymarket, where I could not but take notice of two parties of very fine women, that had placed themselves in the opposite side-boxes, and seemed drawn up in a kind of battle array one against another. After a short survey of them, I found they were patched differently; the faces on one hand, being spotted on the right side of the forehead, and those upon the other on the left. I quickly perceived that they cast hostile glances upon one another; and that their patches were placed in those different situations, as party-signals to distinguish friends from foes. In the middle boxes, between these two opposite bodies, were several ladies who patched indifferently on both sides of their faces, and seemed to sit there with no other intention but to see the opera. Upon inquiry I found, that the body of Amazons on my right hand, were Whigs, and those on my left, Tories; and that those who had placed themselves in the middle boxes were a neutral party, whose faces had not yet declared themselves. These last, however, as I afterwards found, diminished daily, and took their party with one side or the other; insomuch that I observed in several of them, the patches, which were before dispersed equally, are now all gone over to the Whig or Tory side of the face. The censorious say, that the men, whose hearts are aimed at, are very often the occasions that one part of the face is thus dishonoured, and lies under a kind of disgrace, while the other is so much set off and adorned by the owner; and that the patches turn to the right or to the left, according to the principles of the man who is most in favour. But whatever may be the motives of a few fantastical coquettes, who do not patch for the public good so much as for their own private advantage, it is certain, that there are several women of honour who patch out of

THE SPECTATOR

principle, and with an eye to the interest of their country. Nay, I am informed that some of them adhere so stedfastly to their party, and are so far from sacrificing their zeal for the public to their passion for any particular person, that in a late draft of marriage articles a lady has stipulated with her husband, that, whatever his opinions are, she shall be at liberty to patch on which side she pleases.

I must here take notice, that Rosalinda, a famous Whig partisan, has most unfortunately a very beautiful mole on the Tory part of her forehead; which being very conspicuous, has occasioned many mistakes, and given a handle to her enemies to misrepresent her face, as though it had revolted from the Whig interest. But, whatever this natural patch may seem to intimate, it is well known that her notions of government are still the same. This unlucky mole, however, has misled several coxcombs; and like the hanging out of false colours, made some of them converse with Rosalinda in what they thought the spirit of her party, when on a sudden she has given them an unexpected fire, that has sunk them all at once. If Rosalinda is unfortunate in her mole, Nigranilla is as unhappy in a pimple, which forces her, against her inclinations, to patch on the Whig side.

I am told that many virtuous matrons, who formerly have been taught to believe that this artificial spotting of the face was unlawful, are now reconciled by a zeal for their cause, to what they could not be prompted by a concern for their beauty. This way of declaring war upon one another, puts me in mind of what is reported of the tigress, that several spots rise in her skin when she is angry, or as Mr. Cowley has imitated the verses that stand as the motto on this paper,

—— She swells with angry pride,
And calls forth all her spots on ev'ry side.

When I was in the theatre the time above-mentioned, I had the curiosity to count the patches on both sides, and found the Tory patches to be about twenty stronger than the Whig; but to make amends for this small inequality, I the next morning found the whole puppet-show filled with faces spotted after the Whiggish manner. Whether or no the ladies had retreated hither in order to rally their forces I cannot tell; but the next night they came in so great a body to the opera, that they outnumbered the enemy.

THE SPECTATOR

This account of party patches will, I am afraid, appear improbable to those who live at a distance from the fashionable world; but as it is a distinction of a very singular nature, and what perhaps may never meet with a parallel, I think I should not have discharged the office of a faithful Spectator, had I not recorded it.

I have, in former papers, endeavoured to expose this party-rage in women, as it only serves to aggravate the hatreds and animosities that reign among men, and in a great measure deprive the fair sex of those peculiar charms with which nature has endowed them.

When the Romans and Sabines were at war, and just upon the point of giving battle, the women, who were allied to both of them, interposed with so many tears and entreaties, that they prevented the mutual slaughter which threatened both parties, and united them together in a firm and lasting peace.

I would recommend this noble example to our British ladies, at a time when their country is torn with so many unnatural divisions, that if they continue, it will be a misfortune to be born in it. The Greeks thought it so improper for women to interest themselves in competitions and contentions, that for this reason, among others, they forbad them, under pain of death, to be present at the Olympic games, notwithstanding these were the public diversions of all Greece.

As our English women excel those of all nations in beauty, they should endeavour to outshine them in all other accomplishments proper to the sex, and to distinguish themselves as tender mothers, and faithful wives, rather than as furious partisans. Female virtues are of a domestic turn. The family is the proper province for private women to shine in. If they must be showing their zeal for the public, let it not be against those who are perhaps of the same family, or at least of the same religion or nation, but against those who are the open, professed, undoubted enemies of their faith, liberty, and country. When the Romans were pressed with a foreign enemy, the ladies voluntarily contributed all their rings and jewels to assist the government under a public exigence, which appeared so laudable an action in the eyes of their countrymen, that from thenceforth it was permitted by a law to pronounce public orations at the funeral of a woman in praise of the deceased person, which till that time was peculiar to men. Would our English ladies, instead of sticking on a patch against those of their own country, show themselves so truly public-spirited as to sacrifice every one her necklace against the common enemy, what decrees ought not to be made in favour of them?

Since I am recollecting upon this subject such passages as occur to my memory out of ancient authors, I cannot omit a sentence in the celebrated funeral oration of Pericles, which he made in honour of those brave Athenians that were slain in a fight with the Lacedæmonians. After having addressed himself to the several ranks and orders of his countrymen, and shown them how they should behave themselves in the public cause, he turns to the female part of his audience: "And as for you (says he) I shall advise you in very few words: Aspire only to those virtues that are peculiar to your sex; follow your natural modesty, and think it your greatest commendation not to be talked of one way or other."

C.

ON PHYSIOGNOMY

No. 86.] FRIDAY, JUNE 8, 1711. [ADDISON.]

Heu quam difficile est crimen non prodere vultu! — OVID.

THERE are several arts which all men are in some measure masters of, without having been at the pains of learning them. Every one that speaks or reasons is a grammarian and a logician, though he may be wholly unacquainted with the rules of grammar or logic, as they are delivered in books and systems. In the same manner, every one is in some degree a master of that art which is generally distinguished by the name of physiognomy; and naturally forms to himself the character or fortune of a stranger, from the features and lineaments of his face. We are no sooner presented to any one we never saw before, but we are immediately struck with the idea of a proud, a reserved, an affable, or a good-natured man; and upon our first going into a company of strangers, our benevolence or aversion, awe or contempt, rises naturally towards several particular persons, before we have heard them speak a single word, or so much as know who they are.

Every passion gives a particular cast to the countenance, and is apt to discover itself in some feature or other. I have seen an eye curse for half an hour together, and an eye-brow call a man scoundrel.

THE SPECTATOR

Nothing is more common than for lovers to complain, resent, languish, despair, and die, in dumb show. For my own part, I am so apt to frame a notion of every man's humour or circumstances by his looks, that I have sometimes employed myself from Charing-Cross to the Royal Exchange in drawing the characters of those who have passed by me. When I see a man with a sour, rivelled face, I cannot forbear pitying his wife; and when I meet with an open, ingenuous countenance, think on the happiness of his friends, his family, and relations.

I cannot recollect the author of a famous saying to a stranger who stood silent in his company, "Speak, that I may see thee." But, with submission, I think we may be better known by our looks than by our words, and that a man's speech is much more easily disguised than his countenance. In this case, however, I think the air of the whole face is much more expressive than the lines of it: the truth of it is, the air is generally nothing else but the inward disposition of the mind made visible.

Those who have established physiognomy into an art, and laid down rules of judging men's tempers by their faces, have regarded the features much more than the air. Martial has a pretty epigram on this subject.

> Crine ruber, niger ore, brevis pede, lumine læsus;
> Rem magnam præstas, Zoile, si bonus es.
>
> Thy beard and head are of a different dye;
> Short of one foot, distorted in an eye;
> With all these tokens of a knave complete,
> Should'st thou be honest, thou'rt a dev'lish cheat.

I have seen a very ingenious author on this subject, who founds his speculations on the supposition, that as a man hath in the mould of his face a remote likeness to that of an ox, a sheep, a lion, an hog, or any other creature, he hath the same resemblance in the frame of his mind, and is subject to those passions which are predominate in the creature that appears in his countenance. Accordingly he gives the prints of several faces that are of a different mould, and by a little overcharging the likeness, discovers the figures of these several kinds of brutal faces in human features. I remember in the Life of the famous Prince of Condé, the writer observes, the face of that prince was like the face of an eagle, and that the prince was very well pleased to be told so. In this case, therefore, we may be sure, that he had in his mind some general, implicit notion of this art of physiognomy which I have just now mentioned; and that when his courtiers told him his face was made like an eagle's, he understood them in the same manner as if they had told him, there was something in his looks which showed him to be strong, active, piercing, and of a royal descent. Whether or no the different motions of the animal spirits in different passions, may have any effect on the mould of the face when the lineaments are pliable and tender, or whether the same kind of souls require the same kind of habitations, I shall leave to the consideration of the curious. In the mean time I think nothing can be more glorious than for a man to give the lie to his face, and to be an honest, just, and good-natured man, in spite of all those marks and signatures which nature seems to have set upon him for the contrary. This very often happens among those, who, instead of being exasperated by their own looks, or envying the looks of others, apply themselves entirely to the cultivating of their minds, and getting those beauties which are more lasting, and more ornamental. I have seen many an amiable piece of deformity: and have observed a certain cheerfulness in as bad a system of features as ever was clapped together, which hath appeared more lovely than all the blooming charms of an insolent beauty. There is a double praise due to virtue, when it is lodged in a body that seems to have been prepared for the reception of vice; in many such cases the soul and the body do not seem to be fellows.

Socrates was an extraordinary instance of this nature. There chanced to be a great physiognomist in his time at Athens, who had made strange discoveries of men's tempers and inclinations by their outward appearances. Socrates's disciples, that they might put this artist to the trial, carried him to their master, whom he had never seen before, and did not know he was then in company with him. After a short examination of his face, the physiognomist pronounced him the most rude, libidinous, drunken old fellow that he had ever met with in his whole life. Upon which the disciples all burst out a laughing, as thinking they had detected the falsehood and vanity of his art. But Socrates told them, that the principles of his art might be very true, notwithstanding his present mistake; for that he himself was naturally inclined to those particular vices which the physiognomist had discovered in his countenance, but that he had conquered the strong dispositions he was born with, by the dictates of philosophy.

We are indeed told by an ancient author, that Socrates very much resembled Silenus in his face; which we find to have been very rightly observed from the statues and busts of both that are still extant; as well as on several antique seals and precious stones, which are frequently enough to be met with in the cabinets of the curious. But, however observations of this nature may sometimes hold, a wise man should be particularly cautious how he gives credit to a man's outward appearance. It is an irreparable injustice we are guilty of towards one another, when we are prejudiced by the looks and features of those whom we do not know. How often do we conceive hatred against a person of worth; or fancy a man to be proud and ill-natured by his aspect, whom we think we cannot esteem too much when we are acquainted with his real character! Dr. Moore in his admirable System of Ethics, reckons this particular inclination to take a prejudice against a man for his looks, among the smaller vices in morality, and, if I remember, gives it the name of a Prosopolepsia.

ADVENTURE OF M. PONTIGNAN

No. 90.] WEDNESDAY, JUNE 13, 1711. [ADDISON.]

——— Magnus sine viribus ignis
Incassum furit. — VIRG.

THERE is not, in my opinion, a consideration more effectual to extinguish inordinate desires in the soul of man, than the notions of Plato and his followers upon that subject. They tell us, that every passion which has been contracted by the soul during her residence in the body, remains with her in a separate state; and that the soul in the body, or out of the body, differs no more than the man does from himself when he is in his house, or in open air. When, therefore, the obscene passions in particular have once taken root, and spread themselves in the soul, they cleave to her inseparably, and remain in her for ever, after the body is cast off and thrown aside. As an argument to confirm this their doctrine, they observe, that a lewd youth, who goes on in a continued course of voluptuousness, advances by degrees into a libidinous old man; and that the passion survives in the mind when it is altogether dead

THE SPECTATOR

in the body; nay, that the desire grows more violent, and (like all other habits) gathers strength by age, at the same time that it has no power of executing its own purposes. If, say they, the soul is the most subject to these passions at a time when she has the least instigation from the body, we may well suppose she will still retain them when she is entirely divested of it. The very substance of the soul is festered with them; the gangrene is gone too far to be ever cured: the inflammation will rage to all eternity.

In this, therefore, (say the Platonists,) consists the punishment of a voluptuous man after death: he is tormented with desires which it is impossible for him to gratify, solicited by a passion that has neither objects nor organs adapted to it: he lives in a state of invincible desire and impotence, and always burns in the pursuit of what he always despairs to possess. It is for this reason (says Plato) that the souls of the dead appear frequently in cemeteries, and hover about the places where their bodies are buried, as still hankering after their old brutal pleasures, and desiring again to enter the body that gave them an opportunity of fulfilling them.

Some of our most eminent divines have made use of this Platonic notion, so far as it regards the subsistence of our passions after death, with great beauty and strength of reason. Plato, indeed, carries his thought very far, when he grafts upon it his opinion of ghosts appearing in places of burial. Though, I must confess, if one did believe that the departed souls of men and women wandered up and down these lower regions, and entertained themselves with the sight of their species, one could not devise a more proper hell for an impure spirit than that which Plato has touched upon.

The ancients seem to have drawn such a state of torments in the description of Tantalus, who was punished with the rage of an eternal thirst, and set up to the chin in water, that fled from his lips whenever he attempted to drink it.

Virgil, who has cast the whole system of Platonic philosophy, so far as it relates to the soul of man, into beautiful allegories, in the sixth book of his Æneid, gives us the punishment of a voluptuary after death, not unlike that which we are here speaking of.

> —Lucent genialibus altis
> Aurea fulcra toris, epulæque ante ora paratæ
> Regifico luxu; furiarum maxima juxta
> Accubat, et manibus prohibet contingere mensas;
> Exurgitque facem attollens, atque intonat ore.

THE SPECTATOR

> They lie below on golden beds displayed,
> And genial feasts with regal pomp are made.
> The queen of furies by their side is set,
> And snatches from their mouths the untasted meat;
> Which if they touch, her hissing snakes she rears,
> Tossing her torch, and thundering in their ears. DRYDEN.

That I may a little alleviate the severity of this my speculation, (which otherwise may lose me several of my polite readers,) I shall translate a story that has been quoted upon another occasion by one of the most learned men of the present age, as I find it in the original. The reader will see it is not foreign to my present subject, and I dare say will think it a lively representation of a person lying under the torments of such a kind of tantalism, or Platonic hell, as that which we have now under consideration. Monsieur Pontignan, speaking of a love-adventure that happened to him in the country, gives the following account of it.

"When I was in the country last summer, I was often in company with a couple of charming women, who had all the wit and beauty one could desire in female companions, with a dash of coquetry, that from time to time gave me a great many agreeable torments. I was, after my way, in love with both of them, and had such frequent opportunities of pleading my passion to them when they were asunder, that I had reason to hope for particular favours from each of them. As I was walking one evening in my chamber with nothing about me but my night-gown, they both came into my room, and told me they had a very pleasant trick to put upon a gentleman that was in the same house, provided I would bear a part in it. Upon this they told me such a plausible story, that I laughed at their contrivance, and agreed to do whatever they should require of me. They immediately began to swaddle me up in my night-gown with long pieces of linen, which they folded about me till they had wrapt me in above an hundred yards of swathe: my arms were pressed to my sides, and my legs closed together by so many wrappers one over another, that I looked like an Egyptian mummy. As I stood bolt upright upon one end in this antique figure, one of the ladies burst out a laughing. 'And now, *Pontignan*, (says she) we intend to perform the promise that we find you have extorted from each of us. You have often asked the favour of us, and I dare say you are a better bred cavalier than to refuse to go to bed to ladies that desire it of you.' After having stood a fit of laughter,

THE SPECTATOR

I begged them to uncase me, and do with me what they pleased. 'No, no, (say they,) we like you very well as you are;' and upon that ordered me to be carried to one of their houses, and put to bed in all my swaddles. The room was lighted up on all sides; and I was laid very decently between a pair of sheets, with my head (which was, indeed, the only part I could move), upon a very high pillow: this was no sooner done, but my two female friends came into bed to me in their finest night-clothes. You may easily guess at the condition of a man that saw a couple of the most beautiful women in the world undrest and abed with him, without being able to stir hand or foot. I begged them to release me, and struggled all I could to get loose, which I did with so much violence, that about midnight they both leaped out of bed, crying out they were undone. But seeing me safe, they took their posts again, and renewed their raillery. Finding all my prayers and endeavours were lost, I composed myself as well as I could; and told them, that if they would not unbind me, I would fall asleep between them, and by that means disgrace them for ever. But, alas! this was impossible; could I have been disposed to it, they would have prevented me by several little ill-natured caresses and endearments which they bestowed upon me. As much devoted as I am to womankind, I would not pass such another night to be master of the whole sex. My reader will doubtless be curious to know what became of me the next morning: why, truly, my bed-fellows left me about an hour before day, and told me if I would be good, and lie still, they would send somebody to take me up as soon as it was time for me to rise. Accordingly about nine o'clock in the morning an old woman came to unswathe me. I bore all this very patiently, being resolved to take my revenge of my tormentors, and to keep no measures with them as soon as I was at liberty; but upon asking my old woman what was become of the two ladies, she told me she believed they were by that time within sight of Paris, for that they went away in a coach and six before five-a-clock in the morning."

EXERCISE OF THE FAN

No. 102.] WEDNESDAY, JUNE 27, 1711. [ADDISON.]

— Lusus animo debent aliquando dari,
Ad cogitandum melior ut redeat sibi.—PHÆDR.

I DO not know whether to call the following letter a satire upon coquettes, or a representation of their several fantastical accomplishments, or what other title to give it; but as it is I shall communicate it to the public. It will sufficiently explain its own intentions, so that I shall give it my reader at length, without either preface or postscript.

"MR. SPECTATOR,— Women are armed with fans as men with swords, and sometimes do more execution with them. To the end, therefore, that ladies may be entire mistresses of the weapon which they bear, I have erected an Academy for the training up of young women in the Exercise of the Fan, according to the most fashionable airs and motions that are now practised at court. The ladies who carry fans under me are drawn up twice a day in my great hall, where they are instructed in the use of their arms, and exercised by the following words of command:

>*Handle your Fans,*
>*Unfurl your Fans,*
>*Discharge your Fans,*
>*Ground your Fans,*
>*Recover your Fans,*
>*Flutter your Fans,*

By the right observation of these few plain words of command, a woman of tolerable genius who will apply herself diligently to her exercise for the space of one half year, shall be able to give her fan all the graces that can possibly enter into that little modish machine.

"But to the end that my readers may form to themselves a right notion of this exercise, I beg leave to explain it to them in all its parts. When my female regiment is drawn up in array, with every one her weapon in her hand, upon my giving the word to

THE SPECTATOR

Handle their Fans, each of them shakes her fan at me with a smile, then gives her right-hand woman a tap upon the shoulder, then presses her lips with the extremity of her fan, then lets her arms fall in an easy motion, and stands in readiness to receive the next word of command. All this is done with a close fan, and is generally learned in the first week.

"The next motion is that of Unfurling the Fan, in which are comprehended several little flirts and vibrations, as also gradual and deliberate openings, with many voluntary fallings asunder in the fan itself, that are seldom learned under a month's practice. This part of the exercise pleases the spectators more than any other, as it discovers on a sudden an infinite number of Cupids, garlands, altars, birds, beasts, rainbows, and the like agreeable figures, that display themselves to view, whilst every one in the regiment holds a picture in her hand.

"Upon my giving the word to Discharge their Fans, they give one general crack, that may be heard at a considerable distance when the wind sits fair. This is one of the most difficult parts of the exercise; but I have several ladies with me, who at their first entrance could not give a pop loud enough to be heard at the further end of a room, who can now Discharge a Fan in such a manner, that it shall make a report like a pocket-pistol. I have likewise taken care (in order to hinder young women from letting off their fans in wrong places or unsuitable occasions) to show upon what subject the crack of a fan may come in properly. I have likewise invented a fan, with which a girl of sixteen, by the help of a little wind which is enclosed about one of the largest sticks, can make as loud a crack as a woman of fifty with an ordinary fan.

"When the fans are thus discharged, the word of command in course is to Ground their Fans. This teaches a lady to quit her fan gracefully when she throws it aside, in order to take up a pack of cards, adjust a curl of hair, replace a fallen pin, or apply herself to any other matter of importance. This part of the exercise, as it only consists in tossing a fan with an air upon a long table (which stands by for that purpose) may be learnt in two days' time as well as in a twelvemonth.

"When my female regiment is thus disarmed, I generally let them walk about the room for some time; when on a sudden (like ladies that look upon their watches after a long visit) they all of them hasten to their arms, catch them up in a hurry, and place themselves in their proper stations, upon my calling out Recover your Fans. This part of the exercise is not difficult, provided a woman applies her thoughts to it.

"The Fluttering of the Fan is the last, and, indeed, the masterpiece of the whole exercise; but if a lady does not misspend her time, she may make herself mistress of it in three months. I generally lay aside the dog-days and the hot time of the summer for the teaching of this part of the exercise; for as soon as ever I pronounce Flutter your Fans, the place is filled with so many zephyrs and gentle breezes as are very refreshing in that season of the year, though they might be dangerous to ladies of a tender constitution in any other.

"There is an infinite variety of motions to be made use of in the Flutter of a Fan: there is the angry flutter, the modest flutter, the timorous flutter, the confused flutter, the merry flutter, and the amorous flutter. Not to be tedious, there is scarce any emotion in the mind which does not produce a suitable agitation in the fan; insomuch, that if I only see the fan of a disciplined lady, I know very well whether she laughs, frowns, or blushes. I have seen a fan so very angry, that it would have been dangerous for the absent lover who provoked it to have come within the wind of it; and at other times so very languishing, that I have been glad for the lady's sake the lover was at a sufficient distance from it. I need not add, that a fan is either a prude or coquette, according to the nature of the person who bears it. To conclude my letter, I must acquaint you, that I have from my own observations compiled a little treatise for the use of my scholars, entitled, The Passions of the Fan; which I will communicate to you, if you think it may be of use to the public. I shall have a general review on Thursday next; to which you shall be very welcome if you will honour it with your presence.

"I am," &c.

"P. S. I teach young gentlemen the whole art of gallanting a fan.

"N. B. I have several little plain fans made for this use, to avoid expense."

THE SPECTATOR

ON PEDANTRY

No. 105.] SATURDAY, JUNE 30, 1711. [ADDISON.]

——— Id arbitror
Adprime in vita esse utile, NE QUID NIMIS.
TER. Andr. Act 1, Sc. 1.

I take it to be a principal rule of life not to be too much addicted to one thing.
Too much of any thing, is good for nothing.

MY friend Will Honeycomb values himself very much upon what he calls the knowledge of mankind, which has cost him many disasters in his youth; for Will reckons every misfortune that he has met with among the women, and every rencounter among the men, as parts of his education; and fancies he should never have been the man he is had he not broke windows, knocked down constables, disturbed honest people with his midnight serenades, and beat up a lewd woman's quarters when he was a young fellow. The engaging in adventures of this nature Will calls the studying of mankind; and terms this knowledge of the town the knowledge of the world. Will ingeniously confesses that for half his life his head ached every morning with reading of men over-night; and at present comforts himself under certain pains which he endures from time to time, that without them he could not have been acquainted with the gallantries of the age. This Will looks upon as the learning of a gentleman, and regards all other kind of science as the accomplishments of one whom he calls a scholar, a bookish man, or a philosopher.

For these reasons Will shines in mixed company, where he has the discretion not to go out of his depth, and has often a certain way of making his real ignorance appear a seeming one. Our club, however, has frequently caught him tripping, at which times they never spare him. For as Will often insults us with the knowledge of the town, we sometimes take our revenge upon him by our knowledge of books.

He was last week producing two or three letters which he writ in his youth to a coquette lady. The raillery of them was natural, and well enough for a mere man of the town; but very unluckily several of the words were wrong spelt. Will laughed this off at first as well as he could; but finding himself pushed on all sides, and especially by the Templar, he told us with a little passion that he never liked pedantry in spelling, and that he spelt like a gentleman and not like a scholar. Upon this Will had recourse to his old topic of showing the narrow-spiritedness, the pride, and ignorance of pedants; which he carried so far that, upon my retiring to my lodgings, I could not forbear throwing together such reflections as occurred to me upon the subject.

A man who has been brought up among books, and is able to talk of nothing else, is a very indifferent companion, and what we call a pedant. But methinks we should enlarge the title, and give it every one that does not know how to think out of his profession and particular way of life.

What is a greater pedant than a mere man of the town? Bar him the play-houses, a catalogue of the reigning beauties, and an account of a few fashionable distempers that have befallen him, and you strike him dumb. How many a pretty gentleman's knowledge lies all within the verge of the court? He will tell you the names of the principal favourites, repeat the shrewd sayings of a man of quality, whisper an intrigue that is not yet blown upon by common fame; or, if the sphere of his observations is a little larger than ordinary, will perhaps enter into all the incidents, turns, and revolutions in a game of *ombre*. When he has gone thus far, he has shown you the whole circle of his accomplishments, his parts are drained, and he is disabled from any farther conversation. What are these but rank pedants? and yet these are the men who value themselves most on their exemption from the pedantry of colleges.

I might here mention the military pedant who always talks in a camp, and in storming towns, making lodgments and fighting battles from one end of the year to the other. Everything he speaks smells of gunpowder; if you take away his artillery from him, he has not a word to say for himself. I might likewise mention the law pedant, that is perpetually putting cases, repeating the transactions of Westminster-hall, wrangling with you upon the most indifferent circumstances of life, and not to be convinced of the distance of a place, or of the most trivial point in conversation, but by dint of argument. The state pedant is wrapt up in news, and lost in politics. If you mention either of the kings of Spain or Poland, he talks very notably; but if you go out of the *Gazette* you drop him. In short, a mere courtier, a mere soldier, a mere scholar, a mere anything, is an insipid pedantic character, and equally ridiculous.

Of all the species of pedants which I have mentioned, the book pedant is much the most supportable; he has at least an exercised understanding, and a head which is full though confused, so that a man who converses with him may often receive from him hints of things that are worth knowing, and what he may possibly turn to his own advantage, though they are of little use to the owner. The worst kind of pedants among learned men are such as are naturally endued with a very small share of common sense, and have read a great number of books without taste or distinction.

The truth of it is, learning, like travelling, and all other methods of improvement, as it finishes good sense, so it makes a silly man ten thousand times more insufferable, by supplying variety of matter to his impertinence, and giving him an opportunity of abounding in absurdities.

Shallow pedants cry up one another much more than men of solid and useful learning. To read the titles they give an editor or collator of a manuscript, you would take him for the glory of the commonwealth of letters, and the wonder of his age, when perhaps upon examination you find that he has only rectified a Greek particle, or laid out a whole sentence in proper commas.

They are obliged indeed to be thus lavish of their praises, that they may keep one another in countenance; and it is no wonder if a great deal of knowledge, which is not capable of making a man wise, has a natural tendency to make him vain and arrogant. L.

THE MAN OF PLEASURE

No. 151.] THURSDAY, AUGUST 23, 1711. [STEELE.]

Maximas virtutes jacere omnes necesse est voluptate dominante.
TULL. de Fin.
Where pleasure prevails, all the greatest virtues will lose their power.

I KNOW no one character that gives reason a greater shock at the same time that it presents a good ridiculous image to the imagination, than that of a man of wit and pleasure about the town. This description of a man of fashion, spoken by some with a mixture of scorn and ridicule, by others with great gravity as a laudable distinction, is in everybody's mouth that spends any time in conversation. My friend Will Honeycomb has this expression very frequently; and I never could understand by the story which follows, upon his mention of such a one, but that this man of wit and pleasure was either a drunkard too old for wenching, or a young lewd fellow with some liveliness, who would converse with you, receive kind offices of you, and at the same time debauch your sister, or lie with your wife. According to his description a man of wit, when he could have wenches for crowns a-piece, which he liked quite as well, would be so extravagant as to bribe servants, make false friendships, fight relations: I say, according to him, plain and simple vice was too little for a man of wit and pleasure; but he would leave an easy and accessible wickedness to come at the same thing with only the addition of certain falsehood and possible murder. Will thinks the town grown very dull, in that we do not hear so much as we used to do of these coxcombs, whom (without observing it) he describes as the most infamous rogues in nature, with relation to friendship, love, or conversation.

When pleasure is made the chief pursuit of life, it will necessarily follow that such monsters as these will arise, from a constant application to such blandishments as naturally root out the force of reason and reflection, and substitute in their place a general impatience of thought, and a constant pruriency of inordinate desire.

Pleasure, when it is a man's chief purpose, disappoints itself; and the constant application to it palls the faculty of enjoying it, though it leaves the sense of our inability for that we wish with a disrelish of everything else. Thus the intermediate seasons of the man of pleasure are more heavy than one would impose upon the vilest criminal. Take him when he is awaked too soon after a debauch, or disappointed in following a worthless woman without truth, and there is no man living whose being is such a weight or vexation as his is. He is an utter stranger to the pleasing reflections in the evening of a well-spent day, or the gladness of heart or quickness of spirit in the morning after profound sleep or indolent slumbers. He is not to be at ease any longer than he can keep reason and good sense without his curtains; otherwise he will be haunted with the reflection, that he could not believe such a one the woman that upon trial he found her. What has he got by his conquest, but to think meanly of her for whom a day or two before he

The Rake's Progress, Plate II.

had the highest honour? and of himself, for perhaps wronging the man whom of all men living he himself would least willingly have injured?

Pleasure seizes the whole man who addicts himself to it, and will not give him leisure for any good office in life which contradicts the gaiety of the present hour. You may indeed observe in people of pleasure a certain complacency and absence of all severity, which the habit of a loose unconcerned life gives them: but tell the man of pleasure your secret wants, cares, or sorrows, and you will find he has given up the delicacy of his passions to the cravings of his appetites. He little knows the perfect joy he loses for the disappointing gratifications which he pursues. He looks at Pleasure as she approaches and comes to him with the recommendation of warm wishes, gay looks, and graceful motion; but he does not observe how she leaves his presence with disorder, impotence, down-cast shame, and conscious imperfection. She makes our youth inglorious, our age shameful.

Will Honeycomb gives us twenty intimations in an evening of several hags whose bloom was given up to his arms; and would raise a value to himself for having had, as the phrase is, "very good women." Will's good women are the comfort of his heart, and support him, I warrant, by the memory of past interviews with persons of their condition. No, there is not in the world an occasion wherein vice makes so fantastical a figure, as at the meeting of two old people who have been partners in unwarrantable pleasure. To tell a toothless old lady that she once had a good set, or a defunct wencher that he once was the admired thing of the town, are satires instead of applauses; but, on the other side, consider the old age of those who have passed their days in labour, industry, and virtue, their decays make them but appear the more venerable, and the imperfections of their bodies are beheld as a misfortune to human society that their make is so little durable.

But to return more directly to any man of wit and pleasure. In all orders of men, wherever this is the chief character, the person who wears it is a negligent friend, father, and husband, and entails poverty on his unhappy descendants. Mortgages, diseases, and settlements, are the legacies a man of wit and pleasure leaves to his family. All the poor rogues that make such lamentable speeches after every sessions at Tyburn, were, in their way, men of wit and pleasure before they fell into the adventures which brought them thither.

THE SPECTATOR

Irresolution and procrastination in all a man's affairs, are the natural effects of being addicted to pleasure. Dishonour to the gentleman and bankruptcy to the trader are the portion of either whose chief purpose of life is delight. The chief cause that this pursuit has been in all ages received with so much quarter from the soberer part of mankind has been, that some men of great talents have sacrificed themselves to it. The shining qualities of such people have given a beauty to whatever they were engaged in, and a mixture of wit has recommended madness. For let any man who knows what it is to have passed much time in a series of jollity, mirth, wit, or humorous entertainments, look back at what he was all that while a doing, and he will find that he has been at one instant sharp to some man he is sorry to have offended, impertinent to some one it was cruelty to treat with such freedom, ungracefully noisy at such a time, unmercifully calumnious at such a time; and, from the whole course of his applauded satisfactions, unable in the end to recollect any circumstance which can add to the enjoyment of his own mind alone, or which he would put his character upon with other men. Thus it is with those who are best made for becoming pleasures; but how monstrous is it in the generality of mankind who pretend this way, without genius or inclination towards it! The scene then is wild to an extravagance: this is, as if fools should mimic madmen. Pleasure of this kind is the intemperate meals and loud jollities of the common rate of country gentlemen, whose practice and way of enjoyment is to put an end as fast as they can to that little particle of reason they have when they are sober. These men of wit and pleasure despatch their senses as fast as possible by drinking till they cannot taste, smoking till they cannot see, and roaring till they cannot hear.   T.

THE SPECTATOR

A WOMAN'S MAN

No. 156.] WEDNESDAY, AUGUST 29, 1711. [STEELE.]

> — Sed tu simul obligasti
> Perfidum votis caput, enitescis
> Pulchrior multo.
> HOR. 2 Od. viii. 3.
> — But thou,
> When once thou hast broke some tender vow,
> All perjur'd, dost more charming grow!

I DO not think any thing could make a pleasanter entertainment, than the history of the reigning favourites among the women from time to time about this town. In such an account we ought to have a faithful confession of each lady for what she liked such and such a man, and he ought to tell us by what particular action or dress he believed he would be most successful. As for my part, I have always made as easy a judgment when a man dresses for the ladies, as when he is equipped for hunting or coursing. The woman's man is a person in his air and behaviour quite different from the rest of our species. His garb is more loose and negligent, his manner more soft and indolent; that is to say, in both cases there is an apparent endeavour to appear unconcerned and careless. In catching birds the fowlers have a method of imitating their voices to bring them to the snare; and your women's men have always a similitude of the creature they hope to betray, in their own conversation. A woman's man is very knowing in all that passes from one family to another, has pretty little officiousnesses, in not at a loss what is good for a cold, and it is not amiss if he has a bottle of spirits in his pocket in case of any sudden indisposition.

Curiosity having been my prevailing passion, and indeed the sole entertainment of my life, I have sometimes made it my business to examine the course of intrigues as well as the manners and accomplishments of such as have been most successful in that way. In all my observation, I never knew a man of good understanding a general favourite; some singularity in his behaviour, some whim in his way of life, and what would have made him ridiculous among the men, has recommended him to the other sex. I should be very sorry to offend a people so fortunate as those of whom I am speaking; but let any one look over the old beaux, and he will find the man of success was remarkable for quarrelling impertinently for their sakes, for dressing unlike the rest of the world, or passing his days in an insipid assiduity about the fair sex to gain the figure he made amongst them. Add to this that he must have the reputation of being well with other women, to please any one woman of gallantry; for you are to know, that there is a mighty ambition among the light part of the sex to gain slaves from the dominion of others. My friend Will Honeycomb says it was a common bite with him, to lay suspicions that he was favoured by a lady's enemy, that is, some rival beauty, to be well with herself. A little spite is natural to a great beauty: and it is ordinary to snap up a disagreeable fellow lest another should have him. That impudent toad Bareface fares well among all the ladies he converses with, for no other reason in the world but that he has the skill to keep them from explanation with one another. Did they know there is not one who likes him in her heart, each would declare her scorn of him the next moment; but he is well received by them because it is the fashion, and opposition to each other brings them insensibly into an imitation of each other. What adds to him the greatest grace is, that the pleasant thief, as they call him, is the most inconstant creature living, has a wonderful deal of wit and humour, and never wants something to say; besides all which, he has a most spiteful dangerous tongue if you should provoke him.

To make a woman's man, he must not be a man of sense or a fool; the business is to entertain, and it is much better to have a faculty of arguing, than a capacity of judging right. But the pleasantest of all the woman's equipage are your regular visitants; these are volunteers in their service, without hopes of pay or preferment. It is enough that they can lead out from a public place, that they are admitted on a public day, and can be allowed to pass away part of that heavy load, their time, in the company of the fair. But commend me above all others to those who are known for your ruiners of ladies; these are the choicest spirits which our age produces. We have several of these irresistible gentlemen among us when the company is in town. These fellows are accomplished with the knowledge of the ordinary occurrences about court and town, have that sort of good breeding which is exclusive of all morality, and consists only in being publicly decent, privately dissolute.

THE SPECTATOR

It is wonderful how far a fond opinion of herself can carry a woman, to make her have the least regard to a professed known woman's man; but as scarce one of all the women who are in the tour of gallantries ever hears anything of what is the common sense of sober minds, but are entertained with a continual round of flatteries, they cannot be mistresses of themselves enough to make arguments for their own conduct from the behaviour of these men to others. It is so far otherwise, that a general fame for falsehood in this kind is a recommendation; and the coxcomb, loaded with the favours of many others, is received like a victor that disdains his trophies, to be a victim to the present charmer.

If you see a man more full of gesture than ordinary in a public assembly, if loud upon no occasion, if negligent of the company around him, and yet laying wait for destroying by that negligence, you may take it for granted that he has ruined many a fair one. The woman's man expresses himself wholly in that motion which we call strutting. An elevated chest, a pinched hat, a measurable step, and a sly surveying eye, are the marks of him. Now and then you see a gentleman with all these accomplishments; but alas! any one of them is enough to undo thousands. When a gentleman with such perfections adds to it suitable learning, there should be public warning of his residence in town, that we may remove our wives and daughters. It happens sometimes that such a fine man has read all the miscellany poems, a few of our comedies, and has the translation of Ovid's Epistles by heart. "Oh if it were possible that such a one could be as true as he is charming! but that is too much, the women will share such a dear false man: a little gallantry to hear him talk one would indulge one's self in, let him reckon the sticks of one's fan, say something of the cupids in it; and then call one so many soft names which a man of his learning has at his fingers-ends. There sure is some excuse for frailty, when attacked by force against a weak woman." Such is the soliloquy of many a lady one might name, at the sight of one of these who makes it no iniquity to go on from day to day in the sin of women-slaughter.

It is certain that people are got into a way of affectation, with a manner of overlooking the most solid virtues, and admiring the most trivial excellencies. The woman is so far from expecting to be contemned for being a very injudicious silly animal, that while she can preserve her features and her mien, she knows that she is still

THE SPECTATOR

the object of desire; and there is a sort of secret ambition, from reading frivolous books, and keeping as frivolous company, each side to be amiable in imperfection, and arrive at the characters of the Dear Deceiver and the Perjured Fair.

ACCOUNT OF A GRINNING-MATCH

No. 173.] TUESDAY, SEPTEMBER 18, 1711. [ADDISON.]

— Remove fera monstra, tuæque
Saxificos vultus, quæcunque ea, tolle Medusæ.— OVID. MET.

IN a late paper I mentioned the project of an ingenious author for the erecting of several handicraft prizes to be contended for by our British artisans, and the influence they might have towards the improvement of our several manufactures. I have since been very much surprised by the following advertisement which I find in the Post-Boy of the 11th instant, and again repeated in the Post-Boy of the 15th.

"ON the 9th of October next will be run for upon Coleshill Heath, in Warwickshire, a plate of six guineas value, 3 heats, by any horse, mare, or gelding, that hath not won above the value of 5*l.*, the winning horse to be sold for 10*l.*, to carry 10 stone weight, if 14 hands high; if above or under, to carry or be allowed weight for inches, and to be entered Friday the 15th at the Swan in Coleshill, before 6 in the evening. Also a plate of less value to be run for by asses. The same day a gold ring to be grinned for by men."

The first of these diversions, that is to be exhibited by the 10*l.* race-horses, may probably have its use; but the two last, in which the asses and men are concerned, seem to me altogether extraordinary and unaccountable. Why they should keep running asses at Coleshill, or how making mouths turns to account in Warwickshire, more than in any other parts of England, I cannot comprehend. I have looked over all the Olympic games, and do not find anything in them like an ass-race, or a match at grinning. However it be, I am informed, that several asses are now kept in body-clothes, and sweated every morning upon the heath; and that all the country-fellows within ten miles of the Swan grin an hour or two in their glasses every morning, in order to qualify themselves for the 9th of October. The prize which is proposed to be grinned for, has raised such an ambition among the common people of out-grinning one another, that many very discerning persons are afraid it should spoil most of the faces in the county; and that a Warwickshire man will be known by his grin, as Roman Catholics imagine a Kentish man is by his tail. The gold ring which is made the prize of deformity, is just the reverse of the golden apple that was formerly made the prize of beauty, and should carry for its posie the old motto inverted,

> Detur tetriori.

Or, to accommodate it to the capacity of the combatants,

> The frightfull'st grinner
> Be the winner.

In the mean while I would advise a Dutch painter to be present at this great controversy of faces, in order to make a collection of the most remarkable grins that shall be there exhibited.

I must not here omit an account which I lately received of one of these grinning matches from a gentleman, who, upon reading the above-mentioned advertisement, entertained a coffee-house with the following narrative. Upon the taking of Namur, among other public rejoicings made on that occasion, there was a gold ring given by a Whig justice of the peace to be grinned for. The first competitor that entered the lists, was a black, swarthy Frenchman, who accidentally passed that way, and being a man naturally of a withered look and hard features, promised himself good success. He was placed upon a table in the great point of view, and looking upon the company like Milton's death,

> Grinn'd horribly a ghastly smile.

His muscles were so drawn together on each side of his face that he showed twenty teeth at a grin, and put the country in some pain, lest a foreigner should carry away the honour of the day; but upon a further trial they found he was master only of the merry grin.

The next that mounted the table was a Malecontent in those days, and a great master of the whole art of grinning, but particularly excelled in the angry grin. He did his part so well, that he is said to have made half a dozen women miscarry; but the justice being apprized by one who stood near him, that the fellow who grinned in his face was a Jacobite, and being unwilling that a disaffected person should win the gold ring, and be looked upon as the best grinner in the country, he ordered the oaths to be tendered unto him upon his quitting the table, which the grinner refusing, he was set aside as an unqualified person. There were several other grotesque figures that presented themselves, which it would be too tedious to describe. I must not, however, omit a ploughman, who lived in the further part of the country, and being very lucky in a pair of long lanthorn-jaws, wrung his face into such a hideous grimace, that every feature of it appeared under a different distortion. The whole company stood astonished at such a complicated grin, and were ready to assign the prize to him, had it not been proved by one of his antagonists that he had practised with verjuice for some days before, and had a crab found upon him at the very time of grinning; upon which the best judges of grinning declared it as their opinion, that he was not to be looked upon as a fair grinner, and therefore ordered him to be set aside as a cheat.

The prize, it seems, fell at length upon a cobbler, Giles Gorgon by name, who produced several new grins of his own invention, having been used to cut faces for many years together over his last. At the very first grin he cast every human feature out of his countenance, at the second he became the face of a spout, at the third a baboon, at the fourth the head of a bass-viol, and at the fifth a pair of nut-crackers. The whole assembly wondered at his accomplishments, and bestowed the ring on him unanimously; but, what he esteemed more than all the rest, a country wench whom he had wooed in vain for above five years before, was so charmed with his grins, and the applauses which he received on all sides, that she married him the week following, and to this day wears the prize upon her finger, the cobbler having made use of it as his wedding-ring.

This paper might perhaps seem very impertinent, if it grew serious in the conclusion. I would nevertheless leave it to the consideration of those who are the patrons of this monstrous trial of skill, whether or no they are not guilty, in some measure, of an affront to their species, in treating after this manner the Human Face Divine, and turning that part of us, which has so great an

Southwark Fair.

image impressed upon it, into the image of a monkey; whether the raising such silly competitions among the ignorant, proposing prizes for such useless accomplishments, filling the common people's heads with such senseless ambitions, and inspiring them with such absurd ideas of superiority and pre-eminence, has not in it something immoral as well as ridiculous.

ACCOUNT OF A WHISTLING MATCH

No. 179.]   TUESDAY, SEPTEMBER 25, 1711.   [ADDISON.]

>Centuriæ seniorum agitant expertia frugis:
>Celsi prætereunt austera poemata Rhamnes.
>Omne tulit punctum qui miscuit utile dulci,
>Lectorem delectando, pariterque monendo.—HOR.

I MAY cast my readers under two general divisions, the Mercurial and the Saturnine. The first are the gay part of my disciples, who require speculations of wit and humour; the others are those of a more solemn and sober turn, who find no pleasure but in papers of morality and sound sense. The former call everything that is serious stupid; the latter look upon everything as impertinent that is ludicrous. Were I always grave, one half of my readers would fall off from me: were I always merry, I should lose the other. I make it therefore my endeavour to find out entertainments for both kinds, and by that means perhaps consult the good of both, more than I should do did I always write to the particular taste of either. As they neither of them know what I proceed upon, the sprightly reader, who takes up my paper in order to be diverted, very often finds himself engaged unawares in a serious and profitable course of thinking; as, on the contrary, the thoughtful man, who perhaps may hope to find something solid, and full of deep reflection, is very often insensibly betrayed into a fit of mirth. In a word, the reader sits down to my entertainment without knowing his bill of fare, and has therefore at least the pleasure of hoping there may be a dish to his palate.

I must confess, were I left to myself, I would rather aim at instructing than diverting; but if we will be useful to the world, we must take it as we find it. Authors of professed severity discourage the looser part of mankind from having anything to do with their writings. A man must have virtue in him, before he will enter upon the reading of a eneca or an Epictetus. The very title of a moral treatise has something in it austere and shocking to the careless and inconsiderate.

For this reason several unthinking persons fall in my way, who would give no attention to lectures delivered with a religious seriousness or a philosophic gravity. They are insnared into sentiments of wisdom and virtue when they do not think of it; and if by that means they arrive only at such a degree of consideration as may dispose them to listen to more studied and elaborate discourses, I shall not think my speculations useless. I might likewise observe, that the gloominess in which sometimes the minds of the best men are involved, very often stands in need of such little incitements to mirth and laughter as are apt to disperse melancholy, and put our faculties in good humour. To which some will add, that the British climate more than any other makes entertainments of this nature in a manner necessary.

If what I have here said does not recommend, it will at least excuse, the variety of my speculations. I would not willingly laugh but in order to instruct, or if I sometimes fail in this point, when my mirth ceases to be instructive, it shall never cease to be innocent. A scrupulous conduct in this particular has, perhaps, more merit in it than the generality of readers imagine: did they know how many thoughts occur in a point of humour, which a discreet author in modesty suppresses; how many strokes of raillery present themselves, which could not fail to please the ordinary taste of mankind, but are stifled in their birth by reason of some remote tendency which they carry in them to corrupt the minds of those who read them; did they know how many glances of ill-nature are industriously avoided for fear of doing injury to the reputation of another; they would be apt to think kindly of those writers who endeavour to make themselves diverting without being immoral. One may apply to these authors that passage in Waller,

> Poets lose half the praise they would have got,
> Were it but known what they discreetly blot.

As nothing is more easy than to be a wit with all the above-mentioned liberties, it requires some genius and invention to appear such without them.

THE SPECTATOR

What I have here said is not only in regard to the public, but with an eye to my particular correspondent, who has sent me the following letter which I have castrated in some places upon these considerations.

"SIR, — Having lately seen your discourse upon a match of grinning, I cannot forbear giving you an account of a whistling match, which, with many others, I was entertained with about three years since at the Bath. The prize was a guinea, to be conferred upon the ablest whistler, that is, on him who could whistle clearest, and go through his tune without laughing, to which at the same time he was provoked by the antic postures of a Merry-Andrew, who was to stand upon the stage and play his tricks in the eye of the performer. There were three competitors for the guinea. The first was a ploughman of a very promising aspect; his features were steady, and his muscles composed in so inflexible a stupidity, that upon his first appearance every one gave the guinea for lost. The pickled-herring, however, found the way to shake him, for upon his whistling a country jig, this unlucky wag danced to it with such variety of distortions and grimaces, that the countryman could not forbear smiling upon him, and by that means spoiled his whistle and lost the prize.

"The next that mounted the stage was an under-citizen of the Bath, a person remarkable among the inferior people of that place for his great wisdom and his broad band. He contracted his mouth with much gravity, and, that he might dispose his mind to be more serious than ordinary, begun the tune 'of the Children in the Wood,' and went through part of it with good success; when on a sudden the wit at his elbow, who had appeared wonderfully grave and attentive for some time, gave him a touch upon the left shoulder, and stared him in the face with so bewitching a grin, that the whistler relaxed his fibres into a kind of simper, and at length burst out into an open laugh. The third who entered the lists was a foot-man, who, in defiance of the Merry-Andrew and all his arts, whistled a Scotch tune and an Italian sonata, with so settled a countenance, that he bore away the prize, to the great admiration of some hundreds of persons, who, as well as myself, were present at this trial of skill. Now, sir, I humbly conceive, whatever you have determined of the grinners, the whistlers ought to be encouraged, not only as their art is practised without distortion, but as it improves country music, promotes gravity, and teaches ordinary people to keep their countenances, if they see anything ridiculous in their betters; besides that, it seems an entertainment very particularly adapted to the Bath, as it is usual for a rider to whistle to his horse when he would make his waters pass.

"I am, sir," &c.

POSTSCRIPT.

"After you have despatched these two important points of grinning and whistling, I hope you will oblige the world with some reflections upon yawning, as I have seen it practised on a twelfth-night, among other Christmas gambols, at the house of a very worthy gentleman, who always entertains his tenants at that time of the year. They yawn for a Cheshire cheese, and begin about midnight, when the whole company is disposed to be drowsy. He that yawns widest, and at the same time so naturally as to produce the most yawns among the spectators, carries home the cheese. If you handle this subject as you ought, I question not but your paper will set half the kingdom a yawning, though I dare promise you it will never make anybody fall asleep."

ON TEMPERANCE

No. 195.]   SATURDAY, OCTOBER 13, 1711.   [ADDISON.]

Νήπιοι οὐδ' ἴσασιν ὅσῳ πλέον ἥμισυ παντός·
Οὐδ' ὅσον ἐν μαλάχῃ τε δὲ ἀσφοδέλῳ μεγ' ὄνειαρ.

HES. Oper. & Dier. l. i. 40.

Fools not to know that half exceeds the whole,
How blest the sparing meal and temperate bowl.

THERE is a story in the Arabian Nights Tales of a king who had long languished under an ill habit of body, and had taken abundance of remedies to no purpose. At length, says the fable, a physician cured him by the following method. He took a hollow ball of wood, and filled it with several drugs; after which he closed it up so artificially that nothing appeared. He likewise took a mall, and after having hollowed the handle, and that part which strikes the ball, he inclosed in them several drugs after the same manner as in the ball itself. He then ordered the sultan, who was his patient, to exercise himself early in the morning with these rightly-prepared instruments, till such time as he should sweat: when, as the story goes, the virtue of the medicaments perspiring through the wood had so good an influence on the sultan's constitution, that they cured him of an indisposition which all the compositions he had taken inwardly had not been able to remove. This eastern allegory is finely contrived to show us how beneficial bodily labour is to health, and that exercise is the most effectual physic. I have described in my hundred and fifteenth paper, from the general structure and mechanism of an human body, how absolutely necessary exercise is for its preservation. I shall in this place recommend another great preservative of health, which in many cases produces the same effects as exercise, and may, in some measure, supply its place, where opportunities of exercise are wanting. The preservative I am speaking of is temperance, which has those particular advantages above all other means of health, that it may be practised by all ranks and conditions, at any season, or in any place. It is a kind of regimen into which every man may put himself, without interruption to business, expense of money, or loss of time. If exercise throws off all superfluities, temperance prevents them; if exercise clears the vessels, temperance neither satiates nor overstrains them; if exercise raises proper ferments in the humours, and promotes the circulation of the blood, temperance gives nature her full play, and enables her to exert herself in all her force and vigour; if exercise dissipates a growing distemper, temperance starves it.

Physic, for the most part, is nothing else but the substitute of exercise or temperance. Medicines are indeed absolutely necessary in acute distempers, that cannot wait the slow operations of these two great instruments of health; but did men live in an habitual course of exercise and temperance, there would be but little occasion for them. Accordingly we find that those parts of the world are the most healthy, where they subsist by the chace; and that men live longest, when their lives were employed in hunting, and when they had little food besides what they caught. Blistering, cupping, bleeding, are seldom of use but to the idle and intemperate; as all those inward applications which are so much in practice among us, are for the most part nothing else but expedients to make luxury consistent with health. The apothecary is perpetually employed in countermining the cook and the vintner. It is said of Diogenes, that meeting a young man who was going to a feast, he took him up in the street and carried him home to his friends, as one who was running into imminent danger, had not he prevented him. What would that philosopher have said had he been present at the gluttony of a modern meal? Would not he have thought the master of a family mad, and have begged his servants to tie down his hands, had he seen him devour fowl, fish, and flesh, swallow oil and vinegar, wines and spices; throw down salads of twenty different herbs, sauces of an hundred ingredients, confections, and fruits of numberless sweets and flavours? What unnatural motions and counter ferments must such a medley of intemperance produce in the body? For my part, when I behold a fashionable table set out in all its magnificence, I fancy that I see gouts and dropsies, fevers and lethargies, with other innumerable distempers lying in ambuscade among the dishes.

Nature delights in the most plain and simple diet. Every animal but man keeps to one dish. Herbs are the food of this species, fish of that, and flesh of a third. Man falls upon everything that comes in his way; not the smallest fruit or excrescence of the earth, scarce a berry or a mushroom, can escape him.

It is impossible to lay down any determined rule for temperance, because what is luxury in one may be temperance in another, but there are few that have lived any time in the world, who are not judges of their own constitutions, so far as to know what kinds and what proportions of food do best agree with them. Were I to consider my readers as my patients, and to prescribe such a kind of temperance as is accommodated to all persons, and such as is particularly suitable to our climate and way of living, I would copy the following rules of a very eminent physician. "Make your whole repast out of one dish. If you indulge in a second, avoid drinking anything strong, until you have finished your meal; at the same time abstain from all sauces, or at least such as are not the most plain and simple." A man could not be well guilty of gluttony if he stuck to these few obvious and easy rules. In the first case, there would be no variety of tastes to solicit his palate, and occasion excess; nor, in the second, any artificial provocatives to relieve satiety, and create a false appetite. Were I to prescribe a rule for drinking, it should be formed upon a saying quoted by sir

THE SPECTATOR

William Temple; "The first glass for myself, the second for my friends, the third for good-humour, and the fourth for mine enemies." But because it is impossible for one who lives in the world to diet himself always in so philosophical a manner, I think every man should have his days of abstinence, according as his constitution will permit. These are great reliefs to nature, as they qualify her for struggling with hunger and thirst, whenever any distemper or duty of life may put her upon such difficulties; and at the same time give her an opportunity of extricating herself from her oppressions, and recovering the several tones and springs of her distended vessels. Besides that, abstinence well-timed often kills a sickness in embryo, and destroys the first seeds of an indisposition. It is observed by two or three ancient authors, that Socrates, notwithstanding he lived in Athens during that great plague which has made so much noise through all ages, and has been celebrated at different times by such eminent hands; I say, notwithstanding that he lived in the time of this devouring pestilence, he never caught the least infection, which those writers unanimously ascribe to that uninterrupted temperance which he always observed.

And here I cannot but mention an observation which I have often made, upon reading the lives of the philosophers, and comparing it with any series of kings or great men of the same number. If we consider these ancient sages, a great part of whose philosophy consisted in a temperate and abstemious course of life, one would think the life of a philosopher and the life of a man were of two different dates. For we find that the generality of these wise men were nearer a hundred than sixty years of age at the time of their respective deaths. But the most remarkable instance of the efficacy of temperance towards the procuring of long life, is what we meet with in a little book published by Lewis Cornaro the Venetian; which I the rather mention, because it is of undoubted credit, as the late Venetian ambassador, who was of the same family, attested more than once in conversation when he resided in England. Cornaro, who was the author of the little treatise I am mentioning, was of an infirm constitution until about forty, when, by obstinately persisting in an exact course of temperance, he recovered a perfect state of health; insomuch that at fourscore he published his book, which has been translated into English under the title of "Sure and Certain Methods of Attaining a Long and Healthy Life." He lived to give a third or fourth edition of it; and, after having passed his hundredth year, died without pain or agony, and like one who falls asleep. The treatise I mention has been taken notice of by several eminent authors, and is written with such a spirit of cheerfulness, religion, and good sense, as are the natural concomitants of temperance and sobriety. The mixture of the old man in it is rather a recommendation than a discredit to it.

Having designed this paper as the sequel to that upon exercise, I have not here considered temperance as it is a moral virtue, which I shall make the subject of a future speculation, but only as it is the means of health. L.

CHARACTER OF THE SALAMANDERS

No. 198.] WEDNESDAY, October 17, 1711. [ADDISON.]

> Cervæ luporum præda rapacium
> Sectamur ultro, quos opimus
> Fallere et effurgere est triumphus.—HOR.

THERE is a species of women, whom I shall distinguish by the name of Salamanders. Now a salamander is a kind of heroine in chastity, that treads upon fire, and lives in the midst of flames, without being hurt. A salamander knows no distinction of sex in those she converses with, grows familiar with a stranger at first sight, and is not so narrow-spirited as to observe whether the person she talks to be in breeches or in petticoats. She admits a male visitant to her bed-side, plays with him a whole afternoon at picquette, walks with him two or three hours by moon-light; and is extremely scandalized at the unreasonableness of an husband, or the severity of a parent, that would debar the sex from such innocent liberties. Your salamander is therefore a perpetual declaimer against jealousy, an admirer of the French good-breeding, and a great stickler for freedom in conversation. In short, the salamander lives in an invincible state of simplicity and innocence: her constitution is *preserved* in a kind of natural frost; she wonders what people mean by temptations, and defies mankind to do their worst. Her chastity is engaged in a constant ordeal, or fiery trial; (like good queen Emma,) the pretty innocent walks blindfold

THE SPECTATOR

among burning plough-shares, without being scorched or singed by them.

It is not therefore for the use of the salamander, whether in a married or single state of life, that I design the following paper; but for such females only as are made of flesh and blood, and find themselves subject to human frailties.

As for this part of the fair sex, who are not of the salamander kind, I would most earnestly advise them to observe a quite different conduct in their behaviour; and to avoid as much as possible what religion calls *temptations*, and the world *opportunities*. Did they but know how many thousands of their sex have been gradually betrayed from innocent freedoms to ruin and infamy; and how many millions of ours have begun with flatteries, protestations, and endearments, but ended with reproaches, perjury, and perfidiousness; they would shun like death the very first approaches of one that might lead them into inextricable labyrinths of guilt and misery. I must so far give up the cause of the male world, as to exhort the female sex in the language of Chamont in the Orphan,

> Trust not a man; we are by nature false,
> Dissembling, subtle, cruel, and unconstant:
> When a man talks of love, with caution trust him;
> But if he swears, he'll certainly deceive thee.

I might very much enlarge upon this subject, but shall conclude it with a story which I lately heard from one of our Spanish officers, and which may show the danger a woman incurs by too great familiarities with a male companion.

An inhabitant of the kingdom of Castile, being a man of more than ordinary prudence, and of a grave, composed behaviour, determined about the fiftieth year of his age to enter upon wedlock. In order to make himself easy in it, he cast his eye upon a young woman who had nothing to recommend her but her beauty and her education, her parents having been reduced to great poverty by the wars which for some years have laid that whole country waste. The Castilian having made his addresses to her and married her, they lived together in perfect happiness for some time; when at length the husband's affairs made it necessary for him to take a voyage to the kingdom of Naples, where a great part of his estate lay. The wife loved him too tenderly to be left behind him. They had not been on shipboard above a day, when they unluckily fell into the hands of an Algerine pirate, who carried the whole company on shore, and made them slaves. The Castilian and his wife had the comfort to be under the same master; who seeing how dearly they loved one another, and gasped after their liberty, demanded a most exorbitant price for their ransom. The Castilian, though he would rather have died in slavery himself than have paid such a sum as he found would go near to ruin him, was so moved with compassion towards his wife, that he sent repeated orders to his friend in Spain (who happened to be his next relation) to sell his estate, and transmit the money to him. His friend, hoping that the terms of his ransom might be made more reasonable, and unwilling to sell an estate which he himself had some prospect of inheriting, formed so many delays, that three whole years passed away without anything being done for the setting of them at liberty.

There happened to live a French renegado in the same place where the Castilian and his wife were kept prisoners. As this fellow had in him all the vivacity of his nation, he often entertained the captives with accounts of his own adventures; to which he sometimes added a song or a dance, or some other piece of mirth, to divert them during their confinement. His acquaintance with the manners of the Algerines enabled him likewise to do them several good offices. The Castilian, as he was one day in conversation with this renegado, discovered to him the negligence and treachery of his correspondent in Castile, and at the same time asked his advice how he should behave himself in that exigency: he further told the renegado, that he found it would be impossible for him to raise the money, unless he himself might go over to dispose of his estate. The renegado, after having represented to him that his Algerine master would never consent to his release upon such a pretence, at length contrived a method for the Castilian to make his escape in the habit of a seaman. The Castilian succeeded in his attempt; and having sold his estate, being afraid lest the money should miscarry by the way, and determining to perish with it rather than lose what was much dearer to him than his life, he returned himself in a little vessel that was going to Algiers. It is impossible to describe the joy he felt upon this occasion, when he considered that he should soon see the wife whom he so much loved, and endear himself more to her by this uncommon piece of generosity.

The renegado, during the husband's absence, so insinuated himself into the graces of his young wife, and so turned her head with stories of gallantry, that she quickly thought him the finest gentleman she had ever conversed with. To be brief, her mind was quite alienated from the honest Castilian, whom she was taught to look upon as a formal old fellow, unworthy the possession of so charming a creature. She had been instructed by the renegado how to manage herself upon his arrival; so that she received him with an appearance of the utmost love and gratitude, and at length persuaded him to trust their common friend the renegado with the money he had brought over for their ransom; as not questioning, but he would beat down the terms of it, and negotiate the affair more to their advantage than they themselves could do. The good man admired her prudence and followed her advice. I wish I could conceal the sequel of this story, but since I cannot, I shall despatch it in as few words as possible. The Castilian having slept longer than ordinary the next morning, upon his awaking found his wife had left him: he immediately rose and inquired after her, but was told that she was seen with the renegado about break of day. In a word, her lover having got all things ready for their departure, they soon made their escape out of the territories of Algiers, carried away the money, and left the Castilian in captivity: who partly through the cruel treatment of the incensed Algerine his master, and partly through the unkind usage of his unfaithful wife, died some few months after.

SATIRE ON WOMEN

No. 209.]   TUESDAY, October 30, 1711.   [Addison.]

> Γυναικὸς οὐδὲ χρῆμ' ἀνὴρ ληίζεται
> Ἐσθλῆς ἄμεινον, οὐδὲ ῥίγιον κακῆς.
>
> Simonides.
>
> Of earthly goods, the best is a good wife;
> A bad, the bitterest curse of human life.

THERE are no authors I am more pleased with, than those who show human nature in a variety of views, and describe the several ages of the world in their different manners. A reader cannot be more rationally entertained, than by comparing the virtues and vices of his own times with those which prevailed in the times of his forefathers; and drawing a parallel in his mind between his own private character, and that of other persons, whether of his own age, or of the ages that went before him. The contemplation of mankind, under these changeable colours, is apt to shame us out of any particular vice, or animate us to any particular virtue; to make us pleased or displeased with ourselves in the most proper points; to clear our minds of prejudice and prepossession; and rectify that narrowness of temper which inclines us to think amiss of those who differ from ourselves.

If we look into the manners of the most remote ages of the world, we discover human nature in her simplicity; and, the more we come downwards towards our own times, may observe her hiding herself in artifices and refinements, polished insensibly out of her original plainness, and at length, entirely lost under form and ceremony, and (what we call) good-breeding. Read the accounts of men and women as they are given us by the most ancient writers, both sacred and profane, and you would think you were reading the history of another species.

Among the writers of antiquity, there are none who instruct us more openly in the manners of their respective times in which they lived, than those who have employed themselves in satire, under what dress soever it may appear; as there are no other authors whose province it is to enter so directly into the ways of men, and set their miscarriages in so strong a light.

Simonides, a poet famous in his generation, is, I think, author of the oldest satire that is now extant; and, as some say, of the first that was ever written. This poet flourished about four hundred years after the siege of Troy; and shows, by his way of writing, the simplicity, or rather coarseness, of the age in which he lived. I have taken notice, in my hundred and sixty-first speculation, that the rule of observing what the French call the *Bienseance* in an allusion, has been found out of later years; and that the ancients, provided there was a likeness in their similitudes, did not much trouble themselves about the decency of the comparison. The satires or iambics of Simonides, with which I shall entertain my readers in the present paper, are a remarkable instance of what I formerly advanced. The subject of this satire is woman. He describes the sex in their several characters, which he derives to them from a fanciful supposition raised upon the doctrine of preexistence. He tells us, that the gods formed the souls of women out of those seeds and principles which compose several kinds of animals and elements; and that their good or bad dispositions arise in them according as such and such seeds and principles predominate in their constitutions. I have translated the author very faithfully, and if not word for word (which our language would not bear), at least so as to comprehend every one of his sentiments, without adding anything of my own. I have already apologized for this author's want of delicacy, and must farther premise, that the following satire affects only some of the lower part of the sex, and not those who have been refined by a polite education, which was not so common in the age of this poet.

"In the beginning God made the souls of womankind out of different materials, and in a separate state from their bodies.

"The souls of one kind of women were formed out of those ingredients which compose a swine. A woman of this make is a slut in her house, and a glutton at her table. She is uncleanly in her person, a slattern in her dress, and her family is no better than a dunghill.

"A second sort of female soul was formed out of the same materials that enter into the composition of a fox. Such an one is what we call a notable discerning woman, who has an insight into every thing whether it be good or bad. In this species of females there are some virtuous and some vicious.

"A third kind of women were made up of canine particles. These are what we commonly call scolds, who imitate the animals out of which they were taken, that are always busy and barking, that snarl at every one who comes in their way, and live in perpetual clamour.

"The fourth kind of women were made out of the earth. These are your sluggards, who pass away their time in indolence and ignorance, hover over the fire a whole winter, and apply themselves with alacrity to no kind of business but eating.

"The fifth species of females were made out of the sea. These are women of variable uneven tempers, sometimes all storm and tempests, sometimes all calm and sunshine. The stranger who sees one of these in her smiles and smoothness, would cry her up for a miracle of good-humour; but on a sudden her looks and words are changed, she is nothing but fury and outrage, noise and hurricane.

"The sixth species were made up of the ingredients which compose an ass, or a beast of burden. These are naturally exceeding slothful, but, upon the husband's exerting his authority, will live upon hard fare, and do every thing to please him. They are, however, far from being averse to venereal pleasure, and seldom refuse a male companion.

"The cat furnished materials for a seventh species of women, who are of a melancholy, froward, unamiable nature, and so repugnant to the offers of love, that they fly in the face of their husband when he approaches them with conjugal endearments. This species of women are likewise subject to little thefts, cheats, and pilferings.

"The mare with a flowing mane, which was never broke to any servile toil and labour, composed an eighth species of women. These are they who have little regard for their husbands; who pass away their time in dressing, bathing, and perfuming; who throw their hair into the nicest curls, and trick it up with the fairest flowers and garlands. A woman of this species is a very pretty thing for a stranger to look upon, but very detrimental to the owner, unless it be a king or a prince who takes a fancy to such a toy.

"The ninth species of females were taken out of the ape. These are such as are both ugly and ill-natured, who have nothing beautiful in themselves, and endeavour to detract from or ridicule every thing which appears so in others.

"The tenth and last species of women were made out of the bee; and happy is the man who gets such an one for his wife. She is altogether faultless and unblameable. Her family flourishes and improves by her good management. She loves her husband, and is beloved by him. She brings him a race of beautiful and virtuous children. She distinguishes herself among her sex. She is surrounded with graces. She never sits among the loose tribe of women, nor passes away her time with them in wanton discourses. She is full of virtue and prudence, and is the best wife that Jupiter can bestow on man."

I shall conclude these iambics with the motto of this paper, which is a fragment of the same author: "A man cannot possess any thing that is better than a good woman, nor any thing that is worse than a bad one."

As the poet has shown great penetration in this diversity of female characters, he has avoided the fault which Juvenal and Monsieur

Boileau are guilty of, the former in his sixth, and the other in his last satire, where they have endeavoured to expose the sex in general, without doing justice to the valuable part of it. Such levelling satires are of no use to the world; and for this reason I have often wondered how the French author, above-mentioned, who was a man of exquisite judgment, and a lover of virtue, could think human nature a proper subject for satire in another of his celebrated pieces, which is called The Satire upon Man. What vice or frailty can a discourse correct which censures the whole species alike, and endeavours to show, by some superficial strokes of wit, that brutes are the more excellent creatures of the two? A satire should expose nothing but what is corrigible, and make a due discrimination between those who are, and those who are not the proper object of it. L.

ON EDUCATION

No. 215.] TUESDAY, NOVEMBER 6, 1711. [ADDISON.]

— Ingenuas didicisse fideliter artes
Emollit mores, nec sinit esse feros.—OVID.

I CONSIDER an human soul without education, like marble in the quarry, which shows none of its inherent beauties, till the skill of the polisher fetches out the colours, makes the surface shine, and discovers every ornamental cloud, spot, and vein, that runs through the body of it. Education, after the same manner, when it works upon a noble mind, draws out to view every latent virtue and perfection, which without such helps are never able to make their appearance.

If my reader will give me leave to change the allusion so soon upon him, I shall make use of the same instance to illustrate the force of education, which Aristotle has brought to explain his doctrine of substantial forms, when he tells us that a statue lies hid in a block of marble; and that the art of the statuary only clears away the superfluous matter, and removes the rubbish. The figure is in the stone, the sculptor only finds it. What sculpture is to a block of marble, education is to an human soul. The philosopher, the saint, or the hero, the wise, the good, or the great man, very often lie hid and concealed in a plebeian, which a proper education might have disinterred, and have brought to light. I am, therefore, much delighted with reading the accounts of savage nations, and with contemplating those virtues which are wild and uncultivated; to see courage exerting itself in fierceness, resolution in obstinacy, wisdom in cunning, patience in sullenness and despair.

Men's passions operate variously, and appear in different kinds of actions, according as they are more or less rectified and swayed by reason. When one hears of negroes, who, upon the death of their masters, or upon changing their service, hang themselves upon the next tree, as it frequently happens in our American plantations, who can forbear admiring their fidelity, though it expresses itself in so dreadful a manner? What might not that savage greatness of soul, which appears in these poor wretches, on many occasions, be raised to, were it rightly cultivated? And what colour of excuse can there be for the contempt with which we treat this part of our species, that we should not put them upon the common foot of humanity, that we should only set an insignificant fine upon the man who murders them; nay, that we should, as much as in us lies, cut them off from the prospect of happiness in another world, as well as in this, and deny them that which we look upon as the proper means for attaining it?

Since I am engaged on this subject, I cannot forbear mentioning a story which I have lately heard, and which is so well attested, that I have no manner of reason to suspect the truth of it: I may call it a kind of wild tragedy that passed about twelve years ago at St. Christopher's, one of our British Leeward Islands. The negroes who were concerned in it were all of them the slaves of a gentleman who is now in England.

This gentleman, among his negroes, had a young woman, who was looked upon as a most extraordinary beauty by those of her own complexion. He had at the same time two young fellows, who were likewise negroes and slaves, remarkable for the comeliness of their persons, and for the friendship which they bore to one another. It unfortunately happened that both of them fell in love with the female negro above-mentioned, who would have been very glad to have taken either of them for her husband, provided they could agree between themselves which should be the man. But they were both so passionately in love with her, that neither of them could think of giving her up to his rival; and at the same time were so true to one another, that neither of them would think of gaining her without his friend's consent. The torments of these two lovers were the discourse of the family to which they belonged, who could not forbear observing the strange complication of passions which perplexed the hearts of the poor negroes, that often dropped expressions of the uneasiness they underwent, and how impossible it was for either of them ever to be happy.

After a long struggle between love and friendship, truth and jealousy, they one day took a walk together into a wood, carrying their mistress along with them; where, after abundance of lamentations, they stabbed her to the heart, of which she immediately died. A slave, who was at his work not far from the place where this astonishing piece of cruelty was committed, hearing the shrieks of the dying person, ran to see what was the occasion of them. He there discovered the woman lying dead upon the ground, with the two negroes on each side of her kissing the dead corpse, weeping over it, and beating their breasts in the utmost agonies of grief and despair. He immediately ran to the English family with the news of what he had seen; who, upon coming to the place, saw the woman dead, and the two negroes expiring by her with wounds they had given themselves.

We see in this amazing instance of barbarity, what strange disorders are bred in the minds of those men whose passions are not regulated by virtue, and disciplined by reason. Though the action which I have recited is in itself full of guilt and horror, it proceeded from a temper of mind which might have produced very noble fruits, had it been formed and guided by a suitable education.

It is, therefore, an unspeakable blessing to be born in those parts of the world where wisdom and knowledge flourish; though it must be confessed, there are, even in these parts, several poor uninstructed persons, who are but little above the inhabitants of those nations of which I have been here speaking; as those who have had the advantages of a more liberal education, rise above one another by several different degrees of perfection. For, to return to our statue in the block of marble, we see it sometimes only begun to be chipped, sometimes rough-hewn, and but just sketched into an human figure; sometimes we see the man appearing distinctly in all his limbs and features, sometimes we find the figure wrought up to a great elegancy, but seldom meet with any to which the hand of a Phidias or a Praxiteles could not give several nice touches and finishings.

THE SPECTATOR

Discourses of morality, and reflections upon human nature, are the best means we can make use of to improve our minds, and gain a true knowledge of ourselves, and consequently to recover our souls out of the vice, ignorance, and prejudice, which naturally cleave to them. I have all along professed myself in this paper a promoter of these great ends; and I flatter myself that I do from day to day contribute something to the polishing of men's minds; at least my design is laudable, whatever the execution may be. I must confess I am not a little encouraged in it by many letters which I receive from unknown hands, in approbation of my endeavours; and must take this opportunity of returning my thanks to those who write them, and excusing myself for not inserting several of them in my papers, which I am sensible would be a very great ornament to them. Should I publish the praises which are so well penned, they would do honour to the persons who write them; but my publishing of them would, I fear, be a sufficient instance to the world, that I did not deserve them.

THE CRIES OF LONDON

No. 251.] TUESDAY, DECEMBER 18, 1711. [ADDISON.]

— Linguæ centum sunt, oraque centum,
Ferrea vox. VIRG. ÆN. vi. 625.

A hundred mouths, a hundred tongues,
And throats of brass inspir'd with iron lungs.

THERE is nothing which more astonishes a foreigner, and frights a country squire, than the Cries of London. My good friend Sir Roger often declares that he cannot get them out of his head, or go to sleep for them, the first week that he is in town. On the contrary, Will Honeycomb calls them the *Ramage de la Ville*, and prefers them to the sounds of larks and nightingales, with all the music of the fields and woods. I have lately received a letter from some very odd fellow upon this subject, which I shall leave with my reader, without saying any thing farther of it.

THE SPECTATOR

"SIR, — I am a man out of all business, and would willingly turn my hand to any thing for an honest livelihood. I have invented several projects for raising many millions of money without burdening the subject, but I cannot get the parliament to listen to me, who look upon me, forsooth, as a crack and a projector; so that, despairing to enrich either myself or my country by this public-spiritedness, I would make some proposals to you relating to a design which I have very much at heart, and which may procure me a handsome subsistence, if you will be pleased to recommend it to the cities of London and Westminster.

"The post I would aim at, is to be Comptroller-General of the London Cries, which are at present under no manner of rules and discipline. I think I am pretty well qualified for this place, as being a man of very strong lungs, of great insight into all the branches of our British trades and manufactures, and of a competent skill in music.

"The Cries of London may be divided into vocal and instrumental. As for the latter, they are at present under a very great disorder. A freeman of London has the privilege of disturbing a whole street for an hour together, with the twanking of a brass kettle or frying-pan. The watchman's thump at midnight startles us in our beds, as much as the breaking in of a thief. The sowgelder's horn has indeed something musical in it, but this is seldom heard within the liberties. I would therefore propose, that no instrument of this nature should be made use of, which I have not tuned and licensed, after having carefully examined in what manner it may affect the ears of her Majesty's liege subjects.

"Vocal cries are of a much larger extent, and indeed so full of incongruities and barbarisms, that we appear a distracted city to foreigners, who do not comprehend the meaning of such enormous outcries. Milk is generally sold in a note above E-la, and in sounds so exceeding shrill, that it often sets our teeth on edge. The chimney-sweeper is confined to no certain pitch; he sometimes utters himself in the deepest base, and sometimes in the sharpest treble; sometimes in the highest, and sometimes in the lowest note of the gamut. The same observation might be made on the retailers of small-coal, not to mention broken glasses or brick-dust. In these, therefore, and the like cases, it should be my care to sweeten and mellow the voices of these itinerant tradesmen, before they make their appearance in our streets, as also to accommodate their cries to their respective wares: and to take care in particular, that those may not make the most noise who have the least to sell, which is very observable in the vendors of card-matches, to whom I cannot but apply the old proverb of 'Much cry but little wool.'

"Some of these last-mentioned musicians are so very loud in the sale of these trifling manufactures, that an honest splenetic gentleman of my acquaintance bargained with one of them never to come into the street where he lived. But what was the effect of this contract? Why, the whole tribe of card match-makers, which frequent that quarter, passed by his door the very next day, in hopes of being bought off after the same manner.

"It is another great imperfection in our London Cries, that there is no just time nor measure observed in them. Our news should indeed be published in a very quick time, because it is a commodity that will not keep cold. It should not, however, be cried with the same precipitation as fire. Yet this is generally the case. A bloody battle alarms the town from one end to another in an instant. Every motion of the French is published in so great a hurry, that one would think the enemy were at our gates. This likewise I would take upon me to regulate in such a manner, that there should be some distinction made between the spreading of a victory, a march, or an encampment, a Dutch, a Portugal, or a Spanish mail. Nor must I omit under this head those excessive alarms with which several boisterous rustics infest our streets in turnip-season; and which are more inexcusable, because these are wares which are in no danger of cooling upon their hands.

"There are others who affect a very slow time, and are in my opinion much more tuneable than the former. The cooper in particular swells his last note in an hollow voice, that is not without its harmony; nor can I forbear being inspired with a most agreeable melancholy, when I hear that sad and solemn air with which the public are very often asked, if they have any chairs to mend? Your own memory may suggest to you many other lamentable ditties of the same nature, in which the music is wonderfully languishing and melodious.

"I am always pleased with that particular time of the year which is proper for the pickling of dill and cucumbers; but, alas! this cry, like the song of the nightingale, is not heard above two months. It would therefore be worth while to consider, whether the same air might not in some cases be adapted to other words.

The Enraged Musician.

THE SPECTATOR

"It might likewise deserve our most serious consideration, how far, in a well-regulated city, those humourists are to be tolerated, who, not contented with the traditional cries of their forefathers, have invented particular songs and tunes of their own; such as was, not many years since, the pastryman, commonly known by the name of the Colly-Molly-Puff; and such as is at this day the vendor of powder and wash-balls, who, if I am rightly informed, goes under the name of Powder-Wat.

"I must not here omit one particular absurdity which runs through this whole vociferous generation, and which renders their cries very often not only incommodious, but altogether useless to the public. I mean that idle accomplishment, which they all of them aim at, of crying so as not to be understood. Whether or not they have learned this from several of our affected singers, I will not take upon me to say; but most certain it is, that people know the wares they deal in rather by their tunes than by their words; insomuch that I have sometimes seen a country boy run out to buy apples of a bellows mender, and ginger-bread from a grinder of knives and scissors. Nay, so strangely infatuated are some very eminent artists of this particular grace in a cry, that none but their acquaintance are able to guess at their profession; for who else can know, that 'work if I had it,' should be the signification of a corn-cutter.

"Forasmuch, therefore, as persons of this rank are seldom men of genius or capacity, I think it would be proper that some man of good sense and profound judgment should preside over these public cries, who should permit none to lift up their voices in our streets, that have not tuneable throats, and are not only able to overcome the noise of the crowd, and the rattling of coaches, but also to vend their respective merchandizes in apt phrases, and in the most distinct and agreeable sounds. I do therefore humbly recommend myself as a person rightly qualified for this post; and, if I meet with fitting encouragement, shall communicate some other projects which I have by me, that may no less conduce to the emolument of the public.

"I am, Sir, &c.·

C.   "RALPH CROTCHET."

THE SPECTATOR

THE SPECTATOR'S SUCCESS

No. 262.] MONDAY, DECEMBER 31, 1711. [ADDISON.]

Nulla venenato littera mista joco est.— OVID.

I THINK myself highly obliged to the public for their kind acceptance of a paper which visits them every morning, and has in it none of those seasonings that recommend so many of the writings which are in vogue among us.

As, on the one side, my paper has not in it a single word of news, a reflection in politics, nor a stroke of party; so, on the other, there are no fashionable touches of infidelity, no obscene ideas, no satires upon priesthood, marriage, and the like popular topics of ridicule; no private scandal, nor anything that may tend to the defamation of particular persons, families, or societies.

There is not one of these above-mentioned subjects that would not sell a very indifferent paper, could I think of gratifying the public by such mean and base methods; but, notwithstanding I have rejected everything that savours of party, everything that is loose and immoral, and everything that might create uneasiness in the minds of particular persons, I find that the demand of my papers has increased every month since their first appearance in the world. This does not, perhaps, reflect so much honour upon myself, as on my readers, who give a much greater attention to discourses of virtue and morality, than ever I expected, or indeed could hope.

When I broke loose from that great body of writers who have employed their wit and parts in propagating of vice and irreligion, I did not question but I should be treated as an odd kind of fellow that had a mind to appear singular in my way of writing: but the general reception I have found, convinces me that the world is not so corrupt as we are apt to imagine; and that if those men of parts who have been employed in vitiating the age had endeavoured to rectify and amend it, they needed not have sacrificed their good sense and virtue to their fame and reputation. No man is so sunk in vice and ignorance, but there are still some hidden seeds of goodness and knowledge in him; which give him a relish of such reflections and speculations as have an aptness to improve the mind, and to make the heart better.

THE SPECTATOR

I have shown in a former paper, with how much care I have avoided all such thoughts as are loose, obscene, or immoral; and I believe my reader would still think the better of me, if he knew the pains I am at in qualifying what I write after such a manner, that nothing may be interpreted as aimed at private persons. For this reason, when I draw any faulty character, I consider all those persons to whom the malice of the world may possibly apply it, and take care to dash it with such particular circumstances as may prevent all such ill-natured applications. If I write anything on a black man, I run over in my mind all the eminent persons in the nation who are of that complexion: when I place an imaginary name at the head of a character, I examine every syllable and letter of it, that it may not bear any resemblance to one that is real. I know very well the value which every man sets upon his reputation, and how painful it is to be exposed to the mirth and derision of the public, and should therefore scorn to divert my reader at the expense of any private man.

As I have been thus tender of every particular person's reputation, so I have taken more than ordinary care not to give offence to those who appear in the higher figures of life. I would not make myself merry even with a piece of pasteboard that is invested with a public character; for which reason I have never glanced upon the late designed procession of his Holiness and his attendants, notwithstanding it might have afforded matter to many ludicrous speculations. Among those advantages which the public may reap from this paper, it is not the least, that it draws men's minds off from the bitterness of party, and furnishes them with subjects of discourse that may be treated without warmth or passion. This is said to have been the first design of those gentlemen who set on foot the Royal Society; and had then a very good effect, as it turned many of the greatest geniuses of that age to the disquisitions of natural knowledge, who, if they had engaged in politics with the same parts and application, might have set their country in a flame. The air-pump, the barometer, the quadrant, and the like inventions, were thrown out to those busy spirits, as tubs and barrels are to a whale, that he may let the ship sail on without disturbance, while he diverts himself with those innocent amusements.

I have been so very scrupulous in this particular of not hurting any man's reputation, that I have forborne mentioning even such

authors as I could not name with honour. This I must confess to
have been a piece of very great self-denial: for as the public relishes
nothing better than the ridicule which turns upon a writer of any
eminence, so there is nothing which a man that has but a very ordinary talent in ridicule may execute with greater ease. One might
raise laughter for a quarter of a year together upon the works of a
person who has published but a very few volumes. For which
reason I am astonished, that those who have appeared against this
paper have made so very little of it. The criticisms which I have
hitherto published, have been made with an intention rather to discover beauties and excellencies in the writers of my own time, than to
publish any of their faults and imperfections. In the mean while,
I should take if for a very great favour from some of my underhand
detractors, it they would break all measures with me so far, as to
give me a pretence for examining their performances with an impartial eye; nor shall I look upon it as a breach of charity to criticise the author, so long as I keep clear of the person.

In the mean while, till I am provoked to such hostilities, I shall from
time to time endeavour to do justice to those who have distinguished
themselves in the politer parts of learning, and to point out such
beauties in their works as may have escaped the observation of others.

As the first place among our English poets is due to Milton, and
as I have drawn more quotations out of him than from any other, I
shall enter into a regular criticism upon his Paradise Lost, which I
shall publish every Saturday, till I have given my thoughts upon
that poem. I shall not, however, presume to impose upon others my
own particular judgment on this author, but only deliver it as my
private opinion. Criticism is of a large extent, and every particular master in this art has his favourite passages in an author, which
do not equally strike the best judges. It will be sufficient for me
if I discover many beauties or imperfections which others have not
attended to, and I should be very glad to see any of our eminent
writers publish their discoveries on the same subject. In short, I
would always be understood to write my papers of criticism in the
spirit which Horace has expressed in those famous lines;

— Si quid novisti rectius istis,
Candidus imperti; si non, his utere mecum.

If you have made any better remarks of your own, communicate
them with candour; if not, make use of these I present you with.

THE SPECTATOR

PIN-MONEY

No. 295.] THURSDAY, FEBRUARY 7, 1711-12. [ADDISON.]

>Prodiga non sentit pereuntem fœmina censum:
>At velut exhaustâ redivivus pullulet arcâ
>Nummus, et è pleno semper tollatur acervo,
>Non unquam reputat quanti sibi gaudia constent.—Juv.

"MR. SPECTATOR,—I am turned of my great climacteric, and am naturally a man of a meek temper. About a dozen years ago I was married, for my sins, to a young woman of a good family, and of an high spirit; but could not bring her to close with me, before I had entered into a treaty with her longer than that of the grand alliance. Among other articles, it was therein stipulated that she should have £400 a year for pin money, which I obliged myself to pay quarterly into the hands of one who acted as her plenipotentiary in that affair. I have ever since religiously observed my part in this solemn agreement. Now, sir, so it is, that the lady has had several children since I married her; to which, if I should credit our malicious neighbours, her pin-money has not a little contributed. The education of these my children, who, contrary to my expectation, are born to me every year, straitens me so much, that I have begged their mother to free me from the obligation of the above-mentioned pin-money, that it may go towards making a provision for her family. This proposal makes her noble blood swell in her veins, insomuch that finding me a little tardy in her last quarter's payment, she threatens me every day to arrest me; and proceeds so far as to tell me, that if I do not do her justice, I shall die in a jail. To this she adds, when her passion will let her argue calmly, that she has several play-debts on her hand, which must be discharged very suddenly, and that she cannot lose her money as becomes a woman of her fashion, if she makes me any abatements in this article. I hope, sir, you will take an occasion from hence to give your opinion upon a subject which you have not yet touched, and inform us if there are any precedents for this usage among our ancestors; or whether you find any mention of pin-money in Grotius, Puffendorf, or any other of the civilians.

"I am ever the humblest of your admirers,
JOSIAH FRIBBLE, Esq."

THE SPECTATOR

As there is no man living who is a more professed advocate for the fair sex than myself, so there is none that would be more unwilling to invade any of their ancient rights and privileges; but as the doctrine of pin-money is of a very late date, unknown to our great-grandmothers, and not yet received by many of our modern ladies, I think it is for the interest of both sexes to keep it from spreading.

Mr. Fribble may not, perhaps, be much mistaken where he intimates, that the supplying a man's wife with pin money, is furnishing her with arms against himself, and in a manner becoming accessory to his own dishonour. We may, indeed, generally observe, that in proportion as a woman is more or less beautiful, and her husband advanced in years, she stands in need of a greater or less number of pins, and upon a treaty of marriage rises or falls in her demands accordingly. It must likewise be owned, that high quality in a mistress does very much inflame this article in the marriage reckoning.

But where the age and circumstances of both parties are pretty much upon a level, I cannot but think the insisting upon pin-money is very extraordinary; and yet we find several matches broken off upon this very head. What would a foreigner, or one who is a stranger to this practice, think of a lover that forsakes his mistress, because he is not willing to keep her in pins; but what would he think of the mistress, should he be informed that she asks five or six hundred pounds a year for this use? Should a man unacquainted with our customs be told the sums which are allowed in Great Britain, under the title of pin-money, what a prodigious consumption of pins would he think there was in this island! "A pin a day (says our frugal proverb) is a great a year;" so that according to this calculation, my friend Fribble's wife must every year make use of eight millions six hundred and forty thousand new pins.

I am not ignorant that our British ladies allege they comprehend under this general term several other conveniences of life; I could therefore wish, for the honour of my country-women, that they had rather called it needle-money, which might have implied something of good-housewifery, and not have given the malicious world occasion to think, that dress and trifle have always the uppermost place in a woman's thoughts.

I know several of my fair readers urge, in defence of this practice, that it is but a necessary provision to make for themselves, in case their husband proves a churl or a miser; so that they consider this allowance as a kind of alimony, which they may lay their claim to without actually separating from their husbands. But with submission, I think a woman who will give up herself to a man in marriage, where there is the least room for such an apprehension, and trust her person to one whom she will not rely on for the common necessaries of life, may very properly be accused (in the phrase of an homely proverb) of being "penny wise and pound foolish."

It is observed of over-cautious generals, that they never engage in a battle without securing a retreat, in case the event should not answer their expectations; on the other hand, the greatest conquerors have burnt their ships, and broke down the bridges behind them, as being determined either to succeed or die in the engagement. In the same manner I should very much suspect a woman who takes such precautions for her retreat, and contrives methods how she may live happily, without the affection of one to whom she joins herself for life. Separate purses between man and wife, are, in my opinion, as unnatural as separate beds. A marriage cannot be happy, where the pleasures, inclinations, and interests of both parties are not the same. There is no greater incitement to love in the mind of man, than the sense of a person's depending upon him for her ease and happiness; as a woman uses all her endeavours to please the person whom she looks upon as her honour, her comfort, and her support.

For this reason I am not very much surprised at the behaviour of a rough country squire, who, being not a little shocked at the proceeding of a young widow that would not recede from her demands of pin-money, was so enraged at her mercenary temper, that he told her in great wrath, "As much as she thought him her slave, he would show all the world he did not care a pin for her." Upon which he flew out of the room, and never saw her more.

Socrates, in Plato's Alcibiades, says, he was informed by one, who had travelled through Persia, that as he passed over a tract of lands and inquired what the name of the place was, they told him it was the queen's girdle; to which he adds, that another wide field which lay by it was called the queen's veil, and that in the same manner there was a large portion of ground set aside for every part of her Majesty's dress. These lands might not be improperly called the Queen of Persia's pin-money.

I remember my friend Sir Roger, who I dare say never read this passage in Plato, told me some time since, that upon his courting the perverse widow, (of whom I have given an account in former papers), he had disposed of an hundred acres in a diamond-ring, which he would have presented her with, had she thought fit to accept it; and that upon her wedding-day she should have carried on her head fifty of the tallest oaks upon his estate. He further informed me that he would have given her a coal-pit to keep her in clean linen, that he would have allowed her the profits of a wind-mill for her fans, and have presented her, once in three years, with the shearing of his sheep for her under-petticoats. To which the knight always adds, that though he did not care for fine clothes himself, there should not have been a woman in the country better dressed than my lady Coverley. Sir Roger, perhaps, may in this, as well as in many other of his devices, appear something odd and singular, but if the humour of pin-money prevails, I think it would be very proper for every gentleman of an estate to mark out so many acres of it under the title of The Pins.

LETTER FROM SIR JOHN ENVIL

No. 299.] TUESDAY, FEBRUARY 12, 1711–12. [ADDISON.]

> Malo Venusinam, quam te, Cornelia, mater
> Gracchorum, si cum magnis virtutibus affers
> Grande supercilium, et numeras in dote triumphos.
> Tolle tuum precor Annibalem victumque Syphacem
> In castris, et cum totâ Carthagine migra.—JUV.

IT is observed, that a man improves more by reading the story of a person eminent for prudence and virtue, than by the finest rules and precepts of morality. In the same manner a representation of those calamities and misfortunes which a weak man suffers from wrong measures and ill-concerted schemes of life, is apt to make a deeper impression upon our minds, than the wisest maxims and instructions that can be given us for avoiding the like follies and indiscretions in our own private conduct. It is for this reason that I lay before my reader the following letter, and leave it with him to make his own use of it, without adding any reflections of my own upon the subject-matter.

THE SPECTATOR

"Mr. Spectator,—Having carefully perused a letter sent you by Josiah Fribble, Esq., with your subsequent discourse upon pin money, I do presume to trouble you with an account of my own case, which I look upon to be no less deplorable than that of Squire Fribble. I am a person of no extraction, having begun the world with a small parcel of rusty iron, and was for some years commonly known by the name of Jack Anvil. I have naturally a very happy genius for getting money, insomuch that by the age of five and twenty, I had scraped together four thousand two hundred pounds, five shillings, and a few odd pence. I then launched out into considerable business, and became a bold trader both by sea and land, which in a few years raised me a very considerable fortune. For these my good services I was knighted in the thirty-fifth year of my age, and lived with great dignity among my city neighbours by the name of Sir John Anvil. Being in my temper very ambitious, I was now bent upon making a family, and accordingly resolved that my descendants should have a dash of good blood in their veins. In order to this I made love to the Lady Mary Oddly, an indigent young woman of quality. To cut short the marriage treaty, I threw her a *charte blanche*, as our newspapers call it, desiring her to write upon it her own terms. She was very concise in her demands, insisting only that the disposal of my fortune, and the regulation of my family, should be entirely in her hands. Her father and brothers appeared exceedingly averse to this match, and would not see me for some time; but at present are so well reconciled, that they dine with me almost every day, and have borrowed considerable sums of me; which my Lady Mary very often twits me with, when she would show me how kind her relations are to me. She had no portion, as I told you before, but what she wanted in fortune she makes up in spirit. She at first changed my name to Sir John Envil, and at present writes herself Mary Enville. I have had some children by her, whom she has christened with the surnames of her family, in order, as she tells me, to wear out the homeliness of their parentage by the father's side. Our eldest son is the Honourable Oddly Enville, Esq., and our eldest daughter, Harriot Enville. Upon her first coming into my family, she turned off a parcel of very careful servants, who had been long with me, and introduced in their stead a couple of Blackamoors, and three or four very genteel fellows in laced liveries, besides her French woman, who is perpetually making a noise in the house in a language which nobody understands, except my Lady Mary. She next set herself to reform every room of my house, having glazed all my chimney-pieces with looking-glass, and planted every corner with such heaps of china, that I am obliged to move about my own house with the greatest caution and circumspection, for fear of hurting some of our brittle furniture. She makes an illumination once a week with wax-candles in one of the largest rooms, in order, as she phrases it, to see company. At which time she always desires me to be abroad, or to confine myself to the cock-loft, that I may not disgrace her among her visitants of quality. Her footmen, as I told you before, are such beaus, that I do not much care for asking them questions; when I do, they answer me with a saucy frown, and say that everything, which I find fault with, was done by my Lady Mary's order. She tells me that she intends they shall wear swords with their next liveries, having lately observed the footmen of two or three persons of quality hanging behind the coach with swords by their sides. As soon as the first honey-moon was over, I represented to her the unreasonableness of those daily innovations which she made in my family; but she told me I was no longer to consider myself as Sir John Anvil, but as her husband; and added with a frown, that I did not seem to know who she was. I was surprised to be treated thus, after such familiarities as had passed between us. But she has since given me to know, that whatever freedoms she may sometimes indulge me in, she expects in general to be treated with the respect that is due to her birth and quality. Our children have been trained up from their infancy with so many accounts of their mother's family, that they know the stories of all the great men and women it had produced. Their mother tells them, that such an one commanded in such a sea engagement, that their great-grandfather had a horse shot under him at Edgehill, that their uncle was at the siege of Buda, and that her mother danced in a ball at court with the Duke of Monmouth; with abundance of fiddle-faddle of the same nature. I was, the other day, a little out of countenance at a question of my little daughter Harriot, who asked me, with a great deal of innocence, why I never told them of the generals and admirals that had been in *my* family. As for my eldest son Oddly, he has been so spirited up by his mother, that if he does not mend his manners I shall go near to disinherit him. He drew his sword upon me before he was nine years old, and told me, that he expected to be used like a gentleman; upon my offering to correct him for his insolence, my Lady Mary stept in between us, and told me, that I ought to consider there was some difference between his mother and mine. She is perpetually finding out the features of her own relations in every one of my children, though, by the way, I have a little chub-faced boy as like me as he can stare, if I durst say so; but what most angers me, when she sees me playing with any of them upon my knee, she has begged me more than once to converse with the children as little as possible, that they may not learn any of my awkward tricks.

"You must further know, since I am opening my heart to you, that she thinks herself my superior in sense, as much as she is in quality, and therefore treats me like a plain well-meaning man, who does not know the world. She dictates to me in my own business, sets me right in a point of trade, and if I disagree with her about any of my ships at sea, wonders that I will dispute with her, when I know very well that her great-grandfather was a flag officer.

"To complete my sufferings, she has teased me for this quarter of a year last past, to remove into one of the Squares at the other end of the town, promising, for my encouragement, that I shall have as good a cock-loft as any gentleman in the Square: to which the Honourable Oddly Enville, Esq. always adds, like a jack-a-napes as he is, that he hopes it will be as near the court as possible.

"In short, MR. SPECTATOR, I am so much out of my natural element, that to recover my old way of life I would be content to begin the world again, and be plain Jack Anvil; but alas! I am in for life, and am bound to subscribe myself, with great sorrow of heart,

"Your humble servant,

JOHN ENVILLE, Knt."

THE SPECTATOR

ON WASTE OF TIME

No. 317.] TUESDAY, MARCH 4, 1711-12. [ADDISON.]

— Fruges consumere nati.

HOR. 1 Ep. ii. 27.

— Born to drink and eat.

AUGUSTUS, a few moments before his death, asked his friends who stood about him, if they thought he had acted his part well; and upon receiving such an answer as was due to his extraordinary merit, "Let me then," says he, "go off the stage with your applause"; using the expression with which the Roman actors made their exit at the conclusion of a dramatic piece. I could wish that men, while they are in health, would consider well the nature of the part they are engaged in, and what figure it will make in the minds of those they leave behind them: whether it was worth coming into the world for: whether it be suitable to a reasonable being; in short, whether it appears graceful in this life, or will turn to an advantage in the next. Let the sycophant or buffoon, the satirist or the good companion, consider with himself, when his body shall be laid in the grave and his soul pass into another state of existence, how much it would redound to his praise to have it said of him, that no man in England ate better, that he had an admirable talent at turning his friend into ridicule, that nobody outdid him at an ill-natured jest, or that he never went to bed before he had dispatched his third bottle. These are, however, very common funeral orations, and eulogiums on deceased persons who have acted among mankind with some figure and reputation.

But if we look into the bulk of our species, they are such as are not likely to be remembered a moment after their disappearance. They leave behind them no traces of their existence, but are forgotten as though they had never been. They are neither wanted by the poor, regretted by the rich, nor celebrated by the learned. They are neither missed in the commonwealth, nor lamented by private persons. Their actions are of no significancy to mankind, and might have been performed by creatures of much less dignity than those who are distinguished by the faculty of reason. An

THE SPECTATOR

eminent French author speaks somewhere to the following purpose: I have often seen from my chamber window two noble creatures, both of them of an erect countenance and endowed with reason. These two intellectual beings are employed from morning to night, in rubbing two smooth stones one upon another; that is, as the vulgar phrase it, in polishing marble.

My friend, Sir Andrew Freeport, as we were sitting in the club last night, gave us an account of a sober citizen who died a few days since. This honest man, being of greater consequence in his own thoughts than in the eye of the world, had for some years past kept a journal of his life. Sir Andrew showed us one week of it. Since the occurrences set down in it mark out such a road of action as that I have been speaking of, I shall present my reader with a faithful copy of it; after having first informed him, that the deceased person had in his youth been bred to trade, but finding himself not so well turned for business, he had for several years last past lived altogether upon a moderate annuity.

MONDAY, eight o'clock. I put on my clothes, and walked into the parlour.

Nine o'clock ditto. Tied my knee-strings, and washed my hands.

Hours, ten, eleven, and twelve. Smoked three pipes of Virginia. Read the Supplement and Daily Courant. Things go ill in the north. Mr. Nisby's opinion thereupon.

One o'clock in the afternoon. Chid Ralph for mislaying mv tobacco-box.

Two o'clock. Sat down to dinner. Mem. Too many plums and no suet.

From three to four took my afternoon's nap.

From four to six. Walked into the fields. Wind S.S.E.

From six to ten. At the club. Mr. Nisby's opinion about the peace.

Ten o'clock. Went to bed, slept sound.

TUESDAY, being holiday, eight o'clock. Rose as usual.

Nine o'clock. Washed hands and face, shaved, put on my double-soaled shoes.

Ten, eleven, twelve. Took a walk to Islington.

One. Took a pot of Mother Cob's mild.

Between two and three. Returned, dined on a knuckle of veal and bacon. Mem. Sprouts wanting.

Three. Nap as usual.

From four to six. Coffee-house. Read the news. A dish of twist. Grand visier strangled.

From six to ten. At the club. Mr. Nisby's account of the Great Turk.

Ten. Dream of the grand visier. Broken sleep.

WEDNESDAY, eight o'clock. Tongue of my shoe-buckle broke. Hands but not face.

Nine. Paid off the butcher's bill. Mem. To be allowed for the last leg of mutton.

Ten, eleven. At the coffee-house. More work in the north. Stranger in a black wig asked me how stocks went.

From twelve to one. Walked in the fields. Wind to the south.

From one to two. Smoked a pipe and a half.

Two. Dined as usual. Stomach good.

Three. Nap broke by the falling of a pewter dish. Mem. Cook-maid in love, and grown careless.

From four to six. At the coffee-house. Advice from Smyrna that the grand visier was first of all strangled, and afterwards beheaded.

Six o'clock in the evening. Was half an hour in the club before anybody else came. Mr. Nisby of opinion that the grand visier was not strangled the sixth instant.

Ten at night. Went to bed. Slept without waking till nine the next morning.

THURSDAY, nine o'clock. Staid within till two o'clock for Sir Timothy; who did not bring me my annuity according to his promise.

Two in the afternoon. Sat down to dinner. Loss of appetite. Small-beer sour. Beef overcorned.

Three. Could not take my nap.

Four and five. Gave Ralph a box on the ear. Turned off my cook-maid. Sent a messenger to Sir Timothy. Mem. I did not go to the club to-night. Went to bed at nine o'clock.

FRIDAY. Passed the morning in meditation upon Sir Timothy, who was with me a quarter before twelve.

THE SPECTATOR

Twelve o'clock. Bought a new head to my cane, and a tongue to my buckle. Drank a glass of purl to recover appetite.

Two and three. Dined and slept well.

From four to six. Went to the coffee-house. Met Mr. Nisby there. Smoked several pipes. Mr. Nisby of opinion that laced coffee is bad for the head.

Six o'clock. At the club as steward. Sat late.

Twelve o'clock. Went to bed, dreamt that I drank small-beer with the grand visier.

SATURDAY. Waked at eleven, walked in the fields, wind N.E.

Twelve. Caught in a shower.

One in the afternoon. Returned home and dried myself.

Two. Mr. Nisby dined with me. First course, marrow-bones; second, ox-cheek, with a bottle of Brooks and Hellier.

Three. Overslept myself.

Six. Went to the club. Like to have fallen into a gutter. Grand visier certainly dead, &c.

I question not but the reader will be surprised to find the above-mentioned journalist taking so much care of a life that was filled with such inconsiderable actions, and received so very small improvements, and yet if we look into the behaviour of many whom we daily converse with, we shall find that most of their hours are taken up in those three important articles of eating, drinking, and sleeping. I do not suppose that a man loses his time, who is not engaged in public affairs or in an illustrious course of action. On the contrary, I believe our hours may very often be more profitably laid out in such transactions as make no figure in the world, than in such as are apt to draw upon them the attention of mankind. One may become wiser and better by several methods of employing one's self in secrecy and silence, and do what is laudable without noise or ostentation. I would, however, recommend to every one of my readers, the keeping a journal of their lives for one week, and setting down punctually their whole series of employments during that space of time. This kind of self-examination, would give them a true state of themselves, and incline them to consider seriously what they are about. One would rectify the omissions of another, and make a man weigh all those indifferent actions, which, though they are easily forgotten, must certainly be accounted for.   L.

THE SPECTATOR

A YOUNG LADY'S JOURNAL OF A WEEK
No. 323.]   TUESDAY, MARCH 11, 1711–12.   [ADDISON.]

— Modo vir, modo fœmina.—VIRG.

THE journal with which I presented my reader on Tuesday last, has brought me in several letters, with accounts of many private lives cast into that form. I have the Rake's Journal, the Sot's Journal, the Whoremaster's Journal, and among several others a very curious piece, entitled, "The Journal of a Mohock." By these instances I find that the intention of my last Tuesday's paper has been mistaken by many of my readers. I did not design so much to expose vice as idleness, and aimed at those persons who pass away their time rather in trifles and impertinence, than in crimes and immoralities. Offences of this latter kind are not to be dallied with, or treated in so ludicrous a manner. In short, my journal only holds up folly to the light, and shows the disagreeableness of such actions as are indifferent in themselves, and blameable only as they proceed from creatures endowed with reason.

My following correspondent, who calls herself Clarinda, is such a journalist as I require: she seems by her letter to be placed in a modish state of indifference between vice and virtue, and to be susceptible of either, were there proper pains taken with her. Had her journal been filled with gallantries, or such occurrences as had shown her wholly divested of her natural innocence, notwithstanding it might have been more pleasing to the generality of readers, I should not have published it; but as it is only the picture of a life filled with a fashionable kind of gaiety and laziness, I shall set down five days of it, as I have received it from the hand of my correspondent.

"DEAR MR. SPECTATOR,— You having set your readers an exercise in one of your last week's papers, I have performed mine according to your orders, and herewith send it you enclosed. You must know, Mr. Spectator, that I am a maiden lady of a good fortune, who have had several matches offered me for these ten years last past, and have at present warm applications made to me by a very pretty fellow. As I am at my own disposal, I come up to town every winter, and pass my time in it after the manner

THE SPECTATOR

you will find in the following journal, which I began to write upon the very day after your Spectator upon that subject.

TUESDAY night. Could not go to sleep till one in the morning for thinking of my journal.

WEDNESDAY. From eight to ten. Drank two dishes of chocolate in bed, and fell asleep after them.

From ten to eleven. Eat a slice of bread and butter, drank a dish of bohea, read the Spectator.

From eleven to one. At my toilette, tried a new head. Gave orders for Veny to be combed and washed. Mem. I look best in blue.

From one till half an hour after two. Drove to the 'Change. Cheapened a couple of fans.

Till four. At dinner. Mem. Mr. Froth passed by in his new liveries.

From four to six. Dressed, paid a visit to old Lady Blithe and her sister, having before heard they were gone out of town that day.

From six to eleven. At Basset. Mem. Never set again upon the ace of diamonds.

THURSDAY. From eleven at night to eight in the morning. Dreamed that I punted to Mr. Froth.

From eight to ten. Chocolate. Read two acts in Aurenzebe a-bed.

From ten to eleven. Tea-table. Sent to borrow Lady Faddle's Cupid for Veny. Read the play-bills. Received a letter from Mr. Froth. Mem. Locked it up in my strong box.

Rest of the morning. Fontange, the tire-woman, her account of Lady Blithe's wash. Broke a tooth in my little tortoise-shell comb. Sent Frank to know how my Lady Hectick rested after her monkey's leaping out at the window. Looked pale. Fontagne tells me my glass is not true. Dressed by three.

From three to four. Dinner cold before I sat down.

From four to eleven. Saw company. Mr. Froth's opinion of Milton. His accounts of the Mohocks. His fancy for a pin-cushion. Picture in the lid of his snuff-box. Old Lady Faddle promises me her woman to cut my hair. Lost five guineas at crimp.

Twelve o'clock at night. Went to bed.

THE SPECTATOR

FRIDAY. Eight in the morning. A-bed. Read over all Mr. Froth's letters. Cupid and Veny.

Ten o'clock. Stayed within all day, not at home.

From ten to twelve. In conference with my mantua-maker. Sorted a suit of ribands. Broke my blue china cup.

From twelve to one. Shut myself up in my chamber, practised Lady Betty Modely's skuttle.

One in the afternoon. Called for my flowered handkerchief. Worked half a violet leaf in it. Eyes ached and head out of order. Threw by my work, and read over the remaining part of Aurenzebe.

From three to four. Dined.

From four to twelve. Changed my mind, dressed, went abroad, and played at crimp till midnight. Found Mrs. Spitely at home. Conversation: Mrs. Brillant's necklace false stones. Old Lady Loveday going to be married to a young fellow that is not worth a groat. Miss Prue gone into the country. Tom Townley has red hair. Mem. Mrs. Spitely whispered in my ear that she had something to tell me about Mr. Froth, I am sure it is not true.

Between twelve and one. Dreamed that Mr. Froth lay at my feet, and called me Indamora.

SATURDAY. Rose at eight o'clock in the morning. Sat down to my toilette.

From eight to nine. Shifted a patch for half an hour before I could determine it. Fixed it above my left eyebrow.

From nine to twelve. Drank my tea, and dressed.

From twelve to two. At chapel. A great deal of good company. Mem. The third air in the new opera. Lady Blithe dressed frightfully.

From three to four. Dined. Mrs. Kitty called upon me to go to the opera before I was risen from table.

From dinner to six. Drank tea. Turned off a footman for being rude to Veny.

Six o'clock. Went to the opera. I did not see Mr. Froth till the beginning of the second act. Mr. Froth talked to a gentleman in a black wig. Bowed to a lady in the front box. Mr. Froth and his friend clapped Nicolini in the third act. Mr. Froth cried out Ancora. Mr. Froth led me to my chair. I think he squeezed my hand.

Eleven at night. Went to bed. Melancholy dreams. Methought Nicolini said he was Mr. Froth.

THE SPECTATOR

SUNDAY. Indisposed.

MONDAY. *Eight o'clock.* Waked by Miss Kitty. Aurenzebe lay upon the chair by me. Kitty repeated without book the eight best lines in the play. Went in our mobs to the dumb man, according to appointment. Told me that my lover's name began with a G. Mem. The conjurer was within a letter of Mr. Froth's name, &c.

"Upon looking back into this my journal, I find that I am at a loss to know whether I pass my time well or ill; and indeed never thought of considering how I did it, before I perused your speculation upon that subject. I scarce find a single action in these five days that I can thoroughly approve of, except the working upon the violet leaf, which I am resolved to finish the first day I am at leisure. As for Mr. Froth and Veny, I did not think they took up so much of my time and thoughts, as I find they do upon my journal. The latter of whom I will turn off if you insist upon it; and if Mr. Froth does not bring matters to a conclusion very suddenly, I will not let my life run away in a dream.

"Your humble servant,
CLARINDA."

To resume one of the morals of my first paper, and to confirm Clarinda in her good inclinations, I would have her consider what a pretty figure she would make among posterity, were the history of her whole life published like these five days of it. I shall conclude my paper with an epitaph written by an uncertain author on Sir Philip Sidney's sister, a lady who seems to have been of a temper very much different from that of Clarinda. The last thought of it is so very noble, that I dare say my reader will pardon the quotation.

On the Countess Dowager of PEMBROKE.

> Underneath this marble hearse
> Lies the subject of all verse,
> Sidney's sister, Pembroke's mother;
> Death, ere thou hast killed another,
> Fair, and learned, and good as she,
> Time shall throw a dart at thee.

THE SPECTATOR

VARIOUS ADVANTAGES OF THE SPECTATORS

No. 367.] THURSDAY MAY 1, 1712. [ADDISON.]

—Perituræ parcite chartæ. —Juv.

I HAVE often pleased myself with considering the two kinds of benefits which accrue to the public from these my Speculations, and which, were I to speak after the manner of logicians, I would distinguish into the material and the formal. By the latter I understand those advantages which my readers receive, as their minds are either improved or delighted by these my daily labours: but having already several times descanted on my endeavours in this light, I shall at present wholly confine myself to the consideration of the former. By the word material I mean those benefits which arise to the public from these my Speculations, as they consume a considerable quantity of our paper manufacture, employ our artisans in printing, and find business for great numbers of indigent persons.

Our paper-manufacture takes into it several mean materials which could be put to no other use, and affords work for several hands in the collecting of them, which are incapable of any other employment. Those poor retailers, whom we see so busy in every street, deliver in their respective gleanings to the merchant. The merchant carries them in loads to the paper-mill, where they pass through a fresh set of hands, and give life to another trade. Those who have mills on their estates by this means considerably raise their rents, and the whole nation is in a great measure supplied with a manufacture, for which formerly she was obliged to her neighbours.

The materials are no sooner wrought into paper, but they are distributed among the presses, where they again set innumerable artists at work, and furnish business to another mystery. From hence, accordingly as they are stained with news or politics, they fly through the town in Post-men, Post-boys, Daily Courants, Reviews, Medleys, and Examiners. Men, women, and children contend who shall be the first bearers of them, and get their daily sustenance by spreading them. In short, when I trace in my mind a bundle of rags to a quire of Spectators, I find so many

THE SPECTATOR

hands employed in every step they take through their whole progress, that while I am writing a Spectator, I fancy myself providing bread for a multitude.

If I do not take care to obviate some of my witty readers, they will be apt to tell me, that my paper, after it is thus printed and published, is still beneficial to the public on several occasions. I must confess I have lighted my pipe with my own works for this twelvemonth past: my landlady often sends up her little daughter to desire some of my old Spectators, and has frequently told me, that the paper they are printed on is the best in the world to wrap spice in. They likewise make a good foundation for a mutton-pie, as I have more than once experienced, and were very much sought for last Christmas by the whole neighbourhood.

It is pleasant enough to consider the changes that a linen fragment undergoes, by passing through the several hands above-mentioned. The finest pieces of Holland, when torn to tatters, assume a new whiteness more beautiful than their first, and often return in the shape of letters to their native country. A lady's shift may be metamorphosed into billet-doux, and come into her possession a second time. A beau may peruse his cravat after it is worn out, with greater pleasure and advantage than ever he did in a glass. In a word, a piece of cloth, after having officiated for some years as a towel or a napkin, may by this means be raised from a dunghill, and become the most valuable piece of furniture in a prince's cabinet.

The politest nations of Europe have endeavoured to vie with one another for the reputation of the finest printing: absolute governments, as well as republics, have encouraged an art which seems to be the noblest and most beneficial that was ever invented among the sons of men. The present king of France, in his pursuits after glory, has particularly distinguished himself by the promoting of this useful art, insomuch that several books have been printed in the *Louvre* at his own expense, upon which he sets so great a value, that he considers them as the noblest presents he can make to foreign princes and ambassadors. If we look into the commonwealths of Holland and Venice, we shall find that in this particular they have made themselves the envy of the greatest monarchies. Elzevir and Aldus are more frequently mentioned than any pensioner of the one or doge of the other.

The several presses which are now in England, and the encouragement which has been given to learning, for some years last past, has made our own nation as glorious upon this account, as for its late triumphs and conquests. The new edition which is given us of Cæsar's Commentaries, has already been taken notice of in foreign gazettes, and is a work that does honour to the English press. It is no wonder that an edition should be very correct, which has passed through the hands of one of the most accurate, learned, and judicious writers this age has produced. The beauty of the paper, of the character, and of the several cuts with which this noble work is illustrated, makes it the finest book that I have ever seen; and is a true instance of the English genius, which, though it does not come the first into any art, generally carries it to greater heights than any other country in the world. I am particularly glad that this author comes from a British printing-house in so great a magnificence, as he is the first who has given us any tolerable account of our country.

My illiterate readers, if any such there are, will be surprised to hear me talk of learning as the glory of a nation, and of printing as an art that gains a reputation to a people among whom it flourishes. When men's thoughts are taken up with avarice and ambition, they cannot look upon anything as great or valuable which does not bring with it an extraordinary power or interest to the person who is concerned in it. But as I shall never sink this paper so far as to engage with Goths and Vandals, I shall only regard such kind of reasoners with that pity which is due to so deplorable a degree of stupidity and ignorance.

HUMOROUS WAY OF SORTING COMPANIES

No. 371.] TUESDAY, MAY 6, 1712. [ADDISON.]

*Jamne igitur laudas quod de sapientibus unus
Ridebat?* —JUV.

I SHALL communicate to my reader the following letter for the entertainment of this day.

"SIR,— You know very well that our nation is more famous for that sort of men who are called Whims and Humourists, than any other country in the world; for which reason it is observed that our English comedy excels that of all other nations in the novelty and variety of its characters.

"Among those innumerable sets of Whims which our country produces, there are none whom I have regarded with more curiosity than those who have invented any particular kind of diversion for the entertainment of themselves or their friends. My letter shall single out those who take delight in sorting a company that has something of burlesque and ridicule in its appearance. I shall make myself understood by the following example. One of the wits of the last age, who was a man of a good estate, thought he never laid out his money better than in a jest. As he was one year at the Bath, observing that in the great confluence of fine people, there were several among them with long chins, a part of the visage by which he himself was very much distinguished, he invited to dinner half a score of these remarkable persons who had their mouths in the middle of their faces. They had no sooner placed themselves about the table, but they began to stare upon one another, not being able to imagine what had brought them together. Our English proverb says,

> 'Tis merry in the hall,
> When beards wag all.

It proved so in an assembly I am now speaking of, who seeing so many peaks of faces agitated with eating, drinking, and discourse, and observing all the chins that were present meeting together very often over the centre of the table, every one grew sensible of the jest, and came into it with so much good-humour, that they lived in strict friendship and alliance from that day forward.

"The same gentleman some time after packed together a set of oglers, as he called them, consisting of such as had an unlucky cast in their eyes. His diversion on this occasion was to see the cross bows, mistaken signs, and wrong connivances that passed amidst so many broken and refracted rays of sight.

"The third feast which this merry gentleman exhibited was to the stammerers, whom he got together in a sufficient body to fill his table. He had ordered one of his servants, who was placed behind a screen, to write down their table-talk, which was very easy to be done without the help of short-hand. It appears by the notes which were taken, that though their conversation never fell, there were not above twenty words spoken during the first course; that upon serving up the second, one of the company was a quarter of an hour in telling them, that the ducklins and sparrow-grass was very good; and that another took up the same time in declaring himself of the same opinion. This jest did not, however, go off so well as the former; for one of the guests being a brave man, and fuller of resentment than he knew how to express, went out of the room, and sent the facetious inviter a challenge in writing, which though it was afterwards dropped by the interposition of friends, put a stop to these ludicrous entertainments.

"Now, sir, I dare say you will agree with me, that as there is no moral in these jests, they ought to be discouraged, and looked upon rather as pieces of unluckiness than wit. However, as it is natural for one man to refine upon the thought of another, and impossible for any single person, 'how great soever his parts may be, to invent an art, and bring it to its utmost perfection; I shall here give you an account of an honest gentleman of my acquaintance, who upon hearing the character of the wit above-mentioned, has himself assumed it, and endeavoured to convert it to the benefit of mankind. He invited half a dozen of his friends one day to dinner, who were each of them famous for inserting several redundant phrases in their discourse, as 'D'ye hear me, D'ye see, That is, And so, sir.' Each of the guests making frequent use of his particular elegance, appeared so ridiculous to his neighbour, that he could not but reflect upon himself as appearing equally ridiculous to the rest of the company: by this means, before they had sat long togther, every one talking with the greatest circumspection, and carefully avoiding his favourite expletive, the conversation was cleared of its redundancies, and had a greater quantity of sense, though less of sound in it.

"The same well-meaning gentleman took occasion at another time, to bring together such of his friends as were addicted to a foolish habitual custom of swearing. In order to show them the absurdity of the practice, he had recourse to the invention above-mentioned, having placed an amanuensis in a private part of the room. After the second bottle, when men open their minds without reserve, my honest friend began to take notice of the many sonorous but unnecessary words that had passed in his house since their sitting down at table, and how much good conversation they had lost by giving way to such superfluous phrases. What a tax, says he, would they have raised for the poor, had we put the laws in execution upon one another? Every one of them took this gentle reproof in good part: upon which he told them, that knowing their conversation would have no secrets in it, he had ordered it to be taken down in writing, and for the humour-sake would read it to them if they pleased. There were ten sheets of it, which might have been reduced to two, had there not been those abominable interpolations I have before mentioned. Upon the reading of it in cold blood, it looked rather like a conference of fiends than of men. In short, every one trembled at himself upon hearing calmly what he had pronounced amidst the heat and inadvertency of discourse.

"I shall only mention another occasion wherein he made use of the same invention to cure a different kind of men, who are the pests of all polite conversation, and murder time as much as either of the two former, though they do it more innocently; I mean that dull generation of story-tellers. My friend got together about half a dozen of his acquaintance, who were infected with this strange malady. The first day one of them sitting down, entered upon the siege of Namur, which lasted till four o'clock, their time of parting. The second day a North Briton took possession of the discourse, which it was impossible to get out of his hands so long as the company staid together. The third day was engrossed after the same manner by a story of the same length. They at last began to reflect upon this barbarous way of treating one another, and by this means awakened out of that lethargy with which each of them had been seized for several years.

"As you have somewhere declared, that extraordinary and uncommon characters of mankind are the game which you delight in, and as I look upon you to be the greatest sportsman, or, if you please, the Nimrod, among this species of writers, I thought this discovery would not be unacceptable to you.

"I am, sir," &c.

THE SPECTATOR

ON COMPASSION

No. 397.] THURSDAY, JUNE 5, 1712. [ADDISON.]

— Dolor ipse disertum
Fecerat.— OVID.

AS the Stoic philosophers discard all passions in general, they will not allow a wise man so much as to pity the afflictions of another. "If thou seest thy friend in trouble, (says Epictetus,) thou mayest put on a look of sorrow, and condole with him, but take care that thy sorrow be not real." The more rigid of this sect would not comply so far as to show even such an outward appearance of grief; but when one told them of any calamity that had befallen even the nearest of their acquaintance, would immediately reply, "What is that to me?" If you aggravated the circumstances of the affliction, and showed how one misfortune was followed by another, the answer was still, "All this may be true, but what is it to me?"

For my own part, I am of opinion, compassion does not only refine and civilize human nature, but has something in it more pleasing and agreeable than what can be met with in such an indolent happiness, such an indifference to mankind, as that in which the Stoics placed their wisdom. As love is the most delightful passion, pity is nothing else but love softened by a degree of sorrow: in short, it is a kind of pleasing anguish, as well as generous sympathy, that knits mankind together, and blends them in the same common lot.

Those who have laid down rules for rhetoric or poetry, advise the writer to work himself up, if possible, to the pitch of sorrow which he endeavours to produce in others. There are none, therefore, who stir up pity so much as those who indite their own sufferings. Grief has a natural eloquence belonging to it, and breaks out in more moving sentiments than can be supplied by the finest imagination. Nature on this occasion dictates a thousand passionate things which cannot be supplied by art.

It is for this reason that the short speeches or sentences which we often meet with in histories, make a deeper impression on the mind of the reader than the most laboured strokes in a well-written tragedy. Truth and matter of fact sets the person actually before us in the one, whom fiction places at a greater distance from us in the other. I do not remember to have seen any ancient or modern story more affecting than a letter of Ann of Bologne, wife to King Henry the Eighth, and mother to Queen Elizabeth, which is still extant in the Cotton library, as written by her own hand.

Shakspeare himself could not have made her talk in a strain so suitable to her condition and character. One sees in it the expostulations of a slighted lover, the resentments of an injured woman, and the sorrows of an imprisoned queen. I need not acquaint my reader that this princess was then under prosecution for disloyalty to the king's bed, and that she was afterwards publicly beheaded upon the same account, though this prosecution was believed by many to proceed, as she herself intimates, rather from the king's love to Jane Seymour, than from any actual crime in Ann of Bologne.

Queen Ann Boleyn's last Letter to King Henry.

"SIR, — Your Grace's displeasure, and my imprisonment, are things so strange unto me, as what to write, or what to excuse, I am altogether ignorant. Whereas you send unto me (willing me to confess a truth, and so obtain your favour) by such an one, whom you know to be mine ancient professed enemy. I no sooner received this message by him than I rightly conceived your meaning; and if, as you say, confessing a truth, indeed may procure my safety, I shall with all willingness and duty perform your command.

"But let not your Grace ever imagine that your poor wife will ever be brought to acknowledge a fault, where not so much as a thought thereof preceded. And to speak a truth, never prince had wife more loyal in all duty, and in all true affection, than you have ever found in Ann Boleyn: with which name and place I could willingly have contented myself, if God and your Grace's pleasure had been so pleased. Neither did I at any time so far forget myself in my exaltation, or received queenship, but that I always looked for such an alteration as now I find; for the ground of my preferment being on no surer foundation than your Grace's fancy, the least alteration I knew was fit and sufficient to draw that fancy to some other subject. You have chosen me, from a low estate, to be your queen and companion, far beyond my desert and desire. If then you found me worthy of such honour, good your Grace let not any light fancy, or bad counsel of mine enemies withdraw your princely favour from me; neither let that stain, that unworthy stain, of a disloyal heart towards your good Grace, ever cast so foul a blot on your most dutiful wife, and the infant princess your daughter. Try me, good king, but let me have a lawful trial, and let not my sworn enemies sit as my accusers and judges; yea, let me receive an open trial, for my truth shall fear no open shame; then shall you see either mine innocency cleared, your suspicion and conscience satisfied, the ignominy and slander of the world stopped, or my guilt openly declared. So that whatsoever God or you may determine of me, your Grace may be freed from an open censure, and mine offence being so lawfully proved, your Grace is at liberty, both before God and man, not only to execute worthy punishment on me as an unlawful wife, but to follow your affection, already settled on that party, for whose sake I am now as I am, whose name I could some good while since have pointed unto, your Grace being not ignorant of my suspicion therein.

"But if you have already determined of me, and that not only my death, but an infamous slander must bring you the enjoying of your desired happiness; then I desire of God, that he will pardon your great sin therein, and likewise mine enemies, the instruments thereof; and that he will not call you to a strict account for your unprincely and cruel usage of me, at his general judgment-seat, where both you and myself must shortly appear, and in whose judgment I doubt not (whatsoever the world may think of me) mine innocence shall be openly known and sufficiently cleared.

"My last and only request shall be, that myself may only bear the burden of your Grace's displeasure, and that it may not touch the innocent souls of those poor gentlemen who (as I understand) are likewise in strait imprisonment for my sake. If ever I have found favour in your sight, if ever the name of Ann Boleyn hath been pleasing in your ears, then let me obtain this request, and I will so leave to trouble your Grace any further, with mine earnest prayers to the Trinity to have your Grace in his good keeping, and to direct you in all your actions. From my doleful prison in the Tower, this sixth of May.

"Your most loyal and ever faithful wife,

ANN BOLEYN."

THE SPECTATOR

ON THE DEATH OF THE KING OF FRANCE

No. 403.] THURSDAY, JUNE 12, 1712. [ADDISON.]

Qui mores hominum multorum vidit.—HOR.

WHEN I consider this great city in its several quarters and divisions, I look upon it as an aggregate of various nations, distinguished from each other by their respective customs, manners, and interests. The courts of two countries do not so much differ from one another, as the court and city in their peculiar ways of life and conversation. In short, the inhabitants of St. James's, notwithstanding they live under the same laws, and speak the same language, are a distinct people from those of Cheapside, who are likewise removed from those of the Temple on the one side, and those of Smithfield on the other, by several climates and degrees in their way of thinking and conversing together.

For this reason, when any public affair is upon the anvil, I love to hear the reflections that arise upon it in the several districts and parishes of London and Westminster, and to ramble up and down a whole day together, in order to make myself acquainted with the opinions of my ingenious countrymen. By this means I know the faces of all the principal politicians within the bills of mortality; and as every coffee-house has some particular statesman belonging to it, who is the mouth of the street where he lives, I always take care to place myself near him, in order to know his judgment on the present posture of affairs. The last progress that I made with this intention, was about three months ago, when we had a current report of the king of France's death. As I foresaw this would produce a new face of things in Europe, and many curious speculations in our British coffee-houses, I was very desirous to learn the thoughts of our most eminent politicians on that occasion.

That I might begin as near the fountain-head as possible, I first of all called in at St. James's, where I found the whole outward room in a buzz of politics. The speculations were but very indifferent towards the door, but grew finer as you advanced to the upper end of the room, and were so very much improved by a knot of theorists who sat in the inner room, within the steams of the coffee-pot, that I there heard the whole Spanish monarchy disposed of, and all the line of Bourbon provided for, in less than a quarter of an hour.

I afterwards called in at Giles's, where I saw a board of French gentlemen sitting upon the life and death of their *Grand Monarque*. Those among them who had espoused the Whig interest, very positively affirmed, that he departed this life about a week since, and therefore proceeded without any further delay to the release of their friends on the galleys, and to their own re-establishment; but finding they could not agree among themselves, I proceeded on my intended progress.

Upon my arrival at Jenny Man's, I saw an alert young fellow that cocked his hat upon a friend of his who entered just at the same time with myself, and accosted him after the following manner: "Well Jack, the old prig is dead at last. Sharp's the word. Now or never boy. Up to the walls of Paris directly." With several other deep reflections of the same nature.

I met with very little variation in the politics between Charing Cross and Covent Garden. And upon my going into Will.'s, I found their discourse was gone off from the death of the French king to that of Monsieur Boileau, Racine, Corneille, and several other poets, whom they regretted on this occasion, as persons who would have obliged the world with very noble elegies on the death of so great a prince, and so eminent a patron of learning.

At a coffee-house near the Temple, I found a couple of young gentlemen engaged very smartly in a dispute on the succession to the Spanish monarchy. One of them seemed to have been retained as advocate for the Duke of Anjou, the other for his Imperial Majesty. They were both for regulating the title to that kingdom by the statute laws of England; but finding them going out of my depth, I passed forward to Paul's Churchyard, where I listened with great attention to a learned man, who gave the company an account of the deplorable state of France during the minority of the deceased king.

I then turned my right hand into Fish Street, where the chief politician of that quarter, upon hearing the news, (after having taken a pipe of tobacco, and ruminating for some time,) "If, (says he,) the king of France is certainly dead, we shall have plenty of mackerel this season; our fishery will not be disturbed by privateers, as it has been for these ten years past." He afterwards considered how the death of this great man would affect our pilchards, and by several other remarks infused a general joy into his whole audience.

I afterwards entered by a coffee-house that stood at the upper end of a narrow lane, where I met with a Nonjuror, engaged very warmly with a Laceman who was the great support of a neighbouring conventicle. The matter in debate was, whether the late French king was most like Augustus Cæsar or Nero. The controversy was carried on with great heat on both sides, and as each of them looked upon me very frequently during the course of their debate, I was under some apprehension that they would appeal to me, and therefore laid down my penny at the bar, and made the best of my way to Cheapside.

I here gazed upon the signs for some time before I found one to my purpose. The first object I met in the coffee-room was a person who expressed a great grief for the death of the French king; but upon his explaining himself, I found his sorrow did not arise from the loss of the monarch, but for his having sold out of the bank about three days before he heard the news of it; upon which a haberdasher, who was the oracle of the coffee-house, and had his circle of admirers about him, called several to witness that he had declared his opinion above a week before, that the French king was certainly dead; to which he added, that considering the late advices we had received from France, it was impossible that it could be otherwise. As he was laying these together, and dictating to his hearers with great authority, there came in a gentleman from Garraway's, who told us that there were several letters from France just come in, with advice that the king was in good health, and was gone out a hunting the very morning the post came away: upon which the haberdasher stole off his hat that hung upon a wooden peg by him, and retired to his shop with great confusion. This intelligence put a stop to my travels, which I had prosecuted with much satisfaction; not being a little pleased to hear so many different opinions upon so great an event, and to observe how naturally upon such a piece of news every one is apt to consider it with a regard to his own particular interest and advantage.

THE SPECTATOR

ON FEMALE EXTRAVAGANCES

No. 435.]   SATURDAY, JULY 19, 1712.   [ADDISON.]

> Nec duo sunt at forma duplex, nec fœmina dici
> Nec puer ut possint, neutrumque et utrumque videntur.
> OVID. Met. iv. 378.
>
> Both bodies in a single body mix,
> A single body with a double sex.

MOST of the papers I give the public are written on subjects that never vary, but are for ever fixed and immutable. Of this kind are all my more serious essays and discourses; but there is another sort of speculations, which I consider as occasional papers, that take their rise from the folly, extravagance, and caprice of the present age. For I look upon myself as one set to watch the manners and behaviour of my countrymen and contemporaries, and to mark down every absurd fashion, ridiculous custom, or affected form of speech, that makes its appearance in the world during the course of my speculations. The petticoat no sooner began to swell, but I observed its motions. The party-patches had not time to muster themselves before I detected them. I had intelligence of the coloured hood the very first time it appeared in a public assembly. I might here mention several other the like contingent subjects, upon which I have bestowed distinct papers. By this means I have so effectually quashed those irregularities which gave occasion to them, that I am afraid posterity will scarce have a sufficient idea of them to relish those discourses which were in no little vogue at the time they were written. They will be apt to think that the fashions and customs I attacked were some fantastic conceits of my own, and that their great grandmothers could not be so whimsical as I have represented them. For this reason, when I think on the figure my several volumes of speculations will make about a hundred years hence, I consider them as so many pieces of old plate, where the weight will be regarded, but the fashion lost.

Among the several female extravagances I have already taken notice of, there is one which still keeps its ground. I mean, that of the ladies who dress themselves in a hat and feather, a riding coat and periwig, or at least tie up their hair in a bag or riband, in imitation of the smart part of the opposite sex. As in my yesterday's paper I gave an account of the mixture of two sexes in one commonwealth, I shall here take notice of this mixture of two sexes in one person. I have already shown my dislike of this immodest custom more than once; but, in contempt of everything I have hitherto said, I am informed that the highways about this great city are still very much infested with these female cavaliers.

I remember when I was at my friend Sir Roger de Coverley's about this time twelvemonth, an equestrian lady of this order appeared upon the plains which lay at a distance from his house. I was at the time walking in the fields with my old friend; and as his tenants ran out on every side to see so strange a sight, sir Roger asked one of them who came by us, what it was? To which the country fellow replied, ' 'Tis a gentlewoman, saving your worship's presence, in a coat and hat.' This produced a great deal of mirth at the knight's house, where we had a story at the same time of another of his tenants, who, meeting this gentleman-like lady on the highway, was asked by her whether that was Coverley-hall? The honest man seeing only the male part of the querist, replied, 'Yes, Sir;' but upon the second question, whether Sir Roger de Coverley was a married man? having dropped his eye upon the petticoat, he changed his note into 'No, Madam.'

Had one of these hermaphrodites appeared in Juvenal's days, with what an indignation should we have seen her described by that excellent satirist! He would have represented her in a riding habit, as a greater monster than the centaur. He would have called for sacrifices of purifying waters, to expiate the appearance of such a prodigy. He would have invoked the shades of Portia or Lucretia, to see into what the Roman ladies had transformed themselves.

For my own part, I am for treating the sex with greater tenderness, and have all along made use of the most gentle methods to bring them off from any little extravagance into which they have sometimes unwarily fallen. I think it however absolutely necessary to keep up the partition between the two sexes, and to take notice of the smallest encroachment which the one makes upon the other. I hope therefore I shall not hear any more complaints on this subject. I am sure my she-disciples, who peruse these my daily lectures, have profited but little by them, if they are capable of giving in to such an amphibious dress. This I should not have mentioned, had I not lately met one of these my female readers in Hyde-park, who looked upon me with a masculine assurance, and cocked her hat full in my face.

For my part, I have one general key to the behaviour of the fair sex. When I see them singular in any part of their dress, I conclude it is not without some evil intention: and therefore question not but the design of this strange fashion is to smite more effectually their male beholders. Now to set them right in this particular, I would fain have them consider for themselves, whether we are not more likely to be struck by a figure entirely female, than with such an one as we may see every day in our glasses. Or, if they please, let them reflect upon their own hearts, and think how they would be affected should they meet a man on horseback, in his breeches and jack-boots, and at the same time dressed up in a commode and a nightrail.

I must observe that this fashion was first of all brought to us from France, a country which has infected all the nations of Europe with its levity. I speak not this in derogation of a whole people, having more than once found fault with those general reflections which strike at kingdoms or commonwealths in the gross: a piece of cruelty, which an ingenious writer of our own compares to that of Caligula, who wished that the Roman people had all but one neck, that he might behead them at a blow. I shall therefore only remark, that, as liveliness and assurance are in a peculiar manner the qualifications of the French nation, the same habits and customs will not give the same offence to that people which they produce among those of our own country. Modesty is our distinguishing character, as vivacity is theirs: and when this our national virtue appears in that female beauty for which our British ladies are celebrated above all others in the universe, it makes up the most amiable object that the eye of man can possibly behold.   C.

THE SPECTATOR

CUSTOM

No. 447.] SATURDAY, AUGUST 2, 1712. [ADDISON.]

Φημὶ πολυχρονίην μελέτην ἔμμεναι, φίλε· καὶ δὴ
Ταύτην ἀνθρωποῖσι τελεύτωσαν φύσιν εἶναι.

Long exercise, my friend, inures the mind;
And what we once disliked, we pleasing find.

THERE is not a common saying which has a better turn of sense in it, than what we often hear in the mouths of the vulgar, that "custom is a second nature." It is indeed able to form the man anew, and to give him inclinations and capacities altogether different from those he was born with. Dr. Plot, in his history of Staffordshire, tells us of an idiot, that, chancing to live within the sound of a clock, and always amusing himself with counting the hour of the day whenever the clock struck, the clock being spoiled by accident, the idiot continued to strike and count the hour without the help of it, in the same manner as he had done when it was entire. Though I dare not vouch for the truth of this story, it is very certain that custom has a mechanical effect upon the body, at the same time that it has a very extraordinary influence upon the mind.

I shall in this paper consider one very remarkable effect which custom has upon human nature, and which, if rightly observed, may lead us into very useful rules of life. What I shall here take notice of in custom, is its wonderful efficacy in making everything pleasant to us. A person who is addicted to play or gaming, though he took but little delight in it at first, by degrees contracts so strong an inclination towards it, and gives himself up so entirely to it, that it seems the only end of his being. The love of a retired or busy life will grow upon a man insensibly, as he is conversant in the one or the other, until he is utterly unqualified for relishing that to which he has been for some time disused. Nay, a man may smoke, or drink, or take snuff, until he is unable to pass away his time without it; not to mention how our delights in any particular study, art, or science, rises and improves in proportion to the application which we bestow upon it. Thus, what was at first an exercise, becomes at length an entertainment. Our employments are changed into our diversions. The mind grows fond of those actions which she is accustomed to, and is drawn with reluctancy from those paths in which she has been used to walk.

Not only such actions as were at first indifferent to us, but even such as are painful, will by custom and practice become pleasant. Sir Francis Bacon observes in his natural philosophy, that our taste is never pleased better than with those things which at first created a disgust in it. He gives particular instances, of claret, coffee, and other liquors, which the palate seldom approves upon the first taste; but, when it has once got a relish for them, generally retains it for life. The mind is constituted after the same manner; and, after having habituated herself to any particular exercise or employment, not only loses her first aversion towards it, but conceives a certain fondness and affection for it. I have heard one of the greatest geniuses this age has produced, who had been trained up in all the polite studies of antiquity, assure me, upon his being obliged to search into several rolls and records, that, notwithstanding such an employment was at first very dry and irksome to him, he at last took an incredible pleasure in it, and preferred it even to the reading of Virgil or Cicero. The reader will observe that I have not here considered custom as it makes things easy, but as it renders them delightful; and though others have often made the same reflections, it is possible they may not have drawn those uses from it, with which I intend to fill the remaining part of this paper.

If we consider attentively this property of human nature, it may instruct us in very fine moralities. In the first place, I would have no man discouraged with that kind of life, or series of action, in which the choice of others, or his own necessities, may have engaged him. It may perhaps be very disagreeable to him at first; but use and application will certainly render it not only less painful, but pleasing and satisfactory.

In the second place, I would recommend to every one that admirable precept which Pythagoras is said to have given to his disciples, and which that philosopher must have drawn from the observation I have enlarged upon. *Optimum vitæ genus eligito, nam consuetudo faciet jucundissimum;* "Pitch upon that course of life which is the most excellent, and custom will render it the most delightful." Men, whose circumstances will permit them to choose their own way of life, are inexcusable if they do not pursue that which their judgment tells them is the most laudable. The voice of reason is more to be regarded than the bent of any present inclination, since, by the rule above-mentioned, inclination will at length come over to reason, though we can never force reason to comply with inclination.

In the third place, this observation may teach the most sensual and irreligious man to overlook those hardships and difficulties which are apt to discourage him from the prosecution of a virtuous life. "The gods," said Hesiod, "have placed labour before virtue; the way to her is at first rough and difficult, but grows more smooth and easy the farther you advance in it." The man who proceeds in it with steadiness and resolution, will in a little time find that "her ways are ways of pleasantness, and that all her paths are peace."

To enforce this consideration, we may further observe, that the practice of religion will not only be attended with that pleasure which naturally accompanies those actions to which we are habituated, but with those supernumerary joys of heart that rise from the consciousness of such a pleasure, from the satisfaction of acting up to the dictates of reason, and from the prospect of an happy immortality.

In the fourth place, we may learn from this observation, which we have made on the mind of man, to take particular care, when we are once settled in a regular course of life, how we too frequently indulge ourselves in any of the most innocent diversions and entertainments; since the mind may insensibly fall off from the relish of virtuous actions, and, by degrees, exchange that pleasure which it takes in the performance of its duty for delights of a much more inferior and unprofitable nature.

The last use which I shall make of this remarkable property in human nature, of being delighted with those actions to which it is accustomed, is to show how absolutely necessary it is for us to gain habits of virtue in this life, if we would enjoy the pleasures of the next. The state of bliss we call heaven will not be capable of affecting those minds which are not thus qualified for it; we must, in this world, gain a relish of truth and virtue, if we would be able to taste that knowledge and perfection which are to make us happy in the next. The seeds of those spiritual joys and raptures, which are to rise up and flourish in the soul to all eternity, must be planted in her during this her present state of probation. In short, heaven is not to be looked upon only as the reward, but as the natural effect of a religious life.

On the other hand, those evil spirits, who, by long custom, have contracted in the body habits of lust and sensuality, malice and revenge, an aversion to everything that is good, just, or laudable, are naturally seasoned and prepared for pain and misery. Their torments have already taken root in them; they cannot be happy when divested of the body, unless we may suppose that Providence will in a manner create them anew, and work a miracle in the rectification of their faculties. They may, indeed, taste a kind of malignant pleasure in those actions to which they are accustomed, whilst in this life; but when they are removed from all those objects which are here apt to gratify them, they will naturally become their own tormentors, and cherish in themselves those painful habits of mind which are called in scripture phrase, "the worm which never dies." This notion of heaven and hell is so conformable to the light of nature, that it was discovered by several of the most exalted heathens. It has been finely improved by many eminent divines of the last age, as in particular by Archbishop Tillotson and Dr. Sherlock: but there is none who has raised such noble speculations upon it as Dr. Scott, in the first book of his Christian Life, which is one of the finest and most rational schemes of divinity that is written in our tongue, or in any other. That excellent author has shown how every particular custom and habit of virtue will, in its own nature, produce the heaven, or a state of happiness, in him who shall hereafter practise it: as, on the contrary, how every custom or habit of vice will be the natural hell of him in whom it subsists. C.

ON NEWS-WRITERS AND READERS

No. 452.] FRIDAY, AUGUST 8, 1712. [ADDISON.]

Est natura hominum novitatis avida.—PLIN. APUD LILLIUM.

THERE is no humour in my countrymen, which I am more inclined to wonder at, than their general thirst after news. There are about half a dozen ingenious men, who live very plentifully upon this curiosity of their fellow-subjects. They all of them receive the same advices from abroad, and very often in the same words; but their way of cooking it is so different, that there is no citizen, who has an eye to the public good, that can leave the coffee-house with peace of mind, before he has given every one of them a reading. These several dishes of news are so very agreeable to the palate of my countrymen, that they are not only pleased with them when they are served up hot, but when they are again set cold before them by those penetrating politicians, who oblige the public with their reflections and observations upon every piece of intelligence that is sent us from abroad. The text is given us by one set of writers, and the comment by another.

But notwithstanding we have the same tale told us in so many different papers, and if occasion requires, in so many articles of the same paper; notwithstanding in a scarcity of foreign posts we hear the same story repeated, by different advices from Paris, Brussels, the Hague, and from every great town in Europe; notwithstanding the multitude of annotations, explanations, reflections, and various readings which it passes through, our time lies heavy on our hands till the arrival of a fresh mail: we long to receive further particulars, to hear what will be the next step, or what will be the consequence of that which has been lately taken. A westerly wind keeps the whole town in suspense, and puts a stop to conversation.

This general curiosity has been raised and inflamed by our late wars, and, if rightly directed, might be of good use to a person who has such a thirst awakened in him. Why should not a man who takes delight in reading everything that is new, apply himself to history, travels, and other writings of the same kind, where he will find perpetual fuel for his curiosity, and meet with much more pleasure and improvement, than in these papers of the week? An honest tradesman, who languishes a whole summer in expectation of a battle, and perhaps is balked at last, may here meet with half a dozen in a day. He may read the news of a whole campaign in less time than he now bestows upon the products of any single post. Fights, conquests, and revolutions lie thick together. The reader's curiosity is raised and satisfied every moment, and his passions disappointed or gratified, without being detained in a state of uncertainty from day to day, or lying at the mercy of sea and wind. In short, the mind is not here kept in a perpetual gape after knowledge, nor punished with that eternal thirst which is the portion of all our modern newsmongers and coffee-house politicians.

All matters of fact, which a man did not know before, are news to him; and I do not see how any haberdasher in Cheapside is more

THE SPECTATOR

concerned in the present quarrel of the Cantons, than he was in that of the League. At least, I believe every one will allow me, it is of more importance to an Englishman to know the history of his ancestors, than that of his contemporaries who live upon the banks of the Danube or the Borysthenes. As for those who are of another mind, I shall recommend to them the following letter, from a projector, who is willing to turn a penny by this remarkable curiosity of his countrymen.

"Mr. Spectator, — You must have observed, that men who frequent coffee-houses, and delight in news, are pleased with everything that is matter of fact, so it be what they have not heard before. A victory, or a defeat, are equally agreeable to them. The shutting of a cardinal's mouth pleases them one post, and the opening of it another. They are glad to hear the French court is removed to Marli, and are afterwards as much delighted with its return to Versailles. They read the advertisements with the same curiosity as the articles of public news; and are as pleased to hear of a piebald horse that is strayed out of a field near Islington, as of a whole troop that has been engaged in any foreign adventure. In short, they have a relish for everything that is news, let the matter of it be what it will; or to speak more properly, they are men of a voracious appetite, but no taste. Now, sir, since the great fountain of news, I mean the war, is very near being dried up; and since these gentlemen have contracted such an inextinguishable thirst after it; I have taken their case and my own into consideration, and have thought of a project which may turn to the advantage of us both. I have thoughts of publishing a daily paper, which shall comprehend in it all the most remarkable occurrences in every little town, village, and hamlet, that lie within ten miles of London, or in other words, within the verge of the penny-post. I have pitched upon this scene of intelligence for two reasons; first, because the carriage of letters will be very cheap; and secondly, because I may receive them every day. By this means my readers will have their news fresh and fresh, and many worthy citizens, who cannot sleep with any satisfaction at present, for want of being informed how the world goes, may go to bed contentedly, it being my design to put out my paper every night at nine-a-clock precisely. I have already established correspondences in these several places, and received very good intelligence.

THE SPECTATOR

"By my last advices from Knightsbridge I hear that a horse was clapped into the pound on the third instant, and that he was not released when the letters came away.

"We are informed from Pankridge, that a dozen weddings were lately celebrated in the mother-church of that place, but are referred to their next letters for the names of the parties concerned.

"Letters from Brompton advise, that the widow Blight had received several visits from John Mildew, which affords great matter of speculation in those parts.

"By a fisherman which lately touched at Hammersmith, there is advice from Putney, that a certain person well known in that place, is like to lose his election for church-warden; but this being boat-news, we cannot give entire credit to it.

"Letters from Paddington bring little more than that William Squeak, the sow-gelder, passed through that place the fifth instant.

"They advise from Fulham, that things remained there in the same state they were. They had intelligence, just as the letters came away, of a tub of excellent ale just set a-broach at Parsons Green; but this wanted confirmation.

"I have here, sir, given you a specimen of the news with which I intend to entertain the town, and which when drawn up regularly in the form of a newspaper, will, I doubt not, be very acceptable to many of those public-spirited readers, who take more delight in acquainting themselves with other people's business than their own. I hope a paper of this kind, which lets us know what is done near home, may be more useful to us than those which are filled with advices from Zug and Bender, and make some amends for that dearth of intelligence, which we may justly apprehend from times of peace. If I find that you receive this project favourably, I will shortly trouble you with one or two more; and in the mean time am, most worthy sir, with all due respect,

"Your most obedient and most humble servant."

THE SPECTATOR

ON TRUE AND FALSE MODESTY

No. 458.] FRIDAY, AUGUST 15, 1712. [ADDISON.]

Αἰδὼς οὐκ ἀγαθή.— HES.

Pudor malus.— HOR.

I COULD not but smile at the account that was yesterday given me of a modest young gentleman, who being invited to an entertainment, though he was not used to drink, had not the confidence to refuse his glass in his turn, when on a sudden he grew so flustered that he took all the talk of the table into his own hands, abused every one of the company, and flung a bottle at the gentleman's head who treated him. This has given me occasion to reflect upon the ill effects of a vicious modesty, and to remember the saying of Brutus, as it is quoted by Plutarch, that "the person has had but an ill education, who has not been taught to deny anything." This false kind of modesty has, perhaps, betrayed both sexes into as many vices as the most abandoned impudence, and is the more inexcusable to reason, because it acts to gratify others rather than itself, and is punished with a kind of remorse, not only like other vicious habits when the crime is over, but even at the very time that it is committed.

Nothing is more amiable than true modesty, and nothing is more contemptible than the false. The one guards virtue, the other betrays it. True modesty is ashamed to do anything that is repugnant to the rules of right reason: false modesty is ashamed to do anything that is opposite to the humour of the company. True modesty avoids everything that is criminal, false modesty everything that is unfashionable. The latter is only a general undetermined instinct; the former is that instinct limited and circumscribed by the rules of prudence and religion.

We may conclude that modesty to be false and vicious, which engages a man to do anything that is ill or indiscreet, or which restrains him from doing any that is of a contrary nature. How many men, in the common concerns of life, lend sums of money which they are not able to spare, are bound for persons whom they have but little friendship for, give recommendatory characters of men whom they are not acquainted with, bestow places on those whom they do not esteem, live in such a manner as they themselves do not approve, and all this merely because they have not the confidence to resist solicitation, importunity, or example.

Nor does this false modesty expose us only to such actions as are indiscreet, but very often to such as are highly criminal. When Xenophanes was called timorous, because he would not venture his money in a game at dice: "I confess, (said he,) that I am exceeding timorous, for I dare not do an ill thing." On the contrary, a man of vicious modesty complies with everything, and is only fearful of doing what may look singular in the company where he is engaged. He falls in with the torrent, and lets himself go to every action or discourse, however unjustifiable in itself, so it be in vogue among the present party. This, though one of the most common, is one of the most ridiculous dispositions in human nature, that men should not be ashamed of speaking or acting in a dissolute or irrational manner, but that one who is in their company should be ashamed of governing himself by the principles of reason and virtue.

In the second place, we are to consider false modesty as it restrains a man from doing what is good and laudable. My reader's own thoughts will suggest to him many instances and examples under this head. I shall only dwell upon one reflection, which I cannot make without a secret concern. We have in England a particular bashfulness in everything that regards religion. A well-bred man is obliged to conceal any serious sentiment of this nature, and very often to appear a greater libertine than he is, that he may keep himself in countenance among the men of mode. Our excess of modesty makes us shame-faced in all the exercises of piety and devotion. This humour prevails upon us daily; insomuch, that at many well-bred tables, the master of the house is so very modest a man, that he has not the confidence to say grace at his own table: a custom which is not only practised by all the nations about us, but was never omitted by the heathens themselves. English gentlemen who travel into Roman Catholic countries, are not a little surprised to meet with people of the best quality kneeling in their churches, and engaged in their private devotions, though it be not at the hours of public worship. An officer of the army, or a man of wit and pleasure, in those countries, would be afraid of passing not only for an irreligious, but an ill-bred man, should he be seen to go to bed, or sit down at table, without offering up his devotions on such occasions.

The same show of religion appears in all the foreign reformed churches, and enters so much into their ordinary conversation, that an Englishman is apt to term them hypocritical and precise.

This little appearance of a religious deportment in our nation, may proceed in some measure from that modesty which is natural to us, but the great occasion of it is certainly this. Those swarms of sectaries that over-ran the nation in the time of the great rebellion, carried their hypocrisy so high, that they had converted our whole language into a jargon of enthusiasm; insomuch, that upon the restoration men thought they could not recede too far from the behaviour and practice of those persons, who had made religion a cloak to so many villanies. This led them into the other extreme, every appearance of devotion was looked upon as puritanical; and falling into the hands of the ridiculers who flourished in that reign, and attacked everything that was serious, it has ever since been out of countenance among us. By this means we are gradually fallen into that vicious modesty which has in some measure worn out from among us the appearance of Christianity in ordinary life and conversation, and which distinguishes us from all our neighbours.

Hypocrisy cannot indeed be too much detested, but at the same time is to be preferred to open impiety. They are both equally destructive to the person who is possessed with them but in regard to others, hypocrisy is not so pernicious as bare-faced irreligion. The due mean to be observed is to be sincerely virtuous, and at the same time to let the world see we are so. I do not know a more dreadful menace in the holy writings, than that which is pronounced against those who have this perverted modesty, to be ashamed before men in a particular of such unspeakable importance.

THE SPECTATOR

MARRIAGE OF WILL HONEYCOMB

No. 530.]   FRIDAY, NOVEMBER 7, 1712.   [ADDISON.]

> Sic visum Veneri; cui placet impares
> Formas atque animos sub juga ahenea
> Sævo mittere cum joco.
>
> HOR. I Od. xxxiii. 10.

> Thus Venus sports: the rich, the base,
> Unlike in fortune and in face,
> To disagreeing love provokes;
>   When cruelly jocose,
>   She ties the fatal noose,
> And binds the unequals to the brazen yokes.

IT is very usual for those who have been severe upon marriage, in some part or other of their lives, to enter into the fraternity which they have ridiculed, and to see their raillery return upon their own heads. I scarce ever knew a woman-hater that did not, sooner or later, pay for it. Marriage, which is a blessing to another man, falls upon such a one as a judgment. Mr. Congreve's Old Bachelor is set forth to us with much wit and humour as an example of this kind. In short, those who have most distinguished themselves by railing at the sex in general, very often make an honourable amends, by choosing one of the most worthless persons of it for a companion and yoke-fellow. Hymen takes his revenge in kind on those who turn his mysteries into ridicule.

My friend Will Honeycomb, who was so unmercifully witty upon the women in a couple of letters which I lately communicated to the public, has given the ladies ample satisfaction by marrying a farmer's daughter; a piece of news which came to our club by the last post. The Templar is very positive that he has married a dairy-maid: but Will, in his letter to me on this occasion, sets the best face upon the matter that he can, and gives a more tolerable account of his spouse. I must confess I suspected something more than ordinary, when upon opening the letter I found that Will was fallen off from his former gaiety, having changed "Dear Spec," which was his usual salute at the beginning of the letter, into "My worthy Friend," and described himself in the latter end at full length William Honeycomb. In short, the gay, the loud, the vain Will Honeycomb, who had made love to every great fortune that has appeared in town for above thirty years together, and boasted of favours from ladies whom he had never seen, is at length wedded to a plain country girl.

His letter gives us the picture of a converted rake. The sober character of the husband is dashed with the man of the town, and enlivened with those little cant-phrases which have made my friend Will often thought very pretty company. But let us hear what he says for himself.

"MY WORTHY FRIEND, — I question not but you, and the rest of my acquaintance, wonder that I, who have lived in the smoke and gallantries of the town for thirty years together, should all on a sudden grow fond of a country life. Had not my dog of a steward run away as he did without making up his accounts, I had still been immersed in sin and sea-coal. But since my late forced visit to my estate, I am so pleased with it, that I am resolved to live and die upon it. I am every day abroad among my acres, and can scarce forbear filling my letter with breezes, shades, flowers, meadows, and purling streams. The simplicity of manners, which I have heard you so often speak of, and which appears here in perfection, charms me wonderfully. As an instance of it I must acquaint you, and by your means the whole club, that I have lately married one of my tenant's daughters. She is born of honest parents, and though she has no portion, she has a great deal of virtue. The natural sweetness and innocence of her behaviour, the freshness of her complexion, the unaffected turn of her shape and person, shot me through and through every time I saw her, and did more execution upon me in grogram than the greatest beauty in town or court had ever done in brocade. In short, she is such a one as promises me a good heir to my estate; and if by her means I cannot leave to my children what are falsely called the gifts of birth, high titles, and alliances, I hope to convey to them the more real and valuable gifts of birth, strong bodies, and healthy constitutions. As for your fine women, I need not tell thee that I know them. I have had my share in their graces; but no more of that. It shall be my business hereafter to live the life of an honest man, and to act as becomes the master of a family. I question not but I shall draw upon me the raillery of the town, and be treated to the tune of 'The Marriage-hater Matched'; but I am prepared for it. I have been as witty upon others in my time. To tell thee truly, I saw such a tribe of fashionable young fluttering coxcombs shot up that I did not think my post of an *homme de ruelle* any longer tenable. I felt a certain stiffness in my limbs which entirely destroyed the jauntiness of air I was once master of. Besides, for I may now confess my age to thee, I have been eight-and-forty above these twelve years. Since my retirement into the country will make a vacancy in the club, I could wish that you would fill up my place with my friend Tom Dapperwit. He has an infinite deal of fire, and knows the town. For my own part, as I have said before, I shall endeavour to live hereafter suitable to a man in my station, as a prudent head of a family, a good husband, a careful father (when it shall so happen), and as

"Your most sincere friend, and humble servant,

"WILLIAM HONEYCOMB."

O.

ON RETIREMENT

No. 549.] TUESDAY, NOVEMBER 29, 1712. [ADDISON.]

Quamvis digressu veteris confusus amici.
Laudo tamen.   JUV. Sat. iii. 1.

Tho' griev'd at the departure of my friend,
His purpose of retiring I commend.

I BELIEVE most people begin the world with a resolution to withdraw from it into a serious kind of solitude or retirement when they have made themselves easy in it. Our happiness is, that we find out some excuse or other for deferring such our good resolutions until our intended retreat is cut off by death. But among all kinds of people there are none who are so hard to part with the world as those who are grown old in the heaping up of riches. Their minds are so warped with their constant attention to gain, that it is very difficult for them to give their souls another bent, and convert them towards those objects, which, though they are proper for every stage of life, are so more especially for the last.

THE SPECTATOR

Horace describes an old usurer as so charmed with the pleasures of a country life, that in order to make a purchase he called in all his money; but what was the event of it? Why in a very few days after he put it out again. I am engaged in this series of thought by a discourse which I had last week with my worthy friend Sir Andrew Freeport, a man of so much natural eloquence, good sense, and probity of mind, that I always hear him with a particular pleasure. As we were sitting together, being the sole remaining members of our club, Sir Andrew gave me an account of the many busy scenes of life in which he had been engaged, and at the same time reckoned up to me abundance of those lucky hits, which at another time he would have called pieces of good fortune; but in the temper of mind he was then he termed them mercies, favours of Providence, and blessings upon an honest industry. "Now," says he, "you must know, my good friend, I am so used to consider myself as creditor and debtor, that I often state my accounts after the same manner with regard to heaven and my own soul. In this case, when I look upon the debtor side, I find such innumerable articles, that I want arithmetic to cast them up; but when I look upon the creditor side, I find little more than blank paper. Now, though I am very well satisfied that it is not in my power to balance accounts with my Maker, I am resolved however to turn all my future endeavours that way. You must not therefore be surprised, my friend, if you hear that I am betaking myself to a more thoughtful kind of life, and if I meet you no more in this place."

I could not but approve so good a resolution, notwithstanding the loss I shall suffer by it. Sir Andrew has since explained himself to me more at large in the following letter, which is just come to my hands:—

"GOOD MR. SPECTATOR,—Notwithstanding my friends at the club have always rallied me when I have talked of retiring from business, and repeated to me one of my own sayings, that 'a merchant has never enough until he has got a little more'; I can now inform you, that there is one in the world who thinks he has enough, and is determined to pass the remainder of his life in the enjoyment of what he has. You know me so well, that I need not tell you, I mean, by the enjoyment of my possessions, the making of them useful to the public. As the greatest part of my estate has been hitherto of an un-

THE SPECTATOR

steady and volatile nature, either tost upon seas or fluctuating in funds, it is now fixed and settled in substantial acres and tenements. I have removed it from the uncertainty of stocks, winds, and waves, and disposed of it in a considerable purchase. This will give me great opportunity of being charitable in my way, that is, in setting my poor neighbours to work, and giving them a comfortable subsistence out of their own industry. My gardens, my fish-ponds, my arable and pasture grounds, shall be my several hospitals, or rather work-houses, in which I propose to maintain a great many indigent persons, who are now starving in my neighbourhood. I have got a fine spread of improveable lands, and in my own thoughts am already ploughing up some of them, fencing others, planting woods, and draining marshes. In fine, as I have my share in the surface of this island, I am resolved to make it as beautiful a spot as any in her Majesty's dominions; at least there is not an inch of it which shall not be cultivated to the best advantage, and do its utmost for its owner. As in my mercantile employment I so disposed of my affairs, that, from whatever corner of the compass the wind blew, it was bringing home one or other of my ships, I hope as a husbandman to contrive it so, that not a shower of rain, or a glimpse of sunshine, shall fall upon my estate without bettering some part of it, and contributing to the products of the season. You know it has been hitherto my opinion of life, that it is thrown away when it is not some way useful to others. But when I am riding out by myself, in the fresh air on the open heath that lies by my house, I find several other thoughts growing up in me. I am now of opinion, that a man of my age may find business enough on himself, by setting his mind in order, preparing it for another world, and reconciling it to the thoughts of death. I must therefore acquaint you, that besides those usual methods of charity, of which I have before spoken, I am at this very instant finding out a convenient place where I may build an alms-house, which I intend to endow very handsomely for a dozen superannuated husbandmen. It will be a great pleasure to me to say my prayers twice a day with men of my own years, who all of them, as well as myself, may have their thoughts taken up how they shall die, rather than how they shall live. I remember an excellent saying that I learned at school, *finis coronat opus*. You know best whether it be in Virgil or in Horace; it is my business to apply it. If your affairs will permit you to take the country air with me sometimes, you shall find an apartment fitted up for you, and shall be every day entertained with beef or mutton of my own feeding, fish out of my own ponds, and fruit out of my own gardens. You shall have free egress and regress about my house, without having any questions asked you; and, in a word, such a hearty welcome as you may expect from

"Your most sincere friend and humble servant,

"ANDREW FREEPORT."

STERNE AND GOLDSMITH

STERNE AND GOLDSMITH

From THACKERAY'S "ENGLISH HUMORISTS"

ROGER STERNE, Sterne's father, was the second son of a numerous race, descendants of Richard Sterne, Archbishop of York, in the reign of James II.; and children of Simon Sterne and Mary Jaques, his wife, heiress of Elvington, near York. Roger was a lieutenant in Handyside's regiment, and engaged in Flanders in Queen Anne's wars. He married the daughter of a noted sutler — "N. B., he was in debt to him," his son writes, pursuing the paternal biography — and marched through the world with this companion; she following the regiment and bringing many children to poor Roger Sterne. The captain was an irascible but kind and simple little man, Sterne says, and informs us that his sire was run through the body at Gibraltar, by a brother officer, in a duel which arose out of a dispute about a goose. Roger never entirely recovered from the effects of this rencontre, but died presently at Jamaica, whither he had followed the drum.

Laurence, his second child, was born at Clonmel, in Ireland, in 1713, and travelled, for the first ten years of his life, on his father's march, from barrack to transport, from Ireland to England.

One relative of his mother's took her and her family under shelter for ten months at Mullingar: another collateral descendant of the Archbishop's housed them for a year at his castle near Carrickfergus. Larry Sterne was put to school at Halifax in England, finally was adopted by his kinsman at Elvington, and parted company with his father, the Captain, who marched on his path of life till he met the fatal goose, which closed his career. The most picturesque and delightful parts of Laurence Sterne's writings, we owe to his recollections of the military life. Trim's montero cap, and Le Fevre's sword, and dear Uncle Toby's roquelaure, are doubtless reminiscences of the boy, who had lived with the followers of William and Marlborough, and had beat time with his little feet to the fifes of

Ramillies in Dublin barrack-yard, or played with the torn flags and halberds of Malplaquet on the parade-ground at Clonmel.

Laurence remained at Halifax school till he was eighteen years old. His wit and cleverness appear to have acquired the respect of his master here; for when the usher whipped Laurence for writing his name on the newly whitewashed schoolroom ceiling, the pedagogue in chief rebuked the understrapper, and said that the name should never be effaced, for Sterne was a boy of genius, and would come to preferment.

His cousin, the Squire of Elvington, sent Sterne to Jesus College, Cambridge, where he remained five years, and taking orders, got, through his uncle's interest, the living of Sutton and the prebendary of York. Through his wife's connections, he got the living of Stillington. He married her in 1741; having ardently courted the young lady for some years previously. It was not until the young lady fancied herself dying, that she made Sterne acquainted with the extent of her liking for him. One evening when he was sitting with her, with an almost broken heart to see her so ill (the Rev. Mr. Sterne's heart was a good deal broken in the course of his life), she said — "My dear Laurey, I never can be yours, for I verily believe I have not long to live; but I have left you every shilling of my fortune:" a generosity which overpowered Sterne. She recovered: and so they were married, and grew heartily tired of each other before many years were over. "Nescio quid est materia cum me," Sterne writes to one of his friends (in dog-Latin, and very sad dog-Latin too); "sed sum fatigatus et ægrotus de meâ uxore plus quam unquam:" which means, I am sorry to say, "I don't know what is the matter with me: but I am more tired and sick of my wife than ever."

This to be sure was five-and-twenty years after Laurey had been overcome by her generosity and she by Laurey's love. Then he wrote to her of the delights of marriage, saying, "We will be merry and as innocent as our first parents in Paradise, before the arch-fiend entered that indescribable scene. The kindest affections will have room to expand in our retirement: let the human tempest and hurricane rage at a distance, the desolation is beyond the horizon of peace. My L. has seen a polyanthus blow in December? — Some friendly wall has sheltered it from the biting wind. No planetary influence shall reach us, but that which presides and cherishes the sweetest flowers. The gloomy family of care and

STERNE AND GOLDSMITH

distrust shall be banished from our dwelling, guarded by thy kind and tutelar deity. We will sing our choral songs of gratitude and rejoice to the end of our pilgrimage. Adieu, my L. Return to one who languishes for thy society! — As I take up my pen, my poor pulse quickens, my pale face glows, and tears are trickling down on my paper as I trace the word L."

And it is about this woman, with whom he finds no fault but that she bores him, that our philanthropist writes, "Sum fatigatus et ægrotus" — *Sum mortaliter in amore* with somebody else! That fine flower of love, that polyanthus over which Sterne snivelled so many tears, could not last for a quarter of a century!

Or rather it could not be expected that a gentleman with such a fountain at command should keep it to *arroser* one homely old lady, when a score of younger and prettier people might be refreshed from the same gushing source. It was in December, 1767, that the Rev. Laurence Sterne, the famous Shandean, the charming Yorick, the delight of the fashionable world, the delicious divine, for whose sermons the whole polite world was subscribing, the occupier of Rabelais's easy chair, only fresh stuffed and more elegant than when in possession of the cynical old curate of Meudon, — the more than rival of the Dean of St. Patrick's, wrote the above-quoted respectable letter to his friend in London: and it was in April of the same year that he was pouring out his fond heart to Mrs. Elizabeth Draper, wife of "Daniel Draper, Esq., Councillor of Bombay, and, in 1775, chief of the factory of Surat — a gentleman very much respected in that quarter of the globe."

"I got thy letter last night, Eliza, Sterne writes, "on my return from Lord Bathurst's, where I dined" — (the letter has this merit in it, that it contains a pleasant reminiscence of better men than Sterne, and introduces us to a portrait of a kind old gentleman) — "I got thy letter last night, Eliza, on my return from Lord Bathurst's; and where I was heard — as I talked of thee an hour within intermission — with so much pleasure and attention, that the good old Lord toasted your health three different times; and now he is in his 85th year, says he hopes to live long enough to be introduced as a friend to my fair Indian disciple, and to see her eclipse all other Nabobesses as much in wealth as she does already in exterior and, what is far better" (for Sterne is nothing without his morality), "in interior merit. This nobleman is an old friend of mine. You know he was always the protector of men of wit and genius, and has

STERNE AND GOLDSMITH

had those of the last century, Addison, Steele, Pope, Swift, Prior, &c., always at his table. The manner in which his notice began of me was as singular as it was polite. He came up to me one day as I was at the Princess of Wales's court, and said, 'I want to know you, Mr. Sterne, but it is fit you also should know who it is that wishes this pleasure. You have heard of an old Lord Bathurst, of whom your Popes and Swifts have sung and spoken so much? I have lived my life with geniuses of that cast; but have survived them; and, despairing ever to find their equals, it is some years since I have shut up my books and closed my accounts; but you have kindled a desire in me of opening them once more before I die: which I now do: so go home and dine with me.' This nobleman, I say, is a prodigy, for he has all the wit and promptness of a man of thirty; a disposition to be pleased, and a power to please others, beyond whatever I knew: added to which a man of learning, courtesy, and feeling.

"He heard me talk of thee, Eliza, with uncommon satisfaction — for there was only a third person, *and of sensibility*, with us: and a most sentimental afternoon till nine o'clock have we passed! But thou, Eliza, wert the star that conducted and enlivened the discourse! And when I talked not of thee, still didst thou fill my mind, and warm every thought I uttered, for I am not ashamed to acknowledge I greatly miss thee. Best of all good girls! — the sufferings I have sustained all night in consequence of thine, Eliza, are beyond the power of words. . . . . And so thou hast fixed thy Bramin's portrait over thy writing-desk, and will consult it in all doubts and difficulties? — grateful and good girl! Yorick smiles contentedly over all thou dost: his picture does not do justice to his own complacency. I am glad your shipmates are friendly beings" (Eliza was at Deal, going back to the Councillor at Bombay, and indeed it was high time she should be off). "You could least dispense with what is contrary to your own nature, which is soft and gentle, Eliza; it would civilize savages — though pity were it thou should'st be tainted with the office. Write to me, my child, thy delicious letters. Let them speak the easy carelessness of a heart that opens itself anyhow, everyhow. Such, Eliza, I write to thee!" (The artless rogue, of course he did!) "And so I should ever love thee, most artlessly, most affectionately, if Providence permitted thy residence in the same section of the globe: for I am all that honor and affection can make me 'THY BRAMIN.'"

STERNE AND GOLDSMITH

The Bramin continues addressing Mrs. Draper, until the departure of the "Earl of Chatham" Indiaman from Deal, on the 2nd of April, 1767. He is amiably anxious about the fresh paint for Eliza's cabin; he is uncommonly solicitous about her companions on board: "I fear the best of your shipmates are only genteel by comparison with the contrasted crew with which thou beholdest them. So was — you know who — from the same fallacy which was put upon your judgment when — but I will not mortify you!"

"You know who" was, of course, Daniel Draper, Esq., of Bombay — a gentleman very much respected in that quarter of the globe, and about whose probable health our worthy Bramin writes with delightful candor: —

"I honor you, Eliza, for keeping secret some things which, if explained, had been a panegyric on yourself. There is a dignity in venerable affliction which will not allow it to appeal to the world for pity or redress. Well have you supported that character, my amiable, my philosophic friend! And, indeed, I begin to think you have as many virtues as my Uncle Toby's widow. Talking of widows — pray, Eliza, if ever you are such, do not think of giving yourself to some wealthy Nabob, because I design to marry you myself. My wife cannot live long, and I know not the woman I should like so well for her substitute as yourself. 'Tis true I am ninety-five in constitution, and you but twenty-five; but what I want in youth, I will make up in wit and good-humour. Not Swift so loved his Stella, Scarron his Maintenon, or Waller his Saccharissa. Tell me, in answer to this, that you approve and honor the proposal."

Approve and honor the proposal! The coward was writing gay letters to his friends this while, with sneering allusions to this poor foolish *Bramine*. Her ship was not out of the Downs, and the charming Sterne was at the "Mount Coffee-house," with a sheet of gilt-edged paper before him, offering that precious treasure his heart to Lady P——, asking whether it gave her pleasure to see him unhappy? whether it added to her triumph that her eyes and lips had turned a man into a fool? — quoting the Lord's Prayer, with a horrible baseness of blasphemy, as a proof that he had desired not to be led into temptation, and swearing himself the most tender and sincere fool in the world. It was from his home at Coxwould that he wrote the Latin letter, which, I suppose, he was ashamed to put into English. I find in my copy of the Letters, that there is a note of I can't call it admiration, at Letter 112, which seems to announce that there was a No. 3 to whom the wretched worn out old scamp was paying his addresses; and the year after, having come back to his lodgings in Bond Street, with his "Sentimental Journey" to launch upon the town, eager as ever for praise and pleasure — as vain, as wicked, as witty, as false as he had ever been — death at length seized the feeble wretch, and, on the 18th of March, 1768, that "bale of cadaverous goods," as he calls his body, was consigned to Pluto. In his last letter there is one sign of grace — the real affection with which he entreats a friend to be a guardian to his daughter Lydia. All his letters to her are artless, kind, affectionate, and *not* sentimental; as a hundred pages in his writings are beautiful, and full, not of surprising humor merely, but of genuine love and kindness. A perilous trade, indeed, is that of a man who has to bring his tears and laughter, his recollections, his personal griefs and joys, his private thoughts and feelings to market, to write them on paper, and sell them for money. Does he exaggerate his grief, so as to get his reader's pity for a false sensibility? feign indignation, so as to establish a character for virtue? elaborate repartees, so that he may pass for a wit? steal from other authors, and put down the theft to the credit side of his own reputation for ingenuity and learning? feign originality? affect benevolence or misanthropy? appeal to the gallery gods with claptraps and vulgar baits to catch applause?

How much of the paint and emphasis is necessary for the fair business of the stage, and how much of the rant and rouge is put on for the vanity of the actor. His audience trusts him: can he trust himself? How much was deliberate calculation and imposture — how much was false sensibility — and how much true feeling? Where did the lie begin, and did he know where? and where did the truth end in the art and scheme of this man of genius, this actor, this quack? Some time since, I was in the company of a French actor, who began after dinner, and at his own request, to sing French songs of the sort called *des chansons grivoises*, and which he performed admirably, and to the dissatisfaction of most persons present. Having finished these, he commenced a sentimental ballad — it was so charmingly sung, that it touched all persons present, and especially the singer himself, whose voice trembled, whose eyes filled with emotion, and who was snivelling and weeping quite genuine tears by the time his own ditty was over. I suppose

STERNE AND GOLDSMITH

Sterne had this artistical sensibility; he used to blubber perpetually in his study, and finding his tears infectious, and that they brought him a great popularity, he exercised the lucrative gift of weeping: he utilized it, and cried on every occasion. I own that I don't value or respect much the cheap dribble of those fountains. He fatigues me with his perpetual disquiet and his uneasy appeals to my risible or sentimental faculties. He is always looking in my face, watching his effect, uncertain whether I think him an impostor or not; posture-making, coaxing, and imploring me. "See what sensibility I have — own now that I'm very clever — do cry now, you can't resist this." The humor of Swift and Rabelais, whom he pretended to succeed, poured from them as naturally as song does from a bird; they lose no manly dignity with it, but laugh their hearty great laugh out of their broad chests as nature bade them. But this man — who can make you laugh, who can make you cry too — never lets his reader alone, or will permit his audience repose: when you are quiet, he fancies he must rouse you, and turns over head and heels, or sidles up and whispers a nasty story. The man is a great jester, not a great humorist. He goes to work systematically and of cold blood; paints his face, puts on his ruff and motley clothes, and lays down his carpet and tumbles on it.

For instance, take the "Sentimental Journey," and see in the writer the deliberate propensity to make points and seek applause. He gets to "Dessein's Hotel," he wants a carriage to travel to Paris, he goes to the inn-yard, and begins what the actors call "business" at once. There is that little carriage (the *désobligeante*). "Four months had elapsed since it had finished its career of Europe in the corner of Monsieur Dessein's coach-yard, and having sallied out thence but a vamped-up business at first, though it had been twice taken to pieces on Mount Sennis, it had not profited much by its adventures, but by none so little as the standing so many months unpitied in the corner of Monsieur Dessein's coach-yard. Much, indeed, was not to be said for it — but something might — and when a few words will rescue misery out of her distress, I hate the man who can be a churl of them."

Le tour est fait! Paillasse has tumbled! Paillasse has jumped over the *désobligeante*, cleared it, hood and all, and bows to the noble company. Does anybody believe that this is a real Sentiment? that this luxury of generosity, this gallant rescue of Misery — out of an old cab, is genuine feeling? It is as genuine as the virtuous oratory of Joseph Surface when he begins, "The man who," &c. &c., and wishes to pass off for a saint with his credulous good-humored dupes.

Our friend purchases the carriage: after turning that notorious old monk to good account, and effecting (like a soft and good-natured Paillasse as he was, and very free with his money when he had it,) an exchange of snuff-boxes with the old Franciscan, jogs out of Calais; sets down in immense figures on the credit side of his account the sous he gives away to the Montreuil beggars; and at Nampont, gets out of the chaise and whimpers over that famous dead donkey, for which any sentimentalist may cry who will. It is agreeably and skilfully done — that dead jackass: like M. de Soubise's cook on the campaign, Sterne dresses it, and serves it up quite tender and with a very piquante sauce. But tears and fine feelings, and a white pocket-handkerchief, and a funeral sermon, and horses and feathers, and a procession of mutes, and a hearse with a dead donkey inside! Psha, mountebank! I'll not give thee one penny more for that trick, donkey and all!

This donkey had appeared once before with signal effect. In 1765, three years before the publication of the "Sentimental Journey," the seventh and eight volumes of "Tristram Shandy" were given to the world, and the famous Lyons donkey makes his entry in those volumes (pp. 315, 316): —

" 'Twas by a poor ass, with a couple of large panniers at his back, who had just turned in to collect eleemosynary turnip-tops and cabbage-leaves, and stood dubious, with his two forefeet at the inside of the threshold, and with his two hinder feet towards the street, as not knowing very well whether he was to go in or no.

"Now 'tis an animal (be in what hurry I may) I cannot bear to strike: there is a patient endurance of suffering wrote so unaffectedly in his looks and carriage which pleads so mightily for him, that it always disarms me, and to that degree that I do not like to speak unkindly to him: on the contrary, meet him where I will, whether in town or country, in cart or under panniers, whether in liberty or bondage, I have ever something civil to say to him on my part; and, as one word begets another (if he has as little to do as I), I generally fall into conversation with him; and surely never is my imagination so busy as in framing responses from the etchings of his countenance; and where those carry me not deep enough, in flying from my own heart into his, and seeing what is natural for

STERNE AND GOLDSMITH

an ass to think — as well as a man upon the occasion. In truth, it is the only creature of all the classes of beings below me with whom I can do this. . . . With an ass I can commune forever.

"'Come, Honesty,' said I, seeing it was impracticable to pass betwixt him and the gate, 'art thou for coming in or going out?'

"The ass twisted his head round to look up the street.

"'Well!' replied I, 'we'll wait a minute for thy driver.'

"He turned his head thoughtful about, and looked wistfully the opposite way.

"'I understand thee perfectly,' answered I: 'if thou takest a wrong step in this affair, he will cudgel thee to death. Well! a minute is but a minute; and if it saves a fellow-creature a drubbing, it shall not be set down as ill spent.'

"He was eating the stem of an artichoke as this discourse went on, and, in the little peevish contentions between hunger and unsavoriness, had dropped it out of his mouth, half a dozen times, and had picked it up again. 'God help thee, Jack!' said I, 'thou hast a bitter breakfast on't — and many a bitter day's labor, and many a bitter blow, I fear, for its wages! 'Tis all, all bitterness to thee — whatever life is to others! And now thy mouth if one knew the truth of it, is as bitter, I dare say, as soot' (for he had cast aside the stem), 'and thou hast not a friend perhaps in all this world that will give thee a macaroon.' In saying this, I pulled out a paper of 'em, which I had just bought, and gave him one; — and, at this moment that I am telling it, my heart smites me that there was more of pleasantry in the conceit of seeing *how* an ass would eat a macaroon, than of benevolence in giving him one, which presided in the act.

"When the ass had eaten his macaroon, I pressed him to come in. The poor beast was heavy loaded — his legs seemed to tremble under him — he hung rather backwards, and, as I pulled at his halter, it broke in my hand. He looked up pensive in my face: 'Don't thrash me with it; but if you will you may.' 'If I do,' said I, 'I'll be d——.'"

A critic who refuses to see in this charming description wit, humor, pathos, a kind nature speaking, and a real sentiment, must be hard indeed to move and to please. A page or two farther we come to a description not less beautiful — a landscape and figures, deliciously painted by one who had the keenest enjoyment and the most tremulous sensibility: —

STERNE AND GOLDSMITH

"'Twas in the road between Nismes and Lunel, where is the best Muscatto wine in all France: the sun was set, they had done their work: the nymphs had tied up their hair afresh, and the swains were preparing for a carousal. My mule made a dead point. ''Tis the pipe and tambourine,' said I — 'I never will argue a point with one of your family as long as I live;' so leaping off his back, and kicking off one boot into this ditch and t'other into that, 'I'll take a dance,' said I, 'so stay you here.'

"A sunburnt daughter of labor rose up from the group to meet me as I advanced towards them; her hair, which was of a dark chestnut approaching to a black, was tied up in a knot, all but a single tress.

"'We want a cavalier,' said she, holding out both her hands, as if to offer them. 'And a cavalier you shall have,' said I, taking hold of both of them. 'We could not have done without you,' said she, letting go one hand, with self-taught politeness, and leading me up with the other.

"A lame youth, whom Apollo had recompensed with a pipe, and to which he had added a tambourine of his own accord, ran sweetly over the prelude, as he sat upon the bank. 'Tie me up this tress instantly,' said Nannette, putting a piece of string into my hand. It taught me to forget I was a stranger. The whole knot fell down — we had been seven years acquainted. The youth struck the note upon the tambourine, his pipe followed, and off we bounded.

"The sister of the youth — who had stolen her voice from heaven — sang alternately with her brother. 'Twas a Gascoigne roundelay: *Viva la joia, fidon la tristessa.*' The nymphs joined in unison, and their swains an octave below them.

"*Viva la joia* was in Nannette's lips, *viva la joia* in her eyes. A transient spark of amity shot across the space betwixt us. She looked amiable. Why could I not live and end my days thus? 'Just Disposer of our joys and sorrows!' cried I, 'why could not a man sit down in the lap of content here, and dance, and sing, and say his prayers, and go to heaven with this nut-brown maid?' Capriciously did she bend her head on one side, and dance up insidious. ' Then 'tis time to dance off,' quoth I."

And with this pretty dance and chorus, the volume artfully concludes. Even here one can't give the whole description. There is not a page in Sterne's writing but has something that were better away, a latent corruption — a hint as of an impure presence.

STERNE AND GOLDSMITH

Some of that dreary *double entendre* may be attributed to freer times and manners than ours, but not all. The foul Satyr's eyes leer out of the leaves constantly: the last words the famous author wrote were bad and wicked — the last lines the poor stricken wretch penned were for pity and pardon. I think of these past writers and of one who lives amongst us now, and am grateful for the innocent laughter and the sweet and unsullied page which the author of "David Copperfield" gives to my children.

> "Jeté sur cette boule,
> Laid, chétif et souffrant;
> Etouffé dans la foule,
> Faute d'être assez grand:
>
> "Une plainte touchante
> De ma bouche sortit.
> Le bon Dieu me dit: Chante,
> Chante, pauvre petit!
>
> "Chanter, ou je m'abuse,
> Est ma tâche ici bas.
> Toux ceux qu'ainsi j'amuse,
> Ne m'aimeront-ils pas?"

In those charming lines of Béranger, one may fancy described the career, the sufferings, the genius, the gentle nature of GOLDSMITH, and the esteem in which we hold him. Who, of the millions whom he has amused, doesn't love him? To be the most beloved of English writers, what a title that is for a man! A wild youth, wayward, but full of tenderness and affection, quits the country village where his boyhood has been passed in happy musing, in idle shelter, in fond longing to see the great world out of doors, and achieve name and fortune; and after years of dire struggle, and neglect and poverty, his heart turning back as fondly to his native place as it had longed eagerly for change when sheltered there, he writes a book and a poem, full of the recollections and feelings of home: he paints the friends and scenes of his youth, and peoples Auburn and Wakefield with remembrances of Lissoy. Wander he must, but he carries away a home-relic with him, and dies with it on his breast. His nature is truant; in repose it longs for change: as on the journey it looks back for friends and quiet. He passes to-day in building an air-castle for to-morrow, or in writing yesterday's elegy; and he would fly away this hour, but that a cage and necessity keep him. What is the charm of his verse, of his style, and humor? His sweet regrets, his delicate compassion, his soft smile, his tremulous sympathy, the weakness which he owns? Your love for him is half pity. You come hot and tired from the day's battle, and this sweet minstrel sings to you. Who could harm the kind vagrant harper? Whom did he ever hurt? He carries no weapon, save the harp on which he plays to you; and with which he delights great and humble, young and old, the captains in the tents, or the soldiers round the fire, or the women and children in the villages, at whose porches he stops and sings his simple songs of love and beauty. With that sweet story of the "Vicar of Wakefield" he has found entry into every castle and every hamlet in Europe. Not one of us, however busy or hard, but once or twice in our lives has passed an evening with him, and undergone the charm of his delightful music.

Goldsmith's father was no doubt the good Doctor Primrose, whom we all of us know. Swift was yet alive, when the little Oliver was born at Pallas, or Pallasmore, in the county of Longford, in Ireland. In 1730, two years after the child's birth, Charles Goldsmith removed his family to Lissoy, in the county Westmeath, that sweet "Auburn" which every person who hears me has seen in fancy. Here the kind parson* brought up his eight children; and loving all the world, as his son says, fancied all the world loved him. He had a crowd of poor dependants besides those hungry children. He kept an open table; round which sat flatterers and poor friends, who laughed at the honest rector's many jokes, and

---

* "At church, with meek and unaffected grace,
His looks adorn'd the venerable place;
Truth from his lips prevail'd with double sway,
And fools who came to scoff remain'd to pray.
The service past, around the pious man,
With steady zeal each honest rustic ran;
E'en children follow'd with endearing wile,
And pluck'd his gown to share the good man's smile.
His ready smile a parent's warmth exprest,
Their welfare pleased him, and their cares distrest;
To them his heart, his love, his griefs were given,
But all his serious thoughts had rest in Heaven.
As some tall cliff that lifts its awful form,
Swells from the vale, and midway leaves the storm,
Though round its breast the rolling clouds are spread,
Eternal sunshine settles on its head."
The Deserted Village.

STERNE AND GOLDSMITH

ate the produce of his seventy acres of farm. Those who have seen an Irish house in the present day can fancy that one of Lissoy. The old beggar still has his allotted corner by the kitchen turf; the maimed old soldier still gets his potatoes and buttermilk; the poor cottier still asks his honor's charity, and prays God bless his reverence for the sixpence: the ragged pensioner still takes his place by right and sufferance. There's still a crowd in the kitchen, and a crowd round the parlor-table, profusion, confusion, kindness, poverty. If an Irishman comes to London to make his fortune, he has a half-dozen of Irish dependants who take a percentage of his earnings. The good Charles Goldsmith left but little provision for his hungry race when death summoned him: and one of his daughters being engaged to a Squire of rather superior dignity, Charles Goldsmith impoverished the rest of his family to provide the girl with a dowry.

The small-pox, which scourged all Europe at that time, and ravaged the roses off the cheeks of half the world, fell foul of poor little Oliver's face, when the child was eight years old, and left him scarred and disfigured for his life. An old woman in his father's village taught him his letters, and pronounced him a dunce: Paddy Byrne, the hedge-schoolmaster, took him in hand; and from Paddy Byrne, he was transmitted to a clergyman at Elphin. When a child was sent to school in those days, the classic phrase was that he was placed under Mr. So-and-so's *ferule*. Poor little ancestors! It is hard to think how ruthlessly you were birched; and how much of needless whipping and tears our small forefathers had to undergo! A relative — kind uncle Contarine, took the main charge of little Noll; who went through his school-days righteously doing as little work as he could: robbing orchards, playing at ball, and making his pocket-money fly about whenever fortune sent it to him. Everybody knows the story of that famous "Mistake of a Night," when the young schoolboy, provided with a guinea and a nag, rode up to the "best house" in Ardagh, called for the landlord's company over a bottle of wine at supper, and for a hot cake for breakfast in the morning; and found, when he asked for the bill, that the best house was Squire Featherstone's, and not the inn for which he mistook it. Who does not know every story about Goldsmith? That is a delightful and fantastic picture of the child dancing and capering about in the kitchen at home, when the old fiddler gibed at him for his ugliness, and called him Æsop; and little Noll made his

STERNE AND GOLDSMITH

repartee of "Heralds proclaim aloud this saying — See Æsop dancing and his monkey playing." One can fancy a queer pitiful look of humor and appeal upon that little scarred face — the funny little dancing figure, the funny little brogue. In his life, and his writings, which are the honest expression of it, he is constantly bewailing that homely face and person; anon, he surveys them in the glass ruefully; and presently assumes the most comical dignity. He likes to deck out his little person in splendor and fine colors. He presented himself to be examined for ordination in a pair of scarlet breeches, and said honestly that he did not like to go into the church, because he was fond of colored clothes. When he tried to practise as a doctor, he got by hook or by crook a black velvet suit, and looked as big and grand as he could, and kept his hat over a patch on the old coat: in better days he bloomed out in plum-color, in blue silk, and in new velvet. For some of those splendors the heirs and assignees of Mr. Filby, the tailor, have never been paid to this day: perhaps the kind tailor and his creditor have met and settled the little account in Hades.

They showed until lately a window at Trinity College, Dublin, on which the name of O. Goldsmith was engraved with a diamond. Whose diamond was it? Not the young sizar's, who made but a poor figure in that place of learning. He was idle, penniless, and fond of pleasure: he learned his way early to the pawnbroker's shop. He wrote ballads, they say, for the street-singers, who paid him a crown for a poem: and his pleasure was to steal out at night and hear his verses sung. He was chastised by his tutor for giving a dance in his rooms, and took the box on the ear so much to heart, that he packed up his all, pawned his books and little property, and disappeared from college and family. He said he intended to go to America, but when his money was spent, the young prodigal came home ruefully, and the good folks there killed their calf — it was but a lean one — and welcomed him back.

After college, he hung about his mother's house, and lived for some years the life of a buckeen — passed a month with this relation and that, a year with one patron, a great deal of time at the public-house. Tired of this life, it was resolved that he should go to London, and study at the Temple; but he got no farther on the road to London and the woolsack than Dublin, where he gambled away the fifty pounds given to him for his outfit, and whence he returned to the indefatigable forgiveness of home. Then he determined to

STERNE AND GOLDSMITH

be a doctor, and uncle Contarine helped him to a couple of years at Edinburgh. Then from Edinburgh he felt that he ought to hear the famous professors of Leyden and Paris, and wrote most amusing pompous letters to his uncle about the great Farheim, Du Petit, and Duhamel du Monceau, whose lectures he proposed to follow. If uncle Contarine believed those letters — if Oliver's mother believed that story which the youth related of his going to Cork, with the purpose of embarking for America, of his having paid his passage-money, and having sent his kit on board; of the anonymous captain sailing away with Oliver's valuable luggage, in a nameless ship, never to return; if uncle Contarine and the mother at Ballymahon believed his stories, they must have been a very simple pair; as it was a very simple rogue indeed who cheated them. When the lad, after failing in his clerical examination, after failing in his plan for studying the law, took leave of these projects and of his parents, and set out for Edinburgh, he saw mother, and uncle, and lazy Ballymahon, and green native turf, and sparkling river for the last time. He was never to look on old Ireland more, and only in fancy revisit her.

> "But me not destined such delights to share,
> My prime of life in wandering spent and care,
> Impelled, with steps unceasing, to pursue
> Some fleeting good that mocks me with the view;
> That like the circle bounding earth and skies
> Allures from far, yet, as I follow, flies:
> My fortune leads to traverse realms alone,
> And find no spot of all the world my own."

I spoke in a former lecture of that high courage which enabled Fielding, in spite of disease, remorse, and poverty, always to retain a cheerful spirit and to keep his manly benevolence and love of truth intact, as if these treasures had been confided to him for the public benefit, and he was accountable to posterity for their honorable employ; and a constancy equally happy and admirable I think was shown by Goldsmith, whose sweet and friendly nature bloomed kindly always in the midst of a life's storm, and rain, and bitter weather. The poor fellow was never so friendless but he could befriend some one; never so pinched and wretched but he could give of his crust, and speak his word of compassion. If he had but his flute left, he could give that, and make the children happy in the dreary London court. He could give the coals in that queer coal-scuttle we read of to his poor neighbor: he could give away his blankets in college to the poor widow, and warm himself as he best might in the feathers: he could pawn his coat to save his landlord from gaol: when he was a school-usher he spent his earnings in treats for the boys, and the good-natured schoolmaster's wife said justly that she ought to keep Mr. Goldsmith's money as well as the young gentlemen's. When he met his pupils in later life, nothing would satisfy the Doctor but he must treat them still. "Have you seen the print of me after Sir Joshua Reynolds?" he asked one of his old pupils. "Not seen it? not bought it? Sure, Jack, if your picture had been published, I'd not have been without it half an hour." His purse and his heart were everybody's, and his friends' as much as his own. When he was at the height of his reputation, and the Earl of Northumberland, going as Lord Lieutenant to Ireland, asked if he could be of any service to Dr. Goldsmith. Goldsmith recommended his brother, and not himself, to the great man. "My patrons," he gallantly said, "are the booksellers, and I want no others." Hard patrons they were, and hard work he did; but he did not complain much: if in his early writings some bitter words escaped him, some allusions to neglect and poverty, he withdrew these expressions when his works were republished, and better days seemed to open for him; and he did not care to complain that printer or publisher had overlooked his merit, or left him poor. The Court face was turned from honest Oliver, the Court patronized Beattie; the fashion did not shine on him — fashion adored Sterne. Fashion pronounced Kelly to be the great writer of comedy of his day. A little — not ill-humour, but plaintiveness — a little betrayal of wounded pride which he showed render him not the less amiable. The author of the "Vicar of Wakefield" had a right to protest when Newbery kept back the MS. for two years; had a right to be a little peevish with Sterne; a little angry when Colman's actors declined their parts in his delightful comedy, when the manager refused to have a scene painted for it, and pronounced its damnation before hearing. He had not the great public with him; but he had the noble Johnson, and the admirable Reynolds, and the great Gibbon, and the great Burke, and the great Fox — friends and admirers illustrious indeed, as famous as those who, fifty years before, sat round Pope's table.

Nobody knows, and I dare say Goldsmith's buoyant temper kept no account of all the pains which he endured during the early period of his literary career. Should any man of letters in our day have to bear up against such, heaven grant he may come out of the period of misfortune with such a pure kind heart as that which Goldsmith obstinately bore in his breast. The insults to which he had to submit are shocking to read of — slander, contumely, vulgar satire, brutal malignity perverting his commonest motives and actions; he had his share of these, and one's anger is roused at reading of them, as it is at seeing a woman insulted or a child assaulted, at the notion that a creature so very gentle and weak, and full of love, should have had to suffer so. And he had worse than insult to undergo — to own to fault and deprecate the anger of ruffians. There is a letter of his extant to one Griffiths, a bookseller, in which poor Goldsmith is forced to confess that certain books sent by Griffiths are in the hands of a friend from whom Goldsmith had been forced to borrow money. "He was wild, sir," Johnson said, speaking of Goldsmith to Boswell, with his great, wise benevolence and noble mercifulness of heart — " Dr. Goldsmith was wild, sir; but he is so no more." Ah! if we pity the good and weak man who suffers undeservedly, let us deal very gently with him from whom misery extorts not only tears, but shame; let us think humbly and charitably of the human nature that suffers so sadly and falls so low. Whose turn may it be to-morrow? What weak heart, confident before trial, may not succumb under temptation invincible? Cover the good man who has been vanquished — cover his face and pass on.

For the last half-dozen years of his life Goldsmith was far removed from the pressure of any ignoble necessity: and in the receipt, indeed, of a pretty large income from the booksellers his patrons. Had he lived but a few years more, his public fame would have been as great as his private reputation, and he might have enjoyed alive a part of that esteem which his country has ever since paid to the vivid and versatile genius who has touched on almost every subject of literature, and touched nothing that he did not adorn. Except in rare instances, a man is known in our profession, and esteemed as a skilful workman, years before the lucky hit which trebles his usual gains, and stamps him a popular author. In the strength of his age, and the dawn of his reputation, having for backers and friends the most illustrious literary men of his time, fame and prosperity might have been in store for Goldsmith, had fate so willed it; and, at forty-six had not sudden disease carried him off. I say prosperity rather than competence, for it is probable that no sum could have put order into his affairs or sufficed for his irreclaimable habits of dissipation. It must be remembered that he owed 2,000*l.* when he died. "Was ever poet," Johnson asked, "so trusted before?" As has been the case with many another good fellow of his nation, his life was tracked and his substance wasted by crowds of hungry beggars and lazy dependants. If they came at a lucky time (and be sure they knew his affairs better than he did himself, and watched his pay-day), he gave them of his money: if they begged on empty-purse days he gave them his promissory bills: or he treated them to a tavern where he had credit; or he obliged them with an order upon honest Mr. Filby for coats, for which he paid as long as he could earn, and until the shears of Filby were to cut for him no more. Staggering under a load of debt and labor, tracked by bailiffs and reproachful creditors, running from a hundred poor dependants, whose appealing looks were perhaps the hardest of all pains for him to bear, devising fevered plans for to-morrow, new histories, new comedies, all sorts of new literary schemes, flying from all these into seclusion, and out of seclusion into pleasure — at last, at five-and-forty, death seized him and closed his career. I have been many a time in the chambers in the Temple which were his, and passed up the staircase, which Johnson, and Burke, and Reynolds trod to see their friend, their poet, their kind Goldsmith — the stair on which the poor women sat weeping bitterly when they heard that the greatest and most generous of all men was dead within the black oak door. Ah, it was a different lot from that for which the poor fellow sighed, when he wrote with heart yearning for home those most charming of all fond verses, in which he fancies he revisits Auburn —

> "Here, as I take my solitary rounds,
> Amidst thy tangling walks and ruined grounds,
> And, many a year elapsed, return to view
> Where once the cottage stood, the hawthorn grew,
> Remembrance wakes, with all her busy train,
> Swells at my breast, and turns the past to pain.
>
> "In all my wanderings round this world of care,
> In all my griefs — and God has given my share —
> I still had hopes my latest hours to crown,
> Amidst these humble bowers to lay me down;
> To husband out life's taper at the close,

STERNE AND GOLDSMITH

> And keep the flame from wasting by repose;
> I still had hopes — for pride attends us still —
> Amidst the swains to show my book-learned skill,
> Around my fire an evening group to draw,
> And tell of all I felt and all I saw;
> And, as a hare, whom hounds and horns pursue,
> Pants to the place from whence at first he flew —
> I still had hopes — my long vexations past,
> Here to return, and die at home at last.
>
> "O blest retirement, friend to life's decline!
> Retreats from care that never must be mine —
> How blest is he who crowns, in shades like these,
> A youth of labor with an age of ease;
> Who quits a world where strong temptations try,
> And, since 'tis hard to combat, learns to fly!
> For him no wretches born to work and weep
> Explore the mine or tempt the dangerous deep;
> No surly porter stands in guilty state
> To spurn imploring famine from the gate:
> But on he moves to meet his latter end,
> Angels around befriending virtue's friend;
> Sinks to the grave with unperceived decay,
> Whilst resignation gently slopes the way;
> And all his prospects brightening to the last,
> His heaven commences ere the world be past."

In these verses, I need not say with what melody, with what touching truth, with what exquisite beauty of comparison — as indeed in hundreds more pages of the writings of this honest soul — the whole character of the man is told — his humble confession of faults and weakness; his pleasant little vanity, and desire that his village should admire him; his simple scheme of good in which everybody was to be happy — no beggar was to be refused his dinner — nobody in fact was to work much, and he to be the harmless chief of the Utopia, and the monarch of the Irish Yvetot. He would have told again, and without fear of their failing, those famous jokes which had hung fire in London; he would have talked of his great friends of the Club — of my Lord Clare and my Lord Bishop, my Lord Nugent — sure he knew them intimately, and was hand and glove with some of the best men in town — and he would have spoken of Johnson and of Burke, and of Sir Joshua who had painted him — and he would have told wonderful sly stories of Ranelagh and the Pantheon, and the masquerades at Madame Cornelis'; and he would have toasted, with a sigh, the Jessamy Bride — the lovely Mary Horneck.

The figure of that charming young lady forms one of the prettiest recollections of Goldsmith's life. She and her beautiful sister, who married Bunbury, the graceful and humorous amateur artist of those days, when Gilray had but just begun to try his powers, were among the kindest and dearest of Goldsmith's many friends, cheered and pitied him, travelled abroad with him, made him welcome at their home, and gave him many a pleasant holiday. He bought his finest clothes to figure at their country-house at Barton — he wrote them droll verses. They loved him, laughed at him, played him tricks and made him happy. He asked for a loan from Garrick, and Garrick kindly supplied him, to enable him to go to Barton: but there were to be no more holidays, and only one brief struggle more for poor Goldsmith. A lock of his hair was taken from the coffin and given to the Jessamy Bride. She lived quite into our time. Hazlitt saw her an old lady, but beautiful still, in Northcote's painting-room, who told the eager critic how proud she always was that Goldsmith had admired her. The younger Colman has left a touching reminiscence of him. Vol. i. 63, 64.

"I was only five years old," he says, "when Goldsmith took me on his knee one evening whilst he was drinking coffee with my father, and began to play with me, which amiable act I returned, with the ingratitude of a peevish brat, by giving him a very smart slap on the face: it must have been a tingler, for it left the marks of my spiteful paw on his cheek. This infantile outrage was followed by summary justice, and I was locked up by my indignant father in an adjoining room to undergo solitary imprisonment in the dark. Here I began to howl and scream most abominably, which was no bad step towards my liberation, since those who were not inclined to pity me might be likely to set me free for the purpose of abating a nuisance.

"At length a generous friend appeared to extricate me from jeopardy, and that generous friend was no other than the man I had so wantonly molested by assault and battery — it was the tender-hearted Doctor himself, with a lighted candle in his hand, and a smile upon his countenance, which was still partially red from the effects of my petulance. I sulked and sobbed as he fondled and soothed, till I began to brighten. Goldsmith seized the propitious moment of returning good-humor, when he put down the candle and began to conjure. He placed three hats, which happened to

STERNE AND GOLDSMITH

be in the room, and a shilling under each. The shillings he told me were England, France, and Spain. 'Hey Presto cockalorum!' cried the Doctor, and lo, on uncovering the shillings, which had been dispersed each beneath a separate hat, they were all found congregated under one. I was no politician at five years old, and therefore might not have wondered at the sudden revolution which brought England, France, and Spain all under one crown; but, as also I was no conjurer, it amazed me beyond measure. . . . From that time, whenever the doctor came to visit my father, 'I plucked his gown to share the good man's smile;' a game at romps constantly ensued, and we were always cordial friends and merry playfellows. Our unequal companionship varied somewhat as to sports as I grew older; but it did not last long: my senior playmate died in his forty-fifth year, when I had attained my eleventh. . . . In all the numerous accounts of his virtues and foibles, his genius and absurdities, his knowledge of nature and ignorance of the world, his 'compassion for another's woe' was always predominant; and my trivial story of his humoring a froward child weighs but as a feather in the recorded scale of his benevolence."

Think of him reckless, thriftless, vain if you like — but merciful, gentle, generous, full of love and pity. He passes out of our life, and goes to render his account beyond it. Think of the poor pensioners weeping at his grave; think of the noble spirits that admired and deplored him; think of the righteous pen that wrote his epitaph — and of the wonderful and unanimous response of affection with which the world has paid back the love he gave it. His humor delighting us still: his song fresh and beautiful as when first he charmed with it; his words in all our mouths: his very weaknesses beloved and familiar — his benevolent spirit seems still to smile upon us: to do gentle kindnesses: to succor with sweet charity: to soothe, caress, and forgive: to plead with the fortunate for the unhappy and the poor.

His name is the last in the list of those men of humor who have formed the themes of the discourses which you have heard so kindly.

Long before I had ever hoped for such an audience, or dreamed of the possibility of the good fortune which has brought me so many friends, I was at issue with some of my literary brethren upon a point — which they held from tradition I think rather than experience

STERNE AND GOLDSMITH

— that our profession was neglected in this country; and that men of letters were ill-received and held in slight esteem. It would hardly be grateful' of me now to alter my old opinion that we do meet with good-will and kindness, with generous helping hands in the time of our necessity, with cordial and friendly recognition. What claim had any one of these of whom I have been speaking, but genius? What return of gratitude, fame, affection, did it not bring to all?

What punishment befell those who were unfortunate among them, but that which follows reckless habits and careless lives? For these faults a wit must suffer like the dullest prodigal that ever ran in debt. He must pay the tailor if he wears the coat; his children must go in rags if he spends his money at the tavern; he can't come to London and be made Lord Chancellor if he stops on the road and gambles away his last shilling at Dublin. And he must pay the social penalty of these follies too, and expect that the world will shun the man of bad habits, that women will avoid the man of loose life, that prudent folks will close their doors as a precaution, and before a demand should be made on their pockets by the needy prodigal. With what difficulty had any one of these men to contend, save that eternal and mechanical one of want of means and lack of capital, and of which thousands of young lawyers, young doctors, young soldiers and sailors, of inventors, manufacturers, shop-keepers, have to complain? Hearts as brave and resolute as ever beat in the breast of any wit or poet, sicken and break daily in the vain endeavor and unavailing struggle against life's difficulty. Don't we see daily ruined inventors, gray-haired midshipmen, balked heroes, blighted curates, barristers pining a hungry life out in chambers, the attorneys never mounting to their garrets, whilst scores of them are rapping at the door of the successful quack below? If these suffer, who is the author, that he should be exempt? Let us bear our ills with the same constancy with which others endure them, accept our manly part in life, hold our own, and ask no more. I can conceive of no kings or laws causing or curing Goldsmith's improvidence, or Fielding's fatal love of pleasure, or Dick Steele's mania for running races with the constable. You never can outrun that sure-footed officer — not by any swiftness or by dodges devised by any genius, however great; and he carries off the Tatler to the spunging-house, or taps the Citizen of the World on the shoulder as he would any other mortal.

STERNE AND GOLDSMITH

Does society look down on a man because he is an author? I suppose if people want a buffoon they tolerate him only in to far as he is amusing; it can hardly be expected that they should respect him as an equal. Is there to be a guard of honor provided for the author of the last new novel or poem? how long is he to reign, and keep other potentates out of possession? He retires, grumbles, and prints a lamentation that literature is despised. If Captain A. is left out of Lady B.'s parties he does not state that the army is despised: if Lord C. no longer asks Counsellor D. to dinner, Counsellor D. does not announce that the bar is insulted. He is not fair to society if he enters it with this suspicion hankering about him; if he is doubtful about his reception, how hold up his head honestly, and look frankly in the face that world about which he is full of suspicion? Is he place-hunting, and thinking in his mind that he ought to be made an Ambassador, like Prior, or a Secretary of State, like Addison? this pretence of equality falls to the ground at once: he is scheming for a patron, not shaking the hand of a friend, when he meets the world. Treat such a man as he deserves; laugh at his buffoonery, and give him a dinner and a *bon jour;* laugh at his self-sufficiency and absurd assumptions of superiority, and his equally ludicrous airs of martyrdom: laugh at his flattery and his scheming, and buy it, if it's worth the having. Let the wag have his dinner and the hireling his pay if you want him, and make a profound bow to the *grand homme incompris,* and the boisterous martyr, and show him the door. The great world, the great aggregate experience, has its good sense as it has its good humor. It detects a pretender, as it trusts a loyal heart. It is kind in the main: how should it be otherwise than kind, when it is so wise and clear headed? To any literary man who says, "It despises my profession," I say, with all my might — no, no, no. It may pass over your individual case — how many a brave fellow has failed in the race, and perished unknown in the struggle! — but it treats you as you merit in the main. If you serve it, it is not unthankful; if you please, it is pleased; if you cringe to it, it detects you, and scorns you if you are mean; it returns your cheerfulness with its good humor; it deals not ungenerously with your weaknesses; it recognizes most kindly your merits; it gives you a fair place and fair play. To any one of those men of whom we have spoken was it in the main ungrateful? A king might refuse Goldsmith a pension, as a publisher might keep his masterpiece and the delight of all the world in his desk for two years; but it was mistake, and not ill-will. Noble and illustrious names of Swift, and Pope, and Addison! dear and honored memories of Goldsmith and Fielding! kind friends, teachers, benefactors! who shall say that our country, which continues to bring you such an unceasing tribute of applause, admiration, love, sympathy, does not do honor to the literary calling in the honor which it bestows upon *you?*

FROM

THE LIFE AND OPINIONS OF
TRISTRAM SHANDY

BY

LAURENCE STERNE

THE STORY OF LE FEVER

IT was some time in the summer of that year in which *Dendermond* was taken by the allies, — which was about seven years before my father came into the country, — and about as many, after the time, that my uncle *Toby* and *Trim* had privately decamped from my father's house in town, in order to lay some of the finest sieges to some of the finest fortified cities in *Europe* —— when my uncle *Toby* was one evening getting his supper, with *Trim* sitting behind him at a small sideboard, — I say, sitting — for in consideration of the corporal's lame knee (which sometimes gave him exquisite pain) — when my uncle *Toby* dined or supped alone, he would never suffer the corporal to stand; and the poor fellow's veneration for his master was such, that, with a proper artillery, my uncle *Toby* could have taken *Dendermond* itself, with less trouble than he was able to gain this point over him; for many a time when my uncle *Toby* supposed the corporal's leg was at rest, he would look back, and detect him standing behind him with the most dutiful respect: this bred more little squabbles betwixt them, than all other causes for five-and-twenty years together — But this this is neither here nor there — why do I mention it? —— Ask my pen, — it governs me, — I govern not it.

He was one evening sitting thus at his supper, when the landlord of a little inn in the village came into the parlour, with an empty phial in his hand, to beg a glass or two of sack; 'Tis for a poor gentleman, — I think, of the army, said the landlord, who has been taken ill at my house four days ago, and has never held up his head since, or had a desire to taste any thing, till just now, that he has a fancy for a glass of sack and a thin toast, ——*I think*, says he, taking his hand from his forehead, *it would comfort me.* ——

——If I could neither beg, borrow, or buy such a thing — added the landlord, — I would almost steal it for the poor gentleman, he is so ill. —— I hope in God he will still mend, continued **he**, — we are all of us concerned for him.

Thou art a good-natured soul, I will answer for thee, cried my uncle *Toby;* and thou shalt drink the poor gentleman's health in a glass of sack thyself, — and take a couple of bottles with my service, and tell him he is heartily welcome to them, and to a dozen more if they will do him good.

Though I am persuaded, said my uncle *Toby*, as the landlord shut the door, he is a very compassionate fellow — *Trim*, — yet I cannot help entertaining a high opinion of his guest too; there must be something more than common in him, that in so short a time should win so much upon the affections of his host;—— And of his whole family, added the corporal, for they are all concerned for him. —— Step after him, said my uncle *Toby*, — do, *Trim*, — and ask if he knows his name.

—— I have quite forgot it truly, said the landlord, coming back into the parlour with the corporal, — but I can ask his son again: —— Has he a son with him then? said my uncle *Toby*. — A boy, replied the landlord, of about eleven or twelve years of age; — but the poor creature has tasted almost as little as his father; he does nothing but mourn and lament for him night and day:——He has not stirred from the bed-side these two days.

My uncle *Toby* laid down his knife and fork, and thrust his plate from before him, as the landlord gave him the account; and *Trim*, without being ordered, took away, without saying one word, and in a few minutes after brought him his pipe and tobacco.

—— Stay in the room a little, said my uncle *Toby*.

Trim! —— said my uncle *Toby*, after he lighted his pipe, and smoak'd about a dozen whiffs. ——*Trim* came in front of his master, and made his bow; — my uncle *Toby* smoak'd on, and said no more. —— Corporal! said my uncle *Toby* —— the corporal made his bow. —— My uncle *Toby* proceeded no farther, but finished his pipe.

Trim! said my uncle *Toby*, I have a project in my head, as it is a bad night, of wrapping myself up warm in my roquelaure, and paying a visit to this poor gentleman. —— Your honour's roquelaure, replied the corporal, has not once been had on, since the night before your honour received your wound, when we mounted guard in the trenches before the gate of St. *Nicholas;* —— and besides, it is so cold and rainy a night, that what with the roquelaure and what with the weather, 'twill be enough to give your honour your death, and bring on your honour's torment in your groin. I fear so, replied my uncle *Toby;* but I am not at rest in my mind, *Trim,* since the account the landlord has given me. —— I wish I had not known so much of this affair, — added my uncle *Toby,* — or that I had known more of it: —— How shall we manage it? Leave it, an't please your honour, to me, quoth the corporal; —— I'll take my hat and stick and go to the house and reconnoitre, and act accordingly; and I will bring your honour a full account in an hour. —— Thou shalt go, *Trim,* said my uncle *Toby,* and here's a shilling for thee to drink with his servant. —— I shall get it all out of him, said the corporal, shutting the door.

My uncle *Toby* filled his second pipe; and had it not been, that he now and then wandered from the point, with considering whether it was not full as well to have the curtain of the tenaille a straight line, as a crooked one, — he might be said to have thought of nothing else but poor *Le Fever* and his boy the whole time he smoaked it.

CHAPTER VII

THE STORY OF LE FEVER CONTINUED

IT was not till my uncle *Toby* had knocked the ashes out of his third pipe, that corporal *Trim* returned from the inn, and gave him the following account.

I despaired, at first, said the corporal, of being able to bring back your honour any kind of intelligence concerning the poor sick lieutenant. — Is he in the army, then? said my uncle *Toby* —— He is, said the corporal —— And in what regiment? said my uncle *Toby* —— I'll tell your honour, replied the corporal, every thing straight forwards, as I learnt it. — Then, *Trim,* I'll fill another pipe, said my uncle *Toby,* and not interrupt thee till thou hast done; so sit down at thy ease, *Trim,* in the window-seat, and begin thy story again. The corporal made his old bow, which generally spoke as plain as a bow could speak it — *Your honour is good:* —— And having done that, he sat down, as he was ordered, — and begun the story to my uncle *Toby* over again in pretty near the same words.

I despaired at first, said the corporal, of being able to bring back any intelligence to your honour, about the lieutenant and his son; for when I asked where his servant was, from whom I made myself sure of knowing every thing which was proper to be asked, — That's a right distinction, *Trim,* said my uncle *Toby* — I was answered, an' please your honour, that he had no servant with him; —— that he had come to the inn with hired horses, which, upon finding himself unable to proceed (to join, I suppose, the regiment), he had dismissed the morning after he came. — If I get better, my dear, said he, as he gave his purse to his son to pay the man, — we can hire horses from hence. —— But alas! the poor gentleman will never get from hence, said the landlady to me, — for I heard the death-watch all night long; —— and when he dies, the youth, his son, will certainly die with him; for he is broken-hearted already.

I was hearing this account, continued the corporal, when the youth came into the kitchen, to order the thin toast the landlord spoke of; —— but I will do it for my father myself, said the youth. —— Pray let me save you the trouble, young gentleman, said I, taking up a fork for the purpose, and offering him my chair to sit down upon by the fire, whilst I did it. —— I believe, Sir, said he, very modestly, I can please him best myself. —— I am sure, said I, his honour will not like the toast the worse for being toasted by an old soldier. —— The youth took hold of my hand, and instantly burst into tears. —— Poor youth! said my uncle *Toby,* — he has been bred up from an infant in the army, and the name of a soldier *Trim,* sounded in his ears like the name of a friend; — I wish I had him here.

—— I never, in the longest march, said the corporal, had so great a mind to my dinner, as I had to cry with him for company: — What could be the matter with me, an' please your honour? Nothing in the world, *Trim,* said my uncle *Toby,* blowing his nose, — but that thou art a good-natured fellow.

When I gave him the toast, continued the corporal, I thought it was proper to tell him I was captain *Shandy's* servant, and that your honour (though a stranger) was extremely concerned for his father; — and that if there was any thing in your house or cellar —— (And thou might'st have added my purse too, said my uncle *Toby*) —— he was heartily welcome to it: —— He made a very low bow (which was meant to your honour), but no answer — for his heart was full — so he went up stairs with the toast; — I warrant you, my dear, said I, as I opened the kitchen-door, your father will be well again. —— Mr. *Yorick's* curate was smoking a pipe by the kitchen fire, — but said not a word good or bad to comfort the youth.—— I thought it wrong; added the corporal —— I think so too, said my uncle *Toby*.

When the lieutenant had taken his glass of sack and toast, he felt himself a little revived, and sent down into the kitchen, to let me know, that in about ten minutes he should be glad if I would step up stairs.—— I believe, said the landlord, he is going to say his prayers,—— for there was a book laid upon the chair by his bedside, and as I shut the door, I saw his son take up a cushion.——

I thought, said the curate, that you gentlemen of the army, Mr. *Trim*, never said your prayers at all.—— I heard the poor gentleman say his prayers last night, said the landlady, very devoutly, and with my own ears, or I could not have believed it.—— Are you sure of it? replied the curate.—— A soldier, an' please your reverence, said I, prays as often (of his own accord) as a parson;—— and when he is fighting for his king, and for his own life, and for his honour too, he has the most reason to pray to God of any one in the whole world.—— 'Twas well said of thee, *Trim*, said my uncle *Toby*.—— But when a soldier, said I, an' please your reverence, has been standing for twelve hours together in the trenches, up to his knees in cold water,— or engaged, said I, for months together in long and dangerous marches;— harassed, perhaps, in his rear to-day;— harassing others to-morrow;— detached here;— countermanded there;— resting this night out upon his arms;— beat up in his shirt the next;— benumbed in his joints;— perhaps without straw in his tent to kneel on;—— must say his prayers *how* and *when* he can.— I believe, said I,— for I was piqued, quoth the corporal, for the reputation of the army,— I believe, an' please your reverence, said I, that when a soldier gets time to pray,— he prays as heartily as a parson,— though not with all his fuss and hypocrisy.—— Thou shouldst not have said that, *Trim*, said my uncle *Toby*,— for God only knows who is a hypocrite, and who is not:—— At the great and general review of us all, corporal, at the day of judgment (and not till then) — it will be seen who has done their duties in this world,— and who has not; and we shall be advanced, *Trim*, accordingly.—— I hope we shall, said *Trim*.—— It is in the Scripture, said my uncle *Toby;* and I will shew it thee to-morrow:— In the mean time we may depend upon it, *Trim*, for our comfort, said my uncle *Toby*, that God Almighty is so good and just a governor of the world, that if we have but done our duties in it, — it will never be enquired into,

THE LIFE AND OPINIONS

whether we have done them in a red coat or a black one:——I hope not, said the corporal——But go on, *Trim*, said my uncle *Toby*, with thy story.

When I went up, continued the corporal, into the lieutenant's room, which I did not do till the expiration of the ten minutes,—he was lying in his bed with his head raised upon his hand, with his elbow upon the pillow, and a clean white cambrick handkerchief beside it:——The youth was just stooping down to take up the cushion, upon which I supposed he had been kneeling,—the book was laid upon the bed,—and, as he rose, in taking up the cushion with one hand, he reached out his other to take it away at the same time.——Let it remain there, my dear, said the lieutenant.

He did not offer to speak to me, till I had walked up close to his bed-side:—If you are captain *Shandy's* servant, said he, you must present my thanks to your master, with my little boy's thanks along with them, for his courtesy to me;—if he was of *Leven's*—said the lieutenant.—I told him your honour was.—Then, said he, I served three campaigns with him in *Flanders*, and remember him,—but 'tis most likely, as I had not the honour of any acquaintance with him, that he knows nothing of me.—You will tell him, however, that the person his good-nature has laid under obligations to him, is one *Le Fever*, a lieutenant in *Angus's*——but he knows me not,—said he, a second time, musing;——possibly he may my story—added he—pray tell the captain I was the ensign at *Breda*, whose wife was most unfortunately killed with a musket-shot, as she lay in my arms in my tent.——I remember the story an't please your honour, said I, very well.——Do you so? said he, wiping his eyes with his handkerchief,—then well may I.—In saying this, he drew a little ring out of his bosom, which seemed tied with a black ribband about his neck, and kiss'd it twice——Here, *Billy*, said he,——the boy flew across the room to the bed-side,—and falling down upon his knee, took the ring in his hand, and kissed it too,—then kissed his father, and sat down upon the bed and wept.

I wish, said my uncle *Toby*, with a deep sigh,—I wish, *Trim*, I was asleep.

Your honour, replied the corporal, is too much concerned;—shall I pour your honour out a glass of sack to your pipe?——Do, *Trim*, said my uncle *Toby*.

I remember, said my uncle *Toby*, sighing again, the story of the ensign and his wife, with a circumstance his modesty omitted; — and particularly well that he, as well as she, upon some account or other (I forget what) was universally pitied by the whole regiment; — but finish the story thou art upon: — 'Tis finished already, said the corporal, — for I could stay no longer, — so wished his honour a good night; young *Le Fever* rose from off the bed, and saw me to the bottom of the stairs; and as we went down together, told me, they had come from *Ireland*, and were on their route to join the regiment in *Flanders*. —— But alas! said the corporal, — the lieutenant's last day's march is over. — Then what is to become of his poor boy? cried my uncle *Toby*.

CHAPTER VIII

THE STORY OF LE FEVER CONTINUED

IT was to my uncle *Toby's* eternal honour, —— though I tell it only for the sake of those, who, when coop'd in betwixt a natural and a positive law, know not, for their souls, which way in the world to turn themselves —— That notwithstanding my uncle *Toby* was warmly engaged at that time in carrying on the siege of *Dendermond*, parallel with the allies, who pressed theirs on so vigorously, that they scarce allowed him time to get his dinner —— that nevertheless he gave up *Dendermond*, though he had already made a lodgment upon the counterscarp; — and bent his whole thoughts towards the private distresses at the inn; and except that he ordered the garden gate to be bolted up, by which he might be said to have turned the siege of *Dendermond* into a blockade, — he left *Dendermond* to itself — to be relieved or not by the *French* king, as the *French* king thought good; and only considered how he himself should relieve the poor lieutenant and his son.

—— That kind BEING, who is a friend to the friendless, shall recompence thee for this.

Thou hast left this matter short, said my uncle *Toby* to the corporal, as he was putting him to bed, —— and I will tell thee in what, *Trim*. —— In the first place, when thou madest an offer of my services to *Le Fever*, —— as sickness and travelling are both expensive, and thou knowest he was but a poor lieutenant, with a son to subsist as well as himself out of his pay, — that thou didst not make an offer to him of my purse; because, had he stood in need, thou knowest, *Trim*, he had been as welcome to it as myself. —— Your honour knows, said the corporal, I had no orders; —— True, quoth my uncle *Toby*, — thou didst very right, *Trim*, as a soldier, — but certainly very wrong as a man.

In the second place, for which, indeed, thou hast the same excuse, continued my uncle *Toby*, —— when thou offeredst him whatever was in my house, —— thou shouldst have offered him my house too: —— A sick brother officer should have the best quarters, *Trim*, and if we had him with us, — we could tend and look to him: —— Thou art an excellent nurse thyself, *Trim*, — and what with thy care of him, and the old woman's, and his boy's, and mine together, we might recruit him again at once, and set him upon his legs.——

—— In a fortnight or three weeks, added my uncle *Toby*, smiling, —— he might march. —— He will never march; an' please your honour, in this world, said the corporal: —— He will march; said my uncle *Toby*, rising up from the side of the bed, with one shoe off: —— An' please your honour, said the corporal, he will never march but to his grave: —— He shall march, cried my uncle *Toby*, marching the foot which had a shoe on, though without advancing an inch, — he shall march to his regiment. —— He cannot stand it, said the corporal; —— He shall be supported, said my uncle *Toby;* —— He'll drop at last, said the corporal, and what will become of his boy? —— He shall not drop, said my uncle *Toby*, firmly. —— A-well-o'day, — do what we can for him, said *Trim*, maintaining his point — the poor soul will die: —— He shall not die, by G——, cried my uncle *Toby*.

— The ACCUSING SPIRIT, which flew up to heaven's chancery with the oath, blush'd as he gave it in; — and the RECORDING ANGEL, as he wrote it down, dropp'd a tear upon the word, and blotted it out for ever.

CHAPTER IX

MY uncle *Toby* went to his bureau, — put his purse into his breeches pocket, and having ordered the corporal to go early in the morning for a physician, — he went to bed, and fell asleep.

OF TRISTRAM SHANDY

CHAPTER X

THE STORY OF LE FEVER CONTINUED

THE sun looked bright the morning after, to every eye in the village but *Le Fever's* and his afflicted son's; the hand of death press'd heavy upon his eyelids,—— and hardly could the wheel at the cistern turn round its circle,— when my uncle *Toby*, who had rose up an hour before his wonted time, entered the lieutenant's room, and without preface or apology, sat himself down upon the chair by the bed-side, and independently of all modes and customs, opened the curtain in the manner an old friend and brother officer would have done it, and asked him how he did,— how he had rested in the night,— what was his complaint,— where was his pain,— and what he could do to help him:—— and without giving him time to answer any one of the enquiries, went on, and told him of the litttle plan which he had been concerting with the corporal the night before for him.——

—— You shall go home directly, *Le Fever*, said my uncle *Toby*, to my house,— and we'll send for a doctor to see what's the matter, — and we'll have an apothecary,— and the corporal shall be your nurse;—— and I'll be your servant, *Le Fever*.

There was a frankness in my uncle *Toby*, — not the *effect* of familiarity,— but the *cause* of it,— which let you at once into his soul, and shewed you the goodness of his nature; to this, there was something in his looks, and voice, and manner, superadded, which eternally beckoned to the unfortunate to come and take shelter under him; so that before my uncle *Toby* had half finished the kind offers he was making to the father, had the son insensibly pressed up close to his knees, and had taken hold of the breast of his coat, and was pulling it towards him.—— The blood and spirits of *Le Fever*, which were waxing cold and slow within him, and were retreating to their last citadel, the heart, — rallied back,— the film forsook his eyes for a moment, — he looked up wishfully in my uncle *Toby's* face, — then cast a look upon his boy, —— and that *ligament*, fine as it was,— was never broken.——

Nature instantly ebb'd again,— the film returned to its place, —— the pulse fluttered —— stopp'd —— went on ——throbb'd —— stopp'd again —— moved —— stopp'd —— shall I go on? —— No.

THE LIFE AND OPINIONS

CHAPTER XI

I AM so impatient to return to my own story, that what remains of young *Le Fever's*, that is, from this turn of his fortune, to the time my uncle *Toby* recommended him for my preceptor, shall be told in a very few words in the next chapter. — All that is necessary to be added to this chapter is as follows. —

That my uncle *Toby*, with young *Le Fever* in his hand, attended the poor lieutenant, as chief mourners, to his grave.

That the governor of *Dendermond* paid his obsequies all military honours, — and that *Yorick*, not to be behind-hand — paid him all ecclesiastic — for he buried him in his chancel: — And it appears likewise, he preached a funeral sermon over him —— I say it *appears*, — for it was *Yorick's* custom, which I suppose a general one with those of his profession, on the first leaf of every sermon which he composed, to chronicle down the time, the place, and the occasion of its being preached: to this, he was ever wont to add some short comment or stricture upon the sermon itself, seldom, indeed, much to its credit: — For instance, *This sermon upon the Jewish dispensation — I don't like it all; — Though I own there is a world of* WATER-LANDISH *knowledge in it, — but 'tis all tritical, and most tritically put together.* —— *This is but a flimsy kind of a composition; what was in my head when I made it?*

—— N. B. *The excellency of this text is, that it will suit any sermon, — and of this sermon,* —— *that it will suit any text.* ——

—— *For this sermon I shall be hanged, — for I have stolen the greatest part of it. Doctor* Paidagunes *found me out.* ☞ *Set a thief to catch a thief.* ——

On the back of half a dozen I find written, *So, so*, and no more —— and upon a couple *Moderato;* by which, as far as one may gather from *Altieri's Italian* dictionary, — but mostly from the authority of a piece of green whipcord, which seemed to have been the unravelling of *Yorick's* whip-lash, with which he has left us the two sermons marked *Moderato*, and the half dozen of *So, so*, tied fast together in one bundle by themselves, — one may safely suppose he meant pretty near the same thing.

There is but one difficulty in the way of this conjecture, which is this, that the *moderato's* are five times better than the *so, so's;* — show ten times more knowledge of the human heart; — have seventy times more wit and spirit in them; — (and, to rise properly in my climax) — discovered a thousand times more genius; — and to crown all, are infinitely more entertaining than those tied up with them: — for which reason, whene'er *Yorick's dramatic* sermons are offered to the world, though I shall admit but one out of the whole number of the *so, so's*, I shall, nevertheless, adventure to print the two *moderato's* without any sort of scruple.

What *Yorick* could mean by the words *lèntamente,* — *tenuté,* — *grave,* — and sometimes *adagio,* — as applied to *theological* compositions, and with which he has characterised some of these sermons, I dare not venture to guess. —— I am more puzzled still upon finding *a l'octava alta!* upon one; —— *Con strepito* upon the back of another; —— *Siciliana* upon a third; —— *Alla capella* upon a fourth; —— *Con l'arco* upon this; —— *Senza l'acro* upon that. —— All I know is, that they are musical terms, and have a meaning; — and as he was a musical man, I will make no doubt, but that by some quaint application of such metaphors to the compositions in hand, they impressed very distinct ideas of their several characters upon his fancy, — whatever they may do upon that of others.

Amongst these, there is that particular sermon which has unaccountably led me into this digression —— The funeral sermon upon poor *Le Fever,* wrote out very fairly, as if from a hasty copy.— I take notice of it the more, because it seems to have been his favourite composition — It is upon mortality; and is tied lengthways and cross-ways with a yarn thrum, and then rolled up and twisted round with a half-sheet of dirty blue paper, which seems to have been once the cast cover of a general review, which to this day smells horribly of horse drugs. —— Whether these marks of humiliation were designed, — I something doubt; —— because at the end of the sermon (and not at the beginning of it) — very different from his way of treating the rest, he had wrote ——

Bravo!

—— Though not very offensively, —— for it is at two inches, at least, and a half's distance from, and below the concluding line of the sermon, at the very extremity of the page, and in the right-hand corner of it, which, you know, is generally covered with your thumb; and, to do it justice, it is wrote besides with a crow's quill so faintly in a small *Italian* hand, as scarce to solicit the eye towards the place, whether your thumb is there or not, — so that from the *manner of it,* it stands half excused; and being wrote moreover with very pale ink, diluted almost to nothing, — 'tis more like a *ritratto* of the shadow of vanity, than of VANITY herself — of the two; resembling rather a faint thought of transient applause, secretly stirring up in the heart of the composer; than a gross mark of it, coarsely obtruded upon the world.

With all these extenuations, I am aware, that in publishing this, I do no service to *Yorick's* character as a modest man; — but all men have their failings! and what lessens this still farther, and almost wipes it away, is this; that the word was struck through sometime afterwards (as appears from a different tint of the ink) with a line quite across it in this manner, BRAVO —— as if he had retracted, or was ashamed of the opinion he had once entertained of it.

These short characters of his sermons were always written, excepting in this one instance, upon the first leaf of his sermon, which served as a cover to it; and usually upon the inside of it, which was turned towards the text; — but at the end of his discourse, where, perhaps, he had five or six pages, and sometimes, perhaps, a whole score to turn himself in, — he took a large circuit, and, indeed, a much more mettlesome one; — as if he had snatched the occasion of unlacing himself with a few more frolicksome strokes at vice, than the straightness of the pulpit allowed. — These, though hussard-like, they skirmish lightly and out of all order, are still auxiliaries on the side of virtue; —tell me then, Mynheer Vander Blonederdondergewdenstronke, why they should not be printed together?

CHAPTER XII

WHEN my uncle *Toby* had turned every thing into money, and settled all accounts betwixt the agent of the regiment and *Le Fever*, and betwixt *Le Fever* and all mankind, —— there remained nothing more in my uncle *Toby's* hands, than an old regimental coat and a sword; so that my uncle *Toby* found little or no opposition from the world in taking administration. The coat my uncle *Toby* gave the corporal; —— Wear it, *Trim*, said my uncle *Toby*, as long as it will hold together, for the sake of the poor lieutenant —— And this, —— said my uncle *Toby*, taking up the sword in his hand, and drawing it out of the scabbard as he spoke — and this, *Le Fever*, I'll save for thee, — 'tis all the fortune, continued my uncle *Toby*, hanging it up upon a crook, and pointing to it, — 'tis all the fortune, my dear *Le Fever*, which God has left thee; but if he has given thee a heart to fight thy way with it in the world, — and thou doest it like a man of honour, — 'tis enough for us.

As soon as my uncle *Toby* had laid a foundation, and taught him to inscribe a regular polygon in a circle, he sent him to a public school, where, excepting *Whitsontide* and *Christmas*, at which times the corporal was punctually dispatched for him, — he remained to the spring of the year, seventeen; when the stories of the emperor's sending his army into *Hungary* against the *Turks*, kindling a spark of fire in his bosom, he left his *Greek* and *Latin* without leave, and throwing himself upon his knees before my uncle *Toby*, begged his father's sword, and my uncle *Toby's* leave along with it, to go and try his fortune under *Eugene*. — Twice did my uncle *Toby* forget his wound and cry out, *Le Fever!* I will go with thee, and thou shalt fight beside me —— And twice he laid his hand upon his groin, and hung down his head in sorrow and disconsolation. ——

My uncle *Toby* took down the sword from the crook, where it had hung untouched ever since the lieutenant's death, and delivered it to the corporal to brighten up; —— and having detained *Le Fever* a single fortnight to equip him, and contract for his passage to *Leghorn*, — he put the sword into his hand. —— If thou art brave, *Le Fever*, said my uncle *Toby*, this will not fail thee, —— but Fortune, said he (musing a little), —— Fortune may —— And if she does, — added my uncle *Toby*, embracing him, come back again to me, *Le Fever*, and we will shape thee another course.

The greatest injury could not have oppressed the heart of *Le Fever* more than my uncle *Toby's* paternal kindness; — he parted from my uncle *Toby*, as the best of sons from the best of fathers —— both dropped tears —— and as my uncle *Toby* gave him his last kiss, he slipped sixty guineas, tied up in an old purse of his father's, in which was his mother's ring, into his hand, — and bid God bless him.

CHAPTER XIII

LE FEVER got up to the Imperial army just time enough to try what metal his sword was made of, at the defeat of the *Turks* before *Belgrade;* but a series of unmerited mischances had pursued him from that moment, and trod close upon his heels for four years together after; he had withstood these buffetings to the last, till sickness overtook him at *Marseilles*, from whence he wrote my uncle *Toby* word, he had lost his time, his services, his health, and, in short, every thing but his sword;—— and was waiting for the first ship to return back to him.

As his letter came to hand about six weeks before *Susannah's* accident, *Le Fever* was hourly expected; and was uppermost in my uncle *Toby's* mind all the time my father was giving him and *Yorick* a description of what kind of a person he would chuse for a preceptor to me: but as my uncle *Toby* thought my father at first somewhat fanciful in the accomplishments he required, he forebore mentioning *Le Fever's* name,—— till the character, by *Yorick's* interposition, ending unexpectedly, in one, who should be gentle-tempered, and generous, and good, it impressed the image of *Le Fever*, and his interest, upon my uncle *Toby* so forcibly, he rose instantly off his chair; and laying down his pipe, in order to take hold of both my father's hands — I beg, brother *Shandy*, said my uncle *Toby*, I may recommend poor *Le Fever's* son to you —— I beseech you do, added *Yorick* —— He has a good heart, said my uncle *Toby* —— And a brave one too, an' please your honour, said the corporal.

—— The best hearts, *Trim*, are ever the bravest, replied my uncle *Toby*. —— And the greatest cowards, an' please your honour, in our regiment, were the greatest rascals in it. —— There was sergeant *Kumber*, and ensign ——

—— We'll talk of them, said my father, another time.

SAUNTERINGS IN FRANCE

BOOK VII

CHAPTER I

NO —— I think, I said, I would write two volumes every year, provided the vile cough which then tormented me, and which to this hour I dread worse than the devil, would but give me leave — and in another place — (but where, I can't recollect now) speaking of my book at a *machine*, and laying my pen and ruler down crosswise upon the table, in order to gain the greater credit to it — I swore it should be kept a going at that rate these forty years, if it pleased but the fountain of life to bless me so long with health and good spirits.

Now as for my spirits, little have I to lay to their charge — nay so very little (unless the mounting me upon a long stick and playing the fool with me nineteen hours out of the twenty-four, be accusations) that on the contrary, I have much — much to thank 'em for: cheerily have ye made me tread the path of life with all the burthens of it (except its cares) upon my back; in no one moment of my existence, that I remember, have ye once deserted me, or tinged the objects which came in my way, either with sable, or with a sickly green; in dangers ye gilded my horizon with hope, and when DEATH himself knocked at my door — ye bad him come again; and in so gay a tone of careless indifference, did ye do it, that he doubted of his commission ——

" — There must certainly be some mistake in this matter," quoth he.

Now there is nothing in this world I abominate worse, than to be interrupted in a story —— and I was that moment telling *Eugenius* a most tawdry one in my way, of a nun who fancied herself a shellfish, and of a monk damn'd for eating a muscle, and was shewing him the grounds and justice of the procedure. ——

"— Did ever so grave a personage get into so vile a scrape?" quoth Death. Thou hast had a narrow escape, *Tristram,* said *Eugenius,* taking hold of my hand as I finished my story. ——

But there is no *living, Eugenius,* replied I, at this rate; for as this *son of a whore* has found out my lodgings ——

— You call him rightly, said *Eugenius,* — for by sin, we are told, he enter'd the world —— I care not which way he enter'd, quoth I, provided he be not in such a hurry to take me out with him — for I have forty volumes to write, and forty thousand things to say and do which no body in the world will say and do for me, except thyself; and as thou seest he has got me by the throat (for *Eugenius* could scarce hear me speak across the table), and that I am no match for him in the open field, had I not better, whilst these few scatter'd spirits remain, and these two spider legs of mine (holding one of them up to him) are able to support me — had I not better, *Eugenius,* fly for my life? 'Tis my advice, my dear *Tristram,* said *Eugenius,* — Then by heaven! I will lead him a dance he little thinks of —— for I will gallop, quoth I, without looking once behind me, to the banks of the *Garonne;* and if I hear him clattering at my heels —— I'll scamper away to mount *Vesuvius* —— from thence to *Jappa,* and from *Jappa* to the world's end; where, if he follows me, I pray God he may break his neck ——

— He runs more risk *there,* said *Eugenius,* than thou.

Eugenius's wit and affection brought blood into the cheek from whence it had been some months banish'd —— 'twas a vile moment to bid adieu in; he led me to my chaise —— *Allons!* said I; the postboy gave a crack with his whip —— off I went like a cannon, and in half a dozen bounds got into *Dover.*

CHAPTER II

NOW hang it! quoth I, as I look'd towards the *French* coast — a man should know something of his own country too, before he goes abroad —— and I never gave a peep into *Rochester* church, or took notice of the dock of *Chatham,* or visited St. *Thomas* at *Canterbury,* though they all three laid in my way ——

— But mine, indeed, is a particular case ——

So without arguing the matter further with *Thomas o' Becket,* or any one else — I skip'd into the boat, and in five minutes we got under sail, and scudded away like the wind.

Pray, captain, quoth I, as I was going down into the cabin, is a man never overtaken by *Death* in this passage?

Why, there is not time for a man to be sick in it, replied he —— What a cursed lyar! for I am sick as a horse, quoth I, already —— what a brain! —— upside down! —— hey-day! the cells are broke loose one into another, and the blood, and the lymph, and the nervous juices, with the fix'd and volatile salts, are all jumbled into one mass —— good G—! every thing turns round in it like a thousand whirlpools —— I'd give a shilling to know if I shan't write the clearer for it ——

Sick! sick! sick! sick! ——

— When shall we get to land? captain — they have hearts like stones —— O I am deadly sick! —— reach me that thing, boy —— 'tis the most discomfiting sickness —— I wish I was at the bottom — Madam! how is it with you? Undone! undone! un —— O! undone! sir —— What the first time? —— No, 'tis the second, third, sixth, tenth time, sir, —— hey-day! — what a trampling over head! — hollo! cabin boy! what's the matter? —

The wind chopp'd about! s'Death! — then I shall meet him full in the face.

What luck! — 'tis chopp'd about again, master —— O the devil chop it ——

Captain, quoth she, for heaven's sake, let us get ashore.

CHAPTER III

IT is a great inconvenience to a man in a haste, that there are three distinct roads between *Calais* and *Paris*, in behalf of which there is so much to be said by the several deputies from the towns which lie along them, that half a day is easily lost in settling which you'll take.

First, the road by *Lisle* and *Arras*, which is the most about —— but most interesting, and instructing.

The second, that by *Amiens*, which you may go, if you would see *Chantilly* ——

And that by *Beauvais*, which you may go, if you will.

For this reason a great many chuse to go by *Beauvais*.

THE LIFE AND OPINIONS

CHAPTER IV

"NOW before I quit *Calais*," a travel-writer would say, "it would not be amiss to give some account of it." — Now I think it very much amiss — that a man cannot go quietly through a town, and let it alone, when it does not meddle with him, but that he must be turning about and drawing his pen at every kennel he crosses over, merely o' my conscience for the sake of drawing it; because, if we may judge from what has been wrote of these things, by all who have *wrote and gallop'd* — or who have *gallop'd and wrote*, which is a different way still; or who, for more expedition than the rest, have *wrote galloping*, which is the way I do at present —— from the great *Addison*, who did it with his satchel of school books hanging at his a —, and galling his beast's crupper at every stroke — there is not a galloper of us all who might not have gone on ambling quietly in his own ground (in case he had any), and have wrote all he had to write, dryshod, as well as not.

For my own part, as heaven is my judge, and to which I shall ever make my last appeal — I know no more of *Calais* (except the little my barber told me of it as he was whetting his razor), than I do this moment of *Grand Cairo;* for it was dusky in the evening when I landed, and dark as pitch in the morning when I set out, and yet by merely knowing what is what, and by drawing this from that in one part of the town, and by spelling and putting this and that together in another — I would lay any travelling odds, that I this moment write a chápter upon *Calais* as long as my arm; and with so distinct and satisfactory a detail of every item, which is worth a stranger's curiosity in the town — that you would take me for the town-clerk of *Calais* itself — and where, sir, would be the wonder? was not *Democritus*, who laughed ten times more than I — town-clerk of *Abdera?* and was not (I forget his name) who had more discretion than us both, town-clerk of *Ephesus?* —— it should be penn'd moreover, sir, with so much knowledge and good sense, and truth, and precision ——

— Nay — if you don't believe me, you may read the chapter for your pains.

OF TRISTRAM SHANDY

CHAPTER V

CALAIS, *Calatium, Calusium, Calesium*

This town, if we may trust its archives, the authority of which I see no reason to call in question in this place — was *once* no more than a small village belonging to one of the first Counts de *Guignes;* and as it boasts at present of no less than fourteen thousand inhabitants, exclusive of four hundred and twenty distinct families in the *basse ville*, or suburbs —— it must have grown up by little and little, I suppose, to its present size.

Though there are four convents, there is but one parochial church in the whole town; I had not an opportunity of taking its exact dimensions, but it is pretty easy to make a tolerable conjecture of 'em — for as there are fourteen thousand inhabitants in the town, if the church holds them all it must be considerably large — and if it will not — 'tis a very great pity they have not another — it is built in form of a cross, and dedicated to the Virgin *Mary;* the steeple, which has a spire to it, is placed in the middle of the church, and stands upon four pillars elegant and light enough, but sufficiently strong at the same time — it is decorated with eleven altars, most of which are rather fine than beautiful. The great altar is a masterpiece in its kind; 'tis of white marble, and, as I was told, near sixty feet high — had it been much higher, it had been as high as mount *Calvary* itself — therefore, I suppose it must be high enough in all conscience.

There was nothing struck me more than the great *Square;* tho' I cannot say 'tis either well paved or well built; but 'tis in the heart of the town, and most of the streets, especially those in that quarter, all terminate in it; could there have been a fountain in all *Calais*, which it seems there cannot, as such an object would have been a great ornament, it is not to be doubted, but that the inhabitants would have had it in the very centre of this square, — not that it is properly a square, — because 'tis forty feet longer from east to west, than from north to south; so that the *French* in general have more reason on their side in calling them *Places* than *Squares*, which, strictly speaking, to be sure, they are not.

The town-house seems to be but a sorry building, and not to be kept in the best repair; otherwise it had been a second great ornament to this place; it answers however its destination, and serves very well for the reception of the magistrates, who assemble in it from time to time; so that 'tis presumable, justice is regularly distributed.

I have heard much of it, but there is nothing at all curious in the *Courgain;* 'tis a distinct quarter of the town, inhabited solely by sailors and fishermen; it consists of a number of small streets, neatly built and mostly of brick; 'tis extremely populous, but as that may be accounted for, from the principles of their diet, — there is nothing curious in that neither. —— A traveller may see it to satisfy himself — he must not omit however taking notice of *La Tour de Guet*, upon any account; 'tis so called from its particular destination, because in war it serves to discover and give notice of the enemies which approach the place, either by sea or land; —— but 'tis monstrous high, and catches the eye so continually, you cannot avoid taking notice of it if you would.

It was a singular disappointment to me, that I could not have permission to take an exact survey of the fortifications, which are the strongest in the world, and which, from first to last, that is, from the time they were set about by *Philip* of *France*, Count of *Boulogne*, to the present war, wherein many reparations were made, have cost (as I leaned afterwards from an engineer in *Gascony*) — above a hundred millions of livres. It is very remarkable, that at the *Tête de Gravelenes*, and where the town is naturally the weakest, they have expended the most money; so that the outworks stretch a great way into the campaign, and consequently occupy a large tract of ground — However, after all that is *said* and *done*, it must be acknowledged that *Calais* was never upon any account so considerable from itself, as from its situation, and that easy entrance which it gave our ancestors, upon all occasions, into *France:* it was not without its conveniences also; being no less troublesome to the *English* in those times, than *Dumkirk* has been to us, in ours; so that it was deservedly looked upon as the key to both kingdoms, which no doubt is the reason that there have arisen so many contentions who should keep it: of these, the siege of *Calais*, or rather the blockade (for it was shut up both by land and sea), was the most memorable, as it withstood the efforts of *Edward* the Third a whole year, and was not terminated at last but by famine and extreme misery; the gallantry of *Eustace de St. Pierre*, who first offered himself a victim for his fellow-citizens, has rank'd his name with heroes. As it will not take up above fifty pages, it would be injustice to the reader, not to give him a minute account of that romantic transaction, as well as of the siege itself, in *Rapin's* own words:

CHAPTER VI

—— BUT courage! gentle reader! —— I scorn it —— 'tis enough to have thee in my power —— but to make use of the advantage which the fortune of the pen has now gained over thee, would be too much —— No —— ! by that all-powerful fire which warms the visionary brain, and lights the spirits through unworldly tracts! ere I would force a helpless creature upon this hard service, and make thee pay, poor soul! for fifty pages, which I have no right to sell thee, —— naked as I am, I would browse upon the mountains, and smile that the north wind brought me neither my tent or my supper.

— So put on, my brave boy! and make the best of thy way to *Boulogne*.

CHAPTER VII

—— BOULOGNE! —— hah! —— so we are all got together —— debtors and sinners before heaven; a jolly set of us — but I can't stay and quaff it off with you — I'm pursued myself like a hundred devils, and shall be overtaken, before I can well change horses: —— for heaven's sake, make haste —— 'Tis for high-treason, quoth a very little man, whispering as low as he could to a very tall man, that stood next him —— Or else for murder; quoth the tall man —— Well thrown, *Size-ace* quoth I. No; quoth a third, the gentleman has been committing ——

Ah! ma chere fille! said I, as she tripp'd by from her matins — you look as rosy as the morning (for the sun was rising, and it made the compliment the more gracious) — No; it can't be that, quoth a fourth —— (she made a curt'sy to me — I kiss'd my hand) 'tis debt, continued he: 'Tis certainly for debt; quoth a fifth; I would not pay that gentleman's debts, quoth *Ace*, for a thousand pounds; nor would I, quoth *Size*, for six times the sum — Well thrown, *Size-ace*, again! quoth I; — but I have no debt but the debt of NATURE, and I want but patience of her, and I will pay her every farthing I owe her —— How can you be so hard-hearted, MADAM, to arrest a poor traveller going along without molestation to any one upon his lawful occasions? do stop that death-looking, long-striding scoundrel of a scare-sinner, who is posting after me — he never would have followed me but for you —— if it be but for a stage or

THE LIFE AND OPINIONS

two, just to give me start of him, I beseech you, madam —— do, dear lady ——

—— Now, in truth, 'tis a great pity, quoth mine *Irish* host, that all this good courtship should be lost; for the young gentlewoman has been after going out of hearing of it all along. ——

—— Simpleton! quoth I.

—— So you have nothing *else* in *Boulogne* worth seeing?

— By Jasus! there is the finest SEMINARY for the HUMANITIES ——

— There cannot be a finer; quoth I.

CHAPTER VIII

WHEN the precipitancy of a man's wishes hurries on his ideas ninety times faster than the vehicle he rides in —— woe be to truth: and woe be to the vehicle and its tackling (let 'em be made of what stuff you will) upon which he breathes forth the disappintment of his soul!

As I never give general characters either of men or things in choler, "*the most haste the worst speed*," was all the reflection I made upon the affair, the first time it happen'd; — the second, third, fourth, and fifth time, I confined it respectively to those times, and accordingly blamed only the second, third, fourth, and fifth post-boy for it, without carrying my reflections further; but the event continuing to befal me from the fifth, to the sixth, seventh, eighth, ninth, and tenth time, and without one exception, I then could not avoid making a national reflection of it, which I do in these words;

That something is always wrong in a French post-chaise, upon first setting out.

Or the proposition may stand thus:

A French postilion has always to alight before he has got three hundred yards out of town.

What's wrong now? —— Diable! —— a rope's broke! —— a knot has slipt! —— a staple's drawn! —— a bolt's to whittle! —— a tag, a rag, a jag, a strap, a buckle, or a buckle's tongue, want altering.

Now true as all this is, I never think myself impowered to excommunicate thereupon either the post-chaise, or its driver —— nor do

OF TRISTRAM SHANDY

I take it into my head to swear by the living G —, I would rather go a-foot ten thousand times —— or that I will be damn'd, if ever I get into another —— but I take the matter cooly before me, and consider, that some tag, or rag, or jag, or bolt, or buckle, or buckle's tongue, will ever be a wanting, or want altering, travel where I will — so I never chaff, but take the good and the bad as they fall in my road, and get on: ——Do so, my lad! said I; he had lost five minutes already, in alighting in order to get at a luncheon of black bread, which he had cramm'd into the chaise-pocket, and was remounted and going leisurely on, to relish it the better —— Get on, my lad, said I, briskly — but in the most persuasive tone imaginable, for I ingled a four-and-twenty sous piece against the glass, taking care to hold the flat side towards him, as he look'd back: the dog grinn'd intelligence from his right ear to his left, and behind his sooty muzzle discovered such a pearly row of teeth that *Soverei nty* would have pawn'd her jewels for them. ——

Just heaven ! { What masticators!
{ What bread! —

and so as he finished the last mouthful of it, we entered the town of *Montreuil.*

CHAPTER IX

THERE is not a town in all *France*, which, in my opinion, looks better in the map, than MONTREUIL: —— I own, it does not look so well in the book of post-roads; but when you come to see it — to be sure it looks most pitifully.

There is one thing, however, in it at present very handsome; and that is, the inn-keeper's daughter: She has been eighteen months at *Amiens*, and six at *Paris*, in going through her classes; so knits, and sews, and dances, and does the little coquetries very well. ——

— A slut! in running them over within these five minutes that I have stood looking at her, she has let fall at least a dozen loops in a white thread stocking——yes, yes — I see, you cunning gipsy! — 'tis long and taper — you need not pin it to your knee — and that 'tis your own — and fits you exactly. ——

—— That Nature should have told this creature a word about a *statue's thumb!*

— But as this sample is worth all their thumbs —— besides, I have her thumbs and fingers in at the bargain, if they can be any guide to me, — and as *Janatone* withal (for that is her name) stands so well for a drawing —— may I never draw more, or rather may I draw like a draught-horse, by main strength all the days of my life, — if I do not draw her in all her proportions, and with as determined a pencil, as if I had her in the wettest drapery. ——

— But your worships chuse rather that I give you the length, breadth, and perpendicular height of the great parish-church, or drawing of the façade of the abbey of Saint *Austreberte* which has been transported from *Artois* hither — every thing is just I suppose as the masons and carpenters left them, — and if the belief in *Christ* continues so long, will be so these fifty years to come — so your worships and reverences may all measure them at your leisures —— but he who measures thee, *Janatone*, must do it now — thou carriest the principles of change within thy frame; and considering the chances of a transitory life, I would not answer for thee a moment; ere twice twelve months are passed and gone, thou mayest grow out like a pumpkin, and lose thy shapes —— or thou mayest go off like a flower, and lose thy beauty — nay, thou mayest go off like a hussy — and lose thyself. — I would not answer for my aunt *Dinah*, was she alive —— 'faith, scarce for her picture —— were it but painted by *Reynolds* —

But if I go on with my drawing, after naming that son of *Apollo* I'll be shot ——

So you must e'en be content with the original; which, if the evening is fine in passing thro' *Montreuil*, you will see at your chaise-door, as you change horses: but unless you have as bad a reason for haste as I have — you had better stop: —— She has a little of the *devote:* but that, sir, is a terce to a nine in your favour ——

— L — help me! I could not count a single point: so had been piqued and repiqued, and capotted to the devil.

CHAPTER X

ALL which being considered, and that Death moreover might be much nearer me than I imagined —— I wish I was at *Abbeville*, quoth I, were it only to see how they card and spin —— so off we set.

de Montreuil à Nampont-poste et demi
de Nampont à Bernay – – – poste
de Bernay à Nouvion – – – poste
de Nouvion à ABBEVILLE – poste
—— but the carders and spinners were all gone to bed.

CHAPTER XI

WHAT a vast advantage is travelling! only it heats one; but there is a remedy for that, which you may pick out of the next chapter.

CHAPTER XII

WAS I in a condition to stipulate with Death, as I am this moment with my apothecary, how and where I will take his clyster —— I should certainly declare against submitting to it before my friends; and therefore I never seriously think upon the mode and manner of this great catastrophe, which generally takes up and torments my thoughts as much as the catastrophe itself; but I constantly draw the curtain across it with this wish, that the Disposer of all things may so order it, that it happen not to me in my own house —— but rather in some decent inn —— at home, I know it, —— the concern of my friends, and the last services of wiping my brows, and smoothing my pillow, which the quivering hand of pale affection shall pay me, will so crucify my soul, that I shall die of a distemper which my physician is not aware of: but in an inn, the few cold offices I wanted, would be purchased with a few guineas, and paid me with an undisturbed, but punctual attention —— but mark. This inn should not be the inn at *Abbeville* —— if there was not another inn in the universe, I would strike that inn out of the capitulation: so

Let the horses be in the chaise exactly by four in the morning —— Yes, by four, Sir, —— or by *Genevieve!* I'll raise a clatter in the house shall wake the dead.

THE LIFE AND OPINIONS

CHAPTER XIII

"MAKE *them like unto a wheel*," is a bitter sarcasm, as all the learned know, against the *grand tour*, and that restless spirit for making it, which *David* prophetically foresaw would haunt the children of men in the latter days; and therefore, as thinketh the great bishop *Hall*, 'tis one of the severest imprecations which *David* ever utter'd against the enemies of the Lord — and, as if he had said, "I wish them no worse luck than always to be rolling about" — So much motion, continues he (for he was very corpulent) — is so much unquietness; and so much of rest, by the same analogy, is so much of heaven.

Now, I (being very thin) think differently; and that so much of motion, is so much of life, and so much of joy —— and that to stand still, or get on but slowly, is death and the devil ——

Hollo! Ho! —— the whole world's asleep! — bring out the horses —— grease the wheels —— tie on the mail —— and drive a nail into that moulding —— I'll not lose a moment ——

Now the wheel we are talking of, and *whereinto* (but not *whereonto*, for that would make an Ixion's wheel of it) he curseth his enemies, according to the bishop's habit of body, should certainly be a post-chaise wheel, whether they were set up in *Palestine* at that time or not —— and my wheel, for the contrary reasons, must as certainly be a cart-wheel groaning round its revolution once in an age; and of which sort, were I to turn commentator, I should make no scruple to affirm, they had great store in that hilly country.

I love the Pythagoreans (much more than ever I dare tell my dear *Jenny*) for their "χωρισμὸν ἀπὸ τοῦ Σώματος, εἰς τὸ καλῶς φιλοσοφεῖν" ——[their] "*getting out of the body, in order to think well.*" No man thinks right, whilst he is in it; blinded as he must be, with his congenital humours, and drawn differently aside, as the bishop and myself have been, with too lax or too tense a fibre——REASON is, half of it, SENSE; and the measure of heaven itself is but the measure of our present appetites and concoctions ——

—— But which of the two, in the present case, do you think to be mostly in the wrong?

You, certainly: quoth she, to disturb a whole family so early.

OF TRISTRAM SHANDY

CHAPTER XIV

—— BUT she did not know I was under a vow not to shave my beard till I got to *Paris;* —— yet I hate to make mysteries of nothing; —— 'tis the cold cautiousness of one of those little souls from which *Lessius* (*lib.* 13, *de moribus divinis, cap.* 24) hath made his estimate, wherein he setteth forth, That one *Dutch* mile, cubically multiplied, will allow room enough, and to spare, for eight hundred thousand millions, which he supposes to be as great a number of souls (counting from the fall of *Adam*) as can possibly be damn'd to the end of the world.

From what he has made this second estimate —— unless from the parental goodness of God — I don't know — I am much more at a loss what could be in *Franciscus Ribbera's* head, who pretends that no less a space than one of two hundred *Italian* miles multiplied into itself, will be sufficient to hold the like number —— he certainly must have gone upon some of the old *Roman* souls, of which he had read, without reflecting how much, by a gradual and most tabid decline, in the course of eighteen hundred years, they must unavoidably have shrunk so as to have come, when he wrote, almost to nothing.

In *Lessius's* time, who seems the cooler man, they were as little as can be imagined ——

—— We find them less *now* ——

And next winter we shall find them less again; so that if we go on from little to less, and from less to nothing, I hesitate not one moment to affirm, that in half a century, at this rate, we shall have no souls at all; which being the period beyond which I doubt likewise of the existence of the Christian faith, 'twill be one advantage that both of 'em will be exactly worn out together.

Blessed *Jupiter!* and blessed every other heathen god and goddess! for now ye will all come into play again, and with *Priapus* at your tails —— what jovial times! —— but where am I? and into what a delicious riot of things am I rushing? I —— I who must be cut short in the midst of my days, and taste no more of 'em than what I borrow from my imagination —— peace to thee, generous fool! and let me go on.

THE LIFE AND OPINIONS

CHAPTER XV

———" SO hating, I say, to make mysteries of *nothing*"———
I intrusted it with the post-boy, as soon as ever I got off the stones; he gave a crack with his whip to balance the compliment; and with the thill-horse trotting, and a sort of an up and a down of the other, we danced it along to *Ailly au clochers*, famed in days of yore for the finest chimes in the world; but we danced through it without music — the chimes being greatly out of order — (as in truth they were through all *France*).

And so making all possible speed, from
Ailly au clochers, I got to *Hixcourt*,
from *Hixcourt*, I got to *Pequignay*, and
from *Pequignay*, I got to AMIENS,
concerning which town I have nothing to inform you, but what I have informed you once before —— and that was — that *Janatone* went there to school.

CHAPTER XVI

IN the whole catalogue of those whiffling vexations which come puffing across a man's canvass, there is not one of a more teasing and tormenting nature, than this particular one which I am going to describe —— and for which (unless you travel with an avance-courier, which numbers do in order to prevent it) —— there is no help: and it is this.

That be you in never so kindly a propensity to sleep —— tho' you are passing perhaps through the finest country — upon the best roads, and in the easiest carriage for doing it in the world —— nay, was you sure you could sleep fifty miles straight forwards, without once opening your eyes — nay, what is more, was you as demonstratively satisfied as you can be of any truth in *Euclid*, that you should upon all accounts be full as well asleep as awake —— nay, perhaps better —— Yet the incessant returns of paying for the horses at every stage, —— with the necessity thereupon of putting your hand into your pocket, and counting out from thence three livres fifteen sous (sous by sous), puts an end to so much of the project, that you cannot execute above six miles of it (or supposing it is a post and a half, that is but nine) —— were it to save your soul from destruction.

—— I'll be even with 'em, quoth I, for I'll put the precise sum in a piece of paper, and hold it ready in my hand all the way: "Now I shall have nothing to do," said I (composing myself to rest), "but to drop this gently into the post-boy's hat, and not say a word."

—— Then there wants two sous more to drink —— or there is a twelve sous piece of *Louis* XIV. which will not pass — or a livre and some odd liards to be brought over from the last stage, which Monsieur had forgot; which altercations (as a man cannot dispute very well asleep) rouse him: still is sweet sleep retrievable; and still might the flesh weigh down the spirit, and recover itself of these blows — but then, by heaven! you have paid but for a single post — whereas 'tis a post and a half; and this obliges you to pull out your book of post-roads, the print of which is so very small, it forces you to open your eyes, whether you will or no: Then Monsieur *le Curé* offers you a pinch of snuff —— or a poor soldier shews you his leg — or a shaveling his box —— or the priestess of the cistern will water your wheels —— they do not want it —— but she swears by her *priesthood* (throwing it back) that they do: —— then you have all these points to argue, or consider over in your mind; in doing of which, the rational powers get so thoroughly awakened —— you may get 'em to sleep again as you can.

It was entirely owing to one of these misfortunes, or I had pass'd clean by the stables of *Chantilly* ——

—— But the postilion first affirming, and then persisting in it to my face, that there was no mark upon the two sous piece, I open'd my eyes to be convinced — and seeing the mark upon it as plain as my nose — I leap'd out of the chaise in a passion, and so saw every thing at *Chantilly* in spite.—— I tried it but for three posts and a half, but believe 'tis the best principle in the world to travel speedily upon; for as few objects look very inviting in that mood — you have little or nothing to stop you; by which means it was that I passed through St. *Dennis*, without turning my head so much as on one side towards the Abby ——

—— Richness of their treasury! stuff and nonsense! —— bating their jewels, which are all false, I would not give three sous for any one thing in it, but *Jaidas's lantern* —— nor for that either, only as it grows dark, it might be of use.

THE LIFE AND OPINIONS

CHAPTER XVII

CRACK, crack —— crack, crack —— crack, crack —— so this is *Paris!* quoth I (continuing in the same mood) — and this is *Paris!* —— humph! —— *Paris!* cried I, repeating the name the third time ——

The first, the finest, the most brilliant ——

The streets however are nasty.

But it looks, I suppose, better than it smells —— crack, crack —— crack, crack —— what a fuss thou makest! — as if it concerned the good people to be informed, that a man with pale face and clad in black, had the honour to be driven into *Paris* at nine o'clock at night, by a postilion in a tawny yellow jerkin, turned up with red calamanco — crack, crack —— crack, crack, —— crack, crack —— I wish thy whip ——

—— But 'tis the spirit of thy nation; so crack — crack on.

Ha! —— and no one gives the wall! —— but in the SCHOOL OF URBANITY herself, the walls are besh-t — how can you do otherwise?

And prithee when do they light the lamps? What? — never in the summer months! —— Ho! 'tis the time of sallads. —— O rare! sallad and soup — soup and sallad — sallad and soup, *encore* —— —— 'Tis *too much* for sinners.

Now I cannot bear the barbarity of it; how can that unconscionable coachman talk so much bawdy to that lean horse? don't you see, friend, the streets are so villainously narrow, that there is not room in all *Paris* to turn a wheelbarrow? In the grandest city of the whole world, it would not have been amiss, if they had been left a thought wider; nay, were it only so much in every single street, as that a man might know (was it only for satisfaction) on which side of it he was walking.

One — two — three — four — five — six — seven — eight — — nine — ten. — Ten cook's shops! and twice the number of barbers! and all within three minutes driving! one would think that all the cooks in the world, on some great merry-meeting with the barbers, by joint consent had said — Come, let us all go live at *Paris:* the *French* love good eating —— they are all *gourmands* —— we shall rank high; if their god is their belly ——their cooks must be gentlemen: and forasmuch as *the periwig maketh the man*, and the periwig-maker maketh the periwig — *ergo*, would the barbers say, we shall rank higher still — we shall be above you all — we shall be *Capitouls* at least — *pardi !* we shall all wear swords ——

— And so, one would swear (that is, by candle light, — but there is no depending upon it) they continue to do, to this day.

CHAPTER XVIII

THE *French* are certainly misunderstood: — but whether the fault is theirs, in not sufficiently explaining themselves; or speaking with that exact limitation and precision which one would expect on a point of such importance, and which, moreover, is so likely to be contested by us —— or whether the fault may not be altogether on our side, in not understanding their language always so critically as to know "what they would be at" —— I shall not decide; but 'tis evident to me, when they affirm, "*That they who have seen* Paris, *have seen every thing*," they must mean to speak of those who have seen it by day-light.

As for candle-light — I give it up —— I have said before, there was no depending upon it — and I repeat it again; but not because the lights and shades are too sharp — or the tints confounded — or that there is neither beauty or keeping, &c. . . . for that's not truth — but it is an uncertain light in this respect, That in all the five hundred grand Hôtels, which they number up to you in *Paris* — and the five hundred good things, at a modest computation (for 'tis only allowing one good thing to a Hôtel), which by candle-light are best to be *seen, felt, heard,* and *understood* (which, by the bye, is a quotation from *Lilly*) —— the devil a one of us out of fifty, can get our heads fairly thrust in amongst them.

This is no part of the *French* computation: 'tis simply this,

That by the last survey taken in the year one thousand seven hundred and sixteen, since which time there have been considerable augmentations, *Paris* doth contain nine hundred streets; (viz.)

In the quarter called the *City* — there are fifty-three streets.

In St. *James* of the Shambles, fifty-five streets.

In St. *Oportune*, thirty-four streets.

In the quarter of the *Louvre*, twenty-five streets.

In the *Palace Royal*, or St. *Honorius*, forty-nine streets.

In *Mont. Martyr*, forty-one streets.

In St. *Eustace*, twenty-nine streets.
In the *Halles*, twenty-seven streets.
In St. *Dennis*, fifty-five streets.
In St. *Martin*, fifty-four streets.
In St. *Paul*, or the *Mortellerie*, twenty-seven streets.
The *Greve*, thirty-eight streets.
In St. *Avoy*, or the *Verrerie*, nineteen streets.
In the *Marais*, or the *Temple*, fifty-two streets.
In St. *Antony's*, sixty-eight streets.
In the *Place Maubert*, eighty-one streets.
In St. *Bennet*, sixty streets.
In St. *Andrews de Arcs*, fifty-one streets.
In the quarter of the *Luxembourg*, sixty-two streets.
And in that of St. Germain, fifty-five streets, into any of which you may walk; and that when you have seen them with all that belongs to them, fairly by day-light — their gates, their bridges, their squares, their statues - - - and have crusaded it moreover, through all their parish-churches, by no means omitting St. *Roche* and *Sulpice* - - - and to crown all, have taken a walk to the four palaces, which you may see, either with or without the statues and pictures, just as you chuse —
——— Then you will have seen ———
——— but, 'tis what no one needeth to tell you, for you will read of it yourself upon the portico of the *Louvre*, in these words,
EARTH NO SUCH FOLKS! — NO FOLKS E'ER SUCH A TOWN AS PARIS IS! — SING, DERRY, DERRY, DOWN.

The *French* have a *gay* way of treating every thing that is Great; and that is all can be said upon it.

CHAPTER XIX

IN mentioning the word *gay* (as in the close of the last chapter) it puts one (*i. e.* an author) in mind of the word *spleen* ——— especially if he has any thing to say upon it: not that by any analysis — or that from any table of interest or genealogy, there appears much more ground of alliance betwixt them, than betwixt light and darkness, or any two of the most unfriendly opposites in nature ——— only 'tis an undercraft of authors to keep up a good understanding amongst words, as politicians do amongst men —

not knowing how near they may be under a necessity of placing them to each other —— which point being now gain'd, and that I may place mine exactly to my mind, I write it down here —

SPLEEN

This, upon leaving *Chantilly*, I declared to be the best principle in the world to travel speedily upon; but I gave it only as matter of opinion. I still continue in the same sentiments — only I had not then experience enough of its working to add this, that though you do get on at a tearing rate, yet you get on but uneasily to yourself at the same time; for which reason I here quit it entirely, and for ever, and 'tis heartily at any one's service — it has spoiled me the digestion of a good supper, and brought on a bilious diarrhœa, which has brought me back again to my first principle on which I set out —— and with which I shall now scamper it away to the banks of the *Garonne* —

—— No; —— I cannot stop a moment to give you the character of the people — their genius —— their manners — their customs — their laws —— their religion — their government — their manufactures — their commerce — their finances, with all the resources and hidden springs which sustain them: qualified as I may be, by spending three days and two nights amongst them, and during all that time making these things the entire subject of my enquiries and reflections ——

Still — still I must away —— the roads are paved — the posts are short — the days are long — 'tis no more than noon — I shall be at *Fontainbleau* before the king ——

— Was he going there? not that I know ——

CHAPTER XX

NOW I hate to hear a person, especially if he be a traveller, complain that we do not get on so fast in *France* as we do in *England;* whereas we get on much faster, *consideratis considerandis;* thereby always meaning, that if you weigh their vehicles with the mountains of baggage which you lay both before and behind upon them — and then consider their puny horses, with the very little they give them — 'tis a wonder they get on at all: their suffering is most unchristian, and 'tis evident thereupon to me, that a *French* post-horse would not know what in the world to do, was it not for the two words ****** and ****** in which there is as much sustenance, as if you gave him a peck of corn: now as these words cost nothing, I long from my soul to tell the reader what they are; but here is the question — they must be told him plainly, and with the most distinct articulation, or it will answer no end — and yet to do it in that plain way — though their reverences may laugh at it in the bed-chamber — full well I wot, they will abuse it in the parlour: for which cause, I have been volving and revolving in my fancy some time, but to no purpose, by what clean device or facette contrivance I might so modulate them, that whilst I satisfy *that ear* which the reader chuses to *lend* me — I might not dissatisfy the other which he keeps to himself.

—— My ink burns my finger to try —— and when I have —— 'twill have a worse consequence —— it will burn (I fear) my paper.

—— No; —— I dare not ——

But if you wish to know how the *abbess* of *Andoüillets* and a novice of her convent got over the difficulty (only first wishing myself all imaginable success) — I'll tell you without the least scruple

CHAPTER XXI

THE abbess of *Andoüillets*, which, if you look into the large set of provincial maps now publishing at *Paris*, you will find situated amongst the hills which divide *Burgundy* from *Savoy*, being in danger of an *Anchylosis* or stiff joint (the *sinovi* of her knee becoming hard by long matins), and having tried every remedy —— first, prayers and thanksgiving; then invocations to all the saints in heaven promiscuously —— then particularly to every saint who had ever had a stiff leg before her —— then touching it with all the reliques of the convent, principally with the thigh-bone of the man of *Lystra*, who had been impotent from his youth —— then wrapping it up in her veil when she went to bed — then crosswise her rosary — then bringing in to her aid the secular arm, and anointing it with oils and hot fat of animals — then treating it with emollient and resolving fomentations —— then with poultices of marsh-mallows, mallows, bonus Henricus, white lilies and fenugreek — then taking the woods, I mean the smoak of 'em, holding her scapulary across her lap —— then decoctions of wild chicory, water-cresses, chervil, sweet cecily and cochlearia —— and nothing all this while answering, was prevailed on at last to try the hot baths of *Bourbon* —— so having first obtain'd leave of the visitor-general to take care of her existence — she ordered all to be got ready for her journey: a novice of the convent of about seventeen, who had been troubled with a whitloe in her middle finger, by sticking it constantly into the abbess's cast poultices, &c. — had gained such an interest, that overlooking a sciatical old nun, who might have been set up for ever by the hot-baths of *Bourbon*, *Margarita*, the little novice, was elected as the companion of the journey.

An old calesh, belonging to the abbess, lined with green frize, was ordered to be drawn out into the sun — the gardener of the convent being chosen muleteer, led out the two old mules, to clip the hair from the rump-ends of their tails, whilst a couple of lay-sisters were busied, the one in darning the lining, and the other in sewing on the shreds of yellow binding, which the teeth of time had unravelled —— the under-gardener dress'd the muleteer's hat in hot wine-lees —— and a taylor sat musically at it, in a shed over-against the convent, in assorting four dozen of bells for the harness, whistling to each bell, as he tied it on with a thong. ——

—— The carpenter and the smith of *Andoüillets* held a council of wheels; and by seven, the morning after, all look'd spruce, and was ready at the gate of the convent for the hot-baths of *Bourbon* — two rows of the unfortunate stood ready there an hour before.

The abbess of *Andoüillets*, supported by *Margarita* the novice, advanced slowly to the calesh, both clad in white, with their black rosaries hanging at their breasts ——

—— There was a simple solemnity in the contrast: they entered the calesh; and nuns in the same uniform, sweet emblem of innocence, each occupied a window, and as the abbess and *Margarita* look'd up — each (the sciatical poor nun excepted) — each stream'd out the end of her veil in the air — then kiss'd the lily hand which let it go: the good abbess and *Margarita* laid their hands saint-wise upon their breasts — look'd up to heaven — then to them — and look'd "God bless you, dear sisters."

I declare I am interested in this story, and wish I had been there.

The gardener, whom I shall now call the muleteer, was a little, hearty, broad-set, good-natured, chattering, toping kind of a fellow, who troubled his head very little with the *hows* and *whens* of life; so had mortgaged a month of his conventical wages in a borrachio, or leathern cask of wine, which he had disposed behind the calesh, with a large russet-coloured riding-coat over it, to guard it from the sun; and as the weather was hot, and he not a niggard of his labours, walking ten times more than he rode — he found more occasions than those of nature, to fall back to the rear of his carriage; till by frequent coming and going, it had so happen'd, that all his wine had leak'd out at the *legal* vent of the borrachio, before one half of the journey was finish'd.

Man is a creature born to habitudes. The day had been sultry — the evening was delicious — the wine was generous — the *Burgundian* hill on which it grew was steep — a little tempting bush over the door of a cool cottage at the foot of it, hung vibrating in full harmony with the passions — a gentle air rustled distinctly through the leaves — "Come — come, thirsty muleteer — come in."

— The muleteer was a son of *Adam;* I need not say a word more. He gave the mules, each of 'em, a sound lash, and looking in the abbess's and *Margarita's* faces (as he did it) — as much as to say "here I am" — he gave a second good crack — as much as to say to his mules, "get on" —— so slinking behind, he enter'd the little inn at the foot of the hill.

The muleteer, as I told you, was a little, joyous, chirping fellow, who thought not of to-morrow, nor of what had gone before, or what was to follow it, provided he got but his scantling of Burgundy, and a little chit-chat along with it; so entering into a long conversation, as how he was chief gardener to the convent of *Andoüillets,* &c. &c., and out of friendship for the abbess and Mademoiselle *Margarita,* who was only in her noviciate, he had come along with them from the confines of *Savoy,* &c. &c. — and as how she had got a white swelling by her devotions — and what a nation of herbs he had procured to mollify her humours, &c. &c., and that if the waters of *Bourbon* did not mend that leg — she might as well be lame of both — &c. &c. &c. — He so contrived his story, as absolutely to forget the heroine of it — and with her the little novice, and what was a more ticklish point to be forgot than both — the two mules; who being creatures that take advantage of the world, inasmuch as their parents took it of them — and they not being in a condition to return the obligation *downwards* (as men and women and beasts are) — they do it side-ways, and long-ways, and back-ways — and up hill, and down hill, and which way they can. ——

Philosophers, with all their ethicks, have never considered this rightly — how should the poor muleteer, then in his cups, consider it at all? he did not in the least — 'tis time we do; let us leave him then in the vortex of his element, the happiest and most thoughtless of mortal men —— and for a moment let us look after the mules, the abbess, and *Margarita*.

By virtue of the muleteer's two last strokes the mules had gone quietly on, following their own consciences up the hill, till they had conquer'd about one half of it; when the elder of them, a shrewd crafty old devil, at the turn of an angle, giving a side glance, and no muleteer behind them ——

By my fig! said she, swearing, I'll go no further —— And if I do, replied the other, they shall make a drum of my hide. ——

And so with one consent they stopp'd thus ——

CHAPTER XXII

——GET on with you, said the abbess. —— Wh - - - - ysh —— ysh —— cried *Margarita*.

She - - - a —— shu - —— shu - - u — sh - - aw —— shaw'd the abbess.

—— Whu — v — w —— whew — w — w — whuv'd *Margarita*, pursing up her sweet lips betwixt a hoot and a whistle.

Thump — thump — thump — obstreperated the abbess of *Andoüillets* with the end of her gold-headed cane against the bottom of the calesh ——

The old mule let a f —

CHAPTER XXIII

WE are ruin'd and undone, my child, said the abbess to *Margarita*, —— we shall be here all night —— we shall be plunder'd —— we shall be ravish'd ——

—— We shall be ravish'd, said *Margarita*, as sure as a gun.

Sancta Maria! cried the abbess (forgetting the *O!*) — why was I govern'd by this wicked stiff joint? why did I leave the convent of *Andoüillets?* and why didst thou not suffer thy servant to go unpolluted to her tomb?

O my finger! my finger! cried the novice, catching fire at the word *servant* — why was I not content to put it here, or there, any where rather than be in this strait?

Strait! said the abbess.

Strait —— said the novice; for terror had struck their understandings —— the one knew not what she said —— the other what she answer'd.

O my virginity! virginity! cried the abbess.

—— inity! —— inity! said the novice, sobbing.

CHAPTER XXIV

MY dear mother, quoth the novice, coming a little to herself, —— there are two certain words, which I have been told will force any horse, or ass, or mule, to go up a hill whether he will or no; be he never so obstinate or ill-will'd, the moment he hears them utter'd, he obeys. They are words magic! cried the abbess in the utmost horror — No; replied *Margarita* calmly — but they are words sinful — What are they? quoth the abbess, interrupting her: They are sinful in the first degree, answered *Margarita*, — they are mortal — and if we are ravish'd and die unabsolved of them, we shall both —— but you may pronounce them to me, quoth the abbess of *Andoüillets* —— They cannot, my dear mother, said the novice, be pronounced at all; they will make all the blood in one's body fly up into one's face — But you may whisper them in my ear, quoth the abbess.

Heaven! hadst thou no guardian angel to delegate to the inn at the bottom of the hill? was there no generous and friendly spirit unemployed —— no agent in nature, by some monitory shivering, creeping along the artery which led to his heart, to rouse the muleteer from his banquet? —— no sweet minstrelsy to bring back the fair idea of the abbess and *Margarita*, with their black rosaries!

Rouse! rouse! —— but 'tis too late — the horrid words are pronounced this moment ——

—— and how to tell them — Ye, who can speak of every thing existing, with unpolluted lips — instruct me —— guide me ——

CHAPTER XXV

ALL sins whatever, quoth the abbess, turning casuist in the distress they were under, are held by the confessor of our convent to be either mortal or venial: there is no further division. Now a venial sin being the slightest and least of all sins — being halved — by taking either only the half of it, and leaving the rest — or, by taking it all, and amicably halving it betwixt yourself and another person — in course becomes diluted into no sin at all.

Now I see no sin in saying, *bou, bou, bou, bou, bou,* a hundred times together; nor is there any turpitude in pronouncing the syllable *ger, ger, ger, ger, ger,* were it from our matins to our vespers: Therefore, my dear daughter, continued the abbess of *Andoüillets* — I will say *bou,* and thou shalt say *ger;* and then alternately, as there is no more sin in *fou* than in *bou* — Thou shalt say *fou* — and I will come in (like fa, sol, la, re, mi, ut, at our complines) with *ter.* And accordingly the abbess, giving the pitch note, set off thus:

Abbess,   } Bou - - bou - - bou - -
Margarita, } ——— ger, - - ger, - - ger.
Margarita, } Fou - - fou - - fou - -
Abbess,   } ——— ter, - - ter, - - ter.

The two mules acknowledged the notes by a mutual lash of their tails; but it went no further ——— 'Twill answer by an' by, said the novice.

Abbess,   } Bou- bou- bou- bou- bou- bou-
Margarita, } — ger, ger, ger, ger, ger, ger.

Quicker still, cried *Margarita.*

Fou, fou, fou, fou, fou, fou, fou, fou, fou.

Quicker still, cried *Margarita.*

Bou, bou, bou, bou, bou, bou, bou, bou, bou.

Quicker still — God preserve me; said the abbess — They do not understand us, cried *Margarita* — But the Devil does, said the abbess of *Andoüillets.*

CHAPTER XXVI

WHAT a tract of country have I run! — how many degrees nearer to the warm sun am I advanced, and how many fair and goodly cities have I seen, during the time you have been reading, and reflecting, Madam, upon this story! There's FONTAIN-

THE LIFE AND OPINIONS

BLEAU, and SENS, and JOIGNY, and AUXERRE, and DIJON the capital of *Burgundy*, and CHALLON, and *Mâcon* the capital of the *Mâconese*, and a score more upon the road to LYONS —— and now I have run them over —— I might as well talk to you of so many market towns in the moon, as tell you one word about them: it will be this chapter at the least, if not both this and the next entirely lost, do what I will ——

— Why, 'tis a strange story! *Tristram*.

—— Alas! Madam, had it been upon some melancholy lecture of the cross — the peace of meekness, or the contentment of resignation —— I had not been incommoded: or had I thought of writing it upon the purer abstractions of the soul, and that food of wisdom and holiness and contemplation, upon which the spirit of man (when separated from the body) is to subsist for ever —— You would have come with a better appetite from it ——

—— I wish I never had wrote it: but as I never blot any thing out —— let us use some honest means to get it out of our heads directly.

—— Pray reach me my fool's cap —— I fear you sit upon it, Madam —— 'tis under the cushion —— I'll put it on ——

Bless me! you have had it upon your head this half hour. —— There then let it stay, with a

Fa-ra diddle di
and a fa-ri diddle d
and a high-dum — dye-dum
  fiddle - - - dumb - c.

And now, Madam, we may venture, I hope, a little to go on.

CHAPTER XXVII

—— ALL you need say of *Fontainbleau* (in case you are ask'd) is, that it stands about forty miles (south *something*) from *Paris*, in the middle of a large forest —— That there is something great in it —— That the king goes there once every two or three years, with his whole court, for the pleasure of the chase — and that, during that carnival of sporting, any *English* gentleman of fashion (you need not forget yourself) may be accommodated with a nag or two, to partake of the sport, taking care only not to out-gallop the king ——

Though there are two reasons why you need not talk loud of this to every one.

First, Because 'twill make the said nags the harder to be got; and Secondly, 'Tis not a word of it true. —— *Allons !*

As for SENS —— you may dispatch — in a word —— *"'Tis an archiepiscopal see."*

—— For JOIGNY — the less, I think, one says of it the better.

But for AUXERRE — I could go on for ever: for in my *grand tour* through *Europe*, in which, after all, my father (not caring to trust me with any one) attended me himself, with my uncle *Toby*, and *Trim*, and *Obadiah*, and indeed most of the family, except my mother, who being taken up with a project of knitting my father a pair of large worsted breeches — (the thing is common sense) — and she not caring to be put out of her way, she staid at home, at SHANDY HALL, to keep things right during the expedition; in which, I say, my father stopping us two days at *Auxerre*, and his researches being ever of such a nature, that they would have found fruit even in a desert —— he has left me enough to say upon AUXERRE: in short, wherever my father went —— but 'twas more remarkably so, in this journey through *France* and *Italy*, than in any other stages of his life —— his road seemed to lie so much on one side of that, wherein all other travellers have gone before him — he saw kings and courts and silks of all colours, in such strange lights —— and his remarks and reasonings upon the characters, the manners, and customs of the countries we pass'd over, were so opposite to those of all other mortal men, particularly those of my uncle *Toby* and *Trim* — (to say nothing of myself) — and to crown all — the occurrences and scrapes which we were perpetually meeting and getting into, in consequence of his systems and opiniatry — they were of so odd, so mix'd and tragi-comical a contexture — That the whole put together, it appears of so different a shade and tint from any tour of *Europe*, which was ever executed — that I will venture to pronounce — the fault must be mine and mine only — if it be not read by all travellers and travel-readers, till travelling is no more, — or which comes to the same point — till the world, finally, takes it into its head to stand still. ——

—— But this rich bale is not to be open'd now; except a small thread or two of it, merely to unravel the mystery of my father's stay at AUXERRE.

—— As I have mentioned it — 'tis too slight to be kept suspended; and when 'tis wove in, there is an end of it.

We'll go, brother *Toby*, said my father, whilst dinner is coddling — to the abby of Saint *Germain*, if it be only to see these bodies, of which Monsieur *Sequier* has given such a recommendation. —— I'll go see any body, quoth my uncle *Toby;* for he was all compliance through every step of the journey —— Defend me! said my father — they are all mummies —— Then one need not shave; quoth my uncle *Toby* —— Shave! no — cried my father — 'twill be more like relations to go with our beards on — So out we sallied, the corporal lending his master his arm, and bringing up the rear, to the abby of Saint *Germain*.

Every thing is very fine, and very rich, and very superb, and very magnificent, said my father, addressing himself to the sacristan, who was a younger brother of the order of *Benedictines* — but our curiosity has led us to see the bodies, of which Monsieur *Sequier* has given the world so exact a description. — The sacristan made a bow, and lighting a torch first, which he had always in the vestry ready for the purpose; he led us into the tomb of St. *Heribald* —— This, said the sacristan, laying his hand upon the tomb, was a renowned prince of the house of *Bavaria,* who under the successive reigns of *Charlemagne, Louis le Debonnair,* and *Charles the Bald,* bore a great sway in the government, and had a principal hand in bringing every thing into order and discipline ——

Then he has been as great, said my uncle, in the field, as in the cabinet —— I dare say he has been a gallant soldier —— He was a monk — said the sacristan.

My uncle *Toby* and *Trim* sought comfort in each other's faces — but found it not: my father clapped both his hands upon his codpiece, which was a way he had when any thing hugely tickled him: for though he hated a monk and the very smell of a monk worse than all the devils in hell —— yet the shot hitting my uncle *Toby* and *Trim* so much harder than him, 'twas a relative triumph; and put him into the gayest humour in the world.

—— And pray what do you call this gentleman? quoth my father, rather sportingly: This tomb, said the young *Benedictine*, looking downwards, contains the bones of Saint MAXIMA, who came from *Ravenna* on purpose to touch the body ——

—— Of Saint MAXIMUS, said my father, popping in with his saint before him, — they were two of the greatest saints in the whole martyrology, added my father —— Excuse me, said the sacristan —— 'twas to touch the bones of Saint *Germain*, the builder of the abby —— And what did she get by it? said my uncle *Toby* —— What does any woman get by it? said my father —— MARTYRDOME; replied the young *Benedictine*, making a bow down to the ground, and uttering the word with so humble, but decisive a cadence, it disarmed my father for a moment. 'Tis supposed, continued the *Benedictine*, that St. *Maxima* has lain in this tomb four hundred years, and two hundred before her canonization —— 'Tis but a slow rise, brother *Toby*, quoth my father, in this self-same army of martyrs. —— A desperate slow one, an' please your honour, said *Trim*, unless one could purchase —— I should rather sell out entirely, quoth my uncle *Toby* —— I am pretty much of your opinion, brother *Toby*, said my father.

—— Poor St. *Maxima!* said my uncle *Toby* low to himself, as we turn'd from her tomb: She was one of the fairest and most beautiful ladies either of *Italy* or *France*, continued the sacristan —— But who the duce has got lain down here, besides her? quoth my father, pointing with his cane to a large tomb as we walked on —— It is Saint *Optat*, Sir, answered the sacristan —— And properly is Saint *Optat* plac'd! said my father: And what is Saint *Optat's* story? continued he. Saint *Optat*, replied the sacristan, was a bishop ——

—— I thought so, by heaven! cried my father, interrupting him —— Saint *Optat* —— how should Saint *Optat* fail? so snatching out his pocket-book, and the young *Benedictine* holding him the torch as he wrote, he set it down as a new prop to his system of Christian names, and I will be bold to say, so disinterested was he in the search of truth, that had he found a treasure in Saint *Optat's* tomb, it would not have made him half so rich: 'Twas as successful a short visit as ever was paid to the dead; and so highly was his fancy pleas'd with all that had passed in it, — that he determined at once to stay another day in *Auxerre*.

— I'll see the rest of these good gentry to-morrow, said my father, as we cross'd over the square — And while you are paying that visit, brother *Shandy*, quoth my uncle *Toby* — the corporal and I will mount the ramparts.

CHAPTER XXVIII

―― NOW this is the most puzzled skein of all―― for in this last chapter, as far at least as it has help'd me through *Auxerre*, I have been getting forwards in two different journies together, and with the same dash of the pen — for I have got entirely out of *Auxerre* in this journey which I am writing now, and I am got half way out of *Auxerre* in that which I shall write hereafter―― There is but a certain degree of perfection in every thing; and by pushing at something beyond that, I have brought myself into such a situation, as no traveller ever stood before me; for I am this moment walking across the market-place of *Auxerre* with my father and my uncle *Toby*, in our way back to dinner―― and I am this moment also entering *Lyons* with my post-chaise broke into a thousand pieces — and I am moreover this moment in a handsome pavillion built by *Pringello*, upon the banks of the *Garonne*, which Mons. *Sligniac* has lent me, and where I now sit rhapsodising all these affairs.

―― Let me collect myself, and pursue my journey.

CHAPTER XXIX

I AM glad of it, said I, settling the account with myself, as I walk'd into *Lyons*―― my chaise being all laid higgledy-piggledy with my baggage in a cart, which was moving slowly before me―― I am heartily glad, said I, that 'tis all broke to pieces; for now I can go directly by water to *Avignon*, which will carry me on a hundred and twenty miles of my journey, and not cost me seven livres―― and from thence, continued I, bringing forwards the account, I can hire a couple of mules — or asses, if I like, (for nobody knows me) and cross the plains of *Languedoc* for almost nothing―― I shall gain four hundred livres by the misfortune clear into my purse: and pleasure! worth — worth double the money by it. With what velocity, continued I, clapping my two hands together, shall I fly down the rapid *Rhone*, with the Vivares on my right hand, and Dauphiny on my left, scarce seeing the ancient cities of Vienne, *Valence*, and *Vivieres*. What a flame will it rekindle in the lamp, to snatch a blushing grape from the *Hermitage* and *Côte roti*, as I shoot by the foot of them! and what a fresh spring in the blood! to behold upon the banks advancing and retiring, the castles of romance, whence courteous knights have whilome rescued the distress'd —— and see vertiginous, the rocks, the mountains, the cataracts, and all the hurry which Nature is in with all her great works about her.

As I went on thus, methought my chaise, the wreck of which look'd stately enough at the first, insensibly grew less and less in its size; the freshness of the painting was no more — the gilding lost its lustre — and the whole affair appeared so poor in my eyes — so sorry! — so contemptible! and, in a word, so much worse than the abbess of *Andoüillets'* itself — that I was just opening my mouth to give it to the devil — when a pert vamping chaise-undertaker, stepping nimbly across the street, demanded if Monsieur would have his chaise refitted —— No, no, said I, shaking my head sideways — Would Monsieur chuse to sell it? rejoined the undertaker — With all my soul, said I — the iron work is worth forty livres — and the glasses worth forty more — and the leather you may take to live on.

What a mine of wealth, quoth I, as he counted me the money, has this post-chaise brought me in? And this is my usual method of book-keeping, at least with the disasters of life — making a penny of every one of 'em as they happen to me ——

—— Do, my dear *Jenny*, tell the world for me, how I behaved under one, the most oppressive of its kind, which could befal me as a man, proud as he ought to be of his manhood ——

'Tis enough, saidst thou, coming close up to me, as I stood with my garters in my hand, reflecting upon what had *not* pass'd —— 'Tis enough, *Tristram*, and I am satisfied, saidst thou, whispering these words in my ear, **** ** **** *** ****** ; — **** ** ** —— any other man would have sunk down to the center ——

—— Every thing is good for something, quoth I.

—— I'll go into *Wales* for six weeks, and drink goat's whey — and I'll gain seven years longer life for the accident. For which reason I think myself inexcusable, for blaming fortune so often as I have done, for pelting me all my life long, like an ungracious duchess, as I call'd her, with so many small evils: surely, if I have any cause to be angry with her, 'tis that she has not sent me great ones — a score of good cursed, bouncing losses, would have been as good as a pension to me.

—— One of a hundred a year, or so, is all I wish — I would not be at the plague of paying land-tax for a larger.

THE LIFE AND OPINIONS

CHAPTER XXX

TO those who call vexations, VEXATIONS, as knowing what they are, there could not be a greater, than to be the best part of a day at *Lyons*, the most opulent and flourishing city in *France*, enriched with the most fragments of antiquity — and not be able to see it. To be withheld upon *any* account, must be a vexation; but to be withheld *by* a vexation —— must certainly be, what philosophy justly calls

VEXATION
UPON
VEXATION

I had got my two dishes of milk coffee (which by the bye is excellently good for a consumption, but you must boil the milk and coffee together — otherwise 'tis only coffee and milk) — and as it was no more than eight in the morning, and the boat did not go off till noon, I had time to see enough of *Lyons* to tire the patience of all the friends I had in the world with it. I will take a walk to the cathedral, said I, looking at my list, and see the wonderful mechanism of this great clock of *Lippius* of *Basil*, in the first place ——

Now, of all things in the world, I understand the least of mechanism —— I have neither genius, or taste, or fancy — and have a brain so entirely unapt for every thing of that kind, that I solemnly declare I was never yet able to comprehend the principles of motion of a squirrel cage, or a common knife-grinder's wheel — tho' I have many an hour of my life look'd up with great devotion at the one — and stood by with as much patience as any christian ever could do, at the other ——

I'll go see the surprising movements of this great clock, said I, the very first thing I do: and then I will pay a visit to the great library of the Jesuits, and procure, if possible, a sight of the thirty volumes of the general history of *China*, wrote (not in the *Tartarean*, but) in the *Chinese* language, and in the *Chinese* character too.

Now I almost know as little of the *Chinese* language, as I do of the mechanism of *Lippius's* clock-work; so, why these should have jostled themselves into the two first articles of my list —— I leave to the curious as a problem of Nature. I own it looks like one of her ladyship's obliquities; and they who court her, are interested in finding out her humour as much as I.

OF TRISTRAM SHANDY

When these curiosities are seen, quoth I, half addressing myself to my *valet de place*, who stood behind me —— 'twill be no hurt if we go to the church of St. *Irenæus*, and see the pillar to which *Christ* was tied —— and after that, the house where *Pontius Pilate* lived——'Twas at the next town, said the *valet de place* — at *Vienne*; I am glad of it, said I, rising briskly from my chair, and walking across the room with strides twice as long as my usual pace —— " for so much the sooner shall I be at the *Tomb of the two lovers*."

What was the cause of this movement, and why I took such long strides in uttering this —— I might leave to the curious too; but as no principle of clock-work is concerned in it —— 'twill be as well for the reader if I explain it myself.

CHAPTER XXXI

O THERE is a sweet æra in the life of man, when (the brain being tender and fibrillous, and more like pap than any thing else) —— a story read of two fond lovers, separated from each other by cruel parents, and by still more cruel destiny ——

Amandus —— He
Amanda —— She ——

each ignorant of the other's course,

He —— east
She —— west

Amandus taken captive by the *Turks*, and carried to the emperor of *Morocco's* court, where the princess of *Morocco* falling in love with him, keeps him twenty years in prison for the love of his *Amanda*. ——

She — (*Amanda*) all the time wandering barefoot, and with dishevell'd hair, o'er rocks and mountains, enquiring for *Amandus!* —— *Amandus! Amandus!* — making every hill and valley to echo back his name ——

Amandus! Amandus!

at every town and city, sitting down forlorn at the gate —— Has *Amandus!* — has my *Amandus* enter'd? —— till,—— going round, and round, and round the world —— chance unexpected bringing them at the same moment of the night, though by different ways, to the gate of *Lyons*, their native city, and each in well-known accents calling out aloud.

Is *Amandus* }
Is my *Amanda* } still alive?

they fly into each other's arms, and both drop down dead for joy.

There is a soft æra in every gentle mortal's life, where such a story affords more *pabulum* to the brain, than all the *Frusts*, and *Crusts*, and *Rusts* of antiquity, which travellers can cook up for it.

———'Twas all that stuck on the right side of the cullender in my own, of what *Spon* and others, in their accounts of *Lyons*, had *strained* into it; and finding, moreover, in some Itinerary, but in what God knows——— That sacred to the fidelity of *Amandus* and *Amanda*, a tomb was built without the gates, where, to this hour, lovers called upon them to attest their truths——— I never could get into a scrape of that kind in my life, but this *tomb of the lovers* would, somehow or other, come in at the close ——— nay such a kind of empire had it establish'd over me, that I could seldom think or speak of *Lyons* — and sometimes not so much as see even a *Lyons-waistcoat*, but this remnant of antiquity would present itself to my fancy; and I have often said in my wild way of running on ——— tho' I fear with some irreverence ——— "I thought this shrine (neglected as it was) as valuable as that of *Mecca*, and so little short, except in wealth, of the *Santa Casa* itself, that some time or other, I would go a pilgrimage (though I had no other business at *Lyons*) on purpose to pay it a visit."

In my list, therefore, of *Videnda* at *Lyons*, this, tho' *last,* — was not, you see, *least;* so taking a dozen or two of longer strides than usual across my room, just whilst it passed my brain, I walked down calmly into the *Basse Cour*, in order to sally forth; and having called for my bill — as it was uncertain whether I should return to my inn, I had paid it ——— had moreover given the maid ten sous, and was just receiving the dernier compliments of Monsieur *Le Blanc*, for a pleasant voyage down the *Rhône* ——— when I was stopped at the gate ———

CHAPTER XXXII

———'TWAS by a poor ass, who had just turned in with a couple of large panniers upon his back, to collect eleemosynary turnip-tops and cabbage-leaves; and stood dubious, with his two fore-feet on the inside of the threshold, and with his two hinder feet towards the street, as not knowing very well whether he was to go in or no.

OF TRISTRAM SHANDY

Now, 'tis an animal (be in what hurry I may) I cannot bear to strike —— there is a patient endurance of sufferings, wrote so una-affectedly in his looks and carriage, which pleads so mightily for him, that it always disarms me; and to that degree, that I do not like to speak unkindly to him: on the contrary, meet him where I will — whether in town or country — in cart or under panniers — whether in liberty or bondage —— I have ever something civil to say to him on my part; and as one word begets another (if he has as little to do as I) —— I generally fall into conversation with him; and surely never is my imagination so busy as in framing his responses from the etchings of his countenance — and where those carry me not deep enough —— in flying from my own heart into his, and seeing what is natural for an ass to think — as well as a man, upon the occasion. In truth, it is the only creature of all the classes of beings below me, with whom I can do this: for parrots, jackdaws, &c.
—— I never exchange a word with them —— nor with the apes, &c., for pretty near the same reason; they act by rote, as the others speak by it, and equally make me silent: nay my dog and my cat, though I value them both —— (and for my dog he would speak if he could) — yet somehow or other, they neither of them possess the talents for conversation —— I can make nothing of a discourse with them, beyond the *proposition*, the *reply*, and *rejoinder*, which terminated my father's and my mother's conversations, in his beds of justice —— and those utter'd —— there's an end of the dialogue

— But with an ass, I can commune for ever.
Come, *Honesty!* said I, —— seeing it was impracticable to pass betwixt him and the gate —— art thou for coming in, or going out?
The ass twisted his head round to look up the street ——
Well — replied I — we'll wait a minute for thy driver:
—— He turned his head thoughtfully about, and looked wistfully the opposite way ——
I understand thee perfectly, answered I —— If thou takest a wrong step in this affair, he will cudgel thee to death —— Well! a minute is but a minute, and if it saves a fellow-creature a drubbing, it shall not be set down as ill spent.
He was eating the stem of an artichoke as this discourse went on, and in the little peevish contentions of nature betwixt hunger and unsavouriness, had dropt it out of his mouth half a dozen times, and pick'd it up again —— God help thee, *Jack!* said I, thou hast

a bitter breakfast on't — and many a bitter day's labour, — and many a bitter blow, I fear, for its wages —— 'tis all — all bitterness to thee, whatever life to is others. —— And now thy mouth, if one knew the truth of it, is as bitter, I dare say, as soot — (for he had cast aside the stem) and thou hast not a friend perhaps in all this world, that will give thee a macaroon. —— In saying this, I pull'd out a paper of 'em, which I had just purchased, and gave him one — and at this moment that I am telling it, my heart smites me, that there was more of pleasantry in the conceit, of seeing *how* an ass would eat a macaroon —— than of benevolence in giving him one, which presided in the act.

When the ass had eaten his macaroon, I press'd him to come in —— the poor beast was heavy loaded —— his legs seem'd to tremble under him —— he hung rather backwards, and as I pull'd at his halter, it broke short in my hand —— he look'd up pensive in my face — "Don't thrash me with it — but if you will, you may" —— If I do, said I, I'll be d —— d.

The word was but one-half of it pronounced, like the abbess of *Andoüillets'* — (so there was no sin in it) — when a person coming in, let fall a thundering bastinado upon the poor devil's crupper, which put an end to the ceremony.

Out upon it!
cried I —— but the interjection was equivocal —— and, I think, wrong placed too — for the end of an osier which had started out from the contexture of the ass's pannier, had caught hold of my breeches pocket, as he rush'd by me, and rent it in the most disastrous direction you can imagine —— so that the

Out upon it! in my opinion, should have come in here —— but this I leave to be settled by

THE

REVIEWERS

OF

MY BREECHES,

which I have brought over along with me for that purpose.

OF TRISTRAM SHANDY

CHAPTER XXXIII

WHEN all was set to rights, I came down stairs again into the *basse cour* with my *valet de place*, in order to sally out towards the tomb of the two lovers, &c. —— and was a second time stopp'd at the gate —— not by the ass — but by the person who struck him; and who, by that time, had taken possession (as is not uncommon after a defeat) of the very spot of ground where the ass stood.

It was a commissary sent to me from the post-office, with a rescript in his hand for the payment of some six livres odd sous.

Upon what account? said I. —— 'Tis upon the part of the king, replied the commissary, heaving up both his shoulders ——

—— My good friend, quoth I —— as sure as I am I — and you are you ——

—— And who are you? said he —— Don't puzzle me; said I.

CHAPTER XXXIV

——BUT it is an indubitable verity, continued I, addressing myself to the commissary, changing only the form of my asserveration —— that I owe the king of *France* nothing but my good-will; for he is a very honest man, and I wish him all health and pastime in the world ——

Pardonnez moi — replied the commissary, you are indebted to him six livres four sous, for the next post from hence to St. *Fons*, in your route to *Avignon* — which being a post royal, you pay double for the horses and postillion — otherwise 'twould have amounted to no more than three livres two sous ——

—— But I don't go by land; said I.

—— You may if you please; replied the commissary ——

Your most obedient servant —— said I, making him a low bow ——

The commissary, with all the sincerity of grave good breeding — made me one, as low again. —— I never was more disconcerted with a bow in my life.

—— The devil take the serious character of these people! quoth I — (aside) they understand no more of IRONY than this ——

The comparison was standing close by with his panniers — but something seal'd up my lips — I could not pronounce the name —

. Sir, said I, collecting myself — it is not my intention to take post ——

— But you may — said he, persisting in his first reply — you may take post if you chuse ——

— And I may take salt to my pickled herring, said I, if I chuse ——

— But I do not chuse —

— But you must pay for it, whether you do or no. Aye! for the salt; said I (I know) ——

— And for the post too; added he. Defend me! cried I ——

I travel by water — I am going down the *Rhône* this very afternoon — my baggage is in the boat — and I have actually paid nine livres for my passage ——

C'est tout egal — 'tis all one; said he.

Bon Dieu! what, pay for the way I go! and for the way I do *not* go!

—— *C'est tout egal;* replied the commissary ——

—— The devil it is! said I — but I will go to ten thousand Bastiles first ——

O England! England! thou land of liberty, and climate of good sense, thou tenderest of mothers — and gentlest of nurses, cried I, kneeling upon one knee, as I was beginning my apostrophè.

When the director of Madam *Le Blanc's* conscience coming in at that instant, and seeing a person in black, with a face as pale as ashes, at his devotions — looking still paler by the contrast and distress of his drapery — ask'd, if I stood in want of the aids of the church ——

I go by WATER — said I — and here's another will be for making me pay for going by OIL.

CHAPTER XXXV

AS I perceived the commissary of the post-office would have his six livres four sous, I had nothing else for it, but to say some smart thing upon the occasion, worth the money

And so I set off thus: ——

—— And pray, Mr. Commissary, by what law of courtesy is a defenceless stranger to be used just the reverse from what you use a *Frenchman* in this matter?

By no means; said he.

Excuse me; said I — for you have begun, Sir, with first tearing off my breeches — and now you want my pocket ——

Whereas — had you first taken my pocket, as you do with your own people — and then left me bare a—'d after — I had been a beast to have complain'd ——

As it is ——

—— 'Tis contrary to the *law of nature.*

—— 'Tis contrary to *reason.*

—— 'Tis contrary to the GOSPEL.

But not to this —— said he — putting a printed paper into my hand,

PAR LE ROY

—— 'Tis a pithy prolegomenon, quoth I — and so read on
—— —— —— —— —— —— —— —— —— —— ——
—— —— —— —— —— —— —— —— —— —— ——
—— ——

—— By all which it appears, quoth I, having read it over, a little too rapidly, that if a man sets out in a post-chaise from *Paris* — he must go on travelling in one, all the days of his life — or pay for it.— Excuse me, said the commissary, the spirit of the ordinance is this— That if you set out with an intention of running post from *Paris* to *Avignon*, &c., you shall not change that intention or mode of travelling, without first satisfying the fermiers for two posts further than the place you repent at — and 'tis founded, continued he, upon this, that the REVENUES are not to fall short through your *fickleness*—

—— O by heavens! cried I — if fickleness is taxable in *France* — we have nothing to do but to make the best peace with you we can —

AND SO THE PEACE WAS MADE;

—— And if it is a bad one — as *Tristram Shandy* laid the corner-stone of it — nobody but *Tristram Shandy* ought to be hanged.

THE LIFE AND OPINIONS

CHAPTER XXXVI

THOUGH I was sensible I had said as many clever things to the commissary as came to six livres four sous, yet I was determined to note down the imposition amongst my remarks before I retired from the place; so putting my hand into my coat-pocket for my remarks — (which, by the bye, may be a caution to travellers to take a little more care of *their* remarks for the future) "my remarks were *stolen*" ——— Never did sorry traveller make such a pother and racket about his remarks as I did about mine, upon the occasion.

Heaven! earth! sea! fire! cried I, calling in every thing to my aid but what I should ——— My remarks are stolen! — what shall I do? ——— Mr. Commissary! pray did I drop any remarks, as I stood besides you? ———

You dropp'd a good many very singular ones; replied he ——— Pugh! said I, those were but a few, not worth above six livres two sous — but these are a large parcel ——— He shook his head ——— Monsieur *Le Blanc!* Madam *Le Blanc!* did you see any papers of mine? — you maid of the house! run up stairs — *François!* run up after her ———

— I must have my remarks ——— they were the best remarks, cried I, that ever were made — the wisest — the wittiest — What shall I do? — which way shall I turn myself?

Sancho Pança, when he lost his ass's FURNITURE, did not exclaim more bitterly.

CHAPTER XXXVII

WHEN the first transport was over, and the registers of the brain were beginning to get a little out of the confusion into which this jumble of cross accidents had cast them — it then presently occurr'd to me, that I had left my remarks in the pocket of the chaise — and that in selling my chaise, I had sold my remarks along with it, to the chaise-vamper.   I leave this void space that the reader may swear into it any oath that he is most accustomed to ——— For my own part, if ever I swore a *whole* oath into a vacancy in my life, I think it was into that ——— *********, said I — and so my remarks through *France,* which were as full of wit, as an egg is full of meat, and as well worth four hundred guineas, as the said egg is worth a penny — have I been selling here to a chaise-vamper — for four *Louis d'Ors* — and giving him a post-chaise (by heaven) worth six into the bargain; had it been to *Dodsley*, or *Becket*, or any creditable bookseller, who was either leaving off business, and wanted a post-chaise — or who was beginning it — and wanted my remarks, and two or three guineas along with them — I could have borne it —— but to a chaise-vamper! — shew me to him this moment, *François*, — said I — The valet de place put on his hat, and led the way — and I pull'd off mine, as I pass'd the commissary, and followed him.

CHAPTER XXXVIII

WHEN we arrived at the chaise-vamper's house, both the house and the shop were shut up; it was the eighth of *September*, the nativity of the blessed Virgin *Mary*, mother of God —

—— Tantarra-ra-tan-tivi —— the whole world was gone out a May-poling — frisking here — capering there —— nobody cared a button for me or my remarks; so I sat me down upon a bench by the door, philosophating upon my condition: by a better fate than usually attends me, I had not waited half an hour, when the mistress came in to take the papilliotes from off her hair, before she went to the May-poles ——

The *French* women, by the bye, love May-poles, *à la jolie* — that is, as much as their matins —— give 'em but a May-pole, whether in *May*, *June*, *July*, or *September* — they never count the times —— down it goes —— 'tis meat, drink, washing, and lodging to 'em —— and had we but the policy, an' please your worships (as wood is a little scarce in *France*), to send them but plenty of May-poles ——

The women would set them up; and when they had done, they would dance round them (and the men for company) till they were all blind.

The wife of the chaise-vamper stepp'd in, I told you, to take the papilliotes from off her hair —— the toilet stands still for no man — so she jerk'd off her cap, to begin with them as she open'd the door, in doing which, one of them fell upon the ground —— I instantly saw it was my own writing ——

THE LIFE AND OPINIONS

O Seigneur! cried I — you have got all my remarks upon your head, Madam! —— *J'en suis bien mortifiée,* said she —— 'tis well, thinks I, they have stuck there — for could they have gone deeper, they would have made such confusion in a *French* woman's noddle — She had better have gone with it unfrizled to the day of eternity.

Tenez — said she — so without any idea of the nature of my suffering, she took them from her curls, and put them gravely one by one into my hat —— one was twisted this way —— another twisted that —— ey! by my faith; and when they are published, quoth I, ——

They will be worse twisted still.

CHAPTER XXXIX

AND now for *Lippius's* clock! said I, with the air of a man, who had got thro' all his difficulties —— nothing can prevent us seeing that, and the *Chinese* history, &c., except the time, said *François* —— for 'tis almost eleven — Then we must speed the faster, said I, striding it away to the cathedral.

I cannot say, in my heart, that it gave me any concern in being told by one of the minor canons, as I was entering the west door, — That *Lippius's* great clock was all out of joints, and had not gone for some years —— It will give me the more time, thought I, to peruse the *Chinese* history; and besides I shall be able to give the world a better account of the clock in its decay, than I could have done in its flourishing condition ——

—— And so away I posted to the college of the Jesuits.

Now it is with the project of getting a peep at the history of *China* in *Chinese* characters — as with many others I could mention, which strike the fancy only at a distance; for as I came nearer and nearer to the point — my blood cool'd — the freak gradually went off, till at length I would not have given a cherrystone to have it gratified —— The truth was, my time was short, and my heart was at the Tomb of the Lovers —— I wish to God, said I, as I got the rapper in my hand, that the key of the library may be but lost; it fell out as well ——

For all the JESUITS *had got the cholic* — and to that degree, as never was known in the memory of the oldest practitioner.

OF TRISTRAM SHANDY

CHAPTER XL

AS I knew the geography of the Tomb of the Lovers, as well as if I had lived twenty years in *Lyons*, namely, that it was upon the turning of my right hand, just without the gate, leading to the *Fauxbourg de Vaise* —— I dispatched *François* to the boat, that I might pay the homage I so long ow'd it, without a witness of my weakness — I walk'd with all imaginable joy towards the place —— when I saw the gate which intercepted the tomb, my heart glowed within me ——

— Tender and faithful spirits! cried I, addressing myself to *Amandus* and *Amanda* — long — long have I tarried to drop this tear upon your tomb ——— I come ——— I come ———

When I came — there was no tomb to drop it upon.

What would I have given for my uncle *Toby*, to have whistled Lillo bullero!

CHAPTER XLI

NO matter how, or in what mood — but I flew from the tomb of the lovers — or rather I did not fly *from* it — (for there was no such thing existing) and just got time enough to the boat to save my passage; — and ere I had sailed a hundred yards, the *Rhône* and the *Saôn* met together, and carried me down merrily betwixt them.

But I have described this voyage down the *Rhône*, before I made it ——

—— So now I am at *Avignon*, and as there is nothing to see but the old house, in which the duke of *Ormond* resided, and nothing to stop me but a short remark upon the place, in three minutes you will see me crossing the bridge upon a mule, with *François* upon a horse with my portmanteau behind him, and the owner of both, striding the way before us, with a long gun upon his shoulder, and a sword under his arm, lest peradventure we should run away with his cattle. Had you seen my breeches in entering *Avignon*, —— Though you'd have seen them better, I think, as I mounted — you would not have thought the precaution amiss, or found in your heart to have taken it in dudgeon; for my own part, I took it most kindly; and determined to make him a present of them, when we got to the end of our journey, for the trouble they had put him to, of arming himself at all points against them.

THE LIFE AND OPINIONS

Before I go further, let me get rid of my remark upon *Avignon*, which is this: That I think it wrong, merely because a man's hat has been blown off his head by chance the first night he comes to *Avignon,* —— that he should therefore say, "*Avignon* is more subject to high winds than any town in all *France :*" for which reason I laid no stress upon the accident till I had enquired of the master of the inn about it, who telling me seriously it was so —— and hearing, moreover, the windiness of *Avignon* spoke of in the country about as a proverb —— I set it down, merely to ask the learned what can be the cause —— the consequence I saw — for they are all Dukes, Marquisses, and Counts, there —— the duce a Baron, in all *Avignon* —— so that there is scarce any talking to them on a windy day.

Prithee, friend, said I, take hold of my mule for a moment —— for I wanted to pull off one of my jack-boots, which hurt my heel — the man was standing quite idle at the door of the inn, and as I had taken it into my head, he was someway concerned about the house or stable, I put the bridle into his hand — so begun with the boot: — when I had finished the affair, I turned about to take the mule from the man, and thank him ——

But *Monsieur le Marquis* had walked in ——

CHAPTER XLII

I HAD now the whole south of *France*, from the banks of the *Rhône* to those of the *Garonne*, to traverse upon my mule at my own leisure — *at my own leisure* —— for I had left Death, the Lord knows —— and He only — how far behind me —— " I have followed many a man thro' *France*, quoth he — but never at this mettlesome rate." —— Still he followed, —— and still I fled him —— but I fled him chearfully —— still he pursued —— but, like one who pursued his prey without hope —— as he lagg'd, every step he lost, soften'd his looks —— why should I fly him at this rate?

So notwithstanding all the commissary of the post-office had said, I changed the *mode* of my travelling once more; and, after so precipitate and rattling a course as I had run, I flattered my fancy with thinking of my mule, and that I should traverse the rich plains of *Languedoc* upon his back, as slowly as foot could fall.

There is nothing more pleasing to a traveller —— or more terrible to travel-writers, than a large rich plain; especially if it is without great rivers or bridges; and presents nothing to the eye, but one unvaried picture of plenty: for after they have once told you, that 'tis delicious! or delightful! (as the case happens) — that the soil was grateful, and that nature pours out all her abundance, &c. . . . they have then a large plain upon their hands, which they know not what to do with — and which is of little or no use to them but to carry them to some town; and that town, perhaps of little more, but a new place to start from to the next plain —— and so on.

—— This is most terrible work; judge if I don't manage my plains better.

CHAPTER XLIII

I HAD not gone above two leagues and a half, before the man with his gun began to look at his priming.

I had three several times loiter'd *terribly* behind; half a mile at least every time; once, in deep conference with a drum-maker, who was making drums for the fairs of *Baucaira* and *Tarascone* — I did not understand the principles ——

The second time, I cannot so properly say, I stopp'd —— for meeting a couple of *Franciscans* straitened more for time than myself, and not being able to get to the bottom of what I was about —— I had turn'd back with them ——

The third, was an affair of trade with a gossip, for a hand-basket of *Provence* figs for four sous; this would have been transacted at once; but for a case of conscience at the close of it; for when the figs were paid for, it turn'd out, that there were two dozen of eggs cover'd over with vine-leaves at the bottom of the basket — as I had no intention of buying eggs — I made no sort of claim of them — as for the space they had occupied — what signified it? I had figs enow for my money ——

— But it was my intention to have the basket — it was the gossip's intention to keep it, without which, she could do nothing with her eggs —— and unless I had the basket, I could do as little with my figs, which were too ripe already, and most of 'em burst at the side: this brought on a short contention, which terminated in sundry proposals, what we should both do ——

—— How we disposed of our eggs and figs, I defy you, or the

Devil himself, had he not been there (which I am persuaded he was), to form the least probable conjecture: You will read the whole of it —— not this year, for I am hastening to the story of my uncle *Toby's* amours — but you will read it in the collection of those which have arose out of the journey across this plain — and which, therefore, I call my

PLAIN STORIES

How far my pen has been fatigued, like those of other travellers, in this journey of it, over so barren a track — the world must judge — but the traces of it, which are now all set o' vibrating together this moment, tell me 'tis the most fruitful and busy period of my life; for as I had made no convention with my man with the gun, as to time — by stopping and talking to every soul I met, who was not in a full trot — joining all parties before me — waiting for every soul behind — hailing all those who were coming through cross-roads — arresting all kinds of beggars, pilgrims, fiddlers, friars — not passing by a woman in a mulberry-tree without commending her legs, and tempting her into conversation with a pinch of snuff —— In short, by seizing every handle, of what size or shape soever, which chance held out to me in this journey — I turned my *plain* into a *city* — I was always in company, and with great variety too; and as my mule loved society as much as myself, and had some proposals always on his part to offer to every beast he met — I am confident we could have passed through *Pall-Mall* or St. *James's*-Street for a month together, with fewer adventures — and seen less of human nature.

O! there is that sprightly frankness, which at once unpins every plait of a *Languedocian's* dress — that whatever is beneath it, it looks so like the simplicity which poets sing of in better days — I will delude my fancy, and believe it is so.

'Twas in the road betwixt *Nismes* and *Lunel*, where there is the best *Muscatto* wine in all France, and which by the bye belongs to the honest canons of MONTPELLIER — and foul befal the man who has drank it at their table, who grudges them a drop of it.

—— The sun was set — they had done their work; the nymphs had tied up their hair afresh — and the swains were preparing for a carousal —— my mule made a dead point —— 'Tis the fife and tabourin, said I —— I'm frighten'd to death, quoth he —— They are running at the ring of pleasure, said I, giving him a prick ——

OF TRISTRAM SHANDY

By saint *Boogar*, and all the saints at the backside of the door of purgatory, said he — (making the same resolution with the abbesse of *Andoüillets*) I'll not go a step further —— 'Tis very well, sir, said I —— I never will argue a point with one of your family, as long as I live; so leaping off his back, and kicking off one boot into this ditch, and t'other into that — I'll take a dance, said I — so stay you here.

A sun-burnt daughter of Labour rose up from the groupe to meet me, as I advanced towards them; her hair, which was a dark chesnut approaching rather to a black, was tied up in a knot, all but a single tress.

We want a cavalier, said she, holding out both her hands, as if to offer them — And a cavalier ye shall have; said I, taking hold of both of them.

Hadst thou, *Nannette*, been array'd like a dutchesse!

—— But that cursed slit in thy petticoat!

Nannette cared not for it.

We could not have done without you, said she, letting go one hand, with self-taught politeness, leading me up with the other.

A lame youth, whom *Apollo* had recompensed with a pipe, and to which he had added a tabourin of his own accord, ran sweetly over the prelude, as he sat upon the bank —— Tie me up this tress instantly, said *Nannette*, putting a piece of string into my hand — It taught me to forget I was a stranger —— The whole knot fell down — We had been seven years acquainted.

The youth struck the note upon the tabourin — his pipe followed, and off we bounded —— "the duce take that slit!"

The sister of the youth, who had stolen her voice from heaven, sung alternately with her brother —— 'twas a *Gascoigne* roundelay.

VIVA LA JOIA!
FIDON LA TRISTESSA!

The nymphs join'd in unison, and their swains an octave below them ——

I would have given a crown to have it sew'd up — *Nannette* would not have given a sous —*Viva la joia !* was in her lips — *Viva la joia!* was in her eyes. A transient spark of amity shot across the space betwixt us —— She look'd amiable! —— Why could I not live, and end my days thus? Just Disposer of our joys and sorrows, cried I, why could not a man sit down in the lap of content here —— and dance, and sing, and say his prayers, and go to heaven with this nut-brown maid? Capriciously did she bend her head on one side, and dance up insidious —— Then 'tis time to dance off, quoth I; so changing only partners and tunes, I danced it away from *Lunel* to *Montpellier* —— from thence to *Pesçnas, Beziers* —— I danced it along through *Narbonne, Carcasson,* and *Castle Naudairy,* till at last I danced myself into *Perdrillo's* pavillion, where pulling out a paper of black lines, that I might go on straight forwards, without digression or parenthesis, in my uncle *Toby's* amours ——

I begun thus ——

PAPERS FROM
THE
CITIZEN OF THE WORLD
BY
OLIVER GOLDSMITH

LETTERS FROM A CITIZEN OF THE WORLD TO HIS FRIENDS IN THE EAST

LETTER I

To Mr. ——, Merchant, in London
INTRODUCTION
AMSTERDAM.

SIR, — Yours of the 13th instant, covering two bills, one on Messrs. R. and D. value £478, 10s., and the other on Mr. ****, value £285, duly came to hand, the former of which met with honour, but the other has been trifled with, and I am afraid will be returned protested.

The bearer of this is my friend, therefore let him be yours. He is a native of Honan in China, and one who did me signal services, when he was a mandarine, and I a factor, at Canton. By frequently conversing with the English there, he has learned the language, though he is entirely a stranger to their manners and customs. I am told he is a philosopher — I am sure he is an honest man: that to you will be his best recommendation, next to the consideration of his being the friend of, Sir, yours, &c.

LETTER II

From Lien Chi Altangi, to ——, Merchant in Amsterdam
ARRIVAL OF THE CHINESE PHILOSOPHER IN LONDON — HIS MOTIVES FOR THE JOURNEY — SOME DESCRIPTION OF THE STREETS AND HOUSES

LONDON.

FRIEND OF MY HEART, — *May the wings of peace rest upon thy dwelling, and the shield of conscience preserve thee from vice and misery!* For all thy favours accept my gratitude and esteem, the only tributes a poor philosophic wanderer can return. Sure, fortune is resolved to make me unhappy, when she gives others a power of testifying their friendship by actions, and leaves me only words to express the sincerity of mine.

I am perfectly sensible of the delicacy with which you endeavour to lessen your own merit and my obligations. By calling your late instances of friendship only a return for former favours, you would induce me to impute to your justice what I owe to your generosity.

The services I did you at Canton, justice, humanity, and my office, bade me perform; those you have done me since my arrival at Amsterdam, no laws obliged you to, no justice required. Even half your favours would have been greater than my most sanguine expectations.

The sum of money, therefore, which you privately conveyed into my baggage, when I was leaving Holland, and which I was ignorant of till my arrival in London, I must beg leave to return. You have been bred a merchant, and I a scholar; you consequently love money better than I. You can find pleasure in superfluity; I am perfectly content with what is sufficient. Take therefore what is yours; it may give you some pleasure, even though you have no occasion to use it; my happiness it cannot improve, for I have already all that I want.

My passage by sea from Rotterdam to England was more painful to me than all the journeys I ever made on land. I have traversed the immeasurable wilds of Mogul Tartary; felt all the rigours of Siberian skies; I have had my repose a hundred times disturbed by invading savages, and have seen, without shrinking, the desert sands rise like a troubled ocean all around me. Against these calamities I was armed with resolution; but in my passage to England, though nothing occurred that gave the mariners any uneasiness, to one who was never at sea before, all was a subject of astonishment and terror. To find the land disappear — to see our ship mount the waves, swift as an arrow from the Tartar bow — to hear the wind howling through the cordage — to feel a sickness which depresses even the spirits of the brave, — these were unexpected distresses, and, consequently, assaulted me, unprepared to receive them.

You men of Europe think nothing of a voyage by sea. With us of China, a man who has been from sight of land is regarded upon his return with admiration. I have known some provinces where there is not even a name for the ocean. What a strange people, therefore, am I got amongst, who have founded an empire on this unstable element, who build cities upon billows that rise higher

Morning.

than the mountains of Tipertala, and make the deep more formidable than the wildest tempest!

Such accounts as these, I must confess, were my first motives for seeing England. These induced me to undertake a journey of seven hundred painful days, in order to examine its opulence, buildings, sciences, arts, and manufactures on the spot. Judge, then, how great is my disappointment on entering London, to see no signs of that opulence so much talked of abroad: wherever I turn, I am presented with a gloomy solemnity in the houses, the streets, and the inhabitants: none of that beautiful gilding which makes a principal ornament in Chinese architecture. The streets of Nankin are sometimes strewed with gold leaf; very different are those of London: in the midst of their pavements a great lazy puddle moves muddily along; heavy-laden machines, with wheels of unwieldy thickness, crowd up every passage; so that a stranger, instead of finding time for observation, is often happy if he has time to escape from being crushed to pieces.

The houses borrow very few ornaments from architecture; their chief decoration seems to be a paltry piece of painting, hung out at their doors or windows, at once a proof of their indigence and vanity, in each having one of those pictures exposed to public view; and their indigence in being unable to get them better painted. In this respect, the fancy of their painters is also deplorable. Could you believe it? I have seen five black lions and three blue boars in less than the circuit of half a mile; and yet you know that animals of these colours are nowhere to be found except in the wild imaginations of Europe.

From these circumstances in their buildings, and from the dismal looks of the inhabitants, I am induced to conclude that the nation is actually poor; and that, like the Persians, they make a splendid figure everywhere but at home. The proverb of Xixofou is, that a man's riches may be seen in his eyes: if we judge of the English by this rule, there is not a poorer nation under the sun.

I have been here but two days, so will not be hasty in my decisions. Such letters as I shall write to Fipsihi in Moscow, I beg you'll endeavour to forward with all diligence; I shall send them open, in order that you may take copies or translations, as you are equally versed in the Dutch and Chinese languages. Dear friend, think of my absence with regret, as I sincerely regret yours; even while I write, I lament our separation. Farewell.

CITIZEN OF THE WORLD

LETTER III

From Lien Chi Altangi, to the care of Fipsihi, resident in Moscow, to be forwarded by the Russian caravan to Fum Hoam, First President of the Ceremonial Academy at Pekin, in China

THE DESCRIPTION OF LONDON CONTINUED — THE LUXURY OF THE ENGLISH — ITS BENEFITS — THE FINE GENTLEMAN — THE FINE LADY

THINK not, O thou guide of my youth! that absence can impair my respect, or interposing trackless deserts blot your reverend figure from my memory. The farther I travel, I feel the pain of separation with stronger force; those ties that bind me to my native country and you, are still unbroken. By every remove, I only drag a greater length of chain.

Could I find aught worth transmitting from so remote a region as this to which I have wandered, I should gladly send it; but, instead of this, you must be contented with a renewal of my former professions, and an imperfect account of a people with whom I am as yet but superficially acquainted. The remarks of a man who has been but three days in the country, can only be those obvious circumstances which force themselves upon the imagination. I consider myself here as a newly created being, introduced into a new world. Every object strikes with wonder and surprise. The imagination, still unsated, seems the only active principle of the mind. The most trifling occurrences give pleasure, till the gloss of novelty is worn away. When I have ceased to wonder, I may possibly grow wise; I may then call the reasoning principle to my aid, and compare those objects with each other, which were before examined without reflection.

Behold me, then, in London, gazing at the strangers, and they at me. It seems they find somewhat absurd in my figure; and had I been never from home, it is possible I might find an infinite fund of ridicule in theirs, but by long travelling, I am taught to laugh at folly alone, and to find nothing truly ridiculous but villainy and vice.

When I had just quitted my native country, and crossed the Chinese wall, I fancied every deviation from the customs and manners of China was a departing from nature. I smiled at the blue lips and red foreheads of the Tonguese; and could hardly contain when I saw the Daures dress their heads with horns: the Ostiacs powdered with red earth; and the Calmuck beauties tricked out in all the finery of sheepskin, appeared highly ridiculous. But I soon perceived that the ridicule lay not in them, but in me; that I falsely condemned others for absurdity, because they happened to differ from a standard originally founded in prejudice or partiality.

I find no pleasure, therefore, in taxing the English with departing from nature in their external appearance, which is all I yet know of their character: it is possible they only endeavour to improve her simple plan, since every extravagance in dress proceeds from a desire of becoming more beautiful than nature made us; and this is so harmless a vanity, that I not only pardon, but approve it. A desire to be more excellent than others is what actually makes us so; and as thousands find a livelihood in society by such appetites, none but the ignorant inveigh against them.

You are not insensible, most reverend Fum Hoam, what numberless trades, even among the Chinese, subsist by the harmless pride of each other. Your nose-borers, feet-swathers, teeth-stainers, eyebrow-pluckers, would all want bread, should their neighbours want vanity. These vanities, however, employ much fewer hands in China than in England; and a fine gentleman, or a fine lady, here, dressed up to the fashion, seems scarcely to have a single limb that does not suffer some distortions from art.

To make a fine gentleman, several trades are required, but chiefly a barber. You have undoubtedly heard of the Jewish champion, whose strength lay in his hair. One would think the English were for placing all wisdom there. To appear wise, nothing more is requisite here than for a man to borrow hair from the heads of all his neighbours, and clap it, like a bush, on his own. The distributors of law and physic stick on such quantities, that it is almost impossible, even in idea, to distinguish between the head and the hair.

Those whom I have been now describing affect the gravity of the lion; those I am going to describe more resemble the pert vivacity of smaller animals. The barber, who is still master of the ceremonies, cuts their hair close to the crown; and then, with a composition of meal and hog's-lard, plasters the whole in such a manner as to make it impossible to distinguish whether the patient wears a cap or a plaster: but, to make the picture more perfectly striking, conceive the tail of some beast, a grey-hound's tail, or a pig's tail, for instance, appended to the back of the head, and reaching down to the place where tails in other animals are generally seen to begin: thus betailed and bepowdered, the man of taste fancies he improves in beauty, dresses up his hard-featured face in smiles, and attempts to look hideously tender. Thus equipped, he is qualified to make love, and hopes for success more from the powder on the outside of his head, than the sentiments within.

Yet when I consider what sort of a creature the fine lady is, to whom he is supposed to pay his addresses, it is not strange to find him thus equipped in order to please. She is herself every whit as fond of powder, and tails, and hog's-lard, as he. To speak my secret sentiments, most reverend Fum, the ladies here are horridly ugly; I can hardly endure the sight of them; they no way resemble the beauties of China: the Europeans have a quite different idea of beauty from us. When I reflect on the small-footed perfections of an Eastern beauty, how is it possible I should have eyes for a woman whose feet are ten inches long? I shall never forget the beauties of my native city of Nangfew. How very broad their faces; how very short their noses; how very little their eyes; how very thin their lips; how very black their teeth; the snow on the tops of Bao is not fairer than their cheeks; and their eyebrows are small as the line by the pencil of Quamsi. Here a lady with such perfections would be frightful. Dutch and Chinese beauties, indeed, have some resemblance, but English women are entirely different: red cheeks, big eyes, and teeth of a most odious whiteness, are not only seen here, but wished for; and then they have such masculine feet, as actually serve *some* for walking!

Yet uncivil as Nature has been, they seem resolved to outdo her in unkindness: they use white powder, blue powder, and black powder for their hair, and a red powder for the face on some particular occasions.

They like to have the face of various colours, as among the Tartars of Koreki, frequently sticking on, with spittle, little black patches on every part of it, except on the tip of the nose, which I have never seen with a patch. You'll have a better idea of their manner of placing these spots, when I have finished a map of an English face patched up to the fashion, which shall shortly be sent to increase your curious collection of paintings, medals, and monsters.

Noon.

But what surprises more than all the rest is what I have just now been credibly informed of by one of this country. "Most ladies here," says he, "have two faces; one face to sleep in, and another to show in company. The first is generally reserved for the husband and family at home; the other put on to please strangers abroad: the family face is often indifferent enough, but the outdoor one looks something better; this is always made at the toilet, where the looking-glass and toad-eater sit in council, and settle the complexion of the day."

I cannot ascertain the truth of this remark: however, it is actually certain, that they wear more clothes within doors than without; and I have seen a lady, who seemed to shudder at a breeze in her own apartment, appear half naked in the streets. Farewell.

LETTER IV

To the Same

ENGLISH PRIDE — LIBERTY — AN INSTANCE OF BOTH — NEWSPAPERS — POLITENESS

THE English seem as silent as the Japanese, yet vainer than the inhabitants of Siam. Upon my arrival I attributed that reserve to modesty, which, I now find, has its origin in pride. Condescend to address them first, and you are sure of their acquaintance; stoop to flattery, and you conciliate their friendship and esteem. They bear hunger, cold, fatigue, and all the miseries of life without shrinking; danger only calls forth their fortitude; they even exult in calamity; but contempt is what they cannot bear. An Englishman fears contempt more than death; he often flies to death as a refuge from its pressure; and dies when he fancies the world has ceased to esteem him.

Pride seems the source not only of their national vices, but of their national virtues also. An Englishman is taught to love his king as his friend, but to acknowledge no other master than the laws which himself has contributed to enact. He despises those nations who, that one may be free, are all content to be slaves; who first lift a tyrant into terror, and then shrink under his power as if delegated from Heaven. Liberty is echoed in all their assemblies; and thousands might be found ready to offer up their lives for the sound, though perhaps not one of all the number understands its meaning. The lowest mechanic, however, looks upon it as his duty to be a watchful guardian of his country's freedom, and often uses a language that might seem haughty, even in the mouth of the Great Emperor who traces his ancestry to the moon.

A few days ago, passing by one of their prisons, I could not avoid stopping, in order to listen to a dialogue which I thought might afford me some entertainment. The conversation was carried on between a debtor, through the grate of his prison, a porter, who had stopped to rest his burthen, and a soldier at the window. The subject was upon a threatened invasion from France, and each seemed extremely anxious to rescue his country from the impending danger. "For my part," cries the prisoner, "the greatest of my apprehensions is for our freedom; if the French should conquer, what would become of English liberty? My dear friends, liberty is the Englishman's prerogative; we must preserve that at the expense of our lives; of that the French shall never deprive us. It is not to be expected that men who are slaves themselves would preserve our freedom should they happen to conquer." — "Ay, slaves," cries the porter, "they are all slaves, fit only to carry burthens, every one of them. Before I would stoop to slavery, may this be my poison," (and he held the goblet in his hand), "may this be my poison — but I would sooner 'list for a soldier."

The soldier, taking the goblet from his friend, with much awe, fervently cried out, "It is not so much our liberties, as our religion, that would suffer by such a change: ay, our religion, my lads. May the devil sink me into flames," (such was the solemnity of his adjuration), "if the French should come over, but our religion would be utterly undone!" — So saying, instead of a libation, he applied the goblet to his lips, and confirmed his sentiments with a ceremony of the most persevering devotion.

In short, every man here pretends to be a politician; even the fair sex are sometimes found to mix the severity of national altercation with the blandishments of love, and often become conquerors, by more weapons of destruction than their eyes.

This universal passion for politics is gratified by Daily Gazettes, as with us in China. But as in ours the Emperor endeavours to instruct his people, in theirs the people endeavour to instruct the administration. You must not, however, imagine, that they who compile these papers have any actual knowledge of the politics, or

England, Plate II.

the government, of a state; they only collect their materials from the oracle of some coffee-house, which oracle has himself gathered them the night before from a beau at a gaming-table, who has pillaged his knowledge from a great man's porter, who has had his information from the great man's gentleman, who has invented the whole story for his own amusement the night preceding.

The English, in general, seem fonder of gaining the esteem than the love of those they converse with. This gives a formality to their amusements: their gayest conversations have something too wise for innocent relaxation: though in company you are seldom disgusted with the absurdity of a fool, you are seldom lifted into rapture by those strokes of vivacity, which give instant, though not permanent, pleasure.

What they want, however, in gaiety, they make up in politeness. You smile at hearing me praise the English for their politeness; you who have heard very different accounts from the missionaries at Pekin, who have seen such a different behaviour in their merchants and seamen at home. But I must still repeat it, the English seem more polite than any of their neighbours: their great art in this respect lies in endeavouring, while they oblige, to lessen the force of the favour. Other countries are fond of obliging a stranger; but seem desirous that he should be sensible of the obligation. The English confer their kindness with an appearance of indifference, and give away benefits with an air as if they despised them.

Walking, a few days ago, between an English and a Frenchman in the suburbs of the city, we were overtaken by a heavy shower of rain. I was unprepared; but they had each large coats, which defended them from what seemed to me a perfect inundation. The Englishman, seeing me shrink from the weather, accosted me thus: "Psha, man, what dost shrink at? here, take this coat; I don't wan't it; I find it no way useful to me; I had as lief be without it." The Frenchman began to show his politeness in turn. "My dear friend," cries he, "why won't you oblige me by making use of my coat? you see how well it defends me from the rain; I should not choose to part with it to others, but to such a friend as you I could even part with my skin to do him service."

From such minute instances as these, most reverend Fum Hoam, I am sensible your sagacity will collect instruction. The volume of nature is the book of knowledge; and he becomes most wise who makes the most judicious selection. Farewell.

CITIZEN OF THE WORLD

LETTER V

To the Same

ENGLISH PASSION FOR POLITICS — A SPECIMEN OF A NEWSPAPER — CHARACTERISTICS OF THE MANNERS OF DIFFERENT COUNTRIES

I HAVE already informed you of the singular passion of this nation for politics. An Englishman, not satisfied with finding, by his own prosperity, the contending powers of Europe properly balanced, desires also to know the precise value of every weight in either scale. To gratify this curiosity, a leaf of political instruction is served up every morning with tea. When our politician has feasted upon this, he repairs to a coffee-house, in order to ruminate upon what he has read, and increase his collection; from thence he proceeds to the ordinary, enquires what news, and, treasuring up every acquisition there, hunts about all the evening in quest of more, and carefully adds it to the rest. Thus at night he retires home, full of the important advices of the day: when lo! awaking next morning, he finds the instructions of yesterday a collection of absurdity, or palpable falsehood. This one would think a mortifying repulse in the pursuit of wisdom; yet our politician, no way discouraged, hunts on, in order to collect fresh materials, and in order to be again disappointed.

I have often admired the commercial spirit which prevails over Europe; have been surprised to see them carry on a traffic with productions that an Asiatic stranger would deem entirely useless. It is a proverb in China that a European suffers not even his spittle to be lost; the maxim, however, is not sufficiently strong, since they sell even their lies to great advantage. Every nation drives a considerable trade in this commodity with their neighbours.

An English dealer in this way, for instance, has only to ascend to his work-house, and manufacture a turbulent speech, averred to be spoken in the senate; or a report supposed to be dropt at court; a piece of scandal that strikes at a popular mandarine; or a secret treaty between two neighbouring powers. When finished, these goods are baled up, and consigned to a factor abroad, who sends in return two battles, three sieges, and a shrewd letter filled with dashes —— blanks, and stars * * * of great importance.

Thus, you perceive, that a single Gazette is the joint manufacture of Europe; and he who would peruse it with a philosophical eye, might perceive in every paragraph something characteristic of the nation to which it belongs. A map does not exhibit a more distinct view of the boundaries and situation of every country, than its news does a picture of the genius and the morals of its inhabitants. The superstition and erroneous delicacy of Italy, the formality of Spain, the cruelty of Portugal, the fears of Austria, the confidence of Prussia, the levity of France, the avarice of Holland, the pride of England, the absurdity of Ireland, and the national partiality of Scotland, are all conspicuous in every page.

But, perhaps, you may find more satisfaction in a real newspaper, than in my description of one; I therefore send a specimen, which may serve to exhibit the manner of their being written, and distinguish the characters of the various nations which are united in its composition.

NAPLES. — We have lately dug up here a curious Etruscan monument, broke in two in the raising. The characters are scarce visible: but Nugosi, the learned antiquary, supposes it to have been erected in honour of Picus, a Latin king, as one of the lines may be plainly distinguished to begin with a P. It is hoped this discovery will produce something valuable, as the literati of our twelve academies are deeply engaged in the disquisition.

PISA. — Since Father Fudgi, prior of St. Gilbert's, has gone to reside at Rome, no miracles have been performed at the shrine of St. Gilbert: the devout begin to grow uneasy, and some begin actually to fear that St. Gilbert has forsaken them with the reverend father.

LUCCA. — The administrators of our serene republic have frequent conferences upon the part they shall take in the present commotions of Europe. Some are for sending a body of their troops, consisting of one company of foot and six horsemen, to make a diversion in favour of the empress-queen; others are as strenuous asserters of the Prussian interest: what turn these debates may take, time only can discover. However, certain it is, we shall be able to bring into the field, at the opening of the next campaign, seventy-five armed men, a commander-in-chief, and two drummers of great experience.

SPAIN. — Yesterday the new king showed himself to his subjects, and, after having stayed half an hour in his balcony, retired to the royal apartment. The night concluded, on this extraordinary occasion, with illuminations and other demonstrations of joy.

The queen is more beautiful than the rising sun, and reckoned one of the first wits in Europe. She had a glorious opportunity of displaying the readiness of her invention and her skill in repartee, lately at court. The Duke of Lerma coming up to her with a low bow and a smile, and presenting a nosegay set with diamonds, "Madame," cries he, "I am your most obedient humble servant." "O, Sir," replies the queen, without any prompter, or the least hesitation, "I'm very proud of the very great honour you do me." Upon which she made a low courtsy, and all the courtiers fell a-laughing at the readiness and the smartness of her reply.

LISBON. — Yesterday we had an *auto da fe*, at which were burned three young women, accused of heresy, one of them of exquisite beauty, two Jews, and an old woman, convicted of being a witch. One of the friars who attended the last, reports, that he saw the devil fly out of her at the stake in the shape of a flame of fire. The populace behaved on this occasion with great good-humour, joy, and sincere devotion.

Our merciful sovereign has been for some time past recovered of his fright: though so atrocious an attempt deserved to exterminate half the nation, yet he has been graciously pleased to spare the lives of his subjects, and not above five hundred have been broke upon the wheel, or otherwise executed, upon this horrid occasion.

VIENNA. — We have received certain advices that a party of twenty thousand Austrians, having attacked a much superior body of Prussians, put them all to flight, and took the rest prisoners of war.

BERLIN. — We have received certain advices that a party of twenty thousand Prussians, having attacked a much superior body of Austrians, put them to flight, and took a great number of prisoners, with their military chest, cannon, and baggage.

Though we have not succeeded this campaign to our wishes, yet, when we think of him who commands us, we rest in security: while we sleep, our king is watchful for our safety.

PARIS. — We shall soon strike a signal blow. We have seventeen flat-bottomed boats at Havre. The people are in excellent spirits, and our ministers make no difficulty in raising the supplies.

We are all undone; the people are discontented to the last degree; the ministers are obliged to have recourse to the most rigorous methods to raise the expenses of the war.

Our distresses are great; but Madame Pompadour continues to

The Election, Plate II, Canvassing for Votes.

supply our king, who is now growing old, with a fresh lady every night. His health, thank Heaven, is still pretty well; nor is he in the least unfit, as was reported, for any kind of royal exercitation. He was so frightened at the affair of Damien, that his physicians were apprehensive lest his reason should suffer; but that wretch's tortures soon composed the kingly terrors of his breast.

ENGLAND. — Wanted an usher to an academy. — N. B. — He must be able to read, dress hair, and must have had the small-pox.

DUBLIN. — We hear that there is a benevolent subscription on foot among the nobility and gentry of this kingdom, who are great patrons of merit, in order to assist Black and All Black, in his contest with the Paddereen mare.

We hear from Germany that Prince Ferdinand has gained a complete victory, and taken twelve kettle-drums, five standards, and four waggons of ammunition, prisoners of war.

EDINBURGH. — We are positive when we say that Saunders M'Gregor, who was lately executed for horse-stealing, is not a Scotsman, but born in Carrickfergus. — Farewell.

LETTER XII

To the Same

THE FUNERAL SOLEMNITIES OF THE ENGLISH — THEIR PASSION FOR FLATTERING EPITAPHS

FROM the funeral solemnities of the Daures, who think themselves the politest people in the world, I must make a transition to the funeral solemnities of the English, who think themselves as polite as they. The numberless ceremonies which are used here when a person is sick appear to me so many evident marks of fear and apprehension. Ask an Englishman, however, whether he is afraid of death, and he boldly answers in the negative; but observe his behaviour in circumstances of approaching sickness, and you will find his actions give his assertions the lie.

The Chinese are very sincere in this respect; they hate to die, and they confess their terrors: a great part of their life is spent in preparing things proper for their funeral. A poor artisan shall spend half his income in providing himself a tomb twenty years before he wants it; and denies himself the necessaries of life, that he may be amply provided for when he shall want them no more.

But people of distinction in England really deserve pity, for they die in circumstances of the most extreme distress. It is an established rule, never to let a man know that he is dying: physicians are sent for, the clergy are called, and every thing passes in silent solemnity round the sick-bed. The patient is in agonies, looks round for pity, yet not a single creature will say that he is dying. If he is possessed of fortune, his relations entreat him to make his will, as it may restore the tranquillity of his mind. He is desired to undergo the rites of the church, for decency requires it. His friends take their leave, only because they do not care to see him in pain. In short, a hundred stratagems are used to make him do what he might have been induced to perform only by being told, "Sir, you are past all hopes, and had as good think decently of dying."

Besides all this, the chamber is darkened, the whole house echoes to the cries of the wife, the lamentations of the children, the grief of the servants, and the sighs of friends. The bed is surrounded with priests and doctors in black, and only flambeaux emit a yellow gloom. Where is the man, how intrepid soever, that would not shrink at such a hideous solemnity? For fear of affrighting their expiring friends, the English practise all that can fill them with terror. Strange effect of human prejudice, thus to torture, merely from mistaken tenderness!

You see, my friend, what contradictions there are in the tempers of those islanders: when prompted by ambition, revenge, or disappointment, they meet death with the utmost resolution: the very man who in his bed would have trembled at the aspect of a doctor, shall go with intrepidity to attack a bastion, or deliberately noose himself up in his garters.

The passion of the Europeans for magnificent interments, is equally strong with that of the Chinese. When a tradesman dies, his frightful face is painted up by an undertaker, and placed in a proper situation to receive company: this is called lying in state. To this disagreeable spectacle all the idlers in town flock, and learn to loath the wretch dead whom they despised when living. In this manner, you see some who would have refused a shilling to save the life of their dearest friend, bestow thousands on adorning their putrid corpse. I have been told of a fellow, who, grown rich by the price of blood, left it in his will that he should lie in state; and thus unknowingly gibbeted himself into infamy, when he might have otherwise quietly retired into oblivion.

When the person is buried, the next care is to make his epitaph: they are generally reckoned best which flatter most; such relations, therefore, as have received most benefits from the defunct, discharge this friendly office, and generally flatter in proportion to their joy. When we read those monumental histories of the dead, it may be justly said, that "all men are equal in the dust"; for, they all appear equally remarkable for being the most sincere Christians, the most benevolent neighbours, and the honestest men of their time. To go through a European cemetery, one would be apt to wonder how mankind could have so basely degenerated from such excellent ancestors. Every tomb pretends to claim your reverence and regret; some are praised for piety in those inscriptions, who never entered the temple until they were dead; some are praised for being excellent poets, who were never mentioned, except for their dulness when living; others for sublime orators, who were never noted except for their impudence; and others still, for military achievements, who were never in any other skirmishes but with the watch. Some even make epitaphs for themselves, and bespeak the reader's good-will. It were indeed to be wished, that every man would early learn this manner to make his own; that he would draw it up in terms as flattering as possible, and that he would make it the employment of his whole life to deserve it!

I have not yet been in a place called Westminster Abbey, but soon intend to visit it. There, I am told, I shall see justice done to deceased merit: none, I am told, are permitted to be buried there, but such as have adorned as well as improved mankind. There, no intruders, by the influence of friends or fortune, presume to mix their unhallowed ashes with philosophers, heroes, and poets. Nothing but true merit has a place in that awful sanctuary. The guardianship of the tombs is committed to several reverend priests, who are never guilty, for a superior reward, of taking down the names of good men, to make room for others of equivocal character, nor ever profane the sacred walls with pageants that posterity cannot know, or shall blush to own.

I always was of opinion, that sepulchral honours of this kind should be considered as a national concern, and not trusted to the care of the priest of any country, how respectable soever: but from the conduct of the reverend personages, whose disinterested patriotism I shall shortly be able to discover, I am taught to retract my former sentiments. It is true, the Spartans and the Persians made a fine political use of sepulchral vanity: they permitted none to be thus interred, who had not fallen in the vindication of their country. A monument thus became a real mark of distinction; it nerved the hero's arm with tenfold vigor, and he fought without fear, who only fought for a grave. Farewell.

LETTER XIII

To the Same

AN ACCOUNT OF WESTMINSTER ABBEY — [FIRST APPEARANCE OF THE "MAN IN BLACK"]

I AM just returned from Westminster Abbey, the place of sepulture for the philosophers, heroes, and kings of England. What a gloom do monumental inscriptions, and all the venerable remains of deceased merit inspire? Imagine a temple marked with the hand of antiquity, solemn as religious awe, adorned with all the magnificence of barbarous profusion, dim windows, fretted pillars, long colonnades, and dark ceilings. Think, then, what were my sensations at being introduced to such a scene. I stood in the midst of the temple, and threw my eyes round on the walls, filled with the statues, the inscriptions, and the monuments of the dead.

Alas! I said to myself, how does pride attend the puny child of dust even to the grave! Even humble as I am, I possess more consequence in the present scene than the greatest hero of them all: they have toiled for an hour to gain a transient immortality, and are at length retired to the grave, where they have no attendant but the worm, none to flatter but the epitaph.

As I was indulging such reflections, a gentleman dressed in black, perceiving me to be a stranger, came up, entered into conversation, and politely offered to be my instructor and guide through the temple. "If any monument," said he, "should particularly excite your curiosity, I shall endeavour to satisfy your demands." I accepted, with thanks, the gentleman's offer, adding, that "I was come to observe the policy, the wisdom, and the justice of the English, in conferring rewards upon deceased merit. If adulation like this," continued I, "be properly conducted, as it can no ways injure those who are flattered, so it may be a glorious incentive to those who are now capable of enjoying it. It is the duty of every good government to turn this monumental pride to its own advantage; to become strong in the aggregate from the weakness of the individual. If none but the truly great have a place in this awful repository, a temple like this will give the finest lessons of morality, and be a strong incentive to true ambition. I am told, that none have a place here but characters of the most distinguished merit." The man in black seemed impatient at my observations, so I discontinued my remarks, and we walked on together to take a view of every particular monument in order as it lay.

As the eye is naturally caught by the finest objects, I could not avoid being particularly curious about one monument, which appeared more beautiful than the rest: "That," said I to my guide, "I take to be the tomb of some very great man. By the peculiar excellence of the workmanship, and the magnificence of the design, this must be a trophy raised to the memory of some king who has saved his country from ruin, or lawgiver who has reduced his fellow-citizens from anarchy into just subjection." — "It is not requisite," replied my companion, smiling, "to have such qualifications in order to have a very fine monument here: more humble abilities will suffice." — "What, I suppose, then, the gaining two or three battles, or the taking half a score towns is thought a sufficient qualification?" — "Gaining battles, or taking towns," replied the man in black, "may be of service; but a gentleman may have a very fine monument here without ever seeing a battle or a siege." — "This, then, is the monument of some poet, I presume — of one whose wit has gained him immortality?" — "No, Sir," replied my guide, "the gentleman who lies here never made verses; and as for wit, he despised it in others, because he had none himself." "Pray tell me, then, in a word," said I, peevishly, "what is the great man who lies here particularly remarkable for?" — "Remarkable, Sir?" said my companion; "why, Sir, the gentleman that lies here is remarkable, very remarkable — for a tomb in Westminster Abbey." — "But, head of my Ancestors! how has he got here? I fancy he could never bribe the guardians of the temple to give him a place: should he not be ashamed to be seen among company where even moderate merit would look like infamy?" — "I suppose," replied the man in black, "the gentleman was rich.

and his friends, as is usual in such a case, told him he was great, He readily believed them; the guardians of the temple, as they got by the self-delusion, were ready to believe him too; so he paid his money for a fine monument; and the workman, as you see, has made him one of the most beautiful. Think not, however, that this gentleman is singular in his desire of being buried among the great; there are several others in the temple, who, hated and shunned by the great while alive, have come here, fully resolved to keep them company now they are dead."

As we walked along to a particular part of the temple, "There," says the gentleman, pointing with his finger, "that is the Poet's Corner; there you see the monuments of Shakespear, and Milton, and Prior, and Drayton." — "Drayton!" I replied; "I never heard of him before; but I have been told of one Pope — is he there?" — "It is time enough," replied my guide, "these hundred years; he is not long dead; people have not done hating him yet." — —"Strange," cried I; "can any be found to hate a man whose life was wholly spent in entertaining and instructing his fellow-creatures?" — "Yes," says my guide, "they hate him for that very reason. There are a set of men called answerers of books, who take upon them to watch the republic of letters, and distribute reputation by the sheet; they somewhat resemble the eunuchs in a seraglio, who are incapable of giving pleasure themselves, and hinder those that would. These answerers have no other employment but to cry out Dunce and Scribbler; to praise the dead, and revile the living; to grant a man of confessed abilities some small share of merit; to applaud twenty blockheads in order to gain the reputation of candour; and to revile the moral character of the man whose writings they cannot injure. Such wretches are kept in pay by some mercenary bookseller, or, more frequently, the bookseller himself takes this dirty work off their hands, as all that is required is to be very abusive and very dull. Every poet of any genius is sure to find such enemies; he feels, though he seems to despise their malice; they make him miserable here, and in the pursuit of empty fame, at last he gains solid anxiety."

"Has this been the case with every poet I see here?" cried I. "Yes, with every mother's son of them," replied he, "except he happened to be born a mandarine. If he has much money, he may buy reputation from your book-answerers, as well as a monument from the guardians of the temple."

"But are there not some men of distinguished taste, as in China, who are willing to patronize men of merit, and soften the rancour of malevolent dulness?"

"I own there are many," replied the man in black; "but, alas! Sir, the book-answerers crowd about them, and call themselves the writers of books; and the patron is too indolent to distinguish. thus poets are kept at a distance, while their enemies eat up all their rewards at the mandarine's table."

Leaving this part of the temple, we made up to an iron gate, through which my companion told me we were to pass, in order to see the monuments of the kings. Accordingly, I marched up without further ceremony, and was going to enter, when a person, who held the gate in his hand, told me I must pay first. I was surprised at such a demand; and asked the man, whether the people of England kept a *show?* — whether the paltry sum he demanded was not a national reproach? — whether it was not more to the honour of the country to let their magnificence, or their antiquities, be openly seen, than thus meanly to tax a curiosity which tended to their own honour? "As for your questions," replied the gate-keeper, "to be sure they may be very right, because I don't understand them; but, as for that there threepence, I farm it from one — who rents it from another — who hires it from a third — who leases it from the guardians of the temple,— and we all must live." I expected, upon paying here, to see something extraordinary, since what I had seen for nothing filled me with so much surprise: but in this I was disappointed; there was little more within than black coffins, rusty armour, tattered standards, and some few slovenly figures in wax. I was sorry I had paid, but I comforted myself by considering it would be my last payment. A person attended us, who, without once blushing, told a hundred lies: he talked of a lady who died by pricking her finger; of a king with a golden head, and twenty such pieces of absurdity. "Look ye there, gentlemen," says he, pointing to an old oak chair, "there's a curiosity for ye; in that chair the kings of England were crowned: you see also a stone underneath, and that stone is Jacob's pillow." I could see no curiosity either in the oak chair or the stone: could I, indeed, behold one of the old kings of England seated in this, or Jacob's head laid upon the other, there might be something curious in the sight; but in the present case, there was no more reason for my surprise, than if I should pick a stone from their streets, and call it a curiosity, merely because one of the kings happened to tread upon it as he passed in a procession.

From hence our conductor led us through several dark walks and winding ways, uttering lies, talking to himself, and flourishing a wand which he held in his hand. He reminded me of the black magicians of Kobi. After we had been almost fatigued with a variety of objects, he at last desired me to consider attentively a certain suit of armour, which seemed to show nothing remarkable. "This armour," said he, "belonged to General Monk."—"Very surprising that a general should wear armour!"—"And pray," added he, "observe this cap; this is General Monk's cap."—"Very strange, indeed, very strange, that a general should have a cap also! Pray, friend, what might this cap have cost originally?"—"That, Sir," says he, "I don't know; but this cap is all the wages I have for my trouble."—"A very small recompense, truly," said I. "Not so very small," replied he, "for every gentleman puts some money into it, and I spend the money."—"What—more money! still more money!"—"Every gentleman gives something, Sir."—"I'll give thee nothing," returned I; "the guardians of the temple should pay you your wages, friend, and not permit you to squeeze thus from every spectator. When we pay our money at the door to see a show, we never give more as we are going out. Sure the guardians of the temple can never think they get enough. Show me the gate; if I stay longer I may probably meet with more of those ecclesiastical beggars."

Thus leaving the temple precipitately, I returned to my lodgings, in order to ruminate over what was great, and to despise what was mean, in the occurrences of the day.

LETTER XIV

To the Same

THE RECEPTION OF THE CHINESE PHILOSOPHER FROM A LADY OF DISTINCTION

I WAS some days ago agreeably surprised by a message from a lady of distinction, who sent me word, that she most passionately desired the pleasure of my acquaintance, and, with the utmost impatience, expected an interview. I will not deny, my dear Fum

CITIZEN OF THE WORLD

Hoam, but that my vanity was raised at such an invitation. I flattered myself that she had seen me in some public place, and had conceived an affection for my person, which thus induced her to deviate from the usual decorums of the sex. My imagination painted her in all the bloom of youth and beauty. I fancied her attended by the Loves and Graces; and I set out with the most pleasing expectations of seeing the conquest I had made.

When I was introduced into her apartment, my expectations were quickly at an end; I perceived a little shrivelled figure indolently reclined on a sofa, who nodded, by way of approbation, at my approach. This, as I was afterwards informed, was the lady herself, a woman equally distinguished for rank, politeness, taste, and understanding. As I was dressed after the fashion of Europe, she had taken me for an Englishman, and consequently saluted me in her ordinary manner: but when the footman informed her grace that I was the gentleman from China, she instantly lifted herself from the couch, while her eyes sparkled with unusual vivacity. "Bless me! can this be the gentleman that was born so far from home? What an unusual share of *somethingness* in his whole appearance! Lord, how I am charmed with the outlandish cut of his face! how bewitching the exotic breadth of his forehead! I would give the world to see him in his own country dress. Pray, turn about, Sir, and let me see you behind. There, there's a travelled air for you! You that attend there, bring up a plate of beef cut into small pieces; I have a violent passion to see him eat. Pray, Sir, have you got your chop-sticks about you? It will be so pretty to see the meat carried to the mouth with a jerk. Pray, speak a little Chinese: I have learned some of the language myself. Lord! have you nothing pretty from China about you; something that one does not know what to do with? I have got twenty things from China that are of no use in the world. Look at those jars; they are of the right pea-green: these are the furniture!" — "Dear Madam," said I, "these, though they may appear fine in your eyes, are but paltry to a Chinese; but, as they are useful utensils, it is proper they should have a place in every apartment." — "Useful, Sir!" replied the lady; "sure you mistake; they are of no use in the world." — "What! are they not filled with an infusion of tea, as in China?" replied I. "Quite empty and useless, upon my honour, Sir." — "Then they are the most cumbrous and clumsy furniture in the world, as nothing is truly elegant but what unites use with beauty." — "I protest," says the lady, "I shall begin to suspect thee of being an actual barbarian. I suppose you hold my two beautiful pagods in contempt." — "What!" cried I, "has Fohi spread his gross superstitions here also? Pagods of all kinds are my aversion." — "A Chinese, a traveller, and want taste! it surprises me. Pray, Sir, examine the beauties of that Chinese temple which you see at the end of the garden. Is there any thing in China more beautiful?" — "Where I stand, I see nothing, Madam, at the end of the garden, that may not as well be called an Egyptian pyramid as a Chinese temple; for that little building in view is as like the one as t'other." — "What, Sir! is not that a Chinese temple? you must surely be mistaken. Mr. Freeze, who designed it, calls it one, and nobody disputes his pretensions to taste." I now found it vain to contradict the lady in any thing she thought fit to advance; so was resolved rather to act the disciple than the instructor. She took me through several rooms, all furnished as she told me, in the Chinese manner; sprawling dragons, squatting pagods, and clumsy mandarines, were stuck upon every shelf: in turning round, one must have used caution not to demolish a part of the precarious furniture.

In a house like this, thought I, one must live continually upon the watch: the inhabitant must resemble a knight in an enchanted castle, who expects to meet an adventure at every turning. "But, Madam," said I, "do not accidents ever happen to all this finery?" — "Man, Sir," replied the lady, "is born to misfortunes, and it is but fit I should have a share. Three weeks ago, a careless servant snapped off the head of a favourite mandarine: I had scarce done grieving for that, when a monkey broke a beautiful jar; this I took the more to heart, as the injury was done me by a friend. However, I survived the calamity; when yesterday crash went half a dozen dragons upon the marble hearth-stone: and yet I live; I survive it all: you can't conceive what comfort I find under afflictions from philosophy. There is Seneca, and Bolingbroke, and some others, who guide me through life, and teach me to support its calamities." I could not but smile at a woman who makes her own misfortunes, and then deplores the miseries of her situation. Wherefore, tired of acting with dissimulation, and willing to indulge my meditations in solitude, I took leave just as the servant was bringing in a plate of beef, pursuant to the directions of his mistress. Adieu.

CITIZEN OF THE WORLD

LETTER XXI
To the Same
THE PHILOSOPHER GOES TO SEE A PLAY

THE English are as fond of seeing plays acted as the Chinese; but there is a vast difference in the manner of conducting them. We play our pieces in the open air, the English theirs under cover; we act by daylight, they by the blaze of torches. One of our plays continues eight or ten days successively; an English piece seldom takes up above four hours in the representation.

My companion in black, with whom I am now beginning to contract an intimacy, introduced me a few nights ago to the playhouse, where we placed ourselves conveniently at the foot of the stage. As the curtain was not drawn before my arrival, I had an opportunity of observing the behaviour of the spectators, and indulging those reflections which novelty generally inspires.

The rich in general were placed in the lowest seats, and the poor rose above them in degrees proportioned to their poverty. The order of precedence seemed here inverted; those who were undermost all the day, now enjoyed a temporary eminence, and became masters of the ceremonies. It was they who called for the music, indulging every noisy freedom, and testifying all the insolence of beggary in exaltation.

They who held the middle region seemed not so riotous as those above them, nor yet so tame as those below: to judge by their looks, many of them seemed strangers there as well as myself. They were chiefly employed, during this period of expectation, in eating oranges, reading the story of the play, or making assignations.

Those who sat in the lowest rows, which are called the pit, seemed to consider themselves as judges of the merit of the poet and the performers; they were assembled partly to be amused, and partly to show their taste; appearing to labour under that restraint which an affectation of superior discernment generally produces. My companion, however, informed me, that not one in a hundred of them knew even the first principles of criticism; that they assumed the right of being censors because there was none to contradict their pretensions; and that every man who now called himself a connoisseur, became such to all intents and purposes.

Those who sat in the boxes appeared in the most unhappy situation of all. The rest of the audience came merely for their own amusement; these, rather to furnish out a part of the entertainment themselves. I could not avoid considering them as acting parts in dumb show — not a courtesy or nod, that was not all the result of art; not a look nor a smile that was not designed for murder. Gentlemen and ladies ogled each other through spectacles; for, my companion observed, that blindness was of late become fashionable; all affected indifference and ease, while their hearts at the same time burned for conquest. Upon the whole, the lights, the music, the ladies in their gayest dresses, the men with cheerfulness and expectation in their looks, all conspired to make a most agreeable picture, and to fill a heart that sympathizes at human happiness with inexpressible serenity.

The expected time for the play to begin at last arrived; the curtain was drawn, and the actors came on. A woman, who personated a queen, came in curtseying to the audience, who clapped their hands upon her appearance. Clapping of hands is, it seems, the manner of applauding in England; the manner is absurd, but every country, you know, has its peculiar absurdities. I was equally surprised, however, at the submission of the actress, who should have considered herself as a queen, as at the little discernment of the audience who gave her such marks of applause before she attempted to deserve them. Preliminaries between her and the audience being thus adjusted, the dialogue was supported between her and a most hopeful youth, who acted the part of her confidant. They both appeared in extreme distress, for it seems the queen had lost a child some fifteen years before, and still kept its dear resemblance next her heart, while her kind companion bore a part in her sorrows.

Her lamentations grew loud; comfort is offered, but she detests the very sound: she bids them preach comfort to the winds. Upon this her husband comes in, who, seeing the queen so much afflicted, can himself hardly refrain from tears, or avoid partaking in the soft distress. After thus grieving through three scenes, the curtain dropped for the first act.

"Truly," said I to my companion, "these kings and queens are very much disturbed at no very great misfortune: certain I am, were people of humbler stations to act in this manner, they would be thought divested of common sense." I had scarcely finished this observation, when the curtain rose, and the king came on in a violent passion. His wife had, it seems, refused his proffered tenderness, had spurned his royal embrace, and he seemed resolved not to survive her fierce disdain. After he had thus fretted, and the queen had fretted through the second act, the curtain was let down once more.

"Now," says my companion, "you perceive the king to be a man of spirit; he feels at every pore: one of your phlegmatic sons of clay would have given the queen her own way, and let her come to herself by degrees; but the king is for immediate tenderness, or instant death: death and tenderness are leading passions of every modern buskined hero; this moment they embrace, and the next stab, mixing daggers and kisses in every period."

I was going to second his remarks, when my attention was engrossed by a new object; a man came in balancing a straw upon his nose, and the audience were clapping their hands in all the raptures of applause. "To what purpose," cried I, "does this unmeaning figure make his appearance? is he a part of the plot?"—"Unmeaning do you call him?" replied my friend in black; "this is one of the most important characters of the whole play; nothing pleases the people more than seeing a straw balanced: there is a good deal of meaning in the straw: there is something suited to every apprehension in the sight; and a fellow possessed of talents like these is sure of making his fortune."

The third act now began with an actor who came to inform us that he was the villain of the play, and intended to show strange things before all was over. He was joined by another who seemed as much disposed for mischief as he: their intrigues continued through this whole division. "If that be a villain," said I, "he must be a very stupid one to tell his secrets without being asked; such soliloquies of late are never admitted in China."

The noise of clapping interrupted me once more; a child of six years old was learning to dance on the stage, which gave the ladies and mandarines infinite satisfaction. "I am sorry," said I, "to see the pretty creature so early learning so very bad a trade; dancing being, I presume, as contemptible here as in China."—"Quite the reverse," interrupted my companion; "dancing is a very reputable and genteel employment here; men have a greater chance for encouragement from the merit of their heels than their heads. One who jumps up and flourishes his toes three times before he comes to the ground, may have three hundred a year; he who flourishes them four times, gets four hundred; but he who arrives at five is inestimable, and may demand what salary he thinks proper. The female dancers, too, are valued for this sort of jumping and crossing; and it is a cant word amongst them, that she deserves most who shows highest. But the fourth act is begun; let us be attentive."

In the fourth act the queen finds her long lost child, now grown up into a youth of smart parts and great qualifications; wherefore she wisely considers that the crown will fit his head better than that of her husband, whom she knows to be a driveller. The king discovers her design, and here comes on the deep distress: he loves the queen, and he loves the kingdom; he resolves, therefore, in order to possess both, that her son must die. The queen exclaims at his barbarity, is frantic with rage, and at length, overcome with sorrow, falls into a fit; upon which the curtain drops, and the act is concluded.

"Observe the art of the poet," cries my companion. "When the queen can say no more, she falls into a fit. While thus her eyes are shut, while she is supported in the arms of Abigail, what horrors do we not fancy! We feel it in every nerve: take my word for it, that fits are the true *aposiopesis* of modern tragedy."

The fifth act began, and a busy piece it was. Scenes shifting, trumpets sounding, mobs hallooing, carpets spreading, guards bustling from one door to another; gods, demons, daggers, racks, and ratsbane. But whether the king was killed, or the queen was drowned, or the son was poisoned, I have absolutely forgotten.

When the play was over, I could not avoid observing, that the persons of the drama appeared in as much distress in the first act as in the last. "How is it possible," said I, "to sympathize with them through five long acts? Pity is but a short lived passion. I hate to hear an actor mouthing trifles. Neither startings, strainings, nor attitudes, affect me, unless there be cause: after I have been once or twice deceived by those unmeaning alarms, my heart sleeps in peace, probably unaffected by the principal distress. There should be one great passion aimed at by the actor as well as the poet; all the rest should be subordinate, and only contribute to make that the greater; if the actor, therefore, exclaims upon every occasion, in the tones of despair, he attempts to move us too soon; he anticipates the blow, he ceases to affect, though he gains our applause."

I scarce perceived that the audience were almost all departed; wherefore, mixing with the crowd, my companion and I got into the street, where, essaying a hundred obstacles from coach-wheels and palanquin poles, like birds in their flight through the branches of a forest, after various turnings, we both at length got home in safety. Adieu.

LETTER XXVI

To the Same

THE CHARACTER OF THE MAN IN BLACK; WITH SOME INSTANCES OF HIS INCONSISTENT CONDUCT

THOUGH fond of many acquaintances, I desire an intimacy only with a few. The man in black, whom I have often mentioned, is one whose friendship I could wish to acquire, because he possesses my esteem. His manners, it is true, are tinctured with some strange inconsistencies, and he may be justly termed a humourist in a nation of humourists. Though he is generous even to profusion, he affects to be thought a prodigy of parsimony and prudence; though his conversation be replete with the most sordid and selfish maxims, his heart is dilated with the most unbounded love. I have known him profess himself a man-hater, while his cheek was glowing with compassion; and, while his looks were softened into pity, I have heard him use the language of the most unbounded ill-nature. Some affect humanity and tenderness, others boast of having such dispositions from nature; but he is the only man I ever knew who seemed ashamed of his natural benevolence. He takes as much pains to hide his feelings, as any hypocrite would to conceal his indifference; but on every unguarded moment the mask drops off, and reveals him to the most superficial observer.

In one of our late excursions into the country, happening to discourse upon the provision that was made for the poor in England, he seemed amazed how any of his countrymen could be so foolishly weak as to relieve occasional objects of charity, when the laws had made much ample provision for their support. "In every parish-house," says he, "the poor are supplied with food, clothes, fire, and a bed to lie on; they want no more, I desire no more myself; yet still they seem discontented. I am surprised at the inactivity of our magistrates, in not talking up such vagrants, who are only a weight upon the industrious; I am surprised that the people are found to relieve them, when they must be at the same time sensible that it, in some measure, encourages idleness, extravagance, and imposture. Were I to advise any man for whom I had the least regard, I would caution him by all means not to be imposed upon by their false pretences: let me assure you, Sir, they are imposters, every one of them, and rather merit a prison than relief."

He was proceeding in this strain, earnestly to dissuade me from an imprudence of which I am seldom guilty, when an old man, who still had about him the remnants of tattered finery, implored our compassion. He assured us that he was no common beggar, but forced into the shameful profession, to support a dying wife, and five hungry children. Being prepossessed against such falsehoods, his story had not the least influence upon me; but it was quite otherwise with the man in black; I could see it visibly operate upon his countenance, and effectually interrupt his harangue. I could easily perceive, that his heart burned to relieve the five starving children, but he seemed ashamed to discover his weakness to me. While he thus hesitated between compassion and pride, I pretended to look another way, and he seized this opportunity of giving the poor petitioner a piece of silver, bidding him at the same time, in order that I should hear, go work for his bread, and not tease passengers with such impertinent falsehoods for the future.

As he had fancied himself quite unperceived, he continued, as we proceeded, to rail against beggars with as much animosity as before; he threw in some episodes on his own amazing prudence and economy, with his profound skill in discovering imposters; he explained the manner in which he would deal with beggars were he a magistrate, hinted at enlarging some of the prisons for their reception, and told two stories of ladies that were robbed by beggarmen. He was beginning a third to the same purpose, when a sailor with a wooden leg once more crossed our walks, desiring our pity, and blessing our limbs. I was for going on without taking any notice, but my friend looking wishfully upon the poor petitioner, bid me stop, and he would show me with how much ease he could at any time detect an impostor.

He now, therefore, assumed a look of importance, and in an angry tone began to examine the sailor, demanding in what engagement he was thus disabled and rendered unfit for service. The sailor replied, in a tone as angrily as he, that he had been an officer on board a private ship of war, and that he had lost his leg abroad, in defence of those who did nothing at home. At this reply, all my friend's importance vanished in a moment; he had not a single question more to ask; he now only studied what method he should take to relieve him unobserved. He had, however, no easy part to act, as he was obliged to preserve the appearance of ill-nature before me, and yet relieve himself by relieving the sailor. Casting, therefore, a furious look upon some bundles of chips which the fellow carried in a string at his back, my friend demanded how he sold his matches; but, not waiting for a reply, desired, in a surly tone, to have a shilling's worth. The sailor seemed at first surprised at his demand, but soon recollected himself, and presenting his whole bundle, "Here, master," says he, "take all my cargo, and a blessing into the bargain."

It is impossible to describe with what an air of triumph my friend marched off with his new purchase: he assured me, that he was firmly of opinion that those fellows must have stolen their goods, who could thus afford to sell them for half value. He informed me of several different uses to which those chips might be applied; he expatiated largely upon the savings that would result from lighting candles with a match, instead of thrusting them into the fire. He averred, that he would as soon have parted with a tooth as his money to those vagabonds, unless for some valuable consideration. I cannot tell how long this panegyric upon frugality and matches might have continued, had not his attention been called off by another object more distressful than either of the former. A woman in rags, with one child in her arms, and another on her back, was attempting to sing ballads, but with such a mournful voice, that it was difficult to determine whether she was singing or crying. A wretch, who in the deepest distress still aimed at good-humour, was an object my friend was by no means capable of withstanding: his vivacity and his discourse were instantly interrupted; upon this occasion, his very dissimulation had forsaken him. Even in my presence he immediately applied his hands to his pockets, in order to relieve her; but guess his confusion when he found he had already given away all the money he carried about him to former objects. The misery painted in the woman's visage was not half so strongly expressed as the agony in his. He continued to search for some time, but to no purpose, till, at length recollecting himself, with a face of ineffable good-nature, as he had no money, he put into her hands his shilling's worth of matches.

CITIZEN OF THE WORLD

LETTER XXVII

To the Same

THE HISTORY OF THE MAN IN BLACK

AS there appeared something reluctantly good in the character of my companion, I must own it surprised me what could be his motives for thus concealing virtues which others take such pains to display. I was unable to repress my desire of knowing the history of a man who thus seemed to act under continual restraint, and whose benevolence was rather the effect of appetite than reason.

It was not, however, till after repeated solicitations he thought proper to gratify my curiosity. "If you are fond," says he, "of hearing hairbreadth 'scapes, my history must certainly please; for I have been for twenty years upon the very verge of starving, without ever being starved.

"My father, the younger son of a good family, was possessed of a small living in the church. His education was above his fortune, and his generosity greater than his education. Poor as he was, he had his flatterers still poorer than himself; for every dinner he gave them, they returned an equivalent in praise; and this was all he wanted. The same ambition that actuates a monarch at the head of an army, influenced my father at the head of his table. He told the story of the ivy-tree, and that was laughed at; he repeated the jest of the two scholars and one pair of breeches, and the company laughed at that; but the story of Taffy in the sedan-chair, was sure to set the table in a roar. Thus his pleasure increased in proportion to the pleasure he gave; he loved all the world, and he fancied all the world loved him.

"As his fortune was but small, he lived up to the very extent of it; he had no intentions of leaving his children money, for that was dross; he was resolved they should have learning; for learning, he used to observe, was better than silver or gold. For this purpose, he undertook to instruct us himself; and took as much pains to form our morals, as to improve our understanding. We were told, that universal benevolence was what first cemented society; we were taught to consider all the wants of mankind as our own; to regard the 'human face divine' with affection and esteem;

he wound us up to be mere machines of pity, and rendered us incapable of withstanding the slightest impulse made either by real or fictitious distress: in a word, we were perfectly instructed in the art of giving away thousands, before we were taught the more necessary qualifications of getting a farthing.

"I cannot avoid imagining, that thus refined by his lessons out of all my suspicion, and divested of even all the little cunning which nature had given me, I resembled, upon my first entrance into the busy and insidious world, one of those gladiators who were exposed without armour in the amphitheatre at Rome. My father, however, who had only seen the world on one side, seemed to triumph in my superior discernment; though my whole stock of wisdom consisted in being able to talk like himself upon subjects that once were useful, because they were then topics of the busy world, but that now were utterly useless, because connected with the busy world no longer.

"The first opportunity he had of finding his expectations disappointed, was in the very middling figure I made in the university; he had flattered himself that he should soon see me rising into the foremost rank in literary reputation, but was mortified to find me utterly unnoticed and unknown. His disappointment might have been partly ascribed to his having overrated my talents, and partly to my dislike of mathematical reasonings, at a time when my imagination and memory, yet unsatisfied, were more eager after new objects, than desirous of reasoning upon those I knew. This did not, however, please my tutor, who observed, indeed, that I was a little dull; but at the same time allowed, that I seemed to be very good-natured, and had no harm in me.

"After I had resided at college seven years, my father died, and left me — his blessing. Thus shoved from shore without ill-nature to protect, or cunning to guide, or proper stores to subsist me in so dangerous a voyage, I was obliged to embark in the wide world at twenty-two. But, in order to settle in life, my friends *advised*, (for they always advise when they begin to despise us) they advised me, I say, to go into orders.

"To be obliged to wear a long wig, when I liked a short one, or a black coat, when I generally dressed in brown, I thought was such a restraint upon my liberty, that I absolutely rejected the proposal. A priest in England is not the same mortified creature with a bonze in China. With us, not he that fasts best, but eats best, is reckoned the best liver; yet I rejected a life of luxury, indolence, and ease, from no other consideration but that boyish one of dress. So that my friends were now perfectly satisfied I was undone; and yet they thought it a pity for one who had not the least harm in him, and was so very good-natured.

"Poverty naturally begets dependence, and I was admitted as flatterer to a great man. At first, I was surprised that the situation of a flatterer at a great man's table could be thought disagreeable: there was no great trouble in listening attentively when his lordship spoke, and laughing when he looked round for applause. This even good manners might have obliged me to perform. I found, however, too soon, that his lordship was a greater dunce than myself; and from that very moment flattery was at an end. I now rather aimed at setting him right, than at receiving his absurdities with submission. To flatter those we do not know is an easy task; but to flatter our intimate acquaintances, all whose foibles are strongly in our eye, is drudgery insupportable. Every time I now opened my lips in praise, my falsehood went to my conscience: his lordship soon perceived me to be very unfit for service; I was therefore discharged; my patron at the same time being graciously pleased to observe, that he believed I was tolerably good-natured, and had not the least harm in me.

"Disappointed in ambition, I had recourse to love. A young lady, who lived with her aunt, and was possessed of a pretty fortune in her own disposal, had given me, as I fancied, some reason to expect success. The symptoms by which I was guided were striking. She had always laughed with me at her awkward acquaintance, and at her aunt among the number; she always observed, that a man of sense would make a better husband than a fool, and I as constantly applied the observation in my own favour. She continually talked, in my company, of friendship and the beauties of the mind, and spoke of Mr. Shrimp my rival's high-heeled shoes with detestation. These were circumstances which I thought strongly in my favour; so, after resolving, and re-resolving, I had courage enough to tell her my mind. Miss heard my proposal with serenity, seeming at the same time to study the figures of her fan. Out at last it came: There was but one small objection to complete our happiness, which was no more than —— that she was married three months before to Mr. Shrimp, with high-heeled shoes! By way of consolation, however, she observed, that, though I was disappointed in her, my addresses to her aunt would probably kindle her into sensibility; as the old lady always allowed me to be very good-natured, and not to have the least share of harm in me.

"Yet still I had friends, numerous friends, and to them I was resolved to apply. O friendship! thou fond soother of the human breast, to thee we fly in every calamity; to thee the wretched seek for succour; on thee the care-tired son of misery fondly relies; from thy kind assistance the unfortunate always hopes relief, and may be ever sure of — disappointment! My first application was to a city scrivener, who had frequently offered to lend me money, when he knew I did not want it. I informed him, that now was the time to put his friendship to the test; that I wanted to borrow a couple of hundreds for a certain occasion, and was resolved to take it up from him. 'And pray, Sir,' cried my friend, 'do you want all this money?' — 'Indeed, I never wanted it more,' returned I. 'I am sorry for that,' cries the scrivener, 'with all my heart; for they who want money when they come to borrow, will always want money when they should come to pay.'

"From him I flew with indignation, to one of the best friends I had in the world, and made the same request. 'Indeed, Mr. Drybone,' cries my friend, 'I always thought it would come to this. You know, Sir, I would not advise you but for your own good; but your conduct has hitherto been ridiculous in the highest degree, and some of your acquaintance always thought you a very silly fellow. Let me see — you want two hundred pounds. Do you only want two hundred, Sir, exactly?' — 'To confess a truth,' returned I, 'I shall want three hundred; but then I have another friend, from whom I can borrow the rest.' — 'Why, then,' replied my friend, 'if you would take my advice, (and you know I should not presume to advise you but for your own good), I would recommend it to you to borrow the whole sum from that other friend, and then one note will serve for all, you know.'

"Poverty now began to come fast upon me; yet instead of growing more provident or cautious as I grew poor, I became every day more indolent and simple. A friend was arrested for fifty pounds; I was unable to extricate him, except by becoming his bail. When at liberty, he fled from his creditors, and left me to take his place. In prison I expected greater satisfactions than I had enjoyed at large. I hoped to converse with men in this new world, simple and believing like myself; but I found them as cunning and as cautious as those in the world I had left behind. They spunged up my money while it lasted, borrowed my coals and never paid for them, and cheated me when I played at cribbage. All this was done because they believed me to be very good-natured, and knew that I had no harm in me.

"Upon my first entrance into this mansion, which is to some the abode of despair, I felt no sensations different from those I experienced abroad. I was now on one side the door, and those who were unconfined were on the other: this was all the difference between us. At first, indeed, I felt some uneasiness, in considering how I should be able to provide this week for the wants of the week ensuing; but, after some time, if I found myself sure of eating one day, I never troubled my head how I was to be supplied another. I seized every precarious meal with the utmost good-humour; indulged no rants of spleen at my situation; never called down heaven and all the stars to behold me dining upon a halfpenny worth of radishes; my very companions were taught to believe that I liked salad better than mutton. I contented myself with thinking, that all my life I should either eat white bread or brown; considered that all that happened was best; laughed when I was not in pain, took the world as it went, and read Tacitus often, for want of more books and company.

"How long I might have continued in this torpid state of simplicity I cannot tell, had I not been roused by seeing an old acquaintance, whom I knew to be a prudent block-head, preferred to a place in the government. I now found that I had pursued a wrong track, and that the true way of being able to relieve others, was first to aim at independence myself. My immediate care, therefore, was to leave my present habitation, and make an entire reformation in my conduct and behaviour. For a free, open, undesigning deportment, I put on that of closeness, prudence, and economy. One of the most heroic actions I ever performed, and for which I shall praise myself as long as I live, was the refusing half-a-crown to an old acquaintance, at the time when he wanted it, and I had it to spare: for this alone I deserve to be decreed an ovation.

"I now therefore pursued a course of uninterrupted frugality, seldom wanted a dinner, and was consequently invited to twenty. I soon began to get the character of a saving hunks that had money, and insensibly grew into esteem. Neighbours have asked my advice in the disposal of their daughters; and I have always taken care not to give any. I have contracted a friendship with an alderman, only by observing, that if we take a farthing from a thousand pounds, it will be a thousand pounds no longer. I have been invited to a pawnbroker's table, by pretending to hate gravy, and am now actually upon treaty of marriage with a rich widow, for only having observed that the bread was rising. If ever I am asked a question, whether I know it or not, instead of answering, I only smile and look wise. If a charity is proposed, I go about with the hat, but put nothing in myself. If a wretch solicits my pity, I observe that the world is filled with impostors, and take a certain method of not being deceived, by never relieving. In short I now find the truest way of finding esteem, even from the indigent is — to give away nothing, and thus have much in our power to give."

LETTER XXVIII

To the Same

ON THE GREAT NUMBER OF OLD MAIDS AND BACHELORS IN LONDON—
SOME OF THE CAUSES

LATELY, in company with my friend in black, whose conversation is now both by amusement and instruction, I could not avoid observing the great numbers of old bachelors and maiden ladies with which this city seems to be overrun. "Sure, marriage," said I, "is not sufficiently encouraged, or we should never behold such crowds of battered beaux and decayed coquettes, still attempting to drive a trade they have been so long unfit for, and swarming upon the gaity of the age. I behold an old bachelor in the most contemptible light, as an animal that lives upon the common stock without contributing his share: he is a beast of prey, and the laws should make use of as many stratagems, and as much force, to drive the reluctant savage into the toils, as the Indians when they hunt the rhinoceros. The mob should be permitted to halloo after him, boys might play tricks on him with impunity, every well-bred company should laugh at him; and if, when turned of sixty, he offered to make love, his mistress might spit in his face, or, what would be perhaps a greater punishment, should fairly grant the favour.

"As for old maids," continued I, "they should not be treated with so much severity, because I suppose none would be so if they could. No lady in her senses would choose to make a subordinate figure at christenings or lyings-in, when she might be the principal herself; nor curry favour with a sister-in-law, when she might command a husband; nor toil in preparing custards, when she might lie a-bed, and give directions how they ought to be made; nor stifle all her sensations in demure formality, when she might, with matrimonial freedom, shake her acquaintance by the hand, and wink at a *double entendre*. No lady could be so very silly as to live single, if she could help it. I consider an unmarried lady, declining into the vale of years, as one of those charming countries bordering on China, that lies waste for want of proper inhabitants. We are not to accuse the country, but the ignorance of its neighbours, who are insensible of its beauties, though at liberty to enter and cultivate the soil."

"Indeed, Sir," replied my companion, "you are very little acquainted with the English ladies, to think they are old maids against their will. I dare venture to affirm, that you can hardly select one of them all, but has had frequent offers of marriage, which either pride or avarice has not made her reject. Instead of thinking it a disgrace, they take every occasion to boast of their former cruelty; a soldier does not exult more when he counts over the wounds he has received, than a female veteran when she relates the wounds she has formerly given: exhaustless when she begins a narrative of the former death-dealing power of her eyes, she tells of the knight in gold lace, who died with a single frown, and never rose again till — he was married to his maid; of the squire who, being cruelly denied, in a rage flew to the window, and lifting up the sash, threw himself, in an agony — into his arm-chair; of the parson, who, crossed in love, resolutely swallowed opium, which banished the stings of despised love by — making him sleep. In short, she talks over her former losses with pleasure, and, like some tradesmen, finds consolation in the many bankruptcies she has suffered.

"For this reason, whenever I see a superannuated beauty still unmarried, I tacitly accuse her either of pride, avarice, coquetry, or affectation. There's Miss Jenny Tinderbox: I once remember her to have had some beauty, and a moderate fortune. Her elder sister happened to marry a man of quality, and this seemed as a statute of virginity against poor Jane. Because there was one lucky hit in the family, she was resolved not to disgrace it by introducing a tradesman; thus, rejecting her equals, and neglected or despised by her superiors, she now acts in the capacity of tutoress to her sister's children, and undergoes the drudgery of three servants without receiving the wages of one.

"Miss Squeeze was a pawnbroker's daughter; her father had early taught her that money was a very good thing, and left her a moderate fortune at his death. She was so perfectly sensible of the value of what she had got, that she was resolved never to part with a farthing without an equality on the part of her suitor; she thus refused several offers made her by people who wanted to better themselves, as the saying is, and grew old and ill-natured, without ever considering that she should have made an abatement in her pretensions, from her face being pale, and marked with the smallpox.

"Lady Betty Tempest, on the contrary, had beauty, with fortune and family. But, fond of conquest, she passed from triumph to triumph: she had read plays and romances, and there had learned, that a plain man of common sense was no better than a fool. Such she refused, and sighed only for the gay, giddy, inconstant, and thoughtless. After she had thus rejected hundreds who liked her, and sighed for hundreds who despised her, she found herself insensibly deserted. At present she is company only for her aunts and cousins, and sometimes makes one in a country-dance, with only one of the chairs for a partner, casts off round a joint-stool, and sets to a corner cupboard. In a word, she is treated with civil contempt from every quarter, and placed, like a piece of old-fashioned lumber, merely to fill up a corner.

"But Sophronia, the sagacious Sophronia! how shall I mention her? She was taught to love Greek, and hate the men from her very infancy. She has rejected fine gentlemen because they were not pedants, and pedants because they were not fine gentlemen; her exquisite sensibility has taught her to discover every fault in every lover, and her inflexible justice has prevented her pardoning them: thus she rejected several offers, till the wrinkles of age had overtaken her; and now, without one good feature in her face, she talks incessantly of the beauties of the mind." — Farewell.

CITIZEN OF THE WORLD

LETTER XXIX

To the Same

A DESCRIPTION OF A CLUB OF AUTHORS

WERE we to estimate the learning of the English by the number of books that are every day published among them, perhaps no country, not even China itself, could equal them in this particular. I have reckoned not less than twenty-three new books published in one day, which, upon computation, makes eight thousand three hundred and ninety-five in one year. Most of these are not confined to one single science, but embrace the whole circle. History, politics, poetry, mathematics, metaphysics, and the philosophy of nature, are all comprised in a manual not larger than that in which our children are taught the letters. If, then, we suppose the learned of England to read but an eighth part of the works which daily come from the press (and surely none can pretend to learning upon less easy terms), at this rate every scholar will read a thousand books in one year. From such a calculation, you may conjecture what an amazing fund of literature a man must be possessed of, who thus reads three new books every day, not one of which but contains all the good things that ever were said or written.

And yet I know not how it happens, but the English are not, in reality, so learned as would seem from this calculation. We meet but few who know all arts and sciences to perfection; whether it is that the generality are incapable of such extensive knowledge, or that the authors of those books are not adequate instructors. In China, the Emperor himself takes cognizance of all the doctors in the kingdom who profess authorship. In England, every man may be an author, that can write; for they have by law a liberty, not only of saying what they please, but of being also as dull as they please.

Yesterday, I testified my surprise, to the man in black, where writers could be found in sufficient number to throw off the books I daily saw crowding from the press. I at first imagined that their learned seminaries might take this method of instructing the world. But to obviate this objection, my companion assured me, that the doctors of colleges never wrote, and that some of them had actually forgot their reading; "but if you desire," continued he, "to see a collection of authors, I fancy I can introduce you this evening to a club, which assembles every Saturday at seven, at the sign of The Broom, near Islington, to talk over the business of the last, and the entertainment of the week ensuing." I accepted his invitation; we walked together, and entered the house some time before the usual hour for the company assembling.

My friend took this opportunity of letting me into the characters of the principal members of the club, not even the host excepted, who, it seems, was once an author himself, but preferred by a bookseller to this situation as a reward for his former services.

"The first person," said he, "of our society, is Doctor Nonentity, a metaphysician. Most people think him a profound scholar; but, as he seldom speaks, I cannot be positive in that particular; he generally spreads himself before the fire, sucks his pipe, talks little, drinks much, and is reckoned very good company. I'm told he writes indexes to perfection: he makes essays on the origin of evil, philosophical enquiries upon any subject, and draws up an answer to any book upon twenty-four hours warning. You may distinguish him from the rest of the company by his long grey wig, and the blue handkerchief round his neck.

"The next to him in merit and esteem is Tim Syllabub, a droll creature: he sometimes shines as a star of the first magnitude among the choice spirits of the age: he is reckoned equally excellent at a rebus, a riddle, a bawdy song, and a hymn for the Tabernacle. You will know him by his shabby finery, his powdered wig, dirty shirt, and broken silk stockings.

"After him succeeds Mr. Tibs, a very *useful hand:* he writes receipts for the bite of a mad dog, and throws off an Eastern tale to perfection; he understands the *business* of an author as well as any man; for no bookseller alive can cheat him. You may distinguish him by the peculiar clumsiness of his figure, and the coarseness of his coat; however, though it be coarse (as he frequently tells the company), he has paid for it.

"Lawyer Squint is the politician of the society: he makes speeches for Parliament, writes addresses to his fellow-subjects, and letters to noble commanders; he gives the history of every new play, and finds *seasonable thoughts* upon every occasion.' My companion was proceeding in his description, when the host came running in, with terror on his countenance, to tell us that the door was beset with bailiffs. "If that be the case, then," says my comp nion, "we had as good be going; for I am positive we shall not see one of the company this night." Wherefore, disappointed, we were both obliged to return home — he to enjoy the oddities which compose his character alone, and I to write as usual to my friend the occurrences of the day. Adieu.

LETTER XXX

To the Same

THE PROCEEDINGS OF THE CLUB OF AUTHORS

BY my last advices from Moscow, I find the caravan has not yet departed for China: I still continue to write, expecting that you may receive a large number of letters at once. In them you will find rather a minute detail of English peculiarities, than a general picture of their manners or disposition. Happy it were for mankind, if all travellers would thus, instead of characterizing a people in general terms, lead us into a detail of those minute circumstances which first influenced their opinion. The genius of a country should be investigated with a kind of experimental enquiry: by this means, we should have more precise and just notions of foreign nations, and detect travellers themselves when they happened to form wrong conclusions.

My friend and I repeated our visit to the club of authors; where, upon our entrance, we found the members all assembled, and engaged in a loud debate.

The poet, in shabby finery, holding a manuscript in his hand, was earnestly endeavouring to persuade the company to hear him read the first book of an heroic poem, which he had composed the day before. But against this all the members very warmly objected. They knew no reason why any member of the club should be indulged with a particular hearing, when many of them had published whole volumes which had never been looked into. They insisted that the law should be observed, where reading in company was expressly noticed. It was in vain that the plaintiff pleaded the peculiar merit of his piece; he spoke to an assembly insensible to all his remonstrances: the book of laws was opened, and read by the

CITIZEN OF THE WORLD

secretary, where it was expressly enacted, "That whatsoever poet, speech-maker, critic, or historian, should presume to engage the company by reading his own works, he was to lay down sixpence previous to opening the manuscript, and should be charged one shilling an hour while he continued reading: the said shilling to be equally distributed among the company, as a recompense for their trouble."

Our poet seemed at first to shrink at the penalty, hesitating for some time whether he should deposit the fine, or shut up the poem; but, looking round, and perceiving two strangers in the room, his love of fame outweighed his prudence, and, laying down the sum by law established, he insisted on his prerogative.

A profound silence ensuing, he began by explaining his design. "Gentlemen," says he, "the present piece is not one of your common epic poems, which come from the press like paper-kites in summer: there are none of your Turnuses or Didos in it; it is an heroical description of nature. I only beg you'll endeavour to make your souls unison with mine, and hear with the same enthusiasm with which I have written. The poem begins with the description of an author's bedchamber: the picture was sketched in my own apartment; for you must know, gentlemen, that I am myself the hero." Then putting himself into the attitude of an orator, with all the emphasis of voice and action, he proceeded:

> "Where the Red Lion, flaring o'er the way,
>   Invites each passing stranger that can pay;
>   Where Calvert's butt, and Parson's black champagne,
> Regale the drabs and bloods of Drury-lane:
> There, in a lonely room, from bailiffs snug,
> The muse found Scroggen stretch'd beneath a rug.
> A window, patch'd with paper, lent a ray,
> That dimly show'd the state in which he lay;
> The sanded floor that grits beneath the tread;
> The humid wall with paltry pictures spread —
> The Royal Game of Goose was there in view
> And the Twelve Rules the Royal Martyr drew;
> The seasons, fram'd with listing, found a place,
> And brave Prince William show'd his lamp-black face.
> The morn was cold: he views with keen desire
> The rusty grate, unconscious of a fire:
> With beer and milk arrears the frieze was scor'd,
> And five crack'd teacups dress'd the chimney board;
> A night-cap deck'd his brows instead of bay,
> A cap by night — a stocking all the day ! "

With this last line he seemed so much elated, that he was unable to proceed. "There, gentlemen," cries he, "there is a description for you; Rabelais's bed-chamber is but a fool to it:

'A cap by night — a stocking all the day!'

There is sound, and sense, and truth, and nature in the trifling compass of ten little syllables."

He was too much employed in self-admiration to observe the company; who, by nods, winks, shrugs, and stifled laughter, testified every mark of contempt. He turned severally to each for their opinion, and found all, however, ready to applaud. One swore it was inimitable; another said it was damn'd fine; and a third cried out in a rapture "*Carissimo!*" At last, addressing himself to the president, "And pray, Mr. Squint," says he, "let us have your opinion." — "Mine!" answered the president (taking the manuscript out of the author's hand); "may this glass suffocate me, but I think it equal to any thing I have seen; and I fancy" (continued he, doubling up the poem and forcing it into the author's pocket) "that you will get great honour when it comes out; so I shall beg leave to put it in. We will not intrude upon your good-nature, in desiring to hear more of it at present; *ex ungue Herculem*, we are satisfied, perfectly satisfied." The author made two or three attempts to pull it out a second time, and the president made as many to prevent him. Thus, though with reluctance, he was at last obliged to sit down, contented with the commendations for which he had paid.

When this tempest of poetry and praise was blown over, one of the company changed the subject, by wondering how any man could be so dull as to write poetry at present, since prose itself would hardly pay. "Would you think it, gentlemen," continued he, "I have actually written, last week, sixteen prayers, twelve bawdy jests, and three sermons, all at the rate of sixpence a-piece; and, what is still more extraordinary, the bookseller has lost by the bargain. Such sermons would once have gained me a prebend's stall; but now, alas! we have neither piety, taste, nor humour among us! Positively, if this season does not turn out better than it has begun, unless the ministry commit some blunders to furnish us with a new topic of abuse, I shall resume my old business of working at the press, instead of finding it employment."

The whole club seemed to join in condemning the season, as one of the worst that had come for some time: a gentleman particularly observed that the nobility were never known to subscribe worse than at present. "I know not how it happens," said he, "though I follow them up as close as possible, yet I can hardly get a single subscription in a week. The houses of the great are as inaccessible as a frontier garrison at midnight. I never see a nobleman's door half opened, that some surly porter or footman does not stand full in the breach. I was yesterday to wait with a subscription proposal upon my Lord Squash, the Creolian. I had posted myself at his door the whole morning, and, just as he was getting into his coach, thrust my proposal snug into his hand, folded up in the form of a letter from myself. He just glanced at the superscription, and not knowing the hand, consigned it to his valet-de-chambre; this respectable personage treated it as his master, and put it into the hands of the porter; the porter grasped my proposal frowning; and, measuring my figure from top to toe, put it back into my own hands unopened."

"To the devil I pitch all the nobility!" cries a little man, in a peculiar accent; "I am sure they have of late used me most scurvily. You must know, gentlemen, some time ago, upon the arrival of a certain noble duke from his travels, I sat myself down, and vamped up a fine flaunting poetical panegyric, which I had written in such a strain, that I fancied it would have even wheedled milk from a mouse. In this I represented the whole kingdom welcoming his grace to his native soil, not forgetting the loss France and Italy would sustain in their arts by his departure. I expected to touch for a bank-bill at least; so, folding up my verses in gilt paper, I gave my last half-crown to a genteel servant to be the bearer. My letter was safely conveyed to his grace, and the servant, after four hours absence, during which time I led the life of a fiend, returned with a letter four times as big as mine. Guess my extasy at the prospect of so fine a return. I eagerly took the packet into my hands, that trembled to receive it. I kept it some time unopened before me, brooding over the expected treasure it contained; when opening it, as I hope to be saved, gentlemen, his grace had sent me in payment for my poem, no bank-bills, but six copies of verses, each longer than mine, addressed to him upon the same occasion."

"A nobleman," cries a member, who had hitherto been silent, "is created as much for the confusion of us authors, as the catchpole. I'll tell you a story, gentlemen, which is as true as that this pipe is made of clay: — When I was delivered of my first book, I owed my tailor for a suit of clothes; but that is nothing new, you know, and may be any man's case as well as mine. Well, owing him for a suit of clothes, and hearing that my book took very well, he sent for his money and insisted upon being paid immediately. Though I was at that time rich in fame — for my book ran like wild-fire — yet I was very short in money, and, being unable to satisfy his demand, prudently resolved to keep my chamber, preferring a prison of my own choosing at home, to one of my tailor's choosing abroad. In vain the bailiffs used all their arts to decoy me from my citadel; in vain they sent to let me know that a gentleman wanted to speak with me at the next tavern; in vain they came with an urgent message from my aunt in the country; in vain I was told that a particular friend was at the point of death, and desired to take his last farewell: — I was deaf, insensible, rock, adamant; the bailiffs could make no impression on my hard heart, for I effectually kept my liberty by never stirring out of the room.

"This was very well for a fortnight; when one morning I received a most splendid message from the Earl of Doomsday, importing, that he had read my book, and was in raptures with every line of it; he impatiently longed to see the author, and had some designs which might turn out greatly to my advantage. I paused upon the contents of this message, and found there could be no deceit, for the card was gilt at the edges, and the bearer, I was told, had quite the looks of a gentleman. Witness, ye powers, how my heart triumphed at my own importance! I saw a long perspective of felicity before me; I applauded the taste of the times which never saw genius forsaken: I had prepared a set introductory speech for the occasion; five glaring compliments for his lordship, and two more modest for myself. The next morning, therefore, in order to be punctual to my appointment, I took coach, and ordered the fellow to drive to the street and house mentioned in his lordship's address. I had the precaution to pull up the windows as I went along, to keep off the busy part of mankind, and, big with expectation, fancied the coach never went fast enough. At length, however, the wished for moment of its stopping arrived: this for some time I impatiently expected, and letting down the window in a transport, in order to take a previous view of his lordship's magnificent palace and situation, I found — poison to my sight! — I found myself not in an elegant street, but a paltry lane: not at a nobleman's door, but the door of a spunging-house: I found the coachman had all this while been just driving me to jail; and I saw the bailiff, with a devil's face, coming out to secure me."

To a philosopher, no circumstance, however trifling, is too minute; he finds instruction and entertainment in occurrences, which are passed over by the rest of mankind, as low, trite, and indifferent; it is from the number of these particulars, which to many appear insignificant, that he is at last enabled to form general conclusions; this, therefore, must be my excuse for sending so far as China, accounts of manners and follies, which, though minute in their own nature, serve more truly to characterize this people, than histories of their public treaties, courts, ministers, negotiations, and ambassadors. Adieu.

LETTER XLI

To the Same

THE BEHAVIOUR OF THE CONGREGATION IN ST. PAUL'S CHURCH AT PRAYERS

SOME time since I sent thee, O holy disciple of Confucius, an account of the grand abbey, or mausoleum, of the kings and heroes of this nation: I have since been introduced to a temple, not so ancient, but far superior in beauty and magnificence. In this, which is the most considerable of the empire, there are no pompous inscriptions, no flattery paid the dead, but all is elegant and awfully simple. There are, however, a few rags hung round the walls, which have, at a vast expense, been taken from the enemy in the present war. The silk of which they are composed, when new, might be valued at half a string of copper money in China; yet this wise people fitted out a fleet and an army in order to seize them, though now grown old, and scarcely capable of being patched up into a handkerchief. By this conquest, the English are said to have gained, and the French to have lost, much honour. Is the honour of European nations placed only in tattered silk?

In this temple I was permitted to remain during the whole service; and were you not already acquainted with the religion of the English, you might, from my description, be inclined to believe them as grossly idolatrous as the disciples of Lao. The idol which they seem to address, strides like a colossus over the door of the inner temple, which here, as with the Jews, is esteemed the most sacred part of the building. Its oracles are delivered in a hundred various tones, which seem to inspire the worshippers with enthusiasm and awe: an old woman, who appeared to be the priestess, was employed in various attitudes, as she felt the inspiration. When it began to speak, all the people remained fixed in silent attention, nodding assent, looking approbation, appearing highly edified by those sounds which to a stranger might seem inarticulate and unmeaning.

When the idol had done speaking, and the priestess had locked up its lungs with a key, observing almost all the company leaving the temple, I concluded the service was over, and taking my hat, was going to walk away with the crowd, when I was stopped by the man in black, who assured me that the ceremony had scarcely yet begun! "What!" cried I, "do I not see almost the whole body of the worshippers leaving the church? Would you persuade me that such numbers who profess religion and morality, would, in this shameless manner, quit the temple before the service was concluded? You surely mistake: not even the Kalmucks would be guilty of such an indecency, though all the object of their worship was but a joint-stool." My friend seemed to blush for his countrymen, assuring me that those whom I saw running away, were only a parcel of musical blockheads, whose passion was merely for sounds, and whose heads are as empty as a fiddle-case: those who remained behind, says he, are the true religious; they make use of music to warm their hearts, and to lift them to a proper pitch of rapture: examine their behaviour, and you will confess there are some among us who practise true devotion.

I now looked round me as directed, but saw nothing of that fervent devotion which he had promised: one of the worshippers appeared to be ogling the company through a glass; another was fervent, not in addresses to Heaven, but to his mistress; a third whispered, a fourth took snuff, and the priest himself, in a drowsy tone, read over the *duties* of the day.

"Bless my eyes!" cried I, as I happened to look towards the doors, "what do I see? one of the worshippers fallen fast asleep, and actually sunk down on his cushion! Is he now enjoying the benefit of a trance, or does he receive the influence of some mysterious vision?" — "Alas! alas!" replied my companion, "no such thing; he has only had the misfortune of eating too hearty a dinner, and finds

The Sleeping Congregation.

it impossible to keep his eyes open." Turning to another part of the temple, I perceived a young lady just in the same circumstances and attitude: "Strange," cried I; "can she, too, have over-eaten herself?" — "Oh, fie!" replied my friend, "you now grow censorious. She grow drowsy from eating too much! that would be profanation! She only sleeps now from having sat up all night at a brag party." — "Turn me where I will, then," says I, "I can perceive no single symptom of devotion among the worshippers, except from that old woman in the corner, who sits groaning behind the long sticks of a mourning fan; she indeed seems greatly edified with what she hears." — "Ay," replied my friend, "I knew we should find some to catch you; I know her; that is the deaf lady who lives in the cloisters."

In short, the remissness of behaviour in almost all the worshippers, and some even of the guardians, struck me with surprise. I had been taught to believe that none were ever promoted to offices in the temple, but men remarkable for their superior sanctity, learning, and rectitude; that there was no such thing heard of, as persons being introduced into the church merely to oblige a senator, or provide for the younger branch of a noble family: I expected, as their minds were continually set upon heavenly things, to see their eyes directed there also; and hoped, from their behaviour, to perceive their inclinations corresponding with their duty. But I am since informed, that some are appointed to preside over temples they never visit; and, while they receive all the money, are contented with letting others do all the goood. Adieu.

LETTER XLV

To the Same

THE ARDOUR OF THE PEOPLE OF LONDON IN RUNNING AFTER SIGHTS
AND MONSTERS

THOUGH the frequent invitations I receive from men of distinction here might excite the vanity of some, I am quite mortified, however, when I consider the motives that inspire their civility. I am sent for not to be treated as a friend, but to satisfy curiosity; not to be entertained so much as wondered at, the same earnestness which excites them to see a Chinese, would have made them equally proud of a visit from the rhinoceros.

CITIZEN OF THE WORLD

From the highest to the lowest, this people seem fond of sights and monsters. I am told of a person here who gets a very comfortable livelihood by making wonders, and then selling or showing them to the people for money: no matter how insignificant they were in the beginning, by locking them up close, and showing for money, they soon become prodigies! His first essay in this way was to exhibit himself as a wax-work figure behind a glass door at a puppet show. Thus, keeping the spectators at a proper distance, and having his head adorned with a copper crown, he looked "extremely natural, and very like the life itself." He continued this exhibition with success, till an involuntary fit of sneezing brought him to life before all the spectators, and consequently rendered him for that time as entirely useless as the peaceable inhabitant of a catacomb.

Determined to act the statue no more, he next levied contributions under the figure of an Indian king; and by painting his face, and counterfeiting the savage howl, he frighted several ladies and children with amazing success: in this manner, therefore, he might have lived very comfortably, had he not been arrested for a debt that was contracted when he was the figure in wax-work: thus his face underwent an involuntary ablution, and he found himself reduced to his primitive complexion and indigence.

After some time, being freed from jail, he was now grown wiser, and instead of making himself a wonder, was resolved only to make wonders. He learned the art of pasting up mummies; was never at a loss for an artificial *lusus naturæ;* nay, it has been reported, that he has sold seven petrified lobsters of his own manufacture to a noted collector of rarities; but this the learned Cracovius Putridus has undertaken to refute in a very elaborate dissertation.

His last wonder was nothing more than a halter, yet by this halter he gained more than by all his former exhibitions. The people, it seems, had got it in their heads, that a certain noble criminal was to be hanged with a silken rope. Now, there was nothing they so much desired to see as this very rope; and he was resolved to gratify their curiosity: he therefore got one made, not only of silk, but, to render it more striking, several threads of gold were intermixed. The people paid their money only to see silk, but were highly satisfied when they found it was mixed with gold into the bargain. It is scarcely necessary to mention, that the projector sold his silken rope for almost what it had cost him, as soon as the criminal was known to be hanged in hempen materials.

CITIZEN OF THE WORLD

By their fondness of sights, one would be apt to imagine that instead of desiring to see things as they should be, they are rather solicitous of seeing them as they ought not to be. A cat with four legs is disregarded, though never so useful; but if it has but two, and is consequently incapable of catching mice, it is reckoned inestimable, and every man of taste is ready to raise the auction. A man, though in his person faultless as an aerial genius, might starve; but if stuck over with hideous warts like a porcupine, his fortune is made for ever, and he may propagate the breed with impunity and applause.

A good woman in my neighbourhood, who was bred a habit-maker, though she handled her needle tolerably well, could scarcely get employment. But being obliged by an accident to have both her hands cut off from the elbows, what would in another country have been her ruin, made her fortune here: she now was thought more fit for her trade than before; business flowed in apace, and all people paid for seeing the mantua-maker who wrought without hands.

A gentleman, showing me his collection of pictures, stopped at one with peculiar admiration: "There," cries he, "is an inestimable piece." I gazed at the picture for some time, but could see none of those graces with which he seemed enraptured; it appeared to me the most paltry piece of the whole collection: I therefore demanded where those beauties lay, of which I was yet insensible. "Sir," cries he, "the merit does not consist in the piece, but in the manner in which it was done. The painter drew the whole with his foot, and held the pencil between his toes: I bought it at a very great price; for peculiar merit should ever be rewarded."

But these people are not more fond of wonders, than liberal in rewarding those who show them. From the wonderful dog of knowledge, at present under the patronage of the nobility, down to the man with the box, who professes to show "the best imitation of Nature that was ever seen," they all live in luxury. A singing woman shall collect subscriptions in her own coach and six; a fellow shall make a fortune by tossing a straw from his toe to his nose; one in particular has found that eating fire was the most ready way to live; and another, who jingles several bells fixed to his cap, is the only man that I know of who has received emolument from the labours of his head.

A young author, a man of good-nature and learning, was complaining to me some nights ago of this misplaced generosity of the times. "Here," says he, "have I spent part of my youth in attempting to instruct and amuse my fellow-creatures, and all my reward has been solitude, and reproach; while a fellow, possessed of even poverty, the smallest share of fiddling merit, or who has perhaps learned to whistle double, is rewarded, applauded, and caressed!" — "Prithee, young man," says I to him, "are you ignorant, that in so large a city as this, it is better to be an amusing than a useful member of society? Can you leap up, and touch your feet four times before you come to the ground?" — "No, sir." — "Can you pimp for a man of quality?" — "No, sir." — "Can you stand upon two horses at full speed?" — "No, sir." — "Can you swallow a penknife?" — "I can do none of these tricks." —" Why then," cried I, "there is no other prudent means of subsistence left, but to apprize the town that you speedily intend to eat up your own nose, by subscription."

I have frequently regretted that none of our Eastern posture-masters, or showmen, have ever ventured to England. I should be pleased to see that money circulate in Asia, which is now sent to Italy and France, in order to bring their vagabonds hither. Several of our tricks would undoubtedly give the English high satisfaction. Men of fashion would be greatly pleased with the postures as well as the condescension of our dancing girls; and the ladies would equally admire the conductors of our fireworks. What an agreeable surprise would it be to see a huge fellow with whiskers flash a charged blunderbuss full in a lady's face, without singeing her hair, or melting her pomatum. Perhaps, when the first surprise was over, she might then grow familiar with danger; and the ladies might vie with each other in standing fire with intrepidity.

But of all the wonders of the East, the most useful, and I should fancy the most pleasing, would be the looking-glass of Lao, which reflects the mind as well as the body. It is said, that the Emperor Chusi used to make his concubines dress their heads and their hearts in one of these glasses every morning: while the lady was at her toilet, he would frequently look over her shoulder; and it is recorded, that among the three hundred which composed his seraglio, not one was found whose mind was not even more beautiful than her person.

I make no doubt but a glass in this country would have the very same effect. The English ladies, concubines and all, would undoubtedly cut very pretty figures in so faithful a monitor. There, should we happen to peep over a lady's shoulder while dressing, we might be able to see neither gaming nor ill-nature; neither pride, debauchery, nor a love of gadding. We should find her, if any sensible defect appeared in the mind, more careful in rectifying it, than plastering up the irreparable decays of the person; nay, I am even apt to fancy, that ladies would find more real pleasure in this utensil in private, than in any other bauble imported from China, though never so expensive or amusing.

LETTER XLVI

To the Same

[THE LOOKING-GLASS OF LAO], A DREAM

UPON finishing my last letter, I retired to rest, reflecting upon the wonders of the glass of Lao, wishing to be possessed of one here, and resolved, in such a case, to oblige every lady with a sight of it for nothing. What fortune denied me waking, fancy supplied in a dream: the glass, I know not how, was put into my possession, and I could perceive several ladies approaching, some voluntarily, others driven forward against their wills, by a set of discontented genii, whom, by intuition, I knew were their husbands.

The apartment in which I was to show away, was filled with several gaming-tables, as if just forsaken; the candles were burnt to the socket, and the hour was five o'clock in the morning. Placed at one end of the room, which was of prodigious length, I could more easily distinguish every female figure as she marched up from the door; but, guess my surprise, when I could scarce perceive one blooming or agreeable face among the number. This, however, I attributed to the early hour, and kindly considered that the face of a lady just risen from bed, ought always to find a compassionate advocate.

The first person who came up in order to view her intellectual face, was a commoner's wife, who, as I afterwards found, being bred up during her virginity in a pawn-broker's shop, now attempted to make up the defects of breeding and sentiment by the magnificence of her dress, and the expensiveness of her amusements. "Mr. Showman," cried she, approaching, "I am told you *has* something to show in *that there* sort of magic lantern, by which folks can see themselves on the inside: I protest, as my Lord Beetle says, I am sure it will be vastly pretty, for I have never seen anything like it before. But how, — Are we to strip off our clothes, and be turned inside out? if so, as Lord Beetle says, I absolutely declare off; for I would not strip for the world before a man's face, and so I *tells* his Lordship almost every night of my life." I informed the lady that I would dispense with the ceremony of stripping, and immediately presented my glass to her view.

As when a first-rate beauty, after having with difficulty escaped the small-pox, revisits her favourite mirror — that mirror which had repeated the flattery of every lover, and even added force to the compliment — expecting to see what had so often given her pleasure, she no longer beholds the cherry lip, the polished forehead, and speaking blush, but a hateful phiz, quilted into a thousand seams by the hand of deformity; grief, resentment, and rage fill her bosom by turns — she blames the fates and stars, but, most of all, the unhappy glass feels her resentment: So it was with the lady in question; she had never seen her own mind before, and was now shocked at its deformity. One single look was sufficient to satisfy her curiosity: I held up the glass to her face, and she shut her eyes; no entreaties could prevail upon her to gaze once more! She was even going to snatch it from my hands, and break it in a thousand pieces. I found it was time, therefore, to dismiss her as incorrigible, and show away to the next that offered.

This was an unmarried lady, who continued in a state of virginity till thirty-six, and then admitted a lover when she despaired of a husband. No woman was louder at a revel than she, perfectly free hearted, and almost, in every respect a man; she understood ridicule to perfection, and was once known even to sally out in order to beat the watch. "Here, you, my dear, with the outlandish face," said she, addressing me, "let me take a single peep. Not that I care three damns what figure I may cut in the glass of such an old-fashioned creature: if I am allowed the beauties of the face by people of fashion, I know the world will be complaisant enough to toss me the beauties of the mind into the bargain." I held my glass before her as she desired, and, must confess, was shocked with the reflection. The lady, however, gazed for some time with the utmost complacency; and, at last, turning to me with the most satisfied smile, said, she never could think she had been half so handsome.

CITIZEN OF THE WORLD

Upon her dismission, a lady of distinction was reluctantly hauled along to the glass by her husband. In bringing her forward, as he came first to the glass himself, his mind appeared tinctured with immoderate jealousy, and I was going to reproach him for using her with such severity; but when the lady came to present herself, I immediately retracted: for, alas! it was seen that he had but too much reason for his suspicions.

The next was a lady who usually teased all her acquaintance, desiring to be told of her faults, and then never mended any. Upon approaching the glass, I could readily perceive vanity, affectation, and some other ill-looking blots on her mind; wherefore, by my advice, she immediately set about mending. But I could easily find she was not earnest in the work; for as she repaired them on one side, they generally broke out on another. Thus, after three or four attempts, she began to make the ordinary use of the glass in settling her hair.

The company now made room for a woman of learning, who approached with a slow pace and a solemn countenance, which, for her own sake, I could wish had been cleaner. "Sir," cried the lady, flourishing her hand, which held a pinch of snuff, "I shall be enraptured by having presented to my view a mind, with which I have so long studied to be acquainted; but, in order to give the sex a proper example, I must insist, that all the company may be permitted to look over my shoulder." I bowed assent, and, presenting the glass, showed the lady a mind by no means so fair as she had expected to see. Ill-nature, ill-placed pride, and spleen, were too legible to be mistaken. Nothing could be more amusing than the mirth of her female companions who had looked over. They had hated her from the beginning, and now the apartment echoed with a universal laugh. Nothing but a fortitude like hers could have withstood their raillery: she stood it, however; and, when the burst was exhausted, with great tranquillity she assured the company, that the whole was a *deceptio visus*, and that she was too well acquainted with her own mind to believe any false representations from another. Thus saying, she retired with a sullen satisfaction, resolved not to mend her faults, but to write a criticism on the mental reflector.

I must own, by this time, I began myself to suspect the fidelity of my mirror; for, as the ladies appeared at least to have the merit of rising early, since they were up at five, I was amazed to find nothing of this good quality pictured upon their minds in the reflection: I was resolved, therefore, to communicate my suspicions to a lady whose intellectual countenance appeared more fair than any of the rest not having above seventy-nine spots in all, besides slips and foibles. "I own, young woman," said I, "that there are some virtues upon that mind of yours; but there is still one which I do not see represented, I mean that of rising betimes in the morning — I fancy the glass false in that particular." The young lady smiled at my simplicity; and, with a blush, confessed, that she and the whole company had been up all night gaming.

By this time all the ladies, except one, had seen themselves successively, and disliked the show, or scolded the showman: I was resolved, however, that she who seemed to neglect herself, and was neglected by the rest, should take a view; and, going up to a corner of the room where she still continued sitting, I presented my glass full in her face. Here it was that I exulted in my success; no blot, no stain appeared on any part of the faithful mirror. As when the large unwritten page presents its snowy spotless bosom to the writer's hand, so appeared the glass to my view. "Here, O ye daughters of English ancestors!" cried I, "turn hither, and behold an object worthy imitation! Look upon the mirror now, and acknowledge its justice, and this woman's pre-eminence!" The ladies, obeying the summons, came up in a group, and looking on, acknowledged there was some truth in the picture, as the person now represented had been deaf, dumb, and a fool from her cradle!

Thus much of my dream I distinctly remember; the rest was filled with chimeras, enchanted castles, and flying dragons as usual. As you, my dear Fum Hoam, are particularly versed in the interpretation of those midnight warnings, what pleasure should I find in your explanation! But that our distance prevents: I make no doubt, however, but that, from my description, you will very much venerate the good qualities of the English ladies in general, since dreams, you know, go always by contraries. Adieu.

CITIZEN OF THE WORLD

LETTER LI

To the Same

A BOOKSELLER'S VISIT TO THE CHINESE PHILOSOPHER

AS I was yesterday seated at breakfast over a pensive dish of tea, my meditations were interrupted by my old friend and companion, who introduced a stranger, dressed pretty much like himself. The gentleman made several apologies for his visit, begged of me to impute his intrusion to the sincerity of his respect, and the warmth of his curiosity.

As I am very suspicious of my company when I find them very civil without any apparent reason, I answered the stranger's caresses at first with reserve; which my friend perceiving, instantly let me into my visitant's trade and character, asking Mr. Fudge, whether he had lately published any thing new? I now conjectured that my guest was no other than a bookseller, and his answer confirmed my suspicions.

"Excuse me, Sir," says he, "it is not the season; books have their time as well as cucumbers. I would no more bring out a new work in summer, than I would sell pork in the dog days. Nothing in my way goes off in summer, except very light goods indeed. A review, a magazine, or a Sessions paper, may amuse a summer reader; but all our stock of value we reserve for a spring and winter trade." "I must confess, Sir," says I, "a curiosity to know what you call a valuable stock, which can only bear a winter perusal." "Sir," replied the bookseller, "it is not my way to cry up my own goods; but, without exaggeration, I will venture to show with any of the trade: my books at least have the peculiar advantage of being always new; and it is my way to clear off my old to the trunk-makers every season. I have ten new title-pages now about me, which only want books to be added to make them the finest things in nature. Others may pretend to direct the vulgar; but that is not my way; I always let the vulgar direct me; wherever popular clamour arises, I always echo the million. For instance, should the people in general say, that such a man is a rogue, I instantly give orders to set him down in print a villain; thus every man buys the book, not to learn new sentiments, but to have the pleasure of seeing his own reflected." — "But, Sir," interrupted I, "you speak as if you yourself wrote the books you publish; may I be so bold as to ask a sight of some of those intended publications which are shortly to surprise the world?" — "As to that, Sir," replied the talkative bookseller, "I only draw out the plans myself; and though I am very cautious of communicating them to any, yet, as in the end I have a favour to ask, you shall see a few of them. Here, Sir, here they are; diamonds of the first water, I assure you. *Imprimis*, a Translation of several Medical precepts for the use of such physicians as do not understand Latin. *Item*, the Young Clergyman's art of placing patches regularly, with a Dissertation on the different manners of smiling without distorting the face. *Item*, the whole Art of Love made perfectly easy, by a broker of 'Change Alley. *Item*, the proper manner of Cutting blacklead pencils, and making crayons, by the Right Hon. the Earl of * * *. *Item*, the Muster-master-general, or the review of reviews." — "Sir," cried I, interrupting him, "my curiosity, with regard to title-pages, is satisfied; I should be glad to see some longer manuscript, a history, or an epic poem." — "Bless me!" cries the man of industry, "now you speak of an epic poem, you shall see an excellent farce. Here it is; dip into it where you will, it will be found replete with true modern humour. Strokes, Sir; it is filled with strokes of wit and satire in every line." — "Do you call these dashes of the pen strokes," replied I, "for I must confess I can see no other?" — "And pray, Sir," returned he, "what do you call them? Do you see any thing good now-a-days, that is not filled with strokes — and dashes? — Sir, a well placed dash makes half the wit of our writers of modern humour. I bought a piece last season that had no other merit upon earth than nine hundred and ninety-five breaks, seventy-two ha-ha's, three good things, and a garter. And yet it played off, and bounced, and cracked, and made more sport than a firework." — "I fancy, then, Sir, you were a considerable gainer?" — "It must be owned the piece did pay; but, upon the whole, I cannot much boast of last winter's success; I gained by two murders; but then I lost by an ill-timed charity sermon. I was a considerable sufferer by my Direct Road to an Estate, but the Infernal Guide brought me up again. Ah, Sir, that was a piece touched off by the hand of a master; filled with good things from one end to the other. The author had nothing but the jest in view; no dull moral lurking beneath, nor ill-natured satire to sour the reader's good-humour; he wisely considered, that moral and humour at the same time were quite overdoing the business." — "To what purpose was the book then published?" cried I. — "Sir, the book was published in order to be sold; and no book sold better, except the criticisms upon it, which came out soon after: of all kinds of writing, that goes off best at present; and I generally fasten a criticism upon every selling book that is published.

"I once had an author who never left the least opening for the critics: close was the word; always very right and very dull; ever on the safe side of an argument; yet, with all his qualifications, incapable of coming into favour. I soon perceived that his bent was for criticism; and, as he was good for nothing else, supplied him with pens and paper, and planted him, at the beginning of every month, as a censor on the works of others. In short, I found him a treasure; no merit could escape him; but what is most remarkable of all, he ever wrote best and bitterest when drunk." "But are there not some works," interrupted I, "that, from the very manner of their composition, must be exempt from criticism; particularly such as profess to disregard its laws?" — "There is no work whatsoever but he can criticise," replied the bookseller; "even though you wrote in Chinese, he would have a pluck at you. Suppose you should take it into your head to publish a book, let it be a volume of Chinese letters, for instance; write how you will, he shall show the world you could have written better. Should you, with the most local exactness, stick to the manners and customs of the country from whence you come; should you confine yourself to the narrow limits of Eastern knowledge, and be perfectly simple, and perfectly natural, he has then the strongest reason to exclaim. He may, with a sneer, send you back to China for readers. He may observe, that after the first or second letter, the iteration of the same simplicity is insupportably tedious. But the worst of all is, the public, in such a case, will anticipate his censures, and leave you, with all your uninstructive simplicity, to be mauled at discretion."

"Yes," cried I, "but in order to avoid his indignation, and, what I should fear more, that of the public, I would, in such a case, write with all the knowledge I was master of. As I am not possessed of much learning, at least I would not suppress what little I had; nor would I appear more stupid than nature made me." — "Here, then," cries the bookseller, "we should have you entirely in our power; unnatural, un-Eastern, quite out of character, erroneously sensible, would be the whole cry. Sir, we should then hunt you down like a rat." — "Head of my father!" said I, "sure there are but two ways; the door must either be shut or it must be open. I must either be natural or unnatural." — "Be what you will, we shall criticise you," returned the bookseller, "and prove you a dunce in spite of your teeth. But, Sir, it is time that I should come to business. I have just now in the press a history of China; and if you will but put your name to it as the author, I shall repay the obligation with gratitude." — "What, Sir!" replied I, "put my name to a work which I have not written? Never, while I retain a proper respect for the public and myself." The bluntness of my reply quite abated the ardour of the bookseller's conversation: and, after about half an hour's disagreeable reserve, he, with some ceremony, took his leave, and withdrew. Adieu.

LETTER LII

To the Same

THE IMPOSSIBILITY OF DISTINGUISHING MEN IN ENGLAND BY THEIR DRESS. TWO INSTANCES OF THIS

IN all other countries, my dear Fum Hoam, the rich are distinguished by their dress. In Persia, China, and most parts of Europe, those who are possessed of much gold or silver, put some of it upon their clothes; but in England, those who carry much upon their clothes, are remarked for having but little in their pockets. A tawdry outside is regarded as a badge of poverty; and those who can sit at home, and gloat over their thousands in silent satisfaction, are generally found to do it in plain clothes.

This diversity of thinking from the rest of the world which prevails here, I was, at first, at a loss to account for; but am since informed, that it was introduced by an intercourse between them and their neighbours the French, who, whenever they came in order to pay these islanders a visit, were generally very well dressed, and very poor, daubed with lace, but all the gilding on the outside. By this means laced clothes have been brought so much into contempt, that, at present, even their mandarines are ashamed of finery.

I must own myself a convert to English simplicity; I am no more for ostentation of wealth than of learning: the person who in company should pretend to be wiser than others, I am apt to regard as illiterate and ill-bred; the person whose clothes are extremely fine, I am too apt to consider as not being possessed of any superiority of fortune, but resembling those Indians who are found to wear all the gold they have in the world in a bob at the nose.

I was lately introduced into a company of the best dressed men I have seen since my arrival. Upon entering the room, I was struck with awe at the grandeur of the different dresses. That personage, thought I, in blue and gold must be some emperor's son; that in green and silver, a prince of the blood; he in embroidered scarlet, a prime minister; all first rate noblemen, I suppose, and well-looking noblemen too. I sat for some time with that uneasiness which conscious inferiority produces in the ingenuous mind, all attention to their discourse. However, I found their conversation more vulgar than I could have expected from personages of such distinction: If these, thought I to myself, be princes, they are the most stupid princes I have ever conversed with: yet still I continued to venerate their dress; for dress has a kind of mechanical influence on the mind.

My friend in black, indeed, did not behave with the same deference, but contradicted the finest of them all in the most peremptory tones of contempt. But I had scarce time to wonder at the imprudence of his conduct, when I found occasion to be equally surprised at the absurdity of theirs; for upon the entrance of a middle-aged man, dressed in a cap, dirty shirt, and boots, the whole circle seemed diminished of their former importance, and contended who should be first to pay their obeisance to the stranger. They somewhat resembled a circle of Kalmucs offering incense to a bear.

Eager to know the cause of so much seeming contradiction, I whispered my friend out of the room, and found that the august company consisted of no other than a dancing master, two fiddlers, and a third-rate actor, all assembled in order to make a set at country dances; as the middle-aged gentleman whom I saw enter, was a 'squire from the country, desirous of learning the new manner of footing, and smoothing up the rudiments of his rural minuet.

I was no longer surprised at the authority which my friend assumed among them — nay, was even displeased (pardon my Eastern education) that he had not kicked every creature of them down stairs. "What," said I, "shall a set of such paltry fellows dress themselves up like sons of kings, and claim even the transitory respect of half an hour! There should be some law to restrain so manifest a breach of privilege; they should go from house to house as in China, with the instruments of their profession strung round their necks; by this means, we might be able to distinguish and treat them in a style of becoming contempt." — "Hold, my friend," replied my companion, "were your reformation to take place, as dancing masters and fiddlers now mimic gentlemen in appearance, we should then find our fine gentlemen conforming to theirs. A beau might be introduced to a lady of fashion with a fiddle-case hanging at his neck by a red riband; and, instead of a cane, might carry a fiddlestick. Though to be as dull as a first-rate dancing master might be used with proverbial justice; yet, dull as he is, many a fine gentleman sets him up as the proper standard of politeness; copies not only the pert vivacity of his air, but the flat insipidity of his conversation. In short, if you make a law against dancing masters imitating the fine gentleman, you should with as much reason enact, that no fine gentleman shall imitate the dancing master."

After I had left my friend, I made towards home, reflecting as I went upon the difficulty of distinguishing men by their appearance. Invited, however, by the freshness of the evening, I did not return directly, but went to ruminate on what had passed in a public garden belonging to the city. Here, as I sat upon one of the benches, and felt the pleasing sympathy which nature in bloom inspires, a disconsolate figure who sat on the other end of the seat, seemed no way to enjoy the serenity of the season.

His dress was miserable beyond description; a thread-bare coat, of the rudest materials; a shirt, though clean, yet extremely coarse; hair that seemed to have been long unconscious of the comb; and all the rest of his equipage impressed with the marks of genuine poverty.

As he continued to sigh, and testify every symptom of despair, I was naturally led, from a motive of humanity, to offer comfort and assistance. You know my heart; and that all who are miserable may claim a place there. The pensive stranger at first declined any conversation; but at last perceiving a peculiarity in my accent and manner of thinking, he began to unfold himself by degrees.

I now found that he was not so very miserable as he at first appeared; upon my offering him a small piece of money, he refused my favour, yet without appearing displeased at my intended generosity. It is true, he sometimes interrupted the conversation with a sigh, and talked pathetically of neglected merit; yet still I could perceive a serenity in his countenance, that, upon a closer inspection, bespoke inward content.

Upon a pause in the conversation, I was going to take my leave, when he begged I would favour him with my company home to supper. I was surprised at such a demand from a person of his appearance, but, willing to indulge curiosity, I accepted his invitation; and, though I felt some repugnance at being seen with one who appeared so very wretched, went along with seeming alacrity.

Still as he approached nearer home, his good humour proportionably seemed to increase. At last he stopped, not at the gate of a hovel, but of a magnificent palace! When I cast my eyes upon all the sumptuous elegance which every where presented upon entering, and then when I looked at my seeming miserable conductor, I could scarce think that all this finery belonged to him; yet in fact it did. Numerous servants ran through the apartments with silent assiduity; several ladies of beauty, and magnificently dressed, came to welcome his return; a most elegant supper was provided: in short, I found the person whom a little before I had sincerely pitied, to be in reality a most refined epicure: — one who courted contempt abroad, in order to feel with keener gust the pleasure of pre-eminence at home. Adieu.

LETTER LIII

To the Same

THE ABSURD TASTE FOR CERTAIN FORMS OF LITERATURE

HOW often have we admired the eloquence of Europe! that strength of thinking, that delicacy of imagination, even beyond the efforts of the Chinese themselves. How were we enraptured with those bold figures which sent every sentiment with force to the heart. How have we spent whole days together, in learning those arts by which European writers got within the passions, and led the reader as if by enchantment.

But though we have learned most of the rhetorical figures of the last age, yet there seems to be one or two of great use here, which have not yet travelled to China. The figures I mean are called *Bawdy* and *Pertness:* none are more fashionable — none so sure of admirers; they are of such a nature, that the merest blockhead, by a proper use of them, shall have the reputation of a wit; they lie level to the meanest capacities, and address those passions which all have, or would be ashamed to disown.

It has been observed, and I believe with some truth, that it is very difficult for a dunce to obtain the reputation of a wit; yet, by the assistance of the figure *Bawdy*, this may be easily effected, and a bawdy blockhead often passes for a fellow of smart parts and pretensions. Every object in nature helps the jokes forward, without scarce any effort of the imagination. If a lady stands, something very good may be said upon that; if she happens to fall, with the help of a little fashionable pruriency, there are forty sly things ready on the occasion. But a prurient jest has always been found to give most pleasure to a few very old gentlemen, who, being in some measure dead to other sensations, feel the force of the allusion with double violence on the organs of risibility.

An author who writes in this manner is generally sure, therefore, of having the very old and the impotent among his admirers; for these he may properly be said to write, and from these he ought to expect his reward; his works being often a very proper succedaneum to cantharides, or an asafœtida pill. His pen should be considered in the same light as the squirt of an apothecary, both being directed at the same generous end.

But though this manner of writing be perfectly adapted to the taste of gentlemen and ladies of fashion here, yet still it deserves greater praise in being equally suited to the most vulgar apprehensions. The very ladies and gentlemen of Benin or Cafraria are in this respect tolerably polite, and might relish a prurient joke of this kind with critical propriety; probably, too, with higher gust, as they wear neither breeches nor petticoats to intercept the application.

It is certain I never could have expected the ladies here, biassed as they are by education, capable at once of bravely throwing off their prejudices, and not only applauding books in which this figure makes the only merit, but even adopting it in their own conversation. Yet so it is; the pretty innocents now carry those books openly in their hands, which formerly were hid under the cushion; they now lisp their double meanings with so much grace, and talk over the raptures they bestow with such little reserve, that I am sometimes reminded of a custom among the entertainers in China, who think it a piece of necessary breeding to whet the appetites of their guests, by letting them smell dinner in the kitchen, before it is served up to table.

The veneration we have for many things, entirely proceeds from their being carefully concealed. Were the idolatrous Tartar permitted to lift the veil which keeps his idol from view, it might be a certain method to cure his future superstition; with what a noble spirit of freedom, therefore, must that writer be possessed, who bravely paints things as they are — who lifts the veil of modesty — who displays the most hidden recesses of the temple, and shows the erring people that the object of their vows is either, perhaps a mouse or a monkey!

However, though this figure be at present so much in fashion — though the professors of it are so much caressed by the great, those perfect judges of literary excellence, — yet it is confessed to be only a revival of what was once fashionable here before. There was a time, when, by this very manner of writing, the gentle Tom Durfey, as I read in English authors, acquired his great reputation, and became the favourite of a king.

The works of this original genius, though they never travelled abroad to China, and scarce have reached posterity at home, were once found upon every fashionable toilet, and made the subject of polite, I mean very polite conversation. "Has your grace seen Mr. Durfey's last new thing, the *Oylet Hole?* — a most facetious piece!" — "Sure, my lord, all the world must have seen it; Durfey is certainly the most comical creature alive. It is impossible to read his things and live. Was there ever anything so natural and pretty, as when the 'Squire and Bridget meet in the cellar? And then the difficulties they both find in broaching the beer barrel, are so arch and so ingenious! We have certainly nothing of this kind in the language." In this manner they spoke then, and in this manner they speak now; for though the successor of Durfey does not excel him in wit, the world must confess he outdoes him in obscenity.

There are several very dull fellows, who, by a few mechanical helps, sometimes learn to become extremely brilliant and pleasing, with a little dexterity in the management of the eyebrows, fingers, and nose. By imitating a cat, a sow and pigs, — by a loud laugh, and a slap on the shoulder, — the most ignorant are furnished out for conversation. But the writer finds it impossible to throw his winks, his shrugs, or his attitudes upon paper; he may borrow some assistance, indeed, by printing his face at the title page; but, without wit, to pass for a man of ingenuity, no other mechanical help but downright obscenity will suffice. By speaking of some peculiar sensations, we are always sure of exciting laughter, for the jest does not lie in the writer, but in the subject.

But *Bawdy* is often helped on by another figure, called *Pertness;* and few indeed are found to excel in one that are not possessed of the other. As in common conversation, the best way to make the audience laugh is by first laughing yourself; so in writing, the properest manner is to show an attempt at humour, which will pass upon most for humour in reality. To effect this, readers must be treated with the most perfect familiarity: in one page the author is to make them a low bow, and in the next to pull them by the nose; he must talk in riddles, and then send them to bed in order to dream for the solution. He must speak of himself, and his chapters, and his manner, and what he would be at, and his own importance, and his mother's importance, with the most unpitying prolixity; now and then testifying his contempt for all but himself, smiling without a jest, and without wit professing vivacity. Adieu.

LETTER LIV

To the Same

THE CHARACTER OF AN IMPORTANT TRIFLER, [BEAU TIBBS]

THOUGH naturally pensive, yet I am fond of gay company, and take every opportunity of thus dismissing the mind from duty. From this motive, I am often found in the centre of a crowd; and wherever pleasure is to be sold, am always a purchaser. In those places, without being remarked by any, I join in whatever goes forward; work my passions into a similitude of frivolous earnestness, shout as they shout, and condemn as they happen to disapprove. A mind thus sunk for a while below its natural standard, is qualified for stronger flights, as those first retire who would spring forward with greater vigour.

Attracted by the serenity of the evening, my friend and I lately went to gaze upon the company in one of the public walks near the city. Here we sauntered together for some time, either praising the beauty of such as were handsome, or the dresses of such as had nothing else to recommend them. We had gone thus deliberately forward for some time, when, stopping on a sudden, my friend caught me by the elbow, and led me out of the public walk. I could perceive by the quickness of his pace, and by his frequently looking behind, that he was attempting to avoid somebody who followed: we now turned to the right, then to the left: as we went forward, he still went faster, but in vain: the person whom he attempted to escape hunted us through every doubling, and gained upon us each moment, so that at last we fairly stood still, resolving to face what we could not avoid.

Our pursuer soon came up, and joined us with all the familiarity of an old acquaintance. "My dear Drybone," cries he, shaking my friend's hand, "where have you been hiding this half a century? Positively I had fancied you were gone down to cultivate matrimony and your estate in the country." During the reply, I had an opportunity of surveying the appearance of our new companion: his hat was pinched up with peculiar smartness; his looks were pale, thin, and sharp; round his neck he wore a broad black riband, and in his bosom a buckle studded with glass; his coat was trimmed with tarnished twist; he wore by his side a sword with a black hilt; and his stockings of silk, though newly washed, were grown yellow by long service. I was so much engaged with the peculiarity of his dress, that I attended only to the latter part of my friend's reply, in which he complimented Mr. Tibbs on the taste of his clothes, and the bloom of his countenance. "Pshaw, pshaw! Will," cried the figure, "no more of that, if you love me: you know I hate flattery, — on my soul I do; and yet, to be sure, an intimacy with the great will improve one's appearance, and a course of venison will fatten; and yet, faith, I despise the great as much as you do; but there are a great many damn'd honest fellows among them, and we must not quarrel with one half, because the other wants weeding. If they were all such as my Lord Mudler, one of the most good-natured creatures that ever squeezed a lemon, I should myself be among the number of their admirers. I was yesterday to dine at the Duchess of Piccadilly's. My lord was there. 'Ned,' says he to me, 'Ned,' says he, 'I'll hold gold to silver I can tell where you were poaching last night.' 'Poaching, my lord?' says I, 'faith you have missed already; for I staid at home, and let the girls poach for me. That's my way: I take a fine woman as some animals do their prey — stand still, and swoop, they fall into my mouth.'"

"Ah, Tibbs, thou art a happy fellow," cried my companion, with looks of infinite pity; "I hope your fortune is as much improved as your understanding in such company." — "Improved," replied the other; "You shall know, — but let it go no further — a great secret — five hundred a-year to begin with. — My lord's word of honour for it. His lordship took me down in his own chariot yesterday, and we had a tête-a-tête dinner in the country, where we talked of nothing else." — "I fancy you forget, Sir," cried I, "you told us but this moment of your dining yesterday in town." — "Did I say so?" replied he cooly; "to be sure if I said so, it was so — Dined in town; egad, now I do remember, I did dine in town; but I dined in the country too; for you must know, my boys, I eat two dinners. By the by, I am grown as nice as the devil in my eating. I'll tell you a pleasant affair about that: — We were a select party of us to dine at Lady Grogram's — an affected piece, but let it go no farther — a secret — Well, there happened to be no asafœtida in the sauce to a turkey, upon which, says I, "I'll hold a thousand guineas, and say done first, that — But, dear Drybone, you are an honest creature; lend me half-a-crown for a minute or two, or so, just till —— but hearkee, ask me for it the next time we meet, or it may be twenty to one but I forget to pay you."

When he left us, our conversation naturally turned upon so extraordinary a character. "His very dress," cries my friend, "is not less extraordinary than his conduct. If you meet him this day, you find him in rags; if the next, in embroidery. With those persons of distinction of whom he talks so familiarly, he has scarce a coffee-house acquaintance. However, both for the interests of society, and perhaps for his own, Heaven has made him poor, and while all the world perceive his wants, he fancies them concealed from every eye. An agreeable companion, because he understands flattery; and all must be pleased with the first part of his conversation, though all are sure of its ending with a demand on their purse. While his youth countenances the levity of his conduct, he may thus earn a precarious subsistence; but when age comes on, the gravity of which is incompatible with buffoonery, then will he find himself forsaken by all; condemned in the decline of life to hang upon some rich family whom he once despised, there to undergo all the ingenuity of studied contempt, to be employed only as a spy upon the servants, or a bugbear to fright the children into obedience." Adieu.

CITIZEN OF THE WORLD

LETTER LV

To the Same

THE CHARACTER OF THE TRIFLER CONTINUED: WITH THAT OF HIS WIFE, HIS HOUSE, AND FURNITURE

I AM apt to fancy I have contracted a new acquaintance whom it will be no easy matter to shake off. My little Beau yesterday overtook me again in one of the public walks, and slapping me on the shoulder, saluted me with an air of the most perfect familiarity. His dress was the same as usual, except that he had more powder in his hair, wore a dirtier shirt, a pair of temple spectacles, and his hat under his arm.

As I knew him to be a harmless, amusing little thing, I could not return his smiles with any degree of severity: so we walked forward on terms of the utmost intimacy, and in a few minutes discussed all the usual topics preliminary to particular conversation. The oddities that marked his character, however, soon began to appear; he bowed to several well-dressed persons, who, by their manner of returning the compliment, appeared perfect strangers. At intervals he drew out a pocket-book, seeming to take memorandums before all the company, with much importance and assiduity. In this manner he led me through the length of the whole walk, fretting at his absurdities, and fancying myself laughed at not less than him by every spectator.

When we were got to the end of our procession, "Blast me," cries he, with an air of vivacity, "I never saw the Park so thin in my life before! There's no company at all to-day; not a single face to be seen." — "No company!" interrupted I, peevishly; "no company where there is such a crowd? why, man, there's too much. What are the thousands that have been laughing at us but company?" "Lord, my dear," returned he, with the utmost good humour, "you seem immensely chagrined; but, blast me, when the world laughs at me, I laugh at the world, and so we are even. My Lord Trip, Bill Squash the Creolian, and I, sometimes make a party at being ridiculous; and so we say and do a thousand things for the joke's sake. But I see you are grave, and if you are for a fine grave sentimental companion, you shall dine with me and my wife to-day; I must insist on't. I'll introduce you to Mrs. Tibbs, a lady of as elegant qualifications as any in nature; she was bred (but that's between ourselves), under the inspection of the Countess of All-night. A charming body of voice; but no more of that, — she will give us a song. You shall see my little girl too, Carolina Wilhelmina Amelia Tibbs, a sweet pretty creature: I design her for my Lord Drumstick's eldest son; but that's in friendship, let it go no further: she's but six years old, and yet she walks a minuet, and plays on the guitar immensely already. I intend she shall be as perfect as possible in every accomplishment. In the first place, I'll make her a scholar: I'll teach her Greek myself, and learn that language purposely to instruct her; but let that be a secret."

Thus saying, without waiting for a reply, he took me by the arm, and hauled me along. We passed through many dark alleys and winding ways; for, from some motives to me unknown, he seemed to have a particular aversion to every frequented street; at last, however, we got to the door of a dismal-looking house in the outlets of the town, where he informed me he chose to reside for the benefit of the air.

We entered the lower door, which ever seemed to lie most hospitably open; and I began to ascend an old and creaking staircase, when, as he mounted to show me the way, he demanded, whether I delighted in prospects; to which answering in the affirmative, "Then," says he, "I shall show you one of the most charming in the world, out of my window; we shall see the ships sailing, and the whole country for twenty miles round, tip top, quite high. My Lord Swamp would give ten thousand guineas for such a one; but, as I sometimes pleasantly tell him, I always love to keep my prospects at home, that my friends may see me the oftener."

By this time we were arrived as high as the stairs would permit us to ascend, till we came to what he was facetiously pleased to call the first floor down the chimney; and knocking at the door, a voice from within demanded, "Who's there?" My conductor answered that it was him. But this not satisfying the querist, the voice again repeated the demand; to which he answered louder than before; and now the door was opened by an old woman with cautious reluctance.

When we were got in, he welcomed me to his house with great ceremony, and turning to the old woman, asked where was her lady? "Good troth," replied she, in a peculiar dialect, "she's washing your twa shirts at the next door, because they have taken an oath against lending out the tub any longer." — "My two shirts!" cried he in a tone that faltered with confusion, "what does the idiot mean?" — "I ken what I mean weel enough," replied the other; "she's washing your twa shirts at the next door, because ———" "Fire and fury, no more of thy stupid explanations!" cried he; "go and inform her we have got company. Were that Scotch hag," continued he, turning to me, "to be for ever in my family, she would never learn politeness, nor forget that absurd poisonous accent of hers, or testify the smallest specimen of breeding of high life; and yet it is very surprising too, as I had her from a Parliament man, a friend of mine from the Highlands, one of the politest men in the world; but that's a secret."

We waited some time for Mrs. Tibbs's arrival, during which interval I had a full opportunity of surveying the chamber and all its furniture, which consisted of four chairs with old wrought bottoms, that he assured me were his wife's embroidery; a square table that had once been japanned; a cradle in one corner, a lumbering cabinet in the other; a broken shepherdess, and a mandarine without a head, were stuck over the chimney; and round the walls several paltry unframed pictures, which, he observed, were all his own drawing. "What do you think, Sir, of that head in the corner, done in the manner of Grisoni? there's the true keeping in it; it is my own face, and though there happens to be no likeness, a Countess offered me a hundred for its fellow: I refused her, for, hang it, that would be mechanical you know."

The wife at last made her appearance, at once a slattern and a coquette; much emaciated, but still carrying the remains of beauty. She made twenty apologies for being seen in such odious dishabille, but hoped to be excused, as she had stayed out all night at the gardens with the Countess, who was excessively fond of the horns. "And, indeed, my dear," added she, turning to her husband, "his lordship drank your health in a bumper." — "Poor Jack!" cries he, "a dear good-natured creature, I know he loves me. But I hope, my dear, you have given orders for dinner; you need make no great preparations neither, there are but three of us; something elegant, and little will do, — a turbot, an ortolan, a ———" "Or what do you think, my dear," interrupts the wife, "of a nice pretty bit of ox-cheek, piping hot, and dressed with a little of my own sauce?" — "The very thing!" replies he; "it will eat best with some smart bottled beer: but be sure to let us have the sauce his

Grace was so fond of. I hate your immense loads of meat; that is country all over; extremely disgusting to those who are in the least acquainted with high life."

By this time my curiosity began to abate, and my appetite to increase; the company of fools may at first make us smile, but at last never fails of rendering us melancholy: I therefore pretended to recollect a prior engagement, and, after having shown my respect to the house, according to the fashion of the English, by giving the old servant a piece of money at the door, I took my leave; Mr. Tibbs assuring me, that dinner, if I stayed, would be ready at least in less than two hours.

LETTER LVIII

To the Same

A VISITATION DINNER DESCRIBED

AS the man in black takes every opportunity of introducing me to such company as may serve to indulge my speculative temper, or gratify my curiosity, I was, by his influence, lately invited to a *visitation* dinner. To understand this term, you must know, that it was formerly the custom here for the principal priests to go about the country once a-year, and examine upon the spot, whether those of subordinate orders did their duty, or were qualified for the task; whether their temples were kept in proper repair or the laity pleased with their administration.

Though a visitation of this nature was very useful, yet it was found to be extremely troublesome, and for many reasons utterly inconvenient; for, as the principal priests were obliged to attend at court, in order to solicit preferment, it was impossible they could at the same time attend in the country, which was quite out of the road to promotion: if we add to this the gout, which has been time immemorial a clerical disorder here, together with the bad wine, and ill-dressed provisions that must infallibly be served up by the way, it was not strange that the custom has been long discontinued. At present, therefore, every head of the church, instead of going about to visit his priests, is satisfied if his priests come in a body once a-year to visit him; by this means the duty of half a-year is despatched in a day. When assembled, he asks each in turn how they have behaved, and are liked; upon which, those who have neglected their duty, or are disagreeable to their congregation, no doubt accuse themselves, and tell him all their faults, for which he reprimands them most severely.

The thoughts of being introduced into a company of philosophers and learned men, (for such I conceived them) gave me no small pleasure. I expected our entertainment would resemble those sentimental banquets, so finely described by Xenophon and Plato: I was hoping some Socrates would be brought in from the door, in order to harangue upon divine love: but as for eating and drinking, I had prepared myself to be disappointed in that particular. I was apprised that fasting and temperance were tenets strongly recommended to the professors of Christianity, and I had seen the frugality and mortification of the priests of the East; so that I expected an entertainment where we should have much reasoning and little meat.

Upon being introduced, I confess I found no great signs of mortification in the faces or persons of the company. However, I imputed their florid looks to temperance, and their corpulency to a sedentary way of living. I saw several preparations, indeed, for dinner, but none for philosophy. The company seemed to gaze upon the table with silent expectation; but this I easily excused. Men of wisdom, thought I, are ever slow of speech; they deliver nothing unadvisedly. "Silence," says Confucius, "is a friend that will never betray." They are now probably inventing maxims or hard sayings for their mutual instruction, when some one shall think proper to begin.

My curiosity was now wrought up to the highest pitch; I impatiently looked round to see if any were going to interrupt the mighty pause; when at last one of the company declared, that there was a sow in his neighbourhood that farrowed fifteen pigs at a litter. This I thought a very preposterous beginning; but just as another was going to second the remark, dinner was served, which interrupted the conversation for that time.

The appearance of dinner, which consisted of a variety of dishes, seemed to diffuse new cheerfulness upon every face; so that I now expected the philosophical conversation to begin, as they improved in good humour. The principal priest, however, opened his mouth with only observing, that the venison had not been kept enough, though he had given strict orders for having it killed ten days before. "I fear," continued he, "it will be found to want the true healthy flavour; you will find nothing of the original wildness in it." A priest, who sat next him, having smelt it, and wiped his nose, "Ah, my good lord," cries he, "you are too modest, it is perfectly fine; everybody knows that nobody understands keeping venison with your lordship." — "Ay, and partridges too," interrupted another; "I never find them right any where else." His lordship was going to reply, when a third took off the attention of the company, by recommending the pig as inimitable. "I fancy, my lord," continues he, "it has been smothered in its own blood." — "If it has been smothered in its blood," cried a facetious member, helping himself, "we'll now smother it in egg sauce." This poignant piece of humour produced a long luod laugh, which the facetious brother observing, and now that he was in luck, willing to second his blow, assured the company he would tell them a good story about that: "As good a story," cries he, bursting into a violent fit of laughter himself, "as you ever heard in your lives. There was a farmer in my parish who used to sup upon wild ducks and flummery; so this farmer——" "Doctor Marrowfat," cried his lordship, interrupting him; "give me leave to drink your health;" "so — being fond of wild ducks and flummery,——" "Doctor," adds a gentleman who sat next him, "let me advise you to a wing of this turkey;" — "so this farmer being fond——" "Hob [and] nob, Doctor, which do you choose, white or red?" — "so, being fond of wild ducks and flummery;——" "Take care of your band, Sir, it may dip in the gravy." The Doctor, now looking round, found not a single *eye* disposed to listen; wherefore, calling for a glass of wine, he gulped down the disappointment and the tale in a bumper.

The conversation now began to be a little more than a rhapsody of exclamations: as each had pretty well satisfied his own appetite, he now found sufficient time to press others. "Excellent! the very thing! let me recommend the pig." "Do but taste the bacon! never ate a better thing in my life: exquisite! delicious!" This edifying discourse continued through three courses, which lasted as many hours, till every one of the company was unable to swallow or utter any thing more.

It is very natural for men, who are abridged in one excess, to break into some other. The clergy here, particularly those who are advanced in years, think if they are abstemious with regard to women and wine, they may indulge their other appetites without censure. Thus some are found to rise in the morning only to a consultation with their cook about dinner, and, when that has been swallowed, make no other use of their faculties (if they have any) but to ruminate on the succeeding meal.

A debauch in wine is even more pardonable than this, since one glass insensibly leads on to another, and, instead of sating, whets the appetite. The progressive steps to it are cheerful and seducing; the grave are animated, the melancholy relieved, and ther is even classic authority to countenance the excess. But in eating, after nature is once satisfied, every additional morsel brings stupidity and distempers with it, and, as one of their own poets expresses it,—

> " The soul subsides, and wickedly inclines
> To seem but mortal, even in sound divines."

Let me suppose, after such a meal as this I have been describing, while all the company are sitting in lethargic silence round the table, grunting under a load of soup, pig, pork, and bacon; let me suppose, I say, some hungry beggar, with looks of want, peeping through one of the windows, and thus addressing the assembly: "Prithee, pluck those napkins from your chins; after nature is satisfied, all that you eat extraordinary is my property, and I claim it as mine. It was given you in order to relieve me, and not to oppress yourselves. How can they comfort or instruct others, who can scarce feel their own existence, except from the unsavoury returns of an ill-digested meal? But though neither you nor the cushions you sit upon will hear me, yet the world regards the excesses of its teachers with a prying eye, and notes their conduct with double severity." I know no other answer any one of the company could make to such an expostulation but this: "Friend, you talk of our losing a character, and being disliked by the world; well, and supposing all this to be true, what then! who cares for the world? We'll preach for the world, and the world shall pay us for preaching, whether we like each other or not."

CITIZEN OF THE WORLD

LETTER LXIV

To the Same

THE GREAT EXCHANGE HAPPINESS FOR SHOW. THEIR FOLLY IN THIS RESPECT OF USE TO SOCIETY

THE princes of Europe have found out a manner of rewarding their subjects who have behaved well, by presenting them with about two yards of blue ribbon, which is worn about the shoulder. They who are honoured with this mark of distinction are called knights, and the king himself is always the head of the order. This is a very frugal method of recompensing the most important services; and it is very fortunate for kings that their subjects are satisfied with such trifling rewards. Should a nobleman happen to lose his leg in battle, the king presents him with two yards of ribbon, and he is paid for the loss of his limb. Should an ambassador spend all his paternal fortune in supporting the honour of his country abroad, the king presents him with two yards of ribbon, which is to be considered as an equivalent to his estate. In short, while an European king has a yard of blue or green riband left, he need be under no apprehensions of wanting statesmen, generals, and soldiers.

I cannot sufficiently admire those kingdoms in which men with large patrimonial estates are willing thus to undergo real hardships for empty favours. A person, already possessed of a competent fortune, who undertakes to enter the career of ambition, feels many real inconveniences from his station, while it procures him no real happiness that he was not possessed of before. He could eat, drink, and sleep, before he became a courtier, as well, perhaps better, than when invested with his authority. He could command flatterers in a private station, as well as in his public capacity, and indulge at home every favourite inclination, uncensured and unseen by the people.

What real good, then, does an addition to a fortune already sufficient procure? Not any. Could the great man, by having his fortune increased, increase also his appetites, then precedence might be attended with real amusement.

Was he, by having his one thousand made two, thus enabled to enjoy two wives, or eat two dinners, then, indeed, he might be excused for undergoing some pain, in order to extend the sphere of his enjoyments. But, on the contrary, he finds his desire for pleasure often lessen, as he takes pains to be able to improve it; and his capacity of enjoyment diminishes as his fortune happens to increase.

Instead, therefore, of regarding the great with envy, I generally consider them with some share of compassion. I look upon them as a set of good-natured, misguided people, who are indebted to us, and not to themselves, for all the happiness they enjoy. For our pleasure, and not their own, they sweat under a cumbrous heap of finery; for our pleasure, the lackeyed train, the slow parading pageant, with all the gravity of grandeur, moves in review: a single coat, or a single footman, answers all the purposes of the most indolent refinement as well; and those who have twenty, may be said to keep one for their own pleasure, and the other nineteen merely for ours. So true is the observation of Confucius, "That we take greater pains to persuade others that we are happy, than in endeavouring to think so ourselves."

But though this desire of being seen, of being made the subject of discourse, and of supporting the dignities of an exalted station, be troublesome enough to the ambitious, yet it is well for society that there are men thus willing to exchange ease and safety for danger and a ribbon. We lose nothing by their vanity, and it would be unkind to endeavour to deprive a child of its rattle. If a duke or a duchess are willing to carry a long train for our entertainment, so much the worse for themselves; if they choose to exhibit in public, with a hundred lackeys and mamelukes in their equipage, for our entertainment, still so much the worse for themselves; it is the spectators alone who give and receive the pleasure; they only [are] the sweating figures that swell the pageant.

A mandarine, who took much pride in appearing with a number of jewels on every part of his robe, was once accosted by an old sly bonze, who, following him through several streets, and bowing often to the ground, thanked him for his jewels. "What does the man mean?" cried the mandarine: "Friend, I never gave thee any of my jewels." — "No," replied the other; "but you have let me look at them, and that is all the use you can make of them yourself; so there is no difference between us, except that you have the trouble of watching them, and that is an employment I don't much desire." Adieu.

CITIZEN OF THE WORLD

LETTER LXV

To the Same

THE HISTORY OF A PHILOSOPHIC COBBLER

THOUGH not very fond of seeing a pageant myself, yet I am generally pleased with being in the crowd which sees it: it is amusing to observe the effect which such a spectacle has upon the variety of faces; the pleasure it excites in some, the envy in others, and the wishes it raises in all. With this design I lately went to see the entry of a foreign ambassador, resolved to make one in the mob, to shout as they shouted, to fix with earnestness upon the same frivolous objects, and participate for a while the pleasures and the wishes of the vulgar.

Struggling here for some time, in order to be first to see the cavalcade as it passed, some one of the crowd unluckily happened to tread upon my shoe, and tore it in such a manner, that I was utterly unqualified to march forward with the main body, and obliged to fall back in the rear. Thus rendered incapable of being a spectator of the show myself, I was at least willing to observe the spectators, and limped behind like one of the invalids which follow the march of an army.

In this plight, as I was considering the eagerness that appeared on every face, how some bustled to get foremost, and others contented themselves with taking a transient peep when they could; how some praised the four black servants that were stuck behind one of the equipages, and some the ribbons that decorated the horses' necks in another, my attention was called off to an object more extraordinary than any I had yet seen: a poor cobbler sat in his stall by the way-side, and continued to work, while the crowd passed by, without testifying the smallest share of curiosity. I own his want of attention excited mine; and as I stood in need of his assistance, I thought it best to employ a philosophic cobbler on this occasion. Perceiving my business, therefore, he desired me to enter and sit down, took my shoe in his lap, and began to mend it with his usual indifference and taciturnity.

"How, my friend," said I to him, "can you continue to work, while all those fine things are passing by your door?" "Very fine they are, master," returned the cobbler, "for those that like them to be sure; but what are all those fine things to me? You don't know what it is to be a cobbler, and so much the better for yourself. Your bread is baked: you may go and see sights the whole day, and eat a warm supper when you come home at night; but for me, if I should run hunting after all these fine folk, what should I get by my journey but an appetite, and, God help me! I have too much of that at home already, without stirring out for it. Your people who may eat four meals a-day, and a supper at night, are but a bad example to such a one as I. No, master, as God has called me into this world in order to mend old shoes, I have no business with fine folk, and they no business with me." I here interrupted him with a smile. "See this last, master," continues he, "and this hammer; this last and hammer are the two best friends I have in this world; nobody else will be my friend, because I want a friend. The great folks you saw pass by just now have five hundred friends, because they have no occasion for them: now, while I stick to my good friends here, I am very contented; but when I ever so little run after sights and fine things, I begin to hate my work; I grow sad, and have no heart to mend shoes any longer."

This discourse only served to raise my curiosity to know more of a man whom nature had thus formed into a philosopher. I therefore insensibly led him into a history of his adventures: "I have lived," said he, "a wandering sort of a life now five-and-fifty years, here to-day, and gone to-morrow; for it was my misfortune, when I was young, to be fond of changing." — "You have been a traveller, then, I presume," interrupted I. "I cannot boast much of travelling," continued he, "for I have never left the parish in which I was born but three times in my life, that I can remember; but then there is not a street in the whole neighbourhood that I have not lived in, at some time or another. When I began to settle and to take to my business in one street, some unforeseen misfortune, or a desire of trying my luck elsewhere, has removed me, perhaps a whole mile away from my former customers, while some more lucky cobbler would come into my place, and make a handsome fortune among friends of my making: there was one who actually died in a stall that I had left, worth seven pounds seven shillings, all in hard gold, which he had quilted into the waistband of his breeches."

I could not but smile at these migrations of a man by the fireside, and continued to ask if he had ever been married. "Ay, that I have, master," replied he, "for sixteen long years; and a weary life I had of it, Heaven knows. My wife took it into her head, that the only way to thrive in this world was to save money; so, though our comings-in were but about three shillings a-week, all that ever she could lay her hands upon she used to hide away from me, though we were obliged to starve the whole week after for it.

"The first three years we used to quarrel about this every day, and I always got the better; but she had a hard spirit, and still continued to hide as usual: so that I was at last tired of quarrelling and getting the better, and she scraped and scraped at pleasure, till I was almost starved to death. Her conduct drove me at last in despair to the alehouse; here I used to sit with people who hated home like myself, drank while I had money left, and ran in score when any body would trust me; till at last the landlady coming one day with a long bill when I was from home, and putting it into my wife's hands, the length of it effectually broke her heart. I searched the whole stall, after she was dead, for money, but she had hidden it so effectually, that, with all my pains, I could never find a farthing."

By this time my shoe was mended, and satisfying the poor artist for his trouble, and rewarding him besides for his information, I took my leave, and returned home to lengthen out the amusement his conversation afforded, by communicating it to my friend. Adieu.

LETTER LXXI

To the Same

THE SHABBY BEAU, THE MAN IN BLACK, THE CHINESE PHILOSOPHER, ETC., AT VAUXHALL

THE people of London are as fond of walking as our friends at Pekin of riding; one of the principal entertainments of the citizens here in summer is to repair about nightfall to a garden not far from town, where they walk about, show their best clothes and best faces, and listen to a concert provided for the occasion.

I accepted an invitation a few evenings ago from my old friend, the man in black, to be one of a party that was to sup there; and at the appointed hour waited upon him at his lodgings. There I found the company assembled, and expecting my arrival. Our party consisted of my friend in superlative finery, his stockings rolled, a black velvet waistcoat, which was formerly new, and a grey wig combed down in imitation of hair; a pawnbroker's widow, of whom, by the by, my friend was a professed admirer, dressed out in green damask, with three gold rings on every finger; Mr. Tibbs, the second-rate beau I have formerly described, together with his lady, in flimsy silk, dirty gauze instead of linen, and a hat as big as an umbrella.

Our first difficulty was in settling how we should set out. Mrs. Tibbs had a natural aversion to the water, and the widow, being a little in flesh, as warmly protested against walking; a coach was therefore agreed upon; which being too small to carry five, Mr. Tibbs consented to sit in his wife's lap.

In this manner, therefore, we set forward, being entertained by the way with the bodings of Mr. Tibbs, who assured us he did not expect to see a single creature for the evening above the degree of a cheesemonger; that this was the last night of the gardens, and that consequently we should be pestered with the nobility and gentry from Thames Street and Crooked Lane; with several other prophetic ejaculations, probably inspired by the uneasiness of his situation.

The illuminations began before we arrived, and I must confess, that upon entering the gardens I found every sense overpaid with more than expected pleasure; the lights every where glimmering through the scarcely-moving trees — the full-bodied concert bursting on the stillness of the night — the natural concert of the birds, in the more retired part of the grove vieing with that which was formed by art; the company gaily dressed, looking satisfaction, and the table spread with various delicacies, all conspired to fill my imagination with the visionary happiness of the Arabian lawgiver, and lifted me into an ecstasy of admiration. "Head of Confucius," cried I to my friend, "this is fine! this unites rural beauty with courtly magnificence! If we expect the virgins of immortality, that hang on every tree, and may be plucked at every desire, I do not see how this falls short of Mahomet's Paradise!" — "As for virgins," cries my friend, "it is true they are a fruit that do not much abound in our gardens here; but if ladies, as plenty as apples in autumn, and as complying as any Houri of them all, can content you, I fancy we have no need to go to heaven for Paradise."

I was going to second his remarks, when we were called to a consultation by Mr. Tibbs and the rest of the company, to know in what manner we were to lay out the evening to the greatest advantage. Mrs. Tibbs was for keeping the genteel walk of the garden, where, she observed, there was always the very best company; the widow, on the contrary, who came but once a season, was for securing a good standing place to see the waterworks, which she assured us would begin in less than an hour at farthest; a dispute therefore began, and as it was managed between two of very opposite characters, it threatened to grow more bitter at every reply. Mrs. Tibbs wondered how people could pretend to know the polite world, who had received all their rudiments of breeding behind a counter; to which the other replied, that though some people sat behind counters, yet they could sit at the head of their own tables too, and carve three good dishes of hot meat whenever they thought proper, which was more than some people could say for themselves, that hardly knew a rabbit and onions from a green goose and gooseberries.

It is hard to say where this might have ended, had not the husband, who probably knew the impetuosity of his wife's disposition, proposed to end the dispute by adjourning to a box, and try if there was any thing to be had for supper that was supportable. To this we all consented; but here a new distress arose; Mr. and Mrs. Tibbs would sit in none but a genteel box — a box where they might see and be seen — one, as they expressed it, in the very focus of public view; but such a box was not easy to be obtained, for though we were perfectly convinced of our own gentility, and the gentility of our appearance, yet we found it a difficult matter to persuade the keepers of the boxes to be of our opinion; they chose to reserve genteel boxes for what they judged more genteel company.

At last, however, we were fixed, though somewhat obscurely, and supplied with the usual entertainment of the place. The widow found the supper excellent, but Mrs. Tibbs thought every thing detestable. "Come, come, my dear," cries the husband, by way of consolation, "to be sure we can't find such dressing here as we have at Lord Crump's or Lady Crimp's; but, for Vauxhall dressing, it is pretty good: it is not their victuals, indeed, I find fault with, but their wine; their wine," cries he, drinking off a glass, "indeed, is most abominable."

By this last contradiction, the widow was fairly conquered in point of politeness. She perceived now that she had no pretensions in the world to taste; her very senses were vulgar, since she had praised detestable custard, and smacked at wretched wine; she was therefore content to yield the victory, and for the rest of the night to listen and improve. It is true, she would now and then forget herself, and confess she was pleased, but they soon brought her back again to miserable refinement. She once praised the painting of the box in which we were sitting, but was soon convinced that such paltry pieces ought rather to excite horror than satisfaction: she ventured again to commend one of the singers, but Mrs. Tibbs soon let her know, in the style of a connoisseur, that the singer in question had neither ear, voice, nor judgment.

Mr. Tibbs, now, willing to prove that his wife's pretensions to music were just, entreated her to favour the company with a song; but to this she gave a positive denial — "for you know very well, my dear," says she, "that I am not in voice to-day, and when one's voice is not equal to one's judgment, what signifies singing? besides, as there is no accompaniment, it would be but spoiling music." All these excuses, however, were overruled by the rest of the company, who, though one would think they already had music enough, joined in the entreaty. But particularly the widow, now willing to convince the company of her breeding, pressed so warmly, that she seemed determined to take no refusal. At last, then, the lady complied, and after humming for some minutes, began with such a voice, and such affectation, as, I could perceive, gave but little satisfaction to any except her husband. He sat with rapture in his eye, and beat time with his hand on the table.

You must observe, my friend, that it is the custom of this country, when a lady or gentleman happens to sing, for the company to sit as mute and motionless as statues. Every feature, every limb, must seem to correspond in fixed attention; and while the song continues, they are to remain in a state of universal petrifaction. In this mortifying situation we had continued for some time, listening to the song, and looking with tranquillity, when the master of the box came to inform us, that the waterworks were going to begin. At this information I could instantly perceive the widow bounce from her seat; but correcting herself, she sat down again, repressed by motives of good breeding. Mrs. Tibbs, who had seen the waterworks a hundred times, resolving not to be interrupted, continued her song without any share of mercy, nor had the smallest pity on our impatience. The widow's face, I own, gave me high entertainment; in it I could plainly read the struggle she felt between good-breeding and curiosity: she talked of the waterworks the whole evening before, and seemed to have come merely in order to see them; but then she could not bounce out in the very middle of a song, for that would be forfeiting all pretensions to high life, or high-lived company, ever after. Mrs. Tibbs, therefore, kept on singing, and we continued to listen, till at last, when the song was just concluded, the waiter came to inform us that the waterworks were over!

"The waterworks over!" cried the widow; "the waterworks over already! that's impossible! they can't be over so soon!"— "It is not my business," replied the fellow, "to contradict your ladyship; I'll run again and see." He went, and soon returned with a confirmation of the dismal tidings. No ceremony could now bind my friend's disappointed mistress; she testified her displeasure in the openest manner: in short, she now began to find fault in turn, and at last insisted upon going home, just at the time that Mr. and Mrs. Tibbs assured the company, that the polite hours were going to begin, and that the ladies would instantaneously be entertained with the horns. Adieu.

LETTER LXXIV

To the Same

THE DESCRIPTION OF A LITTLE GREAT MAN

IN reading the newspapers here, I have reckoned up not less than twenty-five great men, seventeen very great men, and nine very extraordinary men, in less than the compass of half-a-year. "These," say the gazettes, "are the men that posterity are to gaze at with admiration; these the names that Fame will be employed in holding up for the astonishment of succeeding ages." Let me see — forty-six great men in half-a-year, amount to just ninety-two in a year. I wonder how posterity will be able to remember them all, or whether the people in future times will have any other business to mind, but that of getting the catalogue by heart.

Does the mayor of a corporation make a speech?—he is instantly set down for a great man.—Does a pedant digest his commonplace-book into a folio?—he quickly becomes great. Does a poet string up trite sentiments in rhyme? he also becomes the great man of the hour. How diminutive soever the object of admiration, each is followed by a crowd of still more diminutive admirers. The shout begins in his train; onward he marches to immortality; looks back at the pursuing crowd with self-satisfaction; catching all the oddities, the whimsies, the absurdities, and the littlenesses of conscious greatness by the way.

I was yesterday invited by a gentleman to dinner, who promised that our entertainment should consist of a haunch of venison, a turtle, and a great man. I came according to appointment. The venison was fine, the turtle good, but the great man insupportable. The moment I ventured to speak, I was at once contradicted with a snap. I attempted, by a second and a third assault, to retrieve my lost reputation, but was still beat back with confusion. I was resolved to attack him once more from entrenchment, and turned the conversation upon the government of China: but even here he asserted, snapped, and contradicted as before. "Heavens," thought I, "this man pretends to know China even better than myself!" I looked round to see who was on my side; but every eye was fixed in admiration on the great man: I therefore at last thought proper to sit silent, and act the pretty gentleman during the ensuing conversation.

When a man has once secured a circle of admirers, he may be as ridiculous here as he thinks proper; and it all passes for elevation of sentiment, or learned absence. If he trangresses the common forms of breeding, mistakes even a teapot for a tobacco-box, it is said that his thoughts are fixed on more important objects: to speak and to act like the rest of mankind is to be no greater than they. There is something of oddity in the very idea of greatness; for we are seldom astonished at a thing very much resembling ourselves.

When the Tartars make a Lama, their first care is to place him in a dark corner of the temple: here he is to sit half concealed from view, to regulate the motion of his hands, lips, and eyes; but, above all, he is enjoined gravity and silence. This, however, is but the prelude to his apotheosis: a set of emissaries are dispatched among the people, to cry up his piety, gravity, and love of raw flesh; the people take them at their word, approach the Lama, now become an idol, with the most humble prostration; he receives their addresses without motion, commences a god, and is ever after fed by his priests with the spoon of immortality. The same receipt in this country serves to make a great man. The idol only keeps close, sends out his little emissaries to be hearty in his praise; and straight, whether statesman or author, he is set down in the list of fame, continuing to be praised while it is fashionable to praise, or while he prudently keeps his minuteness concealed from the public.

I have visited many countries, and have been in cities without number, yet never did I enter a town which could not produce ten or twelve of those little great men; all fancying themselves known to the rest of the world, and complimenting each other upon their extensive reputation. It is amusing enough when two of those domestic prodigies of learning mount the stage of ceremony, and give and take praise from each other. I have been present when a German doctor, for having pronounced a panegyric upon a certain monk, was thought the most ingenious man in the world; till the monk soon after divided this reputation by returning the compliment; by which means, they both marched off with universal applause.

The same degree of undeserved adulation that attends our great man while living, often also follows him to the tomb. It frequently happens that one of his little admirers sits down, big with the important subject, and is delivered of the history of his life and writings. This may properly be called the revolutions of a life between the fireside and the easy chair. In this we learn the year in which he was born, at what an early age he gave symptoms of uncommon genius and 'application, together with some of his smart sayings, collected by his aunt and mother while yet but a boy. The next book introduces him to the university, where we are informed of his amazing progress in learning, his excellent skill in darning stockings, and his new invention for papering books to save the covers. He next makes his appearance in the republic of letters, and publishes his folio. Now the colossus is reared, his works are eagerly bought up by all the purchasers of scarce books. The learned societies invite him to become a member: he disputes against some foreigner with a long Latin name, conquers in the controversy, is complimented by several authors of gravity and importance, is excessively fond of egg-sauce with his pig, becomes president of a literary club and dies in the meridian of his glory. Happy they who thus have some little faithful attendant, who never forsakes them, but prepares to wrangle and to praise against every opposer; at once ready to increase their pride while living, and their character when dead! For you and me, my friend, who have no humble admirer thus to attend us — we, who neither are, nor never will be, great men, and who do not much care whether we are great men or no, at least let us strive to be honest men, and to have common sense. [Adieu.]

LETTER LXXVII

To the Same

THE BEHAVIOUR OF A SHOPKEEPER AND HIS JOURNEYMAN

THE shops of London are as well furnished as those of Pekin. Those of London have a picture hung at their door, informing the passengers what they have to sell, as those at Pekin have a board to assure the buyer that they have no intentions to cheat him.

I was this morning to buy silk for a nightcap: immediately upon entering the mercer's shop, the master and his two men, with wigs plastered with powder, appeared to ask my commands. They were certainly the civilest people alive; if I but looked, they flew to the place where I cast my eye; every motion of mine sent them running round the whole shop for my satisfaction. I informed them that I wanted what was good, and they showed me not less than forty pieces, and each was better than the former, the prettiest pattern in nature, and the fittest in the world for nightcaps. "My very good friend," said I to the mercer, "you must not pretend to instruct me in silks; I know these in particular to be no better than your mere flimsy Bungees." — "That may be," cried the mercer, who, I afterwards found, had never contradicted a man in his life; "I can't pretend to say but they may; but I can assure you, my Lady Trail has had a sacque from this piece this very morning." — "But friend," said I, "though my lady has chosen a sacque from it, I see no necessity that I should wear it for a nightcap." — "That may be," returned he again, "yet what becomes a pretty lady, will at any time look well on a handsome gentleman." This short compliment was thrown in so very seasonably upon my ugly face, that even though I disliked the silk, I desired him to cut me off the pattern of a nightcap.

While this business was consigned to his journeymen, the master himself took down some pieces of silk still finer than any I had yet seen, and spreading them before me, "There," cries he, "there's beauty; my Lord Snakeskin has bespoke the fellow to this for the birth-night this very morning; it would look charmingly in waistcoats." — "But I don't want a waistcoat," replied I. "Not want a waistcoat!" returned the mercer, "then I would advise you to buy one; when waistcoats are wanted, you may depend upon it they will come dear. Always buy before you want, and you are sure to be well used, as they say in Cheapside." There was so much justice in his advice, that I could not refuse taking it; besides, the silk, which was really a good one, increased the temptation; so I gave orders for that too.

As I was waiting to have my bargains measured and cut, which, I know not how, they executed but slowly, during the interval the mercer entertained me with the modern manner of some of the nobility receiving company in their morning gowns; "Perhaps, Sir," adds he, "you have a mind to see what kind of silk is universally worn." Without waiting for my reply, he spreads a piece before me, which might be reckoned beautiful even in China. "If the nobility," continues he, "were to know I sold this to any under a Right Honourable, I should certainly lose their custom; you see, my Lord, it is at once rich, tasty, and quite the thing." — "I am no Lord," interrupted I. — "I beg pardon," cried he; "but be pleased to remember, when you intend buying a morning gown, that you had an offer from me of something worth money. Conscience, Sir, conscience is my way of dealing; you may buy a morning gown now, or you may stay till they become dearer and less fashionable; but it is not my business to advise." In short, most reverend Fum, he persuaded me to buy a morning gown also, and would probably have persuaded me to have bought half the goods in his shop, if I had stayed long enough, or was furnished with sufficient money.

Upon returning home, I could not help reflecting, with some astonishment, how this very man, with such a confined education and capacity, was yet capable of turning me as he thought proper, and moulding me to his inclinations! I knew he was only answering his own purposes, even while he attempted to appear solicitous about mine: yet, by a voluntary infatuation, a sort of passion compounded of vanity and good-nature, I walked into the snare with my eyes open, and put myself to future pain in order to give him immediate pleasure. The wisdom of the ignorant somewhat resembles the instinct of animals; it is diffused in but a very narrow sphere, but within that circle it acts with vigour, uniformity, and success. Adieu.

CITIZEN OF THE WORLD

LETTER LXXVIII

To the Same

THE FRENCH RIDICULED AFTER THEIR OWN MANNER

FROM my former accounts, you may be apt to fancy the English the most ridiculous people under the sun. They are indeed ridiculous; yet every other nation in Europe is equally so; each laughs at each, and the Asiatic at all.

I may, upon another occasion, point out what is most strikingly absurd in other countries; I shall at present confine myself only to France. The first national peculiarity a traveller meets upon entering that kingdom, is an odd sort of staring vivacity in every eye, not excepting even the children; the people, it seems, have got it into their heads, that they have more wit than others, and so stare, in order to look smart.

I know not how it happens, but there appears a sickly delicacy in the faces of their finest women. This may have introduced the use of paint, and paint produces wrinkles; so that a fine lady shall look like a hag at twenty-three. But as, in some measure, they never appear young, so it may be equally asserted, that they actually think themselves never old; a gentle Miss shall prepare for new conquests at sixty, shall hobble a rigadoon when she can scarce walk out without a crutch; she shall affect the girl, play her fan and her eyes, and talk of sentiments, bleeding hearts, and expiring for love, when actually dying with age. Like a departing philosopher she attempts to make her last moments the most brilliant of her life.

Their civility to strangers is what they are chiefly proud of; and, to confess sincerely, their beggars are the very politest beggars I ever knew: in other places a traveller is addressed with a piteous whine, or a sturdy solemnity, but a French beggar shall ask your charity with a very genteel bow, and thank you for it with a smile and a shrug.

Another instance of this people's breeding I must not forget. An Englishman would not speak his native language in a company of foreigners, where he was sure that none understood him; a travelling Hottentot himself would be silent if acquainted only with the language of his country; but a Frenchman shall talk to you whether you understand his language or not; never troubling

CITIZEN OF THE WORLD

his head whether you have learned French, still he keeps up the conversation, fixes his eye full in your face, and asks a thousand questions, which he answers himself, for want of a more satisfactory reply.

But their civility to foreigners is not half so great as their admiration of themselves. Every thing that belongs to them and their nation is great, magnificent beyond expression, quite romantic! every garden is a paradise, every hovel a palace, and every woman an angel. They shut their eyes close, throw their mouths wide open, and cry out in a rapture, "*Sacre!* what beauty! *O Ciel!* what taste! *Mort de ma vie!* what grandeur! was ever any people like ourselves? we are the nation of men, and all the rest no better than two-legged barbarians."

I fancy the French would make the best cooks in the world if they had but meat; as it is, they can dress you out five different dishes from a nettle-top, seven from a dock-leaf, and twice as many from a frog's haunches; these eat prettily enough when one is a little used to them, are easy of digestion, and seldom overload the stomach with crudities. They seldom dine under seven hot dishes: it is true, indeed, with all this magnificence, they seldom spread a cloth before the guests; but in that I cannot be angry with them, since those who have got no linen on their backs, may very well be excused for wanting it on their tables.

Even religion itself loses its solemnity among them. Upon their roads, at about every five miles distance, you see an image of the Virgin Mary, dressed up in grim head-clothes, painted cheeks, and an old red petticoat; before her a lamp is often kept burning, at which, with the saint's permission, I have frequently lighted my pipe. Instead of the Virgin, you are sometimes presented with a crucifix, at other times with a wooden Saviour, fitted out in complete garniture, with sponge, spear, nails, pincers, hammer, beeswax, and vinegar-bottle. Some of those images, I have been told, came down from heaven; if so, in heaven they have but bungling workmen.

In passing through their towns, you frequently see the men sitting at the doors knitting stockings, while the care of cultivating the ground and pruning the vines falls to the women. This is, perhaps, the reason why the fair sex are granted some peculiar privileges in this country; particularly, when they can get horses, of riding without a side-saddle.

France, Plate I.

CITIZEN OF THE WORLD

But I begin to think you may find this description pert and dull enough; perhaps it is so; yet, in general, it is the manner in which the French usually describe foreigners; and it is but just to *force* a part of that ridicule back upon them, which they attempt to lavish on others. Adieu.

LETTER LXXIX

To the Same

THE PREPARATIONS OF BOTH THEATRES, FOR A WINTER CAMPAIGN

THE two theatres which serve to amuse the citizens here, are again opened for the winter. The mimetic troops, different from those of the state, begin their campaign when all the others quit the field; and, at a time when the Europeans cease to destroy each other in reality, they are entertained with mock battles upon the stage.

The dancing master once more shakes his quivering feet; the carpenter prepares his paradise of pasteboard; the hero resolves to cover his forehead with brass, and the heroine begins to scour up her copper tail, preparative to future operations; in short, all are in motion, from the theatrical letter carrier in yellow clothes, to Alexander the Great that stands on a stool.

Both houses have already commenced hostilities. War, open war, and no quarter received or given! Two singing women, like heralds, have begun the contest; the whole town is divided on this solemn occasion; one has the finest pipe, the other the finest manner; one curtsies to the ground, the other salutes the audience with a smile; one comes on with modesty which asks, the other with boldness which extorts applause; one wears powder, the other has none; one has the longest waist, but the other appears most easy: all, all is important and serious; the town as yet perseveres in its neutrality; a cause of such moment demands the most mature deliberation; they continue to exhibit, and it is very possible this contest may continue to please to the end of the season.

But the generals of either army have, as I am told, several reinforcements to lend occasional assistance. If they produce a pair of diamond buckles at one house, we have a pair of eyebrows that can match them at the other. If we outdo them in our attitude, they can overcome us by a shrug; if we can bring more children on the stage, they can bring more guards in red clothes, who strut and shoulder their swords to the astonishment of every spectator.

They tell me here, that people frequent the theatre in order to be instructed as well as amused. I smile to hear the assertion. If I ever go to one of their playhouses, what with trumpets, hallooing behind the stage, and bawling upon it, I am quite dizzy before the performance is over. If I enter the house with any sentiments in my head, I am sure to have none going away, the whole mind being filled with a dead march, a funeral procession, a cat-call, a jig, or a tempest.

There is, perhaps, nothing more easy than to write properly for the English theatre; I am amazed that none are apprenticed to the trade. The author, when well acquainted with the value of thunder and lightning; when versed in all the mystery of scene-shifting and trap-doors; when skilled in the proper periods to introduce a wire-walker or a waterfall; when instructed in every actor's peculiar talent, and capable of adapting his speeches to the supposed excellence; when thus instructed, he knows all that can give a modern audience pleasure. One player shines in an exclamation, another in a groan, a third in a horror, a fourth in a start, a fifth in a smile, a sixth faints, and a seventh fidgets round the stage with peculiar vivacity; that piece, therefore, will succeed best, where each has a proper opportunity of shining: the actor's business is not so much to adapt himself to the poet, as the poet's to adapt himself to the actor.

The great secret, therefore, of tragedy writing, at present, is a perfect acquaintance with theatrical "ah"'s and "oh"'s; a certain number of these, interspersed with "gods!" "tortures!" "racks!" and "damnation!" shall distort every actor almost into convulsions, and draw tears from every spectator; a proper use of these will infallibly fill the whole house with applause. But, above all, a whining scene must strike most forcibly. I would advise, from my present knowledge of the audience, the two favourite players of the town to introduce a scene of this sort in every play. Towards the middle of the last act, I would have them enter with wild looks and outspread arms: there is no necessity for speaking, they are only to groan at each other; they must vary the tones of exclamation and despair through the whole theatrical gamut, wring their figures into every shape of distress, and, when their calamities have drawn a proper quantity of tears from the sympathetic spectators, they may go off in dumb solemnity at different doors, clasping their hands, or slapping their pocket-holes: this, which may be called a tragic pantomime, will answer every purpose of moving the passions as well as words could have done, and it must save those expenses which go to reward an author.

All modern plays that would keep the audience alive, must be conceived in this manner; and, indeed, many a modern play is made up on no other plan. This is the merit that lifts up the heart, like opium, into a rapture of insensibility, and can dismiss the mind from all the fatigue of thinking: this is the eloquence that shines in many a long forgotten scene, which has been reckoned excessive fine upon acting; this the lightning that flashes no less in the hyperbolical tyrant, *who breakfasts on the wind,* than in little Norval, *as harmless as the babe unborn.* Adieu.

LETTER LXXXI

To the Same

THE LADIES' TRAINS RIDICULED

I HAVE as yet given you but a short and imperfect description of the ladies of England. Woman, my friend, is a subject not easily understood, even in China; what, therefore, can be expected from my knowledge of the sex in a country where they are universally allowed to be ridldes, and I but a stranger?

To confess a truth, I was afraid to begin the description, lest the sex should undergo some new revolution before it was finished, and my picture should thus become old before it could well be said to have ever been new. To-day they are lifted upon stilts; to-morrow they lower their heels, and raise their heads; their clothes at one time are bloated out with whalebone; at present they have laid their hoops aside, and are become as slim as mermaids. All, all is in a state of continual fluctuation, from the mandarine's wife who rattles through the streets in her chariot, to the humble sempstress who clatters over the pavement in iron-shod pattens.

What chiefly distinguishes the sex at present is the train. As a lady's quality or fashion was once determined here by the circumference of her hoop, both are now measured by the length of her tail. Women of moderate fortunes are contented with tails mod-

CITIZEN OF THE WORLD

erately long; but ladies of true taste and distinction set no bounds to their ambition in this particular. I am told the Lady Mayoress, on days of ceremony, carries one longer than a bell-wether of Bantam, whose tail, you know, is trundled along in a wheel-barrow.

Sun of China, what contradictions do we find in this strange world! not only the people of different countries think in opposition to each other, but the inhabitants of a single island are often found inconsistent with themselves. Would you believe it? this very people, my Fum, who are so fond of seeing their women with long tails, at the same time dock their horses to the very rump! ! !

But you may easily guess, that I am no ways displeased with a fashion which tends to increase a demand for the commodities of the East, and is so very beneficial to the country in which I was born. Nothing can be better calculated to increase the price of silk than the present manner of dressing. A lady's train is not bought but at some expense, and after it has swept the public walks for a very few evenings, is fit to be worn no longer: more silk must be bought in order to repair the breach, and some ladies of peculiar economy are thus found to patch up their tails eight or ten times in a season. This unnecessary consumption may introduce poverty here, but then we shall be the richer for it in China.

The man in black, who is a professed enemy to this manner of ornamenting the tail, assures me, there are numberless inconveniences attending it, and that a lady dressed up to the fashion is as much a cripple as any in Nankin. But his chief indignation is levelled at those who dress in this manner without a proper fortune to support it. He assures me, that he has known some who would have a tail though they wanted a petticoat; and others, who, without any other pretensions, fancied they became ladies, merely from the addition of three superfluous yards of ragged silk: — "I know a thrifty good woman," continues he, "who thinking herself obliged to carry a train like her betters, never walks from home without the uneasy apprehension of wearing it out too soon: every excursion she makes, gives her new anxiety; and her train is every bit as importunate, and wounds her peace as much as the bladder we sometimes see tied to the tail of a cat."

Nay, he ventures to affirm, that a train may often bring a lady into the most critical circumstances: "for, should a rude fellow," says he, "offer to come up to ravish a kiss, and the lady attempt to avoid it, in retiring she must necessarily tread upon her train, and thus fall fairly upon her back; by which means, every one knows, — her clothes may be spoiled."

The ladies here make no scruple to laugh at the smallness of a Chinese slipper, but I fancy our wives at China would have a more real cause of laughter, could they but see the immoderate length of a European train. Head of Confucius! to view a human being crippling herself with a great unwieldy tail for our diversion! Backward she cannot go, forward she must move but slowly; and if ever she attempts to turn round, it must be in a circle not smaller than that described by the wheeling crocodile, when it would face an assailant. And yet to think that all this confers importance and majesty! to think that a lady acquires additional respect from fifteen yards of trailing taffety! I cannot contain — ha! ha! ha! this is certainly a remnant of European barbarity: the female Tartar, dressed in sheep skins, is in far more convenient drapery. Their own writers have sometimes inveighed against the absurdity of this fashion, but perhaps it has never been ridiculed so well as upon the Italian theatre, where Pasquariello being engaged to attend on the Countess of Fernambroco, having one of his hands employed in carrying her muff, and the other her lap-dog, he bears her train majestically along, by sticking it in the waistband of his breeches! Adieu.

LETTER LXXXVI

To the Same

THE RACES OF NEWMARKET RIDICULED. DESCRIPTION OF A CART RACE

OF all the places of amusement where gentlemen and ladies are entertained, I have not been yet to visit Newmarket. This, I am told, is a large field, where, upon certain occasions, three or four horses are brought together, then set a-running, and that horse which runs fastest wins the wager.

This is reckoned a very polite and fashionable amusement here, much more followed by the nobility than partridge fighting at Java, or paper kites in Madagascar. Several of the great here, I am told, understand as much of farriery as their grooms; and a horse, with any share of merit, can never want a patron among the nobility.

We have a description of this entertainment almost every day in some of the gazettes, as for instance: "On such a day the Give and Take Plate was run for between his Grace's Crab, his Lordship's Periwinkle, and 'Squire Smackem's Slamerkin. All rode their own horses. There was the greatest concourse of nobility that has been known here for several seasons. The odds were in favour of Crab in the beginning; but Slamerkin, after the first heat, seemed to have the match hollow; however, it was soon seen that Periwinkle improved in wind, which at last turned out accordingly; Crab was run to a stand still, Slamerkin was knocked up, and Periwinkle was brought in with universal applause." Thus, you see, Periwinkle received universal applause, and, no doubt, his lordship came in for some share of that praise which was so liberally bestowed upon Periwinkle. Sun of China! how glorious must the senator appear in his cap and leather breeches, his whip crossed in his mouth, and thus coming to the goal, amongst the shouts of grooms, jockeys, pimps, stable-bred dukes, and degraded generals!

From the description of this princely amusement, now transcribed, and from the great veneration I have for the characters of its principal promoters, I make no doubt but I shall look upon a horse-race with becoming reverence, predisposed as I am by a similar amusement, of which I have lately been a spectator; for just now I happened to have an opportunity of being present at a cart race.

Whether this contention between three carts of different parishes was promoted by a subscription among the nobility, or whether the grand jury, in council assembled, had gloriously combined to encourage plaustral merit, I cannot take upon me to determine; but certain it is, the whole was conducted with the utmost regularity and decorum, and the company, which made a brilliant appearance, were universally of opinion, that the sport was high, the running fine, and the riders influenced by no bribe.

It was run on the road from London, to a village called Brentford, between a turnip-cart, a dust-cart, and a dung-cart; each of the owners condescending to mount, and be his own driver. The odds, at starting, were Dust against Dung, five to four; but, after half a mile's going, the knowing ones found themselves all on the wrong side, and it was Turnip against the field, brass to silver.

Soon, however, the contest became more doubtful; Turnip indeed kept the way, but it was perceived that Dung had better bottom.

CITIZEN OF THE WORLD

The road re-echoed with the shouts of the spectators — "Dung against Turnip! Turnip against Dung!" was now the universal cry; neck and neck; one rode lighter, but the other had more judgment. I could not but particularly observe the ardour with which the fair sex espoused the cause of the different riders on this occasion; one was charmed with the unwashed beauties of Dung; another was captivated with the patibulary aspect of Turnip; while, in the meantime, unfortunate gloomy Dust, who came whipping behind, was cheered by the encouragement of some, and pity of all.

The contention now continued for some time, without a possibility of determining to whom victory designed the prize. The winning post appeared in view, and he who drove the turnip-cart assured himself of success; and successful he might have been, had his horse been as ambitious as he; but, upon approaching a turn from the road, which led homewards, the horse fairly stood still, and refused to move a foot farther. The dung-cart had scarce time to enjoy this temporary triumph, when it was pitched headlong into a ditch by the way-side, and the rider left to wallow in congenial mud. Dust, in the meantime, soon came up, and not being far from the post, came in, amidst the shouts and acclamations of all the spectators, and greatly caressed by all the quality of Brentford. Fortune was kind only to one, who ought to have been favourable to all; each had peculiar merit, each laboured hard to earn the prize, and each richly deserved the cart he drove.

I do not know whether this description may not have anticipated that which I intended giving of Newmarket. I am told, there is little else to be seen even there. There may be some minute differences in the dress of the spectators, but none at all in their understandings: the quality of Brentford are as remarkable for politeness and delicacy as the breeders of Newmarket. The quality of Brentford drive their own carts, and the honourable fraternity of Newmarket ride their own horses. In short, the matches in one place are as rational as those in the other; and it is more than probable, that turnips, dust, and dung, are all that can be found to furnish out description in either.

Forgive me, my friend; but a person like me, bred up in a philosophic seclusion, is apt to regard perhaps with too much asperity, those occurrences which sink man below his station in nature, and diminish the intrinsic value of humanity. Adieu.

CITIZEN OF THE WORLD

LETTER LXXXVIII

To the Same

THE LADIES ADVISED TO GET HUSBANDS. A STORY TO THIS PURPOSE

AS the instruction of the fair sex in this country is entirely committed to the care of foreigners; as their language-masters, music-masters, hair-frizzers, and governesses, are all from abroad, I had some intentions of opening a female academy myself, and made no doubt, as I was quite a foreigner, of meeting a favourable reception.

In this I intended to instruct the ladies in all the conjugal mysteries; wives should be taught the art of managing husbands, and maids the skill of properly choosing them. I would teach a wife how far she might venture to be sick, without giving disgust; she should be acquainted with the great benefits of the cholic in the stomach, and all the thorough-bred insolence of fashion. Maids should learn the secret of nicely distinguishing every competitor; they should be able to know the difference between a pedant and a scholar, a citizen and a prig, a squire and his horse, a beau and his monkey; but chiefly, they should be taught the art of managing their smiles, from the contemptuous simper to the long laborious laugh.

But I have discontinued the project; for what would signify teaching ladies the manner of governing or choosing husbands, when marriage is at present so much out of fashion, that a lady is very well off who can get any husband at all? Celibacy now prevails in every rank of life; the streets are crowded with old bachelors, and the houses with ladies who have refused good offers, and are never likely to receive any for the future.

The only advice, therefore, I could give the fair sex, as things stand at present, is to get husbands as fast as they can. There is certainly nothing in the whole creation, not even Babylon in ruins, more truly deplorable than a lady in the virgin bloom of sixty-three, or a battered unmarried beau, who squibs about from place to place, showing his pigtail wig and his ears. The one appears to my imagination in the form of a double nightcap, or a roll of pomatum; the other in the shape of an electuary, or a box of pills.

I would once more, therefore, advise the ladies to get husbands.

CITIZEN OF THE WORLD

I would desire them not to discard an old lover without very sufficient reasons, nor treat the new with ill-nature till they know him false; let not prudes allege the falseness of the sex, coquettes the pleasures of long courtship, or parents the necessary preliminaries of penny for penny. I have reasons that would silence even a casuist in this particular. In the first place, therefore, I divide the subject into fifteen heads, and then, *sic argumentor*, — But, not to give you and myself the spleen, be contented at present with an Indian tale: —

[THE MAN-FISH.]

IN a winding of the river Amidar, just before it falls into the Caspian Sea, there lies an island unfrequented by the inhabitants of the continent. In this seclusion, blest with all that wild uncultivated nature could bestow, lived a princess and her two daughters. She had been wrecked upon the coast while her children as yet were infants, who, of consequence, though grown up, were entirely unacquainted with man. Yet, inexperienced as the young ladies were in the opposite sex, both early discovered symptoms, the one of prudery, the other of being a coquette. The eldest was ever learning maxims of wisdom and discretion from her mamma, while the youngest employed all her hours in gazing at her own face in a neighbouring fountain.

Their usual amusement in this solitude was fishing. Their mother had taught them all the secrets of the art; she showed them which were the most likely places to throw out the line, what baits were most proper for the various seasons, and the best manner to draw up the finny prey, when they had hooked it. In this manner they spent their time, easy and innocent, till one day, the Princess being indisposed, desired them to go and catch her a sturgeon or a shark for supper, which she fancied might sit easy on her stomach. The daughters obeyed, and clapping on a gold fish, the usual bait on those occasions, went and sat upon one of the rocks, letting the gilded hook glide down with the stream.

On the opposite shore, farther down, at the mouth of the river, lived a diver for pearls, a youth who, by long habit in his trade, was almost grown amphibious; so that he could remain whole hours at the bottom of the water, without ever fetching breath. He happened to be at that very instant diving when the ladies were fishing with the gilded hook. Seeing therefore the bait, which to him had the appearance of real gold, he was resolved to seize the prize, but both his hands being already filled with pearl oysters, he found himself obliged to snap at it with his mouth. The consequence is easily imagined; the hook, before unperceived, was instantly fastened in his jaw, nor could he, with all his efforts, or his floundering, get free.

"Sister," cries the youngest Princess, "I have certainly caught a monstrous fish; I never perceived any thing struggle so at the end of my line before; come and help me to draw it in." They both now, therefore, assisted in fishing up the diver on shore; but nothing could equal their surprise on seeing him. "Bless my eyes!" cries the prude, "what have we got here? this is a very odd fish to be sure; I never saw anything in my life look so queer: what eyes, what terrible claws, what a monstrous snout! I have read of this monster somewhere before — it certainly must be a *tanlang*, that eats women; let us throw it back again into the sea where we found it."

The diver, in the meantime, stood upon the beach at the end of the line, with the hook in his mouth, using every art that he thought could best excite pity, and particularly looking extremely tender, which is usual in such circumstances. The coquette, therefore, in some measure influenced by the innocence of his looks, ventured to contradict her companion. "Upon my word, sister," says she, "I see nothing in the animal so very terrible as you are pleased to apprehend; I think it may serve well enough for a change. Always sharks, and sturgeons, and lobsters, and crawfish, make me quite sick. I fancy a slice of this, nicely grilled, and dressed up with shrimp sauce, would be very pretty eating. I fancy mamma would like a bit with pickles above all things in the world; and if it should not sit easy on her stomach, it will be time enough to discontinue it when found disagreeable, you know." — "Horrid!" cries the prude, "would the girl be poisoned? I tell you it is a *tanlang*; I have read of it in twenty places. It is everywhere described as being the most pernicious animal that ever infested the ocean. I am certain it is the most insidious ravenous creature in the world, and is certain destruction if taken internally." The youngest sister was now therefore obliged to submit: both assisted in drawing the hook with some violence from the diver's jaw; and he, finding himself at liberty, beat his breast against the broad wave, and disappeared in an instant.

Just at this juncture the mother came down to the beach, to know the cause of her daughters' delay; they told her every circumstance, describing the monster they had caught. The old lady was one of the most discreet women in the world; she was called the Black-eyed Princess, from two black eyes she had received in her youth, being a little addicted to boxing in her liquor. "Alas, my children," cries she, "what have you done! the fish you caught was a man-fish; one of the most tame domestic animals in the world. We could have let him run and play about the garden, and he would have been twenty times more entertaining than our squirrel or monkey." — "If that be all," says the young coquette, "we will fish for him again. If that be all, I'll hold three toothpicks to one pound of snuff, I catch him whenever I please." Accordingly they threw in their line once more; but with all their gilding, and paddling, and assiduity, they could never after catch the diver. In this state of solitude and disappointment, they continued for many years, still fishing, but without success; till at last the Genius of the place, in pity to their distresses, changed the prude into a shrimp, and the coquette into an oyster. Adieu.

LETTER XC

To the Same

THE ENGLISH SUBJECT TO THE SPLEEN

WHEN the men of this country are once turned of thirty they regularly retire every year, at proper intervals, to lie in of the *spleen*. The vulgar, unfurnished with the luxurious comforts of the soft cushion, down bed, and easy chair, are obliged, when the fit is on them, to nurse it up by drinking, idleness, and ill-humour. In such dispositions, unhappy is the foreigner who happens to cross them; his long chin, tarnished coat, or pinched hat, are sure to receive no quarter. If they meet no foreigner, however, to fight with, they are, in such cases, generally content with beating each other.

The rich, as they have more sensibility, are operated upon with greater violence by this disorder. Different from the poor, instead of becoming more insolent, they grow totally unfit for opposition. A general here, who would have faced a culverin when well, if the fit be on him, shall hardly find courage to snuff a candle. An admiral, who could have opposed a broadside without shrinking, shall sit whole days in his chamber, mobbed up in double nightcaps, shuddering at the intrusive breeze, and distinguishable from his wife only by his black beard and heavy eyebrows.

In the country, this disorder mostly attacks the fair sex; in town, it is most unfavourable to the men. A lady, who has pined whole years amidst cooing doves and complaining nightingales, in rural retirement, shall resume all her vivacity in one night at a city gaming-table; her husband, who roared, hunted, and got drunk at home, shall grow splenetic in town in proportion to his wife's good humour. Upon their arrival in London, they exchange their disorders. In consequence of her parties and excursions, he puts on the furred cap and scarlet stomacher, and perfectly resembles an Indian husband, who, when his wife is safely delivered, permits her to transact business abroad, while he undergoes all the formality of keeping his bed, and receiving all the condolence in her place.

But those who reside constantly in town, owe this disorder mostly to the influence of the weather. It is impossible to describe what a variety of transmutations an east wind shall produce; it has been known to change a lady of fashion into a parlour couch; an alderman into a plate of custard; and a dispenser of justice into a rat-trap. Even philosophers themselves are not exempt from its influence; it has often converted a poet into a coral and bells, and a patriot senator into a dumb waiter.

Some days ago I went to visit the man in black, and entered his house with that cheerfulness which the certainty of a favourable reception always inspires. Upon opening the door of his apartment, I found him with the most rueful face imaginable, in a morning gown and flannel nightcap, earnestly employed in learning to blow the German flute. Struck with the absurdity of a man in the decline of life thus blowing away all his constitution and spirits, even without the consolation of being musical, I ventured to ask what could induce him to attempt learning so difficult an instrument so late in life? To this he made no reply, but groaning, and still holding the flute to his lips, continued to gaze at me for some moments very angrily, and then proceeded to practise his gamut as before. After having produced a variety of the most hideous tones in nature, at last turning to me, he demanded, whether I did not think he had made a surprising progress **in two days**? "You see," continues he, "I have got the ambusheer already; and as for fingering, my master tells me, I shall have that in a few lessons more." I was so much astonished with this instance of inverted ambition, that I knew not what to reply, but soon discerned the cause of all his absurdities: my friend was under a metamorphosis by the power of spleen, and flute-blowing was unluckily become his adventitious passion.

In order, therefore, to banish his anxiety imperceptibly, by seeming to indulge it, I began to descant on those gloomy topics by which philosophers often get rid of their own spleen, by communicating it: the wretchedness of a man in this life; the happiness of some wrought out of the miseries of others; the necessity that wretches should expire under punishment, that rogues might enjoy affluence in tranquillity: I led him on from the inhumanity of the rich to the ingratitude of the beggar; from the insincerity of refinement to the fierceness of rusticity; and at last had the good fortune to restore him to his usual serenity of temper, by permitting him to expatiate upon all the modes of human misery.

"Some nights ago," says my friend, "sitting alone by my fire, I happened to look into an account of the detection of a set of men called the thief-takers. I read over the many hideous cruelties of those haters of mankind, of their pretended friendship to wretches they meant to betray, of their sending men out to rob, and then hanging them. I could not avoid sometimes interrupting the narrative, by crying out, 'Yet these are men!' As I went on, I was informed that they had lived by this practice several years, and had been enriched by the price of blood: 'And yet,' cried I, 'I have been sent into this world, and am desired to call these men my brothers!' I read, that the very man who led the condemned wretch to the gallows, was he who falsely swore his life away; 'and yet,' continued I, 'that perjurer had just such a nose, such lips, such hands, and such eyes, as Newton!' I at last came to the account of the wretch that was searched after robbing one of the thief-takers of half-a-crown. Those of the confederacy knew that he had got but that single half-crown in the world; after a long search, therefore, which they knew would be fruitless, and taking from him the half-crown, which they knew was all he had, one of the gang compassionately cried out, 'Alas! poor creature, let him keep all the rest he has got, it will do him service in Newgate, where we are sending him.' This was an instance of such complicated guilt and hypocrisy, that I

threw down the book in an agony of rage, and began to think with malice of all the human kind. I sat silent for some minutes, and soon perceiving the ticking of my watch beginning to grow noisy and troublesome, I quickly placed it out of hearing, and strove to resume my serenity. But the watchmen soon gave me a second alarm. I had scarcely recovered from this, when my peace was assaulted by the wind at my window; and when that ceased to blow, I listened for death-watches in the wainscot. I now found my whole system discomposed. I strove to find a resource in philosophy and reason; but what could I oppose, or where direct my blow, when I could see no enemy to combat? I saw no misery approaching, nor knew any I had to fear, yet still I was miserable. Morning came, I sought for tranquillity in dissipation, sauntered from one place of public resort to another, but found myself disagreeable to my acquaintance, and ridiculous to others. I tried at different times dancing, fencing, and riding; I solved geometrical problems, shaped tobacco-stoppers, wrote verses, and cut paper. At last I placed my affections on music, and find, that earnest employment, if it cannot cure, at least will palliate every anxiety."
Adieu

LETTER XCI

To the Same

THE INFLUENCE OF CLIMATE AND SOIL UPON THE TEMPERS AND DISPOSITIONS OF THE ENGLISH. [THE ENGLISH-MAN]

IT is no unpleasing contemplation, to consider the influence which soil and climate have upon the disposition of the inhabitants, the animals, and vegetables, of different countries. That among the brute creation is much more visible than in man, and that in vegetables more than either. In some places, those plants which are entirely poisonous at home lose their deleterious quality by being carried abroad: there are serpents in Macedonia so harmless as to be used as playthings for children; and we are told, that in some parts of Fez, there are lions so very timorous as to be scared, though coming in herds, by the cries of women.

I know of no country where the influence of climate and soil is more visible than in England; the same hidden cause which gives courage to their dogs and cocks, gives also a fierceness to their men.

But chiefly this ferocity appears among the vulgar. The polite of every country pretty nearly resemble each other. But, as in simpling, it is among the uncultivated productions of nature we are to examine the characteristic differences of climate and soil, so in an estimate of the genius of the people, we must look among the sons of unpolished rusticity. The vulgar English, therefore, may be easily distinguished from all the rest of the world, by superior pride, impatience, and a peculiar hardiness of soul.

Perhaps no qualities in the world are more susceptible of a finer polish than these; artificial complaisance, and easy deference, being superinduced over these, generally forms a great character; something at once elegant and majestic, affable, yet sincere. Such, in general, are the better sort; but they who are left in primitive rudeness, are the least disposed for society with others, or comfort internally, of any people under the sun.

The poor, indeed, of every country, are but little prone to treat each other with tenderness; their own miseries are too apt to engross all their pity; and perhaps, too, they give but little commiseration, as they find but little from others. But, in England, the poor treat each other upon every occasion with more than savage animosity, and as if they were in a state of open war by nature. In China, if two porters should meet in a narrow street, they would lay down their burthens, make a thousand excuses to each other for the accidental interruption, and beg pardon on their knees; if two men of the same occupation should meet here, they would first begin to scold, and at last to beat each other. One would think they had miseries enough resulting from penury and labour, not to increase them by ill-nature among themselves, and subjection to new penalties; but such considerations never weigh with them.

But to recompense this strange absurdity, they are in the main generous, brave, and enterprising. They feel the slightest injuries with a degree of ungoverned impatience, but resist the greatest calamities with surprising fortitude. Those miseries under which any other people in the world would sink, they have often showed they were capable of enduring; if accidentally cast upon some desolate coast, their perseverance is beyond what any other nation is capable of sustaining; if imprisoned for crimes, their efforts to escape are greater than among others. The peculiar strength of their prisons, when compared to those elsewhere, argues their hardiness; even the strongest prisons I have ever seen in other countries, would be very insufficient to confine the untameable spirit of an Englishman. In short, what man dares do in circumstances of danger, an Englishman will. His virtues seem to sleep in the calm, and are called out only to combat the kindred storm.

But the greatest eulogy of this people is the generosity of their miscreants; the tenderness, in general, of their robbers and highwaymen. Perhaps no people can produce instances of the same kind, where the desperate mix pity with injustice; still show that they understand a distinction in crimes, and, even in acts of violence, have still some tincture of remaining virtue. In every other country, robbery and murder go almost always together; here, it seldom happens, except upon ill-judged resistance or pursuit. The banditti of other countries are unmerciful to a supreme degree; the highwayman and robber here are generous, at least, in their intercourse among each other. Taking, therefore, my opinion of the English from the virtues and vices practised among the vulgar, they at once present to a stranger all their faults, and keep their virtues up only for the enquiring eye of a philosopher.

Foreigners are generally shocked at their insolence upon first coming among them: they find themselves ridiculed and insulted in every street; they meet with none of those trifling civilities, so frequent elsewhere, which are instances of mutual good-will, without previous acquaintance; they travel through the country, either too ignorant or too obstinate to cultivate a closer acquaintance; meet every moment something to excite their disgust, and return home to characterize this as the region of spleen, insolence, and ill-nature. In short, England would be the last place in the world I would travel to by way of amusement, but the first for instruction. I would choose to have others for my acquaintance, but Englishmen for my friends.

LETTER XCVI

To the Same

THE CONDOLENCE AND CONGRATULATION UPON THE DEATH OF THE LATE KING RIDICULED. ENGLISH MOURNING DESCRIBED

THE manner of grieving for our departed friends in China, is very different from that of Europe. The mourning color of Europe is black; that of China white. When a parent or relation dies here — for they seldom mourn for friends — it is only clapping on a suit of sables, grimacing it for a few days, and all, soon forgotten, goes on as before; not a single creature missing the deceased, except, perhaps a favourite housekeeper, or a favourite cat.

On the contrary, with us in China it is a very serious affair. The piety with which I have seen you behave, on one of these occasions, should never be forgotten. I remember it was upon the death of thy grandmother's maiden sister. The coffin was exposed in the principal hall, in public view. Before it were placed the figures of eunuchs, horses, tortoises, and other animals, in attitudes of grief and respect. The more distant relations of the old lady, and I among the number, came to pay our compliments of condolence, and to salute the deceased, after the manner of our country. We had scarce presented our wax candles and perfumes, and given the howl of departure, when, crawling on his belly from under a curtain, out came the reverend Fum Hoam himself, in all the dismal solemnity of distress. Your looks were set for sorrow; your clothing consisted of a hempen bag tied round the neck with a string. For two long months did this mourning continue. By night, you lay stretched on a single mat, and sat on the stool of discontent by day. Pious man! who could thus set an example of sorrow and decorum to our country. Pious country! where, if we do not grieve at the departure of our friends for their sakes, at least we are taught to regret them for our own.

All is very different here; amazement all! What sort of people am I got amongst? Fum, thou son of Fo, what sort of people am I got amongst? No crawling round the coffin; no dressing up in hempen bags; no lying on mats, or sitting on stools! Gentlemen here shall put on first mourning, with as sprightly an air as if preparing for a birth-night; and widows shall actually dress for another husband in their weeds for the former. The best jest of all is, that our merry mourners clap bits of muslin on their sleeves, and these are called *weepers*. Weeping muslin! alas! alas! very sorrowful truly! These weepers, then, it seems, are to bear the whole burthen of the distress.

But I have had the strongest instance of this contrast, this tragicomical behaviour in distress, upon a recent occasion. Their king, whose departure, though sudden, was not unexpected, died after a reign of many years. His age, and uncertain state of health, served, in some measure, to diminish the sorrow of his subjects; and their expectations from his successor seemed to balance their minds between uneasiness and satisfaction. But how ought they to have behaved on such an occasion? Surely, they ought rather to have endeavoured to testify their *gratitude* to their deceased friend, than to proclaim their *hopes* of the future! Sure, even the successor must suppose their love to wear the face of adulation, which so quickly changed the object! However, the very same day on which the old king died, they made rejoicing for the new!

For my part, I have no conception of this new manner of mourning and rejoicing in a breath; of being merry and sad; of mixing a funeral procession with a jig and a bonfire. At least, it would have been just, that they who flattered the king, while living, for virtues which he had not, should lament him dead, for those he really had.

In this universal cause for national distress, as I had no interest myself, so it is but natural to suppose I felt no real affliction. "In all the losses of our friends," says a European philosopher, "we first consider how much our own welfare is affected by their departure, and moderate our real grief, just in the same proportion." Now, as I had neither received, nor expected to receive, favours from kings or their flatterers; as I had no acquaintance in particular with their late monarch; as I knew that the place of a king is soon supplied; and, as the Chinese proverb has it, that though the world may sometimes want cobblers to mend their shoes, there is no danger of its wanting emperors to rule their kingdoms; from such considerations, I could bear the loss of a king with the most philosophic resignation. However, I thought it my duty at least to appear sorrowful; to put on a melancholy aspect, or to set my face by that of the people.

The first company I came amongst, after the news became general, was a set of jolly companions, who were drinking prosperity to the ensuing reign. I entered the room with looks of despair, and even expected applause for the superlative misery of my countenance. Instead of that, I was universally condemned by the company for a grimacing son of a whore, and desired to take away my penitential phiz to some other quarter. I now corrected my former mistake, and, with the most sprightly air imaginable, entered a company, where they were talking over the ceremonies of the approaching funeral. Here I sat for some time with an air of pert vivacity; when one of the chief mourners immediately observing my good humour, desired me, if I pleased, to go and grin somewhere else;

they wanted no disaffected scoundrels there. Leaving this company, therefore, I was resolved to assume a look perfectly neutral: and have ever since been studying the fashionable air; something between jest and earnest; a complete virginity of face, uncontaminated with the smallest symptom of meaning.

But though grief be a very slight affair here, the mourning, my friend, is a very important concern. When an emperor dies in China, the whole expense of the solemnities is defrayed from the royal coffers. When the great die here, mandarines are ready enough to order mourning; but I do not see that they are so ready to pay for it. If they send me down from court the grey undress frock, or the black coat without pocket-holes, I am willing enough to comply with their commands, and wear both; but, by the head of Confucius! to be obliged to wear black, and buy it into the bargain, is more than my tranquillity of temper can bear. What! order me to wear mourning before they know whether I can buy it or no! Fum, thou son of Fo, what sort of a people am I got amongst? where being out of black is a certain symptom of poverty; where those who have miserable faces cannot have mourning, and those who have mourning will not wear a miserable face! [Adieu.]

LETTER XCVIII

To the Same

A DESCRIPTION OF THE COURTS OF JUSTICE IN WESTMINSTER HALL

I HAD some intentions lately of going to visit Bedlam, the place where those who go mad are confined. I went to wait upon the man in black to be my conductor, but I found him preparing to go to Westminster-hall, where the English hold their courts of justice. It gave me some surprise to find my friend engaged in a law-suit, but more so when he informed me that it had been depending for several years. "How is it possible," cried I, "for a man who knows the world to go to law? I am well acquainted with the courts of justice in China: they resemble rat-traps every one of them; nothing more easy than to get in, but to get out again is attended with some difficulty, and more cunning than rats are generally found to possess!"

"Faith," replied my friend, "I should not have gone to law but that I was assured of success before I began; things were presented to me in so alluring a light, that I thought by barely declaring myself a candidate for the prize, I had nothing more to do but to enjoy the fruits of the victory. Thus have I been upon the eve of an imaginary triumph every term these ten years; have travelled forward with victory ever in my view, but ever out of reach; however, at present, I fancy we have hampered our antagonist in such a manner, that, without some unforeseen demur, we shall this very day lay him fairly on his back."

"If things be so situated," said I, "I do not care if I attend you to the courts, and partake in the pleasure of your success. But prithee," continued I, as we set forward, "what reasons have you to think an affair at last concluded, which has given you so many former disappointments?" — "My lawyer tells me," returned he, "that I have Salkeld and Ventris strong in my favour, and that there are no less than fifteen cases in point." — "I understand," said I, "those are two of your judges who have already declared their opinions." — "Pardon me," replied my friend, "Salkeld and Ventris are lawyers who some hundred years ago gave their opinions on cases similar to mine; these opinions, which make for me, my lawyer is to cite; and those opinions which look another way are cited by the lawyer employed by my antagonist: as I observed, I have Salkeld and Ventris for me; he has Coke and Hales for him; and he that has most opinions is most likely to carry his cause." — "But where is the necessity," cried I, "of prolonging a suit by citing the opinions and reports of others, since the same good sense which determined lawyers in former ages, may serve to guide your judges at this day? They at that time gave their opinions only from the light of reason; your judges have the same light at present to direct them; let me even add, a greater, as in former ages there were many prejudices from which the present is happily free. If arguing from authorities be exploded from every other branch of learning, why should it be particularly adhered to in this? I plainly foresee how such a method of investigation must embarrass every suit, and even perplex the student; ceremonies will be multiplied, formalities must increase, and more time will thus be spent in learning the arts of litigation, than in the discovery of right."

"I see," cries my friend, "that you are for a speedy administration of justice; but all the world will grant, that the more time that is taken up in considering any subject, the better it will be understood. Besides, it is the boast of an Englishman, that his property is secure, and all the world will grant, that a deliberate administration of justice is the best way to *secure his property*. Why have we so many lawyers, but to *secure our property?* why so many formalities, but to *secure our property?* Not less than one hundred thousand families live in opulence, elegance, and ease, merely by *securing our property.*"

"To embarrass justice," returned I, "by a multiplicity of laws, or to hazard it by a confidence in our judges, are, I grant, the opposite rocks on which legislative wisdom has ever split: in one case, the client resembles that emperor, who is said to have been suffocated with the bed-clothes which were only designed to keep him warm; in the other, to that town which let the enemy take possession of its walls, in order to show the world how little they depended upon aught but courage for safety. — But, bless me! what numbers do I see here — all in black! — how is it possible that half this multitude can find employment?" — "Nothing so easily conceived," returned my companion; "they live by watching each other. For instance, the catchpole watches the man in debt, the attorney watches the catchpole, the counsellor watches the attorney, the solicitor the counsellor, and all find sufficient employment." — "I conceive you," interrupted I, "they watch each other, but it is the client that pays them all for watching; it puts me in mind of a Chinese fable, which is entitled, FIVE ANIMALS AT A MEAL. —

"A grasshopper, filled with dew, was merrily singing under a shade; a whangam, that eats grasshoppers, had marked it for its prey, and was just stretching forth to devour it; a serpent, that had for a long time fed only on whangams, was coiled up to fasten on the whangam; a yellow bird was just upon the wing to dart upon the serpent; a hawk had just stooped from above to seize the yellow bird; all were intent on their prey, and unmindful of their danger: so the whangam ate the grasshopper, the serpent ate the whangam, the yellow bird the serpent, and the hawk the yellow bird; when, sousing from on high, a vulture gobbled up the hawk, grasshopper, whangam, and all in a moment."

I had scarce finished my fable, when the lawyer came to inform my friend, that his cause was put off till another term, that money was wanted to retain, and that all the world was of opinion, that the very next hearing would bring him off victorious. "If so, then," cries my friend, "I believe it will be my wisest way to continue the cause for another term; and, in the meantime, my friend here and I will go and see Bedlam." Adieu.

CITIZEN OF THE WORLD

LETTER XCIX

To the Same

A VISIT FROM THE LITTLE BEAU. THE INDULGENCE WITH WHICH THE FAIR SEX ARE TREATED IN SEVERAL PARTS OF ASIA

I LATELY received a visit from the little beau, who, I found, had assumed a new flow of spirits with a new suit of clothes. Our discourse happened to turn upon the different treatment of the fair sex here and in Asia, with the influence of beauty in refining our manners, and improving our conversation.

I soon perceived he was strongly prejudiced in favour of the Asiatic method of treating the sex, and that it was impossible to persuade him, but that a man was happier who had four wives at his command, than he who had only one. "It is true," cries he, "your men of fashion in the East are slaves, and under some terrors of having their throats squeezed by a bow-string; but what then? they can find ample consolation in a seraglio; they make, indeed, an indifferent figure in conversation abroad, but then they have a seraglio to console them at home. I am told they have no balls, drums, nor operas, but then they have got a seraglio; they may be deprived of wine and French cookery, but they have a seraglio: a seraglio — a seraglio, my dear creature, wipes off every inconvenience in the world!

"Besides, I am told, your Asiatic beauties are the most convenient women alive; for they have no souls: positively there is nothing in nature I should like so much as ladies without souls; soul, here, is the utter ruin of half the sex. A girl of eighteen shall have soul enough to spend a hundred pounds in the turning of a trump. Her mother shall have soul enough to ride a sweepstake match at a horse-race; her maiden aunt shall have soul enough to purchase the furniture of a whole toy-shop; and others shall have soul enough to behave as if they had no souls at all."

"With respect to the soul," interrupted I, "the Asiatics are much kinder to the fair sex than you imagine: instead of one soul, Fohi, the idol of China, gives every woman three; the Brahmins give them fifteen; and even Mahomet himself nowhere excludes the sex from Paradise. Abulfeda reports, that an old woman one day importuning him to know what she ought to do in order to gain Paradise — 'My good lady,' answered the prophet, 'old women never get there.' — 'What! never get to Paradise?' returned the matron, in a fury. 'Never,' says he, 'for they always grow young by the way.'

"No, Sir," continued I; "the men of Asia behave with more deference to the sex than you seem to imagine. As you of Europe say grace upon sitting down to dinner, so it is the custom in China to say grace when a man goes to bed to his wife." — "And may I die," returned my companion, "but a very pretty ceremony! for, seriously, Sir, I see no reason why a man should not be as grateful in one situation as in the other. Upon honour, I always find myself much more disposed to gratitude on the couch of a fine woman, than upon sitting down to a sirloin of beef."

"Another ceremony," said I, resuming the conversation, "in favour of the sex, amongst us, is the bride's being allowed, after marriage, *her three days of freedom*. During this interval, a thousand extravagances are practised by either sex. The lady is placed upon the nuptial bed, and numberless monkey tricks are played round to divert her. One gentleman smells her perfumed handkerchief, another attempts to untie her garters, a third pulls off her shoe to play hunt the slipper, another pretends to be an idiot, and endeavours to raise a laugh by grimacing; in the meantime, the glass goes briskly about, till ladies, gentlemen, wife, husband, and all, are mixed together in one inundation of arrack punch."

"Strike me dumb, deaf, and blind," cried my companion, "but very pretty! there's some sense in your Chinese ladies' condescensions! but, among us, you shall scarce find one of the whole sex that shall hold her good-humour for three days together. No later than yesterday, I happened to say some civil things to a citizen's wife of my acquaintance, not because I loved her, but because I had charity; and what do you think was the tender creature's reply? Only that she detested my pig-tail wig, high-heeled shoes, and sallow complexion! That is all. Nothing more! — Yes, by the heavens, though she was more ugly than an unpainted actress, I found her more insolent than a thorough bred woman of quality!"

He was proceeding in this wild manner, when his invective was interrupted by the man in black, who entered the apartment, introducing his niece, a young lady of exquisite beauty. Her very appearance was sufficient to silence the severest satirist of the sex; easy without pride, and free without impudence, she seemed capable of supplying every sense with pleasure. Her looks, her conversation, were natural and unconstrained; she had neither been taught to languish nor ogle, to laugh without a jest, or sigh without sorrow. I found that she had just returned from abroad, and had been conversant in the manners of the world. Curiosity prompted me to ask several questions, but she declined them all. I own I never found myself so strongly prejudiced in favour of apparent merit before, and could willingly have prolonged our conversation, but the company after some time withdrew. Just, however, before the little beau took his leave, he called me aside, and requested I would change him a twenty pound bill; which, as I was incapable of doing, he was contented with borrowing half-a-crown. Adieu.

LETTER CII

To the Same

THE PASSION FOR GAMING AMONG LADIES RIDICULED

THE ladies here are by no means such ardent gamesters as the women of Asia. In this respect I must do the English justice; for I love to praise where applause is justly merited. Nothing [is] more common in China than to see two women of fashion continue gaming till one has won all the other's clothes, and stripped her quite naked; the winner thus marching off in a double suit of finery, and the loser shrinking behind in the primitive simplicity of nature.

No doubt, you remember when Shang, our maiden aunt, played with a sharper. First her money went; then her trinkets were produced; her clothes followed, piece by piece, soon after; when she had thus played herself quite naked, being a woman of spirit, and willing to pursue *her own*, she staked her teeth: fortune was against her even here, and her teeth followed her clothes. At last she played for her left eye; and, oh! hard fate, this too she lost: however, she had the consolation of biting the sharper, for he never perceived that it was made of glass till it became his own.

How happy, my friend, are the English ladies, who never rise to such an inordinance of passion! Though the sex here are naturally fond of games of chance, and are taught to manage games of skill from their infancy, yet they never pursue ill fortune with such amazing intrepidity. Indeed, I may entirely acquit them of ever playing — I mean of playing for their eyes or their teeth.

It is true, they often stake their fortune, their beauty, health, and

Marriage-a-la-mode, Plate II.

reputations, at a gaming table. It even sometimes happens, that they play their husbands into a jail; yet still they preserve a decorum unknown to our wives and daughters in China. I have been present at a rout in this country, where a woman of fashion, after losing her money, has sat writhing in all the agonies of bad luck; and yet, after all, never once attempted to strip a single petticoat, or cover the board, as her last stake, with her head-clothes.

However, though I praise their moderation at play, I must not conceal their assiduity. In China, our women, except upon some great days, are never permitted to finger a dice-box; but here every day seems to be a festival, and night itself, which gives others rest, only serves to increase the female gamester's industry. I have been told of an old lady in the country who, being given over by the physicians, played with the curate of her parish to pass the time away: having won all his money, she next proposed playing for her funeral charges: her proposal was accepted; but unfortunately the lady expired just as she had taken in her game.

There are some passions which, though differently pursued, are attended with equal consequences in every country: here they game with more perseverence, there with greater fury; here they strip their families, there they strip themselves naked. A lady in China who indulges a passion for gaming, often becomes a drunkard; and by flourishing a dice-box in one hand, she generally comes to brandish a dram-cup in the other. Far be it from me to say there are any who drink drams in England; but it is natural to suppose, that when a lady has lost every thing else but her honour, she will be apt to toss that into the bargain; and, grown insensible to nicer feelings, behave like the Spaniard, who, when all his money was gone, endeavoured to borrow more, by offering to pawn his whisker. Adieu.

LETTER CV

To the Same

THE INTENDED CORONATION DESCRIBED. [BEAU TIBBS ON THE PREPARATIONS FOR THE SHOW]

THE time for the young king's coronation approaches. The great and the little world look forward with impatience. A knight from the country, who has brought up his family to see and be seen on this occasion, has taken all the lower part of the house where I lodge. His wife is laying in a large quantity of silks, which the mercer tells her are to be fashionable next season; and Miss, her daughter, has actually had her ears bored previous to the ceremony. In all this bustle of preparation, I am considered as mere lumber, and have been shoved up two stories higher, to make room for others my landlady seems perfectly convinced are my betters; but whom, before me, she is contented with only calling very good company.

The little beau, who has now forced himself into my intimacy, was yesterday giving me a most minute detail of the intended procession. All men are eloquent upon their favourite topic; and this seemed peculiarly adapted to the size and turn of his understanding. His whole mind was blazoned over with a variety of glittering images, — coronets, escutcheons, lace, fringe, tassels, stones, bugles, and spun glass. "Here," cried he, " Garter is to walk; and there Rouge Dragon marches with the escutcheons on his back. Here Clarencieux moves forward; and there Blue Mantle disdains to be left behind. Here the Aldermen march two and two; and there the undaunted Champion of England, no way terrified at the very numerous appearance of gentlemen and ladies, rides forward in complete armour, and, with an intrepid air, throws down his glove. Ah!" continued he, "should any be so hardy as to take up that fatal glove, and so accept the challenge, we should see fine sport; the Champion would show him no mercy; he would soon teach him all his passes, with a witness. However, I am afraid we shall have none willing to try with him upon the approaching occasion, for two reasons, — first, because his antagonist would stand a chance of being killed in the single combat; and, secondly, because if he escapes the Champion's arm, he would certainly be hanged for treason. No, no; I fancy none will be so hardy as to dispute it with a Champion like him, inured to arms; and we shall probably see him prancing unmolested away, holding his bridle thus in one hand, and brandishing his dram-cup in the other."

Some men have a manner of describing, which only wraps the subject in more than former obscurity; thus I was unable, with all my companion's volubility, to form a distinct idea of the intended procession. I was certain that the inauguration of a king should be conducted with solemnity and religious awe; and I could not be persuaded that there was much solemnity in this description. "If this be true," cried I to myself, "the people of Europe surely have a strange manner of mixing solemn and fantastic images together;

pictures, at once replete with burlesque and the sublime. At a time when the king enters into the most solemn compact with his people, nothing, surely, should be admitted to diminish from the real majesty of the ceremony. A ludicrous image, brought in at such a time, throws an air of ridicule upon the whole. It someway resembles a picture I have seen, designed by Albert Durer, where, amidst all the solemnity of that awful scene, a deity judging, and a trembling world awaiting the decree, he has introduced a merry mortal trundling his scolding wife to hell in a wheel-barrow."

My companion, who mistook my silence, during this interval of reflection, for the rapture of astonishment, proceeded to describe those frivolous parts of the show that most struck his imagination; and to assure me, that if I stayed in this country some months longer, I should see fine things. "For my own part," continued he, "I know already of fifteen suits of clothes, that would stand on one end with gold lace, all designed to be first shown there; and as for diamonds, rubies, emeralds, and pearls, we shall see them as thick as brass nails in a sedan chair. And then we are all to walk so majestically thus; this foot always behind the foot before. The ladies are to fling nosegays; the court poets to scatter verses; the spectators are to be all in full dress; Mrs. Tibbs in a new sack, ruffles, and Frenched hair: look where you will, one thing finer than another; Mrs. Tibbs curtsies to the Duchess; her Grace returns the compliment with a bow. 'Largess!' cries the Herald. 'Make room!' cries the Gentleman Usher. 'Knock him down!' cries the guard. Ah!" continued he, amazed at his own description, "what an astonishing scene of grandeur can Art produce from the smallest circumstance, when it thus actually turns to wonder one man putting on another man's hat!"

I now found his mind was entirely set upon the fopperies of the pageant, and quite regardless of the real meaning of such costly preparations. "Pageants," says Bacon, "are pretty things; but we should rather study to make them elegant than expensive." Processions, cavalcades, and all that fund of gay frippery, furnished out by tailors, barbers, and tirewomen, mechanically influence the mind into veneration. An emperor in his nightcap would not meet with half the respect of an emperor with a glittering crown. Politics resemble religion; attempting to divest either of ceremony is the most certain method of bringing either into contempt. The weak must have their inducements to admiration as well as the wise; and it is the business of a sensible government to impress all ranks with a sense of subordination, whether this be effected by a diamond buckle, or a virtuous edict, a sumptuary law, or a glass necklace.

This interval of reflection only gave my companion spirits to begin his description afresh; and, as a greater inducement to raise my curiosity, he informed me of the vast sums that were given by the spectators for places. "That the ceremony must be fine," cries he, "is very evident from the fine price that is paid for seeing it. Several ladies have assured me, they could willingly part with one eye rather than be prevented from looking on with the other. Come, come," continues he, "I have a friend, who, for my sake, will supply us with places at the most reasonable rates; I'll take care you shall not be imposed upon; and he will inform you of the use, finery, rapture, splendour, and enchantment of the whole ceremony, better than I."

Follies often repeated lose their absurdity, and assume the appearance of reason. His arguments were so often and so strongly enforced, that I had actually some thoughts of becoming a spectator. We accordingly went together to bespeak a place; but guess my surprise when the man demanded a purse of gold for a single seat! I could hardly believe him serious upon making the demand. "Prithee, friend," cried I, "after I have paid twenty pounds for sitting here an hour or two, can I bring a part of the coronation back?" — "No, Sir." — "How long can I live upon it, after I have come away?" — "Not long, Sir." — "Can a coronation clothe, feed, or fatten me?" — "Sir," replied the man, "you seem to be under a mistake; all that you can bring away is the pleasure of having it to say, that you saw the coronation." — "Blast me!" cries Tibbs, "if that be all, there is no need of paying for that, since I am resolved to have that pleasure, whether I am there or no!"

I am conscious, my friend, that this is but a very confused descripton of the intended ceremony. You may object, that I neither settle rank, precedency, nor place; that I seem ignorant whether Gules walks before or behind Garter; that I have neither mentioned the dimensions of a lord's cap, nor measured the length of a lady's tail. I know your delight is in minute description: and this I am unhappily disqualified from furnishing; yet, upon the whole, I fancy it will be no way comparable to the magnificence of our late Emperor Whangti's procession, when he was married to the moon, at which Fum Hoam himself presided in person. Adieu.

CITIZEN OF THE WORLD

LETTER CXII

To the Same

AN ELECTION DESCRIBED

THE English are at present employed in celebrating a feast, which becomes general every seventh year; the parliament of the nation being then dissolved, and another appointed to be chosen. This solemnity falls infinitely short of our Feast of the Lanterns in magnificence and splendour; it is also surpassed by others of the East in unanimity and pure devotion; but no festival in the world can compare with it for eating. Their eating, indeed, amazes me. Had I five hundred heads, and were each head furnished with brains, yet would they all be insufficient to compute the number of cows, pigs, geese, and turkeys, which, upon this occasion, die for the good of their country!

To say the truth, eating seems to make a grand ingredient in all English parties of zeal, business, or amusement. When a church is to be built, or an hospital endowed, the directors assemble, and, instead of consulting upon it, they eat upon it, by which means the business goes forward with success. When the poor are to be relieved, the officers appointed to dole out public charity, assemble and eat upon it. Nor has it ever been known that they filled the bellies of the poor, till they had previously satisfied their own. But in the election of magistrates, the people seem to exceed all bounds: the merits of a candidate are often measured by the number of his treats; his constituents assemble, eat upon him, and lend their applause, not to his integrity or sense, but to the quantities of his beef and brandy.

And yet I could forgive this people their plentiful meals on this occasion, as it is extremely natural for every man to eat a great deal when he gets it for nothing; but what amazes me is, that all this good living no way contributes to improve their good humour. On the contrary, they seem to lose their temper as they lose their appetites; every morsel they swallow, and every glass they pour down, serves to increase their animosity. Many an honest man, before as harmless as a tame rabbit, when loaded with a single election dinner, has become more dangerous than a charged culverin. Upon one of these occasions, I have actually seen a bloody-minded man-milliner sally forth at the head of a mob, determined to face a desperate pastry-cook, who was general of the opposite party.

But you must not suppose they are without a pretext for thus beating each other. On the contrary, no man here is so uncivilized as to beat his neighbour without producing very sufficient reasons. One candidate, for instance, treats with gin, a spirit of their own manufacture; another always drinks brandy, imported from abroad. Brandy is a wholesome liquor; gin, a liquor wholly their own. This then, furnishes an obvious cause of quarrel, — Whether it be most reasonable to get drunk with gin, or get drunk with brandy? The mob meet upon the debate, fight themselves sober, and then draw off to get drunk again, and charge for another encounter. So that the English may now properly be said to be engaged in war; since, while they are subduing their enemies abroad, they are breaking each other's heads at home.

I lately made an excursion to a neighbouring village, in order to be a spectator of the ceremonies practised upon this occasion. I left town in company with three fiddlers, nine dozen of hams, and a corporation poet, which were designed as reinforcements to the gin-drinking party. We entered the town with a very good face; the fiddlers, no way intimidated by the enemy, kept handling their arms up the principal street. By this prudent manœuvre, they took peaceable possession of their head-quarters, amidst the shouts of multitudes, who seemed perfectly rejoiced at hearing their music, but, above all, at seeing their bacon.

I must own, I could not avoid being pleased to see all ranks of people, on this occasion, levelled into an equality, and the poor, in some measure, enjoying the primitive privileges of nature. If there was any distinction shown, the lowest of the people seemed to receive it from the rich. I could perceive a cobbler with a levee at his door, and a haberdasher giving audience from behind his counter. But my reflections were soon interrupted by a mob, who demanded whether I was for the distillery or the brewery? As these were terms with which I was totally unacquainted, I chose at first to be silent; however, I know not what might have been the consequence of my reserve, had not the attention of the mob been called off to a skirmish between a brandy-drinker's cow and a gin-drinker's mastiff, which turned out, greatly to the satisfaction of the mob, in favour of the mastiff.

This spectacle, which afforded high entertainment, was at last

The Election. Plate I, The Entertainment.

ended by the appearance of one of the candidates, who came to harangue the mob: he made a very pathetic speech upon the late excessive importation of foreign drams, and the downfall of the distillery; I could see some of the audience shed tears. He was accompanied in his procession by Mrs. Deputy and Mrs. Mayoress. Mrs. Deputy was not in the least in liquor; and as for Mrs. Mayoress, one of the spectators assured me in my ear, that — she was a very fine woman before she had the small-pox.

Mixing with the crowd, I was now conducted to the hall where the magistrates are chosen; but what tongue can describe this scene of confusion! The whole crowd seemed equally inspired with anger, jealousy, politics, patriotism, and punch. I remarked one figure that was carried up by two men upon this occasion. I at first began to pity his infirmities as natural, but soon found the fellow so drunk that he could not stand; another made his appearance to give his vote, but though he could stand, he actually lost the use of his tongue, and remained silent; a third, who, though excessively drunk, could both stand and speak, being asked the candidate's name for whom he voted, could be prevailed upon to make no other answer but "Tobacco and brandy." In short, an election hall seems to be a theatre, where every passion is seen without disguise; a school where fools may readily become worse, and where philosophers may gather wisdom. Adieu.

LETTER CXVII

To the Same

A CITY NIGHT-PIECE

THE clock just struck two, the expiring taper rises and sinks in the socket, the watchman forgets the hour in slumber, the laborious and the happy are at rest, and nothing wakes but meditation, guilt, revelry, and despair. The drunkard once more fills the destroying bowl, the robber walks his midnight round, and the suicide lifts his guilty arm against his own sacred person.

Let me no longer waste the night over the page of antiquity, or the sallies of contemporary genius, but pursue the solitary walk, where vanity, ever changing, but a few hours past walked before me: where she kept up the pageant, and now, like a froward child, seems hushed with her own importunities.

CITIZEN OF THE WORLD

What a gloom hangs all around! The dying lamp feebly emits a yellow gleam; no sound is heard but of the chiming clock, or the distant watch-dog. All the bustle of human pride is forgotten: an hour like this may well display the emptiness of human vanity.

There will come a time, when this temporary solitude may be made continual, and the city itself, like its inhabitants, fade away, and leave a desert in its room.

What cities, as great as this, have once triumphed in existence, had their victories as great, joy as just and as unbounded; and, with short-sighted presumption, promised themselves immortality. Posterity can hardly trace the situation of some: The sorrowful traveller wanders over the awful ruins of others; and, as he beholds, he learns wisdom, and feels the transience of every sublunary possession.

"Here," he cries, "stood their citadel, now grown over with weeds; there their senate-house, but now the haunt of every noxious reptile; temples and theatres stood here, now only an undistinguished heap of ruin. They are fallen, for luxury and avarice first made them feeble. The rewards of the state were conferred on amusing, and not on useful members of society. Their riches and opulence invited the invaders, who, though at first repulsed, returned again, conquered by perseverance, and at last swept the defendants into undistinguished destruction."

How few appear in those streets which but some few hours ago were crowded! and those who appear, now no longer wear their daily mask, nor attempt to hide their lewdness or their misery.

But who are those who make the streets their couch, and find a short repose from wretchedness at the doors of the opulent? These are strangers, wanderers, and orphans, whose circumstances are too humble to expect redress, and whose distresses are too great even for pity. Their wretchedness excites rather horror than pity. Some are without the covering even of rags, and others emaciated with disease; the world has disclaimed them; society turns its back upon their distress, and has given them up to nakedness and hunger. These poor shivering females have once seen happier days, and been flattered into beauty. They have been prostituted to the gay luxurious villain, and are now turned out to meet the severity of winter. Perhaps, now lying at the doors of their betrayers, they sue to wretches whose hearts are insensible, or debauchees who may curse, but will not relieve them.

CITIZEN OF THE WORLD

Why, why was I born a man, and yet see the sufferings of wretches I cannot relieve! Poor houseless creatures! the world will give you reproaches, but will not give you relief. The slightest misfortunes of the great, the most imaginary uneasiness of the rich, are aggravated with all the power of eloquence, and held up to engage our attention and sympathetic sorrow. The poor weep unheeded, persecuted by every subordinate species of tyranny; and every law which gives others security, becomes an enemy to them.

Why was this heart of mine formed with so much sensibility? or why was not my fortune adapted to its impulse? Tenderness, without a capacity of relieving, only makes the man who feels it more wretched than the object which sues for assistance. Adieu.

LETTER CXIX

To the Same

ON THE DISTRESSES OF THE POOR; EXEMPLIFIED IN THE LIFE OF A PRIVATE SENTINEL

THE misfortunes of the great, my friend, are held up to engage our attention, are enlarged upon in tones of declamation, and the world is called upon to gaze at the noble sufferers: they have at once the comfort of admiration and pity.

Yet, where is the magnanimity of bearing misfortunes when the whole world is looking on? Men, in such circumstances, can act bravely even from motives of vanity. He only who in the vale of obscurity, can brave adversity — who, without friends to encourage, acquaintances to pity, or even without hope to alleviate his distresses, can behave with tranquillity and indifference, is truly great: whether peasant or courtier, he deserves admiration, and should be held up for our imitation and respect.

[While the slightest inconveniences of the great are magnified into calamities; while tragedy mouths out their sufferings in all the strains of eloquence], the miseries of the poor are, however, entirely disregarded; though some undergo more real hardships in one day, than the great in their whole lives. It is indeed inconceivable what difficulties the meanest English sailor or soldier endures without murmuring or regret [; without passionately declaiming against Providence, or calling their fellows to be gazers on their intrepidity].

Every day to him is a day of misery, and yet he bears his hard fate without repining.

With what indignation do I hear the heroes of tragedy complain of misfortunes and hardships, whose greatest calamity is founded in arrogance and pride! Their severest distresses are pleasures, compared to what many of the adventuring poor every day sustain without murmuring. These may eat, drink, and sleep; have slaves to attend them, and are sure of subsistence for life; while many of their fellow-creatures are obliged to wander, without a friend to comfort or to assist them, find enmity in every law, and are too poor to obtain even justice.

I have been led into these reflections from accidentally meeting, some days ago, a poor fellow begging at one of the outlets of this town, with a wooden leg. I was curious to learn what had reduced him to his present situation; and, after giving him what I thought proper, desired to know the history of his life and misfortunes, and the manner in which he was reduced to his present distress. The disabled soldier, for such he was, with an intrepidity truly British, leaning on his crutch, put himself into an attitude to comply with my request, and gave me his history as follows: —

"As for misfortunes, Sir, I cannot pretend to have gone through more than others. Except the loss of my limb, and my being obliged to beg, I don't know any reason, thank Heaven, that I have to complain: there are some who have lost both legs and an eye; but, thank Heaven, it is not quite so bad with me.

"My father was a labourer in the country, and died when I was five years old; so I was put upon the parish. As he had been a wandering sort of a man, the parishioners were not able to tell to what parish I belonged, or where I was born; so they sent me to another parish, and that parish sent me to a third: till at last it was thought I belonged to no parish at all. At length, however, they fixed me. I had some disposition to be a scholar, and had actually learned my letters; but the master of the workhouse put me to business as soon as I was able to handle a mallet.

"Here I lived an easy kind of a life for five years. I only wrought ten hours in the day, and had my meat and drink provided for my labour. It is true, I was not suffered to stir far from the house, for fear I should run away: but what of that? I had the liberty of the whole house, and the yard before the door, and that was enough for me.

"I was next bound out to a farmer, where I was up both early and late; but I ate and drank well, and liked my business well enough, till he died. Being then obliged to provide for myself, I was resolved to go and seek my fortune. Thus I lived, and went from town to town, working when I could get employment, and starving when I could get none, and might have lived so still. But happening one day to go through a field belonging to a magistrate, I spied a hare crossing the path just before me. I believe the devil put it in my head to fling my stick at it: well, what will you have on't? I killed the hare, and was bringing it away in triumph, when the Justice himself met me: he called me a villain, and, collaring me, desired I would give an account of myself. I began immediately to give a full account of all that I knew of my breed, seed, and generation; but though I gave a very long account, the Justice said I could give no account of myself; so I was indicted, and found guilty of being poor, and sent to Newgate in order to be transported to the plantations.

"People may say this and that of being in jail; but for my part, I found Newgate as agreeable a place as ever I was in in all my life. I had my bellyful to eat and drink, and did no work; but, alas! this kind of life was too good to last for ever! I was taken out of prison, after five months, put on board of a ship, and sent off with two hundred more. Our passage was but indifferent, for we were all confined in the hold, and died very fast, for want of sweet air and provisions; but, for my part, I did not want meat, because I had a fever all the way: Providence was kind; when provisions grew short, it took away my desire of eating. When we came ashore, we were sold to the planters. I was bound for seven years, and as I was no scholar — for I had forgot my letters — I was obliged to work among the negroes; and served out my time, as in duty bound to do.

"When my time was expired, I worked my passage home, and glad I was to see Old England again, because I loved my country. O, liberty! liberty! liberty! that is the property of every Englishman, and I will die in its defence! I was afraid, however, that I should be indicted for a vagabond once more, so I did not much care to go into the country, but kept about town, and did little jobs when I could get them. I was very happy in this manner for some time; till one evening, coming home from work, two men knocked me down, and then desired me to stand still.

They belonged to a press-gang: I was carried before the Justice, and as I could give no account of myself, (that was the thing that always hobbled me,) I had my choice left, whether to go on board a man-of-war, or list for a soldier. I chose to be a soldier; and in this post of a gentleman I served two campaigns, was at the battles in Flanders, and received but one wound through the breast, which is troublesome to this day.

"When the peace came on, I was discharged; and as I could not work, because my wound was sometimes painful, I listed for a landman in the East India Company's service. I here fought the French in six pitched battles; and verily believe, that if I could read or write, our captain would have given me promotion, and made me a corporal. But that was not my good fortune, I soon fell sick, and when I became good for nothing, got leave to return home again with forty pounds in my pocket, which I saved in the service. This was at the beginning of the present war, so I hoped to be set on shore, and to have the pleasure of spending my money; but the government wanted men, and I was pressed again, before ever I could set foot on shore.

"The boatswain found me, as he said, an obstinate fellow: he swore that I understood my business perfectly well, but that I pretended sickness merely to be idle. God knows, I knew nothing of sea business: he beat me without considering what he was about. But still my forty pounds was some comfort to me under every beating: the money was my comfort, and the money I might have had to this day, but that our ship was taken by the French, and so I lost it all!

"Our crew was carried into a French prison, and many of them died, because they were not used to live in a jail; but for my part, it was nothing to me, for I was seasoned. One night, however, as I was sleeping on a bed of boards, with a warm blanket about me, (for I always loved to lie well,) I was awaked by the boatswain, who had a dark lantern in his hand. 'Jack,' says he to me, 'will you knock out the French sentries' brains?' — 'I don't care,' says I, striving to keep myself awake, 'if I lend a hand.' — 'Then follow me,' says he, 'and I hope we shall do business.' So up I got, and tied my blanket, which was all the clothes I had, about my middle, and went with him to fight the Frenchmen. We had no arms; but one Englishman is able to beat five French at any time; so we went down to the door, where both the sentries were posted, and, rushing upon them, seized their arms in a moment, and knocked them down. From thence, nine of us ran together to the quay, and seizing the first boat we met, got out of the harbour and put to sea. We had not been here three days before we were taken up by an English privateer, who was glad of so many good hands; and we consented to run our chance. However, we had not so much luck as we expected. In three days we fell in with a French man-of-war, of forty guns, while we had but twenty-three; so to it we went. The fight lasted for three hours, and I verily believe we should have taken the Frenchman, but unfortunately, we lost almost all our men, just as we were going to get the victory. I was once more in the power of the French, and I believe it would have gone hard with me, had I been brought back to my old jail in Brest; but, by good fortune, we were retaken, and carried to England once more.

"I had almost forgot to tell you, that in this last engagement I was wounded in two places, — I lost four fingers of the left hand, and my leg was shot off. Had I had the good fortune to have lost my leg and use of my hand on board a king's ship, and not a privateer, I should have been entitled to clothing and maintenance during the rest of my life; but that was not my chance: one man is born with a silver spoon in his mouth, and another with a wooden ladle. However, blessed be God, I enjoy good health, and have no enemy in this world, that I know of, but the French and the Justice of Peace."

Thus saying, he limped off, leaving my friend and me in admiration of his intrepidity and content; nor could we avoid acknowledging, that an habitual acquaintance with misery, is the truest school of fortitude and philosophy. Adieu.

LETTER CXXIII

To the Same

THE CONCLUSION

AFTER a variety of disappointments, my wishes are at length fully satisfied. My son, so long expected, is arrived, at once, by his presence, banishing my anxiety, and opening a new scene of unexpected pleasure. His improvements in mind and person have far surpassed even the sanguine expectations of a father. I left him a boy, but he is returned a man; pleasing in his person, hardened by travel, and polished by adversity. His disappointment in love, however, had infused an air of melancholy into his conversation, which seemed at intervals to interrupt our mutual satisfaction. I expected that this could find a cure only from time; but fortune, as if willing to load us with her favours, has, in a moment, repaid every uneasiness with rapture.

Two days after his arrival, the man in black, with his beautiful niece, came to congratulate us upon this pleasing occasion; but, guess our surprise, when my friend's lovely kinswoman was found to be the very captive my son had rescued from Persia, and who had been wrecked on the Wolga, and was carried by the Russian peasants to the port of Archangel. Were I to hold the pen of a novelist, I might be prolix in describing their feelings at so unexpected an interview; but you may conceive their joy without my assistance: words were unable to express their transports, then how can words describe it?

When two young persons are sincerely enamoured of each other, nothing can give me such pleasure as seeing them married: whether I know the parties or not, I am happy at thus binding one link more in the universal chain. Nature has, in some measure, formed me for a matchmaker, and given me a soul to sympathize with every mode of human felicity. I instantly, therefore, consulted the man in black, whether we might not crown their mutual wishes by marriage: his soul seems formed of similar materials with mine; he instantly gave his consent, and the next day was appointed for the solemnization of the nuptials.

All the acquaintances which I had made since my arrival, were present at this gay solemnity. The little beau was constituted master of the ceremonies, and his wife, Mrs. Tibbs, conducted the entertainment with proper decorum. The man in black, and the pawnbroker's widow, were very sprightly and tender upon this occasion. The widow was dressed up under the direction of Mrs. Tibbs; and as for her lover, his face was set off by the assistance of a pig-tail wig, which was lent by the little beau, to fit him for making love with proper formality. The whole company easily perceived that it would be a double wedding before all was over, and, indeed, my friend and the widow seemed to make no secret of their passion; he even called me aside, in order to know my candid

opinion, whether I did not think him a little too old to be married?
"As for my own part," continued he, "I know I am going to play the fool, but all my friends will praise my wisdom, and produce me as the very pattern of discretion to others."

At dinner, every thing seemed to run on with good-humour, harmony, and satisfaction. Every creature in company thought themselves pretty, and every jest was laughed at. The man in black sat next his mistress, helped her plate, chimed her glass, and jogging her knees and her elbow, he whispered something arch in her ear, on which she patted his cheek: never was antiquated passion so playful, so harmless, and amusing, as between this reverend couple.

The second course was now called for, and, among a variety of other dishes, a fine turkey was placed before the widow. The Europeans, you know, carve as they eat; my friend, therefore, begged his mistress to help him to a part of the turkey. The widow, pleased with an opportunity of showing her skill in carving, an art upon which it seems she piqued herself, began to cut it up by first taking off the leg. "Madam," cries my friend, "if I might be permitted to advise, I would begin by cutting off the wing, and then the leg will come off more easily." — "Sir," replies the widow, "give me leave to understand cutting up a fowl: I always begin with the leg." — "Yes, Madam," replies the lover, "but if the wing be the most convenient manner, I would begin with the wing," — "Sir," interrupts the lady, "when you have fowls of your own, begin with the wing, if you please, but give me leave to take off the leg; I hope I am not to be taught at this time of day." — "Madam," interrupts he, "we are never too old to be instructed." — "Old, Sir!" interrupts the other, "who is old, Sir? when I die of age, I know of some that will quake for fear: If the leg does not come off, take the turkey to yourself." — "Madam," replied the man in black, "I don't care a farthing whether the leg or the wing comes off; if you are for the leg first, why you shall have the argument, even though it be as I say." — "As for the matter of that," cries the widow, "I don't care a fig whether you are for the leg off or on; and, friend, for the future, keep your distance." — "O," replied the other, "that is easily done; it is only removing to the other end of the table; and so, Madam, your most obedient humble servant."

Thus was this courtship of an age destroyed in one moment; for this dialogue effectually broke off the match between this respectable couple, that had been but just concluded. The smallest accidents disappoint the most important treaties. However, though it in some measure interrupted the general satisfaction, it no ways lessened the happiness of the youthful couple; and, by the young lady's looks, I could perceive she was not entirely displeased with this interruption.

In a few hours the whole transaction seemed entirely forgotten, and we have all since enjoyed those satisfactions which result from a consciousness of making each other happy. My son and his fair partner are fixed here for life: the man in black has given them up a small estate in the country, which, added to what I was able to bestow, will be capable of supplying all the real, but not the fictitious demands of happiness. As for myself, the world being but one city to me, I do not much care in which of the streets I happen to reside: I shall, therefore, spend the remainder of my life in examining the manners of different countries, and have prevailed upon the man in black to be my companion. "They must often change," says Confucius, "who would be constant in happiness or wisdom." Adieu.

www.ingramcontent.com/pod-product-compliance
Lightning Source LLC
Chambersburg PA
CBHW020727160426
43192CB00006B/133